Fundamentals of College Mathematics

Second Custom Edition for the University of Nevada, Reno

Taken from:
Mathematics with Applications in the Management, Natural, and Social Sciences, Eleventh Edition
by Margaret L. Lial, Thomas W. Hungerford, John P. Holcomb, Jr., and Bernadette Mullins

Finite Mathematics and Calculus with Applications, Tenth Edition
by Margaret L. Lial, Raymond N. Greenwell, and Nathan P. Ritchey

Cover Art: Courtesy of Pearson Learning Solutions.

Taken from:

Mathematics with Applications in the Management, Natural, and Social Sciences, Eleventh Edition
by Margaret L. Lial, Thomas W. Hungerford, John P. Holcomb, Jr., and Bernadette Mullins
Copyright © 2015, 2011, 2007, 2004 by Pearson Education, Inc.
New York, New York 10013

Finite Mathematics and Calculus with Applications, Tenth Edition
by Margaret L. Lial, Raymond N. Greenwell, and Nathan P. Ritchey
Copyright © 2016, 2012, 2008 by Pearson Education, Inc.
New York, New York 10013

This special edition published in cooperation with Pearson Education, Inc.

All trademarks, service marks, registered trademarks, and registered service marks are the property of their respective owners and are used herein for identification purposes only.

Pearson Education, Inc., 330 Hudson Street, New York, New York 10013
A Pearson Education Company
www.pearsoned.com

Printed in the United States of America

1   16

000200010272041456

ND

ISBN 10: 1-323-43146-2
ISBN 13: 978-1-323-43146-7

MyMathLab

Welcome Students!

MyMathLab is an interactive website where you can:
- Self-test & work through practice exercises with step-by-step help to improve your math skills.
- Study more efficiently with a personalized study plan and exercises that match your book.
- Get help when YOU need it. MyMathLab includes multimedia learning aids, videos, animations, and live tutorial help.

Before You Begin:
To register for MyMathLab, you need:

☑ **A MyMathLab student access code** (packaged with your new text, standalone at your bookstore, or

available for purchase with a major credit card at www.mymathlab.com)

☑ **Your instructors' Course ID:**

☑ **A valid email address**

☑ **Your school zip code:**

Student Registration:
- Enter www.mymathlab.com in your web browser.
- Under Register, click **Student**.
- Enter your **Course ID** exactly as provided by your instructor and click **Continue.** *Your course information appears on the next page. If it does not look correct, contact your instructor to verify the Course ID.*
- Sign in or follow the instructions to create an account. Use an email address that you check regularly and, if possible, use that same email address for your username. Read and accept the License Agreement and Privacy Policy. Click **Access Code**. Enter your **Access Code** in the boxes and click **Next**.

Once your registration is complete, a **Confirmation** page appears. You will also receive this information by email. Make sure you print the Confirmation page as your receipt. Remember to **write down your username and password**. You are now ready to access your resources!

Signing In:
- Go to www.mymathlab.com and click **Sign in**.
- Enter your **username** and **password** and click **Sign In**.
- On the left, click the name of your course.

The first time you enter your course from your own computer and anytime you use a new computer, click the **Installation Wizard** or **Browser Check** on the Announcements page. After completing the installation process and closing the wizard, you will be on your course home page and ready to explore your MyMathLab resources!

Need help?
Contact Product Support at **http://www.mymathlab.com/student-support** for live CHAT, email, or phone support.

Contents

Taken from: *Mathematics with Applications in the Management, Natural, and Social Sciences*, Eleventh Edition by Margaret L. Lial, Thomas W. Hungerford, John P. Holcomb, Jr., and Bernadette Mullins

Algebra and Equations

1

CHAPTER OUTLINE

CASE STUDY 1
Consumers Often Need to Just Do the Math

Mathematics is widely used in business, finance, and the biological, social, and physical sciences, from developing efficient production schedules for a factory to mapping the human genome. Mathematics also plays a role in determining interest on a loan from a bank, the growth of traffic on websites, and the study of falling objects. See Exercises 61 and 67 on page 51 and Exercise 63 on page 59.

Algebra and equations are the basic mathematical tools for handling many applications. Your success in this course will depend on your having the algebraic skills presented in this chapter.

1.1   The Real Numbers

Only real numbers will be used in this book.[*] The names of the most common types of real numbers are as follows.

Taken from: *Mathematics with Applications in the Management, Natural, and Social Sciences*, Eleventh Edition by Margaret L. Lial Thomas W. Hungerford, John P. Holcomb, Jr., and Bernadette Mullins

The Real Numbers

Natural (counting) numbers	$1, 2, 3, 4, \ldots$
Whole numbers	$0, 1, 2, 3, 4, \ldots$

---

[*]Not all numbers are real numbers. For example, $\sqrt{-1}$ is a number that is *not* a real number.

1

Integers	$\dots, -3, -2, -1, 0, 1, 2, 3, \dots$
Rational numbers	All numbers that can be written in the form p/q, where p and q are integers and $q \neq 0$
Irrational numbers	Real numbers that are not rational

As you can see, every natural number is a whole number, and every whole number is an integer. Furthermore, every integer is a rational number. For instance, the integer 7 can be written as the fraction $\frac{7}{1}$ and is therefore a rational number.

One example of an irrational number is π, the ratio of the circumference of a circle to its diameter. The number π can be approximated as $\pi \approx 3.14159$ ($\approx$ means "is approximately equal to"), but there is no rational number that is exactly equal to π.

> **Example 1**   What kind of number is each of the following?
>
> **(a)** 6
>
> **Solution**   The number 6 is a natural number, a whole number, an integer, a rational number, and a real number.
>
> **(b)** $\dfrac{3}{4}$
>
> **Solution**   This number is rational and real.
>
> **(c)** 3π
>
> **Solution**   Because π is not a rational number, 3π is irrational and real.

✓ **Checkpoint 1**

Name all the types of numbers that apply to the following.

(a) -2

(b) $-5/8$

(c) $\pi/5$

Answers to Checkpoint exercises are found at the end of the section.

All real numbers can be written in decimal form. A rational number, when written in decimal form, is either a terminating decimal, such as .5 or .128, or a repeating decimal, in which some block of digits eventually repeats forever, such as 1.3333 . . . or 4.7234234234 . . . .[†] Irrational numbers are decimals that neither terminate nor repeat.

When a calculator is used for computations, the answers it produces are often decimal *approximations* of the actual answers; they are accurate enough for most applications. To ensure that your final answer is as accurate as possible,

> *you should not round off any numbers during long calculator computations.*

It is usually OK to round off the final answer to a reasonable number of decimal places once the computation is finished.

The important basic properties of the real numbers are as follows.

Properties of the Real Numbers

For all real numbers, a, b, and c, the following properties hold true:

Commutative properties	$a + b = b + a$ and $ab = ba$.
Associative properties	$(a + b) + c = a + (b + c)$ and $(ab)c = a(bc)$.

Identity properties	There exists a unique real number 0, called the **additive identity**, such that
	$$a + 0 = a \quad \text{and} \quad 0 + a = a.$$
	There exists a unique real number 1, called the **multiplicative identity**, such that
	$$a \cdot 1 = a \quad \text{and} \quad 1 \cdot a = a.$$
Inverse properties	For each real number a, there exists a unique real number $-a$, called the **additive inverse** of a, such that
	$$a + (-a) = 0 \quad \text{and} \quad (-a) + a = 0.$$
	If $a \neq 0$, there exists a unique real number $1/a$, called the **multiplicative inverse** of a, such that
	$$a \cdot \frac{1}{a} = 1 \quad \text{and} \quad \frac{1}{a} \cdot a = 1.$$
Distributive property	$$a(b + c) = ab + ac \quad \text{and} \quad (b + c)a = ba + ca.$$

The next five examples illustrate the properties listed in the preceding box.

Example 2 The commutative property says that the order in which you add or multiply two quantities doesn't matter.

(a) $(6 + x) + 9 = 9 + (6 + x) = 9 + (x + 6)$ **(b)** $5 \cdot (9 \cdot 8) = (9 \cdot 8) \cdot 5$

Example 3 When the associative property is used, the order of the numbers does not change, but the placement of parentheses does.

(a) $4 + (9 + 8) = (4 + 9) + 8$ **(b)** $3(9x) = (3 \cdot 9)x$ ✓2

Example 4 By the identity properties,

(a) $-8 + 0 = -8$ **(b)** $(-9) \cdot 1 = -9.$

✎ **TECHNOLOGY TIP** To enter -8 on a calculator, use the negation key (labeled $(-)$ or $+/-$), *not* the subtraction key. On most one-line scientific calculators, key in $8\ +/-$. On graphing calculators or two-line scientific calculators, key in either $(-)\ 8$ or $+/-\ 8$.

Example 5 By the inverse properties, the statements in parts (a) through (d) are true.

(a) $9 + (-9) = 0$ **(b)** $-15 + 15 = 0$

(c) $-8 \cdot \left(\dfrac{1}{-8} \right) = 1$ **(d)** $\dfrac{1}{\sqrt{5}} \cdot \sqrt{5} = 1$

📄 **NOTE** There is no real number x such that $0 \cdot x = 1$, so 0 has no multiplicative inverse. ✓3

✓ **Checkpoint 2**

Name the property illustrated in each of the following examples.

(a) $(2 + 3) + 9 = (3 + 2) + 9$

(b) $(2 + 3) + 9 = 2 + (3 + 9)$

(c) $(2 + 3) + 9 = 9 + (2 + 3)$

(d) $(4 \cdot 6)p = (6 \cdot 4)p$

(e) $4(6p) = (4 \cdot 6)p$

✓ **Checkpoint 3**

Name the property illustrated in each of the following examples.

(a) $2 + 0 = 2$

(b) $-\dfrac{1}{4} \cdot (-4) = 1$

(c) $-\dfrac{1}{4} + \dfrac{1}{4} = 0$

(d) $1 \cdot \dfrac{2}{3} = \dfrac{2}{3}$

Example 6 By the distributive property,

(a) $9(6 + 4) = 9 \cdot 6 + 9 \cdot 4$

(b) $3(x + y) = 3x + 3y$

(c) $-8(m + 2) = (-8)(m) + (-8)(2) = -8m - 16$

(d) $(5 + x)y = 5y + xy.$ ✓₄

Order of Operations

Some complicated expressions may contain many sets of parentheses. To avoid ambiguity, the following procedure should be used.

> ## Parentheses
>
> Work separately above and below any fraction bar. Within each set of parentheses or square brackets, start with the innermost set and work outward.

Example 7 Simplify: $[(3 + 2) - 7]5 + 2([6 \cdot 3] - 13).$

Solution On each segment, work from the inside out:

$$[(3 + 2) - 7]5 - 2([6 \cdot 3] - 13)$$
$$= [5 - 7]5 + 2(18 - 13)$$
$$= [-2]5 + 2(5)$$
$$= -10 + 10 = 0.$$

Does the expression $2 + 4 \times 3$ mean

$$(2 + 4) \times 3 = 6 \times 3 = 18?$$

Or does it mean

$$2 + (4 \times 3) = 2 + 12 = 14?$$

To avoid this ambiguity, mathematicians have adopted the following rules (which are also followed by almost all scientific and graphing calculators).

> ## Order of Operations
>
> **1.** Find all powers and roots, working from left to right.
>
> **2.** Do any multiplications or divisions in the order in which they occur, working from left to right.
>
> **3.** Finally, do any additions or subtractions in the order in which they occur, working from left to right.
>
> If sets of parentheses or square brackets are present, use the rules in the preceding box within each set, working from the innermost set outward.

According to these rules, multiplication is done *before* addition, so $2 + 4 \times 3 = 2 + 12 = 14$. Here are some additional examples.

✓ **Checkpoint 4**

Use the distributive property to complete each of the following.

(a) $4(-2 + 5)$

(b) $2(a + b)$

(c) $-3(p + 1)$

(d) $(8 - k)m$

(e) $5x + 3x$

Example 8   Use the order of operations to evaluate each expression if $x = -2$, $y = 5$, and $z = -3$.

(a) $-4x^2 - 7y + 4z$

Solution   Use parentheses when replacing letters with numbers:

$$-4x^2 - 7y + 4z = -4(-2)^2 - 7(5) + 4(-3)$$
$$= -4(4) - 7(5) + 4(-3) = -16 - 35 - 12 = -63.$$

(b) $\dfrac{2(x - 5)^2 + 4y}{z + 4} = \dfrac{2(-2 - 5)^2 + 4(5)}{-3 + 4}$

$$= \frac{2(-7)^2 + 20}{1}$$

$$= 2(49) + 20 = 118. \quad \boxed{5}$$

✓ **Checkpoint 5**

Evaluate the following if $m = -5$ and $n = 8$.

(a) $-2mn - 2m^2$

(b) $\dfrac{4(n - 5)^2 - m}{m + n}$

Example 9   Use a calculator to evaluate

$$\frac{-9(-3) + (-5)}{3(-4) - 5(2)}.$$

Solution   Use extra parentheses (shown here in blue) around the numerator and denominator when you enter the number in your calculator, and be careful to distinguish the negation key from the subtraction key.

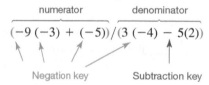

If you don't get -1 as the answer, then you are entering something incorrectly. $\boxed{6}$

✓ **Checkpoint 6**

Use a calculator to evaluate the following.

(a) $4^2 \div 8 + 3^2 \div 3$

(b) $[-7 + (-9)] \cdot (-4) - 8(3)$

(c) $\dfrac{-11 - (-12) - 4 \cdot 5}{4(-2) - (-6)(-5)}$

(d) $\dfrac{36 \div 4 \cdot 3 \div 9 + 1}{9 \div (-6) \cdot 8 - 4}$

Square Roots

There are two numbers whose square is 16, namely, 4 and -4. The positive one, 4, is called the **square root** of 16. Similarly, the square root of a nonnegative number d is defined to be the *nonnegative* number whose square is d; this number is denoted $\sqrt{d}$. For instance,

$$\sqrt{36} = 6 \text{ because } 6^2 = 36, \quad \sqrt{0} = 0 \text{ because } 0^2 = 0, \text{ and}$$
$$\sqrt{1.44} = 1.2 \text{ because } (1.2)^2 = 1.44.$$

No negative number has a square root that is a real number. For instance, there is no real number whose square is -4, so -4 has no square root.

Every nonnegative real number has a square root. Unless an integer is a perfect square (such as $64 = 8^2$), its square root is an irrational number. A calculator can be used to obtain a rational approximation of these square roots.

⬀ **TECHNOLOGY TIP**

On one-line scientific calculators, $\sqrt{40}$ is entered as 40 $\sqrt{\ }$. On graphing calculators and two-line scientific calculators, key in $\sqrt{\ }$ 40 ENTER (or EXE).

Example 10   Estimate each of the given quantities. Verify your estimates with a calculator.

(a) $\sqrt{40}$

Solution   Since $6^2 = 36$ and $7^2 = 49$, $\sqrt{40}$ must be a number between 6 and 7. A typical calculator shows that $\sqrt{40} \approx 6.32455532$.

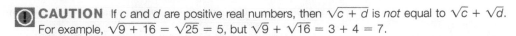 **Checkpoint 7**

Estimate each of the following.

(a) $\sqrt{73}$

(b) $\sqrt{22} + 3$

(c) Confirm your estimates in parts (a) and (b) with a calculator.

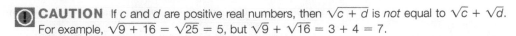 **Checkpoint 8**

Draw a number line, and graph the numbers $-4, -1, 0, 1, 2.5,$ and $13/4$ on it.

(b) $5\sqrt{7}$

Solution $\sqrt{7}$ is between 2 and 3 because $2^2 = 4$ and $3^2 = 9$, so $5\sqrt{7}$ must be a number between $5 \cdot 2 = 10$ and $5 \cdot 3 = 15$. A calculator shows that $5\sqrt{7} \approx 13.22875656$.

! CAUTION If c and d are positive real numbers, then $\sqrt{c + d}$ is *not* equal to $\sqrt{c} + \sqrt{d}$. For example, $\sqrt{9 + 16} = \sqrt{25} = 5$, but $\sqrt{9} + \sqrt{16} = 3 + 4 = 7$.

The Number Line

The real numbers can be illustrated geometrically with a diagram called a **number line.** Each real number corresponds to exactly one point on the line and vice versa. A number line with several sample numbers located (or **graphed**) on it is shown in Figure 1.1.

Figure 1.1

When comparing the sizes of two real numbers, the following symbols are used.

Symbol	Read	Meaning
$a < b$	a is less than b.	a lies to the *left* of b on the number line.
$b > a$	b is greater than a.	b lies to the *right* of a on the number line.

Note that $a < b$ means the same thing as $b > a$. The inequality symbols are sometimes joined with the equals sign, as follows.

Symbol	Read	Meaning
$a \leq b$	a is less than or equal to b.	either $a < b$ or $a = b$
$b \geq a$	b is greater than or equal to a.	either $b > a$ or $b = a$

✈ TECHNOLOGY TIP

If your graphing calculator has inequality symbols (usually located on the TEST menu), you can key in statements such as "5 < 12" or "−2 ≥ 3." When you press ENTER, the calculator will display 1 if the statement is true and 0 if it is false.

Only one part of an "either . . . or" statement needs to be true for the entire statement to be considered true. So the statement $3 \leq 7$ is true because $3 < 7$, and the statement $3 \leq 3$ is true because $3 = 3$.

Example 11 Write *true* or *false* for each of the following.

(a) $8 < 12$

Solution This statement says that 8 is less than 12, which is true.

(b) $-6 > -3$

Solution The graph in Figure 1.2 shows that -6 is to the *left* of -3. Thus, $-6 < -3$, and the given statement is false.

Figure 1.2

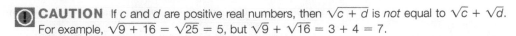 **Checkpoint 9**

Write *true* or *false* for the following.

(a) $-9 \leq -2$

(b) $8 > -3$

(c) $-14 \leq -20$

(c) $-2 \leq -2$

Solution Because $-2 = -2$, this statement is true.

A number line can be used to draw the graph of a set of numbers, as shown in the next few examples.

Example 12   Graph all real numbers x such that $1 < x < 5$.

Solution   This graph includes all the real numbers between 1 and 5, not just the integers. Graph these numbers by drawing a heavy line from 1 to 5 on the number line, as in Figure 1.3. Parentheses at 1 and 5 show that neither of these points belongs to the graph. ☑10

Figure 1.3

A set that consists of all the real numbers between two points, such as $1 < x < 5$ in Example 12, is called an **interval**. A special notation called **interval notation** is used to indicate an interval on the number line. For example, the interval including all numbers x such that $-2 < x < 3$ is written as $(-2, 3)$. The parentheses indicate that the numbers -2 and 3 are *not* included. If -2 and 3 are to be included in the interval, square brackets are used, as in $[-2, 3]$. The following chart shows several typical intervals, where $a < b$.

Intervals

Inequality	Interval Notation	Explanation
$a \le x \le b$	$[a, b]$	Both a and b are included.
$a \le x < b$	$[a, b)$	a is included; b is not.
$a < x \le b$	$(a, b]$	b is included; a is not.
$a < x < b$	(a, b)	Neither a nor b is included.

Interval notation is also used to describe sets such as the set of all numbers x such that $x \ge -2$. This interval is written $[-2, \infty)$. The set of all real numbers is written $(-\infty, \infty)$ in interval notation.

Example 13   Graph the interval $[-2, \infty)$.

Solution   Start at -2 and draw a heavy line to the right, as in Figure 1.4. Use a square bracket at -2 to show that -2 itself is part of the graph. The symbol ∞, read "infinity," *does not* represent a number. This notation simply indicates that *all* numbers greater than -2 are in the interval. Similarly, the notation $(-\infty, 2)$ indicates the set of all numbers x such that $x < 2$. ☑11

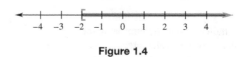

Figure 1.4

Absolute Value

The **absolute value** of a real number a is the distance from a to 0 on the number line and is written $|a|$. For example, Figure 1.5 shows that the distance from 9 to 0 on the number line is 9, so we have $|9| = 9$. The figure also shows that $|-9| = 9$, because the distance from -9 to 0 is also 9.

✓ **Checkpoint 10**

Graph all real numbers x such that
(a) $-5 < x < 1$
(b) $4 < x < 7$.

✓ **Checkpoint 11**

Graph all real numbers x in the given interval.
(a) $(-\infty, 4]$
(b) $[-2, 1]$

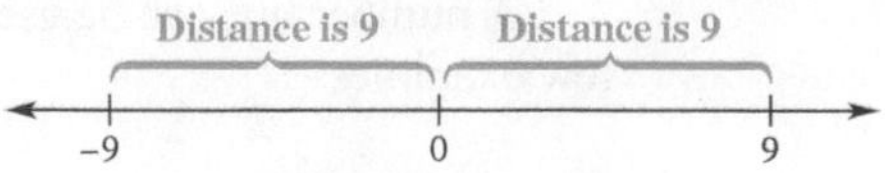

Figure 1.5

The facts that $|9| = 9$ and $|-9| = 9 = -(-9)$ suggest the following algebraic definition of absolute value.

Absolute Value

For any real number a,

$$|a| = a \qquad \text{if } a \geq 0$$
$$|a| = -a \qquad \text{if } a < 0.$$

The first part of the definition shows that $|0| = 0$ (because $0 \geq 0$). It also shows that the absolute value of any positive number a is the number itself, so $|a|$ is positive in such cases. The second part of the definition says that the absolute value of a negative number a is the *negative* of a. For instance, if $a = -5$, then $|-5| = -(-5) = 5$. So $|-5|$ is positive. The same thing works for any negative number—that is, its absolute value (the negative of a negative number) is positive. Thus, we can state the following:

For every nonzero real number a, the number $|a|$ is positive.

✓ **Checkpoint 12**

Find the following.

(a) $|-6|$

(b) $-|7|$

(c) $-|-2|$

(d) $|-3-4|$

(e) $|2 - 7|$

Example 14   Evaluate $|8 - 9|$.

Solution   First, simplify the expression within the absolute-value bars:

$$|8 - 9| = |-1| = 1. \quad \checkmark_{12}$$

1.1 Exercises

In Exercises 1 and 2, label the statement true or false. (See Example 1.)

1. Every integer is a rational number.

2. Every real number is an irrational number.

3. The decimal expansion of the irrational number π begins 3.141592653589793 . . . . Use your calculator to determine which of the following rational numbers is the best approximation for the irrational number π:

$$\frac{22}{7}, \quad \frac{355}{113}, \quad \frac{103,993}{33,102}, \quad \frac{2,508,429,787}{798,458,000}.$$

Your calculator may tell you that some of these numbers are equal to π, but that just indicates that the number agrees with π for as many decimal places as your calculator can handle (usually 10–14). No rational number is exactly equal to π.

Identify the properties that are illustrated in each of the following. (See Examples 2–6.)

4. $0 + (-7) = -7 + 0$

5. $6(t + 4) = 6t + 6 \cdot 4$

6. $3 + (-3) = (-3) + 3$

7. $-5 + 0 = -5$

8. $(-4) \cdot \left(\dfrac{-1}{4} \right) = 1$

9. $8 + (12 + 6) = (8 + 12) + 6$

10. $1 \cdot (-20) = -20$

11. How is the additive inverse property related to the additive identity property? the multiplicative inverse property to the multiplicative identity property?

12. Explain the distinction between the commutative and associative properties.

Evaluate each of the following if $p = -2, q = 3$, and $r = -5$. (See Examples 7–9.)

13. $-3(p + 5q)$

14. $2(q - r)$

15. $\dfrac{q + r}{q + p}$

16. $\dfrac{3q}{3p - 2r}$

Business *The nominal annual percentage rate (APR) reported by lenders has the formula APR = 12r, where r is the monthly interest rate. Find the APR when*

17. $r = 3.8$ **18.** $r = 0.8$

Find the monthly interest rate r when

19. $APR = 11$ **20.** $APR = 13.2$

Evaluate each expression, using the order of operations given in the text. (See Examples 7–9.)

21. $3 - 4 \cdot 5 + 5$ **22.** $8 - (-4)^2 - (-12)$

23. $(4 - 5) \cdot 6 + 6$ **24.** $\dfrac{2(3 - 7) + 4(8)}{4(-3) + (-3)(-2)}$

25. $8 - 4^2 - (-12)$

26. $-(3 - 5) - [2 - (3^2 - 13)]$

27. $\dfrac{2(-3) + 3/(-2) - 2/(-\sqrt{16})}{\sqrt{64} - 1}$

28. $\dfrac{6^2 - 3\sqrt{25}}{\sqrt{6^2 + 13}}$

Use a calculator to help you list the given numbers in order from smallest to largest. (See Example 10.)

29. $\dfrac{189}{37}$, $\dfrac{4587}{691}$, $\sqrt{47}$, 6.735, $\sqrt{27}$, $\dfrac{2040}{523}$

30. $\dfrac{385}{117}$, $\sqrt{10}$, $\dfrac{187}{63}$, π, $\sqrt{\sqrt{85}}$, 2.9884

Express each of the following statements in symbols, using $<$, $>$, $\leq$, or $\geq$.

31. 12 is less than 18.5.

32. -2 is greater than -20.

33. x is greater than or equal to 5.7.

34. y is less than or equal to -5.

35. z is at most 7.5.

36. w is negative.

Fill in the blank with $<$, $=$, or $>$ so that the resulting statement is true.

37. -6 _____ -2 **38.** $3/4$ _____ $.75$

39. 3.14 _____ π **40.** $1/3$ _____ $.33$

Fill in the blank so as to produce two equivalent statements. For example, the arithmetic statement "a is negative" is equivalent to the geometric statement "the point a lies to the left of the point 0."

Arithmetic Statement	Geometric Statement
41. $a \geq b$	_____
42. _____	a lies c units to the right of b
43. _____	a lies between b and c, and to the right of c
44. a is positive	_____

Graph the given intervals on a number line. (See Examples 12 and 13.)

45. $(-8, -1)$ **46.** $[-1, 10]$

47. $(-2, 3]$ **48.** $[-2, 2)$

49. $(-2, \infty)$ **50.** $(-\infty, -2]$

Evaluate each of the following expressions (see Example 14).

51. $|-9| - |-12|$

52. $|8| - |-4|$

53. $-|-4| - |-1 - 14|$

54. $-|6| - |-12 - 4|$

In each of the following problems, fill in the blank with either $=$, $<$, or $>$, so that the resulting statement is true.

55. $|5|$ _____ $|-5|$

56. $-|-4|$ _____ $|4|$

57. $|10 - 3|$ _____ $|3 - 10|$

58. $|6 - (-4)|$ _____ $|-4 - 6|$

59. $|-2 + 8|$ _____ $|2 - 8|$

60. $|3| \cdot |-5|$ _____ $|3(-5)|$

61. $|3 - 5|$ _____ $|3| - |5|$

62. $|-5 + 1|$ _____ $|-5| + |1|$

Write the expression without using absolute-value notation.

63. $|a - 7|$ if $a < 7$ **64.** $|b - c|$ if $b \geq c$

65. If a and b are any real numbers, is it always true that $|a + b| = |a| + |b|$? Explain your answer.

66. If a and b are any two real numbers, is it always true that $|a - b| = |b - a|$? Explain your answer.

67. For which real numbers b does $|2 - b| = |2 + b|$? Explain your answer.

68. **Health** Data from the National Health and Nutrition Examination Study estimates that 95% of adult heights (inches) are in the following ranges for females and males. (Data from: www.cdc.gov/nchs/nhanes.htm.)

Females	63.5 ± 8.4
Males	68.9 ± 9.3

Express the ranges as an absolute-value inequality in which x is the height of the person.

Business *The Consumer Price Index (CPI) tracks the cost of a typical sample of a consumer goods. The following table shows the percentage increase in the CPI for each year in a 10-year period.*

Year	2003	2004	2005	2006	2007
% Increase in CPI	2.3	2.7	2.5	3.2	4.1

Year	2008	2009	2010	2011	2012
% Increase in CPI	0.1	2.7	1.5	3.0	1.7

Let r denote the yearly percentage increase in the CPI. For each of the following inequalities, find the number of years during the given period that r satisfied the inequality. (Data from: U.S. Bureau of Labor Statistics.)

69. $r > 3.2$

70. $r < 3.2$

71. $r \leq 3.2$

72. $r \leq 1.5$

73. $r \geq 2.1$

74. $r \geq 1.3$

Finance *The table presents the 2012 percent change in the stock price for six well-known companies. (Data from: finance. yahoo.com.)*

Company	Percent Change
American Express	+36.5
Coca-Cola	+3.4
ExxonMobil	+0.6
Hewlett-Packard	−46.5
IBM	+4.4
McDonald's	−10.8

Suppose that we wish to determine the difference in percent change between two of the companies in the table and we are interested only in the magnitude, or absolute value, of this difference. Then we subtract the two entries and find the absolute value. For example, the difference in percent change of stock price for American Express and McDonald's is $|36.5\% - (-10.8\%)| = 47.3\%$.

Find the absolute value of the difference between the two indicated changes in stock price.

75. Coca-Cola and Hewlett-Packard

76. IBM and McDonald's

77. ExxonMobil and IBM

78. American Express and ExxonMobil

79. McDonald's and Hewlett-Packard

80. IBM and Coca-Cola

Finance *The following graph shows the per capita amount of disposable income (in thousands of dollars) in the United States. (Data from: U.S. Bureau of Economic Analysis.)*

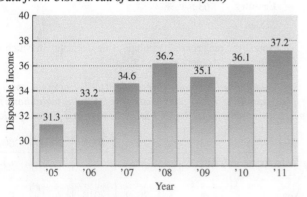

For each of the following, determine the years for which the expression is true where x is the per capita disposable income.

81. $|x - 35,000| > 1000$

82. $|x - 32,000| > 3500$

83. $|x - 36,500| \leq 2200$

84. $|x - 31,500| \leq 4400$

✓ Checkpoint Answers

1. (a) Integer, rational, real

(b) Rational, real

(c) Irrational, real

2. (a) Commutative property

(b) Associative property

(c) Commutative property

(d) Commutative property

(e) Associative property

3. (a) Additive identity property

(b) Multiplicative inverse property

(c) Additive inverse property

(d) Multiplicative identity property

4. (a) $4(-2) + 4(5) = 12$ (b) $2a + 2b$

(c) $-3p - 3$ (d) $8m - km$

(e) $(5 + 3)x = 8x$

5. (a) 30   (b) $\dfrac{41}{3}$

6. (a) 5   (b) 40

(c) $\dfrac{19}{38} = \dfrac{1}{2} = .5$ (d) $-\dfrac{1}{4} = -.25$

7. (a) Between 8 and 9

(b) Between 7 and 8

(c) 8.5440; 7.6904

8.

9. (a) True   (b) True   (c) False

10. (a) ![interval -5 to 1]   (b) ![interval 4 to 7]

11. (a) ![interval to 4]   (b) ![interval -2 to 1]

12. (a) 6   (b) −7

(c) −2   (d) 7

(e) 5

1.2 Polynomials

Polynomials are the fundamental tools of algebra and will play a central role in this course. In order to do polynomial arithmetic, you must first understand exponents. So we begin with them. You are familiar with the usual notation for squares and cubes, such as:

$$5^2 = 5 \cdot 5 \quad \text{and} \quad 6^3 = 6 \cdot 6 \cdot 6.$$

We now extend this convenient notation to other cases.

If n is a natural number and a is any real number, then

a^n denotes the product $a \cdot a \cdot a \cdots a$ (n factors).

The number a is the **base,** and the number n is the **exponent.**

Example 1 4^6, which is read "four to the sixth," or "four to the sixth power," is the number

$$4 \cdot 4 \cdot 4 \cdot 4 \cdot 4 \cdot 4 = 4096.$$

Similarly, $(-5)^3 = (-5)(-5)(-5) = -125$, and

$$\left(\frac{3}{2}\right)^4 = \frac{3}{2} \cdot \frac{3}{2} \cdot \frac{3}{2} \cdot \frac{3}{2} = \frac{81}{16}.$$

Example 2 Use a calculator to approximate the given expressions.

(a) $(1.2)^8$

Solution Key in 1.2 and then use the x^y key (labeled $\wedge$ on some calculators); finally, key in the exponent 8. The calculator displays the (exact) answer 4.29981696.

(b) $\left(\frac{12}{7}\right)^{23}$

Solution Don't compute 12/7 separately. Use parentheses and key in (12/7), followed by the x^y key and the exponent 23 to obtain the approximate answer 242,054.822. ✓₁

✓**Checkpoint 1**

Evaluate the following.
(a) 6^3
(b) 5^{12}
(c) 1^9
(d) $\left(\frac{7}{5}\right)^8$

CAUTION A common error in using exponents occurs with expressions such as $4 \cdot 3^2$. The exponent of 2 applies only to the base 3, so that

$$4 \cdot 3^2 = 4 \cdot 3 \cdot 3 = 36.$$

On the other hand,

$$(4 \cdot 3)^2 = (4 \cdot 3)(4 \cdot 3) = 12 \cdot 12 = 144,$$

so

$$4 \cdot 3^2 \neq (4 \cdot 3)^2.$$

Be careful to distinguish between expressions like -2^4 and $(-2)^4$:

$$-2^4 = -(2^4) = -(2 \cdot 2 \cdot 2 \cdot 2) = -16$$
$$(-2)^4 = (-2)(-2)(-2)(-2) = 16,$$

so

$$-2^4 \neq (-2)^4. ✓₂$$

✓**Checkpoint 2**

Evaluate the following.
(a) $3 \cdot 6^2$
(b) $5 \cdot 4^3$
(c) -3^6
(d) $(-3)^6$
(e) $-2 \cdot (-3)^5$

By the definition of an exponent,

$$3^4 \cdot 3^2 = (3 \cdot 3 \cdot 3 \cdot 3)(3 \cdot 3) = 3^6.$$

Since $6 = 4 + 2$, we can write the preceding equation as $3^4 \cdot 3^2 = 3^{4+2}$. This result suggests the following fact, which applies to any real number a and natural numbers m and n.

Multiplication with Exponents

To multiply a^m by a^n, *add* the exponents:

$$a^m \cdot a^n = a^{m+n}.$$

Example 3   Verify each of the following simplifications.

(a) $7^4 \cdot 7^6 = 7^{4+6} = 7^{10}$

(b) $(-2)^3 \cdot (-2)^5 = (-2)^{3+5} = (-2)^8$

(c) $(3k)^2 \cdot (3k)^3 = (3k)^5$

(d) $(m + n)^2 \cdot (m + n)^5 = (m + n)^7$ ✓ 3

The multiplication property of exponents has a convenient consequence. By definition,

$$(5^2)^3 = 5^2 \cdot 5^2 \cdot 5^2 = 5^{2+2+2} = 5^6.$$

Note that $2 + 2 + 2$ is $3 \cdot 2 = 6$. This is an example of a more general fact about any real number a and natural numbers m and n.

Power of a Power

To find a power of a power, $(a^m)^n$, *multiply* the exponents:

$$(a^m)^n = a^{mn}.$$

Example 4   Verify the following computations.

(a) $(x^3)^4 = x^{3 \cdot 4} = x^{12}$.

(b) $[(-3)^5]^3 = (-3)^{5 \cdot 3} = (-3)^{15}$.

(c) $[(6z)^4]^4 = (6z)^{4 \cdot 4} = (6z)^{16}$. ✓ 4

It will be convenient to give a zero exponent a meaning. If the multiplication property of exponents is to remain valid, we should have, for example, $3^5 \cdot 3^0 = 3^{5+0} = 3^5$. But this will be true only when $3^0 = 1$. So we make the following definition.

Zero Exponent

If a is any nonzero real number, then

$$a^0 = 1.$$

For example, $6^0 = 1$ and $(-9)^0 = 1$. Note that 0^0 is *not* defined. ✓ 5

✓ Checkpoint 3

Simplify the following.

(a) $5^3 \cdot 5^6$

(b) $(-3)^4 \cdot (-3)^{10}$

(c) $(5p)^2 \cdot (5p)^8$

✓ Checkpoint 4

Compute the following.

(a) $(6^3)^7$

(b) $[(4k)^5]^6$

✓ Checkpoint 5

Evaluate the following.

(a) 17^0

(b) 30^0

(c) $(-10)^0$

(d) $-(12)^0$

Polynomials

A **polynomial** is an algebraic expression such as

$$5x^4 + 2x^3 + 6x, \qquad 8m^3 + 9m^2 + \frac{3}{2}m + 3, \qquad -10p, \qquad \text{or} \qquad 8.$$

The letter used is called a **variable,** and a polynomial is a sum of **terms** of the form

$$(\text{constant}) \times (\text{nonnegative integer power of the variable}).$$

We assume that $x^0 = 1$, $m^0 = 1$, etc., so terms such as 3 or 8 may be thought of as $3x^0$ and $8x^0$, respectively. The constants that appear in each term of a polynomial are called the **coefficients** of the polynomial. The coefficient of x^0 is called the **constant term.**

Example 5   Identify the coefficients and the constant term of the given polynomials.

(a) $5x^2 - x + 12$

Solution   The coefficients are 5, -1, and 12, and the constant term is 12.

(b) $7x^3 + 2x - 4$

Solution   The coefficients are 7, 0, 2, and -4, because the polynomial can be written $7x^3 + 0x^2 + 2x - 4$. The constant term is -4.

A polynomial that consists only of a constant term, such as 15, is called a **constant polynomial.** The **zero polynomial** is the constant polynomial 0. The **degree** of a polynomial is the *exponent* of the highest power of x that appears with a *nonzero* coefficient, and the nonzero coefficient of this highest power of x is the **leading coefficient** of the polynomial. For example,

Polynomial	Degree	Leading Coefficient	Constant Term
$6x^7 + 4x^3 + 5x^2 - 7x + 10$	7	6	10
$-x^4 + 2x^3 + \frac{1}{2}$	4	-1	$\frac{1}{2}$
x^3	3	1	0
12	0	12	12

The degree of the zero polynomial is *not defined*, since no exponent of x occurs with nonzero coefficient. First-degree polynomials are often called **linear polynomials.** Second- and third-degree polynomials are called **quadratics** and **cubics,** respectively. ✓6

Addition and Subtraction

Two terms having the same variable with the same exponent are called **like terms;** other terms are called **unlike terms.** Polynomials can be added or subtracted by using the distributive property to combine like terms. Only like terms can be combined. For example,

$$12y^4 + 6y^4 = (12 + 6)y^4 = 18y^4$$

and

$$-2m^2 + 8m^2 = (-2 + 8)m^2 = 6m^2.$$

The polynomial $8y^4 + 2y^5$ has unlike terms, so it cannot be further simplified.

In more complicated cases of addition, you may have to eliminate parentheses, use the commutative and associative laws to regroup like terms, and then combine them.

✓ **Checkpoint 6**

Find the degree of each polynomial.

(a) $x^4 - x^2 + x + 5$

(b) $7x^5 + 6x^3 - 3x^8 + 2$

(c) 17

(d) 0

Example 6 Add the following polynomials.

(a) $(8x^3 - 4x^2 + 6x) + (3x^3 + 5x^2 - 9x + 8)$

Solution $8x^3 - 4x^2 + 6x + 3x^3 + 5x^2 - 9x + 8$ Eliminate parentheses.

$= \underline{(8x^3 + 3x^3)} + \underline{(-4x^2 + 5x^2)} + \underline{(6x - 9x)} + 8$ Group like terms.

$= 11x^3 + x^2 - 3x + 8$ Combine like terms.

(b) $(-4x^4 + 6x^3 - 9x^2 - 12) + (-3x^3 + 8x^2 - 11x + 7)$

Solution

$-4x^4 + 6x^3 - 9x^2 - 12 - 3x^3 + 8x^2 - 11x + 7$ Eliminate parentheses.

$= -4x^4 + \underline{(6x^3 - 3x^3)} + \underline{(-9x^2 + 8x^2)} - 11x + \underline{(-12 + 7)}$ Group like terms.

$= -4x^4 + 3x^3 - x^2 - 11x - 5$ Combine like terms.

Care must be used when parentheses are preceded by a minus sign. For example, we know that

$$-(4 + 3) = -(7) = -7 = -4 - 3.$$

If you simply delete the parentheses in $-(4 + 3)$, you obtain $-4 + 3 = -1$, which is the wrong answer. This fact and the preceding examples illustrate the following rules.

Rules for Eliminating Parentheses

Parentheses preceded by a plus sign (or no sign) may be deleted.

Parentheses preceded by a minus sign may be deleted *provided that* the sign of every term within the parentheses is changed.

Example 7 Subtract: $(2x^2 - 11x + 8) - (7x^2 - 6x + 2)$.

Solution $2x^2 - 11x + 8 - 7x^2 + 6x - 2$ Eliminate parentheses.

$= (2x^2 - 7x^2) + (-11x + 6x) + (8 - 2)$ Group like terms.

$= -5x^2 - 5x + 6$ Combine like terms. ✓7

✓ **Checkpoint 7**

Add or subtract as indicated.

(a) $(-2x^2 + 7x + 9)$
$+ (3x^2 + 2x - 7)$

(b) $(4x + 6) - (13x - 9)$

(c) $(9x^3 - 8x^2 + 2x)$
$- (9x^3 - 2x^2 - 10)$

Multiplication

The distributive property is also used to multiply polynomials. For example, the product of $8x$ and $6x - 4$ is found as follows:

$$8x(6x - 4) = 8x(6x) - 8x(4) \qquad \text{Distributive property}$$
$$= 48x^2 - 32x \qquad x \cdot x = x^2$$

Example 8 Use the distributive property to find each product.

(a) $2p^3(3p^2 - 2p + 5) = 2p^3(3p^2) + 2p^3(-2p) + 2p^3(5)$
$= 6p^5 - 4p^4 + 10p^3$

(b) $(3k - 2)(k^2 + 5k - 4) = 3k(k^2 + 5k - 4) - 2(k^2 + 5k - 4)$
$= 3k^3 + 15k^2 - 12k - 2k^2 - 10k + 8$
$= 3k^3 + 13k^2 - 22k + 8$ ✓8

✓ **Checkpoint 8**

Find the following products.

(a) $-6r(2r - 5)$

(b) $(8m + 3) \cdot (m^4 - 2m^2 + 6m)$

Example 9   The product $(2x - 5)(3x + 4)$ can be found by using the distributive property twice:

$$(2x - 5)(3x + 4) = 2x(3x + 4) - 5(3x + 4)$$
$$= \underline{2x \cdot 3x} + \underline{2x \cdot 4} + \underline{(-5) \cdot 3x} + \underline{(-5) \cdot 4}$$
$$= 6x^2 \quad + \quad 8x \quad - \quad 15x \quad - \quad 20$$
$$= 6x^2 \quad - \quad\quad\quad 7x \quad\quad\quad - \quad 20$$

Observe the pattern in the second line of Example 9 and its relationship to the terms being multiplied:

$$(2x - 5)(3x + 4) = 2x \cdot 3x + 2x \cdot 4 + (-5) \cdot 3x + (-5) \cdot 4$$

First terms

$(2x - 5)(3x + 4)$ Outside terms

$(2x - 5)(3x + 4)$ Inside terms

$(2x - 5)(3x + 4)$ Last terms

This pattern is easy to remember by using the acronym **FOIL** (**F**irst, **O**utside, **I**nside, **L**ast). The FOIL method makes it easy to find products such as this one mentally, without the necessity of writing out the intermediate steps.

Example 10   Use FOIL to find the product of the given polynomials.

(a) $(3x + 2)(x + 5) = 3x^2 + 15x + 2x + 10 = 3x^2 + 17x + 10$

First   Outside   Inside   Last

(b) $(x + 3)^2 = (x + 3)(x + 3) = x^2 + 3x + 3x + 9 = x^2 + 6x + 9$

(c) $(2x + 1)(2x - 1) = 4x^2 - 2x + 2x - 1 = 4x^2 - 1$ ☑₉

✓ **Checkpoint 9**

Use FOIL to find these products.

(a) $(5k - 1)(2k + 3)$

(b) $(7z - 3)(2z + 5)$

Applications

In business, the *revenue* from the sales of an item is given by

Revenue = (price per item) × (number of items sold).

The *cost* to manufacture and sell these items is given by

Cost = Fixed Costs + Variable Costs,

where the fixed costs include such things as buildings and machinery (which do not depend on how many items are made) and variable costs include such things as labor and materials (which vary, depending on how many items are made). Then

Profit = Revenue − Cost.

Example 11   **Business**   A manufacturer of scientific calculators sells calculators for \$12 each (wholesale) and can produce a maximum of 150,000. The variable cost of producing x thousand calculators is $6995x - 7.2x^2$ dollars, and the fixed costs for the manufacturing operation are \$230,000. If x thousand calculators are manufactured and sold, find expressions for the revenue, cost, and profit.

Solution   If x thousand calculators are sold at \$12 each, then

$$\text{Revenue} = (\text{price per item}) \times (\text{number of items sold})$$
$$R = 12 \times 1000x = 12{,}000x,$$

where $x \le 150$ (because only 150,000 calculators can be made). The variable cost of making x thousand calculators is $6995x - 7.2x^2$, so that

$$\text{Cost} = \text{Fixed Costs} + \text{Variable Costs},$$
$$C = 230{,}000 + (6995x - 7.2x^2) \quad (x \le 150).$$

Therefore, the profit is given by

$$P = R - C = 12{,}000x - (230{,}000 + 6995x - 7.2x^2)$$
$$= 12{,}000x - 230{,}000 - 6995x + 7.2x^2$$
$$P = 7.2x^2 + 5005x - 230{,}000 \quad (x \le 150). \quad \boxed{10}$$

✓ **Checkpoint 10**

Suppose revenue is given by $7x^2 - 3x$, fixed costs are \$500, and variable costs are given by $3x^2 + 5x - 25$. Write an expression for

(a) Cost

(b) Profit

1.2 Exercises

Use a calculator to approximate these numbers. (See Examples 1 and 2.)

1. 11.2^6

2. $(-6.54)^{11}$

3. $(-18/7)^6$

4. $(5/9)^7$

5. Explain how the value of -3^2 differs from $(-3)^2$. Do -3^3 and $(-3)^3$ differ in the same way? Why or why not?

6. Describe the steps used to multiply 4^3 and 4^5. Is the product of 4^3 and 3^4 found in the same way? Explain.

Simplify each of the given expressions. Leave your answers in exponential notation. (See Examples 3 and 4.)

7. $4^2 \cdot 4^3$

8. $(-4)^4 \cdot (-4)^6$

9. $(-6)^2 \cdot (-6)^5$

10. $(2z)^5 \cdot (2z)^6$

11. $[(5u)^4]^7$

12. $(6y)^3 \cdot [(6y)^5]^4$

List the degree of the given polynomial, its coefficients, and its constant term. (See Example 5.)

13. $6.2x^4 - 5x^3 + 4x^2 - 3x + 3.7$

14. $6x^7 + 4x^6 - x^3 + x$

State the degree of the given polynomial.

15. $1 + x + 2x^2 + 3x^3$

16. $5x^4 - 4x^5 - 6x^3 + 7x^4 - 2x + 8$

Add or subtract as indicated. (See Examples 6 and 7.)

17. $(3x^3 + 2x^2 - 5x) + (-4x^3 - x^2 - 8x)$

18. $(-2p^3 - 5p + 7) + (-4p^2 + 8p + 2)$

19. $(-4y^2 - 3y + 8) - (2y^2 - 6y + 2)$

20. $(7b^2 + 2b - 5) - (3b^2 + 2b - 6)$

21. $(2x^3 + 2x^2 + 4x - 3) - (2x^3 + 8x^2 + 1)$

22. $(3y^3 + 9y^2 - 11y + 8) - (-4y^2 + 10y - 6)$

Find each of the given products. (See Examples 8–10.)

23. $-9m(2m^2 + 6m - 1)$

24. $2a(4a^2 - 6a + 8)$

25. $(3z + 5)(4z^2 - 2z + 1)$

26. $(2k + 3)(4k^3 - 3k^2 + k)$

27. $(6k - 1)(2k + 3)$

28. $(8r + 3)(r - 1)$

29. $(3y + 5)(2y + 1)$

30. $(5r - 3s)(5r - 4s)$

31. $(9k + q)(2k - q)$

32. $(.012x - .17)(.3x + .54)$

33. $(6.2m - 3.4)(.7m + 1.3)$

34. $2p - 3[4p - (8p + 1)]$

35. $5k - [k + (-3 + 5k)]$

36. $(3x - 1)(x + 2) - (2x + 5)^2$

Business *Find expressions for the revenue, cost, and profit from selling x thousand items. (See Example 11.)*

	Item Price	Fixed Costs	Variable Costs
37.	\$5.00	\$200,000	$1800x$
38.	\$8.50	\$225,000	$4200x$

39. **Business** Beauty Works sells its cologne wholesale for \$9.75 per bottle. The variable costs of producing x thousand bottles is $-3x^2 + 3480x - 325$ dollars, and the fixed costs of manufacturing are \$260,000. Find expressions for the revenue, cost, and profit from selling x thousand items.

40. **Business** A self-help guru sells her book *Be Happy in 45 Easy Steps* for \$23.50 per copy. Her fixed costs are \$145,000 and she estimates the variable cost of printing, binding, and distribution is given by $-4.2x^2 + 3220x - 425$ dollars. Find expressions for the revenue, cost, and profit from selling x thousand copies of the book.

Work these problems.

Business *The accompanying bar graph shows the net earnings (in millions of dollars) of the Starbucks Corporation. The polynomial*

$$-1.48x^4 + 50.0x^3 - 576x^2 + 2731x - 4027$$

gives a good approximation of Starbucks's net earnings in year x, where x = 3 corresponds to 2003, x = 4 to 2004, and so on (3 ≤ x ≤ 12). *For each of the given years,*

(a) *use the bar graph to determine the net earnings;*

(b) *use the polynomial to determine the net earnings.*

(Data from: www.morningstar.com.)

41. 2003   **42.** 2007

43. 2010   **44.** 2012

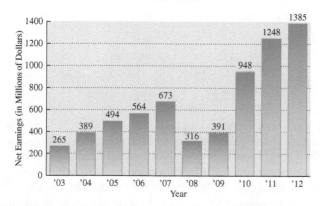

Assuming that the polynomial approximation in Exercises 41–44 remains accurate in later years, use it to estimate Starbucks's net earnings in each of the following years.

45. 2013   **46.** 2014   **47.** 2015

48. Do the estimates in Exercises 45–47 seem plausible? Explain.

Economics *The percentage of persons living below the poverty line in the United States in year x is approximated by the polynomial* $-.0057x^4 + .157x^3 - 1.43x^2 + 5.14x + 6.3$, *where x = 0 corresponds to the year 2000. Determine whether each of the given statements is true or false. (Data from: U.S. Census Bureau, Current Population Survey, Annual Social and Economic Supplements.)*

49. The percentage living in poverty was higher than 13% in 2004.

50. The percentage living in poverty was higher than 14% in 2010.

51. The percentage living in poverty was higher in 2003 than 2006.

52. The percentage living in poverty was lower in 2009 than 2008.

Health *According to data from a leading insurance company, if a person is 65 years old, the probability that he or she will live for another x years is approximated by the polynomial*

$$1 - .0058x - .00076x^2.$$

(Data from: Ralph DeMarr, University of New Mexico.)

Find the probability that a 65-year-old person will live to the following ages.

53. 75 (that is, 10 years past 65)   **54.** 80

55. 87   **56.** 95

57. Physical Science One of the most amazing formulas in all of ancient mathematics is the formula discovered by the Egyptians to find the volume of the frustum of a square pyramid, as shown in the following figure:

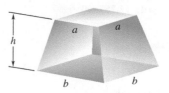

The volume of this pyramid is given by

$$(1/3)h \cdot (a^2 + ab + b^2),$$

where b is the length of the base, a is the length of the top, and h is the height. (Data from: H. A. Freebury, *A History of Mathematics* [New York: MacMillan Company, 1968].)

(a) When the Great Pyramid in Egypt was partially completed to a height h of 200 feet, b was 756 feet and a was 314 feet. Calculate its volume at this stage of construction.

(b) Try to visualize the figure if a = b. What is the resulting shape? Find its volume.

(c) Let a = b in the Egyptian formula and simplify. Are the results the same?

58. Physical Science Refer to the formula and the discussion in Exercise 57.

(a) Use the expression $(1/3)h(a^2 + ab + b^2)$ to determine a formula for the volume of a pyramid with a square base b and height h by letting a = 0.

(b) The Great Pyramid in Egypt had a square base of length 756 feet and a height of 481 feet. Find the volume of the Great Pyramid. Compare it with the volume of the 273-foot-tall Louisiana Superdome, which has an approximate volume of 125 million cubic feet. (Data from: Louisiana Superdome [www.superdome.com].)

(c) The Superdome covers an area of 13 acres. How many acres does the Great Pyramid cover? (*Hint:* 1 acre = 43,560 ft².)

59. Suppose one polynomial has degree 3 and another also has degree 3. Find all possible values for the degree of their

(a) sum;

(b) difference;

(c) product.

Business *Use the table feature of a graphing calculator or use a spreadsheet to make a table of values for the profit function in Example 11, with x = 0, 5, 10, . . . , 150. Use the table to answer the following questions.*

60. What is the profit or loss (negative profit) when 25,000 calculators are sold? when 60,000 are sold? Explain these answers.

61. Approximately how many calculators must be sold in order for the company to make a profit?

62. What is the profit from selling 100,000 calculators? 150,000 calculators?

✓ Checkpoint Answers

1. (a) 216 (b) 244,140,625
   (c) 1 (d) 14.75789056

2. (a) 108 (b) 320 (c) -729
   (d) 729 (e) 486

3. (a) 5^9 (b) $(-3)^{14}$ (c) $(5p)^{10}$

4. (a) 6^{21} (b) $(4k)^{30}$

5. (a) 1 (b) 1 (c) 1 (d) -1

6. (a) 4 (b) 8 (c) 0 (d) Not defined

7. (a) $x^2 + 9x + 2$
   (b) $-9x + 15$
   (c) $-6x^2 + 2x + 10$

8. (a) $-12r^2 + 30r$
   (b) $8m^5 + 3m^4 - 16m^3 + 42m^2 + 18m$

9. (a) $10k^2 + 13k - 3$ (b) $14z^2 + 29z - 15$

10. (a) $C = 3x^2 + 5x + 475$ (b) $P = 4x^2 - 8x - 475$

1.3 Factoring

The number 18 can be written as a product in several ways: $9 \cdot 2$, $(-3)(-6)$, $1 \cdot 18$, etc. The numbers in each product ($9, 2, -3$, etc.) are called **factors,** and the process of writing 18 as a product of factors is called **factoring.** Thus, factoring is the reverse of multiplication.

Factoring of polynomials is a means of simplifying many expressions and of solving certain types of equations. As is the usual custom, factoring of polynomials in this text will be restricted to finding factors with *integer* coefficients (otherwise there may be an infinite number of possible factors).

Greatest Common Factor

The algebraic expression $15m + 45$ is made up of two terms: $15m$ and 45. Each of these terms has 15 as a factor. In fact, $15m = 15 \cdot m$ and $45 = 15 \cdot 3$. By the distributive property,

$$15m + 45 = 15 \cdot m + 15 \cdot 3 = 15(m + 3).$$

Both 15 and $m + 3$ are factors of $15m + 45$. Since 15 divides evenly into all terms of $15m + 45$ and is the largest number that will do so, it is called the **greatest common factor** for the polynomial $15m + 45$. The process of writing $15m + 45$ as $15(m + 3)$ is called **factoring out** the greatest common factor.

Example 1   Factor out the greatest common factor.

(a) $12p - 18q$

Solution   Both $12p$ and $18q$ are divisible by 6, and

$$12p - 18q = 6 \cdot 2p - 6 \cdot 3q$$
$$= 6(2p - 3q).$$

(b) $8x^3 - 9x^2 + 15x$

Solution   Each of these terms is divisible by x:

$$8x^3 - 9x^2 + 15x = (8x^2) \cdot x - (9x) \cdot x + 15 \cdot x$$
$$= x(8x^2 - 9x + 15).$$

(c) $5(4x - 3)^3 + 2(4x - 3)^2$

Solution   The quantity $(4x - 3)^2$ is a common factor. Factoring it out gives

$$5(4x - 3)^3 + 2(4x - 3)^2 = (4x - 3)^2[5(4x - 3) + 2]$$
$$= (4x - 3)^2(20x - 15 + 2)$$
$$= (4x - 3)^2(20x - 13).$$ ✓

✓ Checkpoint 1

Factor out the greatest common factor.

(a) $12r + 9k$

(b) $75m^2 + 100n^2$

(c) $6m^4 - 9m^3 + 12m^2$

(d) $3(2k + 1)^3 + 4(2k + 1)^4$

Factoring Quadratics

If we multiply two first-degree polynomials, the result is a quadratic. For instance, using FOIL, we see that $(x + 1)(x - 2) = x^2 - x - 2$. Since factoring is the reverse of multiplication, factoring quadratics requires using FOIL backward.

Example 2   Factor $x^2 + 9x + 18$.

Solution   We must find integers b and d such that

$$x^2 + 9x + 18 = (x + b)(x + d)$$
$$= x^2 + dx + bx + bd$$
$$x^2 + 9x + 18 = x^2 + (b + d)x + bd.$$

Since the constant coefficients on each side of the equation must be equal, we must have $bd = 18$; that is, b and d are factors of 18. Similarly, the coefficients of x must be the same, so that $b + d = 9$. The possibilities are summarized in this table:

Factors b, d of 18	Sum $b + d$
$18 \cdot 1$	$18 + 1 = 19$
$9 \cdot 2$	$9 + 2 = 11$
$6 \cdot 3$	$6 + 3 = 9$

There is no need to list negative factors, such as $(-3)(-6)$, because their sum is negative. The table suggests that 6 and 3 will work. Verify that

$$(x + 6)(x + 3) = x^2 + 9x + 18.$$

✓ **Checkpoint 2**

Factor the following.
(a) $r^2 + 7r + 10$
(b) $x^2 + 4x + 3$
(c) $y^2 + 6y + 8$

Example 3   Factor $x^2 + 3x - 10$.

Solution   As in Example 2, we must find factors b and d whose product is -10 (the constant term) and whose sum is 3 (the coefficient of x). The following table shows the possibilities.

Factors b, d of -10	Sum $b + d$
$1(-10)$	$1 + (-10) = -9$
$(-1)10$	$-1 + 10 = 9$
$2(-5)$	$2 + (-5) = -3$
$(-2)5$	$-2 + 5 = 3$

The only factors with product -10 and sum 3 are -2 and 5. So the correct factorization is

$$x^2 + 3x - 10 = (x - 2)(x + 5),$$

as you can readily verify.

It is usually not necessary to construct tables as was done in Examples 2 and 3—you can just mentally check the various possibilities. The approach used in Examples 2 and 3 (with minor modifications) also works for factoring quadratic polynomials whose leading coefficient is not 1.

Example 4   Factor $4y^2 - 11y + 6$.

Solution   We must find integers $a, b, c,$ and d such that

$$4y^2 - 11y + 6 = (ay + b)(cy + d)$$
$$= acy^2 + ady + bcy + bd$$
$$4y^2 - 11y + 6 = acy^2 + (ad + bc)y + bd.$$

Since the coefficients of y^2 must be the same on both sides, we see that $ac = 4$. Similarly, the constant terms show that $bd = 6$. The positive factors of 4 are 4 and 1 or 2 and 2. Since the middle term is negative, we consider only negative factors of 6. The possibilities are -2 and -3 or -1 and -6. Now we try various arrangements of these factors until we find one that gives the correct coefficient of y:

$$(2y - 1)(2y - 6) = 4y^2 - 14y + 6 \quad \text{Incorrect}$$
$$(2y - 2)(2y - 3) = 4y^2 - 10y + 6 \quad \text{Incorrect}$$
$$(y - 2)(4y - 3) = 4y^2 - 11y + 6. \quad \text{Correct}$$

The last trial gives the correct factorization. ✓3

✓ **Checkpoint 3**

Factor the following.

(a) $x^2 - 4x + 3$

(b) $2y^2 - 5y + 2$

(c) $6z^2 - 13z + 6$

Example 5 Factor $6p^2 - 7pq - 5q^2$.

Solution Again, we try various possibilities. The positive factors of 6 could be 2 and 3 or 1 and 6. As factors of -5, we have only -1 and 5 or -5 and 1. Try different combinations of these factors until the correct one is found:

$$(2p - 5q)(3p + q) = 6p^2 - 13pq - 5q^2 \quad \text{Incorrect}$$
$$(3p - 5q)(2p + q) = 6p^2 - 7pq - 5q^2. \quad \text{Correct}$$

So $6p^2 - 7pq - 5q^2$ factors as $(3p - 5q)(2p + q)$. ✓4

✓ **Checkpoint 4**

Factor the following.

(a) $r^2 - 5r - 14$

(b) $3m^2 + 5m - 2$

(c) $6p^2 + 13pq - 5q^2$

📄 **NOTE** In Examples 2–4, we chose positive factors of the positive first term. Of course, we could have used two negative factors, but the work is easier if positive factors are used.

Example 6 Factor $x^2 + x + 3$.

Solution There are only two ways to factor 3, namely, $3 = 1 \cdot 3$ and $3 = (-1)(-3)$. They lead to these products:

$$(x + 1)(x + 3) = x^2 + 4x + 3 \quad \text{Incorrect}$$
$$(x - 1)(x - 3) = x^2 - 4x + 3. \quad \text{Incorrect}$$

Therefore, this polynomial cannot be factored.

Factoring Patterns

In some cases, you can factor a polynomial with a minimum amount of guesswork by recognizing common patterns. The easiest pattern to recognize is the *difference of squares*.

$$x^2 - y^2 = (x + y)(x - y). \quad \text{Difference of squares}$$

To verify the accuracy of the preceding equation, multiply out the right side.

Example 7 Factor each of the following.

(a) $4m^2 - 9$

Solution Notice that $4m^2 - 9$ is the difference of two squares, since $4m^2 = (2m)^2$ and $9 = 3^2$. Use the pattern for the difference of two squares, letting $2m$ replace x and 3 replace y. Then the pattern $x^2 - y^2 = (x + y)(x - y)$ becomes

$$4m^2 - 9 = (2m)^2 - 3^2$$
$$= (2m + 3)(2m - 3).$$

(b) $128p^2 - 98q^2$

Solution   First factor out the common factor of 2:

$$128p^2 - 98q^2 = 2(64p^2 - 49q^2)$$
$$= 2[(8p)^2 - (7q)^2]$$
$$= 2(8p + 7q)(8p - 7q).$$

(c) $x^2 + 36$

Solution   The *sum* of two squares cannot be factored. To convince yourself of this, check some possibilities:

$$(x + 6)(x + 6) = (x + 6)^2 = x^2 + 12x + 36;$$
$$(x + 4)(x + 9) = x^2 + 13x + 36.$$

(d) $(x - 2)^2 - 49$

Solution   Since $49 = 7^2$, this is a difference of two squares. So it factors as follows:

$$(x - 2)^2 - 49 = (x - 2)^2 - 7^2$$
$$= [(x - 2) + 7][(x - 2) - 7]$$
$$= (x + 5)(x - 9). \quad \checkmark_5$$

✓ **Checkpoint 5**

Factor the following.

(a) $9p^2 - 49$

(b) $y^2 + 100$

(c) $(x + 3)^2 - 64$

Another common pattern is the *perfect square*. Verify each of the following factorizations by multiplying out the right side.

$$x^2 + 2xy + y^2 = (x + y)^2$$
$$x^2 - 2xy + y^2 = (x - y)^2$$
   Perfect Squares

Whenever you have a quadratic whose first and last terms are squares, it *may* factor as a perfect square. The key is to look at the middle term. To have a perfect square whose first and last terms are x^2 and y^2, the middle term must be $\pm 2xy$. To avoid errors, always check this.

Example 8   Factor each polynomial, if possible.

(a) $16p^2 - 40pq + 25q^2$

Solution   The first and last terms are squares, namely, $16p^2 = (4p)^2$ and $25q^2 = (5q)^2$. So the second perfect-square pattern, with $x = 4p$ and $y = 5q$, might work. To have a perfect square, the middle term $-40pq$ must equal $-2(4p)(5q)$, which it does. So the polynomial factors as

$$16p^2 - 40pq + 25q^2 = (4p - 5q)(4p - 5q),$$

as you can easily verify.

(b) $9u^2 + 5u + 1$

Solution   Again, the first and last terms are squares: $9u^2 = (3u)^2$ and $1 = 1^2$. The middle term is positive, so the first perfect-square pattern might work, with $x = 3u$ and $y = 1$. To have a perfect square, however, the middle term would have to be $2(3u) \cdot 1 = 6u$, which is *not* the middle term of the given polynomial. So it is not a perfect square—in fact, it cannot be factored.

(c) $169x^2 + 104xy^2 + 16y^4$

Solution This polynomial may be factored as $(13x + 4y^2)^2$, since $169x^2 = (13x)^2$, $16y^4 = (4y^2)^2$, and $2(13x)(4y^2) = 104xy^2$. ☑6

✓ **Checkpoint 6**

Factor.

(a) $4m^2 + 4m + 1$

(b) $25z^2 - 80zt + 64t^2$

(c) $9x^2 + 15x + 25$

Example 9 Factor each of the given polynomials.

(a) $12x^2 - 26x - 10$

Solution Look first for a greatest common factor. Here, the greatest common factor is 2: $12x^2 - 26x - 10 = 2(6x^2 - 13x - 5)$. Now try to factor $6x^2 - 13x - 5$. Possible factors of 6 are 3 and 2 or 6 and 1. The only factors of -5 are -5 and 1 or 5 and -1. Try various combinations. You should find that the quadratic factors as $(3x + 1)(2x - 5)$. Thus,

$$12x^2 - 26x - 10 = 2(3x + 1)(2x - 5).$$

(b) $4z^2 + 12z + 9 - w^2$

Solution There is no common factor here, but notice that the first three terms can be factored as a perfect square:

$$4z^2 + 12z + 9 - w^2 = (2z + 3)^2 - w^2.$$

Written in this form, the expression is the difference of squares, which can be factored as follows:

$$(2z + 3)^2 - w^2 = [(2z + 3) + w][(2z + 3) - w]$$
$$= (2z + 3 + w)(2z + 3 - w).$$

(c) $16a^2 - 100 - 48ac + 36c^2$

Solution Factor out the greatest common factor of 4 first:

$$16a^2 - 100 - 48ac + 36c^2 = 4[4a^2 - 25 - 12ac + 9c^2]$$
$$= 4[(4a^2 - 12ac + 9c^2) - 25] \quad \text{Rearrange terms and group.}$$
$$= 4[(2a - 3c)^2 - 25] \quad \text{Factor.}$$
$$= 4(2a - 3c + 5)(2a - 3c - 5) \quad \text{Factor the difference of squares. ☑7}$$

✓ **Checkpoint 7**

Factor the following.

(a) $6x^2 - 27x - 15$

(b) $9r^2 + 12r + 4 - t^2$

(c) $18 - 8xy - 2y^2 - 8x^2$

> ⊘ **CAUTION** Remember always to look first for a greatest common factor.

Higher Degree Polynomials

Polynomials of degree greater than 2 are often difficult to factor. However, factoring is relatively easy in two cases: *the difference and the sum of cubes*. By multiplying out the right side, you can readily verify each of the following factorizations.

$$x^3 - y^3 = (x - y)(x^2 + xy + y^2) \quad \text{Difference of cubes}$$
$$x^3 + y^3 = (x + y)(x^2 - xy + y^2) \quad \text{Sum of cubes}$$

Example 10 Factor each of the following polynomials.

(a) $k^3 - 8$

Solution Since $8 = 2^3$, use the pattern for the difference of two cubes to obtain

$$k^3 - 8 = k^3 - 2^3 = (k - 2)(k^2 + 2k + 4).$$

(b) $m^3 + 125$

Solution $m^3 + 125 = m^3 + 5^3 = (m + 5)(m^2 - 5m + 25)$

(c) $8k^3 - 27z^3$

Solution $8k^3 - 27z^3 = (2k)^3 - (3z)^3 = (2k - 3z)(4k^2 + 6kz + 9z^2)$ ✓₈

✓ **Checkpoint 8**

Factor the following.

(a) $a^3 + 1000$

(b) $z^3 - 64$

(c) $1000m^3 - 27z^3$

Substitution and appropriate factoring patterns can sometimes be used to factor higher degree expressions.

Example 11   Factor the following polynomials.

(a) $x^8 + 4x^4 + 3$

Solution   The idea is to make a substitution that reduces the polynomial to a quadratic or cubic that we can deal with. Note that $x^8 = (x^4)^2$. Let $u = x^4$. Then

$$
\begin{aligned}
x^8 + 4x^4 + 3 &= (x^4)^2 + 4x^4 + 3 && \text{Power of a power} \\
&= u^2 + 4u + 3 && \text{Substitute } x^4 = u. \\
&= (u + 3)(u + 1) && \text{Factor} \\
&= (x^4 + 3)(x^4 + 1). && \text{Substitute } u = x^4.
\end{aligned}
$$

(b) $x^4 - y^4$

Solution   Note that $x^4 = (x^2)^2$, and similarly for the y term. Let $u = x^2$ and $v = y^2$. Then

$$
\begin{aligned}
x^4 - y^4 &= (x^2)^2 - (y^2)^2 && \text{Power of a power} \\
&= u^2 - v^2 && \text{Substitute } x^2 = u \text{ and } y^2 = v. \\
&= (u + v)(u - v) && \text{Difference of squares} \\
&= (x^2 + y^2)(x^2 - y^2) && \text{Substitute } u = x^2 \text{ and } v = y^2. \\
&= (x^2 + y^2)(x + y)(x - y). && \text{Difference of squares} \quad ✓₉
\end{aligned}
$$

✓ **Checkpoint 9**

Factor each of the following.

(a) $2x^4 + 5x^2 + 2$

(b) $3x^4 - x^2 - 2$

Once you understand Example 11, you can often factor without making explicit substitutions.

Example 12   Factor $256k^4 - 625m^4$.

Solution   Use the difference of squares twice, as follows:

$$
\begin{aligned}
256k^4 - 625m^4 &= (16k^2)^2 - (25m^2)^2 \\
&= (16k^2 + 25m^2)(16k^2 - 25m^2) \\
&= (16k^2 + 25m^2)(4k + 5m)(4k - 5m). \quad ✓₁₀
\end{aligned}
$$

✓ **Checkpoint 10**

Factor $81x^4 - 16y^4$.

1.3 Exercises

Factor out the greatest common factor in each of the given polynomials. (See Example 1.)

1. $12x^2 - 24x$

2. $5y - 65xy$

3. $r^3 - 5r^2 + r$

4. $t^3 + 3t^2 + 8t$

5. $6z^3 - 12z^2 + 18z$

6. $5x^3 + 55x^2 + 10x$

7. $3(2y - 1)^2 + 7(2y - 1)^3$ **8.** $(3x + 7)^5 - 4(3x + 7)^3$

9. $3(x + 5)^4 + (x + 5)^6$ **10.** $3(x + 6)^2 + 6(x + 6)^4$

Factor the polynomial. (See Examples 2 and 3.)

11. $x^2 + 5x + 4$

12. $u^2 + 7u + 6$

13. $x^2 + 7x + 12$

14. $y^2 + 8y + 12$

15. $x^2 + x - 6$

16. $x^2 + 4x - 5$

17. $x^2 + 2x - 3$

18. $y^2 + y - 12$

19. $x^2 - 3x - 4$

20. $u^2 - 2u - 8$

21. $z^2 - 9z + 14$ **22.** $w^2 - 6w - 16$

23. $z^2 + 10z + 24$ **24.** $r^2 + 16r + 60$

Factor the polynomial. (See Examples 4–6.)

25. $2x^2 - 9x + 4$ **26.** $3w^2 - 8w + 4$

27. $15p^2 - 23p + 4$ **28.** $8x^2 - 14x + 3$

29. $4z^2 - 16z + 15$ **30.** $12y^2 - 29y + 15$

31. $6x^2 - 5x - 4$ **32.** $12z^2 + z - 1$

33. $10y^2 + 21y - 10$ **34.** $15u^2 + 4u - 4$

35. $6x^2 + 5x - 4$ **36.** $12y^2 + 7y - 10$

Factor each polynomial completely. Factor out the greatest common factor as necessary. (See Examples 2–9.)

37. $3a^2 + 2a - 5$ **38.** $6a^2 - 48a - 120$

39. $x^2 - 81$ **40.** $x^2 + 17xy + 72y^2$

41. $9p^2 - 12p + 4$ **42.** $3r^2 - r - 2$

43. $r^2 + 3rt - 10t^2$ **44.** $2a^2 + ab - 6b^2$

45. $m^2 - 8mn + 16n^2$ **46.** $8k^2 - 16k - 10$

47. $4u^2 + 12u + 9$ **48.** $9p^2 - 16$

49. $25p^2 - 10p + 4$ **50.** $10x^2 - 17x + 3$

51. $4r^2 - 9v^2$ **52.** $x^2 + 3xy - 28y^2$

53. $x^2 + 4xy + 4y^2$ **54.** $16u^2 + 12u - 18$

55. $3a^2 - 13a - 30$ **56.** $3k^2 + 2k - 8$

57. $21m^2 + 13mn + 2n^2$ **58.** $81y^2 - 100$

59. $y^2 - 4yz - 21z^2$ **60.** $49a^2 + 9$

61. $121x^2 - 64$ **62.** $4z^2 + 56zy + 196y^2$

Factor each of these polynomials. (See Example 10.)

63. $a^3 - 64$ **64.** $b^3 + 216$

65. $8r^3 - 27s^3$ **66.** $1000p^3 + 27q^3$

67. $64m^3 + 125$ **68.** $216y^3 - 343$

69. $1000y^3 - z^3$ **70.** $125p^3 + 8q^3$

Factor each of these polynomials. (See Examples 11 and 12.)

71. $x^4 + 5x^2 + 6$ **72.** $y^4 + 7y^2 + 10$

73. $b^4 - b^2$ **74.** $z^4 - 3z^2 - 4$

75. $x^4 - x^2 - 12$ **76.** $4x^4 + 27x^2 - 81$

77. $16a^4 - 81b^4$ **78.** $x^6 - y^6$

79. $x^8 + 8x^2$ **80.** $x^9 - 64x^3$

81. When asked to factor $6x^4 - 3x^2 - 3$ completely, a student gave the following result:

$$6x^4 - 3x^2 - 3 = (2x^2 + 1)(3x^2 - 3).$$

Is this answer correct? Explain why.

82. When can the sum of two squares be factored? Give examples.

83. Explain why $(x + 2)^3$ is not the correct factorization of $x^3 + 8$, and give the correct factorization.

84. Describe how factoring and multiplication are related. Give examples.

✓**Checkpoint Answers**

1. (a) $3(4r + 3k)$ (b) $25(3m^2 + 4n^2)$
    (c) $3m^2(2m^2 - 3m + 4)$ (d) $(2k + 1)^3(7 + 8k)$

2. (a) $(r + 2)(r + 5)$ (b) $(x + 3)(x + 1)$
    (c) $(y + 2)(y + 4)$

3. (a) $(x - 3)(x - 1)$ (b) $(2y - 1)(y - 2)$
    (c) $(3z - 2)(2z - 3)$

4. (a) $(r - 7)(r + 2)$ (b) $(3m - 1)(m + 2)$
    (c) $(2p + 5q)(3p - q)$

5. (a) $(3p + 7)(3p - 7)$ (b) Cannot be factored
    (c) $(x + 11)(x - 5)$

6. (a) $(2m + 1)^2$ (b) $(5z - 8t)^2$
    (c) Does not factor

7. (a) $3(2x + 1)(x - 5)$
    (b) $(3r + 2 + t)(3r + 2 - t)$
    (c) $2(3 - 2x - y)(3 + 2x + y)$

8. (a) $(a + 10)(a^2 - 10a + 100)$
    (b) $(z - 4)(z^2 + 4z + 16)$
    (c) $(10m - 3z)(100m^2 + 30mz + 9z^2)$

9. (a) $(2x^2 + 1)(x^2 + 2)$
    (b) $(3x^2 + 2)(x + 1)(x - 1)$

10. $(9x^2 + 4y^2)(3x + 2y)(3x - 2y)$

1.4 Rational Expressions

A **rational expression** is an expression that can be written as the quotient of two polynomials, such as

$$\frac{8}{x - 1}, \quad \frac{3x^2 + 4x}{5x - 6}, \quad \text{and} \quad \frac{2y + 1}{y^4 + 8}.$$

It is sometimes important to know the values of the variable that make the denominator 0 (in which case the quotient is not defined). For example, 1 cannot be used as a replacement for x in the first expression above and $6/5$ cannot be used in the second one, since these values make the respective denominators equal 0. *Throughout this section, we assume that all denominators are nonzero*, which means that some replacement values for the variables may have to be excluded. ☑₁

Simplifying Rational Expressions

A key tool for simplification is the following fact.

> For all expressions P, Q, R, and S, with $Q \neq 0$ and $S \neq 0$,
>
> $$\frac{PS}{QS} = \frac{P}{Q}.$$ Cancellation Property

Example 1 Write each of the following rational expressions in lowest terms (so that the numerator and denominator have no common factor with integer coefficients except 1 or -1).

(a) $\dfrac{12m}{-18}$

Solution Both $12m$ and -18 are divisible by 6. By the cancellation property,

$$\frac{12m}{-18} = \frac{2m \cdot 6}{-3 \cdot 6}$$
$$= \frac{2m}{-3}$$
$$= -\frac{2m}{3}.$$

(b) $\dfrac{8x + 16}{4}$

Solution Factor the numerator and cancel:

$$\frac{8x + 16}{4} = \frac{8(x + 2)}{4} = \frac{4 \cdot 2(x + 2)}{4} = \frac{2(x + 2)}{1} = 2(x + 2).$$

The answer could also be written as $2x + 4$ if desired.

(c) $\dfrac{k^2 + 7k + 12}{k^2 + 2k - 3}$

Solution Factor the numerator and denominator and cancel:

$$\frac{k^2 + 7k + 12}{k^2 + 2k - 3} = \frac{(k + 4)(k + 3)}{(k - 1)(k + 3)} = \frac{k + 4}{k - 1}.$$ ☑₂

Multiplication and Division

The rules for multiplying and dividing rational expressions are the same fraction rules you learned in arithmetic.

✓ **Checkpoint 1**

What value of the variable makes each denominator equal 0?

(a) $\dfrac{5}{x - 3}$

(b) $\dfrac{2x - 3}{4x - 1}$

(c) $\dfrac{x + 2}{x}$

(d) Why do we need to determine these values?

✓ **Checkpoint 2**

Write each of the following in lowest terms.

(a) $\dfrac{12k + 36}{18}$

(b) $\dfrac{15m + 30m^2}{5m}$

(c) $\dfrac{2p^2 + 3p + 1}{p^2 + 3p + 2}$

For all expressions P, Q, R, and S, with $Q \neq 0$ and $S \neq 0$,

$$\frac{P}{Q} \cdot \frac{R}{S} = \frac{PR}{QS}$$ Multiplication Rule

and

$$\frac{P}{Q} \div \frac{R}{S} = \frac{P}{Q} \cdot \frac{S}{R} \qquad (R \neq 0).$$ Division Rule

Example 2

(a) Multiply $\dfrac{2}{3} \cdot \dfrac{y}{5}$.

Solution   Use the multiplication rule. Multiply the numerators and then the denominators:

$$\frac{2}{3} \cdot \frac{y}{5} = \frac{2 \cdot y}{3 \cdot 5} = \frac{2y}{15}.$$

The result, $2y/15$, is in lowest terms.

(b) Multiply $\dfrac{3y + 9}{6} \cdot \dfrac{18}{5y + 15}$.

Solution   Factor where possible:

$$\frac{3y + 9}{6} \cdot \frac{18}{5y + 15} = \frac{3(y + 3)}{6} \cdot \frac{18}{5(y + 3)}$$

$$= \frac{3 \cdot 18(y + 3)}{6 \cdot 5(y + 3)} \qquad \text{Multiply numerators and denominators.}$$

$$= \frac{3 \cdot 6 \cdot 3(y + 3)}{6 \cdot 5(y + 3)} \qquad 18 = 6 \cdot 3$$

$$= \frac{3 \cdot 3}{5} \qquad \text{Write in lowest terms.}$$

$$= \frac{9}{5}.$$

(c) Multiply $\dfrac{m^2 + 5m + 6}{m + 3} \cdot \dfrac{m^2 + m - 6}{m^2 + 3m + 2}$.

Solution   Factor numerators and denominators:

$$\frac{(m + 2)(m + 3)}{m + 3} \cdot \frac{(m - 2)(m + 3)}{(m + 2)(m + 1)} \qquad \text{Factor.}$$

$$= \frac{(m + 2)(m + 3)(m - 2)(m + 3)}{(m + 3)(m + 2)(m + 1)} \qquad \text{Multiply.}$$

$$= \frac{(m - 2)(m + 3)}{m + 1} \qquad \text{Lowest terms}$$

$$= \frac{m^2 + m - 6}{m + 1}. \quad ✓_3$$

✓ **Checkpoint 3**

Multiply.

(a) $\dfrac{3r^2}{5} \cdot \dfrac{20}{9r}$

(b) $\dfrac{y - 4}{y^2 - 2y - 8} \cdot \dfrac{y^2 - 4}{3y}$

Example 3

(a) Divide $\dfrac{8x}{5} \div \dfrac{11x^2}{20}$.

Solution Invert the second expression and multiply (division rule):

$$\frac{8x}{5} \div \frac{11x^2}{20} = \frac{8x}{5} \cdot \frac{20}{11x^2} \qquad \text{Invert and multiply.}$$

$$= \frac{8x \cdot 20}{5 \cdot 11x^2} \qquad \text{Multiply.}$$

$$= \frac{32}{11x}. \qquad \text{Lowest terms}$$

(b) Divide $\dfrac{9p - 36}{12} \div \dfrac{5(p - 4)}{18}$.

Solution We have

$$\frac{9p - 36}{12} \cdot \frac{18}{5(p - 4)} \qquad \text{Invert and multiply.}$$

$$= \frac{9(p - 4)}{12} \cdot \frac{18}{5(p - 4)} \qquad \text{Factor.}$$

$$= \frac{27}{10}. \qquad \text{Cancel, multiply, and write in lowest terms.} \quad \boxed{4}$$

✓ Checkpoint 4

Divide.

(a) $\dfrac{5m}{16} \div \dfrac{m^2}{10}$

(b) $\dfrac{2y - 8}{6} \div \dfrac{5y - 20}{3}$

(c) $\dfrac{m^2 - 2m - 3}{m(m + 1)} \div \dfrac{m + 4}{5m}$

Addition and Subtraction

As you know, when two numerical fractions have the same denominator, they can be added or subtracted. The same rules apply to rational expressions.

For all expressions P, Q, R, with $Q \neq 0$,

$$\frac{P}{Q} + \frac{R}{Q} = \frac{P + R}{Q} \qquad \text{Addition Rule}$$

and

$$\frac{P}{Q} - \frac{R}{Q} = \frac{P - R}{Q}. \qquad \text{Subtraction Rule}$$

Example 4   Add or subtract as indicated.

(a) $\dfrac{4}{5k} + \dfrac{11}{5k}$

Solution Since the denominators are the same, we add the numerators:

$$\frac{4}{5k} + \frac{11}{5k} = \frac{4 + 11}{5k} = \frac{15}{5k} \qquad \text{Addition rule}$$

$$= \frac{3}{k}. \qquad \text{Lowest terms}$$

(b) $\dfrac{2x^2 + 3x + 1}{x^5 + 1} - \dfrac{x^2 - 7x}{x^5 + 1}$

Solution The denominators are the same, so we subtract numerators, paying careful attention to parentheses:

$$\dfrac{2x^2 + 3x + 1}{x^5 + 1} - \dfrac{x^2 - 7x}{x^5 + 1} = \dfrac{(2x^2 + 3x + 1) - (x^2 - 7x)}{x^5 + 1} \qquad \text{Subtraction rule}$$

$$= \dfrac{2x^2 + 3x + 1 - x^2 - (-7x)}{x^5 + 1} \qquad \text{Subtract numerators.}$$

$$= \dfrac{2x^2 + 3x + 1 - x^2 + 7x}{x^5 + 1}$$

$$= \dfrac{x^2 + 10x + 1}{x^5 + 1}. \qquad \text{Simplify the numerator.}$$

When fractions do not have the same denominator, you must first find a common denominator before you can add or subtract. A common denominator is a denominator that has each fraction's denominator as a factor.

Example 5 Add or subtract as indicated.

(a) $\dfrac{7}{p^2} + \dfrac{9}{2p} + \dfrac{1}{3p^2}$

Solution These three denominators are different, so we must find a common denominator that has each of p^2, $2p$, and $3p^2$ as factors. Observe that $6p^2$ satisfies these requirements. Use the cancellation property to rewrite each fraction as one that has $6p^2$ as its denominator and then add them:

$$\dfrac{7}{p^2} + \dfrac{9}{2p} + \dfrac{1}{3p^2} = \dfrac{6 \cdot 7}{6 \cdot p^2} + \dfrac{3p \cdot 9}{3p \cdot 2p} + \dfrac{2 \cdot 1}{2 \cdot 3p^2} \qquad \text{Cancellation property}$$

$$= \dfrac{42}{6p^2} + \dfrac{27p}{6p^2} + \dfrac{2}{6p^2}$$

$$= \dfrac{42 + 27p + 2}{6p^2} \qquad \text{Addition rule}$$

$$= \dfrac{27p + 44}{6p^2}. \qquad \text{Simplify.}$$

(b) $\dfrac{k^2}{k^2 - 1} - \dfrac{2k^2 - k - 3}{k^2 + 3k + 2}$

Solution Factor the denominators to find a common denominator:

$$\dfrac{k^2}{k^2 - 1} - \dfrac{2k^2 - k - 3}{k^2 + 3k + 2} = \dfrac{k^2}{(k + 1)(k - 1)} - \dfrac{2k^2 - k - 3}{(k + 1)(k + 2)}.$$

A common denominator here is $(k + 1)(k - 1)(k + 2)$, because each of the preceding denominators is a factor of this common denominator. Write each fraction with the common denominator:

$$\frac{k^2}{(k+1)(k-1)} - \frac{2k^2 - k - 3}{(k+1)(k+2)}$$

$$= \frac{k^2(k+2)}{(k+1)(k-1)(k+2)} - \frac{(2k^2 - k - 3)(k-1)}{(k+1)(k-1)(k+2)}$$

$$= \frac{k^3 + 2k^2 - (2k^2 - k - 3)(k-1)}{(k+1)(k-1)(k+2)} \qquad \text{Subtract fractions.}$$

$$= \frac{k^3 + 2k^2 - (2k^3 - 3k^2 - 2k + 3)}{(k+1)(k-1)(k+2)} \qquad \text{Multiply } (2k^2 - k - 3)(k - 1).$$

$$= \frac{k^3 + 2k^2 - 2k^3 + 3k^2 + 2k - 3}{(k+1)(k-1)(k+2)} \qquad \text{Polynomial subtraction}$$

$$= \frac{-k^3 + 5k^2 + 2k - 3}{(k+1)(k-1)(k+2)}. \qquad \text{Combine terms.} \quad \checkmark_5$$

✓ **Checkpoint 5**

Add or subtract.

(a) $\dfrac{3}{4r} + \dfrac{8}{3r}$

(b) $\dfrac{1}{m-2} - \dfrac{3}{2(m-2)}$

(c) $\dfrac{p+1}{p^2 - p} - \dfrac{p^2 - 1}{p^2 + p - 2}$

Complex Fractions

Any quotient of rational expressions is called a **complex fraction.** Complex fractions are simplified as demonstrated in Example 6.

Example 6 Simplify the complex fraction

$$\frac{6 - \dfrac{5}{k}}{1 + \dfrac{5}{k}}.$$

Solution Multiply both numerator and denominator by the common denominator k:

$$\frac{6 - \dfrac{5}{k}}{1 + \dfrac{5}{k}} = \frac{k\left(6 - \dfrac{5}{k}\right)}{k\left(1 + \dfrac{5}{k}\right)} \qquad \text{Multiply by } \dfrac{k}{k}.$$

$$= \frac{6k - k\left(\dfrac{5}{k}\right)}{k + k\left(\dfrac{5}{k}\right)} \qquad \text{Distributive property}$$

$$= \frac{6k - 5}{k + 5}. \qquad \text{Simplify.}$$

1.4 Exercises

Write each of the given expressions in lowest terms. Factor as necessary. (See Example 1.)

1. $\dfrac{8x^2}{56x}$

2. $\dfrac{27m}{81m^3}$

3. $\dfrac{25p^2}{35p^3}$

4. $\dfrac{18y^4}{24y^2}$

5. $\dfrac{5m + 15}{4m + 12}$

6. $\dfrac{10z + 5}{20z + 10}$

7. $\dfrac{4(w - 3)}{(w - 3)(w + 6)}$

8. $\dfrac{-6(x + 2)}{(x + 4)(x + 2)}$

9. $\dfrac{3y^2 - 12y}{9y^3}$

10. $\dfrac{15k^2 + 45k}{9k^2}$

11. $\dfrac{m^2 - 4m + 4}{m^2 + m - 6}$

12. $\dfrac{r^2 - r - 6}{r^2 + r - 12}$

13. $\dfrac{x^2 + 2x - 3}{x^2 - 1}$

14. $\dfrac{z^2 + 4z + 4}{z^2 - 4}$

Multiply or divide as indicated in each of the exercises. Write all answers in lowest terms. (See Examples 2 and 3.)

15. $\dfrac{3a^2}{64} \cdot \dfrac{8}{2a^3}$

16. $\dfrac{2u^2}{8u^4} \cdot \dfrac{10u^3}{9u}$

17. $\dfrac{7x}{11} \div \dfrac{14x^3}{66y}$

18. $\dfrac{6x^2y}{2x} \div \dfrac{21xy}{y}$

19. $\dfrac{2a + b}{3c} \cdot \dfrac{15}{4(2a + b)}$

20. $\dfrac{4(x + 2)}{w} \cdot \dfrac{3w^2}{8(x + 2)}$

21. $\dfrac{15p - 3}{6} \div \dfrac{10p - 2}{3}$

22. $\dfrac{2k + 8}{6} \div \dfrac{3k + 12}{3}$

23. $\dfrac{9y - 18}{6y + 12} \cdot \dfrac{3y + 6}{15y - 30}$

24. $\dfrac{12r + 24}{36r - 36} \div \dfrac{6r + 12}{8r - 8}$

25. $\dfrac{4a + 12}{2a - 10} \div \dfrac{a^2 - 9}{a^2 - a - 20}$

26. $\dfrac{6r - 18}{9r^2 + 6r - 24} \cdot \dfrac{12r - 16}{4r - 12}$

27. $\dfrac{k^2 - k - 6}{k^2 + k - 12} \cdot \dfrac{k^2 + 3k - 4}{k^2 + 2k - 3}$

28. $\dfrac{n^2 - n - 6}{n^2 - 2n - 8} \div \dfrac{n^2 - 9}{n^2 + 7n + 12}$

29. In your own words, explain how to find the least common denominator of two fractions.

30. Describe the steps required to add three rational expressions. You may use an example to illustrate.

Add or subtract as indicated in each of the following. Write all answers in lowest terms. (See Example 4.)

31. $\dfrac{2}{7z} - \dfrac{1}{5z}$

32. $\dfrac{4}{3z} - \dfrac{5}{4z}$

33. $\dfrac{r + 2}{3} - \dfrac{r - 2}{3}$

34. $\dfrac{3y - 1}{8} - \dfrac{3y + 1}{8}$

35. $\dfrac{4}{x} + \dfrac{1}{5}$

36. $\dfrac{6}{r} - \dfrac{3}{4}$

37. $\dfrac{1}{m - 1} + \dfrac{2}{m}$

38. $\dfrac{8}{y + 2} - \dfrac{3}{y}$

39. $\dfrac{7}{b + 2} + \dfrac{2}{5(b + 2)}$

40. $\dfrac{4}{3(k + 1)} + \dfrac{3}{k + 1}$

41. $\dfrac{2}{5(k - 2)} + \dfrac{5}{4(k - 2)}$

42. $\dfrac{11}{3(p + 4)} - \dfrac{5}{6(p + 4)}$

43. $\dfrac{2}{x^2 - 4x + 3} + \dfrac{5}{x^2 - x - 6}$

44. $\dfrac{3}{m^2 - 3m - 10} + \dfrac{7}{m^2 - m - 20}$

45. $\dfrac{2y}{y^2 + 7y + 12} - \dfrac{y}{y^2 + 5y + 6}$

46. $\dfrac{-r}{r^2 - 10r + 16} - \dfrac{3r}{r^2 + 2r - 8}$

In each of the exercises in the next set, simplify the complex fraction. (See Example 6.)

47. $\dfrac{1 + \dfrac{1}{x}}{1 - \dfrac{1}{x}}$

48. $\dfrac{2 - \dfrac{2}{y}}{2 + \dfrac{2}{y}}$

49. $\dfrac{\dfrac{1}{x + h} - \dfrac{1}{x}}{h}$

50. $\dfrac{\dfrac{1}{(x + h)^2} - \dfrac{1}{x^2}}{h}$

Work these problems.

Natural Science *Each figure in the following exercises is a dartboard. The probability that a dart which hits the board lands in the shaded area is the fraction*

$$\frac{\text{area of the shaded region}}{\text{area of the dartboard}} .$$

(a) *Express the probability as a rational expression in x. (Hint: Area formulas are given in Appendix B.)*

(b) *Then reduce the expression to lowest terms.*

51.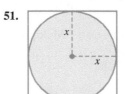

52.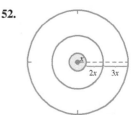

53.
54.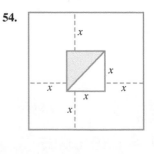

Business *In Example 11 of Section 1.2, we saw that the cost C of producing x thousand calculators is given by*

$$C = -7.2x^2 + 6995x + 230{,}000 \quad (x \le 150).$$

55. Write a rational expression that gives the average cost per calculator when *x* thousand are produced. (*Hint:* The average cost is the total cost *C* divided by the number of calculators produced.)

56. Find the average cost per calculator for each of these production levels: 20,000, 50,000, and 125,000.

Business *The cost (in millions of dollars) for a 30-second ad during the TV broadcast of the Superbowl can be approximated by*

$$\frac{.314x^2 - 1.399x + 15.0}{x + 1}$$

where x = 6 corresponds to the year 2006. (Data from: forbes.com and espn.com.)

57. How much did an ad cost in 2010?

58. How much did an ad cost in 2012?

59. If this trend continues, will the cost of an ad reach $5 million by 2018?

60. If this trend continues, when will the cost of an ad reach $6 million?

Health Economics *The average company cost per hour of an employee's health insurance in year x is approximated by*

$$\frac{.265x^2 + 1.47x + 3.63}{x + 2},$$

where x = 0 corresponds to the year 2000. (Data from: U.S. Bureau of Labor Statistics.)

61. What is the hourly health insurance cost in 2011?

62. What is the hourly health insurance cost in 2012?

63. Assuming that this model remains accurate and that an employee works 2100 hours per year, what is the annual company cost of her health care insurance in 2015?

64. Will annual costs reach $10,000 by 2020?

✓ **Checkpoint Answers**

1. (a) 3   **(b)** 1/4   **(c)** 0
    (d) Because division by 0 is undefined

2. (a) $\dfrac{2(k + 3)}{3}$ or $\dfrac{2k + 6}{3}$

    (b) $3(1 + 2m)$ or $3 + 6m$ **(c)** $\dfrac{2p + 1}{p + 2}$

3. (a) $\dfrac{4r}{3}$ **(b)** $\dfrac{y - 2}{3y}$

4. (a) $\dfrac{25}{8m}$ **(b)** $\dfrac{1}{5}$ **(c)** $\dfrac{5(m - 3)}{m + 4}$

5. (a) $\dfrac{41}{12r}$ **(b)** $\dfrac{-1}{2(m - 2)}$ **(c)** $\dfrac{-p^3 + p^2 + 4p + 2}{p(p - 1)(p + 2)}$

1.5 Exponents and Radicals

Exponents were introduced in Section 1.2. In this section, the definition of exponents will be extended to include negative exponents and rational-number exponents such as $1/2$ and $7/3$.

Integer Exponents

Positive-integer and zero exponents were defined in Section 1.2, where we noted that

$$a^m \cdot a^n = a^{m+n}$$

for nonnegative integers m and n. Now we develop an analogous property for quotients. By definition,

$$\frac{6^5}{6^2} = \frac{6 \cdot 6 \cdot 6 \cdot 6 \cdot 6}{6 \cdot 6} = 6 \cdot 6 \cdot 6 = 6^3.$$

Because there are 5 factors of 6 in the numerator and 2 factors of 6 in the denominator, the quotient has $5 - 2 = 3$ factors of 6. In general, we can make the following statement, which applies to any real number a and nonnegative integers m and n with $m > n$.

Division with Exponents

To divide a^m by a^n, *subtract* the exponents:

$$\frac{a^m}{a^n} = a^{m-n}.$$

Example 1   Compute each of the following.

(a) $\dfrac{5^7}{5^4} = 5^{7-4} = 5^3$.

(b) $\dfrac{(-8)^{10}}{(-8)^5} = (-8)^{10-5} = (-8)^5$.

(c) $\dfrac{(3c)^9}{(3c)^3} = (3c)^{9-3} = (3c)^6$.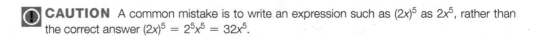

✓**Checkpoint 1**

Evaluate each of the following.

(a) $\dfrac{2^{14}}{2^5}$

(b) $\dfrac{(-5)^9}{(-5)^5}$

(c) $\dfrac{(xy)^{17}}{(xy)^{12}}$

When an exponent applies to the product of two numbers, such as $(7 \cdot 19)^3$, use the definitions carefully. For instance,

$$(7 \cdot 19)^3 = (7 \cdot 19)(7 \cdot 19)(7 \cdot 19) = 7 \cdot 7 \cdot 7 \cdot 19 \cdot 19 \cdot 19 = 7^3 \cdot 19^3.$$

In other words, $(7 \cdot 19)^3 = 7^3 \cdot 19^3$. This is an example of the following fact, which applies to any real numbers a and b and any nonnegative-integer exponent n.

Product to a Power

To find $(ab)^n$, apply the exponent to *every* term inside the parentheses:

$$(ab)^n = a^n b^n.$$

⊘**CAUTION** A common mistake is to write an expression such as $(2x)^5$ as $2x^5$, rather than the correct answer $(2x)^5 = 2^5 x^5 = 32x^5$.

Analogous conclusions are valid for quotients (where a and b are any real numbers with $b \neq 0$ and n is a nonnegative-integer exponent).

Quotient to a Power

To find $\left(\dfrac{a}{b}\right)^n$, apply the exponent to both numerator and denominator:

$$\left(\frac{a}{b}\right)^n = \frac{a^n}{b^n}.$$

Example 2   Compute each of the following.

(a) $(5y)^3 = 5^3 y^3 = 125y^3$ Product to a power

(b) $(c^2 d^3)^4 = (c^2)^4 (d^3)^4$ Product to a power

$\qquad\qquad = c^8 d^{12}$ Power of a power

(c) $\left(\dfrac{x}{2}\right)^6 = \dfrac{x^6}{2^6} = \dfrac{x^6}{64}$ Quotient to a power

(d) $\left(\dfrac{a^4}{b^3}\right)^3 = \dfrac{(a^4)^3}{(b^3)^3}$ Quotient to a power

$\qquad\qquad = \dfrac{a^{12}}{b^9}$ Power of a power

(e) $\left(\dfrac{(rs)^3}{r^4}\right)^2$

Solution   Use several of the preceding properties in succession:

$$\left(\dfrac{(rs)^3}{r^4}\right)^2 = \left(\dfrac{r^3 s^3}{r^4}\right)^2 \qquad \text{Product to a power in numerator}$$

$$= \left(\dfrac{s^3}{r}\right)^2 \qquad \text{Cancel.}$$

$$= \dfrac{(s^3)^2}{r^2} \qquad \text{Quotient to a power}$$

$$= \dfrac{s^6}{r^2}. \qquad \text{Power of a power in numerator}$$

As is often the case, there is another way to reach the last expression. You should be able to supply the reasons for each of the following steps:

$$\left(\dfrac{(rs)^3}{r^4}\right)^2 = \dfrac{[(rs)^3]^2}{(r^4)^2} = \dfrac{(rs)^6}{r^8} = \dfrac{r^6 s^6}{r^8} = \dfrac{s^6}{r^2}. \quad \checkmark_2$$

Negative Exponents

The next step is to define negative-integer exponents. If they are to be defined in such a way that the quotient rule for exponents remains valid, then we must have, for example,

$$\dfrac{3^2}{3^4} = 3^{2-4} = 3^{-2}.$$

However,

$$\dfrac{3^2}{3^4} = \dfrac{3 \cdot 3}{3 \cdot 3 \cdot 3 \cdot 3} = \dfrac{1}{3^2},$$

which suggests that 3^{-2} should be defined to be $1/3^2$. Thus, we have the following definition of a negative exponent.

> ## Negative Exponent
>
> If n is a natural number, and if $a \neq 0$, then
>
> $$a^{-n} = \dfrac{1}{a^n}.$$

✓ Checkpoint 2

Compute each of the following.

(a) $(3x)^4$

(b) $(r^2 s^5)^6$

(c) $\left(\dfrac{2}{z}\right)^5$

(d) $\left(\dfrac{3a^5}{(ab)^3}\right)^2$

✓ Checkpoint 3

Evaluate the following.

(a) 6^{-2}

(b) -6^{-3}

(c) -3^{-4}

(d) $\left(\dfrac{5}{8}\right)^{-1}$

Example 3   Evaluate the following.

(a) $3^{-2} = \dfrac{1}{3^2} = \dfrac{1}{9}.$

(b) $5^{-4} = \dfrac{1}{5^4} = \dfrac{1}{625}.$

(c) $x^{-1} = \dfrac{1}{x^1} = \dfrac{1}{x}.$

(d) $-4^{-2} = -\dfrac{1}{4^2} = -\dfrac{1}{16}.$

(e) $\left(\dfrac{3}{4}\right)^{-1} = \dfrac{1}{\left(\dfrac{3}{4}\right)^1} = \dfrac{1}{\dfrac{3}{4}} = \dfrac{4}{3}. \quad \checkmark_3$

There is a useful property that makes it easy to raise a fraction to a negative exponent. Consider, for example,

$$\left(\frac{2}{3}\right)^{-4} = \frac{1}{\left(\frac{2}{3}\right)^4} = \frac{1}{\left(\frac{2^4}{3^4}\right)} = 1 \cdot \frac{3^4}{2^4} = \left(\frac{3}{2}\right)^4.$$

This example is easily generalized to the following property (in which a/b is a nonzero fraction and n a positive integer).

Inversion Property

$$\left(\frac{a}{b}\right)^{-n} = \left(\frac{b}{a}\right)^{n}.$$

Example 4   Use the inversion property to compute each of the following.

(a) $\left(\frac{2}{5}\right)^{-3} = \left(\frac{5}{2}\right)^3 = \frac{5^3}{2^3} = \frac{125}{8}.$

(b) $\left(\frac{3}{x}\right)^{-5} = \left(\frac{x}{3}\right)^5 = \frac{x^5}{3^5} = \frac{x^5}{243}.$ ✔4

✓ Checkpoint 4

Compute each of the following.

(a) $\left(\frac{5}{8}\right)^{-1}$

(b) $\left(\frac{1}{2}\right)^{-5}$

(c) $\left(\frac{a^2}{b}\right)^{-3}$

When keying in negative exponents on a calculator, be sure to use the negation key (labeled $(-)$ or $+/-$), not the subtraction key. Calculators normally display answers as decimals, as shown in Figure 1.6. Some graphing calculators have a FRAC key that converts these decimals to fractions, as shown in Figure 1.7.

⟋ TECHNOLOGY TIP

The FRAC key is in the MATH menu of TI graphing calculators. A FRAC program for other graphing calculators is in the Program Appendix. Fractions can be displayed on some graphing calculators by changing the number display format (in the MODES menu) to "fraction" or "exact."

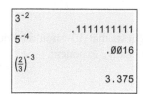

Figure 1.6

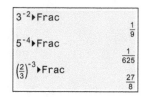

Figure 1.7

Roots and Rational Exponents

There are two numbers whose square is 16: 4 and -4. As we saw in Section 1.1, the positive one, 4, is called the *square root* (or second root) of 16. Similarly, there are two numbers whose fourth power is 16: 2 and -2. We call 2 the **fourth root** of 16. This suggests the following generalization.

> If n is even, the **nth root of a** is the positive real number whose nth power is a.

All nonnegative numbers have nth roots for every natural number n, but *no negative number has a real, even nth root.* For example, there is no real number whose square is -16, so -16 has no square root.

We say that the **cube root** (or third root) of 8 is 2 because $2^3 = 8$. Similarly, since $(-2)^3 = -8$, we say that -2 is the cube root of -8. Again, we can make the following generalization.

If n is odd, the **nth root of a** is the real number whose nth power is a.

Every real number has an nth root for every *odd* natural number n.

We can now define rational exponents. If they are to have the same properties as integer exponents, we want $a^{1/2}$ to be a number such that

$$(a^{1/2})^2 = a^{1/2} \cdot a^{1/2} = a^{1/2+1/2} = a^1 = a.$$

Thus, $a^{1/2}$ should be a number whose square is a, and it is reasonable to *define* $a^{1/2}$ to be the square root of a (if exists). Similarly, $a^{1/3}$ is defined to be the cube root of a, and we have the following definition.

If a is a real number and n is a positive integer, then

$a^{1/n}$ is defined to be the nth root of a (if it exists).

Example 5 Examine the reasoning used to evaluate the following roots.

(a) $36^{1/2} = 6$ because $6^2 = 36$.

(b) $100^{1/2} = 10$ because $10^2 = 100$.

(c) $-(225^{1/2}) = -15$ because $15^2 = 225$.

(d) $625^{1/4} = 5$ because $5^4 = 625$.

(e) $(-1296)^{1/4}$ is not a real number.

(f) $-1296^{1/4} = -6$ because $6^4 = 1296$.

(g) $(-27)^{1/3} = -3$ because $(-3)^3 = -27$.

(h) $-32^{1/5} = -2$ because $2^5 = 32$. ✓5

✓ **Checkpoint 5**

Evaluate the following.

(a) $16^{1/2}$

(b) $16^{1/4}$

(c) $-256^{1/2}$

(d) $(-256)^{1/2}$

(e) $-8^{1/3}$

(f) $243^{1/5}$

A calculator can be used to evaluate expressions with fractional exponents. Whenever it is easy to do so, enter the fractional exponents in their equivalent decimal form. For instance, to find $625^{1/4}$, enter $625^{.25}$ into the calculator. When the decimal equivalent of a fraction is an infinitely repeating decimal, however, it is best to enter the fractional exponent directly. If you use a shortened decimal approximation (such as .333 for $1/3$), you will not get the correct answers. Compare the incorrect answers in Figure 1.9 with the correct ones in Figure 1.8.

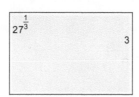

Figure 1.8   Figure 1.9

For other rational exponents, the symbol $a^{m/n}$ should be defined so that the properties for exponents still hold. For example, by the product property, we want

$$(a^{1/3})^2 = a^{1/3} \cdot a^{1/3} = a^{1/3+1/3} = a^{2/3}.$$

This result suggests the following definition.

For all integers m and all positive integers n, and for all real numbers a for which $a^{1/n}$ is a real number,

$$a^{m/n} = (a^{1/n})^m.$$

Example 6 Verify each of the following calculations.

(a) $27^{2/3} = (27^{1/3})^2 = 3^2 = 9.$

(b) $32^{2/5} = (32^{1/5})^2 = 2^2 = 4.$

(c) $64^{4/3} = (64^{1/3})^4 = 4^4 = 256.$

(d) $25^{3/2} = (25^{1/2})^3 = 5^3 = 125.$ ✓₆

✓ Checkpoint 6

Evaluate the following.

(a) $16^{3/4}$

(b) $25^{5/2}$

(c) $32^{7/5}$

(d) $100^{3/2}$

⊘ CAUTION When the base is negative, as in $(-8)^{2/3}$, some calculators produce an error message. On such calculators, you should first compute $(-8)^{1/3}$ and then square the result; that is, compute $[(-8)^{1/3}]^2$.

Since every terminating decimal is a rational number, decimal exponents now have a meaning. For instance, $5.24 = \frac{524}{100}$, so $3^{5.24} = 3^{524/100}$, which is easily approximated by a calculator (Figure 1.10).

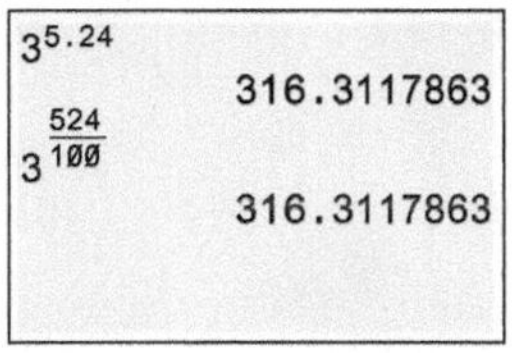

Rational exponents were defined so that one of the familiar properties of exponents remains valid. In fact, it can be proved that *all* of the rules developed earlier for integer exponents are valid for rational exponents. The following box summarizes these rules, which are illustrated in Examples 7–9.

```
3^5.24
           316.3117863
 524
3 100
           316.3117863
```

Figure 1.10

Properties of Exponents

For any rational numbers m and n, and for any real numbers a and b for which the following exist,

(a) $a^m \cdot a^n = a^{m+n}$ Product property

(b) $\dfrac{a^m}{a^n} = a^{m-n}$ Quotient property

(c) $(a^m)^n = a^{mn}$ Power of a power

(d) $(ab)^m = a^m \cdot b^m$ Product to a power

(e) $\left(\dfrac{a}{b}\right)^m = \dfrac{a^m}{b^m}$ Quotient to a power

(f) $a^0 = 1$ Zero exponent

(g) $a^{-n} = \dfrac{1}{a^n}$ Negative exponent

(h) $\left(\dfrac{a}{b}\right)^{-n} = \left(\dfrac{b}{a}\right)^n.$ Inversion property

The power-of-a-power property provides another way to compute $a^{m/n}$ (when it exists):

$$a^{m/n} = a^{m(1/n)} = (a^m)^{1/n}. \tag{1}$$

For example, we can now find $4^{3/2}$ in two ways:

$$4^{3/2} = (4^{1/2})^3 = 2^3 = 8 \quad \text{or} \quad 4^{3/2} = (4^3)^{1/2} = 64^{1/2} = 8.$$

Definition of $a^{m/n}$ Statement (1)

Example 7   Simplify each of the following expressions.

(a) $7^{-4} \cdot 7^6 = 7^{-4+6} = 7^2 = 49.$ Product property

(b) $5x^{2/3} \cdot 2x^{1/4} = 10x^{2/3}x^{1/4}$

$$= 10x^{2/3+1/4} \qquad \text{Product property}$$

$$= 10x^{11/12}. \qquad \frac{2}{3} + \frac{1}{4} = \frac{8}{12} + \frac{3}{12} = \frac{11}{12}$$

(c) $\dfrac{9^{14}}{9^{-6}} = 9^{14-(-6)} = 9^{20}.$ Quotient property

(d) $\dfrac{c^5}{2c^{4/3}} = \dfrac{1}{2} \cdot \dfrac{c^5}{c^{4/3}}$

$$= \frac{1}{2}c^{5-4/3} \qquad \text{Quotient property}$$

$$= \frac{1}{2}c^{11/3} = \frac{c^{11/3}}{2}. \qquad 5 - \frac{4}{3} = \frac{15}{3} - \frac{4}{3} = \frac{11}{3}$$

(e) $\dfrac{27^{1/3} \cdot 27^{5/3}}{27^3} = \dfrac{27^{1/3+5/3}}{27^3}$ Product property

$$= \frac{27^2}{27^3} = 27^{2-3} \qquad \text{Quotient property}$$

$$= 27^{-1} = \frac{1}{27}. \qquad \text{Definition of negative exponent} \quad \checkmark 7$$

You can use a calculator to check numerical computations, such as those in Example 7, by computing the left and right sides separately and confirming that the answers are the same in each case. Figure 1.11 shows this technique for part (e) of Example 7.

Example 8   Perform the indicated operations.

(a) $(2^{-3})^{-4/7} = 2^{(-3)(-4/7)} = 2^{12/7}.$ Power of a power

(b) $\left(\dfrac{3m^{5/6}}{y^{3/4}}\right)^2 = \dfrac{(3m^{5/6})^2}{(y^{3/4})^2}$ Quotient to a power

$$= \frac{3^2(m^{5/6})^2}{(y^{3/4})^2} \qquad \text{Product to a power}$$

$$= \frac{9m^{(5/6)2}}{y^{(3/4)2}} \qquad \text{Power of a power}$$

$$= \frac{9m^{5/3}}{y^{3/2}}. \qquad \frac{5}{6} \cdot 2 = \frac{10}{6} = \frac{5}{3} \text{ and } \frac{3}{4} \cdot 2 = \frac{3}{2}$$

(c) $m^{2/3}(m^{7/3} + 2m^{1/3}) = m^{2/3}m^{7/3} + m^{2/3}2m^{1/3}$ Distributive property

$$= m^{2/3+7/3} + 2m^{2/3+1/3} = m^3 + 2m. \qquad \text{Product rule} \quad \checkmark 8$$

✓ Checkpoint 7

Simplify each of the following.

(a) $9^7 \cdot 9^{-5}$

(b) $3x^{1/4} \cdot 5x^{5/4}$

(c) $\dfrac{8^7}{8^{-3}}$

(d) $\dfrac{5^{2/3} \cdot 5^{-4/3}}{5^2}$

$$\begin{array}{l} 27^{\frac{1}{3}} * 27^{\frac{5}{3}} \\ \overline{\quad\quad 27^3} \\ \qquad\qquad\qquad .037037037 \\ \frac{1}{27} \\ \qquad\qquad\qquad .037037037 \end{array}$$

Figure 1.11

✓ Checkpoint 8

Simplify each of the following.

(a) $(7^{-4})^{-2} \cdot (7^4)^{-2}$

(b) $\dfrac{c^4 c^{-1/2}}{c^{3/2}d^{1/2}}$

(c) $a^{5/8}(2a^{3/8} + a^{-1/8})$

Example 9   Simplify each expression in parts (a)–(c). Give answers with only positive exponents.

(a) $\dfrac{(m^3)^{-2}}{m^4} = \dfrac{m^{-6}}{m^4} = m^{-6-4} = m^{-10} = \dfrac{1}{m^{10}}.$

(b) $6y^{2/3} \cdot 2y^{-1/2} = 12y^{2/3-1/2} = 12y^{1/6}.$

(c) $\dfrac{x^{1/2}(x-2)^{-3}}{5(x-2)} = \dfrac{x^{1/2}}{5} \cdot \dfrac{(x-2)^{-3}}{x-2} = \dfrac{x^{1/2}}{5} \cdot (x-2)^{-3-1}$

$= \dfrac{x^{1/2}}{5} \cdot \dfrac{1}{(x-2)^4} = \dfrac{x^{1/2}}{5(x-2)^4}.$

(d) Write $a^{-1} + b^{-1}$ as a single quotient.

Solution   Be careful here. $a^{-1} + b^{-1}$ does *not* equal $(a+b)^{-1}$; the exponent properties deal only with products and quotients, not with sums. However, using the definition of negative exponents and addition of fractions, we have

$$a^{-1} + b^{-1} = \frac{1}{a} + \frac{1}{b} = \frac{b+a}{ab}. \quad \boxed{9}$$

We can use some functions of the form ax^b where both a and b are constants and b is also an exponent.

Example 10   **Social Science**   The total number of students (in millions) attending institutes of higher education can be approximated by the function

$$5.8x^{0.357} \quad (x \geq 10),$$

where $x = 10$ corresponds to the year 1990. Find the approximate number of students enrolled in higher education in 2012. (Data from: U.S. National Center for Education Statistics.)

Solution   Since 2012 is 22 years after 1990 and $x = 10$ corresponds to 1990, we have that $x = 22 + 10 = 32$ corresponds to 2012. We then obtain

$$5.8(32)^{0.357} \approx 20.0 \text{ million students.} \quad \boxed{10}$$

Radicals

Earlier, we denoted the nth root of a as $a^{1/n}$. An alternative notation for nth roots uses the radical symbol $\sqrt[n]{\ }$.

> If n is an even natural number and $a \geq 0$, or if n is an odd natural number,
>
> $$\sqrt[n]{a} = a^{1/n}.$$

In the radical expression $\sqrt[n]{a}$, a is called the *radicand* and n is called the *index*. When $n = 2$, the familiar square-root symbol $\sqrt{a}$ is used instead of $\sqrt[2]{a}$.

Example 11   Simplify the following radicals.

(a) $\sqrt[4]{16} = 16^{1/4} = 2.$

(b) $\sqrt[5]{-32} = -2.$

(c) $\sqrt[3]{1000} = 10.$

(d) $\sqrt[6]{\dfrac{64}{729}} = \left(\dfrac{64}{729}\right)^{1/6} = \dfrac{64^{1/6}}{729^{1/6}} = \dfrac{2}{3}. \quad \boxed{11}$

✓**Checkpoint 9**

Simplify the given expressions. Give answers with only positive exponents.

(a) $(3x^{2/3})(2x^{-1})(y^{-1/3})^2$

(b) $\dfrac{(t^{-1})^2}{t^{-5}}$

(c) $\left(\dfrac{2k^{1/3}}{p^{5/4}}\right)^2 \cdot \left(\dfrac{4k^{-2}}{p^5}\right)^{3/2}$

(d) $x^{-1} - y^{-2}$

✓**Checkpoint 10**

Assuming the model from Example 10 remains accurate, find the number of students for 2015.

✓**Checkpoint 11**

Simplify.

(a) $\sqrt[3]{27}$

(b) $\sqrt[4]{625}$

(c) $\sqrt[6]{64}$

(d) $\sqrt[3]{\dfrac{64}{125}}$

Recall that $a^{m/n} = (a^{1/n})^m$ by definition and $a^{m/n} = (a^m)^{1/n}$ by statement (**1**) on page 36 (provided that all terms are defined). We translate these facts into radical notation as follows.

> For all rational numbers m/n and all real numbers a for which $\sqrt[n]{a}$ exists,
> $$a^{m/n} = (\sqrt[n]{a})^m \quad \text{or} \quad a^{m/n} = \sqrt[n]{a^m}.$$

Notice that $\sqrt[n]{x^n}$ cannot be written simply as x when n is even. For example, if $x = -5$, then

$$\sqrt{x^2} = \sqrt{(-5)^2} = \sqrt{25} = 5 \neq x.$$

However, $|-5| = 5$, so that $\sqrt{x^2} = |x|$ when x is -5. This relationship is true in general.

> For any real number a and any natural number n,
> $$\sqrt[n]{a^n} = |a| \quad \text{if } n \text{ is even}$$
> and
> $$\sqrt[n]{a^n} = a \quad \text{if } n \text{ is odd}.$$

To avoid the difficulty that $\sqrt[n]{a^n}$ is not necessarily equal to a, we shall assume that all variables in radicands represent only nonnegative numbers, as they usually do in applications.

The properties of exponents can be written with radicals as follows.

> For all real numbers a and b, and for positive integers n for which all indicated roots exist,
> (a) $\sqrt[n]{a} \cdot \sqrt[n]{b} = \sqrt[n]{ab}$ and
> (b) $\dfrac{\sqrt[n]{a}}{\sqrt[n]{b}} = \sqrt[n]{\dfrac{a}{b}}$ $(b \neq 0)$.

Example 12 Simplify the following expressions.

(a) $\sqrt{6} \cdot \sqrt{54} = \sqrt{6 \cdot 54} = \sqrt{324} = 18.$

Alternatively, simplify $\sqrt{54}$ first:
$$\sqrt{6} \cdot \sqrt{54} = \sqrt{6} \cdot \sqrt{9 \cdot 6}$$
$$= \sqrt{6} \cdot 3\sqrt{6} = 3 \cdot 6 = 18.$$

(b) $\sqrt{\dfrac{7}{64}} = \dfrac{\sqrt{7}}{\sqrt{64}} = \dfrac{\sqrt{7}}{8}.$

(c) $\sqrt{75} - \sqrt{12}.$

Solution Note that $12 = 4 \cdot 3$ and that 4 is a perfect square. Similarly, $75 = 25 \cdot 3$ and 25 is a perfect square. Consequently,

$$\sqrt{75} - \sqrt{12} = \sqrt{25 \cdot 3} - \sqrt{4 \cdot 3} \quad \text{Factor.}$$
$$= \sqrt{25}\sqrt{3} - \sqrt{4}\sqrt{3} \quad \text{Property (a)}$$
$$= 5\sqrt{3} - 2\sqrt{3} = 3\sqrt{3}. \quad \text{Simplify.} \quad \boxed{12}$$

✓**Checkpoint 12**

Simplify.
(a) $\sqrt{3} \cdot \sqrt{27}$
(b) $\sqrt{\dfrac{3}{49}}$
(c) $\sqrt{50} + \sqrt{72}$

⚠ **CAUTION** When a and b are nonzero real numbers,

$$\sqrt[n]{a + b} \text{ is NOT equal to } \sqrt[n]{a} + \sqrt[n]{b}.$$

For example,

$$\sqrt{9 + 16} = \sqrt{25} = 5, \text{ but } \sqrt{9} + \sqrt{16} = 3 + 4 = 7,$$

so $\sqrt{9 + 16} \neq \sqrt{9} + \sqrt{16}$.

Multiplying radical expressions is much like multiplying polynomials.

Example 13   Perform the following multiplications.

(a) $(\sqrt{2} + 3)(\sqrt{8} - 5) = \sqrt{2}(\sqrt{8}) - \sqrt{2}(5) + 3\sqrt{8} - 3(5)$ FOIL
$$= \sqrt{16} - 5\sqrt{2} + 3(2\sqrt{2}) - 15$$
$$= 4 - 5\sqrt{2} + 6\sqrt{2} - 15$$
$$= -11 + \sqrt{2}.$$

(b) $(\sqrt{7} - \sqrt{10})(\sqrt{7} + \sqrt{10}) = (\sqrt{7})^2 - (\sqrt{10})^2$
$$= 7 - 10 = -3. \enspace ✓_{13}$$

✓ **Checkpoint 13**

Multiply.

(a) $(\sqrt{5} - \sqrt{2})(3 + \sqrt{2})$

(b) $(\sqrt{3} + \sqrt{7})(\sqrt{3} - \sqrt{7})$

Rationalizing Denominators and Numerators

Before the invention of calculators, it was customary to **rationalize the denominators** of fractions (that is, write equivalent fractions with no radicals in the denominator), because this made many computations easier. Although there is no longer a computational reason to do so, rationalization of denominators (and sometimes numerators) is still used today to simplify expressions and to derive useful formulas.

Example 14   Rationalize each denominator.

(a) $\dfrac{4}{\sqrt{3}}$

Solution   The key is to multiply by 1, with 1 written as a radical fraction:

$$\frac{4}{\sqrt{3}} = \frac{4}{\sqrt{3}} \cdot 1 = \frac{4}{\sqrt{3}} \cdot \frac{\sqrt{3}}{\sqrt{3}} = \frac{4\sqrt{3}}{3}.$$

(b) $\dfrac{1}{3 - \sqrt{2}}$

Solution   The same technique works here, using $1 = \dfrac{3 + \sqrt{2}}{3 + \sqrt{2}}$:

$$\frac{1}{3 - \sqrt{2}} = \frac{1}{3 - \sqrt{2}} \cdot 1 = \frac{1}{3 - \sqrt{2}} \cdot \frac{3 + \sqrt{2}}{3 + \sqrt{2}} = \frac{3 + \sqrt{2}}{(3 - \sqrt{2})(3 + \sqrt{2})}$$

$$= \frac{3 + \sqrt{2}}{9 - 2} = \frac{3 + \sqrt{2}}{7}. \enspace ✓_{14}$$

✓ **Checkpoint 14**

Rationalize the denominator.

(a) $\dfrac{2}{\sqrt{5}}$

(b) $\dfrac{1}{2 + \sqrt{3}}$

Example 15   Rationalize the numerator of

$$\frac{2 + \sqrt{5}}{1 + \sqrt{3}}.$$

Solution   As in Example 14(b), we must write 1 as a suitable fraction. Since we want to rationalize the numerator here, we multiply by the fraction $1 = \dfrac{2 - \sqrt{5}}{2 - \sqrt{5}}$:

$$\frac{2 + \sqrt{5}}{1 + \sqrt{3}} = \frac{2 + \sqrt{5}}{1 + \sqrt{3}} \cdot \frac{2 - \sqrt{5}}{2 - \sqrt{5}} = \frac{4 - 5}{2 - \sqrt{5} + 2\sqrt{3} - \sqrt{3}\sqrt{5}}$$

$$= \frac{-1}{2 - \sqrt{5} + 2\sqrt{3} - \sqrt{15}}.$$

1.5 Exercises

Perform the indicated operations and simplify your answer. (See Examples 1 and 2.)

1. $\dfrac{7^5}{7^3}$

2. $\dfrac{(-6)^{14}}{(-6)^6}$

3. $(4c)^2$

4. $(-2x)^4$

5. $\left(\dfrac{2}{x}\right)^5$

6. $\left(\dfrac{5}{xy}\right)^3$

7. $(3u^2)^3(2u^3)^2$

8. $\dfrac{(5v^2)^3}{(2v)^4}$

Perform the indicated operations and simplify your answer, which should not have any negative exponents. (See Examples 3 and 4.)

9. 7^{-1}

10. 10^{-3}

11. -6^{-5}

12. $(-x)^{-4}$

13. $(-y)^{-3}$

14. $\left(\dfrac{1}{6}\right)^{-2}$

15. $\left(\dfrac{4}{3}\right)^{-2}$

16. $\left(\dfrac{x}{y^2}\right)^{-2}$

17. $\left(\dfrac{a}{b^3}\right)^{-1}$

18. Explain why $-2^{-4} = -1/16$, but $(-2)^{-4} = 1/16$.

Evaluate each expression. Write all answers without exponents. Round decimal answers to two places. (See Examples 5 and 6.)

19. $49^{1/2}$

20. $8^{1/3}$

21. $(5.71)^{1/4}$

22. $12^{5/2}$

23. $-64^{2/3}$

24. $-64^{3/2}$

25. $(8/27)^{-4/3}$

26. $(27/64)^{-1/3}$

Simplify each expression. Write all answers using only positive exponents. (See Example 7.)

27. $\dfrac{5^{-3}}{4^{-2}}$

28. $\dfrac{7^{-4}}{7^{-3}}$

29. $4^{-3} \cdot 4^6$

30. $9^{-9} \cdot 9^{10}$

31. $\dfrac{4^{10} \cdot 4^{-6}}{4^{-4}}$

32. $\dfrac{5^{-4} \cdot 5^6}{5^{-1}}$

Simplify each expression. Assume all variables represent positive real numbers. Write answers with only positive exponents. (See Examples 8 and 9.)

33. $\dfrac{z^6 \cdot z^2}{z^5}$

34. $\dfrac{k^6 \cdot k^9}{k^{12}}$

35. $\dfrac{3^{-1}(p^{-2})^3}{3p^{-7}}$

36. $\dfrac{(5x^3)^{-2}}{x^4}$

37. $(q^{-5}r^3)^{-1}$

38. $(2y^2z^{-2})^{-3}$

39. $(2p^{-1})^3 \cdot (5p^2)^{-2}$

40. $(4^{-1}x^3)^{-2} \cdot (3x^{-3})^4$

41. $(2p)^{1/2} \cdot (2p^3)^{1/3}$

42. $(5k^2)^{3/2} \cdot (5k^{1/3})^{3/4}$

43. $p^{2/3}(2p^{1/3} + 5p)$

44. $3x^{3/2}(2x^{-3/2} + x^{3/2})$

45. $\dfrac{(x^2)^{1/3}(y^2)^{2/3}}{3x^{2/3}y^2}$

46. $\dfrac{(c^{1/2})^3(d^3)^{1/2}}{(c^3)^{1/4}(d^{1/4})^3}$

47. $\dfrac{(7a)^2(5b)^{3/2}}{(5a)^{3/2}(7b)^4}$

48. $\dfrac{(4x)^{1/2}\sqrt{xy}}{x^{3/2}y^2}$

49. $x^{1/2}(x^{2/3} - x^{4/3})$

50. $x^{1/2}(3x^{3/2} + 2x^{-1/2})$

51. $(x^{1/2} + y^{1/2})(x^{1/2} - y^{1/2})$ **52.** $(x^{1/3} + y^{1/2})(2x^{1/3} - y^{3/2})$

Match the rational-exponent expression in Column I with the equivalent radical expression in Column II. Assume that x is not zero.

I	II
53. $(-3x)^{1/3}$	**(a)** $\dfrac{3}{\sqrt[3]{x}}$
54. $-3x^{1/3}$	**(b)** $-3\sqrt[3]{x}$
55. $(-3x)^{-1/3}$	**(c)** $\dfrac{1}{\sqrt[3]{3x}}$
56. $-3x^{-1/3}$	**(d)** $\dfrac{-3}{\sqrt[3]{x}}$
57. $(3x)^{1/3}$	**(e)** $3\sqrt[3]{x}$
58. $3x^{-1/3}$	**(f)** $\sqrt[3]{-3x}$
59. $(3x)^{-1/3}$	**(g)** $\sqrt[3]{3x}$
60. $3x^{1/3}$	**(h)** $\dfrac{1}{\sqrt[3]{-3x}}$

Simplify each of the given radical expressions. (See Examples 11–13.)

61. $\sqrt[3]{125}$

62. $\sqrt[6]{64}$

63. $\sqrt[4]{625}$

64. $\sqrt[7]{-128}$

65. $\sqrt{63}\sqrt{7}$

66. $\sqrt[3]{81} \cdot \sqrt[3]{9}$

67. $\sqrt{81 - 4}$

68. $\sqrt{49 - 16}$

69. $\sqrt{5}\sqrt{15}$

70. $\sqrt{8}\sqrt{96}$

71. $\sqrt{50} - \sqrt{72}$

72. $\sqrt{75} + \sqrt{192}$

73. $5\sqrt{20} - \sqrt{45} + 2\sqrt{80}$ **74.** $(\sqrt{3} + 2)(\sqrt{3} - 2)$

75. $(\sqrt{5} + \sqrt{2})(\sqrt{5} - \sqrt{2})$

76. What is wrong with the statement $\sqrt[3]{4} \cdot \sqrt[3]{4} = 4$?

Rationalize the denominator of each of the given expressions. (See Example 14.)

77. $\dfrac{3}{1 - \sqrt{2}}$

78. $\dfrac{2}{1 + \sqrt{5}}$

79. $\dfrac{9 - \sqrt{3}}{3 - \sqrt{3}}$

80. $\dfrac{\sqrt{3} - 1}{\sqrt{3} - 2}$

Rationalize the numerator of each of the given expressions. (See Example 15.)

81. $\dfrac{3 - \sqrt{2}}{3 + \sqrt{2}}$

82. $\dfrac{1 + \sqrt{7}}{2 - \sqrt{3}}$

The following exercises are applications of exponentiation and radicals.

83. Business The theory of economic lot size shows that, under certain conditions, the number of units to order to minimize total cost is

$$x = \sqrt{\dfrac{kM}{f}},$$

where k is the cost to store one unit for one year, f is the (constant) setup cost to manufacture the product, and M is the total number of units produced annually. Find x for the following values of f, k, and M.

(a) $k = \$1, f = \$500, M = 100,000$

(b) $k = \$3, f = \$7, M = 16,700$

(c) $k = \$1, f = \$5, M = 16,800$

84. Health The threshold weight T for a person is the weight above which the risk of death increases greatly. One researcher found that the threshold weight in pounds for men aged 40–49 is related to height in inches by the equation $h = 12.3T^{1/3}$. What height corresponds to a threshold of 216 pounds for a man in this age group?

Business *The annual domestic revenue (in billions of dollars) generated by the sale of movie tickets can be approximated by the function*

$$8.19x^{0.096} \quad (x \geq 1),$$

where $x = 1$ corresponds to 2001. Assuming the model remains accurate, approximate the revenue in the following years. (Data from: www.the-numbers.com.)

85. 2010

86. 2013

87. 2015

88. 2018

Health *The age-adjusted death rates per 100,000 people for diseases of the heart can be approximated by the function*

$$262.5x^{-.156} \quad (x \geq 1),$$

where $x = 1$ corresponds to 2001. Assuming the model continues to be accurate, find the approximate age-adjusted death rate for

the following years. (Data from: U.S. National Center for Health Statistics.)

89. 2011   **90.** 2013   **91.** 2017   **92.** 2020

Social Science *The number of students receiving financial aid from the federal government in the form of Pell Grants (in millions) can be approximated by the function*

$$3.96x^{0.239} \quad (x \geq 1),$$

where $x = 1$ corresponds to the year 2001. Assuming the model remains accurate, find the number of students receiving a Pell Grant for the following years. (Data from: www.finaid.org.)

93. 2005   **94.** 2010   **95.** 2013   **96.** 2018

Health *A function that approximates the number (in millions) of CT scans performed annually in the United States is*

$$3.5x^{1.04} \quad (x \geq 5),$$

where $x = 5$ corresponds to 1995. Find the approximate number of CT scans performed in the following years. (Data from: The Wall Street Journal.)

97. 1998   **98.** 2005   **99.** 2012   **100.** 2013

✓ Checkpoint Answers

1. (a) 2^9 (b) $(-5)^4$ (c) $(xy)^5$

2. (a) $81x^4$ (b) $r^{12}s^{30}$ (c) $\dfrac{32}{z^5}$ (d) $\dfrac{9a^4}{b^6}$

3. (a) $1/36$ (b) $-1/216$ (c) $-1/81$ (d) $8/5$

4. (a) $8/5$ (b) 32 (c) b^3/a^6

5. (a) 4 (b) 2 (c) -16
    (d) Not a real number   (e) -2 (f) 3

6. (a) 8 (b) 3125 (c) 128 (d) 1000

7. (a) 81 (b) $15x^{3/2}$ (c) 8^{10}
    (d) $5^{-8/3}$ or $1/5^{8/3}$

8. (a) 1 (b) $c^2/d^{1/2}$ (c) $2a + a^{1/2}$

9. (a) $\dfrac{6}{x^{1/3}y^{2/3}}$ (b) t^3

    (c) $32/(p^{10}k^{7/3})$ (d) $\dfrac{y^2 - x}{xy^2}$

10. About 20.6 million

11. (a) 3 (b) 5 (c) 2 (d) $4/5$

12. (a) 9 (b) $\dfrac{\sqrt{3}}{7}$ (c) $11\sqrt{2}$

13. (a) $3\sqrt{5} + \sqrt{10} - 3\sqrt{2} - 2$ (b) -4

14. (a) $\dfrac{2\sqrt{5}}{5}$ (b) $2 - \sqrt{3}$

1.6 First-Degree Equations

An **equation** is a statement that two mathematical expressions are equal; for example,

$$5x - 3 = 13, \qquad 8y = 4, \qquad \text{and} \qquad -3p + 5 = 4p - 8$$

are equations.

The letter in each equation is called the variable. This section concentrates on **first-degree equations,** which are equations that involve only constants and the first power of the variable. All of the equations displayed above are first-degree equations, but neither of the following equations is of first degree:

$$2x^2 = 5x + 6 \qquad \text{(the variable has an exponent greater than 1);}$$
$$\sqrt{x + 2} = 4 \qquad \text{(the variable is under the radical).}$$

A **solution** of an equation is a number that can be substituted for the variable in the equation to produce a true statement. For example, substituting the number 9 for x in the equation $2x + 1 = 19$ gives

$$2x + 1 = 19$$
$$2(9) + 1 \overset{?}{=} 19 \qquad \text{Let } x = 9.$$
$$18 + 1 = 19. \qquad \text{True}$$

This true statement indicates that 9 is a solution of $2x + 1 = 19$. ✓₁

The following properties are used to solve equations.

✓ Checkpoint 1

Is -4 a solution of the equations in parts (a) and (b)?

(a) $3x + 5 = -7$

(b) $2x - 3 = 5$

(c) Is there more than one solution of the equation in part (a)?

Properties of Equality

1. The same number may be added to or subtracted from both sides of an equation:

$$\text{If } a = b, \text{then } a + c = b + c \text{ and } a - c = b - c.$$

2. Both sides of an equation may be multiplied or divided by the same nonzero number:

$$\text{If } a = b \text{ and } c \neq 0, \text{then } ac = bc \text{ and } \frac{a}{c} = \frac{b}{c}.$$

Example 1   Solve the equation $5x - 3 = 12$.

Solution   Using the first property of equality, add 3 to both sides. This isolates the term containing the variable on one side of the equation:

$$5x - 3 = 12$$
$$5x - 3 + 3 = 12 + 3 \qquad \text{Add 3 to both sides.}$$
$$5x = 15.$$

Now arrange for the coefficient of x to be 1 by using the second property of equality:

$$5x = 15$$
$$\frac{5x}{5} = \frac{15}{5} \qquad \text{Divide both sides by 5.}$$
$$x = 3.$$

✓ Checkpoint 2

Solve the following.

(a) $3p - 5 = 19$

(b) $4y + 3 = -5$

(c) $-2k + 6 = 2$

The solution of the original equation, $5x - 3 = 12$, is 3. Check the solution by substituting 3 for x in the original equation. ✓₂

Example 2 Solve $2k + 3(k - 4) = 2(k - 3)$.

Solution First, simplify the equation by using the distributive property on the left-side term $3(k - 4)$ and right-side term $2(k - 3)$:

$$2k + 3(k - 4) = 2(k - 3)$$
$$2k + 3k - 12 = 2(k - 3) \quad \text{Distributive property}$$
$$2k + 3k - 12 = 2k - 6 \quad \text{Distributive property}$$
$$5k - 12 = 2k - 6. \quad \text{Collect like terms on left side.}$$

One way to proceed is to add $-2k$ to both sides:

$$5k - 12 + (-2k) = 2k - 6 + (-2k) \quad \text{Add } -2k \text{ to both sides.}$$
$$3k - 12 = -6$$
$$3k - 12 + 12 = -6 + 12 \quad \text{Add 12 to both sides.}$$
$$3k = 6$$
$$\frac{1}{3}(3k) = \frac{1}{3}(6) \quad \text{Multiply both sides by } \frac{1}{3}.$$
$$k = 2.$$

The solution is 2. Check this result by substituting 2 for k in the original equation. ✓₃

✓ **Checkpoint 3**

Solve the following.

(a) $3(m - 6) + 2(m + 4)$
    $= 4m - 2$

(b) $-2(y + 3) + 4y$
    $= 3(y + 1) - 6$

Example 3 **Business** The percentage y of U.S. households owning Individual Retirement Accounts (IRAs) in year x is approximated by the equation

$$0.096(x - 2000) = 15y - 5.16.$$

Assuming this equation remains valid, use a calculator to determine when 44% of households will own an IRA. (Data from: ProQuest Statistical Abstract of the United States: 2013.)

Solution Since $44\% = .44$, let $y = .44$ in the equation and solve for x. To avoid any rounding errors in the intermediate steps, it is often a good idea to do all the algebra first, before using the calculator:

$$0.096(x - 2000) = 15y - 5.16$$
$$0.096(x - 2000) = 15 \cdot .44 - 5.16 \quad \text{Substitute } y = .44$$
$$.096x - .096 \cdot 2000 = 15 \cdot .44 - 5.16 \quad \text{Distributive property}$$
$$.096x = 15 \cdot .44 - 5.16 + .096 \cdot 2000 \quad \text{Add } .096 \cdot 2000 \text{ to both sides.}$$
$$x = \frac{15 \cdot .44 - 5.16 + .096 \cdot 2000}{.096} \quad \text{Divide both sides by } .096$$

```
15*.44-5.16+.096*2000
           .096
                    2015
```

Figure 1.12

Now use a calculator to determine that $x = 2015$, as shown in Figure 1.12. So 44% of households will own an IRA in 2015. ✓₄

✓ **Checkpoint 4**

In Example 3, in what year will 48% of U.S. households own an IRA?

The next three examples show how to simplify the solution of first-degree equations involving fractions. We solve these equations by multiplying both sides of the equation by a *common denominator*. This step will eliminate the fractions.

Example 4 Solve

$$\frac{r}{10} - \frac{2}{15} = \frac{3r}{20} - \frac{1}{5}.$$

Solution Here, the denominators are 10, 15, 20, and 5. Each of these numbers is a factor of 60; therefore, 60 is a common denominator. Multiply both sides of the equation by 60:

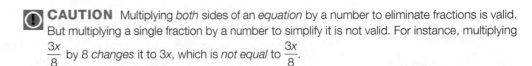

$$60\left(\frac{r}{10} - \frac{2}{15}\right) = 60\left(\frac{3r}{20} - \frac{1}{5}\right)$$

$$60\left(\frac{r}{10}\right) - 60\left(\frac{2}{15}\right) = 60\left(\frac{3r}{20}\right) - 60\left(\frac{1}{5}\right) \qquad \text{Distributive property}$$

$$6r - 8 = 9r - 12$$

$$6r - 8 + (-6r) + 12 = 9r - 12 + (-6r) + 12 \qquad \text{Add } -6r \text{ and 12 to both sides.}$$

$$4 = 3r$$

$$r = \frac{4}{3}. \qquad \text{Multiply both sides by 1/3.}$$

Check this solution in the original equation. ✔5

✔ Checkpoint 5

Solve the following.

(a) $\dfrac{x}{2} - \dfrac{x}{4} = 6$

(b) $\dfrac{2x}{3} + \dfrac{1}{2} = \dfrac{x}{4} - \dfrac{9}{2}$

! CAUTION Multiplying *both* sides of an *equation* by a number to eliminate fractions is valid. But multiplying a single fraction by a number to simplify it is not valid. For instance, multiplying $\dfrac{3x}{8}$ by 8 *changes* it to 3x, which is *not equal* to $\dfrac{3x}{8}$.

The second property of equality (page 43) applies only to *nonzero* quantities. Multiplying or dividing both sides of an equation by a quantity involving the variable (which might be zero for some values) may lead to an **extraneous solution**—that is, a number that does not satisfy the original equation. To avoid errors in such situations, always *check your solutions in the original equation.*

Example 5   Solve

$$\frac{4}{3(k + 2)} - \frac{k}{3(k + 2)} = \frac{5}{3}.$$

Solution   Multiply both sides of the equation by the common denominator $3(k + 2)$. Here, $k \neq -2$, since $k = -2$ would give a 0 denominator, making the fraction undefined. So, we have

$$3(k + 2) \cdot \frac{4}{3(k + 2)} - 3(k + 2) \cdot \frac{k}{3(k + 2)} = 3(k + 2) \cdot \frac{5}{3}.$$

Simplify each side and solve for k:

$$4 - k = 5(k + 2)$$

$$4 - k = 5k + 10 \qquad \text{Distributive property}$$

$$4 - k + k = 5k + 10 + k \qquad \text{Add } k \text{ to both sides.}$$

$$4 = 6k + 10$$

$$4 + (-10) = 6k + 10 + (-10) \qquad \text{Add } -10 \text{ to both sides.}$$

$$-6 = 6k$$

$$-1 = k. \qquad \text{Multiply both sides by } \frac{1}{6}.$$

The solution is -1. Substitute -1 for k in the original equation as a check:

$$\frac{4}{3(-1 + 2)} - \frac{-1}{3(-1 + 2)} \overset{?}{=} \frac{5}{3}$$

$$\frac{4}{3} - \frac{-1}{3} \overset{?}{=} \frac{5}{3}$$

$$\frac{5}{3} = \frac{5}{3}.$$

✔ Checkpoint 6

Solve the equation

$$\frac{5p + 1}{3(p + 1)} = \frac{3p - 3}{3(p + 1)} + \frac{9p - 3}{3(p + 1)}.$$

The check shows that -1 is the solution. ✔6

Example 6 Solve

$$\frac{3x - 4}{x - 2} = \frac{x}{x - 2}.$$

Solution Multiplying both sides by $x - 2$ produces

$$3x - 4 = x$$
$$2x - 4 = 0 \qquad \text{Subtract } x \text{ from both sides.}$$
$$2x = 4 \qquad \text{Add 4 to both sides.}$$
$$x = 2. \qquad \text{Divide both sides by 2.}$$

Substituting 2 for x in the original equation produces fractions with 0 denominators. Since division by 0 is not defined, $x = 2$ is an extraneous solution. So the original equation has no solution. ✓7

Sometimes an equation with several variables must be solved for one of the variables. This process is called **solving for a specified variable.**

Example 7 Solve for x: $3(ax - 5a) + 4b = 4x - 2$.

Solution Use the distributive property to get

$$3ax - 15a + 4b = 4x - 2.$$

Treat x as the variable and the other letters as constants. Get all terms with x on one side of the equation and all terms without x on the other side:

$$3ax - 4x = 15a - 4b - 2 \qquad \text{Isolate terms with } x \text{ on the left.}$$
$$(3a - 4)x = 15a - 4b - 2 \qquad \text{Distributive property}$$
$$x = \frac{15a - 4b - 2}{3a - 4} \qquad \text{Multiply both sides by } \frac{1}{3a - 4}.$$

The final equation is solved for x, as required. ✓8

Absolute-Value Equations

Recall from Section 1.1 that the absolute value of a number a is either a or $-a$, whichever one is nonnegative. For instance, $|4| = 4$ and $|-7| = -(-7) = 7$.

Example 8 Solve $|x| = 3$.

Solution Since $|x|$ is either x or $-x$, the equation says that

$$x = 3 \qquad \text{or} \qquad -x = 3$$
$$x = -3.$$

The solutions of $|x| = 3$ are 3 and -3.

Example 9 Solve $|p - 4| = 2$.

Solution Since $|p - 4|$ is either $p - 4$ or $-(p - 4)$, we have

$$p - 4 = 2 \qquad \text{or} \qquad -(p - 4) = 2$$
$$p = 6 \qquad\qquad -p + 4 = 2$$
$$-p = -2$$
$$p = 2,$$

so that 6 and 2 are possible solutions. Checking them in the original equation shows that both are solutions. ✓9

✓ **Checkpoint 7**

Solve each equation.

(a) $\dfrac{3p}{p + 1} = 1 - \dfrac{3}{p + 1}$

(b) $\dfrac{8y}{y - 4} = \dfrac{32}{y - 4} - 3$

✓ **Checkpoint 8**

Solve for x.

(a) $2x - 7y = 3xk$

(b) $8(4 - x) + 6p = -5k - 11yx$

✓ **Checkpoint 9**

Solve each equation.

(a) $|y| = 9$

(b) $|r + 3| = 1$

(c) $|2k - 3| = 7$

Example 10   Solve $|4m - 3| = |m + 6|$.

Solution   To satisfy the equation, the quantities in absolute-value bars must either be equal or be negatives of one another. That is,

$$4m - 3 = m + 6 \quad \text{or} \quad 4m - 3 = -(m + 6)$$
$$3m = 9 \qquad\qquad 4m - 3 = -m - 6$$
$$m = 3 \qquad\qquad\qquad 5m = -3$$
$$m = -\frac{3}{5}.$$

Check that the solutions for the original equation are 3 and $-3/5$. ✔10

✓ **Checkpoint 10**

Solve each equation.

(a) $|r + 6| = |2r + 1|$

(b) $|5k - 7| = |10k - 2|$

Applications

One of the main reasons for learning mathematics is to be able to use it to solve practical problems. There are no hard-and-fast rules for dealing with real-world applications, except perhaps to use common sense. However, you will find it much easier to deal with such problems if you do not try to do everything at once. After reading the problem carefully, attack it in stages, as suggested in the following guidelines.

Solving Applied Problems

Step 1   Read the problem carefully, focusing on the facts you are given and the unknown values you are asked to find. Look up any words you do not understand. You may have to read the problem more than once, until you understand exactly what you are being asked to do.

Step 2   Identify the unknown. (If there is more than one, choose one of them, and see Step 3 for what to do with the others.) Name the unknown with some variable that you *write down*. Many students try to skip this step. They are eager to get on with the writing of the equation. But this is an important step. If you do not know what the variable represents, how can you write a meaningful equation or interpret a result?

Step 3   Decide on a variable expression to represent any other unknowns in the problem. For example, if x represents the width of a rectangle, and you know that the length is one more than twice the width, then *write down* the fact that the length is $1 + 2x$.

Step 4   Draw a sketch or make a chart, if appropriate, showing the information given in the problem.

Step 5   Using the results of Steps 1–4, write an equation that expresses a condition that must be satisfied.

Step 6   Solve the equation.

Step 7   Check the solution in the words of the *original problem*, not just in the equation you have written.

Example 11   **Finance**   A financial manager has $15,000 to invest for her company. She plans to invest part of the money in tax-free bonds at 5% interest and the remainder in taxable bonds at 8%. She wants to earn $1020 per year in interest from the investments. Find the amount she should invest at each rate.

Solution

Step 1 We are asked to find how much of the $15,000 should be invested at 5% and how much at 8%, in order to earn the required interest.

Step 2 Let x represent the amount to be invested at 5%.

Step 3 After x dollars are invested, the remaining amount is $15,000 - x$ dollars, which is to be invested at 8%.

Step 4 Interest for one year is given by rate $\times$ amount invested. For instance, 5% of x dollars is $.05x$. The given information is summarized in the following chart.

Investment	Amount Invested	Interest Rate	Interest Earned in One Year
Tax-free bonds	x	$5\% = .05$	$.05x$
Taxable bonds	$15,000 - x$	$8\% = .08$	$.08(15,000 - x)$
Totals	$15,000$		1020

Step 5 Because the total interest is to be $1020, the last column of the table shows that

$$.05x + .08(15,000 - x) = 1020.$$

Step 6 Solve the preceding equation as follows:

$$.05x + .08(15,000 - x) = 1020$$
$$.05x + .08(15,000) - .08x = 1020$$
$$.05x + 1200 - .08x = 1020$$
$$-.03x = -180$$
$$x = 6000.$$

The manager should invest $6000 at 5% and $15,000 - \$6000 = \$9000$ at 8%.

Step 7 Check these results in the original problem. If $6000 is invested at 5%, the interest is $.05(6000) = \$300$. If $9000 is invested at 8%, the interest is $.08(9000) = \$720$. So the total interest is $300 + \$720 = \$1020$ as required ✓11

✓ **Checkpoint 11**

An investor owns two pieces of property. One, worth twice as much as the other, returns 6% in annual interest, while the other returns 4%. Find the value of each piece of property if the total annual interest earned is $8000.

Example 12 **Business** Spotify and Rhapsody are digital music streaming services. In 2012, *Time* magazine reported that Spotify acquired in 7 business quarters (a quarter is a 3-month period) the same number of users as Rhapsody acquired in 11 years (44 quarters). Spotify's average rate of user acquisition per quarter was 120,000 more than Rhapsody's average rate per quarter. Find the average rate of user acquisition per quarter for each company.

Solution

Step 1 We must find Spotify's user acquisition rate and Rhapsody's user acquisition rate.

Step 2 Let x represent Rhapsody's rate.

Step 3 Since Spotify's rate is 120,000 users per quarter faster than Rhapsody's, its rate is $x + 120,000$.

Step 4 In general, the number of users can be found by the formula:

Number of users $=$ number of quarters $\times$ rate of users per quarter

So, for Rhapsody, number of users $= 44x$ and for

Spotify, the number of users $= 7(x + 120,000)$

We can collect these facts to make a chart, which organizes the information given in the problem.

	Quarters	Rate	Number of Users
Rhapsody	44	x	$44x$
Spotify	7	$x + 120{,}000$	$7(x + 120{,}000)$

Step 5 Because both companies obtained the *same number of users*, the equation is

$$44x = 7(x + 120{,}000).$$

Step 6 If we distribute the 7 through the quantity on the right side of the equation, we obtain

$$44x = 7x + 840{,}000$$
$$37x = 840{,}000 \qquad \text{Add } -7x \text{ to each side.}$$
$$x \approx 22{,}703 \qquad \text{Divide each side by 37.}$$

Step 7 Since x represents Rhapsody's rate, Rhapsody acquired, on average, 22,702 users per quarter. Spotify's rate is $x + 120{,}000$, or $22{,}702 + 120{,}000 = 142{,}702$ users per quarter. ☑ 12

✓ Checkpoint 12

In Example 12, suppose Spotify had taken 12 quarters and Rhapsody had taken 40 quarters to reach the same number of users. Assuming that Spotify acquired users at a rate 100,000 per quarter more than Rhapsody, find the average rate at which

(a) Rhapsody had acquired users.

(b) Spotify had acquired users.

Example 13 **Business** An oil company needs to fill orders for 89-octane gas, but has only 87- and 93-octane gas on hand. The octane rating is the percentage of isooctane in the standard fuel. How much of each type should be mixed together to produce 100,000 gallons of 89-octane gas?

Solution

Step 1 We must find how much 87-octane gas and how much 93-octane gas are needed for the 100,000 gallon mixture.

Step 2 Let x be the amount of 87-octane gas.

Step 3 Then $100{,}000 - x$ is the amount of 93-octane gas.

Step 4 We can summarize the relevant information in a chart.

Type of Gas	Quantity	% Isooctane	Amount of Isooctane
87-octane	x	87%	$.87x$
93-octane	$100{,}000 - x$	93%	$.93(100{,}000 - x)$
Mixture	$100{,}000$	89%	$.89(100{,}000)$

Step 5 The amount of isooctane satisfies this equation:

$$.87x + .93(100{,}000 - x) = .89(100{,}000).$$

Step 6 Solving this equation yields

$$.87x + 93{,}000 - .93x = .89(100{,}000) \qquad \text{Distribute the left side.}$$
$$.87x + 93{,}000 - .93x = 89{,}000 \qquad \text{Multiply on the right side.}$$
$$-.06x = -4000 \qquad \text{Combine terms and add } -93{,}000 \text{ to each side.}$$
$$x = \frac{-4000}{-.06} \approx 66{,}667.$$

Step 7 So the distributor should mix 66,667 gallons of 87-octane gas with $100{,}000 - 66{,}667 = 33{,}333$ gallons of 93-octane gas. Then the amount of isooctane in the mixture is

$$.87(66{,}667) + .93(33{,}333)$$
$$\approx 58{,}000 + 31{,}000$$
$$= 89{,}000.$$

Hence, the octane rating of the mixture is $\dfrac{89{,}000}{100{,}000} = .89$ as required. ☑ 13

✓ Checkpoint 13

How much 89-octane gas and how much 94-octane gas are needed to produce 1500 gallons of 91-octane gas?

1.6 Exercises

Solve each equation. (See Examples 1–6.)

1. $3x + 8 = 20$

2. $4 - 5y = 19$

3. $.6k - .3 = .5k + .4$

4. $2.5 + 5.04m = 8.5 - .06m$

5. $2a - 1 = 4(a + 1) + 7a + 5$

6. $3(k - 2) - 6 = 4k - (3k - 1)$

7. $2[x - (3 + 2x) + 9] = 3x - 8$

8. $-2[4(k + 2) - 3(k + 1)] = 14 + 2k$

9. $\dfrac{3x}{5} - \dfrac{4}{5}(x + 1) = 2 - \dfrac{3}{10}(3x - 4)$

10. $\dfrac{4}{3}(x - 2) - \dfrac{1}{2} = 2\left(\dfrac{3}{4}x - 1\right)$

11. $\dfrac{5y}{6} - 8 = 5 - \dfrac{2y}{3}$

12. $\dfrac{x}{2} - 3 = \dfrac{3x}{5} + 1$

13. $\dfrac{m}{2} - \dfrac{1}{m} = \dfrac{6m + 5}{12}$

14. $-\dfrac{3k}{2} + \dfrac{9k - 5}{6} = \dfrac{11k + 8}{k}$

15. $\dfrac{4}{x - 3} - \dfrac{8}{2x + 5} + \dfrac{3}{x - 3} = 0$

16. $\dfrac{5}{2p + 3} - \dfrac{3}{p - 2} = \dfrac{4}{2p + 3}$

17. $\dfrac{3}{2m + 4} = \dfrac{1}{m + 2} - 2$

18. $\dfrac{8}{3k - 9} - \dfrac{5}{k - 3} = 4$

Use a calculator to solve each equation. Round your answer to the nearest hundredth. (See Example 3.)

19. $9.06x + 3.59(8x - 5) = 12.07x + .5612$

20. $-5.74(3.1 - 2.7p) = 1.09p + 5.2588$

21. $\dfrac{2.63r - 8.99}{1.25} - \dfrac{3.90r - 1.77}{2.45} = r$

22. $\dfrac{8.19m + 2.55}{4.34} - \dfrac{8.17m - 9.94}{1.04} = 4m$

Solve each equation for x. (See Example 7.)

23. $4(a + x) = b - a + 2x$

24. $(3a - b) - bx = a(x - 2)$ $(a \neq -b)$

25. $5(b - x) = 2b + ax$ $(a \neq -5)$

26. $bx - 2b = 2a - ax$

Solve each equation for the specified variable. Assume that all denominators are nonzero. (See Example 7.)

27. $PV = k$ for V

28. $i = prt$ for p

29. $V = V_0 + gt$ for g

30. $S = S_0 + gt^2 + k$ for g

31. $A = \dfrac{1}{2}(B + b)h$ for B

32. $C = \dfrac{5}{9}(F - 32)$ for F

Solve each equation. (See Examples 8–10.)

33. $|2h - 1| = 5$

34. $|4m - 3| = 12$

35. $|6 + 2p| = 10$

36. $|-5x + 7| = 15$

37. $\left|\dfrac{5}{r - 3}\right| = 10$

38. $\left|\dfrac{3}{2h - 1}\right| = 4$

Solve the following applied problems.

Health   *According to the American Heart Association, the number y of brain neurons (in billions) that are lost in a stroke lasting x hours is given by $y = \dfrac{x}{8}$. Find the length of the stroke for the given number of neurons lost.*

39. 1,250,000,000

40. 2,400,000,000

Natural Science   *The equation that relates Fahrenheit temperature F to Celsius temperature C is*

$$C = \dfrac{5}{9}(F - 32).$$

Find the Fahrenheit temperature corresponding to these Celsius temperatures.

41. -5

42. -15

43. 22

44. 36

Finance   *The gross federal debt y (in trillions of dollars) in year x is approximated by*

$$y = 1.16x + 1.76,$$

where x is the number of years after 2000. Assuming the trend continues, in what year will the federal debt be the given amount? (Data from: U.S. Office of Management and Budget.)

45. $13.36 trillion

46. $16.84 trillion

47. $19.16 trillion

48. $24.96 trillion

Health Economics   *The total health care expenditures E in the United States (in trillions of dollars) can be approximated by*

$$E = .118x + 1.45,$$

where x is the number of years after 2000. Assuming the trend continues, determine the year in which health care expenditures are at the given level. (Data from: U.S. Centers for Medicare and Medicaid Services.)

49. $2.63 trillion

50. $2.866 trillion

51. $3.338 trillion

52. $3.574 trillion

Finance *The percentage y (written as a decimal) of U.S. households who owned Roth Individual Retirement Accounts (IRAs) in year x is given by the equation*

$$.09(x - 2004) = 12y - 1.44.$$

Find the year in which the given percentage of U.S. households own a Roth IRA. (Data from: Proquest Statistical Abstract of the United States: 2013.)

53. 18.0%

54. 19.5%

55. 21%

56. 23.25%

Finance *The total amount A (in millions of dollars) donated within a state for charitable contributions claimed on individual federal tax returns can be modeled by the function*

$$A = 4.35x - 12$$

where x is the total number of returns filed (in thousands) for the state. For the given amounts A donated, determine the number of returns that were filed within the following states. (Data from: Proquest Statistical Abstract of the United States: 2013.)

57. California: $A = \$20{,}777$ million

58. New York: $A = \$13{,}732$ million

59. Texas: $A = \$13{,}360$ million

60. Florida: $A = \$9596$ million

Business *When a loan is paid off early, a portion of the finance charge must be returned to the borrower. By one method of calculating the finance charge (called the rule of 78), the amount of unearned interest (finance charge to be returned) is given by*

$$u = f \cdot \frac{n(n + 1)}{q(q + 1)},$$

where u represents unearned interest, f is the original finance charge, n is the number of payments remaining when the loan is paid off, and q is the original number of payments. Find the amount of the unearned interest in each of the given cases.

61. Original finance charge = $800, loan scheduled to run 36 months, paid off with 18 payments remaining

62. Original finance charge = $1400, loan scheduled to run 48 months, paid off with 12 payments remaining

Business *Solve the following investment problems. (See Example 11.)*

63. Joe Gonzalez received $52,000 profit from the sale of some land. He invested part at 5% interest and the rest at 4% interest. He earned a total of $2290 interest per year. How much did he invest at 5%?

64. Weijen Luan invests $20,000 received from an insurance settlement in two ways: some at 6% and some at 4%. Altogether, she makes $1040 per year in interest. How much is invested at 4%?

65. Maria Martinelli bought two plots of land for a total of $120,000. On the first plot, she made a profit of 15%. On the second, she lost 10%. Her total profit was $5500. How much did she pay for each piece of land?

66. Suppose $20,000 is invested at 5%. How much additional money must be invested at 4% to produce a yield of 4.8% on the entire amount invested?

Solve the given applied problems. (See Example 12.)

According to data from comScore.com, two social media sites, Tumblr.com and Pinterest.com, acquired the same number of unique visitors in 2012. Tumblr.com took 63 months to acquire these visitors while Pinterest.com took 30 months. Pinterest's rate of visitor growth was 450,000 more a month, on average, than Tumblr's average growth per month.

67. Find the average rate of growth of Tumblr.com.

68. Find the average rate of growth of Pinterest.com.

69. Approximately how many unique visitors did Tumblr.com acquire in 63 months?

70. Approximately how many unique visitors did Pinterest.com acquire in 30 months?

Natural Science *Using the same assumptions about octane ratings as in Example 13, solve the following problems.*

71. How many liters of 94-octane gasoline should be mixed with 200 liters of 99-octane gasoline to get a mixture that is 97-octane gasoline?

72. A service station has 92-octane and 98-octane gasoline. How many liters of each gasoline should be mixed to provide 12 liters of 96-octane gasoline for a chemistry experiment?

Solve the following applied problems.

73. **Business** A major car rental firm charges $78 a day for a full-size car in Tampa, Florida, with unlimited mileage. Another firm offers a similar car for $55 a day plus 22 cents per mile. How far must you drive in a day in order for the cost to be the same for both vehicles?

74. **Business** A car radiator contains 8.5 quarts of fluid, 35% of which is antifreeze. How much fluid should be drained and replaced with pure (100%) antifreeze in order that the new mixture be 65% antifreeze?

Business *Massachusetts has a graduated fine system for speeding, meaning you can pay a base fine and then have more charges added on top. For example, the base fine for speeding is $100. But that is just the start. If you are convicted of going more than 10 mph over the speed limit, add $10 for each additional mph you were traveling over the speed limit plus 10 mph. Thus, the amount of the fine y (in dollars) for driving x miles over the speed limit (when the speed limit is 65 miles per hour) can be represented as*

$$y = 10(x - 75) + 100, \quad x \geq 75.$$

(Data from: www.dmv.org.)

75. If Paul was fined $180 for speeding, how fast was he going?

76. If Sarah was fined $120 for speeding, how fast was she going?

Jack borrowed his father's luxury car and promised to return it with a full tank of premium gas, which costs $3.80 per gallon. From experience, he knows that he needs 15.5 gallons. He has, however, only $50 (and no credit card). He decides to get as much premium as possible and fill the remainder of the tank with regular gas, which costs $3.10 per gallon.

77. How much of each type of gas should he get?

78. If he has $53, how much of each type of gas should he get?

✓ **Checkpoint Answers**

1. (a) Yes   **(b)** No   **(c)** No

2. (a) 8   **(b)** −2   **(c)** 2

3. (a) 8   **(b)** −3

4. Early 2021 ($x = 2021.25$)

5. (a) 24   **(b)** −12

6. 1

7. Neither equation has a solution.

8. (a) $x = \dfrac{7y}{2 - 3k}$ **(b)** $x = \dfrac{5k + 32 + 6p}{8 - 11y}$

9. (a) 9, −9   **(b)** −2, −4   **(c)** 5, −2

10. (a) 5, −7/3   **(b)** −1, 3/5

11. 6% return: $100,000; 4% return: $50,000

12. (a) 42,857 per quarter
     (b) 142,857 per quarter

13. 900 gallons of 89-octane gas; 600 gallons of 94-octane gas

1.7 Quadratic Equations

An equation that can be written in the form

$$ax^2 + bx + c = 0,$$

where a, b, and c are real numbers with $a \neq 0$, is called a **quadratic equation.** For example, each of

$$2x^2 + 3x + 4 = 0, \qquad x^2 = 6x - 9, \qquad 3x^2 + x = 6, \qquad \text{and} \qquad x^2 = 5$$

is a quadratic equation. A solution of an equation that is a real number is said to be a **real solution** of the equation.

One method of solving quadratic equations is based on the following property of real numbers.

Zero-Factor Property

If a and b are real numbers, with $ab = 0$, then $a = 0$ or $b = 0$ or both.

Example 1   Solve the equation $(x - 4)(3x + 7) = 0$.

Solution   By the zero-factor property, the product $(x - 4)(3x + 7)$ can equal 0 only if at least one of the factors equals 0. That is, the product equals zero only if $x - 4 = 0$ or $3x + 7 = 0$. Solving each of these equations separately will give the solutions of the original equation:

$$x - 4 = 0 \quad \text{or} \quad 3x + 7 = 0$$
$$x = 4 \quad \text{or} \quad 3x = -7$$
$$x = -\frac{7}{3}.$$

✓ **Checkpoint 1**

Solve the following equations.

(a) $(y - 6)(y + 2) = 0$

(b) $(5k - 3)(k + 5) = 0$

(c) $(2r - 9)(3r + 5) \cdot (r + 3) = 0$

The solutions of the equation $(x - 4)(3x + 7) = 0$ are 4 and −7/3. Check these solutions by substituting them into the original equation. ✓

Example 2   Solve $6r^2 + 7r = 3$.

Solution   Rewrite the equation as

$$6r^2 + 7r - 3 = 0.$$

Now factor $6r^2 + 7r - 3$ to get

$$(3r - 1)(2r + 3) = 0.$$

By the zero-factor property, the product $(3r - 1)(2r + 3)$ can equal 0 only if

$$3r - 1 = 0 \quad \text{or} \quad 2r + 3 = 0.$$

Solving each of these equations separately gives the solutions of the original equation:

$$3r = 1 \quad \text{or} \quad 2r = -3$$
$$r = \frac{1}{3} \qquad\qquad r = -\frac{3}{2}.$$

Verify that both $1/3$ and $-3/2$ are solutions by substituting them into the original equation. ✓₂

An equation such as $x^2 = 5$ has two solutions: $\sqrt{5}$ and $-\sqrt{5}$. This fact is true in general.

✓**Checkpoint 2**

Solve each equation by factoring.

(a) $y^2 + 3y = 10$

(b) $2r^2 + 9r = 5$

(c) $4k^2 = 9k$

Square-Root Property

If $b > 0$, then the solutions of $x^2 = b$ are $\sqrt{b}$ and $-\sqrt{b}$.

The two solutions are sometimes abbreviated $\pm \sqrt{b}$.

Example 3   Solve each equation.

(a) $m^2 = 17$

Solution   By the square-root property, the solutions are $\sqrt{17}$ and $-\sqrt{17}$, abbreviated $\pm\sqrt{17}$.

(b) $(y - 4)^2 = 11$

Solution   Use a generalization of the square-root property, we work as follows.

$$(y - 4)^2 = 11$$
$$y - 4 = \sqrt{11} \quad \text{or} \quad y - 4 = -\sqrt{11}$$
$$y = 4 + \sqrt{11} \qquad\qquad y = 4 - \sqrt{11}.$$

✓**Checkpoint 3**

Solve each equation by using the square-root property.

(a) $p^2 = 21$

(b) $(m + 7)^2 = 15$

(c) $(2k - 3)^2 = 5$

Abbreviate the solutions as $4 \pm \sqrt{11}$. ✓₃

When a quadratic equation cannot be easily factored, it can be solved by using the following formula, which you should memorize.[*]

Quadratic Formula

The solutions of the quadratic equation $ax^2 + bx + c = 0$, where $a \neq 0$, are given by

$$x = \frac{-b \pm \sqrt{b^2 - 4ac}}{2a}.$$

---

[*]A proof of the quadratic formula can be found in many College Algebra books.

! **CAUTION** When using the quadratic formula, remember that the equation must be in the form $ax^2 + bx + c = 0$. Also, notice that the fraction bar in the quadratic formula extends under *both* terms in the numerator. Be sure to add $-b$ to $\pm \sqrt{b^2 - 4ac}$ *before* dividing by $2a$.

Example 4 Solve $x^2 + 1 = 4x$.

Solution First add $-4x$ to both sides to get 0 alone on the right side:

$$x^2 - 4x + 1 = 0.$$

Now identify the values of a, b, and c. Here, $a = 1$, $b = -4$, and $c = 1$. Substitute these numbers into the quadratic formula to obtain

$$x = \frac{-(-4) \pm \sqrt{(-4)^2 - 4(1)(1)}}{2(1)}$$

$$= \frac{4 \pm \sqrt{16 - 4}}{2}$$

$$= \frac{4 \pm \sqrt{12}}{2}$$

$$= \frac{4 \pm 2\sqrt{3}}{2} \qquad \sqrt{12} = \sqrt{4 \cdot 3} = \sqrt{4} \cdot \sqrt{3} = 2\sqrt{3}$$

$$= \frac{2(2 \pm \sqrt{3})}{2} \qquad \text{Factor } 4 \pm 2\sqrt{3}.$$

$$x = 2 \pm \sqrt{3}. \qquad \text{Cancel 2.}$$

The $\pm$ sign represents the two solutions of the equation. First use $+$ and then use $-$ to find each of the solutions: $2 + \sqrt{3}$ and $2 - \sqrt{3}$. ☑ 4

✓ **Checkpoint 4**

Use the quadratic formula to solve each equation.

(a) $x^2 - 2x = 2$

(b) $u^2 - 6u + 4 = 0$

```
2+√3
         3.732050808
2-√3
          .2679491924
```

Figure 1.13

Example 4 shows that the quadratic formula produces exact solutions. In many real-world applications, however, you must use a calculator to find decimal approximations of the solutions. The approximate solutions in Example 4 are

$$x = 2 + \sqrt{3} \approx 3.732050808 \qquad \text{and} \qquad x = 2 - \sqrt{3} \approx .2679491924,$$

as shown in Figure 1.13.

Example 5 **Business** Many companies in recent years saw their net earnings follow a parabolic pattern because of the recession that began in 2008. One such example is Motorola Corporation. The net earnings for Motorola Corporation E (in millions of dollars) can be approximated by the function

$$E = 545.9x^2 - 10{,}408x + 48{,}085 \quad (6 \le x \le 12),$$

where $x = 6$ corresponds to the year 2006. Use the quadratic formula and a calculator to find the year in which net earnings recovered to \$1799 million. (Data from: www.morningstar.com.)

Solution To find the year x, solve the equation above when $E = 1799$:

$$545.9x^2 - 10{,}408x + 48{,}085 = E$$

$$545.9x^2 - 10{,}408x + 48{,}085 = 1799 \qquad \text{Substitute } E = 1799.$$

$$545.9x^2 - 10{,}408x + 46{,}286 = 0 \qquad \text{Subtract 1799 from both sides.}$$

To apply the quadratic formula, first compute the radical part:

$$\sqrt{b^2 - 4ac} = \sqrt{(10{,}408)^2 - 4(545.9)(46{,}286)} = \sqrt{7{,}256{,}354.4}.$$

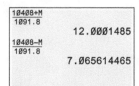

Figure 1.14

Then store $\sqrt{7{,}256{,}354.4}$ (which we denote by M) in the calculator memory. (Check your instruction manual for how to store and recall numbers.) By the quadratic formula, the exact solutions of the equation are

$$x = \frac{-b \pm \sqrt{b^2 - 4ac}}{2a} = \frac{-b \pm M}{2a} = \frac{-(-10{,}408) \pm M}{2(545.9)} = \frac{10{,}408 \pm M}{1091.8}.$$

Figure 1.14 shows that the approximate solutions are

$$\frac{10{,}408 + M}{1091.8} \approx 12.0 \qquad \frac{10{,}408 - M}{1091.8} \approx 7.1.$$

Since we were told that net earnings had recovered, we use the solution later in time and $x = 12$ corresponds to 2012. ✔5

✓ **Checkpoint 5**

Use the equation of Example 5 to find the year in which net earnings were first −$140 million dollars.

Example 6 Solve $9x^2 - 30x + 25 = 0$.

Solution Applying the quadratic formula with $a = 9$, $b = -30$, and $c = 25$, we have

$$x = \frac{-(-30) \pm \sqrt{(-30)^2 - 4(9)(25)}}{2(9)}$$

$$= \frac{30 \pm \sqrt{900 - 900}}{18} = \frac{30 \pm 0}{18} = \frac{30}{18} = \frac{5}{3}.$$

Therefore, the given equation has only one real solution. The fact that the solution is a rational number indicates that this equation could have been solved by factoring.

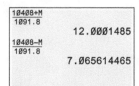/no

📡 **TECHNOLOGY TIP**

You can approximate the solutions of quadratic equations on a graphing calculator by using a quadratic formula program (see the Program Appendix) or using a built-in quadratic equation solver if your calculator has one. Then you need only enter the values of the coefficients a, b, and c to obtain the approximate solutions.

Example 7 Solve $x^2 - 6x + 10 = 0$.

Solution Apply the quadratic formula with $a = 1$, $b = -6$, and $c = 10$:

$$x = \frac{-(-6) \pm \sqrt{(-6)^2 - 4(1)(10)}}{2(1)}$$

$$= \frac{6 \pm \sqrt{36 - 40}}{2}$$

$$= \frac{6 \pm \sqrt{-4}}{2}.$$

Since no negative number has a square root in the real-number system, $\sqrt{-4}$ is not a real number. Hence, the equation has no real solutions. ✔6

✓ **Checkpoint 6**

Solve each equation.
(a) $9k^2 - 6k + 1 = 0$
(b) $4m^2 + 28m + 49 = 0$
(c) $2x^2 - 5x + 5 = 0$

Examples 4–7 show that the number of solutions of the quadratic equation $ax^2 + bx + c = 0$ is determined by $b^2 - 4ac$, the quantity under the radical, which is called the **discriminant** of the equation. ✔7

✓ **Checkpoint 7**

Use the discriminant to determine the number of real solutions of each equation.
(a) $x^2 + 8x + 3 = 0$
(b) $2x^2 + x + 3 = 0$
(c) $x^2 - 194x + 9409 = 0$

The Discriminant

The equation $ax^2 + bx + c = 0$ has either two, or one, or no real solutions.

If $b^2 - 4ac > 0$, there are two real solutions. (*Examples 4 and 5*)
If $b^2 - 4ac = 0$, there is one real solution. (*Example 6*)
If $b^2 - 4ac < 0$, there are no real solutions. (*Example 7*)

Applications

Quadratic equations arise in a variety of settings, as illustrated in the next set of examples. Example 8 depends on the following useful fact from geometry.

The Pythagorean Theorem

In a right triangle with legs of lengths a and b and hypotenuse of length c,

$$a^2 + b^2 = c^2.$$

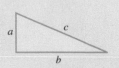

Example 8   **Business**   The size of a flat screen television is the diagonal measurement of its screen. The height of the screen is approximately 63% of its width. Kathy claims that John's 39-inch flat screen has only half of the viewing area that her 46-inch flat screen television has. Is Kathy right?

Solution   First, find the area of Kathy's screen. Let x be its width. Then its height is 63% of x (that is, $.63x$, as shown in Figure 1.15). By the Pythagorean theorem,

$$x^2 + (.63x)^2 = 46^2$$
$$x^2 + .3969x^2 = 2116 \qquad \text{Expand } (.63x)^2 \text{ and } 46^2.$$
$$(1 + .3969)x^2 = 2116 \qquad \text{Distributive property}$$
$$1.3969x^2 = 2116$$
$$x^2 = 1514.78 \qquad \text{Divide both sides by 1.3969.}$$
$$x = \pm\sqrt{1514.78} \qquad \text{Square-root property}$$
$$x \approx \pm38.9.$$

We can ignore the negative solution, since x is a width. Thus, the width is 38.9 inches and the height is $.63x = .63(38.9) \approx 24.5$ inches, so the area is

$$\text{Area} = \text{width} \times \text{height} = 38.9 \times 24.5 = 953.1 \text{ square inches.}$$

Next we find the area of John's television in a similar manner. Let y be the width of John's television. Then its height is 63% of y. By the Pythagorean theorem,

$$y^2 + (.63y)^2 = 39^2$$
$$y^2 + .3969y^2 = 1521 \qquad \text{Expand } (.63y)^2 \text{ and } 39^2.$$
$$(1 + .3969)y^2 = 1521 \qquad \text{Distributive property}$$
$$1.3969y^2 = 1521$$
$$y^2 = 1088.84 \qquad \text{Divide both sides by 1.3969.}$$
$$y = \pm\sqrt{1088.84} \qquad \text{Square-root property}$$
$$y \approx \pm33.0.$$

Again, we can ignore the negative solution, since y is a width. Thus, the width is 33.0 inches and the height is $.63y = .63(33.0) \approx 20.8$ inches, so the area is

$$\text{Area} = \text{width} \times \text{height} = 33.0 \times 20.8 = 686.4 \text{ square inches.}$$

Since half of 953.1 square inches (the area of Kathy's television) is 476.55 square inches, Kathy is wrong because John's viewing area is 686.4 square inches. ✓8

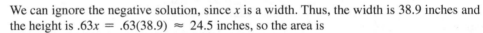

Figure 1.15 appears in the left margin with the following elements:

Figure 1.15

✓ **Checkpoint 8**

If John's television was only a 26-inch flat screen television, would Kathy have been right?

Example 9   **Business**   A landscape architect wants to make an exposed gravel border of uniform width around a small shed behind a company plant. The shed is 10 feet by 6 feet. He has enough gravel to cover 36 square feet. How wide should the border be?

Solution   A sketch of the shed with border is given in Figure 1.16. Let x represent the width of the border. Then the width of the large rectangle is $6 + 2x$, and its length is $10 + 2x$.

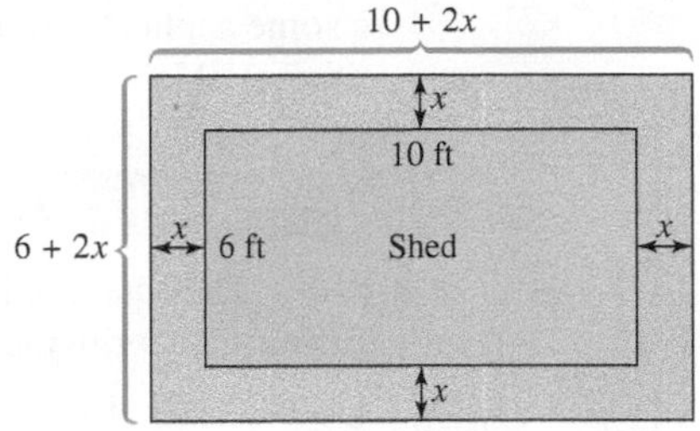

Figure 1.16

We must write an equation relating the given areas and dimensions. The area of the large rectangle is $(6 + 2x)(10 + 2x)$. The area occupied by the shed is $6 \cdot 10 = 60$. The area of the border is found by subtracting the area of the shed from the area of the large rectangle. This difference should be 36 square feet, giving the equation

$$(6 + 2x)(10 + 2x) - 60 = 36.$$

Solve this equation with the following sequence of steps:

$$60 + 32x + 4x^2 - 60 = 36 \qquad \text{Multiply out left side.}$$
$$4x^2 + 32x - 36 = 0 \qquad \text{Simplify.}$$
$$x^2 + 8x - 9 = 0 \qquad \text{Divide both sides by 4.}$$
$$(x + 9)(x - 1) = 0 \qquad \text{Factor.}$$
$$x + 9 = 0 \quad \text{or} \quad x - 1 = 0 \qquad \text{Zero-factor property.}$$
$$x = -9 \quad \text{or} \quad x = 1.$$

The number -9 cannot be the width of the border, so the solution is to make the border 1 foot wide. ✓₉

✓ Checkpoint 9

The length of a picture is 2 inches more than the width. It is mounted on a mat that extends 2 inches beyond the picture on all sides. What are the dimensions of the picture if the area of the mat is 99 square inches?

Example 10 **Physical Science** If an object is thrown upward, dropped, or thrown downward and travels in a straight line subject only to gravity (with wind resistance ignored), the height h of the object above the ground (in feet) after t seconds is given by

$$h = -16t^2 + v_0 t + h_0,$$

where h_0 is the height of the object when $t = 0$ and v_0 is the initial velocity at time $t = 0$. The value of v_0 is taken to be positive if the object moves upward and negative if it moves downward. Suppose that a golf ball is thrown downward from the top of a 625-foot-high building with an initial velocity of 65 feet per second. How long does it take to reach the ground?

Solution In this case, $h_0 = 625$ (the height of the building) and $v_0 = -65$ (negative because the ball is thrown downward). The object is on the ground when $h = 0$, so we must solve the equation

$$h = -16t^2 + v_0 t + h_0$$
$$0 = -16t^2 - 65t + 625. \qquad \text{Let } h = 0, v_0 = -65, \text{ and } h_0 = 625.$$

Using the quadratic formula and a calculator, we see that

$$t = \frac{-(-65) \pm \sqrt{(-65)^2 - 4(-16)(625)}}{2(-16)} = \frac{65 \pm \sqrt{44{,}225}}{-32} \approx \begin{cases} -8.60 \\ \text{or} \\ 4.54 \end{cases}$$

Only the positive answer makes sense in this case. So it takes about 4.54 seconds for the ball to reach the ground.

In some applications, it may be necessary to solve an equation in several variables for a specific variable.

Example 11 Solve $v = mx^2 + x$ for x. (Assume that m and v are positive.)

Solution The equation is quadratic in x because of the x^2 term. Before we use the quadratic formula, we write the equation in standard form:

$$v = mx^2 + x$$
$$0 = mx^2 + x - v.$$

Let $a = m$, $b = 1$, and $c = -v$. Then the quadratic formula gives

$$x = \frac{-1 \pm \sqrt{1^2 - 4(m)(-v)}}{2m}$$

$$x = \frac{-1 \pm \sqrt{1 + 4mv}}{2m}. \quad \checkmark_{10}$$

✓ **Checkpoint 10**

Solve each of the given equations for the indicated variable. Assume that all variables are positive.

(a) $k = mp^2 - bp$ for p

(b) $r = \dfrac{APk^2}{3}$ for k

1.7 Exercises

Use factoring to solve each equation. (See Examples 1 and 2.)

1. $(x + 4)(x - 14) = 0$
2. $(p - 16)(p - 5) = 0$
3. $x(x + 6) = 0$
4. $x^2 - 2x = 0$
5. $2z^2 = 4z$
6. $x^2 - 64 = 0$
7. $y^2 + 15y + 56 = 0$
8. $k^2 - 4k - 5 = 0$
9. $2x^2 = 7x - 3$
10. $2 = 15z^2 + z$
11. $6r^2 + r = 1$
12. $3y^2 = 16y - 5$
13. $2m^2 + 20 = 13m$
14. $6a^2 + 17a + 12 = 0$
15. $m(m + 7) = -10$
16. $z(2z + 7) = 4$
17. $9x^2 - 16 = 0$
18. $36y^2 - 49 = 0$
19. $16x^2 - 16x = 0$
20. $12y^2 - 48y = 0$

Solve each equation by using the square-root property. (See Example 3.)

21. $(r - 2)^2 = 7$
22. $(b + 4)^2 = 27$
23. $(4x - 1)^2 = 20$
24. $(3t + 5)^2 = 11$

Use the quadratic formula to solve each equation. If the solutions involve square roots, give both the exact and approximate solutions. (See Examples 4–7.)

25. $2x^2 + 7x + 1 = 0$
26. $3x^2 - x - 7 = 0$
27. $4k^2 + 2k = 1$
28. $r^2 = 3r + 5$
29. $5y^2 + 5y = 2$
30. $2z^2 + 3 = 8z$
31. $6x^2 + 6x + 4 = 0$
32. $3a^2 - 2a + 2 = 0$
33. $2r^2 + 3r - 5 = 0$
34. $8x^2 = 8x - 3$
35. $2x^2 - 7x + 30 = 0$
36. $3k^2 + k = 6$
37. $1 + \dfrac{7}{2a} = \dfrac{15}{2a^2}$
38. $5 - \dfrac{4}{k} - \dfrac{1}{k^2} = 0$

Use the discriminant to determine the number of real solutions of each equation. You need not solve the equations.

39. $25t^2 + 49 = 70t$
40. $9z^2 - 12z = 1$
41. $13x^2 + 24x - 5 = 0$
42. $20x^2 + 19x + 5 = 0$

Use a calculator and the quadratic formula to find approximate solutions of each equation. (See Example 5.)

43. $4.42x^2 - 10.14x + 3.79 = 0$
44. $3x^2 - 82.74x + 570.4923 = 0$
45. $7.63x^2 + 2.79x = 5.32$
46. $8.06x^2 + 25.8726x = 25.047256$

Solve the following problems. (See Example 3.)

47. **Physical Science** According to the Federal Aviation Administration, the maximum recommended taxiing speed x (in miles per hour) for a plane on a curved runway exit is given by $R = .5x^2$, where R is the radius of the curve (in feet). Find the maximum taxiing speed for planes on such exits when the radius of the exit is

    (a) 450 ft   (b) 615 ft   (c) 970 ft

48. **Social Science** The enrollment E in public colleges and universities (in millions) is approximated by $E = .011x^2 + 10.7$ where x is the number of years since 1990. Find the year when enrollment is the following. (Data from: ProQuest Statistical Abstract of the United States: 2013.)

    (a) 14.7 million   (b) 17.6 million

49. **Social Science** The number of traffic fatalities F (in thousands) where a driver involved in the crash had a blood alcohol level of .08 or higher can be approximated by the function

    $$F = -.079x^2 + .46x + 13.3 \quad (0 \le x \le 10),$$

    where $x = 0$ corresponds to the year 2000. Determine in what year the number of fatalities is approximately the given number. (Data from: National Highway Traffic Safety Administration.)

    (a) 12,600   (b) 11,000

50. Finance The total assets A of private and public pension funds (in trillions of dollars) can be approximated by the function

$$A = .237x^2 - 3.96x + 28.2 \quad (6 \le x \le 11),$$

where $x = 6$ corresponds to the year 2006. (Data from: Board of Governors of the Federal Reserve System.)

(a) What were the assets in 2008?

(b) What year after 2008 produced $12.3 trillion in assets?

51. Finance The assets A of public pension funds (in trillions of dollars) can be approximated by the function

$$A = .169x^2 - 2.85x + 19.6 \quad (6 \le x \le 11),$$

where $x = 6$ corresponds to the year 2006. (Data from: Board of Governors of the Federal Reserve System.)

(a) What were the assets in 2009?

(b) What year before 2008 produced $7.9 trillion in assets?

52. Business The net income for Apple A (in billions) can be approximated by the function

$$A = .877x^2 - 9.33x + 23.4 \quad (6 \le x \le 12),$$

where $x = 6$ corresponds to 2006. Find the year in which net income was the following. (Data from: www.morningstar.com.)

(a) $17.8 billion (b) $37.7 billion

Solve the following problems. (See Examples 8 and 9).

53. Physical Science A 13-foot-long ladder leans on a wall, as shown in the accompanying figure. The bottom of the ladder is 5 feet from the wall. If the bottom is pulled out 2 feet farther from the wall, how far does the top of the ladder move down the wall? [*Hint:* Draw pictures of the right triangle formed by the ladder, the ground, and the wall before and after the ladder is moved. In each case, use the Pythagorean theorem to find the distance from the top of the ladder to the ground.]

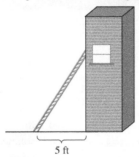

5 ft

54. Physical Science A 15-foot-long pole leans against a wall. The bottom is 9 feet from the wall. How much farther should the bottom be pulled away from the wall so that the top moves the same amount down the wall?

55. Physical Science Two trains leave the same city at the same time, one going north and the other east. The eastbound train travels 20 mph faster than the northbound one. After 5 hours, the trains are 300 miles apart. Determine the speed of each train, using the following steps.

(a) Let x denote the speed of the northbound train. Express the speed of the eastbound train in terms of x.

(b) Write expressions that give the distance traveled by each train after 5 hours.

(c) Use part (b) and the fact that the trains are 300 miles apart after 5 hours to write an equation. (A diagram of the situation may help.)

(d) Solve the equation and determine the speeds of the trains.

56. Physical Science Chris and Josh have received walkie-talkies for Christmas. If they leave from the same point at the same time, Chris walking north at 2.5 mph and Josh walking east at 3 mph, how long will they be able to talk to each other if the range of the walkie-talkies is 4 miles? Round your answer to the nearest minute.

57. Physical Science An ecology center wants to set up an experimental garden. It has 300 meters of fencing to enclose a rectangular area of 5000 square meters. Find the length and width of the rectangle as follows.

(a) Let $x =$ the length and write an expression for the width.

(b) Write an equation relating the length, width, and area, using the result of part (a).

(c) Solve the problem.

58. Business A landscape architect has included a rectangular flower bed measuring 9 feet by 5 feet in her plans for a new building. She wants to use two colors of flowers in the bed, one in the center and the other for a border of the same width on all four sides. If she can get just enough plants to cover 24 square feet for the border, how wide can the border be?

59. Physical Science Joan wants to buy a rug for a room that is 12 feet by 15 feet. She wants to leave a uniform strip of floor around the rug. She can afford 108 square feet of carpeting. What dimensions should the rug have?

60. Physical Science In 2012, Dario Franchitti won the 500-mile Indianapolis 500 race. His speed (rate) was, on average, 92 miles per hour faster than that of the 1911 winner, Ray Haround. Franchitti completed the race in 3.72 hours less time than Harroun. Find Harroun's and Franchitti's rates to the nearest tenth.

Physical Science *Use the height formula in Example 10 to work the given problems. Note that an object that is dropped (rather than thrown downward) has initial velocity $v_0 = 0$.*

61. How long does it take a baseball to reach the ground if it is dropped from the top of a 625-foot-high building? Compare the answer with that in Example 10.

62. After the baseball in Exercise 61 is dropped, how long does it take for the ball to fall 196 feet? (*Hint:* How high is the ball at that time?)

63. You are standing on a cliff that is 200 feet high. How long will it take a rock to reach the ground if

(a) you drop it?

(b) you throw it downward at an initial velocity of 40 feet per second?

(c) How far does the rock fall in 2 seconds if you throw it downward with an initial velocity of 40 feet per second?

64. A rocket is fired straight up from ground level with an initial velocity of 800 feet per second.

(a) How long does it take the rocket to rise 3200 feet?

(b) When will the rocket hit the ground?

65. A ball is thrown upward from ground level with an initial velocity of 64 ft per second. In how many seconds will the ball reach the given height?

(a) 64 ft   (b) 39 ft

(c) Why are two answers possible in part (b)?

66. **Physical Science** A ball is thrown upward from ground level with an initial velocity of 100 feet per second. In how many seconds will the ball reach the given height?

(a) 50 ft   (b) 35 ft

Solve each of the given equations for the indicated variable. Assume that all denominators are nonzero and that all variables represent positive real numbers. (See Example 11.)

67. $S = \dfrac{1}{2}gt^2$ for t

68. $a = \pi r^2$ for r

69. $L = \dfrac{d^4 k}{h^2}$ for h

70. $F = \dfrac{kMv^2}{r}$ for v

71. $P = \dfrac{E^2 R}{(r + R)^2}$ for R

72. $S = 2\pi rh + 2\pi r^2$ for r

73. Solve the equation $z^4 - 2z^2 = 15$ as follows.

(a) Let $x = z^2$ and write the equation in terms of x.

(b) Solve the new equation for x.

(c) Set z^2 equal to each positive answer in part (b) and solve the resulting equation.

Solve each of the given equations. (See Exercise 73.)

74. $6p^4 = p^2 + 2$

75. $2q^4 + 3q^2 - 9 = 0$

76. $4a^4 = 2 - 7a^2$

77. $z^4 - 3z^2 - 1 = 0$

78. $2r^4 - r^2 - 5 = 0$

✓ **Checkpoint Answers**

1. (a) $6, -2$ (b) $3/5, -5$ (c) $9/2, -5/3, -3$

2. (a) $2, -5$ (b) $1/2, -5$ (c) $9/4, 0$

3. (a) $\pm\sqrt{21}$ (b) $-7 \pm \sqrt{15}$ (c) $(3 \pm \sqrt{5})/2$

4. (a) $x = 1 + \sqrt{3}$ or $1 - \sqrt{3}$
(b) $u = 3 + \sqrt{5}$ or $3 - \sqrt{5}$

5. Late 2007

6. (a) $1/3$ (b) $-7/2$ (c) No real solutions

7. (a) 2 (b) 0 (c) 1

8. Yes, area $= 304.92$ sq. in.

9. 5 inches by 7 inches

10. (a) $p = \dfrac{b \pm \sqrt{b^2 + 4mk}}{2m}$

(b) $k = \pm\sqrt{\dfrac{3r}{AP}}$ or $\dfrac{\pm\sqrt{3rAP}}{AP}$

CHAPTER 1 Summary and Review

Key Terms and Symbols

1.1 $\approx$ is approximately equal to
π pi
$|a|$ absolute value of a
real number
natural (counting) number
whole number
integer
rational number
irrational number
properties of real numbers
order of operations
square roots
number line
interval
interval notation
absolute value

1.2 a^n a to the power n
exponent or power

multiplication with exponents
power of a power rule
zero exponent
base
polynomial
variable
coefficient
term
constant term
degree of a polynomial
zero polynomial
leading coefficient
quadratics
cubics
like terms
FOIL
revenue
fixed cost

variable cost
profit

1.3 factor
factoring
greatest common factor
difference of squares
perfect squares
sum and difference of cubes

1.4 rational expression
cancellation property
operations with rational expressions
complex fraction

1.5 $a^{1/n}$ nth root of a
$\sqrt{a}$ square root of a
$\sqrt[n]{a}$ nth root of a
properties of exponents
radical
radicand

index
rationalizing the denominator
rationalizing the numerator

1.6 first-degree equation
solution of an equation
properties of equality
extraneous solution
solving for a specified variable
absolute-value equations
solving applied problems

1.7 quadratic equation
real solution
zero-factor property
square-root property
quadratic formula
discriminant
Pythagorean theorem

Chapter 1 Key Concepts

Factoring

$$x^2 + 2xy + y^2 = (x + y)^2 \qquad x^3 - y^3 = (x - y)(x^2 + xy + y^2)$$
$$x^2 - 2xy + y^2 = (x - y)^2 \qquad x^3 + y^3 = (x + y)(x^2 - xy + y^2)$$
$$x^2 - y^2 = (x + y)(x - y)$$

Properties of Radicals

Let a and b be real numbers, n be a positive integer, and m be any integer for which the given relationships exist. Then

$$a^{m/n} = \sqrt[n]{a^m} = (\sqrt[n]{a})^m; \qquad \sqrt[n]{a^n} = |a| \text{ if } n \text{ is even}; \qquad \sqrt[n]{a^n} = a \text{ if } n \text{ is odd};$$

$$\sqrt[n]{a} \cdot \sqrt[n]{b} = \sqrt[n]{ab}; \qquad \frac{\sqrt[n]{a}}{\sqrt[n]{b}} = \sqrt[n]{\frac{a}{b}} \quad (b \neq 0).$$

Properties of Exponents

Let a, b, r, and s be any real numbers for which the following exist. Then

$$a^{-r} = \frac{1}{a^r} \qquad\qquad a^0 = 1 \qquad\qquad \left(\frac{a}{b}\right)^r = \frac{a^r}{b^r}$$

$$a^r \cdot a^s = a^{r+s} \qquad\qquad (a^r)^s = a^{rs} \qquad\qquad a^{1/r} = \sqrt[r]{a}$$

$$\frac{a^r}{a^s} = a^{r-s} \qquad\qquad (ab)^r = a^r b^r \qquad\qquad \left(\frac{a}{b}\right)^{-r} = \left(\frac{b}{a}\right)^r$$

Absolute Value

Assume that a and b are real numbers with $b > 0$.

The solutions of $|a| = b$ or $|a| = |b|$ are $a = b$ or $a = -b$.

Quadratic Equations

Facts needed to solve quadratic equations (in which a, b, and c are real numbers):

Factoring If $ab = 0$, then $a = 0$ or $b = 0$ or both.

Square-Root Property If $b > 0$, then the solutions of $x^2 = b$ are $\sqrt{b}$ and $-\sqrt{b}$.

Quadratic Formula The solutions of $ax^2 + bx + c = 0$ (with $a \neq 0$) are

$$x = \frac{-b \pm \sqrt{b^2 - 4ac}}{2a}.$$

Discriminant There are two real solutions of $ax^2 + bx + c = 0$ if $b^2 - 4ac > 0$, one real solution if $b^2 - 4ac = 0$, and no real solutions if $b^2 - 4ac < 0$.

Chapter 1 Review Exercises

Name the numbers from the list $-12, -6, -9/10, -\sqrt{7}, -\sqrt{4}$, $0, 1/8, \pi/4, 6,$ and $\sqrt{11}$ that are

1. whole numbers
2. integers
3. rational numbers
4. irrational numbers

Identify the properties of real numbers that are illustrated in each of the following expressions.

5. $9[(-3)4] = 9[4(-3)]$

6. $7(4 + 5) = (4 + 5)7$

7. $6(x + y - 3) = 6x + 6y + 6(-3)$

8. $11 + (5 + 3) = (11 + 5) + 3$

Express each statement in symbols.

9. x is at least 9.
10. x is negative.

Write the following numbers in numerical order from smallest to largest.

11. $|6 - 4|, -|-2|, |8 + 1|, -|3 - (-2)|$

12. $\sqrt{7}, -\sqrt{8}, -|\sqrt{16}|, |-\sqrt{12}|$

Write the following without absolute-value bars.

13. $7 - |-8|$
14. $|-3| - |-9 + 6|$

Graph each of the following on a number line.

15. $x \geq -3$
16. $-4 < x \leq 6$

Use the order of operations to simplify each of the following.

17. $\dfrac{-9 + (-6)(-3) \div 9}{6 - (-3)}$

18. $\dfrac{20 \div 4 \cdot 2 \div 5 - 1}{-9 - (-3) - 12 \div 3}$

Perform each of the indicated operations.

19. $(3x^4 - x^2 + 5x) - (-x^4 + 3x^2 - 6x)$

20. $(-8y^3 + 8y^2 - 5y) - (2y^3 + 4y^2 - 10)$

21. $(5k - 2h)(5k + 2h)$
22. $(2r - 5y)(2r + 5y)$

23. $(3x + 4y)^2$
24. $(2a - 5b)^2$

Factor each of the following as completely as possible.

25. $2kh^2 - 4kh + 5k$
26. $2m^2n^2 + 6mn^2 + 16n^2$

27. $5a^4 + 12a^3 + 4a^2$
28. $24x^3 + 4x^2 - 4x$

29. $144p^2 - 169q^2$
30. $81z^2 - 25x^2$

31. $27y^3 - 1$
32. $125a^3 + 216$

Perform each operation.

33. $\dfrac{3x}{5} \cdot \dfrac{45x}{12}$

34. $\dfrac{5k^2}{24} - \dfrac{70k}{36}$

35. $\dfrac{c^2 - 3c + 2}{2c(c - 1)} \div \dfrac{c - 2}{8c}$

36. $\dfrac{p^3 - 2p^2 - 8p}{3p(p^2 - 16)} \div \dfrac{p^2 + 4p + 4}{9p^2}$

37. $\dfrac{2m^2 - 4m + 2}{m^2 - 1} \div \dfrac{6m + 18}{m^2 + 2m - 3}$

38. $\dfrac{x^2 + 6x + 5}{4(x^2 + 1)} \cdot \dfrac{2x(x + 1)}{x^2 - 25}$

Simplify each of the given expressions. Write all answers without negative exponents. Assume that all variables represent positive real numbers.

39. 5^{-3}

40. 10^{-2}

41. -8^0

42. $\left(-\dfrac{5}{6}\right)^{-2}$

43. $4^6 \cdot 4^{-3}$

44. $7^{-5} \cdot 7^{-2}$

45. $\dfrac{8^{-5}}{8^{-4}}$

46. $\dfrac{6^{-3}}{6^4}$

47. $5^{-1} + 2^{-1}$

48. $5^{-2} + 5^{-1}$

49. $\dfrac{5^{1/3} \cdot 5^{1/2}}{5^{3/2}}$

50. $\dfrac{2^{3/4} \cdot 2^{-1/2}}{2^{1/4}}$

51. $(3a^2)^{1/2} \cdot (3^2 a)^{3/2}$

52. $(4p)^{2/3} \cdot (2p^3)^{3/2}$

Simplify each of the following expressions.

53. $\sqrt[3]{27}$

54. $\sqrt[6]{-64}$

55. $\sqrt[3]{54p^3 q^5}$

56. $\sqrt[4]{64a^5 b^3}$

57. $3\sqrt{3} - 12\sqrt{12}$

58. $8\sqrt{7} + 2\sqrt{63}$

Rationalize each denominator.

59. $\dfrac{\sqrt{3}}{1 + \sqrt{2}}$

60. $\dfrac{4 + \sqrt{2}}{4 - \sqrt{5}}$

Solve each equation.

61. $3x - 4(x - 2) = 2x + 9$

62. $4y + 9 = -3(1 - 2y) + 5$

63. $\dfrac{2m}{m - 3} = \dfrac{6}{m - 3} + 4$

64. $\dfrac{15}{k + 5} = 4 - \dfrac{3k}{k + 5}$

Solve for x.

65. $8ax - 3 = 2x$

66. $b^2 x - 2x = 4b^2$

Solve each equation.

67. $\left|\dfrac{2 - y}{5}\right| = 8$

68. $|4k + 1| = |6k - 3|$

Find all real solutions of each equation.

69. $(b + 7)^2 = 5$

70. $(2p + 1)^2 = 7$

71. $2p^2 + 3p = 2$

72. $2y^2 = 15 + y$

73. $2q^2 - 11q = 21$

74. $3x^2 + 2x = 16$

75. $6k^4 + k^2 = 1$

76. $21p^4 = 2 + p^2$

Solve each equation for the specified variable.

77. $p = \dfrac{E^2 R}{(r + R)^2}$ for r

78. $p = \dfrac{E^2 R}{(r + R)^2}$ for E

79. $K = s(s - a)$ for s

80. $kz^2 - hz - t = 0$ for z

Work these problems.

81. Finance   The percent change in stock price in 2012 for retailers The Gap and J. C. Penny was +67% and −44% respectively. Find the difference in the percent change for these two companies in 2012. (Data from: money.cnn.com.)

82. Finance   The percent change in stock price in 2012 for tech companies Dell and Hewlett-Packard was −31% and −45% respectively. Find the difference in the percent change for these two companies in 2012. (Data from: money.cnn.com.)

83. Business   A new PC is on sale for 20% off. The sale price is $895. What was the original price?

84. Business   The stock price of eBay increased 68% in 2012. If the price was $51 a share at the end of 2012, at what price did it begin the year?

85. Finance   The amount of outlays O of the U.S. government per year (in trillions of dollars) can be approximated by the function

$$O = .2x + 1.5,$$

where $x = 6$ corresponds to the year 2006. Find the year in which the outlays are the following. (Data from: U.S. Office of Management and Budget.)

(a) $3.3 trillion   **(b)** $3.9 trillion

86. Business   Estimated revenue R (in billions of dollars) from the general newspaper industry can be approximated by the function

$$R = -3.6x + 64.4,$$

where $x = 6$ corresponds to the year 2006. In what year was revenue $28.4 billion? (Data from: U.S. Census Bureau.)

87. Business   The number (in millions) of new vehicles V sold or leased in the United States can be approximated by the function $V = .89x^2 - 17.9x + 139.3$ where $x = 6$ corresponds to 2006. Find the total sales for 2012. (Data from: U.S. Bureau of Transportation Statistics.)

88. Business   The total sales (in billions of dollars) of alcoholic beverages A in the United States can be approximated by the function $A = -.023x^3 + .38x^2 + 3.29x + 107$ where $x = 0$ corresponds to the year 2000. (Data from: U.S. Department of Agriculture.)

(a) Find the total sales in 2010.

(b) In what year did sales become greater than $140 billion.

89. Business The number (in millions) of flight departures F within the United States per year can be approximated by the function

$$F = \frac{0.004x^2 + 10.3x + 5.8}{x + 1},$$

where $x = 1$ corresponds to the year 2001. (Data from: U.S. Bureau of Transportation Statistics.)

(a) How many flights departed in 2009?

(b) If the trend continues, when will the number of flights exceed 10 million?

90. Business The total amount of sales from manufacturing (in trillions of dollars) within the United States M can be approximated by

$$M = \frac{.122x^2 + 5.48x + 6.5}{x + 2},$$

where $x = 1$ corresponds to the year 2001. (Data from U.S. Census Bureau.)

(a) What were the sales in 2009?

(b) In what year did sales exceed $6.0 trillion?

91. Economics The total amount (in billions of dollars) of research and development spending by the U.S. government R can be approximated by

$$R = 4.33x^{0.66},$$

where $x = 8$ corresponds to 1998. (Data from: www.nsf.gov/statistics/)

(a) Find the spending in 2000.

(b) Find the spending in 2010.

92. Economics The total number (in millions) of employees within the United States in the service-providing industry E can be approximated by

$$E = 91.5x^{0.07},$$

where $x = 10$ corresponds to the year 2000. Assume the trend continues indefinitely. (Data from: ProQuest Statistical Abstract of the United States: 2013.)

(a) How many employees will there be in the year 2015?

(b) In what year will there be more than 115 million employees?

93. Finance Kinisha borrowed $2000 from a credit union at 12% annual interest and borrowed $500 from her aunt at 7% annual interest. What single rate of interest on $2500 results in the same total amount of interest?

94. Business A butcher makes a blend of stew meat from beef that sells for $2.80 a pound and pork that sells for $3.25 a pound. How many pounds of each meat should be used to get 30 pounds of a mix that can be sold for $3.10 a pound?

95. Business The number of patents P granted for new inventions within each U.S. state in the year 2011 is approximated by

$$P = 18.2x^2 - 26.0x + 789,$$

where x is the population of the state in millions. (Data from: U.S. Patent and Trademark Office).

(a) What is the number of patents granted for the state of New York with a population of 19.47 million?

(b) Approximate the population of Illinois with its number of patents at 3806.

96. Business Within the state of California, the number (in thousands) of patents C granted for new inventions can be approximated by

$$C = .22x^2 - 1.9x + 23.0,$$

where $x = 2$ corresponds to the year 2002. (Data from: U.S. Patent and Trademark Office.)

(a) What was the number of patents issued in California for 2011?

(b) What most recent year saw California hit 24 thousand patents?

97. Business A concrete mixer needs to know how wide to make a walk around a rectangular fountain that is 10 by 15 feet. She has enough concrete to cover 200 square feet. To the nearest tenth of a foot, how wide should the walk be in order to use up all the concrete?

98. Physical Science A new homeowner needs to put up a fence to make his yard secure. The house itself forms the south boundary and the garage forms the west boundary of the property, so he needs to fence only 2 sides. The area of the yard is 4000 square feet. He has enough material for 160 feet of fence. Find the length and width of the yard (to the nearest foot).

99. Physical Science A projectile is launched from the ground vertically upward at a rate of 150 feet per second. How many seconds will it take for the projectile to be 200 feet from the ground on its downward trip?

100. Physical Science Suppose a tennis ball is thrown downward from the top of a 700-foot-high building with an initial velocity of 55 feet per second. How long does it take to reach the ground?

Case Study 1   Consumers Often Need to Just Do the Math

In the late 1960s and early 1970s researchers conducted a series of famous experiments in which children were tested regarding their ability for delayed gratification.[*] In these experiments, a child would be offered a marshmallow, cookie, or pretzel and told that if they did not eat the treat, they could have two of the treats when the researcher returned (after about 15 minutes). Of course, some children would eat the treat immediately, and others would wait and receive two of the treats.

---

[*]Mischel, Walter, Ebbe B. Ebbesen, and Antonette Raskoff Zeiss. (1972). "Cognitive and attentional mechanisms in delay of gratification." *Journal of Personality and Social Psychology*, pp. 204–218.

Similar studies occur in studying consumer behavior among adults. Often when making purchases, consumers will purchase an appliance that initially costs less, but in the long run costs more money when one accounts for the operating expense. Imagine trying to decide whether to buy a new furnace for $4500 that is 80% efficient versus a new furnace that is 90% efficient that costs $5700. Each furnace is expected to last at least 20 years. The furnace with the 90% efficiency is estimated to cost $1800 a year to operate, while the 80% efficiency furnace is estimated to cost $2100 a year to operate—a difference of $300 a year. Thus, the original price differential of $1200 would be made up in four years. Over the course of 16 additional years, the 90% efficiency furnace would end up saving the buyer $4800.

For other appliances, the difference in total expenditures may not be as dramatic, but can still be substantial. The energy guide tags that often accompany new appliances help make it easier for consumers "to do the math" by communicating the yearly operating costs of an appliance. For example, a Kenmore new side-by-side 25.4 cubic foot refrigerator retails for $1128. The energy guide estimates the cost of operation for a year to be $72. A similarly sized new Frigidaire refrigerator retails for $1305, and the energy guide information estimates the annual cost to be $43. Over 10 years, which refrigerator costs the consumer more money?

We can write mathematical expressions to answer this question. With an initial cost of $1128, and an annual operating cost of $72, for x years of operation the cost C for the Kenmore refrigerator is

$$C = 1128 + 72x$$

For 10 years, the Kenmore would cost $C = 1128 + 72(10) = \$1848$. For the Frigidaire model, the cost is

$$C = 1305 + 43x.$$

For 10 years, the Frigidaire would cost $C = 1305 + 43(10) = \$1735$.

Thus, the Frigidaire refrigerator costs $113 less in total costs over 10 years.

Behavior when a consumer seeks the up-front savings sounds very similar to the delayed gratification studies among children. These kinds of behavior are of interest to both psychologists and economists. The implications are also very important in the marketing of energy-efficient appliances that often do have a higher initial cost, but save consumers money over the lifetime of the product.

One tool to help consumers make the best choice in the long run is simply to take the time to "just do the math," as the common expression goes. The techniques of this chapter can be applied to do just that!

Exercises

1. On the homedepot.com website, a General Electric 40-gallon electric hot water tank retails for $218 and the estimated annual cost of operation is $508. Write an expression for the cost to buy and run the hot water tank for x years.

2. On the homedepot.com website, a General Electric 40-gallon gas hot water tank retails for $328 and the estimated annual cost of operation is $309. Write an expression for the cost to buy and run the hot water tank for x years.

3. Over ten years, does the electric or gas hot water tank cost more? By how much?

4. In how many years will the total for the two hot water tanks be equal?

5. On the Lowes website, a Maytag 25-cubic-foot refrigerator was advertised for $1529.10 with an estimated cost per month in electricity of $50 a year. Write an expression for the cost to buy and run the refrigerator for x years.

6. On the HomeDepot website, an LG Electronics 25-cubic-foot refrigerator was advertised for $1618.20 with an estimated cost per month in electricity of $44 a year. Write an expression for the cost to buy and run the refrigerator for x years.

7. Over ten years, which refrigerator (the Maytag or the LG) costs the most? By how much?

8. In how many years will the total for the two refrigerators be equal.

Extended Project

A high-end real estate developer needs to install 50 new washing machines in a building she leases to tenants (with utilities included in the monthly rent). She knows that energy-efficient front loaders cost less per year to run, but they can be much more expensive than traditional top loaders. Investigate by visiting an appliance store or using the Internet, the prices and energy efficiency of two comparable front-loading and top-loading washing machines.

1. Estimate how many years it will take for the total expenditure (including purchase and cost of use) for the 50 front-loading machines to equal the total expenditure for the 50 top-loading machines.

2. The energy guide ratings use data that is often several years old. If the owner believes that current energy costs are 20% higher than what is indicated with the energy guide, redo the calculations for (1) above and determine if it will take less time for the two total expenditures to be equal.

Graphs, Lines, and Inequalities

2

CHAPTER OUTLINE

Data from current and past events is often a useful tool in business and in the social and health sciences. Gathering data is the first step in developing mathematical models that can be used to analyze a situation and predict future performance. For examples of linear models in transportation, business, and health see Exercises 15, 16, and 21 on page 94.

Graphical representations of data are commonly used in business and in the health and social sciences. Lines, equations, and inequalities play an important role in developing mathematical models from such data. This chapter presents both algebraic and graphical methods for dealing with these topics.

2.1 Graphs

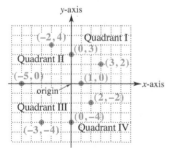

Figure 2.1

Just as the number line associates the points on a line with real numbers, a similar construction in two dimensions associates points in a plane with *ordered pairs* of real numbers. A **Cartesian coordinate system,** as shown in Figure 2.1, consists of a horizontal number line (usually called the **x-axis**) and a vertical number line (usually called the **y-axis**). The point where the number lines meet is called the **origin.** Each point in a Cartesian coordinate system is labeled with an **ordered pair** of real numbers, such as $(-2, 4)$ or $(3, 2)$. Several points and their corresponding ordered pairs are shown in Figure 2.1.

For the point labeled $(-2, 4)$, for example, -2 is the **x-coordinate** and 4 is the **y-coordinate.** You can think of these coordinates as directions telling you how to move to this point from the origin: You go 2 horizontal units to the left (x-coordinate) and 4 vertical

65

✓ **Checkpoint 1**

Locate $(-1, 6), (-3, -5), (4, -3),$ $(0, 2),$ and $(-5, 0)$ on a coordinate system.

Answers to Checkpoint exercises are found at the end of the section.

units upward (y-coordinate). From now on, instead of referring to "the point labeled by the ordered pair $(-2, 4)$," we will say "the point $(-2, 4)$." ✓₁

The x-axis and the y-axis divide the plane into four parts, or **quadrants,** which are numbered as shown in Figure 2.1. The points on the coordinate axes belong to no quadrant.

Equations and Graphs

A **solution of an equation** in two variables, such as

$$y = -2x + 3$$

or

$$y = x^2 + 7x - 2,$$

is an ordered pair of numbers such that the substitution of the first number for x and the second number for y produces a true statement.

Example 1   Which of the following are solutions of $y = -2x + 3$?

(a) $(2, -1)$

Solution   This is a solution of $y = -2x + 3$ because "$-1 = -2 \cdot 2 + 3$" is a true statement.

(b) $(4, 7)$

Solution   Since $-2 \cdot 4 + 3 = -5$, and not 7, the ordered pair $(4, 7)$ is not a solution of $y = -2x + 3$. ✓₂

✓ **Checkpoint 2**

Which of the following are solutions of

$$y = x^2 + 5x - 3?$$

(a) $(1, 3)$

(b) $(-2, -3)$

(c) $(-1, -7)$

Equations in two variables, such as $y = -2x + 3$, typically have an infinite number of solutions. To find one, choose a number for x and then compute the value of y that produces a solution. For instance, if $x = 5$, then $y = -2 \cdot 5 + 3 = -7$, so that the pair $(5, -7)$ is a solution of $y = -2x + 3$. Similarly, if $x = 0$, then $y = -2 \cdot 0 + 3 = 3$, so that $(0, 3)$ is also a solution.

The **graph** of an equation in two variables is the set of points in the plane whose coordinates (ordered pairs) are solutions of the equation. Thus, the graph of an equation is a picture of its solutions. Since a typical equation has infinitely many solutions, its graph has infinitely many points.

Example 2   Sketch the graph of $y = -2x + 5$.

Solution   Since we cannot plot infinitely many points, we construct a table of y-values for a reasonable number of x-values, plot the corresponding points, and make an "educated guess" about the rest. The table of values and points in Figure 2.2 suggests that the graph is a straight line, as shown in Figure 2.3. ✓₃

✓ **Checkpoint 3**

Graph $x = 5y$.

x	$-2x + 5$
-1	7
0	5
2	1
4	-3
5	-5

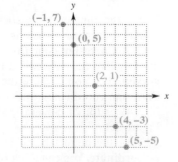

Figure 2.2

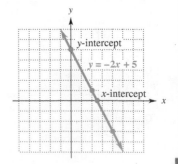

Figure 2.3

An *x*-**intercept** of a graph is the *x*-coordinate of a point where the graph intersects the *x*-axis. The *y*-coordinate of this point is 0, since it is on the axis. Consequently, to find the *x*-intercepts of the graph of an equation, set $y = 0$ and solve for *x*. For instance, in Example 2, the *x*-intercept of the graph of $y = -2x + 5$ (see Figure 2.3) is found by setting $y = 0$ and solving for *x*:

$$0 = -2x + 5$$
$$2x = 5$$
$$x = \frac{5}{2}.$$

Similarly, a *y*-**intercept** of a graph is the *y*-coordinate of a point where the graph intersects the *y*-axis. The *x*-coordinate of this point is 0. The *y*-intercepts are found by setting $x = 0$ and solving for *y*. For example, the graph of $y = -2x + 5$ in Figure 2.3 has *y*-intercept 5. ✓4

✓**Checkpoint 4**

Find the *x*- and *y*-intercepts of the graphs of these equations.

(a) $3x + 4y = 12$

(b) $5x - 2y = 8$

Example 3 Find the *x*- and *y*-intercepts of the graph of $y = x^2 - 2x - 8$, and sketch the graph.

Solution To find the *y*-intercept, set $x = 0$ and solve for *y*:

$$y = x^2 - 2x - 8 = 0^2 - 2 \cdot 0 - 8 = -8.$$

The *y*-intercept is -8. To find the *x*-intercept, set $y = 0$ and solve for *x*.

$$x^2 - 2x - 8 = y$$
$$x^2 - 2x - 8 = 0 \qquad \text{Set } y = 0.$$
$$(x + 2)(x - 4) = 0 \qquad \text{Factor.}$$
$$x + 2 = 0 \quad \text{or} \quad x - 4 = 0 \qquad \text{Zero-factor property}$$
$$x = -2 \quad \text{or} \qquad x = 4$$

The *x*-intercepts are -2 and 4. Now make a table, using both positive and negative values for *x*, and plot the corresponding points, as in Figure 2.4. These points suggest that the entire graph looks like Figure 2.5.

x	$x^2 - 2x - 8$
-3	7
-2	0
-1	-5
0	-8
1	-9
3	-5
4	0
5	7

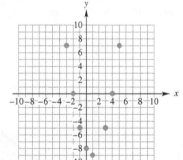

Figure 2.4

Figure 2.5

Example 4 Sketch the graph of $y = \sqrt{x + 2}$.

Solution Notice that $\sqrt{x + 2}$ is a real number only when $x + 2 \geq 0$—that is, when $x \geq -2$. Furthermore, $y = \sqrt{x + 2}$ is always nonnegative. Hence, all points on the graph lie on or above the *x*-axis and on or to the right of $x = -2$. Computing some typical values, we obtain the graph in Figure 2.6.

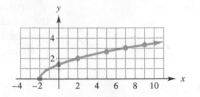

x	$\sqrt{x+2}$
-2	0
0	$\sqrt{2} \approx 1.414$
2	2
5	$\sqrt{7} \approx 2.646$
7	3
9	$\sqrt{11} \approx 3.317$

Figure 2.6

Example 2 shows that the solution of the equation $-2x + 5 = 0$ is the x-intercept of the graph of $y = -2x + 5$. Example 3 shows that the solutions of the equation $x^2 - 2x - 8 = 0$ are the x-intercepts of the graph $y = x^2 - 2x - 8$. Similar facts hold in the general case.

Intercepts and Equations

The real solutions of a one-variable equation of the form

$$\text{expression in } x = 0$$

are the x-intercepts of the graph of

$$y = \text{same expression in } x.$$

Graph Reading

Information is often given in graphical form, so you must be able to read and interpret graphs—that is, translate graphical information into statements in English.

Example 5   **Finance**   Newspapers and websites summarize activity of the S&P 500 Index in graphical form. The results for the 20 trading days for the month of December, 2012 are displayed in Figure 2.7. The first coordinate of each point on the graph is the trading day in December, and the second coordinate represents the closing price of the S&P 500 on that day. (Data from: www.morningstar.com.)

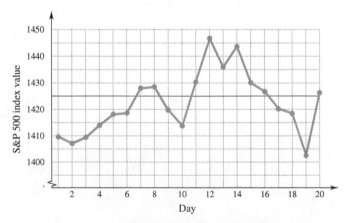

Figure 2.7

(a) What was the value of the S&P 500 Index on day 11 and day 17?

Solution   The point $(11, 1430)$ is on the graph, which means that the value of the index was 1430. The point $(17, 1420)$ is on the graph, which means that the value of the index was 1420 on that day.

(b) On what days was the value of the index above 1425?

Solution Look for points whose second coordinates are greater than 1425—that is, points that lie above the horizontal line through 1425 (shown in red in Figure 2.7). The first coordinates of these points are the days when the index value was above 1425. We see these days occurred on days 7, 8, 11, 12, 13, 14, 15, 16, and 20. ☑️5

The next example deals with the basic business relationship that was introduced in Section 1.2:

$$\text{Profit} = \text{Revenue} - \text{Cost}.$$

✓ **Checkpoint 5**

From Figure 2.7 determine when the S&P 500 had its highest point and its lowest point. What where the index values on those days?

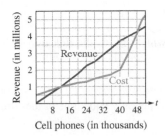

Figure 2.8

| **Example 6** | **Business** Monthly revenue and costs for the Webster Cell Phone Company are determined by the number t of phones produced and sold, as shown in Figure 2.8. |

(a) How many phones should be produced each month if the company is to make a profit (assuming that all phones produced are sold)?

Solution Profit is revenue minus cost, so the company makes a profit whenever revenue is greater than cost—that is, when the revenue graph is above the cost graph. Figure 2.8 shows that this occurs between $t = 12$ and $t = 48$—that is, when 12,000 to 48,000 phones are produced. If the company makes fewer than 12,000 phones, it will lose money (because costs will be greater than revenue.) It also loses money by making more than 48,000 phones. (One reason might be that high production levels require large amounts of overtime pay, which drives costs up too much.)

(b) Is it more profitable to make 40,000 or 44,000 phones?

Solution On the revenue graph, the point with first coordinate 40 has second coordinate of approximately 3.7, meaning that the revenue from 40,000 phones is about 3.7 million dollars. The point with first coordinate 40 on the cost graph is $(40, 2)$, meaning that the cost of producing 40,000 phones is 2 million dollars. Therefore, the profit on 40,000 phones is about $3.7 - 2 = 1.7$ million dollars. For 44,000 phones, we have the approximate points $(44, 4)$ on the revenue graph and $(44, 3)$ on the cost graph. So the profit on 44,000 phones is $4 - 3 = 1$ million dollars. Consequently, it is more profitable to make 40,000 phones. ☑️6

✓ **Checkpoint 6**

In Example 6, find the profit from making

(a) 32,000 phones;

(b) 4000 phones.

◤ Technology and Graphs

A graphing calculator or computer graphing program follows essentially the same procedure used when graphing by hand: The calculator selects a large number of x-values (95 or more), equally spaced along the x-axis, and plots the corresponding points, simultaneously connecting them with line segments. Calculator-generated graphs are generally quite accurate, although they may not appear as smooth as hand-drawn ones. The next example illustrates the basics of graphing on a graphing calculator. (Computer graphing software operates similarly.)

| **Example 7** | Use a graphing calculator to sketch the graph of the equation |

$$2x^3 - 2y - 10x + 2 = 0.$$

Solution *First, set the **viewing window***—the portion of the coordinate plane that will appear on the screen. Press the WINDOW key (labeled RANGE or PLOT-SETUP on some calculators) and enter the appropriate numbers, as in Figure 2.9 (which shows the screen from a TI-84+; other calculators are similar). Then the calculator will display the portion of the plane inside the dashed lines shown in Figure 2.10—that is, the points (x, y) with $-9 \leq x \leq 9$ and $-6 \leq y \leq 6$.

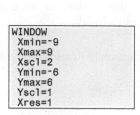

Figure 2.9

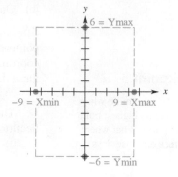

Figure 2.10

In Figure 2.9, we have set Xscl = 2 and Yscl = 1, which means the **tick marks** on the x-axis are two units apart and the tick marks on the y-axis are one unit apart (as shown in Figure 2.10).

Second, enter the equation to be graphed in the equation memory. To do this, you must first solve the equation for y (because a calculator accepts only equations of the form $y = $ expression in x):

$$2y = 2x^3 - 10x + 2$$
$$y = x^3 - 5x + 1.$$

Now press the Y = key (labeled SYMB on some calculators) and enter the equation, using the "variable key" for x. (This key is labeled X, T, θ, n or X, θ, T or x-VAR, depending on the calculator.) Figure 2.11 shows the equation entered on a TI-84+; other calculators are similar. Now press GRAPH (or PLOT or DRW on some calculators), and obtain Figure 2.12.

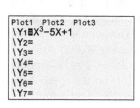

Figure 2.11

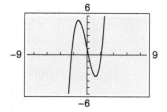

Figure 2.12

Finally, if necessary, change the viewing window to obtain a more readable graph. It is difficult to see the y-intercept in Figure 2.12, so press WINDOW and change the viewing window (Figure 2.13); then press GRAPH to obtain Figure 2.14, in which the y-intercept at $y = 1$ is clearly shown. (It isn't necessary to reenter the equation.)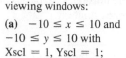

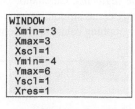

Figure 2.13

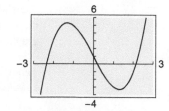

Figure 2.14

✓ **Checkpoint 7**

Use a graphing calculator to graph $y = 18x - 3x^3$ in the following viewing windows:

(a) $-10 \le x \le 10$ and $-10 \le y \le 10$ with Xscl = 1, Yscl = 1;

(b) $-5 \le x \le 5$ and $-20 \le y \le 20$ with Xscl = 1, Yscl = 5.

◤ Technology Tools

In addition to graphing equations, graphing calculators (and graphing software) provide convenient tools for solving equations and reading graphs. For example, when you have graphed an equation, you can readily determine the points the calculator plotted. Press **trace** (a cursor will appear on the graph), and use the left and right arrow keys to move the cursor along the graph. The coordinates of the point the cursor is on appear at the bottom of the screen.

Recall that the solutions of an equation, such as $x^3 - 5x + 1 = 0$, are the x-intercepts of the graph of $y = x^3 - 5x + 1$. (See the box on page 68.) A **graphical root finder** enables you to find these x-intercepts and thus to solve the equation.

✓ Checkpoint 8

Use a graphical root finder to approximate the third solution of the equation in Example 8.

Example 8 Use a graphical root finder to solve $x^3 - 5x + 1 = 0$.

Solution First, graph $y = x^3 - 5x + 1$. The x-intercepts of this graph are the solutions of the equation. To find these intercepts, look for "root" or "zero" in the appropriate menu.* Check your instruction manual for the proper syntax. A typical root finder (see Figure 2.15) shows that two of the solutions (x-intercepts) are $x \approx .2016$ and $x \approx 2.1284$. For the third solution, see Checkpoint 8. ✓₈

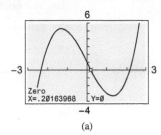 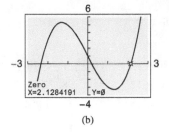

(a)   (b)

Figure 2.15

Many graphs have peaks and valleys (for instance, the graphs in Figure 2.15). A **maximum/minimum finder** provides accurate approximations of the locations of the "tops" of the peaks and the "bottoms" of the valleys.

✓ Checkpoint 9

Use a minimum finder to locate the approximate coordinates of the lowest point on the graph in Figure 2.16.

Example 9 **Business** The net income (in millions of dollars) for Marriott International, Inc. can be approximated by

$$6.159x^3 - 130.9x^2 + 783.4x - 749,$$

where $x = 2$ corresponds to the year 2002. In what year was the net income the highest? What was the net income that year? (Data from: www.morningstar.com.)

Solution The graph of $y = 6.159x^3 - 130.9x^2 + 783.4x - 749$ is shown in Figure 2.16. The highest net income corresponds to the highest point on this graph. To find this point, look for "maximum" or "max" or "extremum" in the same menu as the graphical root finder. Check your instruction manual for the proper syntax. A typical maximum finder (Figure 2.17) shows that the highest point has approximate coordinates (4.29, 688.96). The first coordinate is the year and the second is the net income (in millions). So the largest net income occurred in 2004 and the net income was approximately $689 million. ✓₉

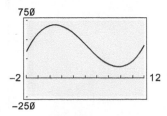 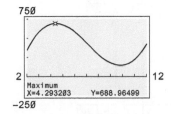

Figure 2.16   **Figure 2.17**

---

*CALC on TI-84+, GRAPH MATH on TI-86, G-SOLV on Casio.

2.1 Exercises

State the quadrant in which each point lies.

1. $(1, -2), (-2, 1), (3, 4), (-5, -6)$

2. $(\pi, 2), (3, -\sqrt{2}), (4, 0), (-\sqrt{3}, \sqrt{3})$

Determine whether the given ordered pair is a solution of the given equation. (See Example 1.)

3. $(1, -3); 3x - y - 6 = 0$

4. $(2, -1); x^2 + y^2 - 6x + 8y = -15$

5. $(3, 4); (x - 2)^2 + (y + 2)^2 = 6$

6. $(1, -1); \dfrac{x^2}{2} + \dfrac{y^2}{3} = -4$

Sketch the graph of each of these equations. (See Example 2.)

7. $4y + 3x = 12$

8. $2x + 7y = 14$

9. $8x + 3y = 12$

10. $9y - 4x = 12$

11. $x = 2y + 3$

12. $x - 3y = 0$

List the x-intercepts and y-intercepts of each graph.

13.

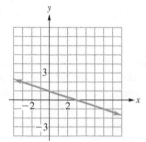

14.

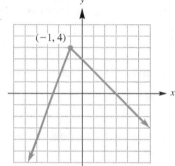

15.

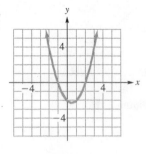

16.

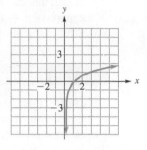

Find the x-intercepts and y-intercepts of the graph of each equation. You need not sketch the graph. (See Example 3.)

17. $3x + 4y = 12$

18. $x - 2y = 5$

19. $2x - 3y = 24$

20. $3x + y = 4$

21. $y = x^2 - 9$

22. $y = x^2 + 4$

23. $y = x^2 + x - 20$

24. $y = 5x^2 + 6x + 1$

25. $y = 2x^2 - 5x + 7$

26. $y = 3x^2 + 4x - 4$

Sketch the graph of the equation. (See Examples 2–4.)

27. $y = x^2$

28. $y = x^2 + 2$

29. $y = x^2 - 3$

30. $y = 2x^2$

31. $y = x^2 - 6x + 5$

32. $y = x^2 + 2x - 3$

33. $y = x^3$

34. $y = x^3 - 3$

35. $y = x^3 + 1$

36. $y = x^3/2$

37. $y = \sqrt{x + 4}$

38. $y = \sqrt{x - 2}$

39. $y = \sqrt{4 - x^2}$

40. $y = \sqrt{9 - x^2}$

Business *An article in the Wall Street Journal on March 17, 2012 spoke of the increase in production of pipe tobacco as stores and consumers found that pipe tobacco is often not subject to the same taxes as cigarette tobacco. The graph below shows the production of pipe tobacco (in millions of pounds) and of roll-your-own tobacco (in millions of pounds). (Data from: Alcohol and Tobacco Tax and Trade Bureau.) (See Examples 5 and 6.)*

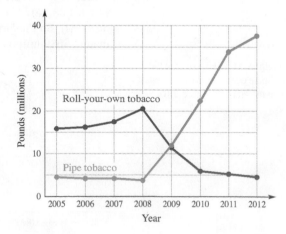

41. In what year did roll-your-own tobacco hit its peak of production? What was that peak production?

42. In what year did both roll-your-own tobacco and pipe tobacco have approximately the same level of production? How much was produced for each?

43. In what year did pipe tobacco production exceed roll-your-own tobacco by at least 25 million pounds?

44. In what years did roll-your-own tobacco production exceed pipe tobacco production by less than 10 million pounds?

Business *Use the revenue and cost graphs for the Webster Cell Phone Company in Example 6 to do Exercises 45–48.*

45. Find the approximate cost of manufacturing the given number of phones.

    (a) 20,000   **(b)** 36,000   **(c)** 48,000

46. Find the approximate revenue from selling the given number of phones.

    (a) 12,000   **(b)** 24,000   **(c)** 36,000

47. Find the approximate profit from manufacturing the given number of phones.

    (a) 20,000   **(b)** 28,000   **(c)** 36,000

48. The company must replace its aging machinery with better, but much more expensive, machines. In addition, raw material prices increase, so that monthly costs go up by $250,000. Owing to competitive pressure, phone prices cannot be increased, so revenue remains the same. Under these new circumstances, find the approximate profit from manufacturing the given number of phones.

    (a) 20,000   **(b)** 36,000   **(c)** 40,000

Business *The graph below gives the annual per-person retail availability of beef, chicken, and pork (in pounds) from 2001 to 2010. Use the graph to answer the following questions. (Data from: U.S. Department of Agriculture.)*

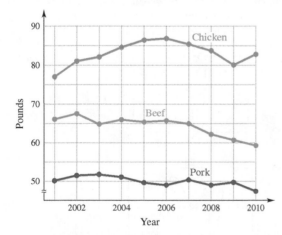

49. What is the approximate annual per-person retail availability of beef, chicken, and pork in 2010?

50. In what year was annual availability of beef the highest?

51. In what year was annual availability of chicken the lowest?

52. How much did the annual availability of beef decrease from 2001 to 2010?

Business *The graph below gives the total sales (in billions of dollars) at grocery stores within the United States from 2005 to 2015. (Years 2011–2015 are projections.) Use the graph to answer the following questions. (Data from: U.S. Census Bureau.)*

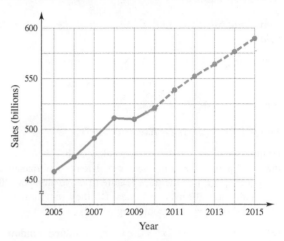

53. What were the total sales at grocery stores in 2008?

54. In what years are total sales below $525 billion (including projections)?

55. In what years are total sales above $500 billion (including projections)?

56. How much are grocery sales projected to increase from 2010 to 2015?

Business *The graph below shows the closing share prices (in dollars) for Hewlett-Packard Corporation and Intel Corporation on the 21 trading days of the month of January, 2013. Use this graph to answer the following questions.*

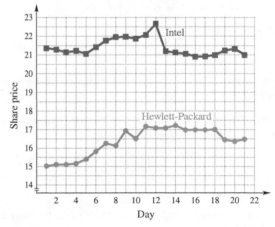

57. What was the approximate closing share price for Hewlett-Packard on day 21? for Intel?

58. What was the approximate closing share price for Hewlett-Packard on day 9? for Intel?

59. What was the highest closing share price for Hewlett-Packard and on what day did this occur?

60. What was the highest closing share price for Intel and on what day did this occur?

61. Was the difference in share price between the two companies ever more than $7.00?

62. Over the course of the month, what was the gain in share price for Hewlett-Packard?

Use a graphing calculator to find the graph of the equation. (See Example 7.)

63. $y = x^2 + x + 1$ **64.** $y = 2 - x - x^2$

65. $y = (x - 3)^3$ **66.** $y = x^3 + 2x^2 + 2$

67. $y = x^3 - 3x^2 + x - 1$ **68.** $y = x^4 - 5x^2 - 2$

Use a graphing calculator for Exercises 69–70.

69. Graph $y = x^4 - 2x^3 + 2x$ in a window with $-3 \le x \le 3$. Is the "flat" part of the graph near $x = 1$ really a horizontal line segment? (*Hint:* Use the trace feature to move along the "flat" part and watch the y-coordinates. Do they remain the same [as they should on a horizontal segment]?)

70. (a) Graph $y = x^4 - 2x^3 + 2x$ in the **standard window** (the one with $-10 \le x \le 10$ and $-10 \le y \le 10$). Use the trace feature to approximate the coordinates of the lowest point on the graph.

     (b) Use a minimum finder to obtain an accurate approximation of the lowest point. How does this compare with your answer in part (a)?

Use a graphing calculator to approximate all real solutions of the equation. (See Example 8.)

71. $x^3 - 3x^2 + 5 = 0$

72. $x^3 + x - 1 = 0$

73. $2x^3 - 4x^2 + x - 3 = 0$

74. $6x^3 - 5x^2 + 3x - 2 = 0$

75. $x^5 - 6x + 6 = 0$

76. $x^3 - 3x^2 + x - 1 = 0$

Use a graphing calculator to work Exercises 77–80. (See Examples 8 and 9.)

Finance *The financial assets of the mutual fund industry (in trillions of dollars) can be approximated by*

$$y = .0556x^3 - 1.286x^2 + 9.76x - 17.4,$$

where $x = 5$ corresponds to 2005. (Data from: Board of Governors of the Federal Reserve System.)

77. Find the maximum value of the total assets between 2005 and 2008.

78. Find the minimum value of the total assets between 2008 and 2011.

Finance *The financial assets of households (in trillions of dollars) can be approximated by*

$$y = .328x^3 - 7.75x^2 + 59.03x - 97.1,$$

where $x = 5$ corresponds to 2005. (Data from: Board of Governors of the Federal Reserve System.)

79. Find the minimum value of the household assets between 2007 and 2011.

80. Find the maximum value of the household assets between 2005 and 2008.

✓ Checkpoint Answers

1.

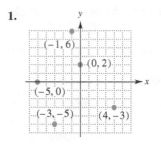

2. (a) and (c)

3.

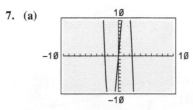

4. (a) x-intercept 4, y-intercept 3

     (b) x-intercept $8/5$, y-intercept -4

5. The highest was 1446 on day 12

     The lowest was 1407 on day 11

6. (a) About $1,200,000 (rounded)

     (b) About $-$500,000
        (that is, a loss of $500,000)

7. (a)

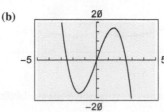

     (b)

8. $x \approx -2.330059$

9. $(9.88, 153.19)$

2.2 Equations of Lines

Straight lines, which are the simplest graphs, play an important role in a wide variety of applications. They are considered here from both a geometric and an algebraic point of view.

The key geometric feature of a nonvertical straight line is how steeply it rises or falls as you move from left to right. The "steepness" of a line can be represented numerically by a number called the *slope* of the line.

To see how the slope is defined, start with Figure 2.18, which shows a line passing through the two different points $(x_1, y_1) = (-5, 6)$ and $(x_2, y_2) = (4, -7)$. The difference in the two x-values,

$$x_2 - x_1 = 4 - (-5) = 9,$$

is called the **change in x.** Similarly, the **change in y** is the difference in the two y-values:

$$y_2 - y_1 = -7 - 6 = -13.$$

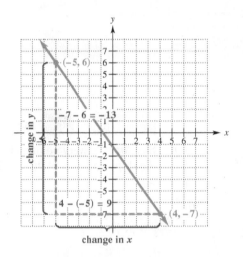

Figure 2.18

The **slope** of the line through the two points (x_1, y_1) and (x_2, y_2), where $x_1 \neq x_2$, is defined as the quotient of the change in y and the change in x:

$$\textbf{slope} = \frac{\textbf{change in } y}{\textbf{change in } x} = \frac{y_2 - y_1}{x_2 - x_1}.$$

The slope of the line in Figure 2.18 is

$$\text{slope} = \frac{-7 - 6}{4 - (-5)} = -\frac{13}{9}.$$

Using similar triangles from geometry, we can show that the slope is independent of the choice of points on the line. That is, the same value of the slope will be obtained for *any* choice of two different points on the line.

Example 1   Find the slope of the line through the points $(-6, 8)$ and $(5, 4)$.

Solution   Let $(x_1, y_1) = (-6, 8)$ and $(x_2, y_2) = (5, 4)$. Use the definition of slope as follows:

$$\text{slope} = \frac{y_2 - y_1}{x_2 - x_1} = \frac{4 - 8}{5 - (-6)} = \frac{-4}{11} = -\frac{4}{11}.$$

The slope can also by found by letting $(x_1, y_1) = (5, 4)$ and $(x_2, y_2) = (-6, 8)$. In that case,

$$\text{slope} = \frac{y_2 - y_1}{x_2 - x_1} = \frac{8 - 4}{-6 - 5} = \frac{4}{-11} = -\frac{4}{11},$$

which is the same answer. ✓₁

✓ Checkpoint 1

Find the slope of the line through the following pairs of points.

(a) $(5, 9), (-5, -3)$

(b) $(-4, 2), (-2, -7)$

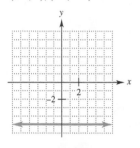

Figure 2.19

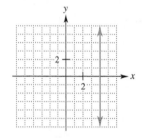

Figure 2.20

CAUTION When finding the slope of a line, be careful to subtract the *x*-values and the *y*-values in the same order. For example, with the points (4, 3) and (2, 9), if you use $9 - 3$ for the numerator, you must use $2 - 4$ (*not* $4 - 2$) for the denominator.

Example 2 Find the slope of the horizontal line in Figure 2.19.

Solution Every point on the line has the same *y*-coordinate, -5. Choose any two of them to compute the slope, say, $(x_1, y_1) = (-3, -5)$ and $(x_2, y_2) = (2, -5)$:

$$\text{slope} = \frac{-5 - (-5)}{2 - (-3)}$$

$$= \frac{0}{5}$$

$$= 0.$$

Example 3 What is the slope of the vertical line in Figure 2.20?

Solution Every point on the line has the same *x*-coordinate, 4. If we attempt to compute the slope with two of these points, say, $(x_1, y_1) = (4, -2)$ and $(x_2, y_2) = (4, 1)$, we obtain

$$\text{slope} = \frac{1 - (-2)}{4 - 4}$$

$$= \frac{3}{0}.$$

Division by 0 is not defined, so the slope of this line is undefined.

The arguments used in Examples 2 and 3 work in the general case and lead to the following conclusion.

The slope of every horizontal line is 0.

The slope of every vertical line is undefined.

Slope–Intercept Form

The slope can be used to develop an algebraic description of nonvertical straight lines. Assume that a line with slope *m* has *y*-intercept *b*, so that it goes through the point $(0, b)$. (See Figure 2.21.) Let (x, y) be any point on the line other than $(0, b)$. Using the definition of slope with the points $(0, b)$ and (x, y) gives

$$m = \frac{y - b}{x - 0}$$

$$m = \frac{y - b}{x}$$

$$mx = y - b \qquad \text{Multiply both sides by } x.$$

$$y = mx + b. \qquad \text{Add } b \text{ to both sides. Reverse the equation.}$$

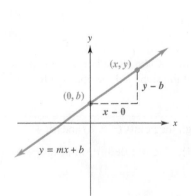

Figure 2.21

In other words, the coordinates of any point on the line satisfy the equation $y = mx + b$.

Slope–Intercept Form

If a line has slope m and y-intercept b, then it is the graph of the equation

$$y = mx + b.$$

This equation is called the **slope–intercept form** of the equation of the line.

Example 4   Find an equation for the line with y-intercept $7/2$ and slope $-5/2$.

Solution   Use the slope–intercept form with $b = 7/2$ and $m = -5/2$:

$$y = mx + b$$

$$y = -\frac{5}{2}x + \frac{7}{2}.$$

✓ **Checkpoint 2**

Find an equation for the line with

(a) y-intercept -3 and slope $2/3$;

(b) y-intercept $1/4$ and slope $-3/2$.

Example 5   Find the equation of the horizontal line with y-intercept 3.

Solution   The slope of the line is 0 (why?) and its y-intercept is 3, so its equation is

$$y = mx + b$$

$$y = 0x + 3$$

$$y = 3.$$

The argument in Example 5 also works in the general case.

If k is a constant, then the graph of the equation $y = k$ is the horizontal line with y-intercept k.

Example 6   Find the slope and y-intercept for each of the following lines.

(a) $5x - 3y = 1$

Solution   Solve for y:

$$5x - 3y = 1$$

$$-3y = -5x + 1 \qquad \text{Subtract } 5x \text{ from both sides.}$$

$$y = \frac{5}{3}x - \frac{1}{3}. \qquad \text{Divide both sides by } -3.$$

This equation is in the form $y = mx + b$, with $m = 5/3$ and $b = -1/3$. So the slope is $5/3$ and the y-intercept is $-1/3$.

(b) $-9x + 6y = 2$

Solution   Solve for y:

$$-9x + 6y = 2$$

$$6y = 9x + 2 \qquad \text{Add } 9x \text{ to both sides.}$$

$$y = \frac{3}{2}x + \frac{1}{3}. \qquad \text{Divide both sides by } 6.$$

✓ **Checkpoint 3**

Find the slope and y-intercept of

(a) $x + 4y = 6$;

(b) $3x - 2y = 1$.

The slope is $3/2$ (the coefficient of x), and the y-intercept is $1/3$. ✓₃

The slope–intercept form can be used to show how the slope measures the steepness of a line. Consider the straight lines A, B, C, and D given by the following equations, where each has y-intercept 0 and slope as indicated:

$$A: y = .5x; \qquad B: y = x; \qquad C: y = 3x; \qquad D: y = 7x.$$
$$\text{Slope .5} \qquad \text{Slope 1} \qquad \text{Slope 3} \qquad \text{Slope 7}$$

For these lines, Figure 2.22 shows that the bigger the slope, the more steeply the line rises from left to right. ✓4

✓ **Checkpoint 4**

(a) List the slopes of the following lines:

$E: y = -.3x;$ $F: y = -x;$

$G: y = -2x;$ $H: y = -5x.$

(b) Graph all four lines on the same set of axes.

(c) How are the slopes of the lines related to their steepness?

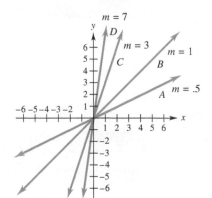

Figure 2.22

The preceding discussion and Checkpoint 4 may be summarized as follows.

Direction of Line (moving from left to right)	Slope
Upward	**Positive** (larger for steeper lines)
Horizontal	**0**
Downward	**Negative** (larger in absolute value for steeper lines)
Vertical	**Undefined**

Example 7   Sketch the graph of $x + 2y = 5$, and label the intercepts.

Solution   Find the x-intercept by setting $y = 0$ and solving for x:

$$x + 2 \cdot 0 = 5$$
$$x = 5.$$

The x-intercept is 5, and $(5, 0)$ is on the graph. The y-intercept is found similarly, by setting $x = 0$ and solving for y:

$$0 + 2y = 5$$
$$y = 5/2.$$

The y-intercept is $5/2$, and $(0, 5/2)$ is on the graph. The points $(5, 0)$ and $(0, 5/2)$ can be used to sketch the graph, as shown on the following page (Figure 2.23). ✓5

✓ **Checkpoint 5**

Graph the given lines and label the intercepts.

(a) $3x + 4y = 12$

(b) $5x - 2y = 8$

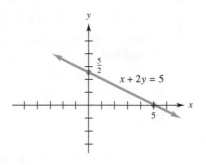

Figure 2.23

✎ **TECHNOLOGY TIP** To graph a linear equation on a graphing calculator, you must first put the equation in slope–intercept form $y = mx + b$ so that it can be entered in the equation memory (called the Y = list on some calculators). Vertical lines cannot be graphed on most calculators.

Slopes of Parallel and Perpendicular Lines

We shall assume the following facts without proof. The first one is a consequence of the fact that the slope measures steepness and that parallel lines have the same steepness.

> Two nonvertical lines are **parallel** whenever they have the same slope.
>
> Two nonvertical lines are **perpendicular** whenever the product of their slopes is -1.

Example 8   Determine whether each of the given pairs of lines are *parallel*, *perpendicular*, or *neither*.

(a) $2x + 3y = 5$ and $4x + 5 = -6y$.

Solution   Put each equation in slope–intercept form by solving for y:

$$3y = -2x + 5 \qquad\qquad -6y = 4x + 5$$
$$y = -\frac{2}{3}x + \frac{5}{3} \qquad\qquad y = -\frac{2}{3}x - \frac{5}{6}.$$

In each case, the slope (the coefficient of x) is $-2/3$, so the lines are parallel. See Figure 2.24(a).

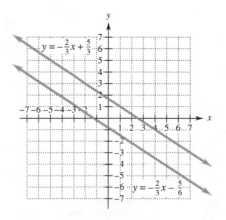

Figure 2.24(a)

(b) $3x = y + 7$ and $x + 3y = 4$.

Solution Put each equation in slope–intercept form to determine the slope of the associated line:

$$3x = y + 7 \qquad\qquad 3y = -x + 4$$

$$y = 3x - 7 \qquad\qquad y = -\frac{1}{3}x + \frac{4}{3}$$

$$\text{slope } 3 \qquad\qquad \text{slope } -1/3.$$

Since $3(-1/3) = -1$, these lines are perpendicular. See Figure 2.24(b).

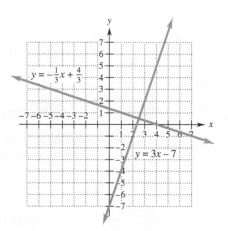

Figure 2.24(b)

(c) $x + y = 4$ and $x - 2y = 3$.

Solution Verify that the slope of the first line is -1 and the slope of the second is $1/2$. The slopes are not equal and their product is not -1, so the lines are neither parallel nor perpendicular. See Figure 2.24(c).

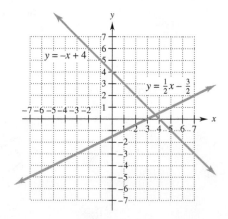

Figure 2.24(c)

✓ Checkpoint 6

Tell whether the lines in each of the following pairs are *parallel, perpendicular*, or *neither*.

(a) $x - 2y = 6$ and $2x + y = 5$

(b) $3x + 4y = 8$ and $x + 3y = 2$

(c) $2x - y = 7$ and $2y = 4x - 5$

◢ TECHNOLOGY TIP Perpendicular lines may not appear perpendicular on a graphing calculator unless you use a *square window*—a window in which a one-unit segment on the y-axis is the same length as a one-unit segment on the x-axis. To obtain such a window on most calculators, use a viewing window in which the y-axis is about two-thirds as long as the x-axis. The SQUARE (or ZSQUARE) key in the ZOOM menu will change the current window to a square window by automatically adjusting the length of one of the axes.

Point–Slope Form

The slope–intercept form of the equation of a line is usually the most convenient for graphing and for understanding how slopes and lines are related. However, it is not always the best way to *find* the equation of a line. In many situations (particularly in calculus), the slope and a point on the line are known and you must find the equation of the line. In such cases, the best method is to use the *point–slope form*, which we now explain.

Suppose that a line has slope m and that (x_1, y_1) is a point on the line. Let (x, y) represent any other point on the line. Since m is the slope, then, by the definition of slope,

$$\frac{y - y_1}{x - x_1} = m.$$

Multiplying both sides by $x - x_1$ yields

$$y - y_1 = m(x - x_1).$$

Point–Slope Form

If a line has slope m and passes through the point (x_1, y_1), then

$$y - y_1 = m(x - x_1)$$

is the **point–slope form** of the equation of the line.

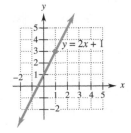

Figure 2.25

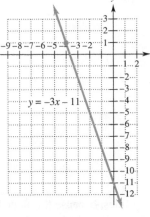

Figure 2.26

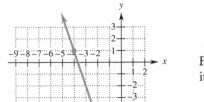 **Checkpoint 7**

Find both the point–slope and the slope–intercept form of the equation of the line having the given slope and passing through the given point.

(a) $m = -3/5, (5, -2)$

(b) $m = 1/3, (6, 8)$

Example 9 Find the equation of the line satisfying the given conditions.

(a) Slope 2; the point $(1, 3)$ is on the line.

Solution Use the point–slope form with $m = 2$ and $(x_1, y_1) = (1, 3)$. Substitute $x_1 = 1, y_1 = 3$, and $m = 2$ into the point–slope form of the equation.

$$y - y_1 = m(x - x_1)$$
$$y - 3 = 2(x - 1). \qquad \text{Point–slope form}$$

For some purposes, this form of the equation is fine; in other cases, you may want to rewrite it in the slope–intercept form.

Using algebra, we obtain the slope–intercept form of this equation:

$$y - 3 = 2(x - 1)$$
$$y - 3 = 2x - 2 \qquad \text{Distributive property}$$
$$y = 2x + 1 \qquad \text{Add 3 to each side to obtain slope-intercept form.}$$

See Figure 2.25 for the graph.

(b) Slope -3; the point $(-4, 1)$ is on the line.

Solution Use the point–slope form with $m = -3$ and $(x_1, y_1) = (-4, 1)$:

$$y - y_1 = m(x - x_1)$$
$$y - 1 = -3[x - (-4)]. \qquad \text{Point–slope form}$$

Using algebra, we obtain the slope–intercept form of this equation:

$$y - 1 = -3(x + 4)$$
$$y - 1 = -3x - 12 \qquad \text{Distributive property}$$
$$y = -3x - 11. \qquad \text{Slope–intercept form}$$

See Figure 2.26. ✔₇

The point–slope form can also be used to find an equation of a line, given two different points on the line. The procedure is shown in the next example.

> **Example 10**   Find an equation of the line through $(5, 4)$ and $(-10, -2)$.
>
> **Solution**   Begin by using the definition of the slope to find the slope of the line that passes through the two points:
>
> $$\text{slope} = m = \frac{-2 - 4}{-10 - 5} = \frac{-6}{-15} = \frac{2}{5}.$$
>
> Use $m = 2/5$ and either of the given points in the point–slope form. If $(x_1, y_1) = (5, 4)$, then
>
> $$y - y_1 = m(x - x_1)$$
>
> $$y - 4 = \frac{2}{5}(x - 5) \qquad \text{Let } y_1 = 4, m = \frac{2}{5}, \text{ and } x_1 = 5.$$
>
> $$y - 4 = \frac{2}{5}x - \frac{10}{5} \qquad \text{Distributive property}$$
>
> $$y = \frac{2}{5}x + 2 \qquad \text{Add 4 to both sides and simplify.}$$
>
> See Figure 2.27. Check that the results are the same when $(x_1, y_1) = (-10, -2)$.

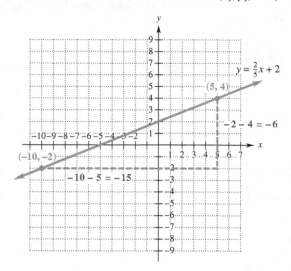

Figure 2.27

✓**Checkpoint 8**

Find an equation of the line through

(a) $(2, 3)$ and $(-4, 6)$;

(b) $(-8, 2)$ and $(3, -6)$.

Vertical Lines

The equation forms we just developed do not apply to vertical lines, because the slope is not defined for such lines. However, vertical lines can easily be described as graphs of equations.

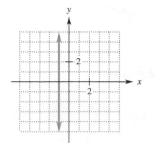

Figure 2.28

> **Example 11**   Find the equation whose graph is the vertical line in Figure 2.28.
>
> **Solution**   Every point on the line has x-coordinate -1 and hence has the form $(-1, y)$. Thus, every point is a solution of the equation $x + 0y = -1$, which is usually written simply as $x = -1$. Note that -1 is the x-intercept of the line.

The argument in Example 11 also works in the general case.

If k is a constant, then the graph of the equation $x = k$ is the vertical line with x-intercept k.

Linear Equations

An equation in two variables whose graph is a straight line is called a **linear equation.** Linear equations have a variety of forms, as summarized in the following table.

Equation	Description
$x = k$	**Vertical line,** x-intercept k, no y-intercept, undefined slope
$y = k$	**Horizontal line,** y-intercept k, no x-intercept, slope 0
$y = mx + b$	**Slope–intercept form,** slope m, y-intercept b
$y - y_1 = m(x - x_1)$	**Point–slope form,** slope m, the line passes through (x_1, y_1)
$ax + by = c$	**General form.** If $a \neq 0$ and $b \neq 0$, the line has x-intercept c/a, y-intercept c/b, and slope $-a/b$.

Note that every linear equation can be written in general form. For example, $y = 4x - 5$ can be written in general form as $4x - y = 5$, and $x = 6$ can be written in general form as $x + 0y = 6$.

Applications

Many relationships are linear or almost linear, so that they can be approximated by linear equations.

Example 12 **Business** The world-wide sales (in billions of dollars) of men's razor blades can be approximated by the linear equation

$$y = .76x + 4.44,$$

where $x = 6$ corresponds to the year 2006. The graph appears in Figure 2.29. (Data from: *Wall Street Journal,* April 12, 2012.)

(a) What were the approximate razor sales in 2011?

Solution   Substitute $x = 11$ in the equation and use a calculator to compute y:

$$y = .76x + 4.44$$
$$y = .76(11) + 4.44 = 12.80.$$

The approximate sales in 2011 were $12.8 billion.

(b) In what year did sales reach $10.5 billion?

Solution   Substitute $y = 10.5$ into the equation and solve for x:

$$10.5 = .76x + 4.44$$
$$10.5 - 4.44 = .76x \qquad \text{Subtract 4.44 from each side.}$$
$$x = \frac{10.5 - 4.44}{.76} \qquad \text{Divide each side by .76 and reverse the equation.}$$
$$x = 8.0.$$

The year was 2008.

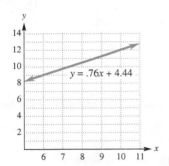

Figure 2.29

Example 13   **Education**   According to the National Center for Education Statistics, the average cost of tuition and fees at public four-year universities was $3768 in the year 2000 and grew in an approximately linear fashion to $8751 in the year 2011.

(a) Find a linear equation for these data.

Solution   Measure time along the x-axis and cost along the y-axis. Then the x-coordinate of each point is a year and the y-coordinate is the average cost of tuition and fees in that year. For convenience, let $x = 0$ correspond to 2000, and so $x = 11$ is 2011. Then the given data points are (0, 3768) and (11, 8751). The slope of the line joining these two points is

$$\frac{8751 - 3768}{11 - 0} = \frac{4983}{11} = 453.$$

Since we already know the y-intercept $b = 3768$ and the slope $m = 453$, we can write the equation as

$$y = mx + b = 453x + 3768.$$

We could also use the point-slope form with the point (11, 8751), to obtain the equation of the line:

$$y - 8751 = 453(x - 11) \quad \text{Point–slope form}$$
$$y - 8751 = 453x - 4983 \quad \text{Distributive property}$$
$$y = 453x + 3768. \quad \text{Add 8751 to both sides.}$$

Figure 2.30 shows the derived equation.

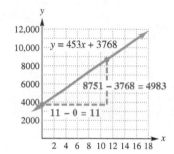

Figure 2.30

✓ **Checkpoint 9**

The average cost of tuition and fees at private four-year universities was $19,307 in 2000 and $34,805 in 2011.

(a) Let $x = 0$ correspond to 2000, and find a linear equation for the given data. (*Hint: Round the slope to the nearest integer.*)

(b) Assuming that your equation remains accurate, estimate the average cost in 2017.

(b) Use this equation to estimate the average cost of tuition and fees in the fall of 2009.

Solution   Since 2009 corresponds to $x = 9$, let $x = 9$ in the equation part of (a). Then

$$y = 453(9) + 3768 = \$7845.$$

(c) Assuming the equation remains valid beyond the fall of 2011, estimate the average cost of tuition and fees in the fall of 2018.

Solution   The year 2018 corresponds to $x = 18$, so the average cost is

$$y = 453(18) + 3768 = \$11,922. \quad ✓_9$$

2.2 Exercises

Find the slope of the given line, if it is defined. (See Examples 1–3.)

1. The line through (2, 5) and (0, 8)

2. The line through (9, 0) and (12, 12)

3. The line through (−4, 14) and (3, 0)

4. The line through (−5, −2) and (−4, 11)

5. The line through the origin and (−4, 10)

6. The line through the origin and (8, −2)

7. The line through (−1, 4) and (−1, 6)

8. The line through (−3, 5) and (2, 5)

Find an equation of the line with the given y-intercept and slope m. (See Examples 4 and 5.)

9. 5, $m = 4$

10. −3, $m = -7$

11. 1.5, $m = -2.3$

12. −4.5, $m = 2.5$

13. 4, $m = -3/4$

14. −3, $m = 4/3$

Find the slope m and the y-intercept b of the line whose equation is given. (See Example 6.)

15. $2x - y = 9$

16. $x + 2y = 7$

17. $6x = 2y + 4$

18. $4x + 3y = 24$

19. $6x - 9y = 16$ **20.** $4x + 2y = 0$

21. $2x - 3y = 0$ **22.** $y = 7$

23. $x = y - 5$

24. On one graph, sketch six straight lines that meet at a single point and satisfy this condition: one line has slope 0, two lines have positive slope, two lines have negative slope, and one line has undefined slope.

25. For which of the line segments in the figure is the slope

(a) largest?   (b) smallest?

(c) largest in absolute value?   (d) closest to 0?

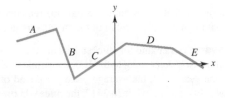

26. Match each equation with the line that most closely resembles its graph. (*Hint*: Consider the signs of m and b in the slope-intercept form.)

(a) $y = 3x + 2$ (b) $y = -3x + 2$

(c) $y = 3x - 2$ (d) $y = -3x - 2$

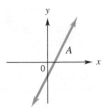
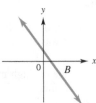
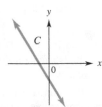
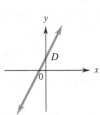

Sketch the graph of the given equation and label its intercepts. (See Example 7.)

27. $2x - y = -2$ **28.** $2y + x = 4$

29. $2x + 3y = 4$ **30.** $-5x + 4y = 3$

31. $4x - 5y = 2$ **32.** $3x + 2y = 8$

Determine whether each pair of lines is parallel, perpendicular, or neither. (See Example 8.)

33. $4x - 3y = 6$ and $3x + 4y = 8$

34. $2x - 5y = 7$ and $15y - 5 = 6x$

35. $3x + 2y = 8$ and $6y = 5 - 9x$

36. $x - 3y = 4$ and $y = 1 - 3x$

37. $4x = 2y + 3$ and $2y = 2x + 3$

38. $2x - y = 6$ and $x - 2y = 4$

39. (a) Find the slope of each side of the triangle with vertices $(9, 6)$, $(-1, 2)$, and $(1, -3)$.

(b) Is this triangle a right triangle? (*Hint*: Are two sides perpendicular?)

40. (a) Find the slope of each side of the quadrilateral with vertices $(-5, -2)$, $(-3, 1)$, $(3, 0)$, and $(1, -3)$.

(b) Is this quadrilateral a parallelogram? (*Hint*: Are opposite sides parallel?)

Find an equation of the line with slope m that passes through the given point. Put the answer in slope–intercept form. (See Example 10.)

41. $(-3, 2), m = -2/3$ **42.** $(-5, -2), m = 4/5$

43. $(2, 3), m = 3$ **44.** $(3, -4), m = -1/4$

45. $(10, 1), m = 0$ **46.** $(-3, -9), m = 0$

47. $(-2, 12)$, undefined slope   **48.** $(1, 1)$, undefined slope

Find an equation of the line that passes through the given points. (See Example 10.)

49. $(-1, 1)$ and $(2, 7)$ **50.** $(2, 5)$ and $(0, 6)$

51. $(1, 2)$ and $(3, 9)$ **52.** $(-1, -2)$ and $(2, -1)$

Find an equation of the line satisfying the given conditions.

53. Through the origin with slope 5

54. Through the origin and horizontal

55. Through $(6, 8)$ and vertical

56. Through $(7, 9)$ and parallel to $y = 6$

57. Through $(3, 4)$ and parallel to $4x - 2y = 5$

58. Through $(6, 8)$ and perpendicular to $y = 2x - 3$

59. x-intercept 6; y-intercept -6

60. Through $(-5, 2)$ and parallel to the line through $(1, 2)$ and $(4, 3)$

61. Through $(-1, 3)$ and perpendicular to the line through $(0, 1)$ and $(2, 3)$

62. y-intercept 3 and perpendicular to $2x - y + 6 = 0$

Business *The lost value of equipment over a period of time is called depreciation. The simplest method for calculating depreciation is straight-line depreciation. The annual straight-line depreciation D of an item that cost x dollars with a useful life of n years is $D = (1/n)x$. Find the depreciation for items with the given characteristics.*

63. Cost: $15,965; life 12 yr

64. Cost: $41,762; life 15 yr

65. Cost: $201,457; life 30 yr

66. Business   Ral Corp. has an incentive compensation plan under which a branch manager receives 10% of the branch's income after deduction of the bonus, but before deduction of income tax. The income of a particular branch before the bonus and income tax was $165,000. The tax rate was 30%. The bonus amounted to

(a) $12,600   (b) $15,000

(c) $16,500   (d) $18,000

67. Business   According to data from the U.S. Centers for Medicare and Medicaid Services, the sales (in billions of dollars) from drug prescriptions can be approximated by

$$y = 13.69x + 133.6,$$

where $x = 1$ corresponds to the year 2001. Find the approximate sales from prescription drugs in the following years.

(a) 2005

(b) 2010

(c) Assuming this model remains accurate, in what year will the prescriptions be $340 billion?

68. Business   The total revenue generated from hospital care (in billions of dollars) can be approximated by

$$y = 40.89x + 405.3,$$

where $x = 1$ corresponds to the year 2001. (Data from: U.S. Centers for Medicare and Medicaid Services.)

(a) What was the approximate revenue generated from hospital stays in 2010?

(b) Assuming the model remains accurate, in what year will revenue be approximately $1 trillion?

69. Business   The number of employees (in thousands) working in the motion picture and sound recording industries can be approximated by

$$y = -1.8x + 384.6,$$

where $x = 0$ corresponds to the year 2000. (Data from: U.S. Bureau of Labor Statistics.)

(a) What was the number of employees in the year 2000?

(b) What was the number of employees in the year 2010?

(c) Assuming the model remains accurate, in what year will the number of employees be 350,000?

70. Business   The number of golf facilities in the United States has been declining and can be approximated with the equation

$$y = -42.1x + 16,288,$$

where $x = 5$ corresponds to the year 2005. (Data from: National Golf Association.)

(a) How many golf facilities were there in 2010?

(b) If the trend continues to hold, in what year will there be 15,500 golf facilities?

71. Business   In the United States, total sales related to lawn care were approximately $35.1 billion in 2005 and $29.7 billion in 2011. (Data from: The National Gardening Association.)

(a) Let the x-axis denote time and the y-axis denote the sales related to lawn care (in billions of dollars). Let $x = 5$ correspond to 2005. Fill in the blanks. The given data is represented by the points (_____, $35.1) and (11, _____).

(b) Find the linear equation determined by the two points in part (a).

(c) Use the equation in part (b) to estimate the sales produced in 2009.

(d) If the model remains accurate, when will lawn care sales reach $25 billion?

72. Business   According the Bureau of Labor Statistics, there were approximately 16.3 million union workers in the year 2000 and 14.9 million union workers in the year 2010.

(a) Consider the change in union workers to be linear and write an equation expressing the number y of union workers in terms of the number x of years since 2000.

(b) Assuming that the equation in part (a) remains accurate, use it to predict the number of union workers in 2015.

73. Business   The demand for chicken legs in the chicken industry has increased. According to the U.S. Department of Agriculture, in the year 2002, the average price per pound of chicken legs was $.40 a pound, while in 2012, the price had risen to $.75 a pound.

(a) Write an equation assuming a linear trend expressing the price per pound of leg meat y in terms of the number x of years since 2002.

(b) Assuming the future accuracy of the equation you found in part (a), predict the price per pound of chicken legs in 2014.

74. Business   Similar to Exercise 73, the price per pound of chicken thighs was $.60 a pound in the year 2002 and $1.25 in 2012.

(a) If the price of thigh meat is linear, express the price per pound of thigh meat y in terms of the number x of years since the year 2002.

(b) Use your expression from (a) to find the price of thigh meat in the year 2010.

75. Social Science   According to data from the U.S. Drug Enforcement Administration, there were 36,845 federal drug arrests in the year 2000 and 27,200 in the year 2010.

(a) Write a linear equation expressing the number of federal drug arrests y in terms of the number x of years since 2000.

(b) Using the equation you found in (a), find the number of federal drug arrests in 2006.

76. Social Science   According to data from the U.S. Drug Enforcement Administration, the total seizure of drugs (in millions of pounds) was 1.5 in the year 2000 and 4.5 in the year 2010.

(a) Write a linear equation expressing the weight in pounds from the seizure of drugs y in terms of the number x of years since 2000.

(b) How much was seized in 2007?

(c) If the trend continues, in what year will the total of seized drugs be 5.7 million pounds?

77. Physical Science   The accompanying graph shows the winning time (in minutes) at the Olympic Games from 1952 to 2008 for the men's 5000-meter run, together with a linear approximation of the data. (Data from: *The World Almanac and Book of Facts*: 2009.)

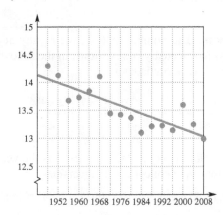

(a) The equation for the linear approximation is

$$y = -.01723x + 47.61.$$

What does the slope of this line represent? Why is the slope negative?

(b) Use the approximation to estimate the winning time in the 2012 Olympics. If possible, check this estimate against the actual time.

78. Business The accompanying graph shows the number of civilians in the U.S. labor force (in millions) in selected years (with the year 2020 projected). (Data from: U.S. Bureau of Labor Statistics.)

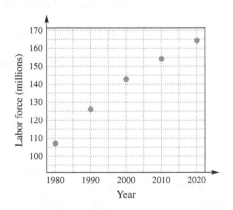

(a) Use the data points (1980, 106.9) and (2010, 153.9) to estimate the slope of the line shown. Interpret this number.

(b) Use part (a) and the point (2010, 153.9) to approximate the civilian labor force in 2015.

✓ **Checkpoint Answers**

1. (a) $6/5$ (b) $-9/2$

2. (a) $y = \dfrac{2}{3}x - 3$ (b) $y = -\dfrac{3}{2}x + \dfrac{1}{4}$

3. (a) Slope $-1/4$; y-intercept $3/2$
   (b) Slope $3/2$; y-intercept $-1/2$

4. (a) Slope of $E = -.3$; slope of $F = -1$; slope of $G = -2$; slope of $H = -5$.
   (b)

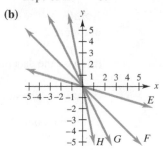

   (c) The larger the slope in absolute value, the more steeply the line falls from left to right.

5. (a)
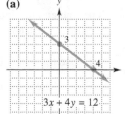
   (b)
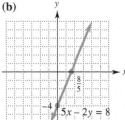

6. (a) Perpendicular   (b) Neither   (c) Parallel

7. (a) $y + 2 = -\dfrac{3}{5}(x - 5); y = -\dfrac{3}{5}x + 1.$

   (b) $y - 8 = \dfrac{1}{3}(x - 6); y = \dfrac{1}{3}x + 6.$

8. (a) $2y = -x + 8$ (b) $11y = -8x - 42$

9. (a) $y = 1409x + 19,307$ (b) $\$43,260$

2.3 Linear Models

In business and science, it is often necessary to make judgments on the basis of data from the past. For instance, a stock analyst might use a company's profits in previous years to estimate the next year's profits. Or a life insurance company might look at life expectancies of people born in various years to predict how much money it should expect to pay out in the next year.

In such situations, the available data is used to construct a mathematical model, such as an equation or a graph, which is used to approximate the likely outcome in cases where complete data is not available. In this section, we consider applications in which the data can be modeled by a linear equation.

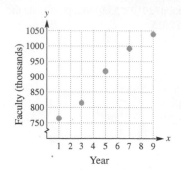

Figure 2.31

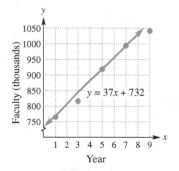

Figure 2.32

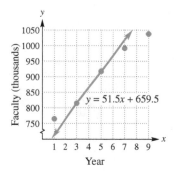

Figure 2.33

✓**Checkpoint 1**

Use the points (5, 917) and (9, 1038) to find another model for the data in Example 1.

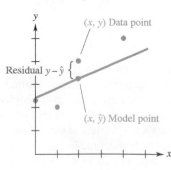

Figure 2.34

The simplest way to construct a linear model is to use the line determined by two of the data points, as illustrated in the following example.

Example 1 **Social Science** The number of full-time faculty at four-year colleges and universities (in thousands) in selected years is shown in the following table. (Data from: U.S. National Center for Education Statistics.)

Year	2001	2003	2005	2007	2009
Number of Faculty	764	814	917	991	1038

(a) Let $x = 1$ correspond to 2001, and plot the points (x, y), where x is the year and y is the number of full-time faculty at four-year colleges and universities.

Solution The data points are (1, 764), (3, 814), (5, 917), (7, 991), and (9, 1038), as shown in Figure 2.31.

(b) Use the data points (5, 917) and (9, 991) to find a line that models the data.

Solution The slope of the line through (5, 917) and (7, 991) is $\dfrac{991 - 917}{7 - 5} = \dfrac{74}{2} = 37$.

Using the point (5, 917) and the slope 37, we find that the equation of this line is

$$y - 917 = 37(x - 5) \qquad \text{Point–slope form for the equation of a line}$$
$$y - 917 = 37x - 185 \qquad \text{Distributive property}$$
$$y = 37x + 732 \qquad \text{Slope–intercept form}$$

The line and the data points are shown in Figure 2.32. Although the line fits the two points we used to calculate the slope perfectly, it overestimates the remaining three data points.

(c) Use the points (3, 814) and (5, 917) to find another line that models the data.

The slope of the line is $\dfrac{917 - 814}{5 - 3} = \dfrac{103}{2} = 51.5$. Using the point (3, 814) and the slope 51.5, we find that the equation of this line is

$$y - 814 = 51.5(x - 3) \qquad \text{Point–slope form for the equation of a line}$$
$$y - 814 = 51.5x - 154.5 \qquad \text{Distributive property}$$
$$y = 51.5x + 659.5 \qquad \text{Slope–intercept form}$$

The line and the data points are shown in Figure 2.33. This line passes through two data points, but significantly underestimates the number of faculty in 2001 and overestimates the number of faculty in 2009. ✓

Opinions may vary as to which of the lines in Example 1 best fits the data. To make a decision, we might try to measure the amount of error in each model. One way to do this is to compute the difference between the number of faculty y and the amount $\hat{y}$ given by the model. If the data point is (x, y) and the corresponding point on the line is $(x, \hat{y})$, then the difference $y - \hat{y}$ measures the error in the model for that particular value of x. The number $y - \hat{y}$ is called a **residual**. As shown in Figure 2.34, the residual $y - \hat{y}$ is the vertical distance from the data point to the line (positive when the data point is above the line, negative when it is below the line, and 0 when it is on the line).

One way to determine how well a line fits the data points is to compute the sum of its residuals—that is, the sum of the individual errors. Unfortunately, however, the sum of the residuals of two different lines might be equal, thwarting our effort to decide which is the better fit. Furthermore, the residuals may sum to 0, which doesn't mean that there is no error, but only that the positive and negative errors (which might be quite large) cancel each other out. (See Exercise 11 at the end of this section for an example.)

To avoid this difficulty, mathematicians use the sum of the *squares* of the residuals to measure how well a line fits the data points. When the sum of the squares is used, a smaller sum means a smaller overall error and hence a better fit. The error is 0 only when all the data points lie on the line (a perfect fit).

Example 2 **Social Science** Two linear models for the number of full-time faculty at four-year colleges and universities were constructed in Example 1:

$$y = 37x + 732 \quad \text{and} \quad y = 51.5x + 659.5.$$

For each model, determine the five residuals, square of each residual, and the sum of the squares of the residuals.

Solution The information for each model is summarized in the following tables:

$$y = 37x + 732$$

Data Point (x, y)	Model Point $(x, \hat{y})$	Residual $y - \hat{y}$	Squared Residual $(y - \hat{y})^2$
(1, 764)	(1, 769)	−5	25
(3, 814)	(3, 843)	−29	841
(5, 917)	(5, 917)	0	0
(7, 991)	(7, 991)	0	0
(9, 1038)	(9, 1065)	−27	729
			Sum = 1595

$$y = 51.5x + 659.5$$

Data Point (x, y)	Model Point $(x, \hat{y})$	Residual $y - \hat{y}$	Squared Residual $(y - \hat{y})^2$
(1, 764)	(1, 711)	53	2809
(3, 814)	(3, 814)	0	0
(5, 917)	(5, 917)	0	0
(7, 991)	(7, 1020)	−29	841
(9, 1038)	(9, 1123)	−85	7225
			Sum = 10,875

✓**Checkpoint 2**

Another model for the data in Examples 1 and 2 is $y = 34.25x + 729.75$. Use this line to find

(a) the residuals and

(b) the sum of the squares of the residuals.

(c) Does this line fit the data better than the two lines in Example 2?

According to this measure of the error, the line $y = 37x + 732$ is a better fit for the data because the sum of the squares of its residuals is smaller than the sum of the squares of the residuals for $y = 51.5x + 659.5$. ✓₂

Linear Regression (Optional)*

Mathematical techniques from multivariable calculus can be used to prove the following result.

> For any set of data points, there is one, and only one, line for which the sum of the squares of the residuals is as small as possible.

---

*Examples 3–6 require either a graphing calculator or a spreadsheet program.

This *line of best fit* is called the **least-squares regression line,** and the computational process for finding its equation is called **linear regression.** Linear-regression formulas are quite complicated and require a large amount of computation. Fortunately, most graphing calculators and spreadsheet programs can do linear regression quickly and easily.

📄 **NOTE** The process outlined here works for most TI graphing calculators. Other graphing calculators and spreadsheet programs operate similarly, but check your instruction manual or see the Graphing Calculator Appendix.

Example 3   Social Science   Recall the number of full-time faculty at four-year colleges and universities (in thousands) in selected years was as follows.

Year	2001	2003	2005	2007	2009
Number of Faculty	764	814	917	991	1038

Use a graphing calculator to do the following:

(a) Plot the data points with $x = 1$ corresponding to 2001.

Solution The data points are (1, 764), (3, 814), (5, 917), (7, 991), and (9, 1038). Press STAT EDIT to bring up the statistics editor. Enter the x-coordinates as list L_1 and the corresponding y-coordinates as L_2, as shown in Figure 2.35. To plot the data points, go to the STAT PLOT menu, choose a plot (here it is Plot 1), choose ON, and enter the lists L_1 and L_2 as shown in Figure 2.36. Then set the viewing window as usual and press GRAPH to produce the plot in Figure 2.37.

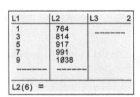

Figure 2.35

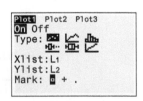

Figure 2.36

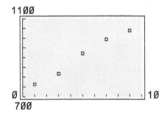

Figure 2.37

(b) Find the least squares regression line for these data.

Solution Go to the STAT CALC menu and choose LINREG, which returns you to the home screen. As shown in Figure 2.38, enter the list names and the place where the equation of the regression line should be stored (here, Y_1 is chosen; it is on the VARS Y-VARS FUNCTION menu); then press ENTER. Figure 2.39 shows that the equation of the regression line is

$$y = 36.25x + 723.55.$$

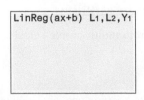

Figure 2.38

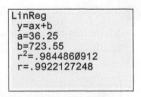

Figure 2.39

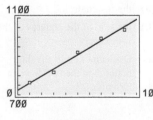

Figure 2.40

✓ Checkpoint 3

Use the least-squares regression line $y = 36.25x + 723.55$ and the data points of Example 3 to find

(a) the residuals and

(b) the sum of the squares of the residuals.

(c) How does this line compare with those in Example 1 and Checkpoint 2?

(c) Graph the data points and the regression line on the same screen.

Solution Press GRAPH to see the line plotted with the data points (Figure 2.40).

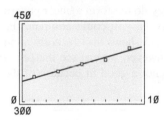

Figure 2.41

Figure 2.42

✓ **Checkpoint 4**

Using only the data from 2005 and later in Example 4, find the equation of the least-squares regression line. Round the coefficients to two decimal places.

Example 4 **Social Science** The following table gives the number (in thousands) of full-time faculty at two-year colleges. (Data from: U.S. National Center for Education Statistics.)

Year	2001	2003	2005	2007	2009
Number of Faculty	349	359	373	381	401

(a) Let $x = 1$ correspond to the year 2001. Use a graphing calculator or spreadsheet program to find the least-squares regression line that models the data in the table.

Solution The data points are $(1, 349)$, $(3, 359)$, $(5, 373)$, $(7, 381)$, and $(9, 401)$. Enter the x-coordinates as list L_1 and the corresponding y-coordinates as list L_2 in a graphing calculator and then find the regression line as in Figure 2.41.

(b) Plot the data points and the regression line on the same screen.

Solution See Figure 2.42, which shows that the line is a reasonable model for the data.

(c) Assuming the trend continues, estimate the number of faculty in the year 2015.

Solution The year 2015 corresponds to $x = 15$. Substitute $x = 15$ into the regression-line equation:

$$y = 6.3(15) + 341.1 = 435.6.$$

This model estimates that the number of full-time faculty at two-year colleges will be approximately 435,600 in the year 2015. ✓ 4

⬈ Correlation

Although the "best fit" line can always be found by linear regression, it may not be a good model. For instance, if the data points are widely scattered, no straight line will model the data accurately. We calculate a value called the **correlation coefficient** to assess the fit of the regression line to the scatterplot. It measures how closely the data points fit the regression line and thus indicates how good the regression line is for predictive purposes.

The correlation coefficient r is always between -1 and 1. When $r = \pm 1$, the data points all lie on the regression line (a perfect fit). When the absolute value of r is close to 1, the line fits the data quite well, and when r is close to 0, the line is a poor fit for the data (but some other curve might be a good fit). Figure 2.43 shows how the value of r varies, depending on the pattern of the data points.

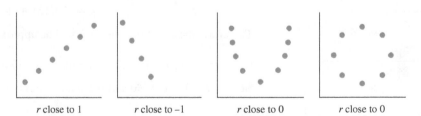

| r close to 1 | r close to -1 | r close to 0 | r close to 0 |

Figure 2.43

⬈ **Example 5** **Business** The number of unemployed people in the U.S. labor force (in millions) in recent years is shown in the table. (Data from: U.S. Department of Labor, Bureau of Labor Statistics.)

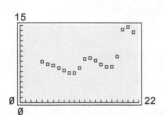

Figure 2.44

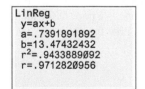

Figure 2.45

✓**Checkpoint 5**

Using only the data from 2002 and later in Example 5, find

(a) the equation of the least-squares regression line and

(b) the correlation coefficient.

(c) How well does this line fit the data?

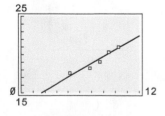

Figure 2.46

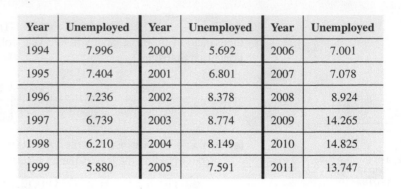

Year	Unemployed	Year	Unemployed	Year	Unemployed
1994	7.996	2000	5.692	2006	7.001
1995	7.404	2001	6.801	2007	7.078
1996	7.236	2002	8.378	2008	8.924
1997	6.739	2003	8.774	2009	14.265
1998	6.210	2004	8.149	2010	14.825
1999	5.880	2005	7.591	2011	13.747

Determine whether a linear equation is a good model for these data or not.

Solution Let $x = 4$ correspond to 1994, and plot the data points (4, 7.996), etc., either by hand or with a graphing calculator, as in Figure 2.44. They do not form a linear pattern (because unemployment tends to rise and fall). Alternatively, you could compute the regression equation for the data, as in Figure 2.45. Figure 2.45 shows that the correlation coefficient is $r \approx .69$, which is a relatively high value. However, we can see that, even though the correlation is somewhat high, a straight line is not a good fit because of the peaks and valleys in Figure 2.44. ✓₅

⬈ **Example 6** **Education** Enrollment projections (in millions) for all U.S. colleges and universities in selected years are shown in the following table: (Data from: U.S. Center for Educational Statistics.)

Year	2005	2007	2008	2009	2010
Enrollment	17.5	18.2	19.1	20.4	21.0

(a) Let $x = 5$ correspond to the year 2005. Use a graphing calculator or spreadsheet program to find a linear model for the data and determine how well it fits the data points.

Solution The least-squares regression line (with coefficients rounded) is

$$y = .74x + 13.5,$$

as shown in Figure 2.46. The correlation coefficient is $r \approx .97$, which is very close to 1, and Figure 2.47 shows a linear trend. Thus, the line fits the data well.

(b) Assuming the trend continues, predict the enrollment in 2015.

Solution Let $x = 15$ (corresponding to 2015) in the regression equation:

$$y = .74(15) + 13.5 = 24.6.$$

Therefore, the enrollment in 2015 will be approximately 24.6 million students.

(c) According to this model, in what year will enrollment reach 30 million?

Solution Let $y = 30$ and solve the regression equation for x:

$$y = .74x + 13.5$$
$$30 = .74x + 13.5 \qquad \text{Let } y = 30.$$
$$16.5 = .74x \qquad \text{Subtract 13.5 from both sides.}$$
$$x \approx 22.3. \qquad \text{Divide both sides by 0.74.}$$

Since these enrollment figures change once a year, use the nearest integer value for x, namely, 22. So enrollment will reach 30 million in 2022.

25

15

Figure 2.47

2.3 Exercises

1. **Physical Science** The following table shows equivalent Fahrenheit and Celsius temperatures:

Degrees Fahrenheit	32	68	104	140	176	212
Degrees Celsius	0	20	40	60	80	100

   (a) Choose any two data points and use them to construct a linear equation that models the data, with x being Fahrenheit and y being Celsius.

   (b) Use the model in part (a) to find the Celsius temperature corresponding to

   $$50° \text{ Fahrenheit and } 75° \text{ Fahrenheit.}$$

Physical Science *Use the linear equation derived in Exercise 1 to work the following problems.*

2. Convert each temperature.

   (a) 58°F to Celsius   (b) 50°C to Fahrenheit

   (c) −10°C to Fahrenheit   (d) −20°F to Celsius

3. According to the *World Almanac and Book of Facts*, 2008, Venus is the hottest planet, with a surface temperature of 867° Fahrenheit. What is this temperature in degrees Celsius?

4. Find the temperature at which Celsius and Fahrenheit temperatures are numerically equal.

In each of the next set of problems, assume that the data can be modeled by a straight line and that the trend continues indefinitely. Use two data points to find such a line and then answer the question. (See Example 1.)

5. **Business** The Consumer Price Index (CPI), which measures the cost of a typical package of consumer goods, was 201.6 in the year 2006 and 224.9 in the year 2011. Let $x = 6$ correspond to 2006, and estimate the CPI in 2008 and 2015. (Data from: U.S. Bureau of Labor Statistics.)

6. **Finance** The approximate number (in millions) of individual tax returns filed with the Internal Revenue Service in the year 2001 was 127.1 and in the year 2011 it was 140.8. Let $x = 1$ correspond to 2001, and estimate the number of returns filed in 2005 and 2012. (Data from: U.S. Internal Revenue Service.)

7. **Business** The number (in millions) of employees working in the finance and insurance industries was 6.0 in the year 2000 and 6.5 in the year 2008. Let $x = 0$ correspond to 2000, and estimate the number of employees in 2010. (Data from: U.S. Census Bureau.)

8. **Business** The number (in millions) of employees working in the health care and social assistance industries was 14.1 in the year 2000 and 17.2 in the year 2008. Let $x = 0$ correspond to 2000, and estimate the number of employees in 2014. (Data from: U.S. Census Bureau.)

9. **Physical Science** Suppose a baseball is thrown at 85 miles per hour. The ball will travel 320 feet when hit by a bat swung at 50 miles per hour and will travel 440 feet when hit by a bat swung at 80 miles per hour. Let y be the number of feet traveled by the ball when hit by a bat swung at x miles per hour. (*Note:* The preceding data are valid for $50 \le x \le 90$, where the bat is 35 inches long, weighs 32 ounces, and strikes a waist-high pitch so that the place of the swing lies at 10° from the diagonal). [Data from: Robert K. Adair, *The Physics of Baseball* (HarperCollins, 1990)]. How much farther will a ball travel for each mile-per-hour increase in the speed of the bat?

10. **Physical Science** Ski resorts require large amounts of water in order to make snow. Snowmass Ski Area in Colorado plans to pump at least 1120 gallons of water per minute for at least 12 hours a day from Snowmass Creek between mid-October and late December. Environmentalists are concerned about the effects on the ecosystem. Find the minimum amount of water pumped in 30 days. [*Hint:* Let y be the total number of gallons pumped x days after pumping begins. Note that $(0, 0)$ is on the graph of the equation.] (Data from: York Snow, Inc.)

In each of the next two problems, two linear models are given for the data. For each model,

(a) *find the residuals and their sum;*

(b) *find the sum of the squares of the residuals;*

(c) *decide which model is the better fit. (See Example 2.)*

11. **Finance** The following table shows the number of operating federal credit unions in the United States for several years.

Year	2007	2008	2009	2010	2011
Number of federal credit unions	5036	4847	4714	4589	4447

   Let $x = 7$ correspond to the year 2007. Two equations that model the data are $y = -143.6x + 6019$ and $y = -170.2x + 6250$. (Data from: National Credit Union Association.)

12. **Business** The percentage of households using direct deposit for selected years is shown in the following table. (Data from: Board of Governors of the Federal Reserve System.)

Year	1995	1998	2001	2004	2007
Percent of households	53	67	71	75	80

   Let $x = 5$ correspond to the year 1995. Two equations that model the data are $y = 2.1x + 47$ and $y = 2.8x + 44$.

☑ *In each of the following problems, determine whether a straight line is a good model for the data. Do this visually by plotting the data points and by finding the correlation coefficient for the least-squares regression line. (See Examples 5 and 6.)*

13. **Business** The accompanying table gives the total sales (in billions of dollars) for the aerospace industry. Let $x = 6$

correspond to the year 2006. (Data from: ProQuest Statistical Abstract of the United States 2013.)

Year	2006	2007	2008	2009	2010	2011
Total Sales	177.3	192.0	194.7	203.0	203.6	210.0

14. Business The accompanying table gives the number (in thousands) of new houses built for each of the years. Let $x = 6$ correspond to the year 2006. (Data from: U.S. Census Bureau.)

Year	2006	2007	2008	2009	2010	2011
Total Sales	1801	1355	906	554	587	609

In Exercises 15–18 find the required linear model using least-squares regression. (See Examples 3–6.)

15. Business Use the data on sales of the aerospace industry in Exercise 13.

   (a) Find a linear model for the data with $x = 6$ corresponding to the year 2006.

   (b) Assuming the trend continues, estimate the total sales for the year 2015.

16. Health The accompanying table shows the number of deaths per 100,000 people from heart disease in selected years. (Data from: U.S. National Center for Health Statistics.)

Year	1985	1990	1995	2000	2005	2010
Deaths	375.0	321.8	293.4	257.6	211.1	178.5

   (a) Find a linear model for the data with $x = 5$ corresponding to the year 1985.

   (b) Assuming the trend continues, estimate the number of deaths per 100,000 people for the year 2015.

17. Business The accompanying table shows the revenue (in billions of dollars) from newspaper publishers. (Data from: U.S. Census Bureau.)

Year	2006	2007	2008	2009	2010
Revenue	48.9	47.6	43.9	36.4	34.7

   (a) Find a linear model for the data with $x = 6$ corresponding to the year 2006.

   (b) Assuming the trend continues, estimate the revenue in 2016.

18. Health Researchers wish to determine if a relationship exists between age and systolic blood pressure (SBP). The accompanying table gives the age and systolic blood pressure for 10 adults.

Age (x)	35	37	42	46	53	57	61	65	69	74
SBP (y)	102	127	120	131	126	137	140	130	148	147

   (a) Find a linear model for these data using age (x) to predict systolic blood pressure (y).

   (b) Use the results from part (a) to predict the systolic blood pressure for a person who is 42-years-old, 53-years-old, and 69-years-old. How well do the actual data agree with the predicted values?

   (c) Use the results from part (a) to predict the systolic blood pressure for a person who is 45-years-old and 70-years-old.

Work these problems.

19. Business The estimated operating revenue (in billions of dollars) from Internet publishing and broadcasting is given in the accompanying table. (Data from: U.S. Census Bureau.)

Year	2006	2007	2008	2009	2010
Revenue	11.5	15.0	17.8	19.1	21.3

   (a) Find the least squares regression line that models these data with $x = 6$ corresponding to the year 2006.

   (b) Assuming the trend continues, estimate the operating revenue in the years 2012 and 2014.

20. Business The number of basic cable television subscribers (in millions) is shown in the following table for various years. (Data from: ProQuest Statistical Abstract of the United States 2013.)

Year	2002	2004	2006	2008	2010
Subscribers	66.5	65.7	65.3	64.3	61.0

   (a) Find the least-squares regression line that models these data with $x = 2$ corresponding to the year 2002.

   (b) Find the number of subscribers for the year 2009.

   (c) If the trend continues indefinitely, determine in what year there will be 55 million subscribers.

   (d) Find the correlation coefficient.

21. Social Science The number (in thousands) of traffic fatalities by year is displayed in the accompanying table. (Data from: U.S. National Highway Traffic Administration.)

Year	2005	2007	2008	2009	2010
Traffic Fatalities	43.5	41.3	37.4	33.9	32.9

   (a) Find the least-squares regression line that models these data with $x = 5$ corresponding to the year 2005.

   (b) Find the number of deaths for the year 2006.

   (c) If the trend continues indefinitely, determine in what year there will be 28 thousand deaths.

   (d) Find the correlation coefficient.

22. Health The following table shows men's and women's life expectancy at birth (in years) for selected birth years in the United States: (Data from: U.S. Center for National Health Statistics.)

| | Life Expectancy | |
Birth Year	Men	Women
1970	67.1	74.7
1975	68.8	76.6
1980	70.0	77.4
1985	71.1	78.2
1990	71.8	78.8
1995	72.5	78.9
1998	73.8	79.5
2000	74.3	79.7
2001	74.4	79.8
2004	75.2	80.4
2010	75.6	81.4

(a) Find the least-squares regression line for the men's data, with $x = 70$ corresponding to 1970.

(b) Find the least-squares regression line for the women's data, with $x = 70$ corresponding to 1970.

(c) Suppose life expectancy continues to increase as predicted by the equations in parts (a) and (b). Will men's life expectancy ever be the same as women's? If so, in what birth year will this occur?

✓**Checkpoint Answers**

1. $y = 30.25x + 765.75$

2. **(a)** 0, −18.5, 16, 21.5, 0

   (b) 1060.5

   (c) Yes, because the sum of the squares of the residuals is lower.

3. **(a)** 4.2, −18.3, 12.2, 13.7, −11.8

   (b) 828.30

   (c) It fits the data best because the sum of the squares of its residuals is smallest.

4. $y = 7x + 336$

5. **(a)** $y = .76x − 2.66$

   (b) $r \approx .74$

   (c) It fits reasonably well because $|r|$ is close to 1 and the pattern is linear.

2.4 Linear Inequalities

An **inequality** is a statement that one mathematical expression is greater than (or less than) another. Inequalities are very important in applications. For example, a company wants revenue to be *greater than* costs and must use *no more than* the total amount of capital or labor available.

Inequalities may be solved by algebraic or geometric methods. In this section, we shall concentrate on algebraic methods for solving **linear inequalities**, such as

$$4 - 3x \le 7 + 2x \quad \text{and} \quad -2 < 5 + 3m < 20,$$

and absolute-value inequalities, such as $|x - 2| < 5$. The following properties are the basic algebraic tools for working with inequalities.

> **Properties of Inequality**
>
> For real numbers a, b, and c,
>
> **(a)** if $a < b$, then $a + c < b + c$;
>
> **(b)** if $a < b$, and if $c > 0$, then $ac < bc$;
>
> **(c)** if $a < b$, and if $c < 0$, then $ac > bc$.

Throughout this section, definitions are given only for $<$, but they are equally valid for $>$, $\le$, and $\ge$.

CAUTION Pay careful attention to part (c) in the previous box; if both sides of an inequality are multiplied by a negative number, the direction of the inequality symbol must be reversed. For example, starting with the true statement $-3 < 5$ and multiplying both sides by the positive number 2 gives

$$-3 \cdot 2 < 5 \cdot 2,$$

or

$$-6 < 10,$$

still a true statement. However, starting with $-3 < 5$ and multiplying both sides by the negative number -2 gives a true result only if the direction of the inequality symbol is reversed:

$$-3(-2) > 5(-2)$$
$$6 > -10. \quad ✓_1$$

✓**Checkpoint 1**

(a) First multiply both sides of $-6 < -1$ by 4, and then multiply both sides of $-6 < -1$ by -7.

(b) First multiply both sides of $9 \geq -4$ by 2, and then multiply both sides of $9 \geq -4$ by -5.

(c) First add 4 to both sides of $-3 < -1$, and then add -6 to both sides of $-3 < -1$.

Example 1 Solve $3x + 5 > 11$. Graph the solution.

Solution First add -5 to both sides:

$$3x + 5 + (-5) > 11 + (-5)$$
$$3x > 6.$$

Now multiply both sides by $1/3$:

$$\frac{1}{3}(3x) > \frac{1}{3}(6)$$
$$x > 2.$$

(Why was the direction of the inequality symbol not changed?) In interval notation (introduced in Section 1.1), the solution is the interval $(2, \infty)$, which is graphed on the number line in Figure 2.48. The parenthesis at 2 shows that 2 is not included in the solution.

Figure 2.48

As a partial check, note that 0, which is not part of the solution, makes the inequality false, while 3, which is part of the solution, makes it true:

$$\overset{?}{3(0) + 5 > 11} \qquad \overset{?}{3(3) + 5 > 11}$$
$$5 > 11 \quad \text{False} \qquad 14 > 11. \quad \text{True} \ ✓_2$$

✓**Checkpoint 2**

Solve these inequalities. Graph each solution.

(a) $5z - 11 < 14$

(b) $-3k \leq -12$

(c) $-8y \geq 32$

Example 2 Solve $4 - 3x \leq 7 + 2x$.

Solution Add -4 to both sides:

$$4 - 3x + (-4) \leq 7 + 2x + (-4)$$
$$-3x \leq 3 + 2x.$$

Add $-2x$ to both sides (remember that *adding* to both sides never changes the direction of the inequality symbol):

$$-3x + (-2x) \leq 3 + 2x + (-2x)$$
$$-5x \leq 3.$$

Multiply both sides by $-1/5$. Since $-1/5$ is negative, change the direction of the inequality symbol:

$$-\frac{1}{5}(-5x) \geq -\frac{1}{5}(3)$$

$$x \geq -\frac{3}{5}.$$

Figure 2.49 shows a graph of the solution, $[-3/5, \infty)$. The bracket in Figure 2.49 shows that $-3/5$ is included in the solution.

Checkpoint 3

Solve these inequalities. Graph each solution.

(a) $8 - 6t \geq 2t + 24$

(b) $-4r + 3(r + 1) < 2r$

Figure 2.49

Example 3   Solve $-2 < 5 + 3m < 20$. Graph the solution.

Solution   The inequality $-2 < 5 + 3m < 20$ says that $5 + 3m$ is between -2 and 20. We can solve this inequality with an extension of the properties given at the beginning of this section. Work as follows, first adding -5 to each part:

$$-2 + (-5) < 5 + 3m + (-5) < 20 + (-5)$$

$$-7 < 3m < 15.$$

Now multiply each part by $1/3$:

$$-\frac{7}{3} < m < 5.$$

Checkpoint 4

Solve each of the given inequalities. Graph each solution.

(a) $9 < k + 5 < 13$

(b) $-6 \leq 2z + 4 \leq 12$

A graph of the solution, $(-7/3, 5)$, is given in Figure 2.50.

Figure 2.50

Example 4   The formula for converting from Celsius to Fahrenheit temperature is

$$F = \frac{9}{5}C + 32.$$

What Celsius temperature range corresponds to the range from 32°F to 77°F?

Solution   The Fahrenheit temperature range is $32 < F < 77$. Since $F = (9/5)C + 32$, we have

$$32 < \frac{9}{5}C + 32 < 77.$$

Solve the inequality for C:

$$32 < \frac{9}{5}C + 32 < 77$$

$$0 < \frac{9}{5}C < 45 \qquad \text{Subtract 32 from each part.}$$

$$\frac{5}{9} \cdot 0 < \frac{5}{9} \cdot \frac{9}{5}C < \frac{5}{9} \cdot 45 \qquad \text{Multiply each part by } \frac{5}{9}.$$

$$0 < C < 25.$$

Checkpoint 5

In Example 4, what Celsius temperatures correspond to the range from 5°F to 95°F?

The corresponding Celsius temperature range is 0°C to 25°C.

A product will break even or produce a profit only if the revenue R from selling the product at least equals the cost C of producing it—that is, if $R \geq C$.

Example 5   **Business**   A company analyst has determined that the cost to produce and sell x units of a certain product is $C = 20x + 1000$. The revenue for that product is $R = 70x$. Find the values of x for which the company will break even or make a profit on the product.

Solution   Solve the inequality $R \geq C$:

$$R \geq C$$
$$70x \geq 20x + 1000 \qquad \text{Let } R = 70x \text{ and } C = 20x + 1000.$$
$$50x \geq 1000 \qquad \text{Subtract } 20x \text{ from both sides.}$$
$$x \geq 20. \qquad \text{Divide both sides by 50.}$$

The company must produce and sell 20 items to break even and more than 20 to make a profit.

Example 6   **Business**   A pretzel manufacturer can sell a 6-ounce bag of pretzels to a wholesaler for $.35 a bag. The variable cost of producing each bag is $.25 per bag, and the fixed cost for the manufacturing operation is $110,000.[*] How many bags of pretzels need to be sold in order to break even or earn a profit?

Solution   Let x be the number of bags produced. Then the revenue equation is

$$R = .35x,$$

and the cost is given by

$$\text{Cost} = \text{Fixed Costs} + \text{Variable Costs}$$
$$C = 110,000 + .25x.$$

We now solve the inequality $R \geq C$:

$$R \geq C$$
$$.35x \geq 110,000 + .25x$$
$$.1x \geq 110,000$$
$$x \geq 1,110,000.$$

The manufacturer must produce and sell 1,110,000 bags of pretzels to break even and more than that to make a profit.

Absolute-Value Inequalities

You may wish to review the definition of absolute value in Section 1.1 before reading the following examples, which show how to solve inequalities involving absolute values.

Example 7   Solve each inequality.

(a) $|x| < 5$

Solution   Because absolute value gives the distance from a number to 0, the inequality $|x| < 5$ is true for all real numbers whose distance from 0 is less than 5. This includes all numbers between -5 and 5, or numbers in the interval $(-5, 5)$. A graph of the solution is shown in Figure 2.51 on the following page.

---

[*]Variable costs, fixed costs, and revenue were discussed on page 15.

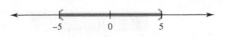

Figure 2.51

(b) $|x| > 5$

Solution   The solution of $|x| > 5$ is given by all those numbers whose distance from 0 is *greater* than 5. This includes the numbers satisfying $x < -5$ or $x > 5$. A graph of the solution, all numbers in

$$(-\infty, -5) \qquad \text{or} \qquad (5, \infty),$$

is shown in Figure 2.52. ✓6

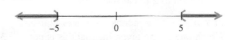

Figure 2.52

The preceding examples suggest the following generalizations.

> Assume that a and b are real numbers and that b is positive.
>
> **1.** Solve $|a| < b$ by solving $-b < a < b$.
> **2.** Solve $|a| > b$ by solving $a < -b$ or $a > b$.

Example 8   Solve $|x - 2| < 5$.

Solution   Replace a with $x - 2$ and b with 5 in property (1) in the box above. Now solve $|x - 2| < 5$ by solving the inequality

$$-5 < x - 2 < 5.$$

Add 2 to each part, getting the solution

$$-3 < x < 7,$$

which is graphed in Figure 2.53. ✓7

Example 9   Solve $|2 - 7m| - 1 > 4$.

Solution   First add 1 to both sides:

$$|2 - 7m| > 5$$

Now use property (2) from the preceding box to solve $|2 - 7m| > 5$ by solving the inequality

$$2 - 7m < -5 \qquad \text{or} \qquad 2 - 7m > 5.$$

Solve each part separately:

$$-7m < -7 \qquad \text{or} \qquad -7m > 3$$
$$m > 1 \qquad \text{or} \qquad m < -\frac{3}{7}.$$

The solution, all numbers in $\left(-\infty, -\dfrac{3}{7}\right)$ or $(1, \infty)$, is graphed in Figure 2.54. ✓8

Figure 2.54

✓**Checkpoint 6**

Solve each inequality. Graph each solution.

(a) $|x| \le 1$

(b) $|y| \ge 3$

Figure 2.53

✓**Checkpoint 7**

Solve each inequality. Graph each solution.

(a) $|p + 3| < 4$

(b) $|2k - 1| \le 7$

✓**Checkpoint 8**

Solve each inequality. Graph each solution.

(a) $|y - 2| > 5$

(b) $|3k - 1| \ge 2$

(c) $|2 + 5r| - 4 \ge 1$

✓ **Checkpoint 9**

Solve each inequality.

(a) $|5m - 3| > -10$

(b) $|6 + 5a| < -9$

(c) $|8 + 2r| > 0$

| **Example 10** | Solve $|3 - 7x| \geq -8$. |

Solution The absolute value of a number is always nonnegative. Therefore, $|3 - 7x| \geq -8$ is always true, so the solution is the set of all real numbers. Note that the inequality $|3 - 7x| \leq -8$ has no solution, because the absolute value of a quantity can never be less than a negative number. ✓₉

2.4 Exercises

1. Explain how to determine whether a parenthesis or a bracket is used when graphing the solution of a linear inequality.

2. The three-part inequality $p < x < q$ means "p is less than x and x is less than q." Which one of the given inequalities is not satisfied by any real number x? Explain why.

    (a) $-3 < x < 5$ (b) $0 < x < 4$

    (c) $-7 < x < -10$ (d) $-3 < x < -2$

Solve each inequality and graph each solution. (See Examples 1–3.)

3. $-8k \leq 32$ 4. $-4a \leq 36$

5. $-2b > 0$ 6. $6 - 6z < 0$

7. $3x + 4 \leq 14$ 8. $2y - 7 < 9$

9. $-5 - p \geq 3$ 10. $5 - 3r \leq -4$

11. $7m - 5 < 2m + 10$ 12. $6x - 2 > 4x - 10$

13. $m - (4 + 2m) + 3 < 2m + 2$

14. $2p - (3 - p) \leq -7p - 2$

15. $-2(3y - 8) \geq 5(4y - 2)$

16. $5r - (r + 2) \geq 3(r - 1) + 6$

17. $3p - 1 < 6p + 2(p - 1)$

18. $x + 5(x + 1) > 4(2 - x) + x$

19. $-7 < y - 2 < 5$ 20. $-3 < m + 6 < 2$

21. $8 \leq 3r + 1 \leq 16$ 22. $-6 < 2p - 3 \leq 5$

23. $-4 \leq \dfrac{2k - 1}{3} \leq 2$ 24. $-1 \leq \dfrac{5y + 2}{3} \leq 4$

25. $\dfrac{3}{5}(2p + 3) \geq \dfrac{1}{10}(5p + 1)$

26. $\dfrac{8}{3}(z - 4) \leq \dfrac{2}{9}(3z + 2)$

In the following exercises, write a linear inequality that describes the given graph.

27.
    $-6\ -4\ -2\ \ 0\ \ 2\ \ 4\ \ 6$

28.
    $-6\ -4\ -2\ \ 0\ \ 2\ \ 4\ \ 6$

29.
    $-6\ -4\ -2\ \ 0\ \ 2\ \ 4\ \ 6$

30.
    $-6\ -4\ -2\ \ 0\ \ 2\ \ 4\ \ 6$

Business   *In Exercises 31–36, find all values of x for which the given products will at least break even. (See Examples 5 and 6.)*

31. The cost to produce x units of wire is $C = 50x + 6000$, while the revenue is $R = 65x$.

32. The cost to produce x units of squash is $C = 100x + 6000$, while the revenue is $R = 500x$.

33. $C = 85x + 1000; R = 105x$

34. $C = 70x + 500; R = 60x$

35. $C = 1000x + 5000; R = 900x$

36. $C = 25{,}000x + 21{,}700{,}000; R = 102{,}500x$

Solve each inequality. Graph each solution. (See Examples 7–10.)

37. $|p| > 7$ 38. $|m| < 2$

39. $|r| \leq 5$ 40. $|a| < -2$

41. $|b| > -5$ 42. $|2x + 5| < 1$

43. $\left| x - \dfrac{1}{2} \right| < 2$ 44. $|3z + 1| \geq 4$

45. $|8b + 5| \geq 7$ 46. $\left| 5x + \dfrac{1}{2} \right| - 2 < 5$

Work these problems.

Physical Science   *The given inequality describes the monthly average high daily temperature T in degrees Fahrenheit in the given location. (Data from: Weatherbase.com.) What range of temperatures corresponds to the inequality?*

47. $|T - 83| \leq 7$; Miami, Florida

48. $|T - 63| \leq 27$; Boise, Idaho

49. $|T - 61| \leq 21$; Flagstaff, Arizona

50. $|T - 43| \leq 22$; Anchorage, Alaska

51. **Natural Science**   Human beings emit carbon dioxide when they breathe. In one study, the emission rates of carbon dioxide by college students were measured both during lectures and during exams. The average individual rate R_L (in grams per hour) during a lecture class satisfied the inequality $|R_L - 26.75| \leq 1.42$, whereas during an exam, the rate R_E satisfied the inequality $|R_E - 38.75| \leq 2.17$. (Data from: T.C. Wang, *ASHRAE Transactions* 81 [Part 1], 32 [1975].)

    (a) Find the range of values for R_L and R_E.

    (b) A class had 225 students. If T_L and T_E represent the total amounts of carbon dioxide (in grams) emitted during a one-hour lecture and one-hour exam, respectively, write inequalities that describe the ranges for T_L and T_E.

52. **Social Science** When administering a standard intelligence quotient (IQ) test, we expect about one-third of the scores to be more than 12 units above 100 or more than 12 units below 100. Describe this situation by writing an absolute value inequality.

53. **Social Science** A Gallup poll found that among Americans aged 18–34 years who consume alcohol, between 35% and 43% prefer beer. Let B represent the percentage of American alcohol consumers who prefer beer. Write the preceding information as an inequality. (Data from: Gallup.com.)

54. **Social Science** A Gallup poll in February 2013 found that between 17% and 19% of Americans considered themselves underemployed (working part-time or not working at all, but wanting to work full-time). Let U represent the percentage of underemployed workers. Write the preceding information as an inequality. (Data from: Gallup.com.)

55. **Finance** The following table shows the 2012 federal income tax for a single person. (Data from: Internal Revenue Service.)

If Taxable Income Is Over	But Not Over	Tax Rate
$0	$8700	10%
$8700	$35,350	15%
$35,350	$85,650	25%
$85,650	$178,650	28%
$178,650	$388,350	33%
$388,350	No limits	35%

Let x denote the taxable income. Write each of the six income ranges in the table as an inequality.

56. **Health** Federal guidelines require drinking water to have less than .050 milligrams per liter of lead. A test using 21 samples of water in a Midwestern city found that the average amount of lead in the samples was 0.040 milligrams per liter. All samples had lead content within 5% of the average.

   (a) Select a variable and write down what it represents.

   (b) Write an inequality to express the results obtained from the sample.

   (c) Did all the samples meet the federal requirement?

✓ **Checkpoint Answers**

1. **(a)** $-24 < -4; 42 > 7$ **(b)** $18 \geq -8; -45 \leq 20$
   (c) $1 < 3; -9 < -7$

2. **(a)** $z < 5$ **(b)** $k \geq 4$

   (c) $y \leq -4$

3. **(a)** $t \leq -2$ **(b)** $r > 1$

4. **(a)** $4 < k < 8$ **(b)** $-5 \leq z \leq 4$

5. $-15°C$ to $35°C$

6. **(a)** $[-1, 1]$

   (b) All numbers in $(-\infty, -3]$ or $[3, \infty)$

7. **(a)** $(-7, 1)$ **(b)** $[-3, 4]$

8. **(a)** All numbers in $(-\infty, -3)$ or $(7, \infty)$

   (b) All numbers in $\left(-\infty, -\dfrac{1}{3}\right]$ or $[1, \infty)$

   (c) All numbers in $\left(-\infty, -\dfrac{7}{5}\right]$ or $\left[\dfrac{3}{5}, \infty\right)$

9. **(a)** All real numbers
   (b) No solution
   (c) All real numbers except -4

2.5 Polynomial and Rational Inequalities

This section deals with the solution of polynomial and rational inequalities, such as

$$r^2 + 3r - 4 \geq 0, \quad x^3 - x \leq 0, \quad \text{and} \quad \frac{2x - 1}{3x + 4} < 5.$$

We shall concentrate on algebraic solution methods, but to understand why these methods work, we must first look at such inequalities from a graphical point of view.

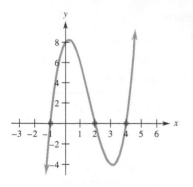

Figure 2.55

Example 1 Use the graph of $y = x^3 - 5x^2 + 2x + 8$ in Figure 2.55 to solve each of the given inequalities.

(a) $x^3 - 5x^2 + 2x + 8 > 0$

Solution Each point on the graph has coordinates of the form $(x, x^3 - 5x^2 + 2x + 8)$. The number x is a solution of the inequality exactly when the second coordinate of this point is positive—that is, when the point lies *above* the x-axis. So to solve the inequality, we need only find the first coordinates of points on the graph that are above the x-axis. This information can be read from Figure 2.55. The graph is above the x-axis when $-1 < x < 2$ and when $x > 4$. Therefore, the solutions of the inequality are all numbers x in the interval $(-1, 2)$ or the interval $(4, \infty)$.

(b) $x^3 - 5x^2 + 2x + 8 < 0$

Solution The number x is a solution of the inequality exactly when the second coordinate of the point $(x, x^3 - 5x^2 + 2x + 8)$ on the graph is negative—that is, when the point lies *below* the x-axis. Figure 2.55 shows that the graph is below the x-axis when $x < -1$ and when $2 < x < 4$. Hence, the solutions are all numbers x in the interval $(-\infty, -1)$ or the interval $(2, 4)$.

The solution process in Example 1 depends only on knowing the graph and its x-intercepts (that is, the points where the graph intersects the x-axis). This information can often be obtained algebraically, without doing any graphing.

Steps for Solving an Inequality Involving a Polynomial

1. Rewrite the inequality so that all the terms are on the left side and 0 is on the right side.
2. Find the x-intercepts by setting $y = 0$ and solving for x.
3. Divide the x-axis (number line) into regions using the solutions found in Step 2.
4. Test a point in each region by choosing a value for x and substituting it into the equation for y.
5. Determine which regions satisfy the original inequality and graph the solution.

Example 2 Solve each of the given quadratic inequalities.

(a) $x^2 - x < 12$

Solution

Step 1 Rewrite the inequality so that all the terms are on the left side and 0 is on the right side.
Hence we add –12 to each side and obtain $x^2 - x - 12 < 0$.

Step 2 Find the x-intercepts by setting $y = 0$ and solving for x.
We find the x-intercepts of $y = x^2 - x - 12$ by setting $y = 0$ and solving for x:

$$x^2 - x - 12 = 0$$
$$(x + 3)(x - 4) = 0$$
$$x + 3 = 0 \quad \text{or} \quad x - 4 = 0$$
$$x = -3 \qquad\qquad x = 4.$$

Step 3 Divide the x-axis (number line) into regions using the solutions found in Step 2.
These numbers divide the x-axis into three regions, as indicated in Figure 2.56.

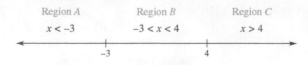

Figure 2.56

Step 4 Test a point in each region by choosing a value for x and substituting it in to the equation for y.

In each region, the graph of $y = x^2 - x - 12$ is an unbroken curve, so it will be entirely above or entirely below the axis. It can pass from above to below the x-axis only at the x-intercepts. To see whether the graph is above or below the x-axis when x is in region A, choose a value of x in region A, say, $x = -5$, and substitute it into the equation:

$$y = x^2 - x - 12 = (-5)^2 - (-5) - 12 = 18.$$

Therefore, the point $(-5, 18)$ is on the graph. Since its y-coordinate 18 is positive, this point lies above the x-axis; hence, the entire graph lies above the x-axis in region A.

Similarly, we can choose a value of x in region B, say, $x = 0$. Then

$$y = x^2 - x - 12 = 0^2 - 0 - 12 = -12,$$

so that $(0, -12)$ is on the graph. Since this point lies below the x-axis (why?), the entire graph in region B must be below the x-axis. Finally, in region C, let $x = 5$. Then $y = 5^2 - 5 - 12 = 8$, so that $(5, 8)$ is on the graph, and the entire graph in region C lies above the x-axis. We can summarize the results as follows:

Interval	$x < -3$	$-3 < x < 4$	$x > 4$
Test value in interval	-5	0	5
Value of $x^2 - x - 12$	18	-12	8
Graph	above x-axis	below x-axis	above x-axis
Conclusion	$x^2 - x - 12 > 0$	$x^2 - x - 12 < 0$	$x^2 - x - 12 > 0$

Step 5 Determine which regions satisfy the original inequality and graph the solution.

The last row shows that the only region where $x^2 - x - 12 < 0$ is region B, so the solutions of the inequality are all numbers x with $-3 < x < 4$—that is, the interval $(-3, 4)$, as shown in the number line graph in Figure 2.57.

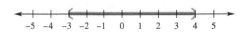

Figure 2.57

(b) $x^2 - x - 12 > 0$

Solution Use the chart in part (a). The last row shows that $x^2 - x - 12 > 0$ only when x is in region A or region C. Hence, the solutions of the inequality are all numbers x with $x < -3$ or $x > 4$—that is, all numbers in the interval $(-\infty, -3)$ or the interval $(4, \infty)$. ✓ 1

✓ **Checkpoint 1**

Solve each inequality. Graph the solution on the number line.

(a) $x^2 - 2x < 15$

(b) $2x^2 - 3x - 20 < 0$

Example 3 Solve the quadratic inequality $r^2 + 3r \geq 4$.

Solution

Step 1 First rewrite the inequality so that one side is 0:

$$r^2 + 3r \geq 4$$

$$r^2 + 3r - 4 \geq 0. \quad \text{Add } -4 \text{ to both sides.}$$

Step 2   Now solve the corresponding equation (which amounts to finding the x-intercepts of $y = r^3 + 3r - 4$):

$$r^2 + 3r - 4 = 0$$
$$(r - 1)(r + 4) = 0$$
$$r = 1 \quad \text{or} \quad r = -4.$$

Step 3   These numbers separate the number line into three regions, as shown in Figure 2.58. Test a number from each region:

Step 4   Let $r = -5$ from region **A**: $(-5)^2 + 3(-5) - 4 = 6 > 0$.

Let $r = 0$ from region **B**: $(0)^2 + 3(0) - 4 = -4 < 0$.

Let $r = 2$ from region **C**: $(2)^2 + 3(2) - 4 = 6 > 0$.

Step 5   We want the inequality to be positive or 0. The solution includes numbers in region A and in region C, as well as -4 and 1, the endpoints. The solution, which includes all numbers in the interval $(-\infty, -4]$ or the interval $[1, \infty)$, is graphed in Figure 2.58. ☑2

✓**Checkpoint 2**

Solve each inequality. Graph each solution.

(a) $k^2 + 2k - 15 \geq 0$

(b) $3m^2 + 7m \geq 6$

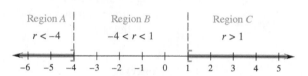

Figure 2.58

Example 4   Solve $q^3 - 4q > 0$.

Solution

Step 1   Step 1 is already complete in the statement of the problem.

Step 2   Solve the corresponding equation by factoring:

$$q^3 - 4q = 0$$
$$q(q^2 - 4) = 0$$
$$q(q + 2)(q - 2) = 0$$
$$q = 0 \quad \text{or} \quad q + 2 = 0 \quad \text{or} \quad q - 2 = 0$$
$$q = 0 \qquad\qquad q = -2 \qquad\qquad q = 2.$$

Step 3   These three numbers separate the number line into the four regions shown in Figure 2.59.

Step 4   Test a number from each region:

$$\textbf{A:} \quad \text{If } q = -3, (-3)^3 - 4(-3) = -15 < 0.$$
$$\textbf{B:} \quad \text{If } q = -1, (-1)^3 - 4(-1) = 3 > 0.$$
$$\textbf{C:} \quad \text{If } q = 1, (1)^3 - 4(1) = -3 < 0.$$
$$\textbf{D:} \quad \text{If } q = 3, (3)^3 - 4(3) = 15 > 0.$$

Step 5   The numbers that make the polynomial positive are in the interval $(-2, 0)$ or the interval $(2, \infty)$, as graphed in Figure 2.59. ☑3

✓**Checkpoint 3**

Solve each inequality. Graph each solution.

(a) $m^3 - 9m > 0$

(b) $2k^3 - 50k \leq 0$

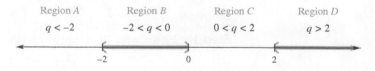

Figure 2.59

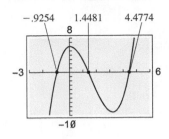

−.9254   1.4481   4.4774

Figure 2.60

✓**Checkpoint 4**

Use graphical methods to find approximate solutions of these inequalities.

(a) $x^2 - 6x + 2 > 0$

(b) $x^2 - 6x + 2 < 0$

A graphing calculator can be used to solve inequalities without the need to evaluate at a test number in each interval. It is also useful for finding approximate solutions when the *x*-intercepts of the graph cannot be found algebraically.

Example 5   Use a graphing calculator to solve $x^3 - 5x^2 + x + 6 > 0$.

Solution   Begin by graphing $y = x^3 - 5x^2 + x + 6$ (Figure 2.60). Find the *x*-intercepts by solving $x^3 - 5x^2 + x + 6 = 0$. Since this cannot readily be done algebraically, use the graphical root finder to determine that the solutions (*x*-intercepts) are approximately −.9254, 1.4481, and 4.4774.

The graph is above the *x*-axis when $-.9254 < x < 1.4481$ and when $x > 4.4774$. Therefore, the approximate solutions of the inequality are all numbers in the interval $(-.9254, 1.4481)$ or the interval $(4.4774, \infty)$. ✓4

Example 6   **Business**   A company sells wholesale portable DVD players for $39 each. The variable cost of producing *x* thousand players is $5.5x - 4.9x^2$ (in thousands of dollars), and the fixed cost is $550 (in thousands). Find the values of *x* for which the company will break even or make a profit on the product.

Solution   If *x* thousand DVD players are sold at $39 each, then

$$R = 39 \times x = 39x.$$

The cost function (in thousands of dollars) is

$$Cost = Fixed\ Costs + Variable\ Costs$$
$$C = 550 + (5.5x - 4.9x^2).$$

Therefore, to break even or earn a profit, we need Revenue (*R*) greater than or equal to Cost (*C*).

$$R \geq C$$
$$39x \geq 550 + 5.5x - 4.9x^2$$
$$4.9x^2 + 33.5x - 550 \geq 0.$$

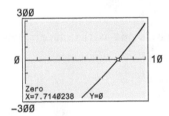

Figure 2.61

Now graph $4.9x^2 + 33.5x - 550$. Since *x* has to be positive in this situation (why?), we need only look at the graph in the right half of the plane. Here, and in other cases, you may have to try several viewing windows before you find one that shows what you need. Once you find a suitable window, such as in Figure 2.61, use the graphical root finder to determine the relevant *x*-intercept. Figure 2.61 shows the intercept is approximately $x \approx 7.71$. Hence, the company must manufacture at least $7.71 \times 1000 = 7710$ portable DVD players to make a profit.

Rational Inequalities

Inequalities with quotients of algebraic expressions are called **rational inequalities**. These inequalities can be solved in much the same way as polynomial inequalities can.

> ### Steps for Solving Inequalities Involving Rational Expressions
>
> 1. Rewrite the inequality so that all the terms are on the left side and the 0 is on the right side.
> 2. Write the left side as a single fraction.
> 3. Set the numerator and the denominator equal to 0 and solve for *x*.
> 4. Divide the *x*-axis (number line) into regions using the solutions found in Step 3.
> 5. Test a point in each region by choosing a value for *x* and substituting it into the equation for *y*.
> 6. Determine which regions satisfy the original inequality and graph the solution.

Example 7   Solve the rational inequality

$$\frac{5}{x + 4} \geq 1.$$

Solution

Step 1   Write an equivalent inequality with one side equal to 0:

$$\frac{5}{x + 4} \geq 1$$

$$\frac{5}{x + 4} - 1 \geq 0.$$

Step 2   Write the left side as a single fraction:

$$\frac{5}{x + 4} - \frac{x + 4}{x + 4} \geq 0 \qquad \text{Obtain a common denominator.}$$

$$\frac{5 - (x + 4)}{x + 4} \geq 0 \qquad \text{Subtract fractions.}$$

$$\frac{5 - x - 4}{x + 4} \geq 0 \qquad \text{Distributive property}$$

$$\frac{1 - x}{x + 4} \geq 0.$$

Step 3   The quotient can change sign only at places where the denominator is 0 or the numerator is 0. (In graphical terms, these are the only places where the graph of $y = \dfrac{1 - x}{x + 4}$ can change from above the x-axis to below.) This happens when

$$1 - x = 0 \qquad \text{or} \qquad x + 4 = 0$$
$$x = 1 \qquad \text{or} \qquad x = -4.$$

Step 4   As in the earlier examples, the numbers -4 and 1 divide the x-axis into three regions:

$$x < -4, \quad -4 < x < 1, \quad x > 1.$$

Step 5   Test a number from each of these regions:

$$\text{Let } x = -5: \quad \frac{1 - (-5)}{-5 + 4} = -6 < 0.$$

$$\text{Let } x = 0: \quad \frac{1 - 0}{0 + 4} = \frac{1}{4} > 0.$$

$$\text{Let } x = 2: \quad \frac{1 - 2}{2 + 4} = -\frac{1}{6} < 0.$$

Step 6   The test shows that numbers in $(-4, 1)$ satisfy the inequality. With a quotient, the endpoints must be considered individually to make sure that no denominator is 0. In this inequality, -4 makes the denominator 0, while 1 satisfies the given inequality. Write the solution in interval notation as $(-4, 1]$ and graphically as in Figure 2.62.

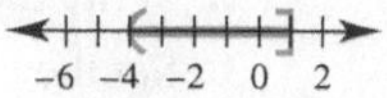

Figure 2.62

✓ **Checkpoint 5**

Solve each inequality.

(a) $\dfrac{3}{x - 2} \geq 4$

(b) $\dfrac{p}{1 - p} < 3$

(c) Why is 2 excluded from the solution in part (a)?

⊘ **CAUTION** As suggested by Example 7, be very careful with the endpoints of the intervals in the solution of rational inequalities. ✓5

Example 8 Solve

$$\frac{2x - 1}{3x + 4} < 5.$$

Solution

Step 1 Write an equivalent inequality with 0 on one side by adding -5 to each side.

$$\frac{2x - 1}{3x + 4} - 5 < 0 \qquad \text{Get 0 on the right side.}$$

Step 2 Write the left side as a single fraction by using $3x + 4$ as a common denominator.

$$\frac{2x - 1 - 5(3x + 4)}{3x + 4} < 0 \qquad \text{Obtain a common denominator.}$$

$$\frac{-13x - 21}{3x + 4} < 0 \qquad \text{Distribute in the numerator and combine terms.}$$

Step 3 Set the numerator and denominator each equal to 0 and solve the two equations:

$$-13x - 21 = 0 \qquad \text{or} \qquad 3x + 4 = 0$$

$$x = -\frac{21}{13} \qquad \text{or} \qquad x = -\frac{4}{3}$$

Step 4 The values $-21/13$ and $-4/3$ divide the x-axis into three regions:

$$x < -\frac{21}{13}, \quad -\frac{21}{13} < x < -\frac{4}{3}, \quad x > -\frac{4}{3}.$$

Steps 5 and 6 Testing points from each interval yields that the quotient is negative for numbers in the interval $(-\infty, -21/13)$ or $(-4/3, \infty)$. Neither endpoint satisfies the given inequality. 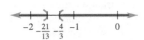 6

Figure 2.63

✓ **Checkpoint 6**

Solve each rational inequality.

(a) $\dfrac{3y - 2}{2y + 5} < 1$

(b) $\dfrac{3c - 4}{2 - c} \geq -5$

✓ **Checkpoint 7**

(a) Solve the inequality

$$\frac{10}{x + 2} \geq 3$$

by first multiplying both sides by $x + 2$.

(b) Show that this method produces a wrong answer by testing $x = -3$.

⓵ **CAUTION** In problems like those in Examples 7 and 8, you should *not* begin by multiplying both sides by the denominator to simplify the inequality. Doing so will usually produce a wrong answer. For the reason, see Exercise 38. For an example, see Checkpoint 7. ✓ 7

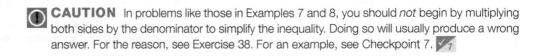

↗ **TECHNOLOGY TIP** Rational inequalities can also be solved graphically. In Example 7, for instance, after rewriting the original inequality in the form $\dfrac{1 - x}{x + 4} \geq 0$, determine the values of x that make the numerator and denominator 0 (namely, $x = 1$ and $x = -4$). Then graph $\dfrac{1 - x}{x + 4}$. Figure 2.64 shows that the graph is above the x-axis when it is between the vertical asymptote at $x = -4$ and the x-intercept at $x = 1$. So the solution of the inequality is the interval $(-4, 1]$. (When the values that make the numerator and denominator 0 cannot be found algebraically, as they were here, you can use the root finder to approximate them.)

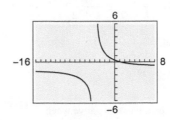

Figure 2.64

2.5 Exercises

Solve each of these quadratic inequalities. Graph the solutions on the number line. (See Examples 2 and 3.)

1. $(x + 4)(2x - 3) \le 0$

2. $(5y - 1)(y + 3) > 0$

3. $r^2 + 4r > -3$

4. $z^2 + 6z > -8$

5. $4m^2 + 7m - 2 \le 0$

6. $6p^2 - 11p + 3 \le 0$

7. $4x^2 + 3x - 1 > 0$

8. $3x^2 - 5x > 2$

9. $x^2 \le 36$

10. $y^2 \ge 9$

11. $p^2 - 16p > 0$

12. $r^2 - 9r < 0$

Solve these inequalities. (See Example 4.)

13. $x^3 - 9x \ge 0$

14. $p^3 - 25p \le 0$

15. $(x + 7)(x + 2)(x - 2) \ge 0$

16. $(2x + 4)(x^2 - 9) \le 0$

17. $(x + 5)(x^2 - 2x - 3) < 0$

18. $x^3 - 2x^2 - 3x \le 0$

19. $6k^3 - 5k^2 < 4k$

20. $2m^3 + 7m^2 > 4m$

21. A student solved the inequality $p^2 < 16$ by taking the square root of both sides to get $p < 4$. She wrote the solution as $(-\infty, 4)$. Is her solution correct?

Use a graphing calculator to solve these inequalities. (See Example 5.)

22. $6x + 7 < 2x^2$

23. $.5x^2 - 1.2x < .2$

24. $3.1x^2 - 7.4x + 3.2 > 0$

25. $x^3 - 2x^2 - 5x + 7 \ge 2x + 1$

26. $x^4 - 6x^3 + 2x^2 < 5x - 2$

27. $2x^4 + 3x^3 < 2x^2 + 4x - 2$

28. $x^5 + 5x^4 > 4x^3 - 3x^2 - 2$

Solve these rational inequalities. (See Examples 7 and 8.)

29. $\dfrac{r - 4}{r - 1} \ge 0$

30. $\dfrac{z + 6}{z + 4} > 1$

31. $\dfrac{a - 2}{a - 5} < -1$

32. $\dfrac{1}{3k - 5} < \dfrac{1}{3}$

33. $\dfrac{1}{p - 2} < \dfrac{1}{3}$

34. $\dfrac{7}{k + 2} \ge \dfrac{1}{k + 2}$

35. $\dfrac{5}{p + 1} > \dfrac{12}{p + 1}$

36. $\dfrac{x^2 - 4}{x} > 0$

37. $\dfrac{x^2 - x - 6}{x} < 0$

38. Determine whether $x + 4$ is positive or negative when

(a) $x > -4$;

(b) $x < -4$.

(c) If you multiply both sides of the inequality $\dfrac{1 - x}{x + 4} \ge 0$ by $x + 4$, should you change the direction of the inequality sign? If so, when?

(d) Explain how you can use parts (a)–(c) to solve $\dfrac{1 - x}{x + 4} \ge 0$ correctly.

Use a graphing calculator to solve these inequalities. You may have to approximate the roots of the numerators or denominators.

39. $\dfrac{2x^2 + x - 1}{x^2 - 4x + 4} \le 0$

40. $\dfrac{x^3 - 3x^2 + 5x - 29}{x^2 - 7} > 3$

41. **Business** An analyst has found that her company's profits, in hundreds of thousands of dollars, are given by $P = 2x^2 - 12x - 32$, where x is the amount, in hundreds of dollars, spent on advertising. For what values of x does the company make a profit?

42. **Business** The commodities market is highly unstable; money can be made or lost quickly on investments in soybeans, wheat, and so on. Suppose that an investor kept track of his total profit P at time t, in months, after he began investing, and he found that $P = 4t^2 - 30t + 14$. Find the time intervals during which he has been ahead.

43. **Business** The manager of a 200-unit apartment complex has found that the profit is given by

$$P = x^2 + 300x - 18,000,$$

where x is the number of apartments rented. For what values of x does the complex produce a profit?

Use a graphing calculator or other technology to complete Exercises 44–48. You may need to find a larger viewing window for some of these problems.

44. **Business** A door-to-door knife salesman finds that his weekly profit can be modeled by the equation

$$P = x^2 + 5x - 530$$

where x is the number of pitches he makes in a week. For what values of x does the salesman need to make in order to earn a profit?

45. **Business** The number of subscribers for cellular telecommunications (in millions) can be approximated by $.79x^2 + 5.4x + 178$ where $x = 7$ corresponds to the year 2007. Assuming the model to be valid indefinitely, in what years was the number of subscribers higher than 300 million? (Data from: ProQuest Statistical Abstract of the United States 2013.)

46. **Business** The percentage of delinquent real estate loans can be approximated by $-.65x^2 + 13.6x - 61.1$ where $x = 7$ corresponds to the year 2007. Assuming the model holds up to and including 2014, find the years in which the percentage of delinquent real estate loans was greater than 8%. (Data from: U.S. Federal Reserve.)

47. Finance The amount of outstanding mortgage debt (in trillions of dollars) can be approximated by $-.2x^2 + 3.44x + .16$ where $x = 4$ corresponds to the year 2004. Assuming the model holds up to and including 2014, find the years in which the amount of outstanding mortgage debt was higher than $13 trillion. (Data from: Board of Governors of the Federal Reserve.)

48. Finance Similar to Exercise 47, the amount of outstanding debt for home mortgages (in trillions of dollars) can be approximated by $-.15x^2 + 2.53x + .66$ where $x = 4$ corresponds to the year 2004. Assuming the model holds up to and including 2014, find the years in which the amount of outstanding home mortgage debt was higher than $9 trillion. (Data from: Board of Governors of the Federal Reserve.)

✓ Checkpoint Answers

1. (a) $(-3, 5)$

(b) $(-5/2, 4)$

2. (a) All numbers in $(-\infty, -5]$ or $[3, \infty)$

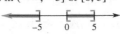

(b) All numbers in $(-\infty, -3]$ or $[2/3, \infty)$

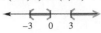

3. (a) All numbers in $(-3, 0)$ or $(3, \infty)$

(b) All numbers in $(-\infty, -5]$ or $[0, 5]$

4. (a) All numbers in $(-\infty, .3542)$ or $(5.6458, \infty)$

(b) All numbers in $(.3542, 5.6458)$

5. (a) $(2, 11/4]$

(b) All numbers in $(-\infty, 3/4)$ or $(1, \infty)$

(c) When $x = 2$, the fraction is undefined.

6. (a) $(-5/2, 7)$

(b) All numbers in $(-\infty, 2)$ or $[3, \infty)$

7. (a) $x \le \dfrac{4}{3}$

(b) $x = -3$ is a solution of $x \le \dfrac{4}{3}$, but not of the original inequality $\dfrac{10}{x + 2} \ge 3$.

CHAPTER 2 Summary and Review

Key Terms and Symbols*

2.1 Cartesian coordinate system
x-axis
y-axis
origin
ordered pair
x-coordinate
y-coordinate
quadrant
solution of an equation
graph

x-intercept
y-intercept
[viewing window]
[trace]
[graphical root finder]
[maximum and minimum finder]
graph reading
2.2 change in x
change in y

slope
slope–intercept form
parallel and perpendicular lines
point–slope form
linear equations
general form
2.3 linear models
residual
[least-squares regression line]

[linear regression]
[correlation coefficient]
2.4 linear inequality
properties of inequality
absolute-value inequality
2.5 polynomial inequality
algebraic solution methods
[graphical solution methods]
rational inequality

Chapter 2 Key Concepts

Slope of a Line   The **slope** of the line through the points (x_1, y_1) and (x_2, y_2), where $x_1 \ne x_2$, is $m = \dfrac{y_2 - y_1}{x_2 - x_1}$.

Equation of a Line   The line with equation $y = mx + b$ has slope m and y-intercept b.

The line with equation $y - y_1 = m(x - x_1)$ has slope m and goes through (x_1, y_1).

The line with equation $ax + by = c$ (with $a \ne 0, b \ne 0$) has x-intercept c/a and y-intercept c/b.

---

*Terms in brackets deal with material in which a graphing calculator or other technology is used.

The line with equation $x = k$ is vertical, with x-intercept k, no y-intercept, and undefined slope.

The line with equation $y = k$ is horizontal, with y-intercept k, no x-intercept, and slope 0.

Parellel and Perpendicular Lines   Nonvertical **parallel lines** have the same slope, and **perpendicular lines,** if neither is vertical, have slopes with a product of -1.

Chapter 2 Review Exercises

Which of the ordered pairs $(-2, 3), (0, -5), (2, -3), (3, -2),$
(4, 3), and (7, 2) are solutions of the given equation?

1. $y = x^2 - 2x - 5$ **2.** $x - y = 5$

Sketch the graph of each equation.

3. $5x - 3y = 15$ **4.** $2x + 7y - 21 = 0$

5. $y + 3 = 0$ **6.** $y - 2x = 0$

7. $y = .25x^2 + 1$ **8.** $y = \sqrt{x + 4}$

9. The following temperature graph was recorded in Bratenahl, Ohio:

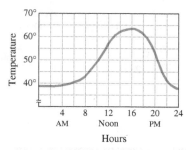

(a) At what times during the day was the temperature over 55°?

(b) When was the temperature below 40°?

10. Greenville, South Carolina, is 500 miles south of Bratenahl, Ohio, and its temperature is 7° higher all day long. (See the graph in Exercise 9.) At what time was the temperature in Greenville the same as the temperature at noon in Bratenahl?

11. In your own words, define the slope of a line.

In Exercises 12–21, find the slope of the line defined by the given conditions.

12. Through $(-1, 3)$ and $(2, 6)$

13. Through $(4, -5)$ and $(1, 4)$

14. Through $(8, -3)$ and the origin

15. Through $(8, 2)$ and $(0, 4)$

16. $3x + 5y = 25$ **17.** $6x - 2y = 7$

18. $x - 2 = 0$ **19.** $y = -4$

20. Parallel to $3x + 8y = 0$

21. Perpendicular to $x = 3y$

22. Graph the line through $(0, 5)$ with slope $m = -2/3$.

23. Graph the line through $(-4, 1)$ with $m = 3$.

24. What information is needed to determine the equation of a line?

Find an equation for each of the following lines.

25. Through $(5, -1)$, slope $2/3$

26. Through $(8, 0)$, slope $-1/4$

27. Through $(5, -2)$ and $(1, 3)$

28. Through $(2, -3)$ and $(-3, 4)$

29. Undefined slope, through $(-1, 4)$

30. Slope 0, through $(-2, 5)$

31. x-intercept -3, y-intercept 5

32. Here is a sample SAT question: Which of the following is an equation of the line that has a y-intercept of 2 and an x-intercept of 3?

    (a) $-2x + 3y = 4$ **(b)** $-2x + 3y = 6$

    (c) $2x + 3y = 4$ **(d)** $2x + 3y = 6$

    (e) $3x + 2y = 6$

33. Business   According to the U.S. Department of Agriculture, in 2005, the United States exported 14.0 million hectoliters of fruit juices and wine. In 2011, that number was 17.3 million hectoliters.

    (a) Assuming the increase in exports of fruit juice and wine is linear, write an equation that gives the amount exported in year x, with $x = 5$ corresponding to the year 2005.

    (b) Is the slope of the line positive or negative? Why?

    (c) Assuming the linear trend continues, estimate the amount exported in the year 2014.

34. Business   In the year 2005, the total domestic fish and shellfish catch was 9.7 billion pounds. In 2010, the total was 8.2 billion pounds. (Data from: U.S. National Oceanic and Atmospheric Administration.)

    (a) Assuming the decline in fish and shellfish catch is linear, write an equation that gives the amount of the catch produced in year x, where $x = 5$ corresponds to the year 2005.

    (b) Graph the equation for the years 2005 through 2010.

    (c) Assuming the trend continues, estimate the total fish and shellfish catch in the year 2013.

35. Business   The following table gives the total compensation (in dollars) per full-time employee for various years. (Data from: U.S. Bureau of Economic Analysis.)

Year	2000	2005	2010	2011
Compensation	47,059	56,620	66,249	68,129

(a) Use the data from the years 2000 and 2010 to find a linear model for the data, with $x = 0$ corresponding to the year 2000.

(b) Find the least-squares regression line for the data.

(c) Use the models from part (a) and (b) to estimate the compensation for the year 2011. Compare the estimates to the actual compensation of $68,129 for the year 2011.

(d) Assume the trend continues and use the model for (b) to estimate the compensation per full-time employee in the year 2015.

36. Business If current trends continue, the median weekly earnings (in dollars) that a male can expect to earn is approximated by the equation $y = 17.4x + 639$, where $x = 0$ corresponds to the year 2000. The equation $y = 17.3x + 495$ approximates median weekly earnings for females. (Data from: U.S. Bureau of Labor Statistics.)

(a) In what year will males achieve median weekly earnings of $900?

(b) In what year will females achieve median weekly earnings of $900?

37. Business The following table shows the total private philanthropy donations (in billions of dollars) for various years. (Data from: Center on Philanthropy at Indiana University.)

Year	1990	1995	2000	2005	2010
Philanthropy	101	124	230	288	287

(a) Let $x = 0$ correspond to the year 1990, and find the least-squares regression line for the data.

(b) Graph the data from the years 1990 to 2010 with the least-squares regression line.

(c) Does the least-squares regression line form a good fit?

(d) What is the correlation coefficient?

38. Economics According to the U.S. Department of Education, the average financial aid award (in dollars) for a full-time student is given in the following table for various years:

Year	2000	2005	2008	2009	2010	2011
Amount	2925	3407	3791	4056	4232	4341

(a) Let $x = 0$ correspond to the year 2000, and find the least-squares regression line for the data.

(b) Graph the data from the years 2000 to 2011 with the least-squares regression line.

(c) Does the least-squares regression line form a good fit?

(d) What is the correlation coefficient?

Solve each inequality.

39. $-6x + 3 < 2x$

40. $12z \geq 5z - 7$

41. $2(3 - 2m) \geq 8m + 3$

42. $6p - 5 > -(2p + 3)$

43. $-3 \leq 4x - 1 \leq 7$

44. $0 \leq 3 - 2a \leq 15$

45. $|b| \leq 8$

46. $|a| > 7$

47. $|2x - 7| \geq 3$

48. $|4m + 9| \leq 16$

49. $|5k + 2| - 3 \leq 4$

50. $|3z - 5| + 2 \geq 10$

51. Natural Science Here is a sample SAT question: For pumpkin carving, Mr. Sephera will not use pumpkins that weigh less than 2 pounds or more than 10 pounds. If x represents the weight of a pumpkin (in pounds) that he will *not* use, which of the following inequalities represents all possible values of x?

(a) $|x - 2| > 10$ **(b)** $|x - 4| > 6$

(c) $|x - 5| > 5$ **(d)** $|x - 6| > 4$

(e) $|x - 10| > 4$

52. Business Prices at several retail outlets for a new 24-inch, 2-cycle snow thrower were all within $55 of $600. Write this information as an inequality, using absolute-value notation.

53. Business The amount of renewable energy consumed by the industrial sector of the U.S. economy (in trillion BTUs) was 1873 in the year 2005 and 2250 in the year 2010. Assume the amount of energy consumed is increasing linearly. (Data from: U.S. Energy Information Administration.)

(a) Find the linear equation that gives the number of BTUs consumed with $x = 5$ corresponding to the year 2005.

(b) Assume the linear equation that gives the amount of energy consumed continues indefinitely. Determine when the consumption will exceed 2500.

54. Business One car rental firm charges $125 for a weekend rental (Friday afternoon through Monday morning) and gives unlimited mileage. A second firm charges $95 plus $.20 a mile. For what range of miles driven is the second firm cheaper?

Solve each inequality.

55. $r^2 + r - 6 < 0$

56. $y^2 + 4y - 5 \geq 0$

57. $2z^2 + 7z \geq 15$

58. $3k^2 \leq k + 14$

59. $(x - 3)(x^2 + 7x + 10) \leq 0$

60. $(x + 4)(x^2 - 1) \geq 0$

61. $\dfrac{m + 2}{m} \leq 0$

62. $\dfrac{q - 4}{q + 3} > 0$

63. $\dfrac{5}{p + 1} > 2$

64. $\dfrac{6}{a - 2} \leq -3$

65. $\dfrac{2}{r + 5} \leq \dfrac{3}{r - 2}$

66. $\dfrac{1}{z - 1} > \dfrac{2}{z + 1}$

67. Business The net income (in millions of dollars) generated by the satellite radio company SiriusXM can be approximated by the equation $y = 340.1x^2 - 5360x + 18,834$, where $x = 6$ corresponds to the year 2006. In what years between 2006 and 2012 did SiriusXM have positive net income? (Data from: www.morningstar.com.)

68. Business The net income (in millions of dollars) generated by Xerox corporation can be approximated by the equation $y = 89.29x^2 - 1577x + 7505$, where $x = 6$ corresponds to the year 2006. In what years between 2006 and 2012 did Xerox have net income higher than $1000 million? (Data from: www.morningstar.com.)

Case Study 2 Using Extrapolation and Interpolation for Prediction

One reason for developing a mathematical model is to make predictions. If your model is a least-squares line, you can predict the y-value corresponding to some new x-value by substituting that x-value into an equation of the form $\hat{y} = mx + b$. (We use $\hat{y}$ to remind us that we're getting a predicted value rather than an actual data value.) Data analysts distinguish between two very different kinds of prediction: *interpolation* and *extrapolation*. An interpolation uses a new x inside the x-range of your original data. For example, if you have inflation data at five-year intervals from 1950 to 2010, estimating the rate of inflation in 1957 is an interpolation problem. But if you use the same data to estimate what the inflation rate was in 1920, or what it will be in 2020, you are extrapolating.

In general, interpolation is much safer than extrapolation, because data that are approximately linear over a short interval may be nonlinear over a larger interval. Let us examine a case of the dangers of extrapolation. Figure 1 shows the net income (in millions of dollars) for the Starbucks Corporation from the years 2001–2007. Also on Figure 1, we see the least-squares regression line. (Data from: www.morningstar.com.)

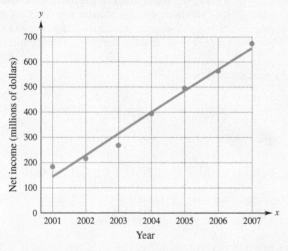

Figure 1

As we can see from graph, the fit is quite good and the linear trend seems quite clear. Additionally, the correlation coefficient is $r \approx .99$, which is quite high. The least-squares regression equation is

$$y = 85.7x + 55.3,$$

where $x = 1$ corresponds to 2001. If we extrapolate to the next two years, we predict the net earnings for Starbucks to be

$$2008\text{: } 85.7(8) + 55.3 = \$740.9 \text{ million}$$
$$2009\text{: } 85.7(9) + 55.3 = \$826.6 \text{ million}$$

As we know, however, the year 2008 saw the start of a deep recession in the United States, and the net earnings for Starbucks were actually $316 million in the year 2008 and $391 million in the year 2009—substantially lower than the predictions.

Using the past to predict the future is generally a dangerous business because we often cannot foresee events with major impact such as recessions, natural disasters, etc. Predictions into the future are often made, however, because planning has to occur and we use the best data we have available. One merely needs to realize that predictions into the future are highly likely to be inaccurate.

One way to determine if a model is likely to be inaccurate in the future is to examine the residuals. In Section 2.3, we defined a residual to be the difference between the actual value y and its predicted value $\hat{y}$.

$$\text{Residual} = y - \hat{y}.$$

Graphing these residuals on the y-axis and the predictor variable on the x-axis can be illuminating. Let's look at another historical example. Figure 2 shows the total household debt (in trillions of dollars) from the years 2004 through 2010. (Data from: Federal Reserve Bank of New York.)

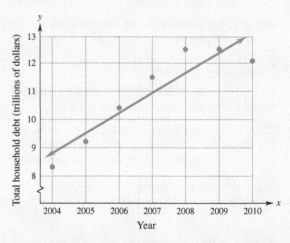

Figure 2

The regression equation for the least-squares line in Figure 2 is

$$y = .7x + 5.9,$$

where $x = 4$ corresponds to the year 2004. Since the correlation coefficient r is approximately .93, our linear model appears to fit the data well. We notice, however, that the predictions overpredict, then underpredict, and then overpredict. We can get a better look at this pattern by plotting the residuals. To find them, we put each value of the independent variable into the regression equation, calculate the predicted value $\hat{y}$, and subtract it from the actual value of y as in the table.

Year	2004	2005	2006	2007	2008	2009	2010
x	4	5	6	7	8	9	10
y	8.3	9.2	10.4	11.5	12.5	12.5	12.1
$\hat{y}$	8.7	9.4	10.1	10.8	11.5	12.2	12.9
Residual $y - \hat{y}$	−.4	−.2	.3	.7	1.0	.3	−.8

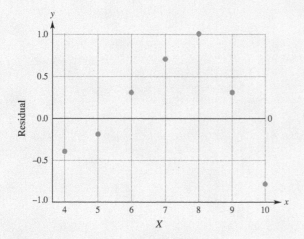

Figure 3

The residuals in Figure 3 indicate that our data have a nonlinear U-shaped component that is not captured by a linear model. When a residual plot shows a pattern such as this (or a similar pattern with an upside down U), extrapolating from the data is probably not a good idea. Our prediction for the year 2011, for example, would be

$$\hat{y} = .7(11) + 5.9 = \$13.6 \text{ trillion,}$$

which is far higher than the actual value of \$11.8 trillion.

Exercises

Business   The following table gives the number of completed new single family homes (in thousands) from the years 2002 to 2012. (Data from: U.S. Census Bureau.)

Year	Housing Units	Year	Housing Units
2002	1648	2008	1120
2003	1679	2009	794
2004	1842	2010	652
2005	1931	2011	585
2006	1979	2012	650
2007	1503		

1. If you have access to the appropriate technology, verify that the least-squares regression line that models these data (with rounded coefficients) is $y = -146.1x + 2330$, where $x = 2$ corresponds to the year 2002.

2. Use the model from Exercise 1 to calculate the predicted values $\hat{y}$ for each year in the table.

3. Use your answers from Exercise 2 to calculate the residuals for each year in the table. Make a graph of the residuals similar to Figure 3.

4. Do you think the linear model of Exercise 1 is a good fit for these data? Why or why not?

Business   The following table gives the average hourly earnings (in dollars) of U.S. production workers from 1970 to 2010. (Data from: U.S. Bureau of Labor Statistics.)

Year	Average Hourly Wage (Dollars)
1970	3.40
1975	4.73
1980	6.85
1985	8.74
1990	10.20
1995	11.65
2000	14.02
2005	16.13
2010	16.26

5. If you have appropriate technology, verify that the least-squares regression line that models these data (with coefficients rounded) is $y = .343x - 20.65$, where y is the average hourly wage in year x and $x = 0$ corresponds to 1900.

6. Use the model from Exercise 5 to interpolate a prediction of the hourly wage in 2002. The actual value was \$14.97. How close was your prediction?

7. Use the model from Exercise 5 to extrapolate to 1960 and predict the hourly average wage. Why is this prediction nonsensical?

8. Using the model from Exercise 5, find the average hourly wage for each year in the table, and subtract it from the actual value in the second column. This gives you a table of the residuals. Plot your residuals as points on a graph.

9. What will happen if you try linear regression on the *residuals*? If you're not sure, use technology such as a graphing calculator to find the regression equation for the residuals. Why does this result make sense?

Extended Project

Go the library or use the Internet to obtain the average amount of student loan debt for the most recent years available.

1. Create a scatterplot of the data with the amount on the y-axis and the year on the x-axis and assess the trend.
2. Fit a linear model to the data and predict the loan debt amount for each year.

3. Calculate the residuals from each year in the data set. Graph the residuals.
4. Do the residuals show a U-shape?
5. Find the correlation coefficient for your data.

Functions and Graphs

3

CHAPTER

CHAPTER OUTLINE

The modern world is overwhelmed with data—from the cost of college to mortgage rates, health care expenditures, and hundreds of other pieces of information. Functions enable us to construct mathematical models that can sometimes be used to estimate outcomes. Graphs of functions allow us to visualize a situation and to detect trends more easily. See Example 11 on page 129 and Exercises 57 and 58 on page 179.

Functions are an extremely useful way of describing many real-world situations in which the value of one quantity varies with, depends on, or determines the value of another. In this chapter, you will be introduced to functions, learn how to use functional notation, develop skills in constructing and interpreting the graphs of functions, and, finally, learn to apply this knowledge in a variety of situations.

3.1   Functions

To understand the origin of the concept of a function, we consider some real-life situations in which one numerical quantity depends on, corresponds to, or determines another.

> **Example 1**   The amount of the electric bill you pay depends on the amount of kilowatt hours (kWh) consumed. The way in which the usage determines the bill is given by the rate per kWh.

Example 2   Economics   The graph in Figure 3.1 shows the poverty rate from the years 1959 to 2011. The blue vertical bands indicate times of economic recession. The graph displays the percentage living in poverty that corresponds to each year. (Source: DeNavas-Walt, Carmen, Bernadette D. Proctor, and Jessica C. Smith, U.S. Census Bureau, Current Population Reports, P60-243, Income, Poverty, and Health Insurance Coverage in the United States: 2011, U.S. Government Printing Office, Washington, DC, 2012.)

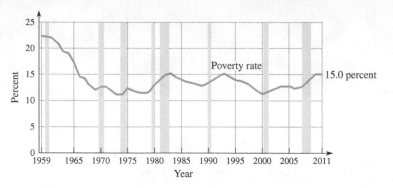

Figure 3.1

Example 3   Physical Science   Suppose a rock is dropped straight down from a high point. From physics, we know that the distance traveled by the rock in t seconds is $16t^2$ feet. So the distance depends on the time.

These examples share a couple of features. First, each involves two sets of numbers, which we can think of as inputs and outputs. Second, in each case, there is a rule by which each input determines an output, as summarized here:

	Set of Inputs	Set of Outputs	Rule
Example 1	All usages	All bill amounts	The rate per kWh
Example 2	Year	Poverty rate	Time-rate graph
Example 3	Seconds elapsed after dropping the rock	Distances the rock travels	Distance $= 16t^2$

Each of these examples may be mentally represented by an idealized calculator that has a single operation key: A number is entered [*input*], the rule key is pushed [*rule*], and an answer is displayed [*output*]. The formal definition of a function incorporates these same common features (input–rule–output), with a slight change in terminology.

A **function** consists of a set of inputs called the **domain,** a set of outputs called the **range,** and a rule by which each input determines *exactly one* output.

✓ **Checkpoint 1**

Find the domain and range of the function in Example 3, assuming (unrealistically) that the rock can fall forever.

Answers to Checkpoint exercises are found at the end of the section.

Example 4   Find the domains and ranges for the functions in Examples 1 and 2.

Solution   In Example 1, the domain consists of all possible usage amounts and the range consists of all possible bill amounts.

In Example 2, the domain is the set of years from 1959 to 2011, all real numbers in the interval [1959, 2011]. The range consists of the poverty rates that actually occur during those years. Figure 3.1 suggests that these are all numbers in the interval [11, 22].

Be sure that you understand the phrase "exactly one output" in the definition of the rule of a function. In Example 2, for instance, each year (input) determines exactly one poverty rate (output)—you can't have two different rates at the same time. However, it is quite possible to have the same rate (output) at two different times (inputs). In other words, we can say the following:

> **In a function, each input produces a single output, but different inputs may produce the same output.**

Example 5   Which of the following rules describe functions?

(a) Use the optical reader at the checkout counter of the supermarket to convert codes to prices.

Solution   For each code, the reader produces exactly one price, so this is a function.

(b) Enter a number in a calculator and press the x^2 key.

Solution   This is a function, because the calculator produces just one number x^2 for each number x that is entered.

(c) Assign to each number x the number y given by this table:

x	1	1	2	2	3	3
y	3	-3	-5	-5	8	-8

Solution   Since $x = 1$ corresponds to more than one y-value (as does $x = 3$), this table does not define a function.

(d) Assign to each number x the number y given by the equation $y = 3x - 5$.

Solution   Because the equation determines a unique value of y for each value of x, it defines a function. ✓₂

The equation $y = 3x - 5$ in part (d) of Example 5 defines a function, with x as input and y as output, because each value of x determines a *unique* value of y. In such a case, the equation is said to **define y as a function of x.**

Example 6   Decide whether each of the following equations defines y as a function of x.

(a) $y = -4x + 11$

Solution   For a given value of x, calculating $-4x + 11$ produces exactly one value of y. (For example, if $x = -7$, then $y = -4(-7) + 11 = 39$). Because one value of the input variable leads to exactly one value of the output variable, $y = -4x + 11$ defines y as a function of x.

(b) $y^2 = x$

Solution   Suppose $x = 36$. Then $y^2 = x$ becomes $y^2 = 36$, from which $y = 6$ or $y = -6$. Since one value of x can lead to two values of y, $y^2 = x$ does *not* define y as a function of x. ✓₃

Almost all the functions in this text are defined by formulas or equations, as in part (a) of Example 6. The domain of such a function is determined by the following **agreement on domains.**

✓ **Checkpoint 2**

Do the following define functions?

(a) The correspondence defined by the rule $y = x^2 + 5$, where x is the input and y is the output.

(b) The correspondence defined by entering a nonzero number in a calculator and pressing the $1/x$ key.

(c) The correspondence between a computer, x, and several users of the computer, y.

✓ **Checkpoint 3**

Do the following define y as a function of x?

(a) $y = -6x + 1$

(b) $y = x^2$

(c) $x = y^2 - 1$

(d) $y < x + 2$

> Unless otherwise stated, assume that the domain of any function defined by a formula or an equation is the largest set of real numbers (inputs) that each produces a real number as output.

Example 7   Each of the given equations defines y as a function of x. Find the domain of each function.

(a) $y = x^4$

Solution   Any number can be raised to the fourth power, so the domain is the set of all real numbers, which is sometimes written as $(-\infty, \infty)$.

(b) $y = \sqrt{x - 6}$

Solution   For y to be a real number, $x - 6$ must be nonnegative. This happens only when $x - 6 \geq 0$—that is, when $x \geq 6$. So the domain is the interval $[6, \infty)$.

(c) $y = \sqrt{4 - x}$

Solution   For y to be a real number here, we must have $4 - x \geq 0$, which is equivalent to $x \leq 4$. So the domain is the interval $(-\infty, 4]$.

(d) $y = \dfrac{1}{x + 3}$

Solution   Because the denominator cannot be 0, $x \neq -3$ and the domain consists of all numbers in the intervals,

$$(-\infty, -3) \quad \text{or} \quad (-3, \infty).$$

(e) $y = \dfrac{\sqrt{x}}{x^2 - 3x + 2}$

Solution   The numerator is defined only when $x \geq 0$. The domain cannot contain any numbers that make the denominator 0—that is, the numbers that are solutions of

$$x^2 - 3x + 2 = 0.$$
$$(x - 1)(x - 2) = 0 \qquad \text{Factor.}$$
$$x - 1 = 0 \quad \text{or} \quad x - 2 = 0 \qquad \text{Zero-factor property}$$
$$x = 1 \quad \text{or} \qquad x = 2.$$

Therefore, the domain consists of all nonnegative real numbers except 1 and 2. ✓₄

✓ **Checkpoint 4**

Give the domain of each function.

(a) $y = 3x + 1$

(b) $y = x^2$

(c) $y = \sqrt{-x}$

(d) $y = \dfrac{3}{x^2 - 1}$

Functional Notation

In actual practice, functions are seldom presented in the style of domain–rule–range, as they have been here. Functions are usually denoted by a letter such as f. If x is an input, then $f(x)$ denotes the output number that the function f produces from the input x. The symbol $f(x)$ is read "f of x." The rule is usually given by a formula, such as $f(x) = \sqrt{x^2 + 1}$. This formula can be thought of as a set of directions:

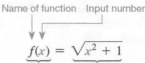

Name of function   Input number

$$\underline{f(x)} = \sqrt{x^2 + 1}$$

Output number   Directions that tell you what to do with input x in order to produce the corresponding output $f(x)$—namely, "square it, add 1, and take the square root of the result."

For example, to find $f(3)$ (the output number produced by the input 3), simply replace x by 3 in the formula:

$$f(3) = \sqrt{3^2 + 1}$$
$$= \sqrt{10}.$$

Similarly, replacing x respectively by -5 and 0 shows that

$$f(-5) = \sqrt{(-5)^2 + 1} \quad \text{and} \quad f(0) = \sqrt{0^2 + 1}$$
$$= \sqrt{26} \qquad\qquad\qquad = 1.$$

These directions can be applied to any quantities, such as $a + b$ or c^4 (where a, b, and c are real numbers). Thus, to compute $f(a + b)$, the output corresponding to input $a + b$, we square the input [obtaining $(a + b)^2$], add 1 [obtaining $(a + b)^2 + 1$], and take the square root of the result:

$$f(a + b) = \sqrt{(a + b)^2 + 1}$$
$$= \sqrt{a^2 + 2ab + b^2 + 1}.$$

Similarly, the output $f(c^4)$, corresponding to the input c^4, is computed by squaring the input $[(c^4)^2]$, adding 1 $[(c^4)^2 + 1]$, and taking the square root of the result:

$$f(c^4) = \sqrt{(c^4)^2 + 1}$$
$$= \sqrt{c^8 + 1}.$$

Example 8   Let $g(x) = -x^2 + 4x - 5$. Find each of the given outputs.

(a) $g(-2)$

Solution   Replace x with -2:

$$g(-2) = -(-2)^2 + 4(-2) - 5$$
$$= -4 - 8 - 5$$
$$= -17.$$

(b) $g(x + h)$

Solution   Replace x by the quantity $x + h$ in the rule of g:

$$g(x + h) = -(x + h)^2 + 4(x + h) - 5$$
$$= -(x^2 + 2xh + h^2) + (4x + 4h) - 5$$
$$= -x^2 - 2xh - h^2 + 4x + 4h - 5.$$

(c) $g(x + h) - g(x)$

Solution   Use the result from part (b) and the rule for $g(x)$:

$$g(x + h) - g(x) = \overbrace{(-x^2 - 2xh - h^2 + 4x + 4h - 5)}^{g(x + h)} - \overbrace{(-x^2 + 4x - 5)}^{g(x)}$$
$$= -2xh - h^2 + 4h.$$

(d) $\dfrac{g(x + h) - g(x)}{h}$ (assuming that $h \neq 0$)

Solution   The numerator was found in part (c). Divide it by h as follows:

$$\frac{g(x + h) - g(x)}{h} = \frac{-2xh - h^2 + 4h}{h}$$
$$= \frac{h(-2x - h + 4)}{h}$$
$$= -2x - h + 4.$$

The quotient found in Example 8(d),

$$\frac{g(x + h) - g(x)}{h},$$

is called the **difference quotient** of the function g. Difference quotients are important in calculus. ☑5

Let $f(x) = 5x^2 - 2x + 1$. Find the following.

(a) $f(1)$

(b) $f(3)$

(c) $f(1 + 3)$

(d) $f(1) + f(3)$

(e) $f(m)$

(f) $f(x + h) - f(x)$

(g) $\dfrac{f(x + h) - f(x)}{h} (h \neq 0)$

CAUTION Functional notation is *not* the same as ordinary algebraic notation. You cannot simplify an expression such as $f(x + h)$ by writing $f(x) + f(h)$. To see why, consider the answers to Checkpoints 5(c) and (d), which show that

$$f(1 + 3) \neq f(1) + f(3).$$

Applications

Example 9 **Finance** If you were a single person in Connecticut in 2013 with a taxable income of x dollars and $x \leq \$500,000$ then your state income tax T was determined by the rule

$$T(x) = \begin{cases} .03x & \text{if } 0 \leq x \leq 10{,}000 \\ 300 + .05(x - 10{,}000) & \text{if } 10{,}000 \leq x \leq 500{,}00 \end{cases}$$

Find the income tax paid by a single person with the given taxable income. (Data from: www.taxbrackets.org.)

(a) $9200

Solution We must find $T(9200)$. Since 9200 is less than 10,000, the first part of the rule applies:

$$T(x) = .03x$$
$$T(9200) = .03(9200) = \$276. \quad \text{Let } x = 9200.$$

(b) $30,000

Solution Now we must find $T(30,000)$. Since 30,000 is greater than \$10,000, the second part of the rule applies:

$$T(x) = 300 + .05(x - 10{,}000)$$
$$T(30{,}000) = 300 + .05(30{,}000 - 10{,}000) \quad \text{Let } x = 30{,}000.$$
$$= 300 + .05(20{,}000) \quad \text{Simplify.}$$
$$= 300 + 1000 = \$1300. \ ☑6$$

Use Example 9 to find the tax on each of these incomes.

(a) $48,750

(b) $7345

A function with a multipart rule, as in Example 9, is called a **piecewise-defined function.**

Example 10 **Business** Suppose the projected sales (in thousands of dollars) of a small company over the next 10 years are approximated by the function

$$S(x) = .07x^4 - .05x^3 + 2x^2 + 7x + 62.$$

(a) What are the projected sales for the current year?

Solution The current year corresponds to $x = 0$, and the sales for this year are given by $S(0)$. Substituting 0 for x in the rule for S, we see that $S(0) = 62$. So the current projected sales are $62,000.

✓ **Checkpoint 7**

A developer estimates that the total cost of building x large apartment complexes in a year is approximated by

$$A(x) = x^2 + 80x + 60,$$

where $A(x)$ represents the cost in hundred thousands of dollars. Find the cost of building

(a) 4 complexes;

(b) 10 complexes.

(b) What will sales be in four years?

Solution The sales in four years from now are given by $S(4)$, which can be computed by hand or with a calculator:

$$S(x) = .07x^4 - .05x^3 + 2x^2 + 7x + 62$$
$$S(4) = .07(4)^4 - .05(4)^3 + 2(4)^2 + 7(4) + 62 \qquad \text{Let } x = 4.$$
$$= 136.72.$$

Thus, sales are projected to be \$136,720. ✓7

X	Y1
5	184.5
6	255.92
7	359.92
8	507.12
9	709.82
10	982
11	1339.3

X=5

Figure 3.2

↗ **Example 11**   **Business**   Use the table feature of the graphing calculator to find the projected sales of the company in Example 10 for years 5 through 10.

Solution Enter the sales equation $y = .07x^4 - .05x^3 + 2x^2 + 7x + 62$ into the equation memory of the calculator (often called the Y = list). Check your instruction manual for how to set the table to start at $x = 5$ and go at least through $x = 10$. Then display the table, as in Figure 3.2. The figure shows that sales are projected to rise from \$184,500 in year 5 to \$982,000 in year 10.

3.1 Exercises

For each of the following rules, state whether it defines y as a function of x or not. (See Examples 5 and 6.)

1.

x	3	2	1	0	−1	−2	−3
y	9	4	1	0	1	4	9

2.

x	9	4	1	0	1	4	9
y	3	2	1	0	−1	−2	−3

3. $y = x^3$

4. $y = \sqrt{x - 1}$

5. $x = |y + 2|$

6. $x = y^2 + 3$

7. $y = \dfrac{-1}{x - 1}$

8. $y = \dfrac{4}{2x + 3}$

State the domain of each function. (See Example 7.)

9. $f(x) = 4x - 1$

10. $f(x) = 2x + 7$

11. $f(x) = x^4 - 1$

12. $f(x) = (2x + 5)^2$

13. $f(x) = \sqrt{-x} + 3$

14. $f(x) = \sqrt{5 - x}$

15. $g(x) = \dfrac{1}{x - 2}$

16. $g(x) = \dfrac{x}{x^2 + x - 2}$

17. $g(x) = \dfrac{x^2 + 4}{x^2 - 4}$

18. $g(x) = \dfrac{x^2 - 1}{x^2 + 1}$

19. $h(x) = \dfrac{\sqrt{x + 4}}{x^2 + x - 12}$

20. $h(x) = |5 - 4x|$

21. $g(x) = \begin{cases} 1/x & \text{if } x < 0 \\ \sqrt{x^2 + 1} & \text{if } x \geq 0 \end{cases}$

22. $f(x) = \begin{cases} 2x + 3 & \text{if } x < 4 \\ x^2 - 1 & \text{if } 4 \leq x \leq 10 \end{cases}$

For each of the following functions, find

(a) $f(4)$;   **(b)** $f(-3)$;   **(c)** $f(2.7)$;   **(d)** $f(-4.9)$.

(See Examples 8 and 9.)

23. $f(x) = 8$

24. $f(x) = 0$

25. $f(x) = 2x^2 + 4x$

26. $f(x) = x^2 - 2x$

27. $f(x) = \sqrt{x + 3}$

28. $f(x) = \sqrt{5 - x}$

29. $f(x) = |x^2 - 6x - 4|$

30. $f(x) = |x^3 - x^2 + x - 1|$

31. $f(x) = \dfrac{\sqrt{x - 1}}{x^2 - 1}$

32. $f(x) = \sqrt{-x} + \dfrac{2}{x + 1}$

33. $f(x) = \begin{cases} x^2 & \text{if } x < 2 \\ 5x - 7 & \text{if } x \geq 2 \end{cases}$

34. $f(x) = \begin{cases} -2x + 4 & \text{if } x \leq 1 \\ 3 & \text{if } 1 < x < 4 \\ x + 1 & \text{if } x \geq 4 \end{cases}$

For each of the following functions, find

(a) $f(p)$;   **(b)** $f(-r)$;   **(c)** $f(m + 3)$.

(See Example 8.)

35. $f(x) = 6 - x$ **36.** $f(x) = 3x + 5$

37. $f(x) = \sqrt{4 - x}$ **38.** $f(x) = \sqrt{-2x}$

39. $f(x) = x^3 + 1$ **40.** $f(x) = 3 - x^3$

41. $f(x) = \dfrac{3}{x - 1}$ **42.** $f(x) = \dfrac{-1}{5 + x}$

For each of the following functions, find the difference quotient

$$\frac{f(x + h) - f(x)}{h} \quad (h \neq 0).$$

(See Example 8.)

43. $f(x) = 2x - 4$ **44.** $f(x) = 2 + 4x$

45. $f(x) = x^2 + 1$ **46.** $f(x) = x^2 - x$

If you have a graphing calculator with table-making ability, display a table showing the (approximate) values of the given function at x = 3.5, 3.9, 4.3, 4.7, 5.1, and 5.5. (See Example 11.)

47. $g(x) = 3x^4 - x^3 + 2x$

48. $f(x) = \sqrt{x^2 - 2.4x + 8}$

Use a calculator to work these exercises. (See Examples 9 and 10.)

49. Finance The Minnesota state income tax for a single person in 2013 was determined by the rule

$$T(x) = \begin{cases} .0535x & \text{if } 0 \le x \le 23{,}100 \\ 1235.85 + .0705(x - 23{,}100) & \text{if } 23{,}100 < x \le 75{,}891 \\ 4957.62 + .0785(x - 75{,}891) & \text{if } x > 75{,}891, \end{cases}$$

where x is the person's taxable income. Find the tax on each of these incomes. (Data from: www.taxbrackets.org.)

(a) $20,000

(b) $70,000

(c) $120,000

50. Economics The gross domestic product (GDP) of the United States, which measures the overall size of the U.S. economy in trillions of dollars, is approximated by the function

$$f(x) = -.017x^2 + .68x + 9.6,$$

where $x = 0$ corresponds to the year 2000. Estimate the GDP in the given years. (Data from: U.S. Bureau of Economic Analysis.)

(a) 2005   **(b)** 2009

(c) 2011

51. Business The net revenue for Ford Motor Company (in billions of dollars) between the years 2006 and 2012 is approximated by

$$R(x) = -.722x^3 + 19.23x^2 - 161.2x + 421.8,$$

where $x = 6$ corresponds to the year 2006. (Data from: www. morningstar.com.)

(a) What was the net revenue in 2008?

(b) What was the net revenue in 2011?

52. Business The number of passengers enplaned (in millions) for the years 2000–2011 can be approximated by the function

$$f(x) = .377x^4 - 9.23x^3 + 71.4x^2 - 163x + 666,$$

where $x = 0$ corresponds to the year 2000. Find the number of enplaned passengers in the following years. (Data from: Airlines for America.)

(a) 2004   **(b)** 2009

(c) 2010

53. Business The value (in millions of dollars) of electric household ranges and ovens shipped in the United States can be approximated by the function

$$g(x) = -21.1x^2 + 205x + 2164,$$

where $x = 0$ corresponds to the year 2000. (Data from: U.S. Census Bureau.)

(a) What is the value of the ranges and ovens shipped in 2001?

(b) What is the value of the ranges and ovens shipped in 2009?

54. Natural Science High concentrations of zinc ions in water are lethal to rainbow trout. The function

$$f(x) = \left(\frac{x}{1960}\right)^{-.833}$$

gives the approximate average survival time (in minutes) for trout exposed to x milligrams per liter (mg/L) of zinc ions. Find the survival time (to the nearest minute) for the given concentrations of zinc ions.

(a) 110   **(b)** 525   **(c)** 1960   **(d)** 4500

55. Physical Science The distance from Chicago to Sacramento, California, is approximately 2050 miles. A plane flying directly to Sacramento passes over Chicago at noon. If the plane travels at 500 mph, find the rule of the function $f(t)$ that gives the distance of the plane from Sacramento at time t hours (with $t = 0$ corresponding to noon).

56. Physical Science The distance from Toronto, Ontario to Dallas, Texas is approximately 1200 miles. A plane flying directly to Dallas passes over Toronto at 2 p.m. If the plane travels at 550 mph, find the rule of the function $f(t)$ that gives the distance of the plane from Dallas at time t hours (with $t = 0$ corresponding to 2 pm).

57. Business A pretzel factory has daily fixed costs of $1800. In addition, it costs 50 cents to produce each bag of pretzels. A bag of pretzels sells for $1.20.

(a) Find the rule of the cost function $c(x)$ that gives the total daily cost of producing x bags of pretzels.

(b) Find the rule of the revenue function $r(x)$ that gives the daily revenue from selling x bags of pretzels.

(c) Find the rule of the profit function $p(x)$ that gives the daily profit from x bags of pretzels.

58. Business An aluminum can factory has daily fixed costs of $120,000 per day. In addition, it costs $.03 to produce each can. They can sell a can to a soda manufacturer for $.05 a can.

(a) Find the rule of the cost function $c(x)$ that gives the total daily cost of producing x aluminum cans.

(b) Find the rule of the revenue function $r(x)$ that gives the daily revenue from selling x aluminum cans.

(c) Find the rule of the profit function $p(x)$ that gives the daily profit from x aluminum cans.

⬈ Use the table feature of a graphing calculator to do these exercises. (See Example 11.)

59. Business The value (in millions of dollars) of new orders for all manufacturing industries can be approximated by the function

$$h(x) = -4.83x^3 + 50.3x^2 + 25.5x + 4149,$$

where $x = 0$ corresponds to the year 2000. Create a table that gives the value of the sales for the years 2005–2010. (Data from: U.S. Census Bureau.)

60. Business The value added to the economy (in billions of dollars) for agricultural production can be approximated by the function

$$g(x) = -.35x^3 + 5.34x^2 - 5.17x + 217.3,$$

where $x = 0$ corresponds to 2000. Create a table that gives the value added to the economy for the years 2007–2010. (Data from: U.S. Department of Agriculture.)

✓**Checkpoint Answers**

1. The domain consists of all possible times—that is, all nonnegative real numbers. The range consists of all possible distances; thus, the range is also the set of all nonnegative real numbers.

2. (a) Yes   (b) Yes   (c) No

3. (a) Yes   (b) Yes   (c) No   (d) No

4. (a) $(-\infty, \infty)$ (b) $(-\infty, \infty)$ (c) $(-\infty, 0]$
   (d) All real numbers except 1 and -1

5. (a) 4   (b) 40   (c) 73   (d) ·44
   (e) $5m^2 - 2m + 1$ (f) $10xh + 5h^2 - 2h$
   (g) $10x + 5h - 2$

6. (a) $2237.50   (b) $220.35

7. (a) $39,600,000   (b) $96,000,000

3.2 Graphs of Functions

The **graph** of a function $f(x)$ is defined to be the graph of the *equation* $y = f(x)$. It consists of all points $(x, f(x))$—that is, every point whose first coordinate is an input number from the domain of f and whose second coordinate is the corresponding output number.

> **Example 1** The graph of the function $g(x) = .5x - 3$ is the graph of the equation $y = .5x - 3$. So the graph is a straight line with slope .5 and y-intercept -3, as shown in Figure 3.3.
>
>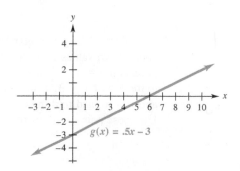
>
> **Figure 3.3**

A function whose graph is a straight line, as in Example 1, is called a **linear function.** The rule of a linear function can always be put into the form

$$f(x) = ax + b$$

for some constants a and b.

Piecewise Linear Functions

We now consider functions whose graphs consist of straight-line segments. Such functions are called **piecewise linear functions** and are typically defined with different equations for different parts of the domain.

Example 2   Graph the following function:

$$f(x) = \begin{cases} x + 1 & \text{if } x \le 2 \\ -2x + 7 & \text{if } x > 2. \end{cases}$$

Solution   Consider the two parts of the rule of f. The graphs of $y = x + 1$ and $y = -2x + 7$ are straight lines. The graph of f consists of

the part of the line $y = x + 1$ with $x \le 2$ and

the part of the line $y = -2x + 7$ with $x > 2$.

Each of these line segments can be graphed by plotting two points in the appropriate interval, as shown in Figure 3.4.

$x \le 2$		
x	0	2
$y = x + 1$	1	3

$x > 2$		
x	3	4
$y = -2x + 7$	1	-1

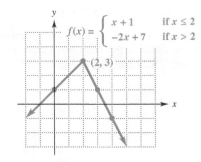

Figure 3.4

Note that the left and right parts of the graph each extend to the vertical line through $x = 2$, where the two halves of the graph meet at the point (2, 3). ✓

✓Checkpoint 1

Graph

$$f(x) = \begin{cases} x + 2 & \text{if } x < 0 \\ 2 - x & \text{if } x \ge 0. \end{cases}$$

Example 3   Graph the function

$$f(x) = \begin{cases} x - 2 & \text{if } x \le 3 \\ -x + 8 & \text{if } x > 3. \end{cases}$$

Solution   The graph consists of parts of two lines. To find the left side of the graph, choose two values of x with $x \le 3$, say, $x = 0$ and $x = 3$. Then find the corresponding points on $y = x - 2$, namely, (0, −2) and (3, 1). Use these points to draw the line segment to the left of $x = 3$, as in Figure 3.5. Next, choose two values of x with $x > 3$, say, $x = 4$ and $x = 6$, and find the corresponding points on $y = -x + 8$, namely, (4, 4) and (6, 2). Use these points to draw the line segment to the right of $x = 3$, as in Figure 3.5.

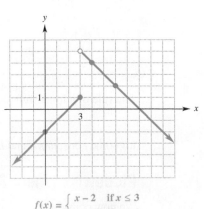

$$f(x) = \begin{cases} x - 2 & \text{if } x \le 3 \\ -x + 8 & \text{if } x > 3 \end{cases}$$

Figure 3.5

Note that both line segments of the graph of f extend to the vertical line through $x = 3$. The closed circle at $(3, 1)$ indicates that this point is on the graph of f, whereas the open circle at $(3, 5)$ indicates that this point is *not* on the graph of f (although it is on the graph of the line $y = -x + 8$). ✔₂

✓Checkpoint 2

Graph

$$f(x) = \begin{cases} -2x - 3 & \text{if } x < 1 \\ x - 2 & \text{if } x \geq 1. \end{cases}$$

Example 4   Graph the **absolute-value function,** whose rule is $f(x) = |x|$.

Solution   The definition of absolute value on page 8 shows that the rule of f can be written as

$$f(x) = \begin{cases} x & \text{if } x \geq 0 \\ -x & \text{if } x < 0. \end{cases}$$

So the right half of the graph (that is, where $x \geq 0$) will consist of a portion of the line $y = x$. It can be graphed by plotting two points, say, $(0, 0)$ and $(1, 1)$. The left half of the graph (where $x < 0$) will consist of a portion of the line $y = -x$, which can be graphed by plotting $(-2, 2)$ and $(-1, 1)$, as shown in Figure 3.6. ✔₃

✓Checkpoint 3

Graph $f(x) = |3x - 4|$.

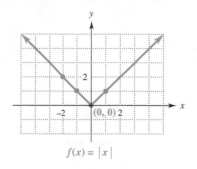

$$f(x) = |x|$$

Figure 3.6

TECHNOLOGY TIP   To graph most piecewise linear functions on a graphing calculator, you must use a special syntax. For example, on TI calculators, the best way to obtain the graph in Example 3 is to graph two separate equations on the same screen:

$$y_1 = (x - 2)/(x \leq 3) \quad \text{and} \quad y_2 = (-x + 8)/(x > 3).$$

The inequality symbols are in the TEST (or CHAR) menu. However, most calculators will graph absolute-value functions directly. To graph $f(x) = |x + 2|$, for instance, graph the equation $y = abs(x + 2)$. "Abs" (for absolute value) is on the keyboard or in the MATH menu.

Step Functions

The **greatest-integer function,** usually written $f(x) = [x]$, is defined by saying that $[x]$ denotes the largest integer that is less than or equal to x. For example, $[8] = 8, [7.45] = 7, [\pi] = 3, [-1] = -1, [-2.6] = -3$, and so on.

Example 5   Graph the greatest-integer function $f(x) = [x]$.

Solution   Consider the values of the function between each two consecutive integers—for instance,

x	$-2 \leq x < -1$	$-1 \leq x < 0$	$0 \leq x < 1$	$1 \leq x < 2$	$2 \leq x < 3$
$[x]$	-2	-1	0	1	2

Thus, between $x = -2$ and $x = -1$, the value of $f(x) = [x]$ is always -2, so the graph there is a horizontal line segment, all of whose points have second coordinate -2. The rest of the graph is obtained similarly (Figure 3.7). An open circle in that figure indicates that the endpoint of the segment is *not* on the graph, whereas a closed circle indicates that the endpoint *is* on the graph. ✓4

✓**Checkpoint 4**

Graph $y = [\frac{1}{2}x + 1]$.

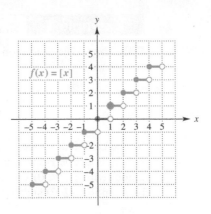

Figure 3.7

Functions whose graphs resemble the graph of the greatest-integer function are sometimes called **step functions.**

Example 6   **Business**   In 2013, the U.S. Post Office charged to ship a flat envelope first class to Eastern Europe, Europe, or Australia a fee of $2.05 for up to and including the first ounce, $.85 for each additional ounce or fraction of an ounce up to and including 8 ounces, and then $1.70 for each additional four ounces or less, up to a peak of 64 ounces. Let $D(x)$ represent the cost to send a flat envelope weighing x ounces. Graph $D(x)$ for x in the interval $(0, 20]$.

Solution   For x in the interval $(0, 1]$, $y = 2.05$. For x in $(1, 2]$, $y = 2.05 + .85 = 2.90$. For x in $(2, 3]$, $y = 2.90 + .85 = 3.75$, and so on up to x in $(7, 8]$, $y = 7.15 + .85 = 8.00$. Then for x in $(8, 12]$, $y = 8.00 + 1.70 = 9.70$. For x in $(12, 16]$, $y = 9.70 + 1.70 = 11.40$, and x in $(16, 20]$, $y = 11.40 + 1.70 = 13.10$. The graph, which is that of a step function, is shown in Figure 3.8. ✓5

✓**Checkpoint 5**

To mail a letter to the regions described in Example 6, the U.S. Post Office charges $1.10 for up to and including the first ounce, an additional $.95 for up to and including 2 ounces, an additional $.95 for up to and including 3 ounces, and then an additional $.95 to a maximum weight of 3.5 ounces. Let $L(x)$ represent the cost of sending a letter to those regions where x represents the weight of the letter in ounces. Graph $L(x)$ for x in the interval $(0, 3.5]$.

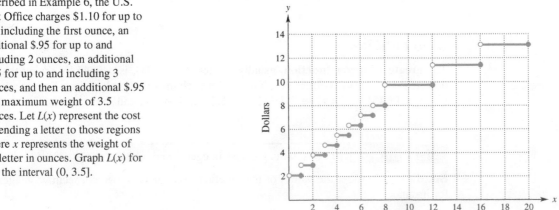

Ounces

Figure 3.8

TECHNOLOGY TIP On most graphing calculators, the greatest-integer function is denoted INT or FLOOR. (Look on the MATH menu or its NUM submenu.) Casio calculators use INTG for the greatest-integer function and INT for a different function. When graphing these functions, put your calculator in "dot" graphing mode rather than the usual "connected" mode to avoid erroneous vertical line segments in the graph.

Other Functions

The graphs of many functions do not consist only of straight-line segments. As a general rule when graphing functions by hand, you should follow the procedure introduced in Section 2.1 and summarized here.

Graphing a Function by Plotting Points

1. Determine the domain of the function.

2. Select a few numbers in the domain of f (include both negative and positive ones when possible), and compute the corresponding values of $f(x)$.

3. Plot the points $(x, f(x))$ computed in Step 2. Use these points and any other information you may have about the function to make an educated guess about the shape of the entire graph.

4. Unless you have information to the contrary, assume that the graph is continuous (unbroken) wherever it is defined.

This method was used to find the graphs of the functions $f(x) = x^2 - 2x - 8$ and $g(x) = \sqrt{x + 2}$ in Examples 3 and 4 of Section 2.1. Here are some more examples.

Example 7   Graph $g(x) = \sqrt{x - 1}$.

Solution   Because the rule of the function is defined only when $x - 1 \geq 0$ (that is, when $x \geq 1$), the domain of g is the interval $[1, \infty)$. Use a calculator to make a table of values such as the one in Figure 3.9. Plot the corresponding points and connect them to get the graph in Figure 3.9. ✓ 6

✓**Checkpoint 6**

Graph $f(x) = \sqrt{5 - 2x}$.

x	$g(x) = \sqrt{x - 1}$
1	0
2	1
3	$\sqrt{2} \approx 1.414$
5	2
7	$\sqrt{6} \approx 2.449$
10	3

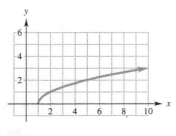

Figure 3.9

Example 8   Graph the function whose rule is

$$f(x) = 3 - \frac{x^3}{4}.$$

Solution   Make a table of values and plot the corresponding points. They suggest the graph in Figure 3.10.

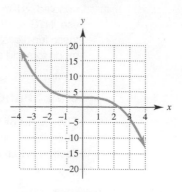

x	$f(x) = 3 - \dfrac{x^3}{4}$
-4	19.0
-3	9.8
-2	5.0
-1	3.3
0	3.0
1	2.8
2	1.0
3	-3.8
4	-13.0

Figure 3.10

> **Example 9** Graph the piecewise defined function
>
> $$f(x) = \begin{cases} x^2 & \text{if } x \le 2 \\ \sqrt{x - 1} & \text{if } x > 2. \end{cases}$$

Solution When $x \le 2$, the rule of the function is $f(x) = x^2$. Make a table of values such as the one in Figure 3.11. Plot the corresponding points and connect them to get the left half of the graph in Figure 3.11. When $x > 2$, the rule of the function is $f(x) = \sqrt{x - 1}$, whose graph is shown in Figure 3.9. In Example 7, the entire graph was given, beginning at $x = 1$. Here we use only the part of the graph to the right of $x = 2$, as shown in Figure 3.11. The open circle at $(2, 1)$ indicates that this point is not part of the graph of f (why?).

x	x^2
-2	4
-1	1
0	0
1	1
2	4

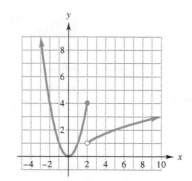

Figure 3.11

Graph Reading

Graphs are often used in business and the social sciences to present data. It is just as important to know how to *read* such graphs as it is to construct them.

> **Example 10** **Business** Figure 3.12, on the following page, shows the median sales prices (in thousands of dollars) of new privately owned one-family houses by region of the United States (northeast, midwest, south, and west) from the years 2005 to 2011. (Data from: U.S. Census Bureau and U.S. Department of Housing and Urban Development.)

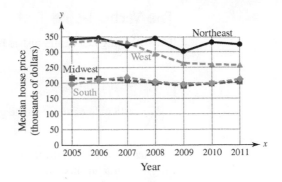

Figure 3.12

(a) How do prices in the west compare with those in the midwest over the period shown in the graph?

Solution The prices of the houses in the west started out approximately $100,000 higher than those in the midwest. In both regions prices declined until 2009 when prices in the midwest inched higher while those in the west continued to decline. In 2011, the gap between the two regions had shrunk to just over $50,000.

(b) Which region typically had the highest price?

Solution The northeast had the highest median price for all years except for 2007 when the west had the highest price.

Example 11 Figure 3.13 is the graph of the function f whose rule is $f(x) =$ average interest rate on a 30-year fixed-rate mortgage for a new home in year x. (Data from: www.fhfa.gov.)

Figure 3.13

(a) Find the function values of $f(1988)$ and $f(2009)$.

Solution The point (1988, 10) is on the graph, which means that $f(1988) = 10$. Similarly, $f(2009) = 5$, because the point (2009, 5) is on the graph. These values tell us the average mortgage rates were 10% in the year 1988 and 5% in the year 2009.

(b) During what period were mortgage rates at or above 7%?

Solution Look for points on the graph whose second coordinates are 7 or more—that is, points on or above the horizontal line through 7. These points represent the period from 1985 to 2001.

(c) During what period were mortgage rates at or below 5%?

Solution Look for points that are at or below the horizontal line through 5—that is, points with second coordinates less than or equal to 5. They occur from 2009 to 2011.

The Vertical-Line Test

The following fact distinguishes function graphs from other graphs.

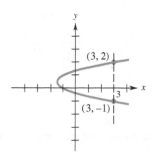

Figure 3.14

> ### Vertical-Line Test
>
> No vertical line intersects the graph of a function $y = f(x)$ at more than one point.

In other words, if a vertical line intersects a graph at more than one point, the graph is not the graph of a function. To see why this is true, consider the graph in Figure 3.14. The vertical line $x = 3$ intersects the graph at two points. If this were the graph of a function f, it would mean that $f(3) = 2$ (because $(3, 2)$ is on the graph) and that $f(3) = -1$ (because $(3, -1)$ is on the graph). This is impossible, because a *function* can have only one value when $x = 3$ (because each input determines exactly one output). Therefore, the graph in Figure 3.14 cannot be the graph of a function. A similar argument works in the general case.

Example 12   Use the vertical-line test to determine which of the graphs in Figure 3.15 are the graphs of functions.

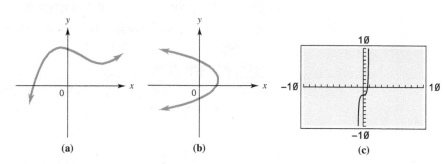

(a)   **(b)**   **(c)**

Figure 3.15

Solution   To use the vertical-line test, imagine dragging a ruler held vertically across the graph from left to right. If the graph is that of a function, the edge of the ruler would hit the graph only once for every x-value. If you do this for graph (a), every vertical line intersects the graph in at most one point, so this graph is the graph of a function. Many vertical lines (including the y-axis) intersect graph (b) twice, so it is not the graph of a function.

Graph (c) appears to fail the vertical-line test near $x = 1$ and $x = -1$, indicating that it is not the graph of a function. But this appearance is misleading because of the low resolution of the calculator screen. The table in Figure 3.16 and the very narrow segment of the graph in Figure 3.17 show that the graph actually rises as it moves to the right. The same thing happens near $x = -1$. So this graph *does* pass the vertical-line test and *is* the graph of a function. (Its rule is $f(x) = 15x^{11} - 2$). The moral of this story is that you can't always trust images produced by a graphing calculator. When in doubt, try other viewing windows or a table to see what is really going on. ✔ 7

✓ **Checkpoint 7**

Find a viewing window that indicates the actual shape of the graph of the function $f(x) = 15x^{11} - 2$ of Example 12 near the point $(-1, -17)$.

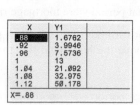

Figure 3.16

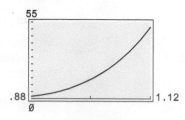

Figure 3.17

3.2 Exercises

Graph each function. (See Examples 1–4.)

1. $f(x) = -.5x + 2$ **2.** $g(x) = 3 - x$

3. $f(x) = \begin{cases} x + 3 & \text{if } x \le 1 \\ 4 & \text{if } x > 1 \end{cases}$

4. $g(x) = \begin{cases} 2x - 1 & \text{if } x < 0 \\ -1 & \text{if } x \ge 0 \end{cases}$

5. $y = \begin{cases} 4 - x & \text{if } x \le 0 \\ 3x + 4 & \text{if } x > 0 \end{cases}$

6. $y = \begin{cases} x + 5 & \text{if } x \le 1 \\ 2 - 3x & \text{if } x > 1 \end{cases}$

7. $f(x) = \begin{cases} |x| & \text{if } x < 2 \\ -2x & \text{if } x \ge 2 \end{cases}$

8. $g(x) = \begin{cases} -|x| & \text{if } x \le 1 \\ 2x & \text{if } x > 1 \end{cases}$

9. $f(x) = |x - 4|$ **10.** $g(x) = |4 - x|$

11. $f(x) = |3 - 3x|$ **12.** $g(x) = -|x|$

13. $y = -|x - 1|$ **14.** $f(x) = |x| - 2$

15. $y = |x - 2| + 3$

16. $|x| + |y| = 1$ (*Hint:* This is not the graph of a function, but is made up of four straight-line segments. Find them by using the definition of absolute value in these four cases: $x \ge 0$ and $y \ge 0$; $x \ge 0$ and $y < 0$; $x < 0$ and $y \ge 0$; $x < 0$ and $y < 0$).

Graph each function. (See Examples 5 and 6.)

17. $f(x) = [x - 3]$ **18.** $g(x) = [x + 3]$

19. $g(x) = [-x]$

20. $f(x) = [x] + [-x]$ (The graph contains horizontal segments, but is *not* a horizontal line.)

21. Business   The accompanying table gives rates charged by the U.S. Postal Service for first-class letters in March 2013. Graph the function $f(x)$ that gives the price of mailing a first-class letter, where x represents the weight of the letter in ounces and $0 \le x \le 3.5$.

Weight Not Over	Price
1 ounce	$0.46
2 ounces	$0.66
3 ounces	$0.86
3.5 ounces	$1.06

22. Business   The accompanying table gives rates charged by the U.S. Postal Service for first-class large flat envelopes in March, 2013. Graph the function $f(x)$ that gives the price of mailing a first-class large flat envelope, where x represents the weight of the envelope in ounces and $0 \le x \le 6$.

Weight Not Over	Price
1 ounce	$0.92
2 ounces	$1.12
3 ounces	$1.32
4 ounces	$1.53
5 ounces	$1.72
6 ounces	$1.92

Graph each function. (See Examples 7–9.)

23. $f(x) = 3 - 2x^2$

24. $g(x) = 2 - x^2$

25. $h(x) = x^3/10 + 2$

26. $f(x) = x^3/20 - 3$

27. $g(x) = \sqrt{-x}$

28. $h(x) = \sqrt{x} - 1$

29. $f(x) = \sqrt[3]{x}$

30. $g(x) = \sqrt[3]{x - 4}$

31. $f(x) = \begin{cases} x^2 & \text{if } x < 2 \\ -2x + 2 & \text{if } x \ge 2 \end{cases}$

32. $g(x) = \begin{cases} \sqrt{-x} & \text{if } x \le -4 \\ \dfrac{x^2}{4} & \text{if } x > -4 \end{cases}$

Determine whether each graph is a graph of a function or not. (See Example 12.)

33.

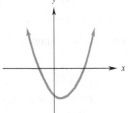

34.

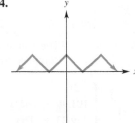

35.

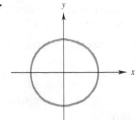

36.

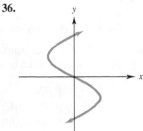

37.

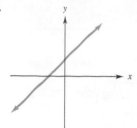

38.

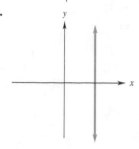

Use a graphing calculator or other technology to graph each of the given functions. If the graph has any endpoints, indicate whether they are part of the graph or not.

39. $f(x) = .2x^3 - .8x^2 - 4x + 9.6$

40. $g(x) = .1x^4 - .3x^3 - 1.3x^2 + 1.5x$

41. $g(x) = \begin{cases} 2x^2 + x & \text{if } x < 1 \\ x^3 - x - 1 & \text{if } x \geq 1 \end{cases}$ (*Hint:* See the Technology Tip on page 125)

42. $f(x) = \begin{cases} x|x| & \text{if } x \leq 0 \\ -x^2|x| + 2 & \text{if } x > 0 \end{cases}$

Use a graphical root finder to determine the x-intercepts of the graph of

43. f in Exercise 39;   **44.** g in Exercise 40.

Use a maximum–minimum finder to determine the location of the peaks and valleys in the graph of

45. g in Exercise 40;   **46.** f in Exercise 39.

See Examples 2, 3, 10, and 11 as you do Exercises 47–52.

47. Finance The Maine state income tax for a single person in 2013 was determined by the rule

$$T(x) = \begin{cases} .02x & \text{if } 0 \leq x \leq 5099 \\ 101.98 + .045(x - 5099) & \text{if } 5099 < x \leq 10,149 \\ 329.23 + .07(x - 10,149) & \text{if } 10,149 < x \leq 20,349 \\ 1043.23 + .085(x - 20,349) & \text{if } x > 20,349, \end{cases}$$

where x is the person's taxable income in dollars. Graph the function $T(x)$ for taxable incomes between 0 and $24,000.

48. Finance The Alabama state income tax for a single person in 2013 was determined by the rule

$$T(x) = \begin{cases} .02x & \text{if } 0 \leq x \leq 500 \\ 10 + .04(x - 500) & \text{if } 500 < x \leq 3000 \\ 110 + .05(x - 3000) & \text{if } x > 3000 \end{cases}$$

where x is the person's taxable income in dollars. Graph the function $T(x)$ for taxable incomes between 0 and $5000.

49. Finance The price of KeyCorp stock can be approximated by the function

$$f(x) = \begin{cases} 9.04 - .027x & \text{if } 0 < x \leq 43 \\ 7.879 + .032(x - 43) & \text{if } 43 < x \leq 113 \end{cases}$$

where x represents the number of trading days past September 14, 2012. (Data from: www.morningstar.com.)

(a) Graph $f(x)$.

(b) What is the lowest stock price during the period defined by $f(x)$?

50. Natural Science The number of minutes of daylight in Washington, DC, can be modeled by the function

$$g(x) = \begin{cases} .0106x^2 + 1.24x + 565 & \text{if } 1 \leq x < 84 \\ -.0202x^2 + 6.97x + 295 & \text{if } 84 \leq x < 263 \\ .0148x^2 - 11.1x + 2632 & \text{if } 263 \leq x \leq 365, \end{cases}$$

where x represents the number of days of the year, starting on January 1. Find the number of minutes of daylight on

(a) day 32.   **(b)** day 90.

(c) day 200.   **(d)** day 270.

(e) Graph $g(x)$.

(f) On what day is the number of minutes of daylight the greatest?

51. Health The following table shows the consumer price index (CPI) for medical care in selected years: (Data from: U.S. Bureau of Labor Statistics.)

Year	Medical-Care CPI
1950	15.1
1980	74.9
2010	388.4

(a) Let $x = 0$ correspond to 1950. Find the rule of a piecewise linear function that models these data—that is, a piecewise linear function f with $f(0) = 15.1$, $f(30) = 74.9$, and $f(60) = 388.4$. Round all coefficients in your final answer to one decimal place.

(b) Graph the function f for $0 \leq x \leq 65$.

(c) Use the function to estimate the medical-care CPI in 2004.

(d) Assuming that this model remains accurate after 2010, estimate the medical-care CPI for 2015.

52. Business The graph on the following page from the U.S. Office of Management and Budget shows the federal debt from the year 2007 to the year 2012 (in billions of dollars), with $x = 7$ corresponding to the year 2007. Find the rule of a linear function g that passes through the two points corresponding to 2007 and 2012. Draw the graph of g.

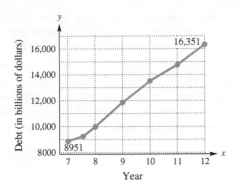

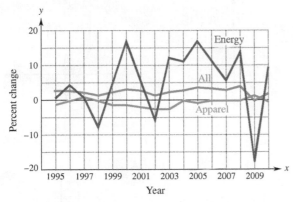

Finance *Use the accompanying graph to answer Exercises 53 and 54. The graph shows the annual percent change in various consumer price indexes (CPIs). (See Examples 10 and 11.) (Data from: U.S. Census Bureau.)*

53. (a) Was there any period between 1995 and 2010 when all three indexes showed a decrease?

(b) During what years did the CPI for energy show a decrease?

(c) When was the CPI for energy decreasing at the fastest rate?

54. (a) During what years did the CPI for apparel show an increase?

(b) When was the CPI for apparel increasing at the greatest rate?

55. Finance The following graph shows the number of FDIC-insured financial institutions in the United States for the year 1990 through the year 2010. (Data from: U.S. Federal Deposit Insurance Corporation.)

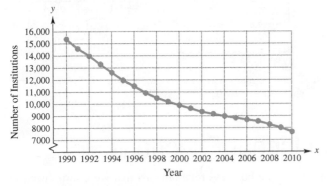

(a) Is this the graph of a function?

(b) What does the domain represent?

(c) Estimate the range.

56. Finance The following graph shows the percent-per-year yield of the 10-year U.S. Treasury Bond from the year 2000 to the year 2010. (Data from: Board of Governors of the Federal Reserve System.)

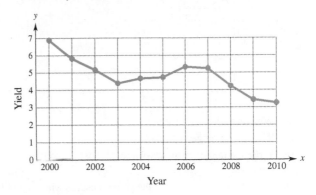

(a) Is this the graph of a function?

(b) What does the domain represent?

(c) Estimate the range.

57. Business Whenever postage rates change, some newspaper publishes a graph like this one, which shows the price of a first-class stamp from 1982 to 2008:

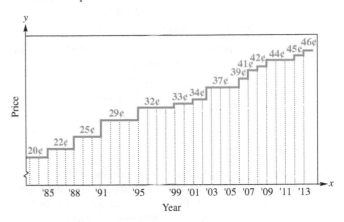

(a) Let f be the function whose rule is

$$f(x) = \text{cost of a first-class stamp in year } x.$$

Find $f(2000)$ and $f(2011)$.

(b) Explain why the graph in the figure is not the graph of the *function* f. What must be done to the figure to make it an accurate graph of the function f?

58. Business A chain-saw rental firm charges $20 per day or fraction of a day to rent a saw, plus a fixed fee of $7 for resharpening the blade. Let $S(x)$ represent the cost of renting a saw for x days. Find each of the following.

(a) $S\left(\dfrac{1}{2}\right)$ **(b)** $S(1)$ **(c)** $S\left(1\dfrac{2}{3}\right)$ **(d)** $S\left(4\dfrac{3}{4}\right)$

(e) What does it cost to rent for $5\dfrac{7}{8}$ days?

(f) A portion of the graph of $y = S(x)$ is shown on the following page. Explain how the graph could be continued.

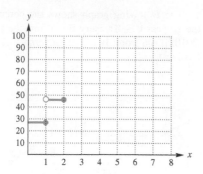

(g) What is the domain variable?

(h) What is the range variable?

(i) Write a sentence or two explaining what (c) and its answer represent.

(j) We have left $x = 0$ out of the graph. Discuss why it should or should not be included. If it were included, how would you define $S(0)$?

59. Business Sarah Hendrickson needs to rent a van to pick up a new couch she has purchased. The cost of the van is $19.99 for the first 75 minutes and then an additional $5 for each block of 15 minutes beyond 75. Find the cost to rent a van for

(a) 2 hours;   **(b)** 1.5 hours;

(c) 3.5 hours;   **(d)** 4 hours.

(e) Graph the ordered pairs (hours, cost).

60. Business A delivery company charges $25 plus 60¢ per mile or part of a mile. Find the cost for a trip of

(a) 3 miles;   **(b)** 4.2 miles;

(c) 5.9 miles;   **(d)** 8 miles.

(e) Graph the ordered pairs (miles, cost).

(f) Is this a function?

Work these problems.

61. Natural Science A laboratory culture contains about 1 million bacteria at midnight. The culture grows very rapidly until noon, when a bactericide is introduced and the bacteria population plunges. By 4 p.m., the bacteria have adapted to the bactericide and the culture slowly increases in population until 9 p.m., when the culture is accidentally destroyed by the cleanup crew. Let $g(t)$ denote the bacteria population at time t (with $t = 0$ corresponding to midnight). Draw a plausible graph of the function g. (Many correct answers are possible.)

62. Physical Science A plane flies from Austin, Texas, to Cleveland, Ohio, a distance of 1200 miles. Let f be the function whose rule is

$f(t) = $ distance (in miles) from Austin at time t hours,

with $t = 0$ corresponding to the 4 p.m. takeoff. In each part of this exercise, draw a plausible graph of f under the given circumstances. (There are many correct answers for each part.)

(a) The flight is nonstop and takes between 3.5 and 4 hours.

(b) Bad weather forces the plane to land in Dallas (about 200 miles from Austin) at 5 p.m., remain overnight, and leave at 8 a.m. the next day, flying nonstop to Cleveland.

(c) The plane flies nonstop, but due to heavy traffic it must fly in a holding pattern for an hour over Cincinnati (about 200 miles from Cleveland) and then go on to Cleveland.

✓**Checkpoint Answers**

1.

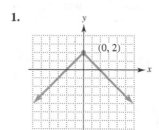

2.

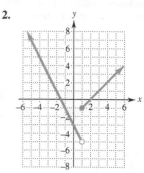

3.

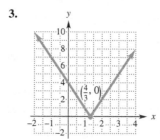

4.

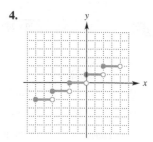

5.

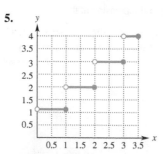

6.

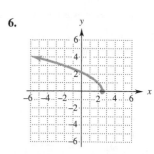

7. There are many correct answers, including, $-1.4 \le x \le -.6$ and $-30 \le y \le 0$.

3.3 Applications of Linear Functions

Most of this section deals with the basic business relationships that were introduced in Section 1.2:

$$\text{Revenue} = (\textbf{Price per item}) \times (\textbf{Number of items});$$
$$\text{Cost} = \textbf{Fixed Costs} + \textbf{Variable Costs};$$
$$\text{Profit} = \textbf{Revenue} - \textbf{Cost}.$$

The examples will use only linear functions, but the methods presented here also apply to more complicated functions.

Cost Analysis

Recall that fixed costs are for such things as buildings, machinery, real-estate taxes, and product design. Within broad limits, the fixed cost is constant for a particular product and does not change as more items are made. Variable costs are for labor, materials, shipping, and so on, and depend on the number of items made.

If $C(x)$ is the cost of making x items, then the fixed cost (the cost that occurs even when no items are produced) can be found by letting $x = 0$. For example, for the cost function $C(x) = 45x + 250,000$, the fixed cost is

$$C(0) = 45(0) + 250,000 = \$250,000.$$

In this case, the variable cost of making x items is $45x$—that is, $45 per item manufactured.

Example 1   **Business**   An anticlot drug can be made for $10 per unit. The total cost to produce 100 units is $1500.

(a) Assuming that the cost function is linear, find its rule.

Solution   Since the cost function $C(x)$ is linear, its rule is of the form $C(x) = mx + b$. We are given that m (the cost per item) is 10, so the rule is $C(x) = 10x + b$. To find b, use the fact that it costs $1500 to produce 100 units, which means that

$$C(100) = 1500$$
$$10(100) + b = 1500 \qquad C(x) = 10x + b.$$
$$1000 + b = 1500$$
$$b = 500.$$

So the rule of the cost function is $C(x) = 10x + 500$.

(b) What are the fixed costs?

Solution   The fixed costs are $C(0) = 10(0) + 500 = \$500$. ☑₁

✓ **Checkpoint 1**

The total cost of producing 10 calculators is $100. The variable costs per calculator are $4. Find the rule of the linear cost function.

If $C(x)$ is the total cost to produce x items, then the **average cost** per item is given by

$$\overline{C}(x) = \frac{C(x)}{x}.$$

As more and more items are produced, the average cost per item typically decreases.

Example 2   **Business**   Find the average cost of producing 100 and 1000 units of the anticlot drug in Example 1.

Solution   The cost function is $C(x) = 10x + 500$, so the average cost of producing 100 units is

$$\overline{C}(100) = \frac{C(100)}{100} = \frac{10(100) + 500}{100} = \frac{1500}{100} = \$15.00 \text{ per unit.}$$

The average cost of producing 1000 units is

✓ **Checkpoint 2**

In Checkpoint 1, find the average cost per calculator when 100 are produced.

$$\overline{C}(1000) = \frac{C(1000)}{1000} = \frac{10(1000) + 500}{1000} = \frac{10,500}{1000} = \$10.50 \text{ per unit.} ☑₂$$

x	$f(x) = 3x + 5$
1	8
2	11
3	14
4	17
5	20

Rates of Change

The rate at which a quantity (such as revenue or profit) is changing can be quite important. For instance, if a company determines that the rate of change of its revenue is decreasing, then sales growth is slowing down, a trend that may require a response.

The rate of change of a linear function is easily determined. For example, suppose $f(x) = 3x + 5$ and consider the table of values in the margin. The table shows that each time x changes by 1, the corresponding value of $f(x)$ changes by 3. Thus, the rate of change of $f(x) = 3x + 5$ with respect to x is 3, which is the slope of the line $y = 3x + 5$. The same thing happens for any linear function:

> **The rate of change of a linear function $f(x) = mx + b$ is the slope m.**

In particular, the rate of change of a linear function is constant.

The value of a computer, or an automobile, or a machine *depreciates* (decreases) over time. **Linear depreciation** means that the value of the item at time x is given by a linear function $f(x) = mx + b$. The slope m of this line gives the rate of depreciation.

Example 3   **Business**   According to the *Kelley Blue Book*, a Ford Mustang two-door convertible that is worth $14,776 today will be worth $10,600 in two years (if it is in excellent condition with average mileage).

(a) Assuming linear depreciation, find the depreciation function for this car.

Solution   We know the car is worth $14,776 now ($x = 0$) and will be worth $10,600 in two years ($x = 2$). So the points $(0, 14{,}776)$ and $(2, 10{,}600)$ are on the graph of the linear-depreciation function and can be used to determine its slope:

$$m = \frac{10{,}600 - 14{,}776}{2} = \frac{-4176}{2} = -2088.$$

Using the point $(0, 14{,}776)$, we find that the equation of the line is

$$y - 14{,}776 = -2088(x - 0) \qquad \text{Point–slope form}$$
$$y = -2088x + 14{,}776. \qquad \text{Slope–intercept form}$$

Therefore, the rule of the depreciation function is $f(x) = -2088x + 14{,}776$.

(b) What will the car be worth in 4 years?

Solution   Evaluate f when $x = 4$:

$$f(x) = -2088x + 14{,}776$$
$$f(4) = -2088(4) + 14{,}776 = \$6424.$$

(c) At what rate is the car depreciating?

Solution   The depreciation rate is given by the slope of $f(x) = -2088x + 14{,}776$, namely, -2088. This negative slope means that the car is decreasing in value an average of $2088 a year. ✔3

✓ **Checkpoint 3**

Using the information from Example 3, determine what the car will be worth in 6 years.

In economics, the rate of change of the cost function is called the **marginal cost.** Marginal cost is important to management in making decisions in such areas as cost control, pricing, and production planning. When the cost function is linear, say, $C(x) = mx + b$, the marginal cost is the number m (the slope of the graph of C). Marginal cost can also be thought of as the cost of producing one more item, as the next example demonstrates.

Example 4   **Business**   An electronics company manufactures handheld PCs. The cost function for one of its models is $C(x) = 160x + 750,000$.

(a) What are the fixed costs for this product?

Solution   The fixed costs are $C(0) = 160(0) + 750,000 = \$750,000$.

(b) What is the marginal cost?

Solution   The slope of $C(x) = 160x + 750,000$ is 160, so the marginal cost is \$160 per item.

(c) After 50,000 units have been produced, what is the cost of producing one more?

Solution   The cost of producing 50,000 is

$$C(50,000) = 160(50,000) + 750,000 = \$8,750,000.$$

The cost of 50,001 units is

$$C(50,001) = 160(50,001) + 750,000 = \$8,750,160.$$

The cost of the additional unit is the difference

$$C(50,001) - C(50,000) = 8,750,160 - 8,750,000 = \$160.$$

Thus, the cost of one more item is the marginal cost. ✓₄

Similarly, the rate of change of a revenue function is called the **marginal revenue**. When the revenue function is linear, the marginal revenue is the slope of the line, as well as the revenue from producing one more item.

Example 5   **Business**   The energy company New York State Electric and Gas charges each residential customer a basic fee for electricity of \$15.11, plus \$.0333 per kilowatt hour (kWh).

(a) Assuming there are 700,000 residential customers, find the company's revenue function.

Solution   The monthly revenue from the basic fee is

$$15.11(700,000) = \$10,577,000.$$

If x is the total number of kilowatt hours used by all customers, then the revenue from electricity use is $.0333x$. So the monthly revenue function is given by

$$R(x) = .0333x + 10,577,000.$$

(b) What is the marginal revenue?

Solution   The marginal revenue (the rate at which revenue is changing) is given by the slope of the rate function: \$0.0333 per kWh. ✓₅

Examples 4 and 5 are typical of the general case, as summarized here.

In a **linear cost function** $C(x) = mx + b$, the marginal cost is m (the slope of the cost line) and the fixed cost is b (the y-intercept of the cost line). The marginal cost is the cost of producing one more item.

Similarly, in a **linear revenue function** $R(x) = kx + d$, the marginal revenue is k (the slope of the revenue line), which is the revenue from selling one more item.

✓ Checkpoint 4

The cost in dollars to produce x kilograms of chocolate candy is given by $C(x) = 3.5x + 800$. Find each of the following.

(a) The fixed cost

(b) The total cost for 12 kilograms

(c) The marginal cost of the 40th kilogram

(d) The marginal cost per kilogram

✓ Checkpoint 5

Assume that the average customer in Example 5 uses 1600 kWh in a month.

(a) What is the total number of kWh used by all customers?

(b) What is the company's monthly revenue?

Break-Even Analysis

A typical company must analyze its costs and the potential market for its product to determine when (or even whether) it will make a profit.

Example 6   **Business**   A company manufactures a 42-inch plasma HDTV that sells to retailers for \$550. The cost of making x of these TVs for a month is given by the cost function $C(x) = 250x + 213{,}000$.

(a) Find the function R that gives the revenue from selling x TVs.

Solution   Since revenue is the product of the price per item and the number of items, $R(x) = 550x$.

(b) What is the revenue from selling 600 TVs?

Solution   Evaluate the revenue function R at 600:

$$R(600) = 550(600) = \$330{,}000.$$

(c) Find the profit function P.

Solution   Since Profit = Revenue − Cost,

$$P(x) = R(x) - C(x) = 550x - (250x + 213{,}000) = 300x - 213{,}000.$$

(d) What is the profit from selling 500 TVs?

Solution   Evaluate the profit function at 500 to obtain

$$P(500) = 300(500) - 213{,}000 = -63{,}000,$$

that is, a loss of \$63,000.

A company can make a profit only if the revenue on a product exceeds the cost of manufacturing it. The number of units at which revenue equals cost (that is, profit is 0) is the **break-even point.**

Example 7   **Business**   Find the break-even point for the company in Example 6.

Solution   The company will break even when revenue equals cost—that is, when

$$R(x) = C(x)$$
$$550x = 250x + 213{,}000$$
$$300x = 213{,}000$$
$$x = 710.$$

The company breaks even by selling 710 TVs. The graphs of the revenue and cost functions and the break-even point (where $x = 710$) are shown in the Figure 3.18. The company must sell more than 710 TVs ($x > 710$) in order to make a profit. ✓6

✓ **Checkpoint 6**

For a certain newsletter, the cost equation is $C(x) = 0.90x + 1500$, where x is the number of newsletters sold. The newsletter sells for \$1.25 per copy. Find the break-even point.

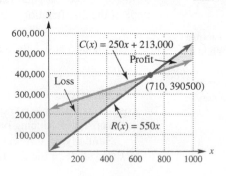

Figure 3.18

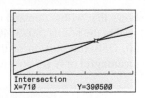

Intersection
X=710   Y=390500

Figure 3.19

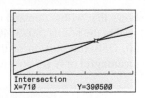 **TECHNOLOGY TIP** The break-even point in Example 7 can be found on a graphing calculator by graphing the cost and revenue functions on the same screen and using the calculator's intersection finder, as shown in Figure 3.19. Depending on the calculator, the intersection finder is in the CALC or G-SOLVE menu or in the MATH or FCN submenu of the GRAPH menu.

Supply and Demand

The supply of and demand for an item are usually related to its price. Producers will supply large numbers of the item at a high price, but consumer demand will be low. As the price of the item decreases, consumer demand increases, but producers are less willing to supply large numbers of the item. The curves showing the quantity that will be supplied at a given price and the quantity that will be demanded at a given price are called **supply and demand curves,** respectively. In supply-and-demand problems, we use p for price and q for quantity. We will discuss the economic concepts of supply and demand in more detail in later chapters.

Example 8   **Economics**   Joseph Nolan has studied the supply and demand for aluminum siding and has determined that the price per unit,[*] p, and the quantity demanded, q, are related by the linear equation

$$p = 60 - \frac{3}{4}q.$$

(a) Find the demand at a price of $40 per unit.

Solution   Let $p = 40$. Then we have

$$p = 60 - \frac{3}{4}q$$

$$40 = 60 - \frac{3}{4}q \qquad \text{\textit{Let} p = 40.}$$

$$-20 = -\frac{3}{4}q \qquad \text{Add} -60 \text{ to both sides.}$$

$$\frac{80}{3} = q. \qquad \text{Multiply both sides by} -\frac{4}{3}.$$

At a price of $40 per unit, 80/3 (or $26\frac{2}{3}$) units will be demanded.

(b) Find the price if the demand is 32 units.

Solution   Let $q = 32$. Then we have

$$p = 60 - \frac{3}{4}q$$

$$p = 60 - \frac{3}{4}(32) \qquad \text{\textit{Let} q = 32.}$$

$$p = 60 - 24$$

$$p = 36.$$

With a demand of 32 units, the price is $36.

(c) Graph $p = 60 - \frac{3}{4}q$.

Solution   It is customary to use the horizontal axis for the quantity q and the vertical axis for the price p. In part (a), we saw that 80/3 units would be demanded at a price of

[*]An appropriate unit here might be, for example, one thousand square feet of siding.

$40 per unit; this gives the ordered pair (80/3, 40). Part (b) shows that with a demand of 32 units, the price is $36, which gives the ordered pair (32, 36). Using the points (80/3, 40) and (32, 36) yields the demand graph depicted in Figure 3.20. Only the portion of the graph in Quadrant I is shown, because supply and demand are meaningful only for positive values of p and q. ✓₇

✓ **Checkpoint 7**

Suppose price and quantity demanded are related by $p = 100 - 4q$.

(a) Find the price if the quantity demanded is 10 units.

(b) Find the quantity demanded if the price is $80.

(c) Write the corresponding ordered pairs.

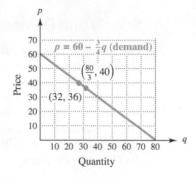

Figure 3.20

(d) From Figure 3.20, at a price of $30, what quantity is demanded?

Solution Price is located on the vertical axis. Look for 30 on the p-axis, and read across to where the line $p = 30$ crosses the demand graph. As the graph shows, this occurs where the quantity demanded is 40.

(e) At what price will 60 units be demanded?

Solution Quantity is located on the horizontal axis. Find 60 on the q-axis, and read up to where the vertical line $q = 60$ crosses the demand graph. This occurs where the price is about $15 per unit.

(f) What quantity is demanded at a price of $60 per unit?

Solution The point (0, 60) on the demand graph shows that the demand is 0 at a price of $60 (that is, there is no demand at such a high price).

Example 9 **Economics** Suppose the economist in Example 8 concludes that the supply q of siding is related to its price p by the equation

$$p = .85q.$$

(a) Find the supply if the price is $51 per unit.

Solution $51 = .85q$ Let $p = 51$.

           $60 = q$.   Divide both sides by .85

If the price is $51 per unit, then 60 units will be supplied to the marketplace.

(b) Find the price per unit if the supply is 20 units.

Solution $p = .85(20) = 17$.   Let $q = 20$.

If the supply is 20 units, then the price is $17 per unit.

(c) Graph the supply equation $p = .85q$.

Solution As with demand, each point on the graph has quantity q as its first coordinate and the corresponding price p as its second coordinate. Part (a) shows that the ordered pair (60, 51) is on the graph of the supply equation, and part (b) shows that (20, 17) is on the graph. Using these points, we obtain the supply graph in Figure 3.21.

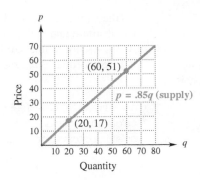

Figure 3.21

(d) Use the graph in Figure 3.21 to find the approximate price at which 35 units will be supplied. Then use algebra to find the exact price.

Solution The point on the graph with first coordinate $q = 35$ is approximately $(35, 30)$. Therefore, 35 units will be supplied when the price is approximately $30. To determine the exact price algebraically, substitute $q = 35$ into the supply equation:

$$p = .85q = .85(35) = \$29.75.$$

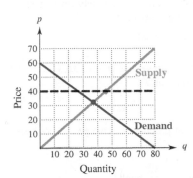

Figure 3.22

Example 10 **Economics** The supply and demand curves of Examples 8 and 9 are shown in Figure 3.22. Determine graphically whether there is a surplus or a shortage of supply at a price of $40 per unit.

Solution Find 40 on the vertical axis in Figure 3.22 and read across to the point where the horizontal line $p = 40$ crosses the supply graph (that is, the point corresponding to a price of $40). This point lies above the demand graph, so supply is greater than demand at a price of $40, and there is a surplus of supply.

Supply and demand are equal at the point where the supply curve intersects the demand curve. This is the **equilibrium point.** Its second coordinate is the **equilibrium price,** the price at which the same quantity will be supplied as is demanded. Its first coordinate is the quantity that will be demanded and supplied at the equilibrium price; this number is called the **equilibrium quantity.**

Example 11 **Economics** In the situation described in Examples 8–10, what is the equilibrium quantity? What is the equilibrium price?

Solution The equilibrium point is where the supply and demand curves in Figure 3.22 intersect. To find the quantity q at which the price given by the demand equation $p = 60 - .75q$ (Example 8) is the same as that given by the supply equation $p = .85q$ (Example 9), set these two expressions for p equal to each other and solve the resulting equation:

$$60 - .75q = .85q$$
$$60 = 1.6q$$
$$37.5 = q.$$

Therefore, the equilibrium quantity is 37.5 units, the number of units for which supply will equal demand. Substituting $q = 37.5$ into either the demand or supply equation shows that

$$p = 60 - .75(37.5) = 31.875 \quad \text{or} \quad p = .85(37.5) = 31.875.$$

Checkpoint 8

The demand for a certain commodity is related to the price by $p = 80 - (2/3)q$. The supply is related to the price by $p = (4/3)q$. Find

(a) the equilibrium quantity;

(b) the equilibrium price.

So the equilibrium price is \$31.875 (or \$31.88, rounded). (To avoid error, it is a good idea to substitute into both equations, as we did here, to be sure that the same value of p results; if it does not, a mistake has been made.) In this case, the equilibrium point—the point whose coordinates are the equilibrium quantity and price—is (37.5, 31.875). ✓8

✎ **TECHNOLOGY TIP** The equilibrium point (37.5, 31.875) can be found on a graphing calculator by graphing the supply and demand curves on the same screen and using the calculator's intersection finder to locate their point of intersection.

3.3 Exercises

Business   *Write a cost function for each of the given scenarios. Identify all variables used. (See Example 1.)*

1. A chain-saw rental firm charges \$25, plus \$5 per hour.

2. A trailer-hauling service charges \$95, plus \$8 per mile.

3. A parking garage charges \$8.00, plus \$2.50 per half hour.

4. For a 1-day rental, a car rental firm charges \$65, plus 45¢ per mile.

Business   *Assume that each of the given situations can be expressed as a linear cost function. Find the appropriate cost function in each case. (See Examples 1 and 4.)*

5. Fixed cost, \$200; 50 items cost \$2000 to produce.

6. Fixed cost, \$2000; 40 items cost \$5000 to produce.

7. Marginal cost, \$120; 100 items cost \$15,800 to produce.

8. Marginal cost, \$90; 150 items cost \$16,000 to produce.

Business   *In Exercises 9–12, a cost function is given. Find the average cost per item when the required numbers of items are produced. (See Example 2.)*

9. $C(x) = 12x + 1800$; 50 items, 500 items, 1000 items

10. $C(x) = 80x + 12{,}000$; 100 items, 1000 items, 10,000 items

11. $C(x) = 6.5x + 9800$; 200 items, 2000 items, 5000 items

12. $C(x) = 8.75x + 16{,}500$; 1000 items, 10,000 items, 75,000 items

Business   *Work these exercises. (See Example 3.)*

13. A Volkswagen Beetle convertible sedan is worth \$16,615 now and is expected to be worth \$8950 in 4 years.

   (a) Find a linear depreciation function for this car.

   (b) Estimate the value of the car 5 years from now.

   (c) At what rate is the car depreciating?

14. A computer that cost \$1250 new is expected to depreciate linearly at a rate of \$250 per year.

   (a) Find the depreciation function f.

   (b) Explain why the domain of f is [0, 5].

15. A machine is now worth \$120,000 and will be depreciated linearly over an 8-year period, at which time it will be worth \$25,000 as scrap.

   (a) Find the rule of the depreciation function f.

   (b) What is the domain of f?

   (c) What will the machine be worth in 6 years?

16. A house increases in value in an approximately linear fashion from \$222,000 to \$300,000 in 6 years.

   (a) Find the *appreciation function* that gives the value of the house in year x.

   (b) If the house continues to appreciate at this rate, what will it be worth 12 years from now?

Business   *Work these problems. (See Example 4.)*

17. The total cost (in dollars) of producing x college algebra books is $C(x) = 42.5x + 80{,}000$.

   (a) What are the fixed costs?

   (b) What is the marginal cost per book?

   (c) What is the total cost of producing 1000 books? 32,000 books?

   (d) What is the average cost when 1000 are produced? when 32,000 are produced?

18. The total cost (in dollars) of producing x DVDs is $C(x) = 6.80x + 450{,}000$.

   (a) What are the fixed costs?

   (b) What is the marginal cost per DVD?

   (c) What is the total cost of producing 50,000 DVDs? 600,000 DVDs?

   (d) What is the average cost per DVD when 50,000 are produced? when 500,000 are produced?

19. The manager of a restaurant found that the cost of producing 100 cups of coffee is \$11.02, while the cost of producing 400 cups is \$40.12. Assume that the cost $C(x)$ is a linear function of x, the number of cups produced.

   (a) Find a formula for $C(x)$.

   (b) Find the total cost of producing 1000 cups.

   (c) Find the total cost of producing 1001 cups.

   (d) Find the marginal cost of producing the 1000th cup.

   (e) What is the marginal cost of producing *any* cup?

20. In deciding whether to set up a new manufacturing plant, company analysts have determined that a linear function is a reasonable estimation for the total cost $C(x)$ in dollars of producing x items. They estimate the cost of producing 10,000 items as \$547,500 and the cost of producing 50,000 items as \$737,500.

    (a) Find a formula for $C(x)$.

    (b) Find the total cost of producing 100,000 items.

    (c) Find the marginal cost of the items to be produced in this plant.

Business *Work these problems. (See Example 5.)*

21. For the year 2013, a resident of the city of Dallas, Texas with a 5/8 inch water meter pays \$4.20 per month plus \$1.77 per 1000 gallons of water used (up to 4000 gallons). If the city of Dallas has 550,000 customers that use less than 4000 gallons a month, find its monthly revenue function $R(x)$, where the total number of gallons x is measured in thousands.

22. The Lacledge Gas Company in St. Louis, Missouri in the winter of 2012–2013 charged customers \$21.32 per month plus \$1.19071 per therm for the first 30 therms of gas used and \$.57903 for each therm above 30.

    (a) How much revenue does the company get from a customer who uses exactly 30 therms of gas in a month?

    (b) Find the rule of the function $R(x)$ that gives the company's monthly revenue from one customer, where x is the number of therms of gas used. (*Hint:* $R(x)$ is a piecewise-defined function that has a two-part rule, one part for $x \le 30$ and the other for $x > 30$.)

Business *Assume that each row of the accompanying table has a linear cost function. Find (a) the cost function; (b) the revenue function; (c) the profit function; (d) the profit on 100 items. (See Example 6.)*

	Fixed Cost	Marginal Cost per Item	Item Sells For
23.	\$750	\$10	\$35
24.	\$150	\$11	\$20
25.	\$300	\$18	\$28
26.	\$17,000	\$30	\$80
27.	\$20,000	\$12.50	\$30

28. Business In the following profit–volume chart, *EF* and *GH* represent the profit–volume graphs of a single-product company for, 2012 and 2013, respectively. (Adapted from: Uniform CPA Examination, American Institute of Certified Public Accountants.)

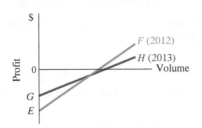

If the 2012 and 2013 unit sales prices are identical, how did the total fixed costs and unit variable costs of 2013 change compared with their values in 2012? Choose one:

	2012 Total Fixed Costs	2013 Unit Variable Costs
(a)	Decreased	Increased
(b)	Decreased	Decreased
(c)	Increased	Increased
(d)	Increased	Decreased

Use algebra to find the intersection points of the graphs of the given equations. (See Examples 7 and 11.)

29. $2x - y = 7$ and $y = 8 - 3x$

30. $6x - y = 2$ and $y = 4x + 7$

31. $y = 3x - 7$ and $y = 7x + 4$

32. $y = 3x + 5$ and $y = 12 - 2x$

Business *Work the following problems. (See Example 7.)*

33. An insurance company claims that for x thousand policies, its monthly revenue in dollars is given by $R(x) = 125x$ and its monthly cost in dollars is given by $C(x) = 100x + 5000$.

    (a) Find the break-even point.

    (b) Graph the revenue and cost equations on the same axes.

    (c) From the graph, estimate the revenue and cost when $x = 100$ (100,000 policies).

34. The owners of a parking lot have determined that their weekly revenue and cost in dollars are given by $R(x) = 80x$ and $C(x) = 50x + 2400$, where x is the number of long-term parkers.

    (a) Find the break-even point.

    (b) Graph $R(x)$ and $C(x)$ on the same axes.

    (c) From the graph, estimate the revenue and cost when there are 60 long-term parkers.

35. The revenue (in millions of dollars) from the sale of x units at a home supply outlet is given by $R(x) = .21x$. The profit (in millions of dollars) from the sale of x units is given by $P(x) = .084x - 1.5$.

    (a) Find the cost equation.

    (b) What is the cost of producing 7 units?

    (c) What is the break-even point?

36. The profit (in millions of dollars) from the sale of x million units of Blue Glue is given by $P(x) = .7x - 25.5$. The cost is given by $C(x) = .9x + 25.5$.

(a) Find the revenue equation.

(b) What is the revenue from selling 10 million units?

(c) What is the break-even point?

Business *Suppose you are the manager of a firm. The accounting department has provided cost estimates, and the sales department sales estimates, on a new product. You must analyze the data they give you, determine what it will take to break even, and decide whether to go ahead with production of the new product. (See Example 7.)*

37. Cost is estimated by $C(x) = 80x + 7000$ and revenue is estimated by $R(x) = 95x$; no more than 400 units can be sold.

38. Cost is $C(x) = 140x + 3000$ and revenue is $R(x) = 125x$.

39. Cost is $C(x) = 125x + 42{,}000$ and revenue is $R(x) = 165.5x$; no more than 2000 units can be sold.

40. Cost is $C(x) = 1750x + 95{,}000$ and revenue is $R(x) = 1975x$; no more than 600 units can be sold.

41. **Business** The accompanying graph shows the percentage of females in the workforce for Ireland and South Korea for the years 1980 through 2010. Estimate the break-even point (the point at which the two countries had the same percentage of females in the workforce.) (Data from: Organisation for Economic Co-operation and Development.)

42. **Social Science** Gallup conducts an annual poll of residents of 130 countries around the world to ask about approval of world leadership. The graph below shows the percentage of respondents who approve of the job performance of the leadership of the United States and Great Britain from the years 2007 to 2012. Estimate the year in which the break-even point (the year in which the opinion on leadership was the same) occurred.

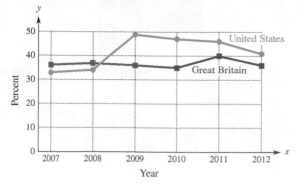

43. **Social Science** The population (in millions of people) of Florida from the year 2000 to the year 2010 can be approximated by the function $f(x) = .292x + 16.17$. Similarly, the population of (in millions of people) of New York can be approximated by the function $g(x) = .026x + 19.04$. For both of these models, let $x = 0$ correspond to the year 2000. (Data from: U.S. Census Bureau.)

(a) Graph both functions on the same coordinate axes for $x = 0$ to $x = 10$.

(b) Do the graphs intersect in this window?

(c) If trends continue at the same rate, will Florida overtake New York in population? If so, estimate what year that will occur.

44. **Social Science** The population (in millions of people) of Massachusetts from the year 2000 to the year 2010 can be approximated by the function $f(x) = .019x + 6.36$. Similarly, the population (in millions of people) of Arizona can be approximated by the function $g(x) = .130x + 5.15$. For both of these models, let $x = 0$ correspond to the year 2000. (Data from: U.S. Census Bureau.)

(a) Graph both functions on the same coordinate axes for $x = 0$ to $x = 10$.

(b) Do the graphs intersect in this window?

(c) If trends continue at the same rate, will Arizona overtake Massachusetts in population? If so, estimate what year that will occur.

Business *Use the supply and demand curves in the accompanying graph to answer Exercises 45–48. (See Examples 8–11.)*

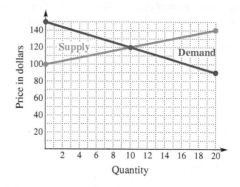

45. At what price are 20 items supplied?

46. At what price are 20 items demanded?

47. Find the equilibrium quantity.

48. Find the equilibrium price.

Economics *Work the following exercises. (See Examples 8–11.)*

49. Suppose that the demand and price for a certain brand of shampoo are related by

$$p = 16 - \frac{5}{4}q,$$

where p is price in dollars and q is demand. Find the price for a demand of

(a) 0 units; **(b)** 4 units; **(c)** 8 units.

Find the demand for the shampoo at a price of

(d) $6;   **(e)** $11;   **(f)** $16.

(g) Graph $p = 16 - (5/4)q$.

Suppose the price and supply of the shampoo are related by

$$p = \frac{3}{4}q,$$

where q represents the supply and p the price. Find the supply when the price is

(h) $0;   **(i)** $10;   **(j)** $20.

(k) Graph $p = (3/4)q$ on the same axes used for part (g).

(l) Find the equilibrium quantity.

(m) Find the equilibrium price.

50. Let the supply and demand for radial tires in dollars be given by

$$\text{supply: } p = \frac{3}{2}q; \quad \text{demand: } p = 81 - \frac{3}{4}q.$$

(a) Graph these equations on the same axes.

(b) Find the equilibrium quantity.

(c) Find the equilibrium price.

51. Let the supply and demand for bananas in cents per pound be given by

$$\text{supply: } p = \frac{2}{5}q; \quad \text{demand: } p = 100 - \frac{2}{5}q.$$

(a) Graph these equations on the same axes.

(b) Find the equilibrium quantity.

(c) Find the equilibrium price.

(d) On what interval does demand exceed supply?

52. Let the supply and demand for sugar be given by

$$\text{supply: } p = 1.4q - .6$$

and

$$\text{demand: } p = -2q + 3.2,$$

where p is in dollars.

(a) Graph these on the same axes.

(b) Find the equilibrium quantity.

(c) Find the equilibrium price.

(d) On what interval does supply exceed demand?

53. Explain why the graph of the (total) cost function is always above the x-axis and can never move downward as you go from left to right. Is the same thing true of the graph of the average cost function?

54. Explain why the graph of the profit function can rise or fall (as you go from left to right) and can be below the x-axis.

✓**Checkpoint Answers**

1. $C(x) = 4x + 60$.   **2.** $4.60   **3.** $2248

4. **(a)** $800   **(b)** $842   **(c)** $3.50   **(d)** $3.50

5. **(a)** 1,120,000,000   **(b)** $47,873,000

6. 4286 newsletters

7. **(a)** $60   **(b)** 5 units   **(c)** (10, 60); (5, 80)

8. **(a)** 40   **(b)** $160/3 \approx $53.33

3.4 Quadratic Functions and Applications

A **quadratic function** is a function whose rule is given by a quadratic polynomial, such as

$$f(x) = x^2, \quad g(x) = 3x^2 + 30x + 67, \quad \text{and} \quad h(x) = -x^2 + 4x.$$

Thus, a quadratic function is a function whose rule can be written in the form

$$f(x) = ax^2 + bx + c$$

for some constants a, b, and c, with $a \neq 0$.

Example 1   Graph each of these quadratic functions:

$$f(x) = x^2; \qquad g(x) = 4x^2; \qquad h(x) = -.2x^2.$$

Solution   In each case, choose several numbers (negative, positive, and 0) for x, find the values of the function at these numbers, and plot the corresponding points. Then connect the points with a smooth curve to obtain Figure 3.23, on the next page.

$f(x) = x^2$				
x	-2	-1	0	1	2
x^2	4	1	0	1	4

$g(x) = 4x^2$				
x	-2	-1	0	1	2
$4x^2$	16	4	0	4	16

$h(x) = -.2x^2$					
x	-5	-3	-1	0	2	4
$-.2x^2$	-5	-1.8	$-.2$	0	$-.8$	-3.2

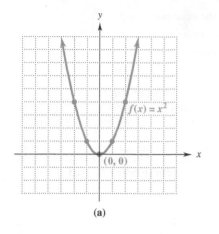

(a)

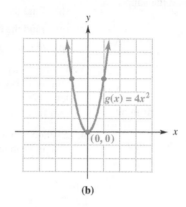

(b)

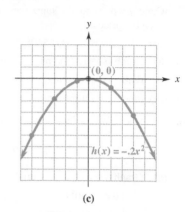

(c)

Figure 3.23

Each of the curves in Figure 3.23 is a **parabola.** It can be shown that the graph of every quadratic function is a parabola. Parabolas have many useful properties. Cross sections of radar dishes and spotlights form parabolas. Disks often visible on the sidelines of televised football games are microphones having reflectors with parabolic cross sections. These microphones are used by the television networks to pick up the signals shouted by the quarterbacks.

All parabolas have the same basic "cup" shape, although the cup may be broad or narrow and open upward or downward. The general shape of a parabola is determined by the coefficient of x^2 in its rule, as summarized here and illustrated in Example 1. ✓₁

✓ **Checkpoint 1**

Graph each quadratic function.

(a) $f(x) = x^2 - 4$

(b) $g(x) = -x^2 + 4$

The graph of a quadratic function $f(x) = ax^2 + bx + c$ is a parabola.

If $a > 0$, the parabola opens upward.   [*Figure 3.23(a) and 3.23(b)*]

If $a < 0$, the parabola opens downward.   [*Figure 3.23(c)*]

If $|a| < 1$, the parabola appears wider than the graph of $y = x^2$. [*Figure 3.23(c)*]

If $|a| > 1$, the parabola appears narrower than the graph of $y = x^2$.
   [*Figure 3.23(b)*]

When a parabola opens upward [as in Figure 3.23(a), (b)], its lowest point is called the **vertex.** When a parabola opens downward [as in Figure 3.23(c)], its highest point is called the **vertex.** The vertical line through the vertex of a parabola is called the **axis of the parabola.** For example, (0, 0) is the vertex of each of the parabolas in Figure 3.23, and the axis of each parabola is the y-axis. If you were to fold the graph of a parabola along its axis, the two halves of the parabola would match exactly. This means that a parabola is *symmetric* about its axis.

Although the vertex of a parabola can be approximated by a graphing calculator's maximum or minimum finder, its exact coordinates can be found algebraically, as in the following examples.

Example 2   Consider the function $g(x) = 2(x - 3)^2 + 1$.

(a) Show that g is a quadratic function.

Solution   Multiply out the rule of g to show that it has the required form:

$$g(x) = 2(x - 3)^2 + 1$$
$$= 2(x^2 - 6x + 9) + 1$$
$$= 2x^2 - 12x + 18 + 1$$
$$g(x) = 2x^2 - 12x + 19.$$

According to the preceding box, the graph of g is a somewhat narrow, upward-opening parabola.

(b) Show that the vertex of the graph of $g(x) = 2(x - 3)^2 + 1$ is $(3, 1)$.

Solution   Since $g(3) = 2(3 - 3)^2 + 1 = 0 + 1 = 1$, the point $(3, 1)$ is on the graph. The vertex of an upward-opening parabola is the lowest point on the graph, so we must show that $(3, 1)$ is the lowest point. Let x be any number except 3 (so that $x - 3 \neq 0$). Then the quantity $2(x - 3)^2$ is positive, and hence

$$g(x) = 2(x - 3)^2 + 1 = (\text{a positive number}) + 1,$$

which means that $g(x) > 1$. Therefore, every point $(x, g(x))$ on the graph, where $x \neq 3$, has second coordinate $g(x)$ greater than 1. Hence $(x, g(x))$ lies *above* $(3, 1)$. In other words, $(3, 1)$ is the lowest point on the graph—the vertex of the parabola.

(c) Graph $g(x) = 2(x - 3)^2 + 1$.

Solution   Plot some points on both sides of the vertex $(3, 1)$ to obtain the graph in Figure 3.24. The vertical line $x = 3$ through the vertex is the axis of the parabola.

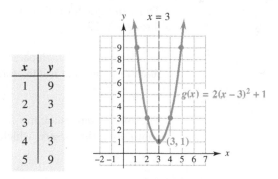

x	y
1	9
2	3
3	1
4	3
5	9

Figure 3.24

In Example 2, notice how the rule of the function g is related to the coordinates of the vertex:

$$g(x) = 2(x - 3)^2 + 1. \qquad (3, 1).$$

Arguments similar to those in Example 2 lead to the following fact.

> The graph of the quadratic function $f(x) = a(x - h)^2 + k$ is a parabola with vertex (h, k). It opens upward when $a > 0$ and downward when $a < 0$.

Example 3   Determine algebraically whether the given parabola opens upward or downward, and find its vertex.

(a) $f(x) = -3(x - 4)^2 - 7$

Solution   The rule of the function is in the form $f(x) = a(x - h)^2 + k$ (with $a = -3, h = 4$, and $k = -7$). The parabola opens downward ($a < 0$), and its vertex is $(h, k) = (4, -7)$.

(b) $g(x) = 2(x + 3)^2 + 5$

Solution   Be careful here: The vertex is *not* $(3, 5)$. To put the rule of $g(x)$ in the form $a(x - h)^2 + k$, we must rewrite it so that there is a minus sign inside the parentheses:

$$g(x) = 2(x + 3)^2 + 5$$
$$= 2(x - (-3))^2 + 5.$$

This is the required form, with $a = 2, h = -3$, and $k = 5$. The parabola opens upward, and its vertex is $(-3, 5)$. ✓₂

✓ **Checkpoint 2**

Determine the vertex of each parabola, and graph the parabola.

(a) $f(x) = (x + 4)^2 - 3$

(b) $f(x) = -2(x - 3)^2 + 1$

Example 4   Find the rule of a quadratic function whose graph has vertex $(3, 4)$ and passes through the point $(6, 22)$.

Solution   The graph of $f(x) = a(x - h)^2 + k$ has vertex (h, k). We want $h = 3$ and $k = 4$, so that $f(x) = a(x - 3)^2 + 4$. Since $(6, 22)$ is on the graph, we must have $f(6) = 22$. Therefore,

$$f(x) = a(x - 3)^2 + 4$$
$$f(6) = a(6 - 3)^2 + 4$$
$$22 = a(3)^2 + 4$$
$$9a = 18$$
$$a = 2.$$

Thus, the graph of $f(x) = 2(x - 3)^2 + 4$ is a parabola with vertex $(3, 4)$ that passes through $(6, 22)$.

The vertex of each parabola in Examples 2 and 3 was easily determined because the rule of the function had the form

$$f(x) = a(x - h)^2 + k.$$

The rule of *any* quadratic function can be put in this form by using the technique of **completing the square**, which is illustrated in the next example.

Example 5   Determine the vertex of the graph of $f(x) = x^2 - 4x + 2$. Then graph the parabola.

Solution   In order to get $f(x)$ in the form $a(x - h)^2 + k$, take half the coefficient of x, namely $\frac{1}{2}(-4) = -2$, and *square it:* $(-2)^2 = 4$. Then proceed as follows.

$$f(x) = x^2 - 4x + 2$$
$$= x^2 - 4x + \underline{\quad} + 2 \qquad \text{Leave space for the squared term and its negative.}$$
$$= x^2 - 4x + 4 - 4 + 2 \qquad \text{Add and subtract 4.}$$
$$= (x^2 - 4x + 4) - 4 + 2 \qquad \text{Insert parentheses.}$$
$$= (x - 2)^2 - 2 \qquad \text{Factor expression in parentheses and add.}$$

✓ **Checkpoint 3**

Rewrite the rule of each function by completing the square, and use this form to find the vertex of the graph.

(a) $f(x) = x^2 + 6x + 5$

(*Hint:* add and subtract the square of half the coefficient of x.)

(b) $g(x) = x^2 - 12x + 33$

Adding and subtracting 4 did not change the rule of $f(x)$, but did make it possible to have a perfect square as part of its rule: $f(x) = (x - 2)^2 - 2$. Now we can see that the graph is an upward-opening parabola, as shown in Figure 3.25, on the following page. ✓₃

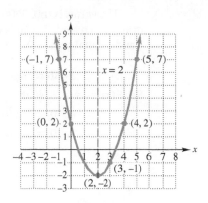

Figure 3.25

⚠ **CAUTION** The technique of completing the square only works when the coefficient of x^2 is 1. To find the vertex of a quadratic function such as

$$f(x) = 2x^2 + 12x - 19,$$

you must first factor out the coefficient of x^2 and write the rule as

$$f(x) = 2(x^2 + 6x - \tfrac{19}{2}).$$

Now complete the square on the expression in parentheses by adding and subtracting 9 (the square of half the coefficient of x), and proceed as in Example 5.

The technique of completing the square can be used to rewrite the general equation $f(x) = ax^2 + bx + c$ in the form $f(x) = a(x - h)^2 + k$. When this is done, we obtain a formula for the coordinates of the vertex.

The graph of $f(x) = ax^2 + bx + c$ is a parabola with vertex (h, k), where

$$h = \frac{-b}{2a} \quad \text{and} \quad k = f(h).$$

Additionally, the fact that the vertex of a parabola is the highest or lowest point on the graph can be used in applications to find a maximum or minimum value.

Example 6   **Business**   Lynn Wolf owns and operates Wolf's microbrewery. She has hired a consultant to analyze her business operations. The consultant tells her that her daily profits from the sale of x cases of beer are given by

$$P(x) = -x^2 + 120x.$$

Find the vertex, determine if it is a maximum or minimum, write the equation of the axis of the parabola, and compute the x- and y-intercepts of the profit function $P(x)$.

Solution   Since $a = -1$ and $b = 120$, the x-value of the vertex is

$$\frac{-b}{2a} = \frac{-120}{2(-1)} = 60.$$

The y-value of the vertex is

$$P(60) = -(60)^2 + 120(60) = 3600.$$

The vertex is (60, 3600) and since *a* is negative, it is a maximum because the parabola opens downward. The axis of the parabola is $x = 60$. The intercepts are found by setting *x* and *y* equal to 0.

x-intercepts	**y-intercept**
Set $P(x) = y = 0$, so that	Set $x = 0$ to obtain

$$0 = -x^2 + 120x$$
$$0 = x(-x + 120)$$
$$x = 0 \quad \text{or} \quad -x + 120 = 0$$
$$-x = -120$$
$$x = 120$$

Set $x = 0$ to obtain
$$P(0) = 0^2 + 120(0) = 0$$
The *y*-intercept is 0.

The *x*–intercepts are 0 and 120.

Figure 3.26 shows the profit function $P(x)$.

✓**Checkpoint 4**

When a company sells *x* units of a product, its profit is
$P(x) = -2x^2 + 40x + 280$. Find

(a) the number of units which should be sold so that maximum profit is received;

(b) the maximum profit.

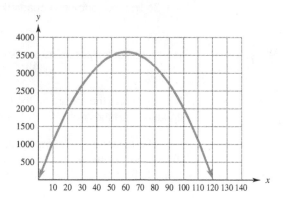

Figure 3.26

⬧ **TECHNOLOGY TIP** The maximum or minimum finder on a graphing calculator can approximate the vertex of a parabola with a high degree of accuracy. The max–min finder is in the CALC menu or in the MATH or FCN submenu of the GRAPH menu. Similarly, the calculator's graphical root finder can approximate the *x*-intercepts of a parabola.

⟳ Supply and demand curves were introduced in Section 3.3. Here is a quadratic example.

Example 7 **Economics** Suppose that the price of and demand for an item are related by

$$p = 150 - 6q^2, \qquad \text{Demand function}$$

where *p* is the price (in dollars) and *q* is the number of items demanded (in hundreds). Suppose also that the price and supply are related by

$$p = 10q^2 + 2q, \qquad \text{Supply function}$$

where *q* is the number of items supplied (in hundreds). Find the equilibrium quantity and the equilibrium price.

Solution The graphs of both of these equations are parabolas (Figure 3.27), as seen on the following page. Only those portions of the graphs which lie in the first quadrant are included, because none of supply, demand, or price can be negative.

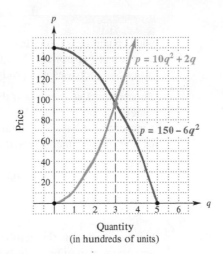

Figure 3.27

The point where the demand and supply curves intersect is the equilibrium point. Its first coordinate is the equilibrium quantity, and its second coordinate is the equilibrium price. These coordinates may be found in two ways.

Algebraic Method   At the equilibrium point, the second coordinate of the demand curve must be the same as the second coordinate of the supply curve, so that

$$150 - 6q^2 = 10q^2 + 2q.$$

Write this quadratic equation in standard form as follows:

$$0 = 16q^2 + 2q - 150 \qquad \text{Add} -150 \text{ and } 6q^2 \text{ to both sides.}$$
$$0 = 8q^2 + q - 75. \qquad \text{Multiply both sides by } \frac{1}{2}.$$

This equation can be solved by the quadratic formula, given in Section 1.7. Here, $a = 8$, $b = 1$, and $c = -75$:

$$q = \frac{-1 \pm \sqrt{1 - 4(8)(-75)}}{2(8)}$$
$$= \frac{-1 \pm \sqrt{1 + 2400}}{16} \qquad -4(8)(-75) = 2400$$
$$= \frac{-1 \pm 49}{16} \qquad \sqrt{1 + 2400} = \sqrt{2401} = 49$$
$$q = \frac{-1 + 49}{16} = \frac{48}{16} = 3 \quad \text{or} \quad q = \frac{-1 - 49}{16} = -\frac{50}{16} = -\frac{25}{8}.$$

It is not possible to make $-25/8$ units, so discard that answer and use only $q = 3$. Hence, the equilibrium quantity is 300. Find the equilibrium price by substituting 3 for q in either the supply or the demand function (and check your answer by using the other one). Using the supply function gives

$$p = 10q^2 + 2q$$
$$p = 10 \cdot 3^2 + 2 \cdot 3 \qquad \text{Let } q = 3.$$
$$= 10 \cdot 9 + 6$$
$$p = \$96.$$

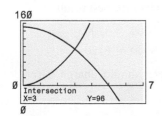

Figure 3.28

✓**Checkpoint 5**

The price and demand for an item are related by $p = 32 - x^2$, while price and supply are related by $p = x^2$. Find

(a) the equilibrium quantity;

(b) the equilibrium price.

⬧ **Graphical Method**   Graph the two functions on a graphing calculator, and use the intersection finder to determine that the equilibrium point is (3, 96), as in Figure 3.28. ✓₅

Example 8   **Business**   The rental manager of a small apartment complex with 16 units has found from experience that each $40 increase in the monthly rent results in an empty apartment. All 16 apartments will be rented at a monthly rent of $500. How many $40 increases will produce maximum monthly income for the complex?

Solution   Let x represent the number of $40 increases. Then the number of apartments rented will be $16 - x$. Also, the monthly rent per apartment will be $500 + 40x$. (There are x increases of $40, for a total increase of $40x$.) The monthly income, $I(x)$, is given by the number of apartments rented times the rent per apartment, so

$$I(x) = (16 - x)(500 + 40x)$$
$$= 8000 + 640x - 500x - 40x^2$$
$$= 8000 + 140x - 40x^2.$$

Since x represents the number of $40 increases and each $40 increase causes one empty apartment, x must be a whole number. Because there are only 16 apartments, $0 \le x \le 16$. Since there is a small number of possibilities, the value of x that produces maximum income may be found in several ways.

Brute Force Method   Use a scientific calculator or the table feature of a graphing calculator (as in Figure 3.29) to evaluate $I(x)$ when $x = 1, 2, \ldots, 16$ and find the largest value.

X	Y1				X	Y1				X	Y1	
0	8000				7	7020				14	2120	
1	8100				8	6560				15	1100	
2	8120				9	6020				16	0	
3	8060				10	5400				17	−1180	
4	7920				11	4700				18	−2440	
5	7700				12	3920				19	−3780	
6	7400				13	3060				20	−5200	
X=0					X=7					X=14		

Figure 3.29

The tables show that a maximum income of $8120 occurs when $x = 2$. So the manager should charge rent of $500 + 2(40) = \$580$, leaving two apartments vacant.

Algebraic Method   The graph of $I(x) = 8000 + 140x - 40x^2$ is a downward-opening parabola (why?), and the value of x that produces maximum income occurs at the vertex. The methods of Section 3.4 show that the vertex is $(1.75, 8122.50)$. Since x must be a whole number, evaluate $I(x)$ at $x = 1$ and $x = 2$ to see which one gives the best result:

If $x = 1$, then $I(1) = -40(1)^2 + 140(1) + 8000 = 8100$.

If $x = 2$, then $I(2) = -40(2)^2 + 140(2) + 8000 = 8120$.

So maximum income occurs when $x = 2$. The manager should charge a rent of $500 + 2(40) = \$580$, leaving two apartments vacant.

Quadratic Models

Real-world data can sometimes be used to construct a quadratic function that approximates the data. Such **quadratic models** can then be used (subject to limitations) to predict future behavior.

Example 9   **Business**   The number of physical compact disks (CDs, in millions of units) shipped are given in the following table for the years 1997 through 2011. (Data from: Recording Industry Association of America.)

Year	1997	1998	1999	2000	2001	2002	2003	2004
CDs shipped	753	847	939	943	882	803	746	767
Year		2005	2006	2007	2008	2009	2010	2011
CDs shipped		705	620	511	369	293	253	241

(a) Let $x = 7$ correspond to the year 1997. Display the information graphically.

Solution   Plot the points (7, 753), (8, 847), and so on—as in Figure 3.30.

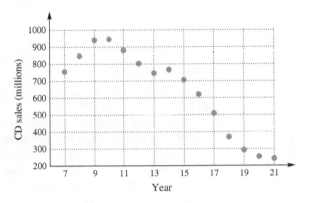

Figure 3.30

(b)   The shape of the data points in Figure 3.31 resembles a downward-opening parabola. Using the year 2000 as the maximum, find a quadratic model $f(x) = a(x - h)^2 + k$ for these data.

Solution   Recall that when a quadratic function is written in the form $f(x) = a(x - h)^2 + k$, the vertex of its graph is (h, k). On the basis of Figure 3.30, let (10, 943) be the vertex, so that

$$f(x) = a(x - 10)^2 + 943.$$

To find a, choose another data point (15, 705). Assume this point lies on the parabola so that

$$f(x) = a(x - 10)^2 + 943$$
$$705 = a(15 - 10)^2 + 943 \qquad \text{Substitute 15 for } x \text{ and 705 for } f(x).$$
$$705 = 25a + 943 \qquad \text{Subtract inside the parentheses and then square.}$$
$$-238 = 25a \qquad \text{Subtract 943 from both sides.}$$
$$a = -9.52. \qquad \text{Divide both sides by 25.}$$

Therefore, $f(x) = -9.52(x - 10)^2 + 943$ is a quadratic model for these data. If we expand the form into $f(x) = ax^2 + bx + c$, we obtain

$$f(x) = -9.52(x - 10)^2 + 943$$
$$= -9.52(x^2 - 20x + 100) + 943 \qquad \text{Expand inside the parentheses.}$$
$$= -9.52x^2 + 190.4x - 952 + 943 \qquad \text{Distribute the } -9.52.$$
$$= -9.52x^2 + 190.4x - 9. \qquad \text{Add the last two terms together.}$$

✓ **Checkpoint 6**

Find another quadratic model in Example 9(b) by using (10, 943) as the vertex and (19, 293) as the other point.

Figure 3.31, on the following page, shows the original data with the graph of $f(x)$. It appears to fit the data rather well except for the last two points. (We find a better fitting model in Example 10.) ✓ 6

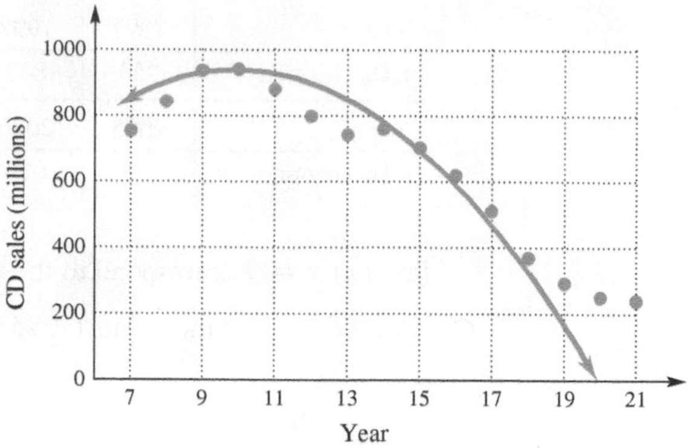

Figure 3.31

Quadratic Regression

Linear regression was used in Section 2.3 to construct a linear function that modeled a set of data points. When the data points appear to lie on a parabola rather than on a straight line (as in Example 9), a similar least-squares regression procedure is available on most graphing calculators and spreadsheet programs to construct a quadratic model for the data. Simply follow the same steps as in linear regression, with one exception: Choose quadratic, rather than linear, regression. (Both options are on the same menu.)

Example 10 Use a graphing calculator to find a quadratic-regression model for the data in Example 9.

Solution Enter the first coordinates of the data points as list L_1 and the second coordinates as list L_2. Performing the quadratic regression, as in Figure 3.32, leads to the model

$$g(x) = -5.034x^2 + 90.25x + 461.8.$$

The number R^2 in Figure 3.32 is fairly close to 1, which indicates that this model fits the data fairly well. Figure 3.33 shows the data with the quadratic regression curve.

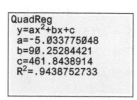

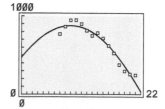

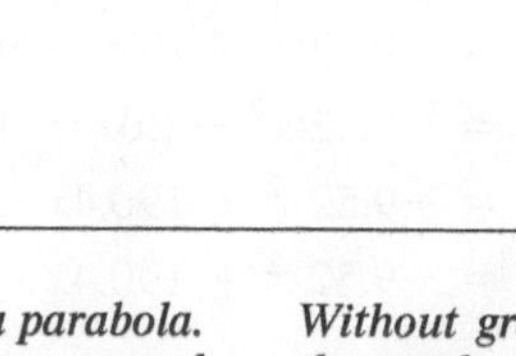

Figure 3.32

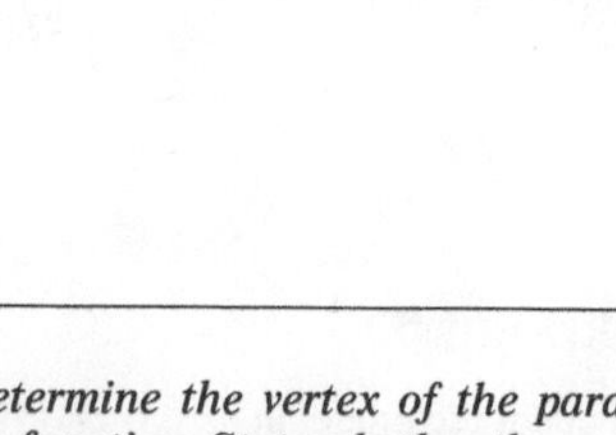

Figure 3.33

3.4 Exercises

The graph of each of the functions in Exercises 1–4 is a parabola. Without graphing, determine whether the parabola opens upward or downward. (See Example 1.)

1. $f(x) = x^2 - 3x - 12$ **2.** $g(x) = -x^2 + 5x + 15$

3. $h(x) = -3x^2 + 14x + 1$ **4.** $f(x) = 6.5x^2 - 7.2x + 4$

Without graphing, determine the vertex of the parabola that is the graph of the given function. State whether the parabola opens upward or downward. (See Examples 2 and 3.)

5. $f(x) = -2(x - 5)^2 + 7$ **6.** $g(x) = -7(x - 8)^2 - 3$

7. $h(x) = 4(x + 1)^2 - 9$ **8.** $f(x) = -8(x + 12)^2 + 9$

Match each function with its graph, which is one of those shown.
(See Examples 1–3.)

9. $f(x) = x^2 + 2$ **10.** $g(x) = x^2 - 2$

11. $g(x) = (x - 2)^2$ **12.** $f(x) = -(x + 2)^2$

13. $f(x) = 2(x - 2)^2 + 2$

14. $g(x) = -2(x - 2)^2 - 2$

15. $g(x) = -2(x + 2)^2 + 2$

16. $f(x) = 2(x + 2)^2 - 2$

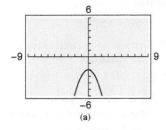
(a)

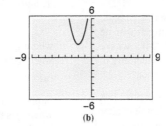
(b)

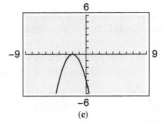
(c)

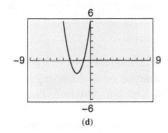
(d)

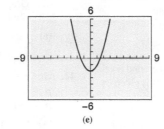
(e)

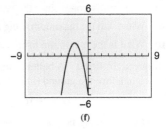
(f)

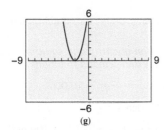
(g)

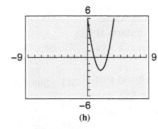
(h)

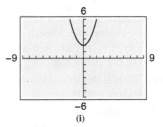
(i)

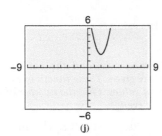
(j)

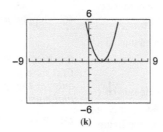
(k)

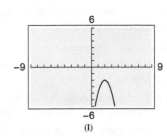
(l)

Find the rule of a quadratic function whose graph has the given
vertex and passes through the given point. (See Example 4.)

17. Vertex $(1, 2)$; point $(5, 6)$

18. Vertex $(-3, 2)$; point $(2, 1)$

19. Vertex $(-1, -2)$; point $(1, 2)$

20. Vertex $(2, -4)$; point $(5, 2)$

Without graphing, find the vertex of the parabola that is the graph
of the given function. (See Examples 5 and 6.)

21. $f(x) = -x^2 - 6x + 3$ **22.** $g(x) = x^2 + 10x + 9$

23. $f(x) = 3x^2 - 12x + 5$ **24.** $g(x) = -4x^2 - 16x + 9$

Without graphing, determine the x- and y-intercepts of each of the
given parabolas. (See Example 6.)

25. $f(x) = 3(x - 2)^2 - 3$ **26.** $f(x) = x^2 - 4x - 1$

27. $g(x) = 2x^2 + 8x + 6$ **28.** $g(x) = x^2 - 10x + 20$

Graph each parabola and find its vertex and axis of symmetry. (See
Examples 1–6.)

29. $f(x) = (x + 2)^2$

30. $f(x) = -(x + 5)^2$

31. $f(x) = x^2 - 4x + 6$

32. $f(x) = x^2 + 6x + 3$

Use a calculator to work these problems.

33. Social Science According to data from the National Safety Council, the fatal-accident rate per 100,000 licensed drivers can be approximated by the function $f(x) = .0328x^2 - 3.55x + 115$, where x is the age of the driver ($16 \leq x \leq 88$). At what age is the rate the lowest?

34. Social Science Using data from the U.S. Census Bureau, the population (in thousands) of Detroit, Michigan can be approximated by $g(x) = -.422x^2 + 48.84x + 248$, where $x = 0$ corresponds to the year 1900. In what year, according to the given model, did Detroit have its highest population?

35. Natural Science A researcher in physiology has decided that a good mathematical model for the number of impulses fired after a nerve has been stimulated is given by $y = -x^2 + 20x - 60$, where y is the number of responses per millisecond and x is the number of milliseconds since the nerve was stimulated.

(a) When will the maximum firing rate be reached?

(b) What is the maximum firing rate?

36. Physical Science A bullet is fired upward from ground level. Its height above the ground (in feet) at time t seconds is given by

$$H = -16t^2 + 1000t.$$

Find the maximum height of the bullet and the time at which it hits the ground.

37. Business Pat Kan owns a factory that manufactures souvenir key chains. Her weekly profit (in hundreds of dollars) is given by $P(x) = -2x^2 + 60x - 120$, where x is the number of cases of key chains sold.

(a) What is the largest number of cases she can sell and still make a profit?

(b) Explain how it is possible for her to lose money if she sells more cases than your answer in part (a).

(c) How many cases should she make and sell in order to maximize her profits?

38. Business The manager of a bicycle shop has found that, at a price (in dollars) of $p(x) = 150 - \frac{x}{4}$ per bicycle, x bicycles will be sold.

(a) Find an expression for the total revenue from the sale of x bicycles. (*Hint:* Revenue = Demand × Price.)

(b) Find the number of bicycle sales that leads to maximum revenue.

(c) Find the maximum revenue.

Work the following problems. (See Example 7.)

39. Business Suppose the supply of and demand for a certain textbook are given by

$$\text{supply: } p = \frac{1}{5}q^2 \quad \text{and} \quad \text{demand: } p = -\frac{1}{5}q^2 + 40,$$

where p is price and q is quantity. How many books are demanded at a price of

(a) 10?   (b) 20?   (c) 30?   (d) 40?

How many books are supplied at a price of

(e) 5?   (f) 10?   (g) 20?   (h) 30?

(i) Graph the supply and demand functions on the same axes.

40. Business Find the equilibrium quantity and the equilibrium price in Exercise 39.

41. Business Suppose the price p of widgets is related to the quantity q that is demanded by

$$p = 640 - 5q^2,$$

where q is measured in hundreds of widgets. Find the price when the number of widgets demanded is

(a) 0;   (b) 5;   (c) 10.

Suppose the supply function for widgets is given by $p = 5q^2$, where q is the number of widgets (in hundreds) that are supplied at price p.

(d) Graph the demand function $p = 640 - 5q^2$ and the supply function $p = 5q^2$ on the same axes.

(e) Find the equilibrium quantity.

(f) Find the equilibrium price.

42. Business The supply function for a commodity is given by $p = q^2 + 200$, and the demand function is given by $p = -10q + 3200$

(a) Graph the supply and demand functions on the same axes.

(b) Find the equilibrium point.

(c) What is the equilibrium quantity? the equilibrium price?

Business *Find the equilibrium quantity and equilibrium price for the commodity whose supply and demand functions are given.*

43. Supply: $p = 45q$; demand: $p = -q^2 + 10,000$.

44. Supply: $p = q^2 + q + 10$; demand: $p = -10q + 3060$.

45. Supply: $p = q^2 + 20q$; demand: $p = -2q^2 + 10q + 3000$.

46. Supply: $p = .2q + 51$; demand: $p = \dfrac{3000}{q + 5}$.

Business *The revenue function $R(x)$ and the cost function $C(x)$ for a particular product are given. These functions are valid only for the specified domain of values. Find the number of units that must be produced to break even.*

47. $R(x) = 200x - x^2; C(x) = 70x + 2200; 0 \leq x \leq 100$

48. $R(x) = 300x - x^2; C(x) = 65x + 7000; 0 \leq x \leq 150$

49. $R(x) = 400x - 2x^2; C(x) = -x^2 + 200x + 1900; 0 \leq x \leq 100$

50. $R(x) = 500x - 2x^2; C(x) = -x^2 + 270x + 5125; 0 \leq x \leq 125$

Business *Work each problem. (See Example 8.)*

51. A charter flight charges a fare of $200 per person, plus $4 per person for each unsold seat on the plane. If the plane holds 100 passengers and if x represents the number of unsold seats, find the following:

(a) an expression for the total revenue received for the flight. (*Hint:* Multiply the number of people flying, $100 - x$, by the price per ticket);

(b) the graph for the expression in part (a);

(c) the number of unsold seats that will produce the maximum revenue;

(d) the maximum revenue.

52. The revenue of a charter bus company depends on the number of unsold seats. If 100 seats are sold, the price is $50 per seat. Each unsold seat increases the price per seat by $1. Let x represent the number of unsold seats.

(a) Write an expression for the number of seats that are sold.

(b) Write an expression for the price per seat.

(c) Write an expression for the revenue.

(d) Find the number of unsold seats that will produce the maximum revenue.

(e) Find the maximum revenue.

53. A hog farmer wants to find the best time to take her hogs to market. The current price is 88 cents per pound, and her hogs weigh an average of 90 pounds. The hogs gain 5 pounds per week, and the market price for hogs is falling each week by 2 cents per pound. How many weeks should the farmer wait before taking her hogs to market in order to receive as much money as possible? At that time, how much money (per hog) will she get?

54. The manager of a peach orchard is trying to decide when to arrange for picking the peaches. If they are picked now, the average yield per tree will be 100 pounds, which can be sold for 40¢ per pound. Past experience shows that the yield per tree will increase about 5 pounds per week, while the price will decrease about 2¢ per pound per week.

(a) Let x represent the number of weeks that the manager should wait. Find the price per pound.

(b) Find the number of pounds per tree.

(c) Find the total revenue from a tree.

(d) When should the peaches be picked in order to produce the maximum revenue?

(e) What is the maximum revenue?

Work these exercises. (See Example 9.)

55. **Health** The National Center for Catastrophic Sport Injury Research keeps data on the number of fatalities directly related to football each year. These deaths occur in sandlot, pro and semipro, high school, and college-level playing. The following table gives selected years and the number of deaths. (Data from: www.unc.edu/depts/nccsi/FootballAnnual.pdf.)

Year	Deaths
1970	29
1975	15
1980	9
1985	7
1990	0
1995	4
2000	3
2005	3
2010	5

(a) Let $x = 0$ correspond to 1970. Use $(20, 0)$ as the vertex and the data from 2005 to find a quadratic function $g(x) = a(x - h)^2 + k$ that models the data.

(b) Use the model to estimate the number of deaths in 2008.

56. **Natural Science** The acreage (in millions) consumed by forest fires in the United States is given in the following table. (Data from: National Interagency Fire Center.)

Year	Acres
1985	2.9
1988	5.0
1991	3.0
1994	4.1
1997	2.9
2000	7.4
2003	4.0
2006	9.9
2009	5.9
2012	9.2

(a) Let $x = 5$ correspond to the year 1985. Use $(5, 2.9)$ as the vertex and the data for the year 1994 to find a quadratic function $f(x) = a(x - h)^2 + k$ that models the data.

(b) Use the model to estimate the acreage destroyed by forest fires in the year 2009.

57. **Business** The following table shows China's gross domestic expenditures on research and development (in billions of U.S. dollars) for the years 2004 through 2010. (Data from: National Science Foundation, *National Patterns of R & D Resources* [annual series].)

Year	Acres
2004	57.8
2005	71.1
2006	86.7
2007	102.4
2008	120.8
2009	154.1
2010	179.0

(a) Let $x = 4$ correspond to the year 2004. Use $(4, 57.8)$ as the vertex and the data from 2008 to find a quadratic function $f(x) = a(x - h)^2 + k$ that models these data.

(b) Use the model to estimate the expenditures in the year 2012.

58. **Economics** The amount (in billions of dollars) of personal health care expenditures for hospital care for various years is given in the table on the following page. (Data from: U.S. Centers for Medicare and Medicaid Services.)

Year	Expenditures
1990	250
1995	339
2000	416
2005	609
2006	652
2007	693
2008	729
2009	776
2010	814

(a) Let $x = 0$ correspond to the year 1990. Use $(0, 250)$ as the vertex and the data from the year 2007 to find a quadratic function $f(x) = a(x - h)^2 + k$ that models these data.

(b) Use the model to estimate the expenditures in 1997 and 2012.

In Exercises 59–62, plot the data points and use quadratic regression to find a function that models the data. (See Example 10.)

59. Health Use the data in Exercise 55, with $x = 0$ corresponding to 1970. What number of injuries does this model estimate for 2008? Compare your answer with that for Exercise 55.

60. Natural Science Use the data from Exercise 56, with $x = 5$ corresponding to the year 1985. How much acreage does this model estimate for the year 2009? Compare your answer with that for Exercise 56.

61. Business Use the data from Exercise 57, with $x = 4$ corresponding to the year 2004. What is the estimate of the amount of R&D expenditures for China in the year 2012? Compare your answer with that for Exercise 57.

62. Economics Use the data from Exercise 58, with $x = 0$ corresponding to the year 1990. What is the amount of expenditures for hospital care estimated by this model for the years 1997 and 2012? Compare your answers with those for Exercise 58.

Business *Recall that profit equals revenue minus cost. In Exercises 63 and 64, find the following:*

(a) *The break-even point (to the nearest tenth)*

(b) *The x-value that makes profit a maximum*

(c) *The maximum profit*

(d) *For what x-values will a loss occur?*

(e) *For what x-values will a profit occur?*

63. $R(x) = 400x - 2x^2$ and $C(x) = 200x + 2000$, with $0 \leq x \leq 100$

64. $R(x) = 900x - 3x^2$ and $C(x) = 450x + 5000$, with $20 \leq x \leq 150$

✓**Checkpoint Answers**

1. (a)

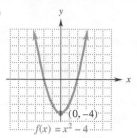

(b)

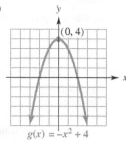

2. (a)

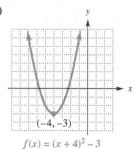

(b)

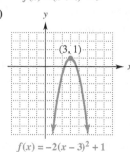

3. (a) $f(x) = (x + 3)^2 - 4; (-3, -4)$

  (b) $g(x) = (x - 6)^2 - 3; (6, -3)$

4. (a) 10 units   **(b)** $480

5. (a) 4   **(b)** 16

6. $f(x) = -8.02x^2 + 160.4x + 141$

3.5 Polynomial Functions

A **polynomial function of degree n** is a function whose rule is given by a polynomial of degree n.[*] For example

$$f(x) = 3x - 2 \qquad \text{polynomial function of degree 1;}$$

$$g(x) = 3x^2 + 4x - 6 \qquad \text{polynomial function of degree 2;}$$

$$h(x) = x^4 + 5x^3 - 6x^2 + x - 3 \qquad \text{polynomial function of degree 4.}$$

[*]The degree of a polynomial was defined on page 13.

Basic Graphs

The simplest polynomial functions are those whose rules are of the form $f(x) = ax^n$ (where a is a constant).

Example 1   Graph $f(x) = x^3$.

Solution   First, find several ordered pairs belonging to the graph. Be sure to choose some negative x-values, $x = 0$, and some positive x-values in order to get representative ordered pairs. Find as many ordered pairs as you need in order to see the shape of the graph. Then plot the ordered pairs and draw a smooth curve through them to obtain the graph in Figure 3.34.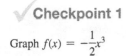

✓ **Checkpoint 1**

Graph $f(x) = -\dfrac{1}{2}x^3$

x	y
2	8
1	1
0	0
−1	−1
−2	−8

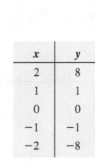

Figure 3.34

Example 2   Graph

$$f(x) = \frac{3}{2}x^4.$$

Solution   The following table gives some typical ordered pairs and leads to the graph in Figure 3.35.

✓ **Checkpoint 2**

Graph $g(x) = -2x^4$

x	$f(x)$
−2	24
−1	3/2
0	0
1	3/2
2	24

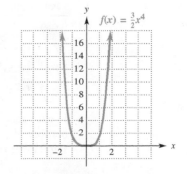

Figure 3.35

The graph of $f(x) = ax^n$ has one of the four basic shapes illustrated in Examples 1 and 2 and in Checkpoints 1 and 2. The basic shapes are summarized on the next page.

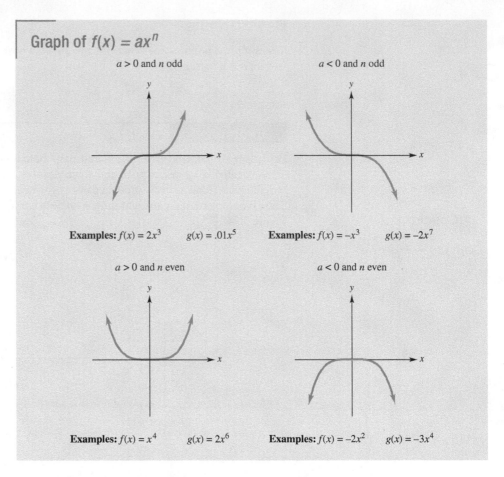

Graph of $f(x) = ax^n$

$a > 0$ and n odd

$a < 0$ and n odd

Examples: $f(x) = 2x^3$ $g(x) = .01x^5$ **Examples:** $f(x) = -x^3$ $g(x) = -2x^7$

$a > 0$ and n even

$a < 0$ and n even

Examples: $f(x) = x^4$ $g(x) = 2x^6$ **Examples:** $f(x) = -2x^2$ $g(x) = -3x^4$

Properties of Polynomial Graphs

Unlike the graphs in the preceding figures, the graphs of more complicated polynomial functions may have several "peaks" and "valleys," as illustrated in Figure 3.36, on the following page. The locations of the peaks and valleys can be accurately approximated by a maximum or minimum finder on a graphing calculator. Calculus is needed to determine their exact location.

The total number of peaks and valleys in a polynomial graph, as well as the number of the graph's x-intercepts, depends on the degree of the polynomial, as shown in Figure 3.36 and summarized here.

Polynomial	Degree	Number of peaks & valleys	Number of x-intercepts
$f(x) = x^3 - 4x + 2$	3	2	3
$f(x) = x^5 - 5x^3 + 4x$	5	4	5
$f(x) = 1.5x^4 + x^3 - 4x^2 - 3x + 4$	4	3	2
$f(x) = -x^6 + x^5 + 2x^4 + 1$	6	3	2

In each case, the number of x-intercepts is *at most* the degree of the polynomial. The total number of peaks and valleys is at most *one less than* the degree of the polynomial. The same thing is true in every case.

1. The total number of peaks and valleys on the graph of a polynomial function of degree n is at most $n - 1$.

2. The number of x-intercepts on the graph of a polynomial function of degree n is at most n.

(a) $f(x) = x^3 - 4x + 2$
1 peak $\left.\right\}$ total 2
1 valley
3 x-intercepts

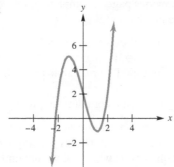

(b) $f(x) = x^5 - 5x^3 + 4x$
2 peaks $\left.\right\}$ total 4
2 valleys
5 x-intercepts

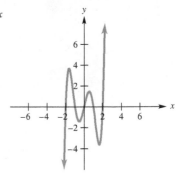

(c) $f(x) = 1.5x^4 + x^3 - 4x^2 - 3x + 4$
1 peak $\left.\right\}$ total 3
2 valleys
2 x-intercepts

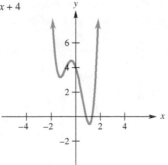

(d) $f(x) = -x^6 + x^5 + 2x^4 + 1$
2 peaks $\left.\right\}$ total 3
1 (shallow) valley
2 x-intercepts

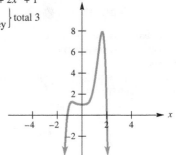

Figure 3.36

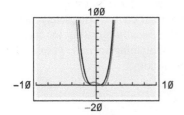

Figure 3.37

The domain of every polynomial function is the set of all real numbers, which means that its graph extends forever to the left and right. We indicate this by the arrows on the ends of polynomial graphs.

Although there may be peaks, valleys, and bends in a polynomial graph, the far ends of the graph are easy to describe: *they look like the graph of the highest-degree term of the polynomial.* Consider, for example, $f(x) = 1.5x^4 + x^3 - 4x^2 - 3x + 4$, whose highest-degree term is $1.5x^4$ and whose graph is shown in Figure 3.36(c). The ends of the graph shoot upward, just as the graph of $y = 1.5x^4$ does in Figure 3.35. When $f(x)$ and $y = 1.5x^4$ are graphed in the same large viewing window of a graphing calculator (Figure 3.37), the graphs look almost identical, except near the origin. This is an illustration of the following facts.

> The graph of a polynomial function is a smooth, unbroken curve that extends forever to the left and right. When $|x|$ is large, the graph resembles the graph of its highest-degree term and moves sharply away from the x-axis.

Example 3 Let $g(x) = x^3 - 11x^2 - 32x + 24$, and consider the graph in Figure 3.38.

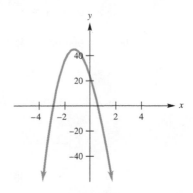

Figure 3.38

(a) Is Figure 3.38, on the previous page, a complete graph of $g(x)$; that is, does it show all the important features of the graph?

Solution The far ends of the graph of $g(x)$ should resemble the graph of its highest-degree term x^3. The graph of $f(x) = x^3$ in Figure 3.34 moves upward at the far right, but the graph in Figure 3.38 does not. So Figure 3.38 is *not* a complete graph.

 **(b)** Use a graphing calculator to find a complete graph of $g(x)$.

Solution Since the graph of $g(x)$ must eventually start rising on the right side (as does the graph of x^3), a viewing window that shows a complete graph must extend beyond $x = 4$. By experimenting with various windows, we obtain Figure 3.39. This graph shows a total of two peaks and valleys and three x-intercepts (the maximum possible for a polynomial of degree 3). At the far ends, the graph of $g(x)$ resembles the graph of $f(x) = x^3$. Therefore, Figure 3.39 is a complete graph of $g(x)$.

✓ **Checkpoint 3**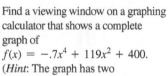

Find a viewing window on a graphing calculator that shows a complete graph of
$f(x) = -.7x^4 + 119x^2 + 400$.
(*Hint*: The graph has two x-intercepts and the maximum possible number of peaks and valleys.)

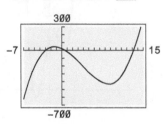

Figure 3.39

Graphing Techniques

Accurate graphs of first- and second-degree polynomial functions (lines and parabolas) are easily found algebraically, as we saw in Sections 2.2 and 3.4. All polynomial functions of degree 3, and some of higher degree, can be accurately graphed by hand by using calculus and algebra to locate the peaks and valleys. When a polynomial can be completely factored, the general shape of its graph can be determined algebraically by using the basic properties of polynomial graphs, as illustrated in Example 4. Obtaining accurate graphs of other polynomial functions generally requires the use of technology.

> **Example 4** Graph $f(x) = (2x + 3)(x - 1)(x + 2)$.

Solution Note that $f(x)$ is a polynomial of degree 3. (If you don't see why, do Checkpoint 4.) Begin by finding any x-intercepts. Set $f(x) = 0$ and solve for x:

$$f(x) = 0$$
$$(2x + 3)(x - 1)(x + 2) = 0.$$

✓ **Checkpoint 4**

Multiply out the expression for $f(x)$ in Example 4 and determine its degree.

Solve this equation by setting each of the three factors equal to 0:

$$2x + 3 = 0 \qquad \text{or} \qquad x - 1 = 0 \qquad \text{or} \qquad x + 2 = 0$$
$$x = -\frac{3}{2} \qquad\qquad\qquad x = 1 \qquad\qquad\qquad x = -2.$$

The three numbers $-3/2$, 1, and -2 divide the x-axis into four intervals:

$$x < -2, \qquad -2 < x < -\frac{3}{2}, \qquad -\frac{3}{2} < x < 1, \qquad \text{and} \qquad 1 < x.$$

These intervals are shown in Figure 3.40.

Figure 3.40

Since the graph is an unbroken curve, it can change from above the x-axis to below it only by passing through the x-axis. As we have seen, this occurs only at the x-intercepts: $x = -2, -3/2$, and 1. Consequently, in the interval between two intercepts (or to the left of $x = -2$ or to the right of $x = 1$), the graph of $f(x)$ must lie entirely above or entirely below the x-axis.

We can determine where the graph lies over an interval by evaluating $f(x) = (2x + 3)(x - 1)(x + 2)$ at a number in that interval. For example, $x = -3$ is in the interval where $x < -2$, and

$$f(-3) = (2(-3) + 3)(-3 - 1)(-3 + 2)$$
$$= -12.$$

Therefore, $(-3, -12)$ is on the graph. Since this point lies below the x-axis, all points in this interval (that is, all points with $x < -2$) must lie below the x-axis. By testing numbers in the other intervals, we obtain the following table.

Interval	$x < -2$	$-2 < x < -3/2$	$-3/2 < x < 1$	$x > 1$
Test Number	-3	$-7/4$	0	2
Value of $f(x)$	-12	$11/32$	-6	28
Sign of $f(x)$	Negative	Positive	Negative	Positive
Graph	Below x-axis	Above x-axis	Below x-axis	Above x-axis

Since the graph intersects the x-axis at the intercepts and is above the x-axis between these intercepts, there must be at least one peak there. Similarly, there must be at least one valley between $x = -3/2$ and $x = 1$, because the graph is below the x-axis there. However, a polynomial function of degree 3 can have a total of at most $3 - 1 = 2$ peaks and valleys. So there must be exactly one peak and exactly one valley on this graph.

Furthermore, when $|x|$ is large, the graph must resemble the graph of $y = 2x^3$ (the highest-degree term). The graph of $y = 2x^3$, like the graph of $y = x^3$ in Figure 3.34, moves upward to the right and downward to the left. Using these facts and plotting the x-intercepts shows that the graph must have the general shape shown in Figure 3.41. Plotting additional points leads to the reasonably accurate graph in Figure 3.42. We say "reasonably accurate" because we cannot be sure of the exact locations of the peaks and valleys on the graph without using calculus.

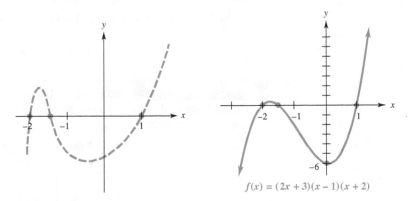

Figure 3.41   **Figure 3.42**

$f(x) = (2x + 3)(x - 1)(x + 2)$

✓ **Checkpoint 5**

Graph $f(x) = .4(x - 2)(x + 3)(x - 4)$.

🔁 ✈ Polynomial Models

Regression procedures similar to those presented for linear regression in Section 2.3 and quadratic regression in Section 3.5 can be used to find cubic and quartic (degree 4) polynomial models for appropriate data.

Example 5 **Social Science** The following table shows the population of the city of San Francisco, California in selected years.

Year	1950	1960	1970	1980	1990	2000	2010
Population	775,357	740,316	715,674	678,974	723,959	776,733	805,863

(a) Plot the data on a graphing calculator, with $x = 0$ corresponding to the year 1950.

Solution The points in Figure 3.43 suggest the general shape of a fourth-degree (quartic) polynomial.

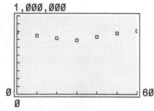

Figure 3.43

(b) Use quartic regression to obtain a model for these data.

Solution The procedure is the same as for linear regression; just choose "quartic" in place of "linear." It produces the function

$$f(x) = -.137x^4 + 16.07x^3 - 470.34x^2 + 542.65x + 773,944.$$

Its graph, shown in Figure 3.44, appears to fit the data well.

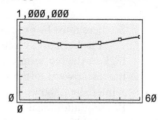

Figure 3.44

(c) Use the model to estimate the population of San Francisco in the years 1985 and 2005.

Solution The years 1985 and 2005 correspond to $x = 35$ and $x = 55$, respectively. Verify that

$$f(35) \approx 700,186 \quad \text{and} \quad f(55) \approx 801,022.$$

Example 6 **Business** The following table shows the revenue and costs (in millions of dollars) for Ford Motor Company for the years 2004–2012. (Data from: www.morningstar.com.)

Year	Revenue	Costs
2004	171,652	168,165
2005	177,089	175,065
2006	160,123	172,736
2007	172,455	175,178
2008	146,277	160,949
2009	118,308	115,346
2010	128,954	122,397
2011	136,264	116,042
2012	134,252	128,588

(a) Let $x = 4$ correspond to the year 2004. Use cubic regression to obtain models for the revenue data $R(x)$ and the costs $C(x)$.

Solution The functions obtained using cubic regression from a calculator or software are

$$R(x) = 551.1x^3 - 12,601x^2 + 82,828x + 7002;$$
$$C(x) = 885.5x^3 - 21,438x^2 + 154,283x - 166,074.$$

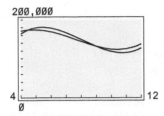

200,000

4   12
0

Figure 3.45

(b) Graph $R(x)$ and $C(x)$ on the same set of axes. Did costs ever exceed revenues?

Solution The graph is shown in Figure 3.45. Since the lines cross twice, we can say that costs exceeded revenues in various periods.

(c) Find the profit function $P(x)$ and show its graph.

Solution The profit function is the difference between the revenue function and the cost function. We subtract the coefficients of the cost function from the respective coefficients of the revenue function.

$$\begin{aligned}
P(x) &= R(x) - C(x) \\
&= (551.1 - 885.5)x^3 + (-12,601 + 21,438)x^2 \\
&\quad + (82,828 - 154,283)x + (7002 + 166,074) \qquad \text{Subtract like terms.} \\
&= -334.4x^3 + 8837x^2 - 71,455x + 173,076.
\end{aligned}$$

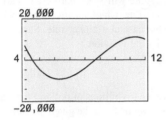

20,000

4   12

−20,000

Figure 3.46

The graph of $P(x)$ appears in Figure 3.46.

(d) According to the model of the profit function $P(x)$, in what years was Ford Motor Company profitable?

Solution The motor company was profitable in 2004, 2009, 2010, 2011, and 2012 because that is where the graph is positive.

3.5 Exercises

Graph each of the given polynomial functions. (See Examples 1 and 2.)

1. $f(x) = x^4$

2. $g(x) = -.5x^6$

3. $h(x) = -.2x^5$

4. $f(x) = x^7$

In Exercises 5–8, state whether the graph could possibly be the graph of (a) some polynomial function; (b) a polynomial function of degree 3; (c) a polynomial function of degree 4; (d) a polynomial function of degree 5. (See Example 3.)

5.

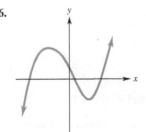

6.

7.

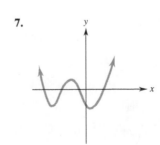

8.

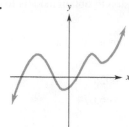

In Exercises 9–14, match the given polynomial function to its graph [(a)–(f)], without using a graphing calculator. (See Example 3 and the two boxes preceding it.)

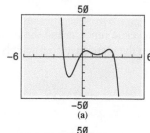
(a)

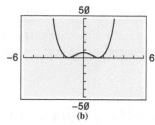
(b)

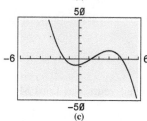
(c)

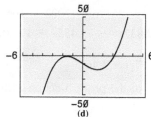
(d)

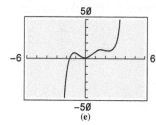
(e)

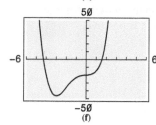
(f)

9. $f(x) = x^3 - 7x - 9$

10. $f(x) = -x^3 + 4x^2 + 3x - 8$

11. $f(x) = x^4 - 5x^2 + 7$

12. $f(x) = x^4 + 4x^3 - 20$

13. $f(x) = .7x^5 - 2.5x^4 - x^3 + 8x^2 + x + 2$

14. $f(x) = -x^5 + 4x^4 + x^3 - 16x^2 + 12x + 5$

Graph each of the given polynomial functions. (See Example 4.)

15. $f(x) = (x + 3)(x - 4)(x + 1)$

16. $f(x) = (x - 5)(x - 1)(x + 1)$

17. $f(x) = x^2(x + 3)(x - 1)$

18. $f(x) = x^2(x + 2)(x - 2)$

19. $f(x) = x^3 - x^2 - 20x$

20. $f(x) = x^3 + 2x^2 - 10x$

21. $f(x) = x^3 + 4x^2 - 7x$

22. $f(x) = x^4 - 6x^2$

Exercises 23–26 require a graphing calculator. Find a viewing window that shows a complete graph of the polynomial function (that is, a graph that includes all the peaks and valleys and that indicates how the curve moves away from the x-axis at the far left and far right). There are many correct answers. Consider your answer correct if it shows all the features that appear in the window given in the answers. (See Example 3.)

23. $g(x) = x^3 - 3x^2 - 4x - 5$

24. $f(x) = x^4 - 10x^3 + 35x^2 - 50x + 24$

25. $f(x) = 2x^5 - 3.5x^4 - 10x^3 + 5x^2 + 12x + 6$

26. $g(x) = x^5 + 8x^4 + 20x^3 + 9x^2 - 27x - 7$

In Exercises 27–31, use a calculator to evaluate the functions. Generate the graph by plotting points or by using a graphing calculator.

27. **Finance**   An idealized version of the Laffer curve (originated by economist Arthur Laffer) is shown in the accompanying graph. According to this theory, decreasing the tax rate, say, from x_2 to x_1, may actually increase the total revenue to the government. The theory is that people will work harder and earn more if they are taxed at a lower rate, which means higher total tax revenues than would be the case at a higher rate. Suppose that the Laffer curve is given by the function

$$f(x) = \frac{x(x - 100)(x - 160)}{240} \quad (0 \le x \le 100),$$

where $f(x)$ is government revenue (in billions of dollars) from a tax rate of x percent. Find the revenue from the given tax rates.

(a) 20%   **(b)** 40%   **(c)** 50%   **(d)** 70%

(e) Graph $f(x)$.

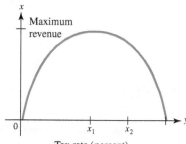

Tax rate (percent)

28. **Health**   A technique for measuring cardiac output depends on the concentration of a dye after a known amount is injected into a vein near the heart. In a normal heart, the concentration of the dye at time x (in seconds) is given by the function defined by

$$g(x) = -.006x^4 + .140x^3 - .053x^2 + 1.79x.$$

(a) Find the following: $g(0)$; $g(1)$; $g(2)$; $g(3)$.

(b) Graph $g(x)$ for $x \ge 0$.

29. **Business**   The revenue for Costco Wholesale Corporation (in millions of dollars) can be approximated by the function

$$R(x) = .141x^3 - 3.11x^2 + 26.98x - 19.99,$$

where $x = 4$ corresponds to the year 2004. (Data from: www.morningstar.com.)

(a) Find the following: $R(5)$; $R(7)$; $R(12)$.

(b) Graph $R(x)$.

(c) Is revenue always increasing in this model?

30. Business The revenue for Target Corporation (in billions of dollars) can be approximated by the function

$$R(x) = .0600x^4 - 1.9766x^3 + 23.155x^2 - 110.22x + 229.42,$$

where $x = 4$ corresponds to the year 2004. (Data from: www.morningstar.com.)

(a) Find the following: $R(6)$; $R(9)$; $R(11)$.

(b) Graph $R(x)$.

31. Business The cost function for Costco Wholesale Corporation (in millions of dollars) can be approximated by the function

$$C(x) = .135x^3 - 2.98x^2 + 25.99x - 18.71,$$

where $x = 4$ corresponds to the year 2004. (Data from: www.morningstar.com.)

(a) Find the following: $C(5)$; $C(7)$; $C(12)$.

(b) Graph $C(x)$.

(c) Are costs always increasing in this model?

32. Business The cost function for Target Corporation (in billions of dollars) can be approximated by the function

$$C(x) = .0697x^4 - 2.296x^3 + 26.947x^2 - 129.49x + 261.86,$$

where $x = 4$ corresponds to the year 2004. (Data from: www.morningstar.com.)

(a) Find the following: $C(6)$; $C(9)$; $C(11)$.

(b) Graph $C(x)$.

33. Business Use the revenue function $R(x)$ from Exercise 29 and the cost function $C(x)$ from Exercise 31 to write the profit function $P(x)$ for Costco Wholesale Corporation. Use your function to find the profit for the year 2012.

34. Business Use the revenue function $R(x)$ from Exercise 30 and the cost function $C(x)$ from Exercise 32 to write the profit function $P(x)$ for Target Corporation. Use your function to find the profit for the year 2011.

⚐ *Use a graphing calculator to do the following problems. (See Example 5.)*

35. Social Science The following table shows the public school enrollment (in millions) in selected years. (Data from: U.S. National Center for Education Statistics.)

Year	Enrollment
1980	50.3
1985	48.9
1990	52.1
1995	55.9
2000	60.0
2005	62.1
2010	64.4

(a) Plot the data with $x = 0$ corresponding to the year 1980.

(b) Use cubic regression to find a third-order polynomial function $g(x)$ that models these data.

(c) Graph $g(x)$ on the same screen as the data points. Does the graph appear to fit the data well?

(d) According to the model, what was the enrollment in the year 2008?

36. Business The following table shows the profit (in billions of dollars) for Intel Corporation. (Data from: www.morningstar.com.)

Year	Profit
2004	7.5
2005	8.7
2006	5.0
2007	7.0
2008	5.3
2009	4.4
2010	11.5
2011	12.9
2012	11.0

(a) Plot the data with $x = 4$ corresponding to the year 2004.

(b) Use quartic regression to find a fourth-order polynomial function $h(x)$ that models these data.

(c) Graph $h(x)$ on the same screen as the data points. Does the graph appear to fit the data well?

(d) According to the model, what were Intel's profits in 2010?

37. Business The accompanying table gives the annual revenue for International Business Machines Corp. (IBM) in billions of dollars for the years 2004–2012. (Data from www.morningstar.com.)

Year	Revenue
2004	96.3
2005	91.1
2006	91.4
2007	98.8
2008	103.6
2009	95.8
2010	99.9
2011	106.9
2012	104.5

(a) Let $x = 4$ correspond to the year 2004. Use cubic regression to find a polynomial function $R(x)$ that models these data.

(b) Graph $R(x)$ on the same screen as the data points. Does the graph appear to fit the data well?

38. Business The accompanying table gives the annual costs for International Business Machines Corp. (IBM) in billions of dollars for the years 2004–2012. (Data from www.morningstar.com.)

Year	Costs
2004	87.9
2005	83.2
2006	81.9
2007	88.4
2008	91.3
2009	82.4
2010	85.1
2011	91.0
2012	87.9

(a) Let $x = 4$ correspond to the year 2004. Use cubic regression to find a polynomial function $C(x)$ that models these data.

(b) Graph $C(x)$ on the screen as the data points. Does the graph appear to fit the data well?

Business *For Exercises 39 and 40, use the functions $R(x)$ and $C(x)$ from the answers to Exercises 37(a) and 38(a).*

39. Find the profit function $P(x)$ for IBM for the years 2004–2012.

40. Find the profits for the year 2008.

✓Checkpoint Answers

1.
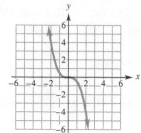

2.
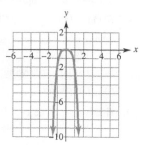

3. Many correct answers, including $-15 \leq x \leq 15$ and $-2000 \leq y \leq 6000$.

4. $f(x) = 2x^3 + 5x^2 - x - 6$; degree 3.

5.
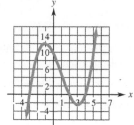

3.6 Rational Functions

A **rational function** is a function whose rule is the quotient of two polynomials, such as

$$f(x) = \frac{2}{1 + x}, \qquad g(x) = \frac{3x + 2}{2x + 4}, \qquad \text{and} \qquad h(x) = \frac{x^2 - 2x - 4}{x^3 - 2x^2 + x}.$$

Thus, a rational function is a function whose rule can be written in the form

$$f(x) = \frac{P(x)}{Q(x)},$$

where $P(x)$ and $Q(x)$ are polynomials, with $Q(x) \neq 0$. The function is undefined for any values of x that make $Q(x) = 0$, so there are breaks in the graph at these numbers.

Linear Rational Functions

We begin with rational functions in which both numerator and denominator are first-degree or constant polynomials. Such functions are sometimes called **linear rational functions.**

Example 1 Graph the rational function defined by

$$y = \frac{2}{1 + x}.$$

Solution This function is undefined for $x = -1$, since -1 leads to a 0 denominator. For that reason, the graph of this function will not intersect the vertical line $x = -1$. Since x can take on any value except -1, the values of x can approach -1 as closely as desired from either side of -1, as shown in the following table of values.

x approaches −1

x	-1.5	-1.2	-1.1	-1.01	$-.99$	$-.9$	$-.8$	$-.5$
$1 + x$	$-.5$	$-.2$	$-.1$	$-.01$	$.01$	$.1$	$.2$	$.5$
$\dfrac{2}{1+x}$	-4	-10	-20	-200	200	20	10	4

$|f(x)|$ gets larger and larger

The preceding table suggests that as x gets closer and closer to -1 from either side, $|f(x)|$ gets larger and larger. The part of the graph near $x = -1$ in Figure 3.47 shows this behavior. The vertical line $x = -1$ that is approached by the curve is called a *vertical asymptote*. For convenience, the vertical asymptote is indicated by a dashed line in Figure 3.47, but this line is *not* part of the graph of the function.

As $|x|$ gets larger and larger, so does the absolute value of the denominator $1 + x$. Hence, $y = 2/(1 + x)$ gets closer and closer to 0, as shown in the following table.

x	-101	-11	-2	0	9	99
$1 + x$	-100	-10	-1	1	10	100
$\dfrac{2}{1+x}$	$-.02$	$-.2$	-2	2	$.2$	$.02$

The horizontal line $y = 0$ is called a *horizontal asymptote* for this graph. Using the asymptotes and plotting the intercept and other points gives the graph of Figure 3.47. ✓

✓ **Checkpoint 1**

Graph the following.

(a) $f(x) = \dfrac{3}{5 - x}$

(b) $f(x) = \dfrac{-4}{x + 4}$

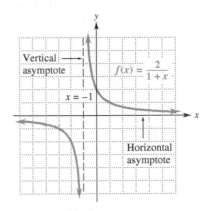

Figure 3.47

Example 1 suggests the following conclusion, which applies to all rational functions.

If a number c makes the denominator zero, but the numerator nonzero, in the expression defining a rational function, then the line $x = c$ is a **vertical asymptote** for the graph of the function.

If the graph of a function approaches a horizontal line very closely when x is very large or very small, we say that this line is a **horizontal asymptote** of the graph.

In Example 1, the horizontal asymptote was the x-axis. This is not always the case, however, as the next example illustrates.

Example 2 Graph

$$f(x) = \frac{3x + 2}{2x + 4}.$$

Solution Find the vertical asymptote by setting the denominator equal to 0 and then solving for x:

$$2x + 4 = 0$$

$$x = -2.$$

In order to see what the graph looks like when $|x|$ is very large, we rewrite the rule of the function. When $x \neq 0$, dividing both numerator and denominator by x does not change the value of the function:

$$f(x) = \frac{3x + 2}{2x + 4} = \frac{\dfrac{3x + 2}{x}}{\dfrac{2x + 4}{x}}$$

$$= \frac{\dfrac{3x}{x} + \dfrac{2}{x}}{\dfrac{2x}{x} + \dfrac{4}{x}} = \frac{3 + \dfrac{2}{x}}{2 + \dfrac{4}{x}}.$$

Now, when $|x|$ is very large, the fractions $2/x$ and $4/x$ are very close to 0. (For instance, when $x = 200, 4/x = 4/200 = .02$.) Therefore, the numerator of $f(x)$ is very close to $3 + 0 = 3$ and the denominator is very close to $2 + 0 = 2$. Hence, $f(x)$ is very close to $3/2$ when $|x|$ is large, so the line $y = 3/2$ is the horizontal asymptote of the graph, as shown in Figure 3.48.

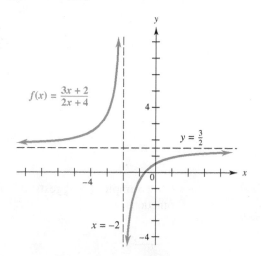

Figure 3.48

✓ **Checkpoint 2**

Graph the following.

(a) $f(x) = \dfrac{2x - 5}{x - 2}$

(b) $f(x) = \dfrac{3 - x}{x + 1}$

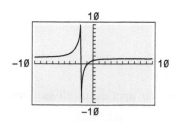

Figure 3.49

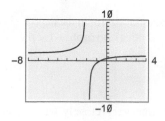

Figure 3.50

TECHNOLOGY TIP Depending on the viewing window, a graphing calculator may not accurately represent the graph of a rational function. For example, the graph of $f(x) = \dfrac{3x + 2}{2x + 4}$ in Figure 3.49, which should look like Figure 3.48, has an erroneous vertical line at the place where the graph has a vertical asymptote. This problem can usually be avoided by using a window that has the vertical asymptote at the center of the x-axis, as in Figure 3.50.

The horizontal asymptotes of a linear rational function are closely related to the coefficients of the x-terms of the numerator and denominator, as illustrated in Examples 1 and 2:

	Function	Horizontal Asymptote
Example 2:	$f(x) = \dfrac{3x + 2}{2x + 4}$	$y = \dfrac{3}{2}$
Example 1:	$f(x) = \dfrac{2}{1 + x} = \dfrac{0x + 2}{1x + 1}$	$y = \dfrac{0}{1} = 0$ (the x-axis)

The same pattern holds in the general case.

The graph of $f(x) = \dfrac{ax + b}{cx + d}$ (where $c \neq 0$ and $ad \neq bc$) has a vertical asymptote at the root of the denominator and has horizontal asymptote $y = \dfrac{a}{c}$.

Other Rational Functions

When the numerator or denominator of a rational function has degree greater than 1, the graph of the function can be more complicated than those in Examples 1 and 2. The graph may have several vertical asymptotes, as well as peaks and valleys.

Example 3   Graph

$$f(x) = \frac{2x^2}{x^2 - 4}.$$

Solution   Find the vertical asymptotes by setting the denominator equal to 0 and solving for x:

$$x^2 - 4 = 0$$
$$(x + 2)(x - 2) = 0 \qquad \text{Factor.}$$
$$x + 2 = 0 \quad \text{or} \quad x - 2 = 0 \qquad \text{Set each term equal to 0.}$$
$$x = -2 \quad \text{or} \quad x = 2. \qquad \text{Solve for } x.$$

Since neither of these numbers makes the numerator 0, the lines $x = -2$ and $x = 2$ are vertical asymptotes of the graph. The horizontal asymptote can be determined by dividing both the numerator and denominator of $f(x)$ by x^2 (the highest power of x that appears in either one):

$$f(x) = \frac{2x^2}{x^2 - 4}$$

$$= \frac{\dfrac{2x^2}{x^2}}{\dfrac{x^2 - 4}{x^2}}$$

$$= \frac{\dfrac{2x^2}{x^2}}{\dfrac{x^2}{x^2} - \dfrac{4}{x^2}}$$

$$= \frac{2}{1 - \dfrac{4}{x^2}}.$$

When $|x|$ is very large, the fraction $4/x^2$ is very close to 0, so the denominator is very close to 1 and $f(x)$ is very close to 2. Hence, the line $y = 2$ is the horizontal asymptote of the graph. Using this information and plotting several points in each of the three regions determined by the vertical asymptotes, we obtain Figure 3.51. ✔️3

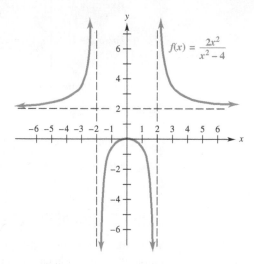

Figure 3.51

✓ **Checkpoint 3**

List the vertical and horizontal asymptotes of the given function.

(a) $f(x) = \dfrac{3x + 5}{x + 5}$

(b) $g(x) = \dfrac{2 - x^2}{x^2 - 4}$

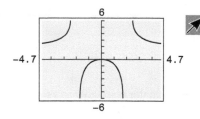

Figure 3.52

🖊️ **TECHNOLOGY TIP** When a function whose graph has more than one vertical asymptote (as in Example 3) is graphed on a graphing calculator, erroneous vertical lines can sometimes be avoided by using a *decimal window* (with the y-range adjusted to show the graph). On TI, use (Z)DECIMAL in the ZOOM or VIEWS menu. On Casio, use INIT in the V-WINDOW menu. Figure 3.52 shows the function of Example 3 graphed in a decimal window on a TI-84+. (The x-range may be different on other calculators.)

The arguments used to find the horizontal asymptotes in Examples 1–3 work in the general case and lead to the following conclusion.

> If the numerator of a rational function $f(x)$ is of *smaller* degree than the denominator, then the x-axis (the line $y = 0$) is the horizontal asymptote of the graph. If the numerator and denominator are of the *same* degree, say, $f(x) = \dfrac{ax^n + \cdots}{cx^n + \cdots}$, then the line $y = \dfrac{a}{c}$ is the horizontal asymptote.*

Applications

Rational functions have a variety of applications, some of which are explored next.

Example 4   **Natural Science** In many situations involving environmental pollution, much of the pollutant can be removed from the air or water at a fairly reasonable cost, but the minute amounts of the pollutant that remain can be very expensive to remove.

Cost as a function of the percentage of pollutant removed from the environment can be calculated for various percentages of removal, with a curve fitted through the resulting data points. This curve then leads to a function that approximates the situation. Rational functions often are a good choice for these **cost–benefit functions.**

---

*When the numerator is of larger degree than the denominator, the graph has no horizontal asymptote, but may have nonhorizontal lines or other curves as asymptotes; see Exercises 32 and 33 at the end of this section for examples.

For example, suppose a cost–benefit function is given by

$$f(x) = \frac{18x}{106 - x},$$

where $f(x)$, or y, is the cost (in thousands of dollars) of removing x percent of a certain pollutant. The domain of x is the set of all numbers from 0 to 100, inclusive; any amount of pollutant from 0% to 100% can be removed. To remove 100% of the pollutant here would cost

$$y = \frac{18(100)}{106 - 100} = 300,$$

or $300,000. Check that 95% of the pollutant can be removed for about $155,000, 90% for about $101,000, and 80% for about $55,000, as shown in Figure 3.53 (in which the displayed y-coordinates are rounded to the nearest integer). ☑4

 Checkpoint 4

Using the function in Example 4, find the cost to remove the following percentages of pollutants.

(a) 70%

(b) 85%

(c) 98%

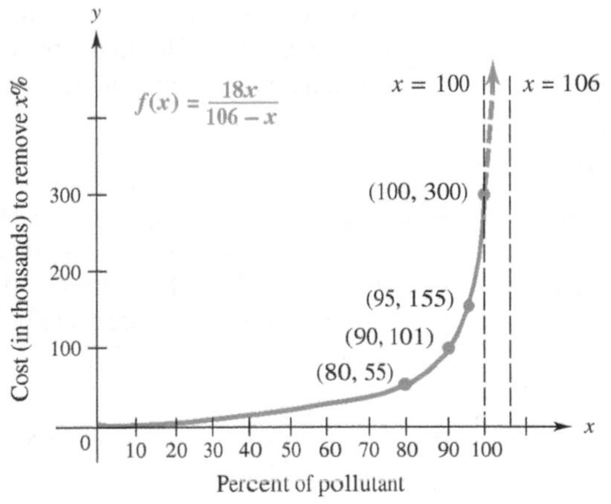

Figure 3.53

In management, **product-exchange functions** give the relationship between quantities of two items that can be produced by the same machine or factory. For example, an oil refinery can produce gasoline, heating oil, or a combination of the two; a winery can produce red wine, white wine, or a combination of the two. The next example discusses a product-exchange function.

Example 5 **Business** The product-exchange function for the Fruits of the Earth Winery for red wine x and white wine y, in number of cases, is

$$y = \frac{150{,}000 - 75x}{1200 + x}.$$

Graph the function and find the maximum quantity of each kind of wine that can be produced.

Solution Only nonnegative values of x and y make sense in this situation, so we graph the function in the first quadrant (Figure 3.54, on the following page). Note that the y-intercept of the graph (found by setting $x = 0$) is 125 and the x-intercept (found by setting $y = 0$ and solving for x) is 2000. Since we are interested only in the portion of the graph in Quadrant I, we can find a few more points in that quadrant and complete the graph as shown in Figure 3.54.

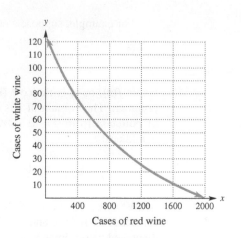

Figure 3.54

The maximum value of y occurs when $x = 0$, so the maximum amount of white wine that can be produced is 125 cases, as given by the y-intercept. The x-intercept gives the maximum amount of red wine that can be produced: 2000 cases. ☑ 5

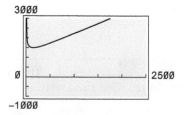

✓ **Checkpoint 5**

Rework Example 5 with the product-exchange function

$$y = \frac{70,000 - 10x}{70 + x}$$

to find the maximum amount of each wine that can be produced.

Example 6   **Business**   A retailer buys 2500 specialty lightbulbs from a distributor each year. In addition to the cost of each bulb, there is a fee for each order, so she wants to order as few times as possible. However, storage costs are higher when there are fewer orders (and hence more bulbs per order to store). Past experience shows that the total annual cost (for the bulbs, ordering fees, and storage costs) is given by the rational function.

$$C(x) = \frac{.98x^2 + 1200x + 22,000}{x},$$

where x is the number of bulbs ordered each time. How many bulbs should be ordered each time in order to have the smallest possible cost?

Solution   Graph the cost function $C(x)$ in a window with $0 \le x \le 2500$ (because the retailer cannot order a negative number of bulbs and needs only 2500 for the year).

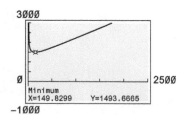

Figure 3.55   **Figure 3.56**

For each point on the graph in Figure 3.55,

>   the x-coordinate is the number of bulbs ordered each time;
>   the y-coordinate is the annual cost when x bulbs are ordered each time.

Use the minimum finder on a graphing calculator to find the point with the smallest y-coordinate, which is approximately (149.83, 1493.67), as shown in Figure 3.56. Since the retailer cannot order part of a lightbulb, she should order 150 bulbs each time, for an approximate annual cost of $1494.

3.6 Exercises

Graph each function. Give the equations of the vertical and horizontal asymptotes. (See Examples 1–3.)

1. $f(x) = \dfrac{1}{x + 5}$

2. $g(x) = \dfrac{-7}{x - 6}$

3. $f(x) = \dfrac{-3}{2x + 5}$

4. $h(x) = \dfrac{-4}{2 - x}$

5. $f(x) = \dfrac{3x}{x - 1}$

6. $g(x) = \dfrac{x - 2}{x}$

7. $f(x) = \dfrac{x + 1}{x - 4}$

8. $f(x) = \dfrac{x - 3}{x + 5}$

9. $f(x) = \dfrac{2 - x}{x - 3}$

10. $g(x) = \dfrac{3x - 2}{x + 3}$

11. $f(x) = \dfrac{3x + 2}{2x + 4}$

12. $f(x) = \dfrac{4x - 8}{8x + 1}$

13. $h(x) = \dfrac{x + 1}{x^2 + 2x - 8}$

14. $g(x) = \dfrac{1}{x(x + 2)^2}$

15. $f(x) = \dfrac{x^2 + 4}{x^2 - 4}$

16. $f(x) = \dfrac{x - 1}{x^2 - 2x - 3}$

Find the equations of the vertical asymptotes of each of the given rational functions.

17. $f(x) = \dfrac{x - 3}{x^2 + x - 2}$

18. $g(x) = \dfrac{x + 2}{x^2 - 1}$

19. $g(x) = \dfrac{x^2 + 2x}{x^2 - 4x - 5}$

20. $f(x) = \dfrac{x^2 - 2x - 4}{x^3 - 2x^2 + x}$

Work these problems. (See Example 4.)

21. Natural Science Suppose a cost–benefit model is given by

$$f(x) = \frac{4.3x}{100 - x},$$

where $f(x)$ is the cost, in thousands of dollars, of removing x percent of a given pollutant. Find the cost of removing each of the given percentages of pollutants.

(a) 50%   **(b)** 70%   **(c)** 80%

(d) 90%   **(e)** 95%   **(f)** 98%

(g) 99%

(h) Is it possible, according to this model, to remove *all* the pollutant?

(i) Graph the function.

22. Business Suppose a cost–benefit model is given by

$$f(x) = \frac{6.2x}{112 - x},$$

where $f(x)$ is the cost, in thousands of dollars, of removing x percent of a certain pollutant. Find the cost of removing the given percentages of pollutants.

(a) 0%   **(b)** 50%

(c) 80%   **(d)** 90%

(e) 95%   **(f)** 99%

(g) 100%   **(h)** Graph the function.

23. Natural Science The function

$$f(x) = \frac{\lambda x}{1 + (ax)^b}$$

is used in population models to give the size of the next generation $f(x)$ in terms of the current generation x. (See J. Maynard Smith, *Models in Ecology* [Cambridge University Press, 1974].)

(a) What is a reasonable domain for this function, considering what x represents?

(b) Graph the function for $\lambda = a = b = 1$ and $x \geq 0$.

(c) Graph the function for $\lambda = a = 1$ and $b = 2$ and $x \geq 0$.

(d) What is the effect of making b larger?

24. Natural Science The function

$$f(x) = \frac{Kx}{A + x}$$

is used in biology to give the growth rate of a population in the presence of a quantity x of food. This concept is called Michaelis–Menten kinetics. (See Leah Edelstein-Keshet, *Mathematical Models in Biology* [Random House, 1988].)

(a) What is a reasonable domain for this function, considering what x represents?

(b) Graph the function for $K = 5$, $A = 2$, and $x \geq 0$.

(c) Show that $y = K$ is a horizontal asymptote.

(d) What do you think K represents?

(e) Show that A represents the quantity of food for which the growth rate is half of its maximum.

25. Social Science The average waiting time in a line (or queue) before getting served is given by

$$W = \frac{S(S - A)}{A},$$

where A is the average rate at which people arrive at the line and S is the average service time. At a certain fast-food restaurant, the average service time is 3 minutes. Find W for each of the given average arrival times.

(a) 1 minute

(b) 2 minutes

(c) 2.5 minutes

(d) What is the vertical asymptote?

(e) Graph the equation on the interval $(0, 3)$.

(f) What happens to W when $A > 3$? What does this mean?

Business *Sketch the portion of the graph in Quadrant I of each of the functions defined in Exercises 26 and 27, and then estimate the maximum quantities of each product that can be produced. (See Example 5.)*

26. The product-exchange function for gasoline x and heating oil y, in hundreds of gallons per day, is

$$y = \frac{125,000 - 25x}{125 + 2x}.$$

27. A drug factory found that the product-exchange function for a red tranquilizer x and a blue tranquilizer y is

$$y = \frac{900,000,000 - 30,000x}{x + 90,000}.$$

28. **Physical Science** The failure of several O-rings in field joints was the cause of the fatal crash of the *Challenger* space shuttle in 1986. NASA data from 24 successful launches prior to *Challenger* suggested that O-ring failure was related to launch temperature by a function similar to

$$N(t) = \frac{600 - 7t}{4t - 100} \quad (50 \leq t \leq 85),$$

where t is the temperature (in °F) at launch and N is the approximate number of O-rings that fail. Assume that this function accurately models the number of O-ring failures that would occur at lower launch temperatures (an assumption NASA did not make).

(a) Does $N(t)$ have a vertical asymptote? At what value of t does it occur?

(b) Without actually graphing the function, what would you conjecture that the graph would look like just to the right of the vertical asymptote? What does this suggest about the number of O-ring failures that might be expected near that temperature? (The temperature at the *Challenger* launching was 31°.)

(c) Confirm your conjecture by graphing $N(t)$ between the vertical asymptote and $t = 85$.

29. **Business** A company has fixed costs of $40,000 and a marginal cost of $2.60 per unit.

(a) Find the linear cost function.

(b) Find the average cost function. (Average cost was defined in Section 3.3.)

(c) Find the horizontal asymptote of the graph of the average cost function. Explain what the asymptote means in this situation. (How low can the average cost be?)

Use a graphing calculator to do Exercises 30–33. (See Example 6.)

30. **Finance** Another model of a Laffer curve (see Exercise 27 of Section 3.5) is given by

$$f(x) = \frac{300x - 3x^2}{10x + 200},$$

where $f(x)$ is government revenue (in billions of dollars) from a tax rate of x percent. Find the revenue from the given tax rates.

(a) 16% (b) 25%

(c) 40% (d) 55%

(e) Graph $f(x)$.

(f) What tax rate produces maximum revenue? What is the maximum revenue?

31. **Business** When no more than 110 units are produced, the cost of producing x units is given by

$$C(x) = .2x^3 - 25x^2 + 1531x + 25,000.$$

How many units should be produced in order to have the lowest possible average cost?

32. (a) Graph $f(x) = \dfrac{x^3 + 3x^2 + x + 1}{x^2 + 2x + 1}$.

(b) Does the graph appear to have a horizontal asymptote? Does the graph appear to have some nonhorizontal straight line as an asymptote?

(c) Graph $f(x)$ and the line $y = x + 1$ on the same screen. Does this line appear to be an asymptote of the graph of $f(x)$?

33. (a) Graph $g(x) = \dfrac{x^3 - 2}{x - 1}$ in the window with $-5 \leq x \leq 5$ and $-6 \leq y \leq 12$.

(b) Graph $g(x)$ and the parabola $y = x^2 + x + 1$ on the same screen. How do the two graphs compare when $|x| \geq 2$?

✓**Checkpoint Answers**

1. (a)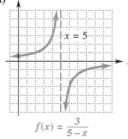

$$f(x) = \frac{3}{5 - x}$$

(b)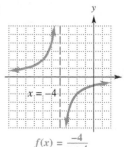

$$f(x) = \frac{-4}{x + 4}$$

2. (a)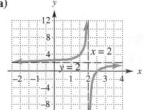

(b)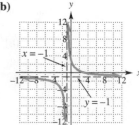

3. (a) Vertical, $x = -5$; horizontal, $y = 3$

(b) Vertical, $x = -2$ and $x = 2$; horizontal, $y = -1$

4. (a) $35,000

(b) About $73,000

(c) About $221,000

5. 7000 cases of red, 1000 cases of white

CHAPTER 3 Summary and Review

Key Terms and Symbols

3.1 function
domain
range
functional notation
piecewise-defined function

3.2 graph
linear function
piecewise linear function
absolute-value function
greatest-integer function
step function

graph reading
vertical-line test

3.3 fixed costs
variable cost
average cost
linear depreciation
rate of change
marginal cost
linear cost function
linear revenue function
break-even point

supply and demand curves
equilibrium point
equilibrium price
equilibrium quantity

3.4 quadratic function
parabola
vertex
axis
quadratic model

3.5 polynomial function
graph of $f(x) = ax^n$

properties of polynomial
   graphs
polynomial models

3.6 rational function
linear rational function
vertical asymptote
horizontal asymptote

Chapter 3 Key Concepts

Functions

A **function** consists of a set of inputs called the **domain,** a set of outputs called the **range,** and a rule by which each input determines exactly one output.

If a vertical line intersects a graph in more than one point, the graph is not that of a function.

Linear Functions

A **linear cost function** has equation $C(x) = mx + b$, where m is the **marginal cost** (the cost of producing one more item) and b is the **fixed cost.**

If $p = f(q)$ gives the price per unit when q units can be supplied and $p = g(q)$ gives the price per unit when q units are demanded, then the **equilibrium price** and **equilibrium quantity** occur at the q-value such that $f(q) = g(q)$.

Quadratic Functions

The **quadratic function** defined by $f(x) = a(x - h)^2 + k$ has a graph that is a **parabola** with vertex (h, k) and axis of symmetry $x = h$. The parabola opens upward if $a > 0$ and downward if $a < 0$.

If the equation is in the form $f(x) = ax^2 + bx + c$, the vertex is $\left(-\dfrac{b}{2a}, f\left(-\dfrac{b}{2a}\right)\right)$.

Polynomial Functions

When $|x|$ is large, the graph of a **polynomial function** resembles the graph of its highest-degree term ax^n. The graph of $f(x) = ax^n$ is described on page 160.

On the graph of a polynomial function of degree n,

  the total number of peaks and valleys is at most $n - 1$;

  the total number of x-intercepts is at most n.

Rational Functions

If a number c makes the denominator of a **rational function** 0, but the numerator nonzero, then the line $x = c$ is a **vertical asymptote** of the graph.

Whenever the values of y approach, but do not equal, some number k as $|x|$ gets larger and larger, the line $y = k$ is a **horizontal asymptote** of the graph.

If the numerator of a rational function is of *smaller* degree than the denominator, then the x-axis is the horizontal asymptote of the graph.

If the numerator and denominator of a rational function are of the *same* degree, say, $f(x) = \dfrac{ax^n + \cdots}{cx^n + \cdots}$, then the line $y = \dfrac{a}{c}$ is the horizontal asymptote of the graph.

Chapter 3 Review Exercises

In Exercises 1–6, state whether the given rule defines a function or not.

1.

x	3	2	1	0	1	2
y	8	5	2	0	−2	−5

2.

x	2	1	0	−1	−2
y	5	3	1	−1	−3

3. $y = \sqrt{x}$

4. $x = |y|$

5. $x = y^2 + 1$

6. $y = 5x - 2$

For the functions in Exercises 7–10, find

(a) $f(6)$;   (b) $f(-2)$;   (c) $f(p)$;   (d) $f(r + 1)$.

7. $f(x) = 4x - 1$ **8.** $f(x) = 3 - 4x$

9. $f(x) = -x^2 + 2x - 4$ **10.** $f(x) = 8 - x - x^2$

11. Let $f(x) = 5x - 3$ and $g(x) = -x^2 + 4x$. Find each of the following:

   (a) $f(-2)$ **(b)** $g(3)$ **(c)** $g(-k)$

   (d) $g(3m)$ **(e)** $g(k - 5)$ **(f)** $f(3 - p)$

12. Let $f(x) = x^2 + x + 1$. Find each of the following:

   (a) $f(3)$ **(b)** $f(1)$ **(c)** $f(4)$

   (d) Based on your answers in parts (a)–(c), is it true that $f(a + b) = f(a) + f(b)$ for all real numbers a and b?

Graph the functions in Exercises 13–24.

13. $f(x) = |x| - 3$ **14.** $f(x) = -|x| - 2$

15. $f(x) = -|x + 1| + 3$ **16.** $f(x) = 2|x - 3| - 4$

17. $f(x) = [x - 3]$ **18.** $f(x) = \left[\frac{1}{2}x - 2\right]$

19. $f(x) = \begin{cases} -4x + 2 & \text{if } x \le 1 \\ 3x - 5 & \text{If } x > 1 \end{cases}$

20. $f(x) = \begin{cases} 3x + 1 & \text{if } x < 2 \\ -x + 4 & \text{if } x \ge 2 \end{cases}$

21. $f(x) = \begin{cases} |x| & \text{if } x < 3 \\ 6 - x & \text{if } x \ge 3 \end{cases}$

22. $f(x) = \sqrt{x^2}$

23. $g(x) = x^2/8 - 3$

24. $h(x) = \sqrt{x} + 2$

25. **Business** Let f be a function that gives the cost to rent a power washer for x hours. The cost is a flat $45 for renting the washer, plus $20 per day or fraction of a day for using the washer.

   (a) Graph f.

   (b) Give the domain and range of f.

   (c) John McDonough wants to rent the washer, but he can spend no more than $90. What is the maximum number of days he can use it?

26. **Business** A tree removal service assesses a $400 fee and then charges $80 per hour for the time on an owner's property.

   (a) Is $750 enough for 5 hours work?

   (b) Graph the ordered pairs (hours, cost).

   (c) Give the domain and range.

27. **Health** The following graph, which tracks the percentage of the female population of the United States who smoke cigarettes, appeared in a report from the Centers for Disease Control and Prevention.

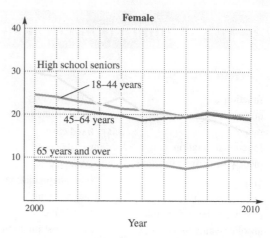

   (a) What is the general trend for female high school seniors? What is the general trend for females 65 years and over?

   (b) Let $x = 0$ correspond to the year 2000. Approximate a linear function for female high school seniors using the points $(0, 30)$ and $(10, 16)$.

   (c) If the trend continues, estimate the percentage of female high school seniors who smoke cigarettes in 2012.

28. **Health** The following graph, which tracks the rate of traumatic brain injury-related deaths per 100,000 people, appeared on a website for the Centers for Disease Control and Prevention.

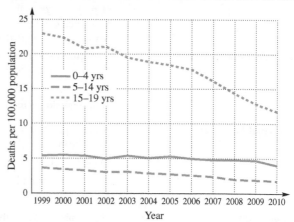

   (a) What is the general trend for youth age 15–19 years?

   (b) Let $x = 9$ correspond to the year 1999. Approximate a linear function to fit the data using 22 as the number of deaths in 2000 and 11 for 2010.

   (c) If the trend continues, estimate the deaths per 100,000 people in the year 2012.

Business *In Exercises 29–32, find the following:*

(a) *the linear cost function;*

(b) *the marginal cost;*

(c) *the average cost per unit to produce 100 units.*

29. Eight units cost $300; fixed cost is $60.

30. Fixed cost is $2000; 36 units cost $8480.

31. Twelve units cost $445; 50 units cost $1585.

32. Thirty units cost $1500; 120 units cost $5640.

33. **Business** The cost of producing x ink cartridges for a printer is given by $C(x) = 24x + 18,000$. Each cartridge can be sold for $28.

    (a) What are the fixed costs?

    (b) Find the revenue function.

    (c) Find the break-even point.

    (d) If the company sells exactly the number of cartridges needed to break even, what is its revenue?

34. **Business** The cost of producing x laser printers is given by $C(x) = 325x + 2,300,000$. Each printer can be sold for $450.

    (a) What are the fixed costs?

    (b) Find the revenue function.

    (c) Find the break-even point.

    (d) If the company sells exactly the number of printers needed to break even, what is its revenue?

35. **Business** Suppose the demand and price for the HBO cable channel are related by $p = -.5q + 30.95$, where p is the monthly price in dollars and q is measured in millions of subscribers. If the price and supply are related by $p = .3q + 2.15$, what are the equilibrium quantity and price?

36. **Business** Suppose the supply and price for prescription-strength Tylenol are related by $p = .0015q + 1$, where p is the price (in dollars) of a 30-day prescription. If the demand is related to price by $p = -.0025q + 64.36$, what are the equilibrium quantity and price?

Without graphing, determine whether each of the following parabolas opens upward or downward, and find its vertex.

37. $f(x) = 3(x - 2)^2 + 6$ 38. $f(x) = 2(x + 3)^2 - 5$

39. $g(x) = -4(x + 1)^2 + 8$ 40. $g(x) = -5(x - 4)^2 - 6$

Graph each of the following quadratic functions, and label its vertex.

41. $f(x) = x^2 - 9$ 42. $f(x) = 5 - 2x^2$

43. $f(x) = x^2 + 2x - 6$ 44. $f(x) = -x^2 + 8x - 1$

45. $f(x) = -x^2 - 6x + 5$ 46. $f(x) = 5x^2 + 20x - 2$

47. $f(x) = 2x^2 - 12x + 10$ 48. $f(x) = -3x^2 - 12x - 2$

Determine whether the functions in Exercises 49–52 have a minimum or a maximum value, and find that value.

49. $f(x) = x^2 + 6x - 2$ 50. $f(x) = x^2 + 4x + 5$

51. $g(x) = -4x^2 + 8x + 3$ 52. $g(x) = -3x^2 - 6x + 3$

Solve each problem.

53. **Business** The weekly future price for a barrel of oil can be approximated by the function $f(x) = -.002x^2 + .644x + 45.32$, where x is the number of weeks since the beginning of the year 2009. How many weeks from the beginning of the year 2009 until the peak oil futures price occurs? What is the peak oil futures price with this model? (Data from: U.S. Energy Information Administration.)

54. **Social Science** The percent of children living below the poverty line can be approximated by the function $f(x) = .096x^2 - 2.40x + 31.7$, where $x = 6$ corresponds to the year 1996. What year saw the lowest percent living in poverty? What was the lowest percent?

55. **Social Science** The declining birth rate in China has demographers believing that the population of China will soon peak. A model for the population (in millions) for China is $g(x) = -.173x^2 + 12.86x + 1152$, where $x = 0$ corresponds to the year 1990. According to this model, what year will China reach its peak population? What is the estimate of the peak population? (Data from: U.S. Census Bureau.)

56. **Business** The amount of energy (in kilowatt hours) a new refrigerator typically used for a year of operation can be approximated by the function $h(x) = -1.44x^2 + 220x - 6953$, where $x = 50$ corresponds to the year 1950. According to this model, what year did peak electrical use occur? What was that amount? (Data from: U.S. Energy Information Administration.)

57. **Business** The following table shows the average cost of tuition and fees at private colleges in various years. (Data from: U.S. Center for Educational Statistics.)

Year	Cost
1975	3672
1980	5470
1985	8885
1990	12,910
1995	17,208
2000	21,373
2005	26,908
2010	32,026

    (a) Let $x = 5$ correspond to the year 1975. Find a quadratic function $f(x) = a(x - h)^2 + k$ that models these data using $(5, 3672)$ as the vertex and the data for 2005.

    (b) Estimate the average tuition and fees at private colleges in 2015.

58. **Social Science** According the U.S. Department of Justice, the following table gives the number (in thousands) of violent crimes committed in the given years.

Year	Crimes
2004	1360
2005	1391
2006	1418
2007	1408
2008	1393
2009	1326
2010	1246

    (a) Let $x = 4$ correspond to the year 2004. Find a quadratic function $f(x) = a(x - h)^2 + k$ that models these data using $(6, 1418)$ as the vertex and the data for 2009.

    (b) Estimate the number of violent crimes in 2012.

59. Business Use the data from Exercise 57 and use quadratic regression to find a function g that models these data.

(a) Give the function.

(b) Graph the function with the data points.

(c) Find the estimated tuition with this model for the year 2015.

60. Business Use the data from Exercise 58 and use quadratic regression to find a function g that models these data.

(a) Give the function.

(b) Graph the function with the data points.

(c) Find the estimated number of violent crimes with this model for the year 2012.

Graph each of the following polynomial functions.

61. $f(x) = x^4 - 5$ **62.** $g(x) = x^3 - 4x$

63. $f(x) = x(x - 4)(x + 1)$

64. $f(x) = (x - 1)(x + 2)(x - 3)$

65. $f(x) = x^4 - 5x^2 - 6$

66. $f(x) = x^4 - 7x^2 - 8$

Use a graphing calculator to do Exercises 67–70.

67. Business The demand equation for automobile oil filters is

$$p = -.000012q^3 - .00498q^2 + .1264q + 1508,$$

where p is in dollars and q is in thousands of items. The supply equation is

$$p = -.000001q^3 + .00097q^2 + 2q.$$

Find the equilibrium quantity and the equilibrium price.

68. Business The average cost (in dollars) per item of manufacturing x thousand cans of spray paint is given by

$$A(x) = -.000006x^4 + .0017x^3 + .03x^2 - 24x + 1110.$$

How many cans should be manufactured if the average cost is to be as low as possible? What is the average cost in that case?

69. Business The revenue (in millions of dollars) for the Exxon Mobil Corporation can be approximated by the function $R(x) = 1558x^3 - 36,587x^2 + 283,469x - 329,027$ where $x = 3$ corresponds to the year 2003. The cost function is approximated by $C(x) = 1261x^3 - 29,686x^2 + 233,069x - 249,868$ again with $x = 3$ corresponding to the year 2003. (Data from: www.morningstar.com.)

(a) Find the revenue for the year 2010.

(b) Find the costs for the year 2010.

(c) Find the profit function $P(x)$.

(d) Find the profit for the years 2010 and 2012.

70. Health The following table shows the average remaining life expectancy (in years) for a person in the United States at selected ages. (Data from: National Center for Health Statistics.)

Current Age	Birth	20	40	60	80	90	100
Life Expectancy	77.8	58.8	39.9	22.6	9.2	5.0	2.6

(a) Let birth = 0, and plot the data points.

(b) Use quartic regression to find a fourth-degree polynomial $f(x)$ that models the data.

(c) What is the remaining life expectancy of a person of age 25? age 35? age 50?

(d) What is the life expectancy of a person who is exactly your age?

List the vertical and horizontal asymptotes of each function, and sketch its graph.

71. $f(x) = \dfrac{1}{x - 3}$ **72.** $f(x) = \dfrac{-2}{x + 4}$

73. $f(x) = \dfrac{-3}{2x - 4}$ **74.** $f(x) = \dfrac{5}{3x + 7}$

75. $g(x) = \dfrac{5x - 2}{4x^2 - 4x - 3}$ **76.** $g(x) = \dfrac{x^2}{x^2 - 1}$

77. Business The average cost per carton of producing x cartons of cocoa is given by

$$A(x) = \frac{650}{2x + 40}.$$

Find the average cost per carton to make the given number of cartons.

(a) 10 cartons   (b) 50 cartons   (c) 70 cartons

(d) 100 cartons   (e) Graph $C(x)$.

78. Business The cost and revenue functions (in dollars) for a frozen-yogurt shop are given by

$$C(x) = \frac{400x + 400}{x + 4} \quad \text{and} \quad R(x) = 100x,$$

where x is measured in hundreds of units.

(a) Graph $C(x)$ and $R(x)$ on the same set of axes.

(b) What is the break-even point for this shop?

(c) If the profit function is given by $P(x)$, does $P(1)$ represent a profit or a loss?

(d) Does $P(4)$ represent a profit or a loss?

79. Business The supply and demand functions for the yogurt shop in Exercise 78 are

$$\text{supply: } p = \frac{q^2}{4} + 25 \quad \text{and} \quad \text{demand: } p = \frac{500}{q},$$

where p is the price in dollars for q hundred units of yogurt.

(a) Graph both functions on the same axes, and from the graph, estimate the equilibrium point.

(b) Give the q-intervals where supply exceeds demand.

(c) Give the q-intervals where demand exceeds supply.

80. Business A cost–benefit curve for pollution control is given by

$$y = \frac{9.2x}{106 - x},$$

where y is the cost, in thousands of dollars, of removing x percent of a specific industrial pollutant. Find y for each of the given values of x.

(a) $x = 50$ (b) $x = 98$

(c) What percent of the pollutant can be removed for $22,000?

Case Study 3 Architectural Arches

From ancient Roman bridges to medieval cathedrals, modern highway tunnels, and fast-food restaurants, arches are everywhere. For centuries builders and architects have used them for both structural and aesthetic reasons. There are arches of almost every material, from stone to steel. Some of the most common arch shapes are the parabolic arch, the semicircular arch, and the Norman arch (a semicircular arch set atop a rectangle, as shown here).

Parabolic   Semicircular   Norman

Note that every arch is symmetric around a vertical line through its center. The part of the arch on the left side of the line is mirror image of the part on the right side, with the line being the mirror. To describe these arches mathematically, suppose that each one is located on a coordinate plane with the origin at the intersection of the verticle symmetry line and a horizontal line at the base of the arch. For a parabolic arch, the situation looks like this, for some numbers k and c:

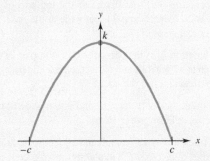

Since $(0, k)$ is the vertex, the arch is the graph of a function of the form

$$f(x) = a(x - 0)^2 + k,$$

or

$$f(x) = ax^2 + k.$$

Note that the point $(c, 0)$ is on the arch, which means that $f(c) = 0$. Therefore, we can make the following derivation:

$$f(x) = ax^2 + k$$
$$f(c) = ac^2 + k \qquad \text{Let } x = c.$$
$$0 = ac^2 + k \qquad f(c) = 0.$$
$$-k = ac^2 \qquad \text{Subtract } k \text{ from both sides.}$$
$$a = \frac{-k}{c^2} \qquad \text{Divide both sides by } c^2.$$

So the function whose graph is the shape of the parabolic arch is

$$f(x) = \frac{-k}{c^2}x^2 + k \qquad (-c \le x \le c),$$

where k is the height of the arch at its highest point and $2c$ (the distance from $-c$ to c) is the width of the arch at its base. For example, a 12-foot-high arch that is 14 feet wide at its base has $k = 12$ and $c = 7$, so it is the graph of

$$f(x) = \frac{-12}{49}x^2 + 12.$$

In order to describe semicircular and Norman arches, we must first find the equation of a circle of radius r with center at the origin. Consider a point (x, y) on the graph and the right triangle it determines:[*]

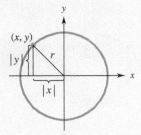

The horizontal side of the triangle has length $|x|$ (the distance from x to 0 on the x-axis), and the vertical side has length $|y|$ (the distance from y to 0 on the y-axis). The hypotenuse has length r (the radius of the circle). By the Pythagorean theorem,

$$|x|^2 + |y|^2 = r^2,$$

which is equivalent to

$$x^2 + y^2 = r^2,$$

because the absolute value of x is either x or $-x$ (see the definition on page 8), so $|x|^2 = (\pm x)^2 = x^2$, and similarly for y. Solving this equation for y shows that

$$y^2 = r^2 - x^2$$
$$y = \sqrt{r^2 - x^2} \quad \text{or} \quad y = -\sqrt{r^2 - x^2}.$$

In the first equation, y is always positive or 0 (because square roots are nonnegative), so its graph is the top half of the circle. Similarly, the second equation gives the bottom half of the circle.

Now consider a semicircle arch of radius r:

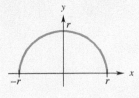

---

[*]The figure shows a point in the second quadrant, where x is negative and y is positive, but the same argument will work for points in other quadrants.

The arch is the top half of a circle with center at the origin. By the preceding paragraph, it is the graph of the function

$$g(x) = \sqrt{r^2 - x^2} \qquad (-r \le x \le r).$$

For instance, a semicircular arch that is 8 feet high has $r = 8$ and is the graph of

$$g(x) = \sqrt{8^2 - x^2} = \sqrt{64 - x^2} \qquad (-8 \le x \le 8).$$

A Norman arch is not the graph of a function (since its sides are vertical lines), but we can describe the semicircular top of the arch.

For example, consider a Norman arch whose top has radius 8 and whose sides are 10 feet high. If the top of the arch were at ground level, then its equation would be $g(x) = \sqrt{64 - x^2}$, as we just saw. But in the actual arch, this semicircular part is raised 10 feet, so it is the graph of

$$h(x) = g(x) + 10 = \sqrt{64 - x^2} + 10 \qquad (-8 \le x \le 8),$$

as shown below.

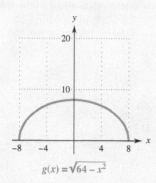

$g(x) = \sqrt{64 - x^2}$

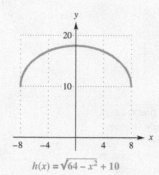

$h(x) = \sqrt{64 - x^2} + 10$

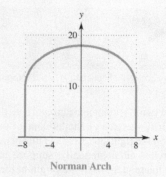

Norman Arch

Exercises

1. Write a function $f(x)$ that describes a parabolic arch which is 20 feet tall and 14 feet wide at the base.

2. Write a function $f(x)$ that describes a parabolic arch that is 25 feet tall and 30 feet wide at its base.

3. Write a function $g(x)$ that describes a semicircular arch that is 25 feet tall. How wide is the arch at its base?

4. Write a function $g(x)$ that describes a semicircular arch that is 40 feet tall. How wide is the arch at its base?

5. Write a function $h(x)$ that describes the top part of a Norman arch that is 20 feet tall and 24 feet wide at the base. How high are the vertical sides of this arch?

6. Write a function $h(x)$ that describes the top part of a Norman arch which is 32 feet tall and 44 feet wide at the base. How high are the vertical sides of this arch?

7. Would a truck that is 12 feet tall and 9 feet wide fit through all of the arches in Exercises 1, 3, and 5?

8. Would a truck that is 13 feet tall and 10 feet wide fit through all of the arches in Exercises 2, 4, and 6?

Extended Projects

1. Find an example of a parabolic, circular, or Norman arch (or all three) on your campus. Measure the dimensions and then write the equation for the arch in a manner similar to Exercises 1–8.

2. Find the dimensions of the fleet of Good Year Blimps that are currently in use. Determine the equation of a semicircular arch that would need to be built for the entrance to a facility that would house the blimps when not in use.

Exponential and Logarithmic Functions

4

CHAPTER

CHAPTER OUTLINE

4.1 Exponential Functions
4.2 Applications of Exponential Functions
4.3 Logarithmic Functions
4.4 Logarithmic and Exponential Equations

CASE STUDY 4
Gapminder.org

Population growth (of humans, fish, bacteria, etc.), compound interest, radioactive decay, and a host of other phenomena can be described by exponential functions. See Exercises 42–50 on page 191. Archeologists sometimes use carbon-14 dating to determine the approximate age of an artifact (such as a dinosaur skeleton or a mummy). This procedure involves using logarithms to solve an exponential equation. See Exercises 70–72 on page 217. The Richter scale for measuring the magnitude of an earthquake is a logarithmic function. See Exercises 73–74 on page 217.

Exponential and logarithmic functions play a key role in management, economics, the social and physical sciences, and engineering. We begin with exponential growth and exponential decay functions.

4.1 Exponential Functions

In polynomial functions such as $f(x) = x^2 + 5x - 4$, the variable is raised to various constant exponents. In **exponential functions,** such as

$$f(x) = 10^x, \quad g(x) = 750(1.05^x), \quad h(x) = 3^{.6x}, \quad \text{and} \quad k(x) = 2^{-x^2},$$

the variable is in the exponent and the **base** is a positive constant. We begin with the simplest type of exponential function, whose rule is of the form $f(x) = a^x$, with $a > 0$.

Example 1 Graph $f(x) = 2^x$, and estimate the height of the graph when $x = 50$.

Solution Either use a graphing calculator or graph by hand: Make a table of values, plot the corresponding points, and join them by a smooth curve, as in Figure 4.1. The graph has y-intercept 1 and rises steeply to the right. Note that the graph gets very close to the x-axis on the left, but always lies *above* the axis (because *every* power of 2 is positive).

x	y
-3	$1/8$
-2	$1/4$
-1	$1/2$
0	1
1	2
2	4
3	8

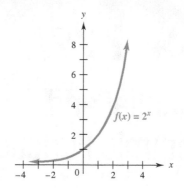

Figure 4.1

The graph illustrates **exponential growth,** which is far more explosive than polynomial growth. At $x = 50$, the graph would be 2^{50} units high. Since there are approximately 6 units to the inch in Figure 4.1, and since there are 12 inches to the foot and 5280 feet to the mile, the height of the graph at $x = 50$ would be approximately

$$\frac{2^{50}}{6 \times 12 \times 5280} \approx 2{,}961{,}647{,}482 \text{ miles!}$$

When $a > 1$, the graph of the exponential function $h(x) = a^x$ has the same basic shape as the graph of $f(x) = 2^x$, as illustrated in Figure 4.2 and summarized in the next box.

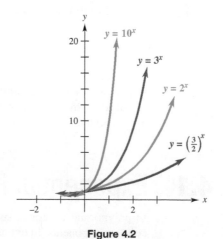

Figure 4.2

When $a > 1$, the function $f(x) = a^x$ has the set of all real numbers as its domain. Its graph has the shape shown on the following page and all five of the properties listed below.

✓ Checkpoint 1

(a) Fill in this table:

x	$g(x) = 3^x$
-3	
-2	
-1	
0	
1	
2	
3	

(b) Sketch the graph of $g(x) = 3^x$.

Answers to Checkpoint exercises are found at the end of the section.

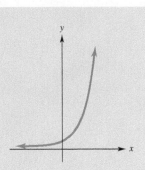

1. The graph is above the *x*-axis.
2. The *y*-intercept is 1.
3. The graph climbs steeply to the right.
4. The negative *x*-axis is a horizontal asymptote.
5. The larger the base *a*, the more steeply the graph rises to the right.

Example 2   Consider the function $g(x) = 2^{-x}$.

(a) Rewrite the rule of *g* so that no minus signs appear in it.

Solution   By the definition of negative exponents,

$$g(x) = 2^{-x} = \frac{1}{2^x} = \left(\frac{1}{2}\right)^x.$$

(b) Graph *g*(*x*).

Solution   Either use a graphing calculator or graph by hand in the usual way, as shown in Figure 4.3.

x	$y = 2^{-x}$
−3	8
−2	4
−1	2
0	1
1	1/2
2	1/4
3	1/8

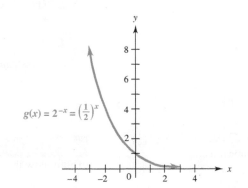

Figure 4.3

The graph falls sharply to the right, but never touches the *x*-axis, because every power of $\frac{1}{2}$ is positive. This is an example of **exponential decay.** ✓2

✓ **Checkpoint 2**

Graph $h(x) = (1/3)^x$.

When $0 < a < 1$, the graph of $k(x) = a^x$ has the same basic shape as the graph of $g(x) = (1/2)^x$, as illustrated in Figure 4.4 and summarized in the next box, on the following page.

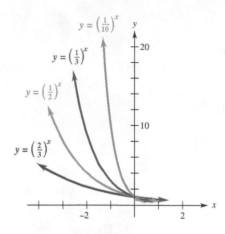

Figure 4.4

When $0 < a < 1$, the function $f(x) = a^x$ has the set of all real numbers as its domain. Its graph has the shape shown here and all five of the properties listed.

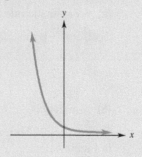

1. The graph is above the x-axis.
2. The y-intercept is 1.
3. The graph falls sharply to the right.
4. The positive x-axis is a horizontal asymptote.
5. The smaller the base a, the more steeply the graph falls to the right.

✓ **Checkpoint 3** ⟋

Use a graphing calculator to graph $f(x) = 4^x$ and $g(x) = \left(\frac{1}{4}\right)^x$ on the same screen.

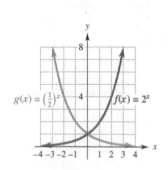

Figure 4.5

Example 3   In each case, graph $f(x)$ and $g(x)$ on the same set of axes and explain how the graphs are related.

(a) $f(x) = 2^x$ and $g(x) = (1/2)^x$

Solution   The graphs of f and g are shown in Figures 4.1 and 4.3, above. Placing them on the same set of axes, we obtain Figure 4.5. It shows that the graph of $g(x) = (1/2)^x$ is the mirror image of the graph of $f(x) = 2^x$, with the y-axis as the mirror. ✓3

(b) $f(x) = 3^{1-x}$ and $g(x) = 3^{-x}$

Solution   Choose values of x that make the exponent positive, zero, and negative, and plot the corresponding points. The graphs are shown in Figure 4.6, on the following page. The graph of $f(x) = 3^{1-x}$ has the same shape as the graph of $g(x) = 3^{-x}$, but is shifted 1 unit to the right, making the y-intercept $(0, 3)$ rather than $(0, 1)$.

(c) $f(x) = 2^{.6x}$ and $g(x) = 2^x$

Solution   Comparing the graphs of $f(x) = 2^{.6x}$ and $g(x) = 2^x$ in Figure 4.7, we see that the graphs are both increasing, but the graph of $f(x)$ rises at a slower rate. This happens because of the .6 in the exponent. If the coefficient of x were greater than 1, the graph would rise at a faster rate than the graph of $g(x) = 2^x$. ✔4

✓Checkpoint 4

Graph $f(x) = 2^{x+1}$.

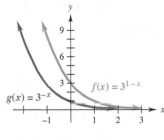

Figure 4.6

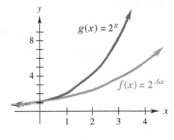

Figure 4.7

When the exponent involves a nonlinear expression in x, the graph of an exponential function may have a much different shape than the preceding ones have.

Example 4   Graph $f(x) = 2^{-x^2}$.

Solution   Either use a graphing calculator or plot points and connect them with a smooth curve, as in Figure 4.8. The graph is symmetric about the y-axis; that is, if the figure were folded on the y-axis, the two halves would match. This graph has the x-axis as a horizontal asymptote. The domain is still all real numbers, but here the range is $0 < y \leq 1$. Graphs such as this are important in probability, where the normal curve has an equation similar to $f(x)$ in this example. ✔5

✓Checkpoint 5

Graph $f(x) = (\frac{1}{2})^{-x^2}$.

x	y
-2	$1/16$
-1.5	$.21$
-1	$1/2$
$-.5$	$.84$
0	1
$.5$	$.84$
1	$1/2$
1.5	$.21$
2	$1/16$

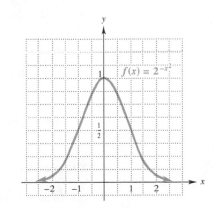

Figure 4.8

The Number e

In Case 5, we shall see that a certain irrational number, denoted e, plays an important role in the compounding of interest. This number e also arises naturally in a variety of other mathematical and scientific contexts. To 12 decimal places,

$$e \approx 2.718281828459.$$

Perhaps the single most useful exponential function is the function defined by $f(x) = e^x$.

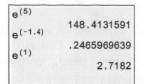

Figure 4.9

✓ 6

✓ **Checkpoint 6**

Evaluate the following powers of e.

(a) $e^{.06}$

(b) $e^{-.06}$

(c) $e^{2.30}$

(d) $e^{-2.30}$

TECHNOLOGY TIP To evaluate powers of e with a calculator, use the e^x key, as in Figure 4.9. The figure also shows how to display the decimal expansion of e by calculating e^1. ✓ 6

In Figure 4.10, the functions defined by

$$g(x) = 2^x, \qquad f(x) = e^x, \qquad \text{and} \qquad h(x) = 3^x$$

are graphed for comparison.

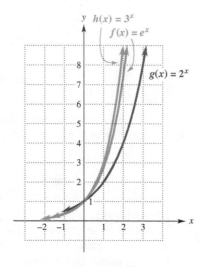

Figure 4.10

Example 5 **Business** The amount of wine (in millions of gallons) consumed in the United States can be approximated by the function

$$f(x) = 139.6e^{.031x},$$

where $x = 0$ corresponds to the year 1950. (Data from: www.wineinstitute.org.)

(a) How much wine was consumed in the year 1970?

Solution Since 1970 corresponds to $x = 20$, we evaluate $f(20)$:

$$f(20) = 139.6e^{.031(20)} \approx 260 \text{ million gallons.}$$

So the consumption was approximately 260 million gallons.

(b) How much wine was consumed in the year 2010?

Solution Since 2010 corresponds to $x = 60$, we evaluate $f(60)$:

$$f(60) = 139.6e^{.031(60)} \approx 897 \text{ million gallons.}$$

So the consumption was approximately 897 million gallons.

(c) Use a graphing calculator to determine when consumption will reach 1000 million gallons.

Solution Since f measures consumption in millions of gallons, we must solve the equation $f(x) = 1000$, that is

$$139.6e^{.031x} = 1000.$$

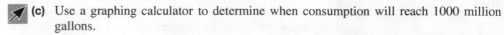

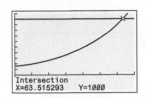

Figure 4.11

 Checkpoint 7

Per-person wine consumption (in gallons) can be approximated by $g(x) = .875e^{.019x}$, where $x = 0$ corresponds to the year 1950.

(a) Estimate the per-person wine consumption in 1990.

(b) Determine when the per-person consumption reached 2.0 gallons.

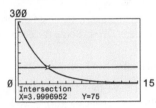

Figure 4.12

One way to do this is to find the intersection point of the graphs of $y = 139.6e^{.031x}$ and $y = 1000$. (The calculator's intersection finder is in the same menu as its root [or zero] finder.) Figure 4.11 shows that this point is approximately $(63.5, 1000)$. Hence, consumption reached 1000 million gallons when $x \approx 63.5$, that is, in 2013. ✔️7

Example 6 Health When a patient is given a 300-mg dose of the drug cimetidine intravenously, the amount C of the drug in the bloodstream t hours later is given by $C(t) = 300e^{-.3466t}$.

(a) How much of the drug is in the bloodstream after 3 hours and after 10 hours?

Solution Evaluate the function at $t = 3$ and $t = 10$:

$$C(3) = 300e^{-.3466*3} \approx 106.1 \text{ mg};$$
$$C(10) = 300e^{-.3466*10} \approx 9.4 \text{ mg}.$$

(b) Doctors want to give a patient a second 300-mg dose of cimetidine when its level in her bloodstream decreases to 75 mg. Use graphing technology to determine when this should be done.

Solution The second dose should be given when $C(t) = 75$, so we must solve the equation

$$300e^{-.3466t} = 75.$$

Using the method of Example 5(c), we graph $y = 300e^{-.3466t}$ and $y = 75$ and find their intersection point. Figure 4.12 shows that this point is approximately $(4, 75)$. So the second dose should be given 4 hours after the first dose.

4.1 Exercises

Classify each function as linear, quadratic, or exponential.

1. $f(x) = 6^x$

2. $g(x) = -5x$

3. $h(x) = 4x^2 - x + 5$

4. $k(x) = 4^{x+3}$

5. $f(x) = 675(1.055^x)$

6. $g(x) = 12e^{x^2+1}$

Without graphing,

(a) *describe the shape of the graph of each function;*

(b) *find the second coordinates of the points with first coordinates 0 and 1. (See Examples 1–3.)*

7. $f(x) = .6^x$

8. $g(x) = 4^{-x}$

9. $h(x) = 2^{.5x}$

10. $k(x) = 5(3^x)$

11. $f(x) = e^{-x}$

12. $g(x) = 3(16^{x/4})$

Graph each function. (See Examples 1–3.)

13. $f(x) = 3^x$

14. $g(x) = 3^{.5x}$

15. $f(x) = 2^{x/2}$

16. $g(x) = e^{x/4}$

17. $f(x) = (1/5)^x$

18. $g(x) = 2^{3x}$

19. Graph these functions on the same axes.

(a) $f(x) = 2^x$ (b) $g(x) = 2^{x+3}$ (c) $h(x) = 2^{x-4}$

(d) If c is a positive constant, explain how the graphs of $y = 2^{x+c}$ and $y = 2^{x-c}$ are related to the graph of $f(x) = 2^x$.

20. Graph these functions on the same axes.

(a) $f(x) = 3^x$ (b) $g(x) = 3^x + 2$ (c) $h(x) = 3^x - 4$

(d) If c is a positive constant, explain how the graphs of $y = 3^x + c$ and $y = 3^x - c$ are related to the graph of $f(x) = 3^x$.

The accompanying figure shows the graphs of $y = a^x$ for $a = 1.8, 2.3, 3.2, .4, .75,$ and $.31$. They are identified by letter, but not necessarily in the same order as the values just given. Use your knowledge of how the exponential function behaves for various powers of a to match each lettered graph with the correct value of a.

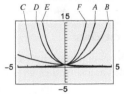

21. A

22. B

23. C

24. D

25. E

26. F

In Exercises 27 and 28, the graph of an exponential function with base a is given. Follow the directions in parts (a)–(f) in each exercise.

27.

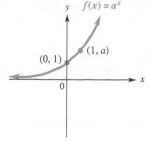

$f(x) = a^x$

(0, 1)

(1, a)

(a) Is $a > 1$ or is $0 < a < 1$?

(b) Give the domain and range of f.

(c) Sketch the graph of $g(x) = -a^x$.

(d) Give the domain and range of g.

(e) Sketch the graph of $h(x) = a^{-x}$.

(f) Give the domain and range of h.

28.

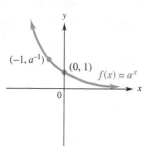

$(-1, a^{-1})$

(0, 1)

$f(x) = a^x$

(a) Is $a > 1$ or is $0 < a < 1$?

(b) Give the domain and range of f.

(c) Sketch the graph of $g(x) = a^x + 2$.

(d) Give the domain and range of g.

(e) Sketch the graph of $h(x) = a^{x+2}$.

(f) Give the domain and range of h.

29. If $f(x) = a^x$ and $f(3) = 27$, find the following values of $f(x)$.

(a) $f(1)$ (b) $f(-1)$ (c) $f(2)$ (d) $f(0)$

30. Give a rule of the form $f(x) = a^x$ to define the exponential function whose graph contains the given point.

(a) $(3, 8)$ (b) $(-3, 64)$

Graph each function. (See Example 4.)

31. $f(x) = 2^{-x^2+2}$ **32.** $g(x) = 2^{x^2-2}$

33. $f(x) = x \cdot 2^x$ **34.** $f(x) = x^2 \cdot 2^x$

Work the following exercises.

35. **Finance** If $1 is deposited into an account paying 6% per year compounded annually, then after t years the account will contain

$$y = (1 + .06)^t = (1.06)^t$$

dollars.

(a) Use a calculator to complete the following table:

t	0	1	2	3	4	5	6	7	8	9	10
y	1					1.34					1.79

(b) Graph $y = (1.06)^t$.

36. **Finance** If money loses value at the rate of 3% per year, the value of $1 in t years is given by

$$y = (1 - .03)^t = (.97)^t.$$

(a) Use a calculator to complete the following table:

t	0	1	2	3	4	5	6	7	8	9	10
y	1					.86					.74

(b) Graph $y = (.97)^t$.

Work these problems. (See Example 5.)

37. **Finance** If money loses value, then as time passes, it takes more dollars to buy the same item. Use the results of Exercise 36(a) to answer the following questions.

(a) Suppose a house costs $105,000 today. Estimate the cost of the same house in 10 years. (*Hint:* Solve the equation $.74t = \$105,000$.)

(b) Estimate the cost of a $50 textbook in 8 years.

38. **Natural Science** Biologists have found that the oxygen consumption of yearling salmon is given by $g(x) = 100e^{.7x}$, where x is the speed in feet per second. Find each of the following.

(a) the oxygen consumption when the fish are still;

(b) the oxygen consumption when the fish are swimming at a speed of 2 feet per second.

39. **Business** The number of cell phone subscribers (in millions) can be approximated by

$$f(x) = 116.75e^{.101x},$$

where $x = 0$ corresponds to the year 2000. Estimate the number of cell phone subscribers in the following years. (Data from: CTIA-The Wireless Association.)

(a) 2004   (b) 2010   (c) 2011

40. **Business** The monthly payment on a car loan at 12% interest per year on the unpaid balance is given by

$$f(n) = \frac{P}{\dfrac{1 - 1.01^{-n}}{.01}},$$

where P is the amount borrowed and n is the number of months over which the loan is paid back. Find the monthly payment for each of the following loans.

(a) $8000 for 48 months   **(b)** $8000 for 24 months

(c) $6500 for 36 months   **(d)** $6500 for 60 months

41. Natural Science The amount of plutonium remaining from 1 kilogram after x years is given by the function $W(x) = 2^{-x/24,360}$. How much will be left after

(a) 1000 years?   **(b)** 10,000 years?   **(c)** 15,000 years?

(d) Estimate how long it will take for the 1 kilogram to decay to half its original weight. Your answer may help to explain why nuclear waste disposal is a serious problem.

Business *The scrap value of a machine is the value of the machine at the end of its useful life. By one method of calculating scrap value, where it is assumed that a constant percentage of value is lost annually, the scrap value is given by*

$$S = C(1 - r)^n,$$

where C is the original cost, n is the useful life of the machine in years, and r is the constant annual percentage of value lost. Find the scrap value for each of the following machines.

42. Original cost, $68,000; life, 10 years; annual rate of value loss, 8%

43. Original cost, $244,000; life, 12 years; annual rate of value loss, 15%

44. Use the graphs of $f(x) = 2^x$ and $g(x) = 2^{-x}$ (not a calculator) to explain why $2^x + 2^{-x}$ is approximately equal to 2^x when x is very large.

Work the following problems. (See Examples 5 and 6.)

45. Social Science There were fewer than a billion people on Earth when Thomas Jefferson died in 1826, and there are now more than 6 billion. If the world population continues to grow as expected, the population (in billions) in year t will be given by the function $P(t) = 4.834(1.01^{(t-1980)})$. (Data from: U.S. Census Bureau.) Estimate the world population in the following years.

(a) 2005   **(b)** 2010   **(c)** 2030

(d) What will the world population be when you reach 65 years old?

46. Business The number of unique monthly visitors (in thousands) for Pinterest.com can be approximated by the function

$$g(x) = 325(1.29^x),$$

where $x = 1$ corresponds to the month of May, 2011. Estimate the number of unique monthly visitors for the following months. (Data from: cnet.com and techcrunch.com.)

(a) September 2011   **(b)** May 2012

(c) If the model remains accurate, find the month in which the number of unique visitors surpasses 40,000,000.

47. Economics Projections of the gross domestic product (GDP—in trillions of U.S. dollars), adjusted for purchasing power parity, are approximated as follows.

China: $f(x) = 10.21(1.103)^x$

United States: $g(x) = 14.28(1.046)^x$,

where $x = 1$ corresponds to the year 2011. (Data from: International Monetary Fund.) Find the projected GDP for the given years.

(a) 2012   **(b)** 2020   **(c)** 2050

(d) Use technology to determine when the Chinese GDP surpasses the U.S. GDP according to these projections. (*Hint:* Either graph both functions and find their intersection point or use the table feature of a graphing calculator.)

48. Business The amount of electricity (in trillion kilowatt hours) generated by natural gas in the United States can be approximated by the function

$$f(x) = .10(1.05)^x,$$

where $x = 0$ corresponds to the year 1960. (Data from: Energy Information Administration.) How many kilowatt hours were generated in the given years?

(a) 1990

(b) 2002

(c) In what year did the kilowatt hours hit 1 trillion?

49. Business The number of total subscribers (in millions) to Netflix, Inc. can be approximated by the function

$$g(x) = 9.78(1.07)^x,$$

where $x = 1$ corresponds to the first quarter of the year 2009, $x = 2$ corresponds to the second quarter of the year 2009, etc. Find the number of subscribers for the following quarters. (Data from: The *Wall Street Journal* and The *Associated Press*.)

(a) First quarter of 2010

(b) Fourth quarter of 2012

(c) Find the quarter and year when total subscribers surpassed 25 million.

50. Business The monthly rate for basic cable (in dollars) can be approximated by the function

$$h(x) = 8.71e^{.06x}, \quad (5 \le x \le 30)$$

where $x = 5$ corresponds to the year 1985. (Data from: ProQuest Statistical Abstract of the United States: 2013.)

(a) Find the rate in the year 2000 and the year 2009.

(b) When did spending reach $40 a month.

51. Business The amount of music (in billions of hours) listened to on the on-line streaming site Pandora can be approximated by the function

$$f(x) = .54e^{.191x},$$

where $x = 1$ corresponds to the first quarter of the year 2011, $x = 2$ corresponds to the second quarter of the year 2011, etc. Find the hours listened for the following quarters. (Data from: The *Wall Street Journal*.)

(a) Fourth quarter of 2011

(b) Third quarter of 2012

(c) When did the hours exceed 2.5 billion hours?

52. Business The stock price (in dollars) for Apple, Inc. can be approximated by the function

$$g(x) = 2.23e^{.404x} \quad (4 \le x \le 13),$$

where $x = 4$ corresponds to the year 2004. Use this model to approximate the price in the following years. (Data from: www.morningstar.com.)

(a) 2007

(b) 2013

(c) In what year, according to the model, did the price reach $300?

53. Health When a patient is given a 20-mg dose of aminophylline intravenously, the amount C of the drug in the bloodstream t hours later is given by $C(t) = 20e^{-.1155t}$. How much aminophylline remains in the bloodstream after the given numbers of hours?

(a) 4 hours

(b) 8 hours

(c) Approximately when does the amount of aminophylline decrease to 3.5 mg?

54. The accompanying figure shows the graph of an exponential growth function $f(x) = Pa^x$.

(a) Find P. [*Hint:* What is $f(0)$?]

(b) Find a. [*Hint:* What is $f(2)$?]

(c) Find $f(5)$.

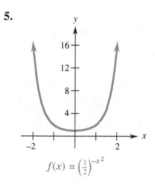

✓ Checkpoint Answers

1. (a) The entries in the second column are 1/27, 1/9, 1/3, 1, 3, 9, 27, respectively.

(b)

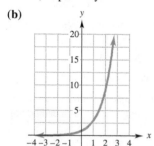

2.

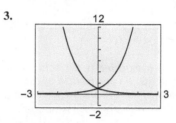

3.

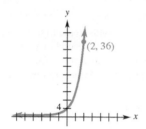

4.

5.

$$f(x) = \left(\tfrac{1}{2}\right)^{-x^2}$$

6. (a) 1.06184   **(b)** .94176

(c) 9.97418   **(d)** .10026

7. (a) About 1.87 gallons per person

(b) 1993

4.2 Applications of Exponential Functions

In many situations in biology, economics, and the social sciences, a quantity changes at a rate proportional to the quantity present. For example, a country's population might be increasing at a rate of 1.3% a year. In such cases, the amount present at time t is given by an **exponential growth function.**

It is understood that growth can involve either growing larger or growing smaller.

Exponential Growth Function

Under normal conditions, growth can be described by a function of the form

$$f(t) = y_0 e^{kt} \quad \text{or} \quad f(t) = y_0 b^t,$$

where $f(t)$ is the amount present at time t, y_0 is the amount present at time $t = 0$, and k and b are constants that depend on the rate of growth.

When $f(t) = y_0 e^{kt}$, and $k > 0$, we describe $f(t)$ as modeling exponential growth, and when $k < 0$, we describe $f(t)$ as modeling exponential decay. When $f(t) = y_0 b^t$, and $b > 1$, we describe $f(t)$ as modeling exponential growth, and when $0 < b < 1$, we describe $f(t)$ as modeling exponential decay.

Example 1   **Finance**   Since the early 1970s, the amount of the total credit market (debt owed by the government, companies, or individuals) as a percentage of gross domestic product (GDP) can be approximated by the exponential function

$$f(t) = y_0 e^{.02t},$$

where t is time in years, $t = 0$ corresponds to the year 1970, and $f(t)$ is a percent. (Data from: Federal Reserve.)

(a) If the amount of total credit market was 155% of the GDP in 1970, find the percent in the year 2005.

Solution   Since y_0 represents the percent when $t = 0$ (that is, in 1970) we have $y_0 = 155$. So the growth function is $f(t) = 155e^{.02t}$. To find the percent of the total credit market in the year 2005, evaluate $f(t)$ at $t = 35$ (which corresponds to the year 2005):

$$f(t) = 155e^{.02t}$$
$$f(35) = 155e^{.02(35)} \approx 312.$$

Hence, the percent of the total credit market in the year 2005 was approximately 312% of GDP.

(b) If the model remains accurate, what percent of GDP will the total credit market be in the year 2015?

Solution   Since 2015 corresponds to $t = 45$, evaluate the function at $t = 45$:

$$f(45) = 155e^{.02(45)} \approx 381\%.$$

✓ **Checkpoint 1**

Suppose the number of bacteria in a culture at time t is

$$y = 500e^{.4t},$$

where t is measured in hours.

(a) How many bacteria are present initially?

(b) How many bacteria are present after 10 hours?

Example 2   **Business**   Cigarette consumption in the United States has been decreasing for some time. Based on data from the Centers for Disease Control and Prevention, the number (in billions) of cigarettes consumed can be approximated by the function

$$g(x) = 436e^{-.036x},$$

with $x = 0$ corresponding to the year 2000.

(a) Find the number of cigarettes consumed in the years 2005 and 2010.

Solution   The years 2005 and 2010 correspond to $x = 5$ and $x = 10$, respectively. We can evaluate $g(x)$ at these values for x:

$$g(5) = 436e^{-.036(5)} \approx 364 \text{ billion in the year 2005};$$
$$g(10) = 436e^{-.036(10)} \approx 304 \text{ billion in the year 2010.}$$

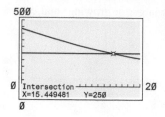

Figure 4.13

(b) If this model remains accurate, when will cigarette consumption fall to 250 billion?

Solution Graph $y = 436e^{-.036x}$ and $y = 250$ on the same screen and find the x-coordinate of their intersection point. Figure 4.13 shows that consumption is expected to be 250 billion in the year 2015 ($x = 15$).

When a quantity is known to grow exponentially, it is sometimes possible to find a function that models its growth from a small amount of data.

Example 3 **Finance** When money is placed in a bank account that pays compound interest, the amount in the account grows exponentially, as we shall see in Chapter 5. Suppose such an account grows from $1000 to $1316 in 7 years.

(a) Find a growth function of the form $f(t) = y_0b^t$ that gives the amount in the account at time t years.

Solution The values of the account at time $t = 0$ and $t = 7$ are given; that is, $f(0) = 1000$ and $f(7) = 1316$. Solve the first of these equations for y_0:

$$f(0) = 1000$$
$$y_0b^0 = 1000 \qquad \text{Rule of } f$$
$$y_0 = 1000. \qquad b^0 = 1$$

So the rule of f has the form $f(t) = 1000b^t$. Now solve the equation $f(7) = 1316$ for b:

$$f(7) = 1316$$
$$1000b^7 = 1316 \qquad \text{Rule of } f$$
$$b^7 = 1.316 \qquad \text{Divide both sides by 1000.}$$
$$b = (1.316)^{1/7} \approx 1.04. \qquad \text{Take the seventh root of each side.}$$

So the rule of the function is $f(t) = 1000(1.04)^t$.

(b) How much is in the account after 12 years?

Solution $f(12) = 1000(1.04)^{12} = \$1601.03.$

✓ Checkpoint 2

Suppose an investment grows exponentially from $500 to $587.12 in three years.

(a) Find a function of the form $f(t) = y_0b^t$ that gives the value of the investment after t years.

(b) How much is the investment worth after 10 years?

Example 4 **Health** Infant mortality rates in the United States are shown in the following table. (Data from: U.S. National Center for Health Statistics.)

Year	Rate	Year	Rate
1920	76.7	1980	12.6
1930	60.4	1990	9.2
1940	47.0	1995	7.6
1950	29.2	2000	6.9
1960	26.0	2005	6.9
1970	20.0	2008	6.6

(a) Let $t = 0$ correspond to 1920. Use the data for 1920 and 2008 to find a function of the form $f(t) = y_0b^t$ that models these data.

Solution Since the rate is 76.7 when $t = 0$, we have $y_0 = 76.7$. Hence, $f(t) = 76.7b^t$. Because 2008 corresponds to $t = 88$, we have $f(88) = 6.6$; that is,

$$76.7b^{88} = 6.6 \qquad \text{Rule of } f$$

$$b^{88} = \frac{6.6}{76.7} \qquad \text{Divide both sides by 76.7.}$$

$$b = \left(\frac{6.6}{76.7}\right)^{\frac{1}{88}} \approx .97251 \qquad \text{Take } 88^{th} \text{ roots on both sides.}$$

Therefore, the function is $f(t) = 76.7(.97251^t)$.

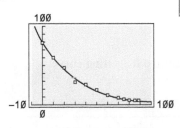

Figure 4.14

(b) Use exponential regression on a graphing calculator to find another model for the data.

Solution The procedure for entering the data and finding the function is the same as that for linear regression (just choose "exponential" instead of "linear"), as explained in Section 2.3. Depending on the calculator, one of the following functions will be produced:

$$g(t) = 79.2092*.9708^t \qquad \text{or} \qquad h(t) = 79.2092e^{-.0296t}.$$

Both functions give the same values (except for slight differences due to rounding of the coefficients). They fit the data reasonably well, as shown in Figure 4.14.

(c) Use the preceding models, and assume they continue to remain accurate, to estimate the infant mortality rate in the years 2012 and 2015.

Solution Evaluating each of the models in parts (a) and (b) at $t = 92$ and $t = 95$ shows that the models give slightly different results.

t	$f(t)$	$g(t)$
92	5.9	5.2
95	5.4	4.7

Other Exponential Models

When a quantity changes exponentially, but does not either grow very large or decrease practically to 0, as in Examples 1–3, different functions are needed.

Example 5 **Business** Sales of a new product often grow rapidly at first and then begin to level off with time. Suppose the annual sales of an inexpensive can opener are given by

$$S(x) = 10,000(1 - e^{-.5x}),$$

where $x = 0$ corresponds to the time the can opener went on the market.

(a) What were the sales in each of the first three years?

Solution At the end of one year ($x = 1$), sales were

$$S(1) = 10,000(1 - e^{-.5(1)}) \approx 3935.$$

Sales in the next two years were

$$S(2) = 10,000(1 - e^{-.5(2)}) \approx 6321 \qquad \text{and} \qquad S(3) = 10,000(1 - e^{-.5(3)}) \approx 7769.$$

(b) What were the sales at the end of the 10th year?

Solution $S(10) = 10,000(1 - e^{-.5(10)}) \approx 9933.$

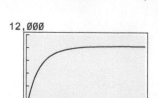

Figure 4.15

✓ **Checkpoint 3**

Suppose the value of the assets (in thousands of dollars) of a certain company after t years is given by

$$V(t) = 100 - 75e^{-.2t}.$$

(a) What is the initial value of the assets?

(b) What is the limiting value of the assets?

(c) Find the value after 10 years.

(d) Graph $V(t)$.

✓ **Checkpoint 4**

In Example 6,

(a) find the number of facts remembered after 10 days;

(b) use the graph to estimate when just one fact will be remembered.

🖈 **TECHNOLOGY TIP**
Many graphing calculators can find a logistic model for appropriate data.

(c) Graph the function S. What does it suggest?

Solution   The graph can be obtained by plotting points and connecting them with a smooth curve or by using a graphing calculator, as in Figure 4.15. The graph indicates that sales will level off after the 12th year, to around 10,000 can openers per year. ✓₃

A variety of activities can be modeled by **logistic functions,** whose rules are of the form

$$f(x) = \frac{c}{1 + ae^{kx}}.$$

The logistic function in the next example is sometimes called a **forgetting curve.**

Example 6   **Social Science**   Psychologists have measured people's ability to remember facts that they have memorized. In one such experiment, it was found that the number of facts, $N(t)$, remembered after t days was given by

$$N(t) = \frac{10.003}{1 + .0003e^{.8t}}.$$

(a) How many facts were remembered at the beginning of the experiment?

Solution   When $t = 0$,

$$N(0) = \frac{10.003}{1 + .0003e^{.8(0)}} = \frac{10.003}{1.0003} = 10.$$

So 10 facts were remembered at the beginning.

(b) How many facts were remembered after one week? after two weeks?

Solution   One and two weeks respectively correspond to $t = 7$ and $t = 14$:

$$N(7) = \frac{10.003}{1 + .0003e^{.8(7)}} = \frac{10.003}{1.0811} \approx 9.25;$$

$$N(14) = \frac{10.003}{1 + .0003e^{.8(14)}} = \frac{10.003}{22.9391} \approx .44.$$

So 9 facts were remembered after one week, but effectively none were remembered after two weeks (because .44 is less than "half a fact"). The graph of the function in Figure 4.16 gives a picture of this forgetting process. ✓₄

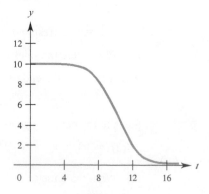

Figure 4.16

4.2 Exercises

1. **Finance** Suppose you owe $800 on your credit card and you decide to make no new purchases and to make the minimum monthly payment on the account. Assuming that the interest rate on your card is 1% per month on the unpaid balance and that the minimum payment is 2% of the total (balance plus interest), your balance after t months is given by

$$B(t) = 800(.9898^t).$$

Find your balance at each of the given times.

(a) six months

(b) one year (remember that t is in months)

(c) five years

(d) eight years

(e) On the basis of your answers to parts (a)–(d), what advice would you give to your friends about minimum payments?

2. **Finance** Suppose you owe $1500 on your credit card and you decide to make no new purchases and to make the minimum monthly payment on the account. Assuming the interest rate on the card is 1.1% per month on the unpaid balance, and the minimum payment is 5% of the total (balance plus interest), your balance after t months is given by

$$B(t) = 1500(.9604)^t.$$

Find the balance at each of the given times.

(a) five months

(b) one year (remember that t is in months)

(c) Is the balance paid off in two years?

3. **Business** The amount (in megawatts) of energy generated in the United States from wind power can be modeled by the function

$$W(t) = w_0(1.30)^t,$$

where $t = 0$ corresponds to the year 2000. (Data from: www.windpoweringamerica.gov.)

(a) The amount generated in the year 2000 was 2540 megawatts. Find w_0.

(b) Estimate the amount of energy generated by wind power in the years 2005 and 2012.

4. **Finance** The percent that public pension funds with assets over $1 billion hold in private-equity investments can be modeled by the function

$$f(t) = 2.214(1.142)^t,$$

where $t = 0$ corresponds to the year 2000. (Data from: The *Wall Street Journal*.)

Find the percent held in private-equity investments in the years:

(a) 2008

(b) 2011

(c) If the model continues to be accurate, project the percent for the year 2015.

In each of the following problems, find an exponential function of the form $f(t) = y_0 b^t$ to model the data. (See Examples 3 and 4.)

5. **Business** The average asking price for rent in San Francisco was $1000 a month in the year 1990 and $2663 in the year 2012. (Data from: The *Wall Street Journal*.)

(a) Find a model for these data in which $t = 0$ corresponds to the year 1990.

(b) If this model remains accurate, what is the predicted average rent in the year 2015?

(c) By experimenting with different values (or using a graphing calculator to solve an appropriate equation), estimate the year in which the average rent hit $2000 a month.

6. **Social Science** The U.S. Census Bureau predicts that the African-American population will increase from 35.3 million in 2000 to 61.8 million in 2060.

(a) Find a model for these data, in which $t = 0$ corresponds to 2000.

(b) What is the projected African-American population in 2020? in 2030?

(c) By experimenting with different values of t (or by using a graphing calculator to solve an appropriate equation), estimate the year in which the African-American population will reach 55 million.

7. **Business** Sales of video and audio equipment, computers, and related services in the United States were about $81.1 billion in the year 1990 and $296 billion in the year 2010.

(a) Let $t = 0$ correspond to the year 1990 and find a model for these data.

(b) According to the model, what were sales in the year 2008?

(c) If the model remains accurate, estimate sales for the year 2015.

8. **Health** Medicare expenditures were $110 billion in the year 1990 and increased to $554 billion in the year 2011.

(a) Find a model for these data in which $t = 0$ corresponds to the year 1990 and expenditures are in billions of dollars.

(b) Estimate Medicare expenditures in 2010.

(c) If the model remains accurate, estimate Medicare expenditures for the year 2016.

In the following exercises, find the exponential model as follows: If you do not have suitable technology, use the first and last data points to find a function. (See Examples 3 and 4.) If you have a graphing calculator or other suitable technology, use exponential regression to find a function. (See Example 4.)

9. **Finance** The table shows the purchasing power of a dollar in recent years, with the year 2000 being the base year. For example, the entry .88 for 2005 means that a dollar in 2005 bought what $.88 did in the year 2000. (Data from: Bureau of Labor Statistics.)

Year	Purchasing Power of $1
2000	$1.00
2001	.97
2002	.96
2003	.94
2004	.91
2005	.88
2006	.85
2007	.83
2008	.79
2009	.80
2010	.79
2011	.77
2012	.75

(a) Find an exponential model for these data, where $t = 0$ corresponds to the year 2000.

(b) Assume the model remains accurate and predict the purchasing power of a dollar in 2015 and 2018.

(c) Use a graphing calculator (or trial and error) to determine the year in which the purchasing power of the 2000 dollar will drop to $.40.

10. Physical Science The table shows the atmospheric pressure (in millibars) at various altitudes (in meters).

Altitude	Pressure
0	1,013
1000	899
2000	795
3000	701
4000	617
5000	541
6000	472
7000	411
8000	357
9000	308
10,000	265

(a) Find an exponential model for these data, in which t is measured in thousands. (For instance, $t = 2$ is 2000 meters.)

(b) Use the function in part (a) to estimate the atmospheric pressure at 1500 meters and 11,000 meters. Compare your results with the actual values of 846 millibars and 227 millibars, respectively.

11. Health The table shows the age-adjusted death rates per 100,000 Americans for heart disease. (Data from: U.S. Center for Health Statistics.)

Year	Death Rate
2000	257.6
2002	240.8
2004	217.0
2006	210.2
2008	186.5
2010	178.5

(a) Find an exponential model for these data, where $t = 0$ corresponds to the year 2000.

(b) Assuming the model remains accurate, estimate the death rate in 2012 and 2016.

(c) Use a graphing calculator (or trial and error) to determine the year in which the death rate will fall to 100.

12. Business The table shows outstanding consumer credit (in billions of dollars) at the beginning of various years. (Data from: U.S. Federal Reserve.)

Year	Credit
1980	350.5
1985	524.0
1990	797.7
1995	1010.4
2000	1543.7
2005	2200.1
2010	2438.7

(a) Find an exponential model for these data, where $t = 0$ corresponds to the year 1980.

(b) If this model remains accurate, what will the outstanding consumer credit be in 2013 and 2016?

(c) In what year will consumer credit reach $6000 billion?

Work the following problems. (See Example 5.)

13. Business Assembly-line operations tend to have a high turnover of employees, forcing the companies involved to spend much time and effort in training new workers. It has been found that a worker who is new to the operation of a certain task on the assembly line will produce $P(t)$ items on day t, where

$$P(t) = 25 - 25e^{-.3t}.$$

(a) How many items will be produced on the first day?

(b) How many items will be produced on the eighth day?

(c) According to the function, what is the maximum number of items the worker can produce?

14. Social Science The number of words per minute that an average person can type is given by

$$W(t) = 60 - 30e^{-.5t},$$

where t is time in months after the beginning of a typing class. Find each of the following.

(a) $W(0)$ (b) $W(1)$

(c) $W(4)$ (d) $W(6)$

Natural Science *Newton's law of cooling says that the rate at which a body cools is proportional to the difference in temperature between the body and an environment into which it is introduced. Using calculus, we can find that the temperature F(t) of the body at time t after being introduced into an environment having constant temperature T_0 is*

$$F(t) = T_0 + Cb^t,$$

where C and b are constants. Use this result in Exercises 15 and 16.

15. Boiling water at 100° Celsius is placed in a freezer at −18° Celsius. The temperature of the water is 50° Celsius after 24 minutes. Find the temperature of the water after 76 minutes.

16. Paisley refuses to drink coffee cooler than 95°F. She makes coffee with a temperature of 170°F in a room with a temperature of 70°F. The coffee cools to 120°F in 10 minutes. What is the longest amount of time she can let the coffee sit before she drinks it?

17. Social Science A sociologist has shown that the fraction $y(t)$ of people in a group who have heard a rumor after t days is approximated by

$$y(t) = \frac{y_0 e^{kt}}{1 - y_0(1 - e^{kt})},$$

where y_0 is the fraction of people who heard the rumor at time $t = 0$ and k is a constant. A graph of $y(t)$ for a particular value of k is shown in the figure.

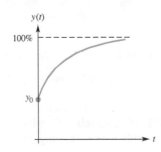

(a) If $k = .1$ and $y_0 = .05$, find $y(10)$.

(b) If $k = .2$ and $y_0 = .10$, find $y(5)$.

(c) Assume the situation in part (b). How many *weeks* will it take for 65% of the people to have heard the rumor?

18. Social Science Data from the National Highway Traffic Safety Administration indicate that, in year t, the approximate percentage of people in the United States who wear seat belts when driving is given by

$$g(t) = \frac{97}{1 + .823e^{-.1401t}},$$

where $t = 0$ corresponds to the year 1994. What percentage used seat belts in

(a) 2000?

(b) 2003?

(c) 2004?

Assuming that this function is accurate after 2004, estimate seat belt use for the following years.

(d) 2011?

(e) 2013?

(f) 2015?

(g) Graph the function. Does the graph suggest that seat belt usage will ever reach 100%?

Use a graphing calculator or other technology to do the following problems. (See Example 6.)

19. Economics The amount of U.S. expenditures on national defense (in billions of dollars) can by approximated by the function

$$f(x) = \frac{1084}{1 + 1.94e^{-.171x}},$$

where $x = 0$ corresponds to the year 2000. (Data from: U.S. Bureau of Economic Analysis.)

(a) Estimate the expenditures in the years 2005 and 2010.

(b) Assume the model remains accurate and graph the function from the year 2000 to the year 2020.

(c) Use the graph to determine the year in which expenditures reach $850 billion.

20. Natural Science The population of fish in a certain lake at time t months is given by the function

$$p(t) = \frac{20,000}{1 + 24(2^{-.36t})}.$$

(a) Graph the population function from $t = 0$ to $t = 48$ (a four-year period).

(b) What was the population at the beginning of the period?

(c) Use the graph to estimate the one-year period in which the population grew most rapidly.

(d) When do you think the population will reach 25,000? What factors in nature might explain your answer?

21. Business The amount (in billions of dollars) spent on legal services in the United States can be approximated by the function

$$g(x) = \frac{99.85}{1 + .527e^{-.258x}},$$

where $x = 0$ corresponds to the year 2000. (Data from: U.S. Bureau of Economic Analysis.)

(a) Estimate the amount spent on legal services in 2007 and 2011.

(b) Assume the model remains accurate and graph $g(x)$ from the year 2000 to the year 2025.

(c) Does the graph ever go over $110 billion dollars?

22. Social Science The probability P percent of having an automobile accident is related to the alcohol level t of the driver's blood by the function $P(t) = e^{21.459t}$.

(a) Graph $P(t)$ in a viewing window with $0 \le t \le .2$ and $0 \le P(t) \le 100$.

(b) At what blood alcohol level is the probability of an accident at least 50%? What is the legal blood alcohol level in your state?

1. **(a)** 500

   (b) About 27,300

2. **(a)** $f(t) = 500(1.055)^t$

   (b) $854.07

3. **(a)** $25,000

   (b) $100,000

   (c) $89,850

(d)

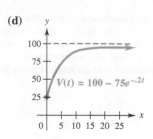

$V(t) = 100 - 75e^{-.2t}$

4. **(a)** 5

   (b) After about 12 days

4.3 Logarithmic Functions

Until the development of computers and calculators, logarithms were the only effective tool for large-scale numerical computations. They are no longer needed for this purpose, but logarithmic functions still play a crucial role in calculus and in many applications.

Common Logarithms

Logarithms are simply *a new language for old ideas*—essentially, a special case of exponents.

> ### Definition of Common (Base 10) Logarithms
>
> $$y = \log x \qquad \text{means} \qquad 10^y = x.$$

Log x, which is read "the logarithm of *x*," is the answer to the question,

To what exponent must 10 be raised to produce *x*?

Find each common logarithm.

(a) log 100

(b) log 1000

(c) log .1

```
log(359)
           2.555094449
10^(2.5551)
             359.004589
log(.026)
            -1.585026652
```

Figure 4.17

Find each common logarithm.

(a) log 27

(b) log 1089

(c) log .00426

Example 1 To find log 10,000, ask yourself, "To what exponent must 10 be raised to produce 10,000?" Since $10^4 = 10,000$, we see that log 10,000 = 4. Similarly,

$$\log 1 = 0 \qquad \text{because} \qquad 10^0 = 1;$$

$$\log .01 = -2 \qquad \text{because} \qquad 10^{-2} = \frac{1}{10^2} = \frac{1}{100} = .01;$$

$$\log \sqrt{10} = 1/2 \qquad \text{because} \qquad 10^{1/2} = \sqrt{10}.$$ ✓₁

Example 2 Log (-25) is the exponent to which 10 must be raised to produce -25. But every power of 10 is positive! So there is no exponent that will produce -25. *Logarithms of negative numbers and 0 are not defined.*

Example 3 **(a)** We know that log 359 must be a number between 2 and 3 because $10^2 = 100$ and $10^3 = 1000$. By using the "log" key on a calculator, we find that log 359 (to four decimal places) is 2.5551. You can verify this statement by computing $10^{2.5551}$; the result (rounded) is 359. See the first two lines in Figure 4.17.

(b) When 10 is raised to a negative exponent, the result is a number less than 1. Consequently, the logarithms of numbers between 0 and 1 are negative. For instance, log .026 = -1.5850, as shown in the third line in Figure 4.17. ✓₂

> 📄 **NOTE** On most scientific calculators, enter the number followed by the log key. On graphing calculators, press the log key followed by the number, as in Figure 4.17.

Natural Logarithms

Although common logarithms still have some uses (one of which is discussed in Section 4.4), the most widely used logarithms today are defined in terms of the number e (whose decimal expansion begins 2.71828 . . .) rather than 10. They have a special name and notation.

Definition of Natural (Base e) Logarithms

$$y = \ln x \quad \text{means} \quad e^y = x.$$

Thus, the number **ln** x (which is sometimes read "el-en x") is the exponent to which e must be raised to produce the number x. For instance, $\ln 1 = 0$ because $e^0 = 1$. Although logarithms to the base e may not seem as "natural" as common logarithms, there are several reasons for using them, some of which are discussed in Section 4.4.

```
ln(85)
              4.442651256
e^4.4427
              85.0041433
ln(.38)
             -.9675840263
```

Figure 4.18

✓ **Checkpoint 3**

Find the following.

(a) $\ln 6.1$

(b) $\ln 20$

(c) $\ln .8$

(d) $\ln .1$

Example 4   **(a)** To find $\ln 85$, use the ⬛ **LN** key of your calculator, as in Figure 4.18. The result is 4.4427. Thus, 4.4427 is the exponent (to four decimal places) to which e must be raised to produce 85. You can verify this result by computing $e^{4.4427}$; the answer (rounded) is 85. See Figure 4.18.

(b) A calculator shows that $\ln .38 = -.9676$ (rounded), which means that $e^{-.9676} \approx .38$. See Figure 4.18. ✓ 3

Example 5   You don't need a calculator to find $\ln e^8$. Just ask yourself, "To what exponent must e be raised to produce e^8?" The answer, obviously, is 8. So $\ln e^8 = 8$.

Other Logarithms

The procedure used to define common and natural logarithms can be carried out with any positive number $a \neq 1$ as the base in place of 10 or e.

Definition of Logarithms to the Base a

$$y = \log_a x \quad \text{means} \quad a^y = x.$$

Read $y = \log_a x$ as "y is the logarithm of x to the base a." As was the case with common and natural logarithms, $\log_a x$ is an *exponent*; it is the answer to the question,

To what power must a be raised to produce x?

For example, suppose $a = 2$ and $x = 16$. Then $\log_2 16$ is the answer to the question,

To what power must 2 be raised to produce 16?

It is easy to see that $2^4 = 16$, so $\log_2 16 = 4$. In other words, the exponential statement $2^4 = 16$ is equivalent to the logarithmic statement $4 = \log_2 16$.

In the definition of a logarithm to base a, note carefully the relationship between the base and the exponent:

Logarithmic form: $y = \log_a x$

Exponential form: $a^y = x$

Common and natural logarithms are the special cases when $a = 10$ and when $a = e$, respectively. Both $\log u$ and $\log_{10} u$ mean the same thing. Similarly, $\ln u$ and $\log_e u$ mean the same thing.

Example 6   This example shows several statements written in both exponential and logarithmic form.

Exponential Form	Logarithmic Form
(a) $3^2 = 9$	$\log_3 9 = 2$
(b) $(1/5)^{-2} = 25$	$\log_{1/5} 25 = -2$
(c) $10^5 = 100{,}000$	$\log_{10} 100{,}000$ (or $\log 100{,}000$) $= 5$
(d) $4^{-3} = 1/64$	$\log_4 (1/64) = -3$
(e) $2^{-4} = 1/16$	$\log_2 (1/16) = -4$
(f) $e^0 = 1$	$\log_e 1$ (or $\ln 1$) $= 0$

✓4 ✓5

✓ **Checkpoint 4**

Write the logarithmic form of
(a) $5^3 = 125$;
(b) $3^{-4} = 1/81$;
(c) $8^{2/3} = 4$.

✓ **Checkpoint 5**

Write the exponential form of
(a) $\log_{16} 4 = 1/2$;
(b) $\log_3 (1/9) = -2$;
(c) $\log_{16} 8 = 3/4$.

Properties of Logarithms

Some of the important properties of logarithms arise directly from their definition.

Let x and a be any positive real numbers, with $a \neq 1$, and r be any real number. Then

(a) $\log_a 1 = 0$;   (b) $\log_a a = 1$;
(c) $\log_a a^r = r$;   (d) $a^{\log_a x} = x$.

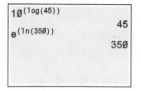

Figure 4.19

Property (a) was discussed in Example 1 (with $a = 10$). Property (c) was illustrated in Example 5 (with $a = e$ and $r = 8$). Property (b) is property (c) with $r = 1$. To understand property (d), recall that $\log_a x$ is the exponent to which a must be raised to produce x. Consequently, when you raise a to this exponent, the result is x, as illustrated for common and natural logarithms in Figure 4.19.

The following properties are part of the reason that logarithms are so useful. They will be used in the next section to solve exponential and logarithmic equations.

The Product, Quotient, and Power Properties

Let x, y, and a be any positive real numbers, with $a \neq 1$. Let r be any real number. Then

$$\log_a xy = \log_a x + \log_a y \qquad \text{Product property}$$

$$\log_a \frac{x}{y} = \log_a x - \log_a y \qquad \text{Quotient property}$$

$$\log_a x^r = r \log_a x \qquad \text{Power property}$$

Each of these three properties is illustrated on a calculator in Figure 4.20.

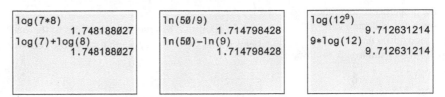

Figure 4.20

To prove the product property, let

$$m = \log_a x \qquad \text{and} \qquad n = \log_a y.$$

Then, by the definition of logarithm,

$$a^m = x \qquad \text{and} \qquad a^n = y.$$

Multiply to get

$$a^m \cdot a^n = x \cdot y,$$

or, by a property of exponents,

$$a^{m+n} = xy.$$

Use the definition of logarithm to rewrite this last statement as

$$\log_a xy = m + n.$$

Replace m with $\log_a x$ and n with $\log_a y$ to get

$$\log_a xy = \log_a x + \log_a y.$$

The quotient and power properties can be proved similarly.

Example 7 Using the properties of logarithms, we can write each of the following as a single logarithm:[*]

(a) $\log_a x + \log_a (x - 1) = \log_a x(x - 1)$;   Product property

(b) $\log_a (x^2 + 4) - \log_a (x + 6) = \log_a \dfrac{x^2 + 4}{x + 6}$;   Quotient property

(c) $\log_a 9 + 5 \log_a x = \log_a 9 + \log_a x^5 = \log_a 9x^5$.   Product and power properties

---

✓ **Checkpoint 6**

Write each expression as a single logarithm, using the properties of logarithms.

(a) $\log_a 5x + \log_a 3x^4$

(b) $\log_a 3p - \log_a 5q$

(c) $4 \log_a k - 3 \log_a m$

---

[*]Here and elsewhere, we assume that variable expressions represent positive numbers and that the base a is positive, with $a \neq 1$.

> **⊘ CAUTION** There is no logarithm property that allows you to simplify the logarithm of a sum, such as $\log_a (x^2 + 4)$. In particular, $\log_a (x^2 + 4)$ is *not* equal to $\log_a x^2 + \log_a 4$. The product property of logarithms shows that $\log_a x^2 + \log_a 4 = \log_a 4x^2$.

Example 8 Assume that $\log_6 7 \approx 1.09$ and $\log_6 5 \approx .90$. Use the properties of logarithms to find each of the following:

(a) $\log_6 35 = \log_6 (7 \cdot 5) = \log_6 7 + \log_6 5 \approx 1.09 + .90 = 1.99$;

(b) $\log_6 5/7 = \log_6 5 - \log_6 7 \approx .90 - 1.09 = -.19$;

(c) $\log_6 5^3 = 3 \log_6 5 \approx 3(.90) = 2.70$;

(d) $\log_6 6 = 1$;

(e) $\log_6 1 = 0.$ ✓₇

✓ **Checkpoint 7**

Use the properties of logarithms to rewrite and evaluate each expression, given that $\log_3 7 \approx 1.77$ and $\log_3 5 \approx 1.46$.

(a) $\log_3 35$

(b) $\log_3 7/5$

(c) $\log_3 25$

(d) $\log_3 3$

(e) $\log_3 1$

In Example 8, several logarithms to the base 6 were given. However, they could have been found by using a calculator and the following formula.

Change-of-Base Theorem

For any positive numbers a and x (with $a \neq 1$),

$$\log_a x = \frac{\ln x}{\ln a}.$$

Example 9 To find $\log_7 3$, use the theorem with $a = 7$ and $x = 3$:

$$\log_7 3 = \frac{\ln 3}{\ln 7} \approx \frac{1.0986}{1.9459} \approx .5646.$$

You can check this result on your calculator by verifying that $7^{.5646} \approx 3$.

Example 10 **Natural Science** Environmental scientists who study the diversity of species in an ecological community use the *Shannon index* to measure diversity. If there are k different species, with n_1 individuals of species 1, n_2 individuals of species 2, and so on, then the Shannon index H is defined as

$$H = \frac{N \log_2 N - [n_1 \log_2 n_1 + n_2 \log_2 n_2 + \cdots + n_k \log_2 n_k]}{N},$$

where $N = n_1 + n_2 + n_3 + \cdots + n_k$. A study of the species that barn owls in a particular region typically eat yielded the following data:

Species	Number
Rats	143
Mice	1405
Birds	452

Find the index of diversity of this community.

Solution In this case, $n_1 = 143, n_2 = 1405, n_3 = 452$, and

$$N = n_1 + n_2 + n_3 = 143 + 1405 + 452 = 2000.$$

So the index of diversity is

$$H = \frac{N \log_2 N - [n_1 \log_2 n_1 + n_2 \log_2 n_2 + \cdots + n_k \log_2 n_k]}{N}$$

$$= \frac{2000 \log_2 2000 - [143 \log_2 143 + 1405 \log_2 1405 + 452 \log_2 452]}{2000}.$$

To compute H, we use the change-of-base theorem:

$$H = \frac{2000 \dfrac{\ln 2000}{\ln 2} - \left[143 \dfrac{\ln 143}{\ln 2} + 1405 \dfrac{\ln 1405}{\ln 2} + 452 \dfrac{\ln 452}{\ln 2} \right]}{2000}$$

$$\approx 1.1149.$$

Logarithmic Functions

For a given *positive* value of x, the definition of logarithm leads to exactly one value of y, so that $y = \log_a x$ defines a function.

> If $a > 0$ and $a \neq 1$, the **logarithmic function** with base a is defined as
>
> $$f(x) = \log_a x.$$

The most important logarithmic function is the natural logarithmic function.

Example 11   Graph $f(x) = \ln x$ and $g(x) = e^x$ on the same axes.

Solution   For each function, use a calculator to compute some ordered pairs. Then plot the corresponding points and connect them with a curve to obtain the graphs in Figure 4.21.

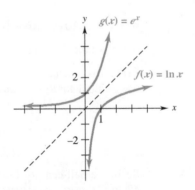

Figure 4.21

The dashed line in Figure 4.21 is the graph of $y = x$. Observe that the graph of $f(x) = \ln x$ is the mirror image of the graph of $g(x) = e^x$, with the line $y = x$ being the mirror. A pair of functions whose graphs are related in this way are said to be **inverses** of each other. A more complete discussion of inverse functions is given in many college algebra books. ✓8

✓ Checkpoint 8

Verify that $f(x) = \log x$ and $g(x) = 10^x$ are inverses of each other by graphing $f(x)$ and $g(x)$ on the same axes.

When the base $a > 1$, the graph of $f(x) = \log_a x$ has the same basic shape as the graph of the natural logarithmic function in Figure 4.21, as summarized on the following page.

Exponential Functions	Logarithmic Functions
$f(x) = a^x$	$f(x) = \log_a x$
domain: set of all real numbers	*domain*: set of all positive real numbers
range: set of all positive real numbers	*range*: set of all real numbers
horizontal asymptote no vertical asymptote	vertical asymptote no horizontal asymptote

As the information in the box suggests, the functions $f(x) = \log_a x$ and $g(x) = a^x$ are inverses of each other. (Their graphs are mirror images of each other, with the line $y = x$ being the mirror.)

Applications

Logarithmic functions are useful for, among other things, describing quantities that grow, but do so at a slower rate as time goes on.

Example 12   **Health**   The life expectancy at birth of a person born in year x is approximated by the function

$$f(x) = 17.6 + 12.8 \ln x,$$

where $x = 10$ corresponds to 1910. (Data from: U.S. National Center for Health Statistics.)

(a) Find the life expectancy of persons born in 1910, 1960, and 2010.

Solution   Since these years correspond to $x = 10, x = 60$, and $x = 110$, respectively, use a calculator to evaluate $f(x)$ at these numbers:

$$f(10) = 17.6 + 12.8 \ln(10) \approx 47.073;$$
$$f(60) = 17.6 + 12.8 \ln(60) \approx 70.008;$$
$$f(110) = 17.6 + 12.8 \ln(110) \approx 77.766.$$

So in the half-century from 1910 to 1960, life expectancy at birth increased from about 47 to 70 years, an increase of 23 years. But in the half-century from 1960 to 2010, it increased less than 8 years, from about 70 to 77.8 years.

(b) If this function remains accurate, when will life expectancy at birth be 80.2 years?

Solution   We must solve the equation $f(x) = 80.2$, that is,

$$17.6 + 12.8 \ln x = 80.2$$

In the next section, we shall see how to do this algebraically. For now, we solve the equation graphically by graphing $f(x)$ and $y = 80.2$ on the same screen and finding their intersection point. Figure 4.22 shows that the x-coordinate of this point is approximately 133. So life expectancy will be 80.2 years in 2033.

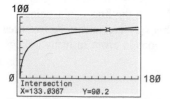

Intersection
X=133.0367   Y=90.2

Figure 4.22

4.3 Exercises

Complete each statement in Exercises 1–4.

1. $y = \log_a x$ means $x =$ _____.

2. The statement $\log_5 125 = 3$ tells us that _____ is the power of _____ that equals _____.

3. What is wrong with the expression $y = \log_b$?

4. Logarithms of negative numbers are not defined because _____.

Translate each logarithmic statement into an equivalent exponential statement. (See Examples 1, 5, and 6.)

5. $\log 100{,}000 = 5$ **6.** $\log .001 = -3$

7. $\log_9 81 = 2$ **8.** $\log_2 (1/8) = -3$

Translate each exponential statement into an equivalent logarithmic statement. (See Examples 5 and 6.)

9. $10^{1.9823} = 96$ **10.** $e^{3.2189} = 25$

11. $3^{-2} = 1/9$ **12.** $16^{1/2} = 4$

Without using a calculator, evaluate each of the given expressions. (See Examples 1, 5, and 6.)

13. $\log 1000$ **14.** $\log .0001$

15. $\log_6 36$ **16.** $\log_3 81$

17. $\log_4 64$ **18.** $\log_5 125$

19. $\log_2 \dfrac{1}{4}$ **20.** $\log_3 \dfrac{1}{27}$

21. $\ln \sqrt{e}$ **22.** $\ln(1/e)$

23. $\ln e^{8.77}$ **24.** $\log 10^{74.3}$

Use a calculator to evaluate each logarithm to three decimal places. (See Examples 3 and 4.)

25. $\log 53$ **26.** $\log .005$

27. $\ln .0068$ **28.** $\ln 354$

29. Why does $\log_a 1$ always equal 0 for any valid base a?

Write each expression as the logarithm of a single number or expression. Assume that all variables represent positive numbers. (See Example 7.)

30. $\log 20 - \log 5$ **31.** $\log 6 + \log 8 - \log 2$

32. $3 \ln 2 + 2 \ln 3$ **33.** $2 \ln 5 - \frac{1}{2} \ln 25$

34. $5 \log x - 2 \log y$ **35.** $2 \log u + 3 \log w - 6 \log v$

36. $\ln(3x + 2) + \ln(x + 4)$ **37.** $2 \ln(x + 2) - \ln(x + 3)$

Write each expression as a sum and/or a difference of logarithms, with all variables to the first degree.

38. $\log 5x^2 y^3$ **39.** $\ln \sqrt{6m^4 n^2}$

40. $\ln \dfrac{3x}{5y}$ **41.** $\log \dfrac{\sqrt{xz}}{z^3}$

42. The calculator-generated table in the figure is for $y_1 = \log(4 - x)$. Why do the values in the y_1 column show ERROR for $x \geq 4$?

X	Y1	
0	.60206	
1	.47712	
2	.30103	
3	0	
4	ERROR	
5	ERROR	
6	ERROR	
X=4		

Express each expression in terms of u and v, where $u = \ln x$ and $v = \ln y$. For example, $\ln x^3 = 3(\ln x) = 3u$.

43. $\ln(x^2 y^5)$ **44.** $\ln(\sqrt{x} \cdot y^2)$

45. $\ln(x^3/y^2)$ **46.** $\ln(\sqrt{x}/y)$

Evaluate each expression. (See Example 9.)

47. $\log_6 384$ **48.** $\log_{30} 78$

49. $\log_{35} 5646$ **50.** $\log_6 60 - \log_{60} 6$

Find numerical values for b and c for which the given statement is FALSE.

51. $\log(b + c) = \log b + \log c$

52. $\dfrac{\ln b}{\ln c} = \ln\left(\dfrac{b}{c}\right)$

Graph each function. (See Example 11.)

53. $y = \ln(x + 2)$ **54.** $y = \ln x + 2$

55. $y = \log(x - 3)$ **56.** $y = \log x - 3$

57. Graph $f(x) = \log x$ and $g(x) = \log(x/4)$ for $-2 \leq x \leq 8$. How are these graphs related? How does the quotient rule support your answer?

In Exercises 58 and 59, the coordinates of a point on the graph of the indicated function are displayed at the bottom of the screen. Write the logarithmic and exponential equations associated with the display.

58.

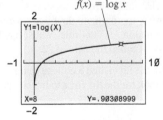

59.

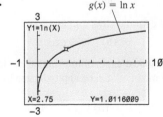

60. Match each equation with its graph. Each tick mark represents one unit.

(a) $y = \log x$ (b) $y = 10^x$

(c) $y = \ln x$ (d) $y = e^x$

(A)

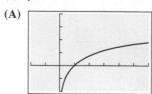

(B)

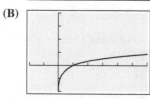

(C)

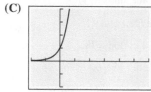

(D)

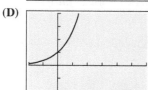

61. Finance The doubling function

$$D(r) = \frac{\ln 2}{\ln(1 + r)}$$

gives the number of years required to double your money when it is invested at interest rate r (expressed as a decimal), compounded annually. How long does it take to double your money at each of the following rates?

(a) 4%   (b) 8%   (c) 18%   (d) 36%

(e) Round each of your answers in parts (a)–(d) to the nearest year, and compare them with these numbers: 72/4, 72/8, 72/18, and 72/36. Use this evidence to state a "rule of thumb" for determining approximate doubling time without employing the function D. This rule, which has long been used by bankers, is called the *rule of 72*.

62. Health Two people with the flu visited a college campus. The number of days, T, that it took for the flu virus to infect n people is given by

$$T = -1.43 \ln\left(\frac{10,000 - n}{4998n}\right).$$

How many days will it take for the virus to infect

(a) 500 people?   (b) 5000 people?

63. Business The average annual expenditure (in dollars) for a consumer of gasoline and motor oil can be approximated by the function

$$g(x) = -771.9 + 1035 \ln x,$$

where $x = 5$ corresponds to the year 1995. (Data from: U.S. Bureau of Labor Statistics.)

(a) Estimate the average expenditure in 2008.

(b) Graph the function g for the period 1995 to 2011.

(c) Assuming the graph remains accurate, what does the shape of the graph suggest regarding the average expenditure on gasoline and motor oil?

64. Physical Science The barometric pressure p (in inches of mercury) is related to the height h above sea level (in miles) by the equation

$$h = -5 \ln\left(\frac{p}{29.92}\right).$$

The pressure readings given in parts (a)–(c) were made by a weather balloon. At what heights were they made?

(a) 29.92 in.   (b) 20.05 in.   (c) 11.92 in.

(d) Use a graphing calculator to determine the pressure at a height of 3 miles.

65. Social Science The number of residents (in millions) of the United States age 65 or older can be approximated by the function

$$h(x) = 1.58 + 10.15 \ln x,$$

where $x = 10$ corresponds to the year 1980. (Data from: U.S. Census Bureau.)

(a) Give the number of residents age 65 or older for the years 1990 and 2005.

(b) Graph the function h for $10 \le x \le 50$.

(c) What does the graph suggest regarding the number of older people as time goes on?

Natural Science *These exercises deal with the Shannon index of diversity. (See Example 10.) Note that in two communities with the same number of species, a larger index indicates greater diversity.*

66. A study of barn owl prey in a particular area produced the following data:

Species	Number
Rats	662
Mice	907
Birds	531

Find the index of diversity of this community. Is this community more or less diverse than the one in Example 10?

67. An eastern forest is composed of the following trees:

Species	Number
Beech	2754
Birch	689
Hemlock	4428
Maple	629

What is the index of diversity of this community?

68. A community has high diversity when all of its species have approximately the same number of individuals. It has low diversity when a few of its species account for most of the total population. Illustrate this fact for the following two communities:

Community 1	Number
Species A	1000
Species B	1000
Species C	1000

Community 2	Number
Species A	2500
Species B	200
Species C	300

69. Business The total assets (in billions of dollars) held by credit unions can be approximated by the function

$$f(x) = -1237 + 580.6 \ln x,$$

where $x = 10$ corresponds to the year 1990. (Data from: U.S. Census Bureau.)

(a) What were the assets held by credit unions in 1998 and 2010?

(b) If the model remains accurate, find the year the assets reach $1000 billion.

70. Finance The amount (in billions of dollars) held in private pension funds can be approximated by the function

$$h(x) = -11,052 + 5742 \ln x,$$

where $x = 10$ corresponds to the year 1990. (Data from: Board of Governors of the Federal Reserve System.)

(a) What was the amount in private pension funds in 2001 and 2009?

(b) If the model remains accurate, when will the amount reach $9000 billion?

71. Business The amount of milk (in gallons) consumed per person annually can be approximated by the function

$$g(x) = 28.29 - 1.948 \ln(x + 1),$$

where $x = 0$ corresponds to the year 1980. (Data from: U.S. Department of Agriculture.)

(a) How many gallons per person were consumed in the years 1985 and 2005?

(b) Assuming the model remains accurate, when will the per-person consumption be at 21 gallons?

72. Economics The median family income is the "middle income"—half the families have this income or more, and half have a lesser income. The median family income can be approximated by

$$f(x) = 22,751 + 8217 \ln(x + 1),$$

where $x = 0$ corresponds to the year 1990. (Data from: U.S. Census Bureau.)

(a) What is the median income in the years 2000 and 2010?

(b) If this model remains accurate, when will the median income reach $52,000?

✓ Checkpoint Answers

1. (a) 2 **(b)** 3 **(c)** −1

2. (a) 1.4314 **(b)** 3.0370 **(c)** −2.3706

3. (a) 1.8083 **(b)** 2.9957 **(c)** −.2231
  (d) −2.3026

4. (a) $\log_5 125 = 3$ **(b)** $\log_3 (1/81) = -4$ **(c)** $\log_8 4 = 2/3$

5. (a) $16^{1/2} = 4$ **(b)** $3^{-2} = 1/9$ **(c)** $16^{3/4} = 8$

6. (a) $\log_a 15x^5$ **(b)** $\log_a (3p/5q)$ **(c)** $\log_a (k^4/m^3)$

7. (a) 3.23 **(b)** .31 **(c)** 2.92
  (d) 1 **(e)** 0

8.

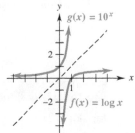

4.4 Logarithmic and Exponential Equations

Many applications involve solving logarithmic and exponential equations, so we begin with solution methods for such equations.

Logarithmic Equations

When an equation involves only logarithmic terms, use the logarithm properties to write each side as a single logarithm. Then use the following fact.

Let u, v, and a be positive real numbers, with $a \neq 1$.

If $\log_a u = \log_a v$, then $u = v$.

Example 1   Solve $\log x = \log(x + 3) - \log(x - 1)$.

Solution   First, use the quotient property of logarithms to write the right side as a single logarithm:

$$\log x = \log(x + 3) - \log(x - 1)$$

$$\log x = \log\left(\frac{x + 3}{x - 1}\right). \qquad \text{Quotient property of logarithms}$$

The fact in the preceding box now shows that

$$x = \frac{x + 3}{x - 1}$$

$$x(x - 1) = x + 3 \qquad \text{Cross multiply.}$$

$$x^2 - x = x + 3$$

$$x^2 - 2x - 3 = 0$$

$$(x - 3)(x + 1) = 0 \qquad \text{Factor.}$$

$$x = 3 \quad \text{or} \quad x = -1.$$

Since $\log x$ is not defined when $x = -1$, the only possible solution is $x = 3$. Use a calculator to verify that 3 actually is a solution. ✔1

✓ **Checkpoint 1**

Solve each equation.

(a) $\log_2(p + 9) - \log_2 p = \log_2(p + 1)$

(b) $\log_3(m + 1) - \log_3(m - 1) = \log_3 m$

When an equation involves constants and logarithmic terms, use algebra and the logarithm properties to write one side as a single logarithm and the other as a constant. Then use the following property of logarithms, which was discussed on pages 202–203.

If a and u are positive real numbers, with $a \neq 1$, then

$$a^{\log_a u} = u.$$

Example 2   Solve each equation.

(a) $\log_5(2x - 3) = 2$

Solution   Since the base of the logarithm is 5, raise 5 to the exponents given by the equation:

$$5^{\log_5(2x-3)} = 5^2$$

On the left side, use the fact in the preceding box (with $a = 5$ and $u = 2x - 3$) to conclude that

$$2x - 3 = 25$$

$$2x = 28$$

$$x = 14.$$

Verify that 14 is a solution of the original equation.

(b) $\log(x - 16) = 2 - \log(x - 1)$

Solution First rearrange the terms to obtain a single logarithm on the left side:

$$\log(x - 16) + \log(x - 1) = 2$$
$$\log[(x - 16)(x - 1)] = 2 \qquad \text{Product property of logarithms}$$
$$\log(x^2 - 17x + 16) = 2.$$

Since the base of the logarithm is 10, raise 10 to the given powers:

$$10^{\log(x^2 - 17x + 16)} = 10^2.$$

On the left side, apply the logarithm property in the preceding box (with $a = 10$ and $u = x^2 - 17x + 16$):

$$x^2 - 17x + 16 = 100$$
$$x^2 - 17x - 84 = 0$$
$$(x + 4)(x - 21) = 0$$
$$x = -4 \qquad \text{or} \qquad x = 21.$$

In the original equation, when $x = -4$, $\log(x - 16) = \log(-20)$, which is not defined. So -4 is not a solution. You should verify that 21 is a solution of the original equation.

(c) $\log_2 x - \log_2 (x - 1) = 1$

Solution Proceed as before, with 2 as the base of the logarithm:

$$\log_2 \frac{x}{x - 1} = 1 \qquad \text{Quotient property of logarithms}$$
$$2^{\log_2 x/(x - 1)} = 2^1 \qquad \text{Exponentiate to the base 2.}$$
$$\frac{x}{x - 1} = 2 \qquad \text{Use the fact in the preceding box.}$$
$$x = 2(x - 1) \qquad \text{Multiply both sides by } x - 1.$$
$$x = 2x - 2$$
$$-x = -2$$
$$x = 2.$$

Verify that 2 is a solution of the original equation. ✓₂

✓ **Checkpoint 2**

Solve each equation.
(a) $\log_5 x + 2 \log_5 x = 3$
(b) $\log_6 (a + 2) - \log_6 \frac{a - 7}{5} = 1$

Exponential Equations

An equation in which all the variables are exponents is called an *exponential equation*. When such an equation can be written as two powers of the same base, it can be solved by using the following fact.

Let a be a positive real number, with $a \neq 1$.

$$\text{If } a^u = a^v, \qquad \text{then} \qquad u = v.$$

Example 3 Solve $9^x = 27$.

Solution First, write both sides as powers of the same base. Since $9 = 3^2$ and $27 = 3^3$, we have

$$9^x = 27$$
$$(3^2)^x = 3^3$$
$$3^{2x} = 3^3.$$

Apply the fact in the preceding box (with $a = 3$, $u = 2x$, and $v = 3$):

$$2x = 3$$

$$x = \frac{3}{2}.$$

✓ **Checkpoint 3**

Solve each equation.

(a) $8^{2x} = 4$

(b) $5^{3x} = 25^4$

(c) $36^{-2x} = 6$

Verify that $x = 3/2$ is a solution of the original equation. ✓₃

Exponential equations involving different bases can often be solved by using the power property of logarithms, which is repeated here for natural logarithms.

> If u and r are real numbers, with u positive, then
>
> $$\ln u^r = r \ln u.$$

Although natural logarithms are used in the following examples, logarithms to any base will produce the same solutions.

Example 4   Solve $3^x = 5$.

Solution   Take natural logarithms on both sides:

$$\ln 3^x = \ln 5.$$

Apply the power property of logarithms in the preceding box (with $r = x$) to the left side:

$$x \ln 3 = \ln 5$$

$$x = \frac{\ln 5}{\ln 3} \approx 1.465. \qquad \text{Divide both sides by the constant ln 3.}$$

To check, evaluate $3^{1.465}$; the answer should be approximately 5, which verifies that the solution of the given equation is 1.465 (to the nearest thousandth). ✓₄

✓ **Checkpoint 4**

Solve each equation. Round solutions to the nearest thousandth.

(a) $2^x = 7$

(b) $5^m = 50$

(c) $3^y = 17$

🛑 **CAUTION**   Be careful: $\dfrac{\ln 5}{\ln 3}$ is *not* equal to $\ln\left(\dfrac{5}{3}\right)$ or $\ln 5 - \ln 3$.

Example 5   Solve $3^{2x-1} = 4^{x+2}$.

Solution   Taking natural logarithms on both sides gives

$$\ln 3^{2x-1} = \ln 4^{x+2}.$$

Now use the power property of logarithms and the fact that $\ln 3$ and $\ln 4$ are constants to rewrite the equation:

$$(2x - 1)(\ln 3) = (x + 2)(\ln 4) \qquad \text{Power property}$$

$$2x(\ln 3) - 1(\ln 3) = x(\ln 4) + 2(\ln 4) \qquad \text{Distributive property}$$

$$2x(\ln 3) - x(\ln 4) = 2(\ln 4) + 1(\ln 3). \qquad \text{Collect terms with } x \text{ on one side.}$$

Factor out x on the left side to get

$$[2(\ln 3) - \ln 4]x = 2(\ln 4) + \ln 3.$$

Divide both sides by the coefficient of x:

$$x = \frac{2(\ln 4) + \ln 3}{2(\ln 3) - \ln 4}.$$

Using a calculator to evaluate this last expression, we find that

$$x = \frac{2 \ln 4 + \ln 3}{2 \ln 3 - \ln 4} \approx 4.774.$$ ✓5

Checkpoint 5

Solve each equation. Round solutions to the nearest thousandth.

(a) $6^m = 3^{2m-1}$

(b) $5^{6a-3} = 2^{4a+1}$

Recall that $\ln e = 1$ (because 1 is the exponent to which e must be raised to produce e). This fact simplifies the solution of equations involving powers of e.

Example 6 Solve $3e^{x^2} = 600$.

Solution First divide each side by 3 to get

$$e^{x^2} = 200.$$

Now take natural logarithms on both sides; then use the power property of logarithms:

$$e^{x^2} = 200$$
$$\ln e^{x^2} = \ln 200$$
$$x^2 \ln e = \ln 200 \quad \text{Power property}$$
$$x^2 = \ln 200 \quad \ln e = 1.$$
$$x = \pm\sqrt{\ln 200}$$
$$x \approx \pm 2.302.$$

Verify that the solutions are ± 2.302, rounded to the nearest thousandth. (The symbol $\pm$ is used as a shortcut for writing the two solutions 2.302 and -2.302.) ✓6

Checkpoint 6

Solve each equation. Round solutions to the nearest thousandth.

(a) $e^{.1x} = 11$

(b) $e^{3+x} = .893$

(c) $e^{2x^2-3} = 9$

TECHNOLOGY TIP Logarithmic and exponential equations can be solved on a graphing calculator. To solve $3^x = 5^{2x-1}$, for example, graph $y = 3^x$ and $y = 5^{2x-1}$ on the same screen. Then use the intersection finder to determine the x-coordinates of their intersection points. Alternatively, graph $y = 3^x - 5^{2x-1}$ and use the root finder to determine the x-intercepts of the graph.

Applications

Some of the most important applications of exponential and logarithmic functions arise in banking and finance. They will be thoroughly discussed in Chapter 5. The applications here are from other fields.

Example 7 **Business** The number of total subscribers (in millions) to Netflix, Inc. can be approximated by the function

$$g(x) = 9.78(1.07)^x,$$

where $x = 1$ corresponds to the first quarter of the year 2009, $x = 2$ corresponds to the second quarter of the year 2009, etc. Assume the model remains accurate and determine when the number of subscribers reached 28 million. (Data from: The *Wall Street Journal* and The *Associated Press.*)

Solution You are being asked to find the value of x for which $g(x) = 28$—that is, to solve the following equation:

$$9.78(1.07)^x = 28$$
$$1.07^x = \frac{28}{9.78} \quad \text{Divide both sides by 9.78.}$$
$$\ln(1.07^x) = \ln\left(\frac{28}{9.78}\right) \quad \text{Take logarithms on both sides.}$$
$$x \ln(1.07) = \ln\left(\frac{28}{9.78}\right) \quad \text{Power property of logarithms}$$
$$x = \frac{\ln(28/9.78)}{\ln(1.07)} \quad \text{Divide both sides by } \ln(1.07).$$
$$x \approx 15.5.$$

The 15th quarter corresponds to the third quarter of the year 2012. Hence, according to this model, Netflix, Inc., reached 28 million subscribers in the third quarter of 2012. ✓7

Checkpoint 7

Use the function in Example 7 to determine when Netflix reached 35 million subscribers.

The **half-life** of a radioactive substance is the time it takes for a given quantity of the substance to decay to one-half its original mass. The half-life depends only on the substance, not on the size of the sample. It can be shown that the amount of a radioactive substance at time t is given by the function

$$f(t) = y_0\left(\frac{1}{2}\right)^{t/h} = y_0(.5^{t/h}),$$

where y_0 is the initial amount (at time $t = 0$) and h is the half-life of the substance.

Radioactive carbon-14 is found in every living plant and animal. After the plant or animal dies, its carbon-14 decays exponentially, with a half-life of 5730 years. This fact is the basis for a technique called *carbon dating* for determining the age of fossils.

Example 8   **Natural Science**   A round wooden table hanging in Winchester Castle (England) was alleged to have belonged to King Arthur, who lived in the fifth century. A recent chemical analysis showed that the wood had lost 9% of its carbon-14.[*] How old is the table?

Solution   The decay function for carbon-14 is

$$f(t) = y_0(.5^{t/5730}),$$

where $t = 0$ corresponds to the time the wood was cut to make the table. (That is when the tree died.) Since the wood has lost 9% of its carbon-14, the amount in the table now is 91% of the initial amount y_0 (that is, $.91y_0$). We must find the value of t for which $f(t) = .91y_0$. So we must solve the equation

$y_0(.5^{t/5730}) = .91y_0$	Definition of $f(t)$
$.5^{t/5730} = .91$	Divide both sides by y_0.
$\ln .5^{t/5730} = \ln .91$	Take logarithms on both sides.
$\left(\dfrac{t}{5730}\right)\ln .5 = \ln .91$	Power property of logarithms
$t \ln .5 = 5730 \ln .91$	Multiply both sides by 5730.
$t = \dfrac{5730 \ln .91}{\ln .5} \approx 779.63.$	Divide both sides by $\ln .5$.

The table is about 780 years old and therefore could not have belonged to King Arthur. ✓8

✓ **Checkpoint 8**

How old is a skeleton that has lost 65% of its carbon-14?

Earthquakes are often in the news. The standard method of measuring their size, the **Richter scale,** is a logarithmic function (base 10).

Example 9   **Physical Science**   The intensity $R(i)$ of an earthquake, measured on the Richter scale, is given by

$$R(i) = \log\left(\frac{i}{i_0}\right),$$

where i is the intensity of the ground motion of the earthquake and i_0 is the intensity of the ground motion of the so-called *zero earthquake* (the smallest detectable earthquake, against which others are measured). The underwater earthquake that caused the disastrous 2004 tsunami in Southeast Asia measured 9.1 on the Richter scale.

---

[*]This is done by measuring the ratio of carbon-14 to nonradioactive carbon-12 in the table (a ratio that is approximately constant over long periods) and comparing it with the ratio in living wood.

(a) How did the ground motion of this tsunami compare with that of the zero earthquake?

Solution   In this case,

$$R(i) = 9.1$$

$$\log\left(\frac{i}{i_0}\right) = 9.1.$$

By the definition of logarithms, 9.1 is the exponent to which 10 must be raised to produce i/i_0, which means that

$$10^{9.1} = \frac{i}{i_0}, \quad \text{or equivalently,} \quad i = 10^{9.1}i_0.$$

So the earthquake that produced the tsunami had $10^{9.1}$ (about 1.26 *billion*) times more ground motion than the zero earthquake.

(b) What is the Richter-scale intensity of an earthquake with 10 times as much ground motion as the 2004 tsunami earthquake?

Solution   From (a), the ground motion of the tsunami quake was $10^{9.1}i_0$. So a quake with 10 times that motion would satisfy

$$i = 10(10^{9.1}i_0) = 10^1 \cdot 10^{9.1}i_0 = 10^{10.1}i_0.$$

Therefore, its Richter scale measure would be

$$R(i) = \log\left(\frac{i}{i_0}\right) = \log\left(\frac{10^{10.1}i_0}{i_0}\right) = \log 10^{10.1} = 10.1.$$

Thus, a tenfold increase in ground motion increases the Richter scale measure by only 1. ✓₉

✓ **Checkpoint 9**

Find the Richter-scale intensity of an earthquake whose ground motion is 100 times greater than the ground motion of the 2004 tsunami earthquake discussed in Example 9.

Example 10   **Economics**   One action that government could take to reduce carbon emissions into the atmosphere is to place a tax on fossil fuels. This tax would be based on the amount of carbon dioxide that is emitted into the air when such a fuel is burned. The *cost–benefit* equation $\ln(1 - P) = -.0034 - .0053T$ describes the approximate relationship between a tax of T dollars per ton of carbon dioxide and the corresponding percent reduction P (in decimals) in emissions of carbon dioxide.*

(a) Write P as a function of T.

Solution   We begin by writing the cost–benefit equation in exponential form:

$$\ln(1 - P) = -.0034 - .0053T$$
$$1 - P = e^{-.0034 - .0053T}$$
$$P = P(T) = 1 - e^{-.0034 - .0053T}.$$

A calculator-generated graph of $P(T)$ is shown in Figure 4.23.

(b) Discuss the benefit of continuing to raise taxes on carbon dioxide emissions.

Solution   From the graph, we see that initially there is a rapid reduction in carbon dioxide emissions. However, after a while, there is little benefit in raising taxes further.

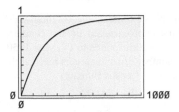

Figure 4.23

---

*"To Slow or Not to Slow: The Economics of The Greenhouse Effect," William D. Nordhaus, *The Economic Journal*, Vol. 101, No. 407 (July, 1991), pp. 920–937.

4.4 Exercises

Solve each logarithmic equation. (See Example 1.)

1. $\ln(x + 3) = \ln(2x - 5)$

2. $\ln(8k - 7) - \ln(3 + 4k) = \ln(9/11)$

3. $\ln(3x + 1) - \ln(5 + x) = \ln 2$

4. $\ln(5x + 2) = \ln 4 + \ln(x + 3)$

5. $2 \ln(x - 3) = \ln(x + 5) + \ln 4$

6. $\ln(k + 5) + \ln(k + 2) = \ln 18k$

Solve each logarithmic equation. (See Example 2.)

7. $\log_3 (6x - 2) = 2$

8. $\log_5 (3x - 4) = 1$

9. $\log x - \log(x + 4) = -1$

10. $\log m - \log(m + 4) = -2$

11. $\log_3 (y + 2) = \log_3 (y - 7) + \log_3 4$

12. $\log_8 (z - 6) = 2 - \log_8 (z + 15)$

13. $\ln(x + 9) - \ln x = 1$

14. $\ln(2x + 1) - 1 = \ln(x - 2)$

15. $\log x + \log(x - 9) = 1$

16. $\log(x - 1) + \log(x + 2) = 1$

Solve each equation for c.

17. $\log(3 + b) = \log(4c - 1)$

18. $\ln(b + 7) = \ln(6c + 8)$

19. $2 - b = \log(6c + 5)$

20. $8b + 6 = \ln(2c) + \ln c$

21. Suppose you overhear the following statement: "I must reject any negative answer when I solve an equation involving logarithms." Is this correct? Write an explanation of why it is or is not correct.

22. What values of x cannot be solutions of the following equation?
$$\log_a (4x - 7) + \log_a (x^2 + 4) = 0.$$

Solve these exponential equations without using logarithms. (See Example 3.)

23. $2^{x-1} = 8$

24. $16^{-x+2} = 8$

25. $25^{-3x} = 3125$

26. $81^{-2x} = 3^{x-1}$

27. $6^{-x} = 36^{x+6}$

28. $16^x = 64$

29. $\left(\dfrac{3}{4}\right)^x = \dfrac{16}{9}$

30. $2^{x^2 - 4x} = \dfrac{1}{16}$

Use logarithms to solve these exponential equations. (See Examples 4–6.)

31. $2^x = 5$

32. $5^x = 8$

33. $2^x = 3^{x-1}$

34. $4^{x+2} = 5^{x-1}$

35. $3^{1-2x} = 5^{x+5}$

36. $4^{3x-1} = 3^{x-2}$

37. $e^{3x} = 6$

38. $e^{-3x} = 5$

39. $2e^{5a+2} = 8$

40. $10e^{3z-7} = 5$

Solve each equation for c.

41. $10^{4c-3} = d$

42. $3 \cdot 10^{2c+1} = 4d$

43. $e^{2c-1} = b$

44. $3e^{5c-7} = b$

Solve these equations. (See Examples 1–6.)

45. $\log_7 (r + 3) + \log_7 (r - 3) = 1$

46. $\log_4 (z + 3) + \log_4 (z - 3) = 2$

47. $\log_3 (a - 3) = 1 + \log_3 (a + 1)$

48. $\log w + \log(3w - 13) = 1$

49. $\log_2 \sqrt{2y^2 - 1} = 3/2$

50. $\log_2 (\log_2 x) = 1$

51. $\log_2 (\log_3 x) = 1$

52. $\dfrac{\ln(2x + 1)}{\ln(3x - 1)} = 2$

53. $5^{-2x} = \dfrac{1}{25}$

54. $5^{x^2+x} = 1$

55. $2^{|x|} = 16$

56. $5^{-|x|} = \dfrac{1}{25}$

57. $2^{x^2-1} = 10$

58. $3^{2-x^2} = 8$

59. $2(e^x + 1) = 10$

60. $5(e^{2x} - 2) = 15$

61. Explain why the equation $4^{x^2+1} = 2$ has no solutions.

62. Explain why the equation $\log(-x) = -4$ does have a solution, and find that solution.

Work these problems. (See Example 7.)

63. **Business**   Gambling revenues (in billions of U.S. dollars) generated in Macau, China can be approximated by the function $g(x) = 1.104(1.346)^x$, where $x = 2$ corresponds to the year 2002. Assume the model remains accurate and find the years in which the gambling revenues reached the indicated amounts. (Data from: The *Wall Street Journal*.)

    (a) $20 billion   (b) $45 billion

64. **Social Science**   The number of centenarians (in thousands) in the United States can be approximated by the function $h(x) = 2(1.056)^x$, where $x = 0$ corresponds to the year 1950. Find the year in which the number of centenarians reached the following levels. (Data from: U.S. Census Bureau.)

    (a) 30,000   (b) 50,000

65. **Health**   As we saw in Example 12 of Section 4.3, the life expectancy at birth of a person born in year x is approximately
$$f(x) = 17.6 + 12.8 \ln x,$$
where $x = 10$ corresponds to the year 1910. Find the birth year of a person whose life expectancy at birth was

    (a) 75.5 years;   (b) 77.5 years;   (c) 81 years.

66. Health A drug's effectiveness decreases over time. If, each hour, a drug is only 90% as effective as during the previous hour, at some point the patient will not be receiving enough medication and must receive another dose. This situation can be modeled by the exponential function $y = y_0(.90)^{t-1}$. In this equation, y_0 is the amount of the initial dose and y is the amount of medication still available t hours after the drug was administered. Suppose 200 mg of the drug is administered. How long will it take for this initial dose to reach the dangerously low level of 50 mg?

67. Economics The percentage of the U.S. income earned by the top one percent of earners can be approximated by the function $f(x) = 7.9e^{.0254x}$, where $x = 0$ corresponds to the year 1970. (Data from: The *New York Times*.)

(a) When did the percentage reach 15%?

(b) If the model remains accurate, when will the percentage reach 30%?

68. Health The probability P percent of having an accident while driving a car is related to the alcohol level t of the driver's blood by the equation $P = e^{kt}$, where k is a constant. Accident statistics show that the probability of an accident is 25% when the blood alcohol level is $t = .15$.

(a) Use the equation and the preceding information to find k (to three decimal places). *Note:* Use $P = 25$, and not .25.

(b) Using the value of k from part (a), find the blood alcohol level at which the probability of having an accident is 50%.

Work these exercises. (See Example 8.)

69. Natural Science The amount of cobalt-60 (in grams) in a storage facility at time t is given by

$$C(t) = 25e^{-.14t},$$

where time is measured in years.

(a) How much cobalt-60 was present initially?

(b) What is the half-life of cobalt-60? (*Hint:* For what value of t is $C(t) = 12.5$?)

70. Natural Science A Native American mummy was found recently. It had 73.6% of the amount of radiocarbon present in living beings. Approximately how long ago did this person die?

71. Natural Science How old is a piece of ivory that has lost 36% of its radiocarbon?

72. Natural Science A sample from a refuse deposit near the Strait of Magellan had 60% of the carbon-14 of a contemporary living sample. How old was the sample?

Natural Science *Work these problems. (See Example 9.)*

73. In May 2008, Sichuan province, China suffered an earthquake that measured 7.9 on the Richter scale.

(a) Express the intensity of this earthquake in terms of i_0.

(b) In July of the same year, a quake measuring 5.4 on the Richter scale struck Los Angeles. Express the intensity of this earthquake in terms of i_0.

(c) How many times more intense was the China earthquake than the one in Los Angeles?

74. Find the Richter-scale intensity of earthquakes whose ground motion is

(a) $1000i_0$; (b) $100,000i_0$;

(c) $10,000,000i_0$.

(d) Fill in the blank in this statement: Increasing the ground motion by a factor of 10^k increases the Richter intensity by _____ units.

75. The loudness of sound is measured in units called decibels. The decibel rating of a sound is given by

$$D(i) = 10 \cdot \log\left(\frac{i}{i_0}\right),$$

where i is the intensity of the sound and i_0 is the minimum intensity detectable by the human ear (the so-called *threshold sound*). Find the decibel rating of each of the sounds with the given intensities. Round answers to the nearest whole number.

(a) Whisper, $115i_0$

(b) Average sound level in the movie *Godzilla*, $10^{10}i_0$

(c) Jackhammer, $31,600,000,000i_0$

(d) Rock music, $895,000,000,000i_0$

(e) Jetliner at takeoff, $109,000,000,000,000i_0$

76. (a) How much more intense is a sound that measures 100 decibels than the threshold sound?

(b) How much more intense is a sound that measures 50 decibels than the threshold sound?

(c) How much more intense is a sound measuring 100 decibels than one measuring 50 decibels?

77. Natural Science Refer to Example 10.

(a) Determine the percent reduction in carbon dioxide when the tax is $60.

(b) What tax will cause a 50% reduction in carbon dioxide emissions?

78. Business The revenue (in billions of dollars) for Walt Disney Company can be approximated by the function $R(x) = 16.20 + 9.992 \ln x$, where $x = 3$ corresponds to the year 2003. Find each of the following. (Data from: www.morningstar.com.)

(a) $R(9)$ (b) $R(12)$

(c) If the model remains accurate, in what year will revenue reach $50 billion?

79. Business Annual box office revenue (in billions of dollars) generated in North America can be approximated by the function $g(x) = 2.0 + 2.768 \ln x$, where $x = 2$ corresponds to the year 1992. (Data from: www.boxofficemojo.com.)

(a) Graph the function g for the years 1992 through 2012.

(b) According to the model, in what year did revenue reach $9 billion?

80. Physical Science The table on the following page gives some of the planets' average distances D from the sun and their period P of revolution around the sun in years. The distances have been normalized so that Earth is one unit from the sun. Thus, Jupiter's distance of 5.2 means that Jupiter's distance from the sun is 5.2 times farther than Earth's.[*]

Planet	D	P
Earth	1	1
Jupiter	5.2	11.9
Saturn	9.54	29.5
Uranus	19.2	84.0

(a) Plot the points (D, P) for these planets. Would a straight line or an exponential curve fit these points best?

(b) Plot the points $(\ln D, \ln P)$ for these planets. Do these points appear to lie on a line?

(c) Determine a linear equation that approximates the data points, with $x = \ln D$ and $y = \ln P$. Use the first and last data points (rounded to 2 decimal places). Graph your line and the data on the same coordinate axes.

(d) Use the linear equation to predict the period of the planet Pluto if its distance is 39.5. Compare your answer with the true value of 248.5 years.

✓ **Checkpoint Answers**

1. (a) 3   (b) $1 + \sqrt{2} \approx 2.414$

2. (a) 5   (b) 52

3. (a) 1/3   (b) 8/3   (c) −1/4

4. (a) 2.807   (b) 2.431   (c) 2.579

5. (a) 2.710   (b) .802

6. (a) 23.979   (b) −3.113   (c) ±1.612

7. Second quarter of 2013.

8. About 8679 years

9. 11.1

[*]C. Ronan, *The Natural History of the Universe.* New York: Macmillan Publishing Co., 1991.

CHAPTER 4 Summary and Review

Key Terms and Symbols

4.1 exponential function
exponential growth and
decay
the number
$e \approx 2.71828\ldots$

4.2 exponential growth function
logistic function

4.3 $\log x$ common (base-10)
logarithm of x

$\ln x$ natural (base-e)
logarithm of x

$\log_a x$ base-a logarithm
of x

product, quotient, and
power properties of
logarithms

change-of-base theorem

Inverse logarithmic
functions

4.4 logarithmic equations
exponential equations
half-life
Richter scale

Chapter 4 Key Concepts

Exponentialic Functions

An important application of exponents is the **exponential growth function,** defined as $f(t) = y_0 e^{kt}$ or $f(t) = y_0 b^t$, where y_0 is the amount of a quantity present at time $t = 0$, $e \approx 2.71828$, and k and b are constants.

Logarithmic Functions

The **logarithm** of x to the base a is defined as follows: For $a > 0$ and $a \neq 1$, $y = \log_a x$ means $a^y = x$. Thus, $\log_a x$ is an *exponent*, the power to which a must be raised to produce x.

Properties of Logarithms

Let x, y, and a be positive real numbers, with $a \neq 1$, and let r be any real number. Then

$$\log_a 1 = 0; \quad \log_a a = 1;$$
$$\log_a a^r = r; \quad a^{\log_a x} = x.$$

Product property $\log_a xy = \log_a x + \log_a y$

Quotient property $\log_a \dfrac{x}{y} = \log_a x - \log_a y$

Power property $\log_a x^r = r \log_a x$

Solving Exponential and Logarithmic Equations

Let $a > 0$, with $a \neq 1$.

If $\log_a u = \log_a v$, then $u = v$.

If $a^u = a^v$, then $u = v$.

Chapter 4 Review Exercises

Match each equation with the letter of the graph that most closely resembles the graph of the equation. Assume that $a > 1$.

1. $y = a^{x+2}$

2. $y = a^x + 2$

3. $y = -a^x + 2$

4. $y = a^{-x} + 2$

(a)

(b)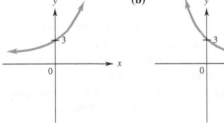

(c)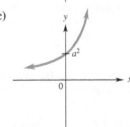

(d)

Consider the exponential function $y = f(x) = a^x$ graphed here. Answer each question on the basis of the graph.

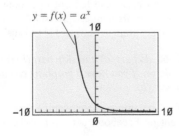

$y = f(x) = a^x$

5. What is true about the value of a in comparison to 1?

6. What is the domain of f?

7. What is the range of f?

8. What is the value of $f(0)$?

Graph each function.

9. $f(x) = 4^x$

10. $g(x) = 4^{-x}$

11. $f(x) = \ln x + 5$

12. $g(x) = \log x - 3$

Work these problems.

13. Economics The cumulative number of retail jobs (in thousands) added each month to the U.S. economy can be approximated by the function $f(x) = 39.61(1.118)^x$, where $x = 1$ corresponds to January, 2011. (Data from: U.S. Bureau of Labor Statistics.)

(a) Estimate the cumulative number of jobs added in September, 2012.

(b) In what month, according to the model, did the cumulative number of jobs hit 300,000?

14. Economics The cumulative number of construction jobs (in thousands) added each month to the U.S. economy can be approximated by the function $f(x) = 28.7(1.120)^x$, where $x = 1$ corresponds to January, 2011. (Data from: U.S. Bureau of Labor Statistics.)

(a) Estimate the cumulative number of jobs added in June, 2012.

(b) In what month, according to the model, did the cumulative number of jobs hit 250,000?

Translate each exponential statement into an equivalent logarithmic one.

15. $10^{2.53148} = 340$

16. $5^4 = 625$

17. $e^{3.8067} = 45$ **18.** $7^{1/2} = \sqrt{7}$

Translate each logarithmic statement into an equivalent exponential one.

19. $\log 10,000 = 4$ **20.** $\log 26.3 = 1.4200$

21. $\ln 81.1 = 4.3957$ **22.** $\log_2 4096 = 12$

Evaluate these expressions without using a calculator.

23. $\ln e^5$ **24.** $\log \sqrt[3]{10}$

25. $10^{\log 8.9}$ **26.** $\ln e^{3t^2}$

27. $\log_8 2$ **28.** $\log_8 32$

Write these expressions as a single logarithm. Assume all variables represent positive quantities.

29. $\log 4x + \log 5x^5$ **30.** $4 \log u - 5 \log u^6$

31. $3 \log b - 2 \log c$ **32.** $7 \ln x - 3(\ln x^3 + 5 \ln x)$

Solve each equation. Round to the nearest thousandth.

33. $\ln(m + 8) - \ln m = \ln 3$

34. $2 \ln(y + 1) = \ln(y^2 - 1) + \ln 5$

35. $\log(m + 3) = 2$ **36.** $\log x^3 = 2$

37. $\log_2 (3k + 1) = 4$ **38.** $\log_5 \left(\dfrac{5z}{z - 2} \right) = 2$

39. $\log x + \log(x - 3) = 1$ **40.** $\log_2 r + \log_2 (r - 2) = 3$

41. $2^{3x} = \dfrac{1}{64}$ **42.** $\left(\dfrac{9}{16} \right)^x = \dfrac{3}{4}$

43. $9^{2y+1} = 27^y$ **44.** $\dfrac{1}{2} = \left(\dfrac{b}{4} \right)^{1/4}$

45. $8^p = 19$ **46.** $3^z = 11$

47. $5 \cdot 2^{-m} = 35$ **48.** $2 \cdot 15^{-k} = 18$

49. $e^{-5-2x} = 5$ **50.** $e^{3x-1} = 12$

51. $6^{2-m} = 2^{3m+1}$ **52.** $5^{3r-1} = 6^{2r+5}$

53. $(1 + .003)^k = 1.089$ **54.** $(1 + .094)^z = 2.387$

Work these problems.

55. A population is increasing according to the growth law $y = 4e^{.03t}$, where y is in thousands and t is in months. Match each of the questions (a), (b), (c), and (d) with one of the solution (A), (B), (C), or (D).

    (a) How long will it take for the population to double?   **(A)** Solve $4e^{.03t} = 12$ for t.

    (b) When will the population reach 12 thousand?   **(B)** Evaluate $4e^{.03(72)}$.

    (c) How large will the population be in 6 months?   **(C)** Solve $4e^{.03t} = 2 \cdot 4$ for t.

    (d) How large will the population be in 6 years?   **(D)** Evaluate $4e^{.03(6)}$.

56. **Natural Science** A population is increasing according to the growth law $y = 2e^{.02t}$, where y is in millions and t is in years. Match each of the questions (a), (b), (c), and (d) with one of the solutions (A), (B), (C), or (D).

    (a) How long will it take for the population to triple?   **(A)** Evaluate $2e^{.02(1/3)}$.

    (b) When will the population reach 3 million?   **(B)** Solve $2e^{.02t} = 3 \cdot 2$ for t.

    (c) How large will the population be in 3 years?   **(C)** Evaluate $2e^{.02(3)}$.

    (d) How large will the population be in 4 months?   **(D)** Solve $2e^{.02t} = 3$ for t.

57. **Natural Science** The amount of polonium (in grams) present after t days is given by

$$A(t) = 10e^{-.00495t}.$$

    (a) How much polonium was present initially?

    (b) What is the half-life of polonium?

    (c) How long will it take for the polonium to decay to 3 grams?

58. **Business** The annual average natural gas price (in dollars per million BTUs) can be approximated by the function $h(x) = 69.54e^{-.264x}$, where $x = 8$ corresponds to the year 2008. (Data from: Energy Information Administration.)

    (a) What was the average price per million BTUs in the year 2010?

    (b) According to the model, in what year did the average price per million BTUs hit $3.00?

59. **Natural Science** In April, 2013, Enarotali, Indonesia suffered an earthquake that measured 7.0 on the Richter scale.

    (a) Express the intensity of this earthquake in terms of i_0.

    (b) In March, 2013, Papua New Guinea suffered an earthquake that registered 6.5 on the Richter scale. Express the intensity of this earthquake in terms of i_0.

    (c) How many times more intense was the earthquake in Indonesia than the one in Papua New Guinea?

60. **Natural Science** One earthquake measures 4.6 on the Richter scale. A second earthquake has ground motion 1000 times greater than the first. What does the second one measure on the Richter scale?

Natural Science Another form of Newton's law of cooling (see Section 4.2, Exercises 15 and 16) is $F(t) = T_0 + Ce^{-kt}$, where C and k are constants.

61. A piece of metal is heated to 300° Celsius and then placed in a cooling liquid at 50° Celsius. After 4 minutes, the metal has cooled to 175° Celsius. Find its temperature after 12 minutes.

62. A frozen pizza has a temperature of 3.4° Celsius when it is taken from the freezer and left out in a room at 18° Celsius. After half an hour, its temperature is 7.2° Celsius. How long will it take for the pizza to thaw to 10° Celsius?

In Exercises 63–66, do part (a) and skip part (b) if you do not have a graphing calculator. If you have a graphing calculator, then skip part (a) and do part (b).

63. **Business** The approximate average times (in minutes per month) spent on Facebook per unique visitor in the United

States on a mobile device are given in the following table for the last six months of 2012 and first two months of 2013. (Data from: www.comScore.com.)

Month	July 2012	Aug. 2012	Sept. 2012	Oct. 2012	Nov. 2012	Dec. 2012	Jan. 2013	Feb. 2013
Minutes	500	510	520	580	615	700	760	785

(a) Let $x = 0$ correspond to July, 2012. Use the data points from July, 2012 and February, 2013 to find a function of the form $f(x) = a(b^x)$ that models these data.

(b) Use exponential regression to find a function g that models these data, with $x = 0$ corresponding to July, 2012.

(c) Assume the model remains accurate and estimate the minutes per month in April, 2013.

(d) According to this model, when will the minutes per month reach 1000?

64. **Physical Science** The atmospheric pressure (in millibars) at a given altitude (in thousands of meters) is listed in the table:

Altitude	0	2000	4000	6000	8000	10,000
Pressure	1013	795	617	472	357	265

(a) Use the data points for altitudes 0 and 10,000 to find a function of the form $f(x) = a(b^x)$ that models these data, where altitude x is measured in thousands of meters. (For example, $x = 4$ means 4000 meters.)

(b) Use exponential regression to find a function $g(x)$ that models these data, with x measured in thousands of meters.

(c) Estimate the pressure at 1500 m and 11,000 m, and compare the results with the actual values of 846 and 227 millibars, respectively.

(d) At what height is the pressure 500 millibars?

65. **Business** The table shows the approximate digital share (in percent) of recorded music sales in the United States in recent years. (Data from: www.statista.com.)

Year	2006	2007	2008	2009	2010	2011	2012
Percent	18	25	39	43	47	50	59

(a) Let $x = 1$ correspond to the year 2006. Use the data points for 2006 and 2012 to find a function of the form $f(x) = a + b \ln x$ that models these data. [*Hint:* Use (1, 18) to find a; then use (7, 59) to find b.]

(b) Use logarithmic regression to find a function g that models these data, with $x = 1$ corresponding to the year 2006.

(c) Assume the model remains accurate and predict the percentage for 2014.

(d) According to the model, when will the share of digital music reach 70%?

66. **Health** The number of kidney transplants (in thousands) in selected years is shown in the table. (Data from: National Network for Organ Sharing.)

Year	1991	1995	2000	2005	2011
Transplants	9.678	11.083	13.613	16.481	16.813

(a) Let $x = 1$ correspond to 1991. Use the data points for 1991 and 2011 to find a function of the form $f(x) = a + b \ln x$ that models these data. [See Exercise 65(a).]

(b) Use logarithmic regression to find a function $g(x)$ that models these data, with $x = 1$ corresponding to 1991.

(c) Estimate the number of kidney transplants in 2013.

(d) If the model remains accurate, when will the number of kidney transplants reach 17,500?

Case Study 4 Gapminder.org

The website www.gapminder.org is committed to displaying economic and health data for countries around the world in a visually compelling way. The goal is to make publicly available data easy for citizens of the world to understand so individuals and policy makers can comprehend trends and make data-driven conclusions. For example, the website uses the size of the bubble on a plot to indicate the population of the country, and the color indicates the region in which the country lies:

Yellow	America
Orange	Europe and Central Asia
Green	Middle East and Northern Africa
Dark Blue	Sub-Saharan Africa
Red	East Asia and the Pacific

Additionally, the website also uses animation to show how variables change over time.

Let's look at an example of two variables of interest as best we can on a printed page. We will use income per-person (in U.S. dollars and measured as gross domestic product per capita) as a measure of a country's wealth as the x-axis variable and life expectancy (in years) at birth as a measure of the health of a country on the y-axis. In Figure 4.24 on the following page we see a bubble for each country in the year 1800.

We see that all the countries are bunched together with quite low income per-person and average life expectancy ranging from 25–40 years. The two large bubbles you see are for the two most populous countries: China (red) and India (light blue). When you visit the website (please do so, it is very cool!) and press the "Play" button at the bottom left, you can see how income per-person and life expectancy change over time for each country. At its conclusion, you obtain Figure 4.25 on the following page, which shows the relationship between income per-person and average life expectancy in the year 2011.

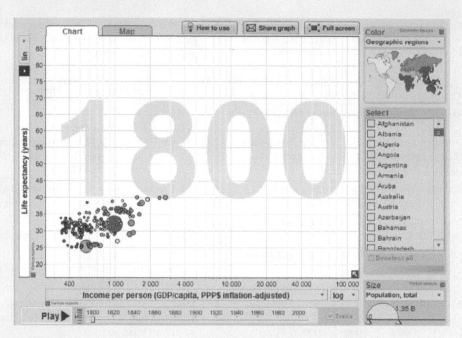

Figure 4.24 Relationship Between Income per Person and Average Life Expectancy in 1800 from Gapminder Foundation. Reproduced by permission of Gapminder Foundation.

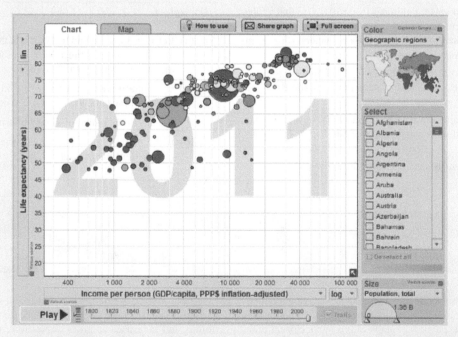

Figure 4.25 Relationship Between Income per Person and Average Life Expectancy in 2011 from Gapminder Foundation. Reproduced by permission of Gapminder Foundation.

We can see that a great deal has changed in 200 years! One great thing is that all countries now have average life expectancy that is over 45 years. This is simply incredible. Also, we see there is a great range of income per-person values for a variety of countries. The country to the far right (the little green dot) is the Middle Eastern country of Qatar. We see that many of the Sub-Sahara countries on the left (in dark blue) have the lowest per-person income and the lowest average life expectancy. The wealthier countries—for example, countries whose per-person income is greater than \$20,000—all have life expectancy over 70 years.

We can actually use the per-person income x to predict the average life expectancy $f(x)$. Note that Gapminder.org has its default showing the income per-person on a logarithmic scale. When we see a linear pattern such as this where the x-axis is on a logarithmic scale and the y-axis is on the regular scale, a model of the form $f(x) = a + b \ln x$ often fits the data well. Since Gapminder.org makes all the data for their graphs available, we can fit a model to find values for a and b. Using regression, we obtain the following model:

$$f(x) = 15.32 + 6.178 \ln x. \tag{1}$$

Gapminder.org will also show the economic development for an individual country. Figure 4.26 shows per capita GDP on the y-axis for the country of Brazil over time. We can see that economic gains began close to the year 1900. The graph shows per-person income on the y-axis (again on a logarithmic scale) and the trend seems approx-

imately linear since 1900. When this is the case, a model of the form $a(b^x)$ usually fits the data well. Letting $x = 0$ correspond to the year 1900, we obtain the following:

$$g(x) = 510.3(1.029)^x \tag{2}$$

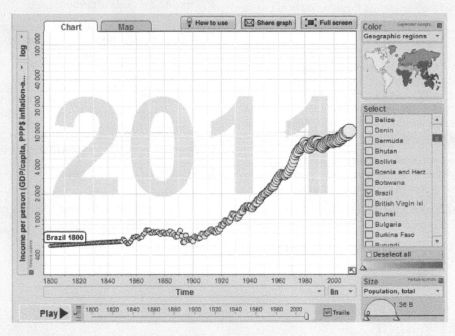

Figure 4.26   Relationship Between Time and per Capita GDP in 2011 from Gapminder Foundation. Reproduced by permission of Gapminder Foundation.

The trajectory of the United States (Figure 4.27) is a bit different, with rising incomes starting in the early 1800s and continuing to the present. Notice the dips that occur in the mid-1930s (the Great Depression) and the early 1940s (World War II). Fitting a model to

the data for the United States (again with $x = 0$ corresponding to the year 1900) yields the model:

$$h(x) = 6229.2(1.018)^x \tag{3}$$

Figure 4.27   Trajectory of United States from Gapminder Foundation. Reproduced by permission of Gapminder Foundation.

Exercises

For Exercises 1–6, use Equation (1) that provides a model using per-person income as the *x*-variable to predict life expectancy as the *y*-variable.

1. Create a graph of the function given in Equation (1) from $x = 0$ to 100,000.

2. Describe the shape of the graph.

3. The country farthest to the left in Figure 4.25 is the Democratic Republic of the Congo. In 2011, its income per-person was $387 and its life expectancy was 48. Suppose that the economic development improved so that the Democratic Republic of the Congo had a per-person income level of $4000. What does the model of Equation (1) predict for life expectancy?

4. In 2011, Russia had per-person income of $14,738 and life expectancy of 69 years. What does the model predict for life expectancy if the per-person income improved to $25,000?

5. According to the model, what per-person income level predicts a life expectancy of 60 years?

6. According to the model, what per-person income level predicts a life expectancy of 75 years?

For Exercises 7–10, use the model in Equation (2) that uses year (with $x = 0$ corresponding to the year 1900) to predict the per-person income for Brazil.

7. Graph the model of Equation (2) from $x = 0$ to 111.

8. Describe the shape of the model.

9. According to the model, what was the per-person income for Brazil in the year 1950? In the year 2000?

10. What year does the model indicate that per-person income reached $4000?

For Exercises 11–14, use the model in Equation (3) that uses year (with $x = 0$ corresponding to the year 1900) to predict the per-person income for the United States.

11. Graph the model of Equation (3) from $x = 0$ to 111.

12. Describe the shape of the model.

13. According to the model, what was the per-person income for the United States in the year 1960? In the year 2010?

14. What year does the model indicate that per-person income reached $20,000?

↗ Extended Project

Go to the website www.gapminder.org and explore different relationships. Examine the relationship between a variety of variables that look at relationships among health, climate, disasters, economy, education, family, global trends, HIV, and poverty. (*Hint:* When you have the graphic display showing, click on the button for "Open Graph Menu" to see a list of options in these areas all ready to be viewed.) When observing the different graphs, notice when the *x*-axis, the *y*-axis, or both are on a logarithmic scale.

1. Find a relationship that appears linear when the *x*-axis is on the logarithmic scale and the *y*-axis is not. Now click on the button to the right of the *x*-axis and observe the graph on a linear scale (rather than the logarithmic scale). Describe the shape.

2. Find a relationship that appears linear when the *x*-axis is not on the logarithmic scale, but the *y*-axis is on the logarithmic scale. Now click on the button above the *y*-axis and observe the graph on a linear scale (rather than the logarithmic scale). Describe the shape.

3. Find a relationship that appears linear when the *x*-axis is on the logarithmic scale, and the *y*-axis is on the logarithmic scale. Now click on the button to the right of the *x*-axis and click on the button above the *y*-axis and observe the graph on a linear scale (rather than the logarithmic scale) for both axes. Describe the shape.

Mathematics of Finance

5
CHAPTER

Most people must take out a loan for a big purchase, such as a car, a major appliance, or a house. People who carry a balance on their credit cards are, in effect, also borrowing money. Loan payments must be accurately determined, and it may take some work to find the "best deal." See Exercise 54 on page 262 and Exercise 57 on page 242. We must all plan for eventual retirement, which usually involves savings accounts and investments in stocks, bonds, and annuities to fund 401K accounts or individual retirement accounts (IRAs). See Exercises 40 and 41 on page 250.

It is important for both businesspersons and consumers to understand the mathematics of finance in order to make sound financial decisions. Interest formulas for borrowing and investing money are introduced in this chapter.

📄 **NOTE** We try to present realistic, up-to-date applications in this text. Because interest rates change so frequently, however, it is very unlikely that the rates in effect when this chapter was written are the same as the rates today when you are reading it. Fortunately, the mathematics of finance is the same regardless of the level of interest rates. So we have used a variety of rates in the examples and exercises. Some will be realistic and some won't by the time you see them—but all of them have occurred in the past several decades.

5.1 Simple Interest and Discount

Interest is the fee paid to use someone else's money. Interest on loans of a year or less is frequently calculated as **simple interest,** which is paid only on the amount borrowed or invested and not on past interest. The amount borrowed or deposited is called the

principal. The **rate** of interest is given as a percent per year, expressed as a decimal. For example, $6\% = .06$ and $11\frac{1}{2}\% = .115$. The **time** during which the money is accruing interest is calculated in years. Simple interest is the product of the principal, rate, and time.

Simple Interest

The simple interest I on P dollars at a rate of interest r per year for t years is

$$I = Prt.$$

It is customary in financial problems to round interest to the nearest cent.

Example 1   To furnish her new apartment, Maggie Chan borrowed \$4000 at 3% interest from her parents for 9 months. How much interest will she pay?

Solution   Use the formula $I = Prt$, with $P = 4000$, $r = 0.03$, and $t = 9/12 = 3/4$ years:

$$I = Prt$$

$$I = 4000 * .03 * \frac{3}{4} = 90.$$

Thus, Maggie pays a total of \$90 in interest. ☑₁

Simple interest is normally used only for loans with a term of a year or less. A significant exception is the case of **corporate bonds** and similar financial instruments. A typical bond pays simple interest twice a year for a specified length of time, at the end of which the bond **matures.** At maturity, the company returns your initial investment to you.

Example 2   **Finance**   On January 8, 2013, Bank of America issued 10-year bonds at an annual simple interest rate of 3.3%, with interest paid twice a year. John Altiere buys a \$10,000 bond. (Data from: www.finra.org.)

(a) How much interest will he earn every six months?

Solution   Use the interest formula, $I = Prt$, with $P = 10,000$, $r = .033$, and $t = \frac{1}{2}$:

$$I = Prt = 10,000 * .033 * \frac{1}{2} = \$165.$$

(b) How much interest will he earn over the 10-year life of the bond?

Solution   Either use the interest formula with $t = 10$, that is,

$$I = Prt = 10,000 * .033 * 10 = \$3300,$$

or take the answer in part (a), which will be paid out every six months for 10 years for a total of twenty times. Thus, John would obtain $\$165 * 20 = \$3300$. ☑₂

✓ **Checkpoint 1**

Find the simple interest for each loan.

(a) \$2000 at 8.5% for 10 months

(b) \$3500 at 10.5% for $1\frac{1}{2}$ years

Answers to Checkpoint exercises are found at the end of the section.

✓ **Checkpoint 2**

For the given bonds, find the semiannual interest payment and the total interest paid over the life of the bond.

(a) \$7500 Time Warner Cable, Inc. 30-year bond at 7.3% annual interest.

(b) \$15,000 Clear Channel Communications 10-year bond at 9.0% annual interest.

Future Value

If you deposit P dollars at simple interest rate r for t years, then the **future value** (or **maturity value**) A of this investment is the sum of the principal P and the interest I it has earned:

$$A = \text{Principal} + \text{Interest}$$
$$= P + I$$
$$= P + Prt \qquad \qquad I = Prt.$$
$$= P(1 + rt). \qquad \qquad \text{Factor out } P.$$

The following box summarizes this result.

Future Value (or Maturity Value) for Simple Interest

The future value (maturity value) A of P dollars for t years at interest rate r per year is

$$A = P + I, \qquad \text{or} \qquad A = P(1 + rt).$$

Example 3   Find each maturity value and the amount of interest paid.

(a) Rick borrows $20,000 from his parents at 5.25% to add a room on his house. He plans to repay the loan in 9 months with a bonus he expects to receive at that time.

Solution   The loan is for 9 months, or $9/12$ of a year, so $t = .75, P = 20{,}000$, and $r = .0525$. Use the formula to obtain

$$A = P(1 + rt)$$
$$= 20{,}000[1 + .0525(.75)]$$
$$\approx 20{,}787.5, \qquad \qquad \text{Use a calculator.}$$

or $20,787.50. The maturity value A is the sum of the principal P and the interest I, that is, $A = P + I$. To find the amount of interest paid, rearrange this equation:

$$I = A - P$$
$$I = \$20{,}787.50 - \$20{,}000 = \$787.50.$$

(b) A loan of $11,280 for 85 days at 9% interest.

Solution   Use the formula $A = P(1 + rt)$, with $P = 11{,}280$ and $r = .09$. Unless stated otherwise, we assume a 365-day year, so the period in years is $t = 85/365$. The maturity value is

$$A = P(1 + rt)$$
$$A = 11{,}280\left(1 + .09 * \frac{85}{365}\right)$$
$$\approx 11{,}280(1.020958904) \approx \$11{,}516.42.$$

As in part (a), the interest is

$$I = A - P = \$11{,}516.42 - \$11{,}280 = \$236.42.$$

✓**Checkpoint 3**

Find each future value.

(a) $1000 at 4.6% for 6 months

(b) $8970 at 11% for 9 months

(c) $95,106 at 9.8% for 76 days

Example 4   Suppose you borrow $15,000 and are required to pay $15,315 in 4 months to pay off the loan and interest. What is the simple interest rate?

Solution   One way to find the rate is to solve for r in the future-value formula when $P = 15,000, A = 15,315$, and $t = 4/12 = 1/3$:

$$P(1 + rt) = A$$

$$15,000\left(1 + r * \frac{1}{3}\right) = 15,315$$

$$15,000 + \frac{15,000r}{3} = 15,315 \qquad \text{Multiply out left side.}$$

$$\frac{15,000r}{3} = 315 \qquad \text{Subtract 15,000 from both sides.}$$

$$15,000r = 945 \qquad \text{Multiply both sides by 3.}$$

$$r = \frac{945}{15,000} = .063. \qquad \text{Divide both sides by 15,000.}$$

Therefore, the interest rate is 6.3%. ✓4

✓**Checkpoint 4**

You lend a friend $500. She agrees to pay you $520 in 6 months. What is the interest rate?

Present Value

A sum of money that can be deposited today to yield some larger amount in the future is called the **present value** of that future amount. Present value refers to the principal to be invested or loaned, so we use the same variable P as we did for principal. In interest problems, P always represents the amount at the beginning of the period, and A always represents the amount at the end of the period. To find a formula for P, we begin with the future-value formula:

$$A = P(1 + rt).$$

Dividing each side by $1 + rt$ gives the following formula for the present value.

> ### Present Value for Simple Interest
>
> The **present value** P of a future amount of A dollars at a simple interest rate r for t years is
>
> $$P = \frac{A}{1 + rt}.$$

Example 5   Find the present value of $32,000 in 4 months at 9% interest.

Solution

$$P = \frac{A}{1 + rt} = \frac{32,000}{1 + (.09)\left(\frac{4}{12}\right)} = \frac{32,000}{1.03} = 31,067.96.$$

✓**Checkpoint 5**

Find the present value of the given future amounts. Assume 6% interest.

(a) $7500 in 1 year

(b) $89,000 in 5 months

(c) $164,200 in 125 days

A deposit of $31,067.96 today at 9% interest would produce $32,000 in 4 months. These two sums, $31,067.96 today and $32,000.00 in 4 months, are equivalent (at 9%) because the first amount becomes the second amount in 4 months. ✓5

Example 6 Because of a court settlement, Jeff Weidenaar owes $5000 to Chuck Synovec. The money must be paid in 10 months, with no interest. Suppose Weidenaar wants to pay the money today and that Synovec can invest it at an annual rate of 5%. What amount should Synovec be willing to accept to settle the debt?

Solution The $5000 is the future value in 10 months. So Synovec should be willing to accept an amount that will grow to $5000 in 10 months at 5% interest. In other words, he should accept the present value of $5000 under these circumstances. Use the present-value formula with $A = 5000$, $r = .05$, and $t = 10/12 = 5/6$:

$$P = \frac{A}{1 + rt} = \frac{5000}{1 + .05 * \dfrac{5}{6}} = 4800.$$

Synovec should be willing to accept $4800 today in settlement of the debt.

✓ **Checkpoint 6**

Jerrell Davis is owed $19,500 by Christine O'Brien. The money will be paid in 11 months, with no interest. If the current interest rate is 10%, how much should Davis be willing to accept today in settlement of the debt?

Example 7 Larry Parks owes $6500 to Virginia Donovan. The loan is payable in one year at 6% interest. Donovan needs cash to pay medical bills, so four months before the loan is due, she sells the note (loan) to the bank. If the bank wants a return of 9% on its investment, how much should it pay Donovan for the note?

Solution First find the maturity value of the loan—the amount (with interest) that Parks must pay Donovan:

$$
\begin{aligned}
A &= P(1 + rt) & &\text{Maturity-value formula}\\
&= 6500(1 + .06 * 1) & &\text{Let } P = 6500, r = .06, \text{ and } t = 1.\\
&= 6500(1.06) = \$6890.
\end{aligned}
$$

In four months, the bank will receive $6890. Since the bank wants a 9% return, compute the present value of this amount at 9% for four months:

$$
\begin{aligned}
P &= \frac{A}{1 + rt} & &\text{Present-value formula}\\[2mm]
&= \frac{6890}{1 + .09\left(\dfrac{4}{12}\right)} = \$6689.32. & &\text{Let } A = 6890, r = .09, \text{ and } t = 4/12.
\end{aligned}
$$

✓ **Checkpoint 7**

A firm accepts a $21,000 note due in 8 months, with interest of 10.5%. Two months before it is due, the firm sells the note to a broker. If the broker wants a 12.5% return on his investment, how much should he pay for the note?

The bank pays Donovan $6689.32 and four months later collects $6890 from Parks. ✓₇

Discount

The preceding examples dealt with loans in which money is borrowed and simple interest is charged. For most loans, both the principal (amount borrowed) and the interest are paid at the end of the loan period. With a corporate bond (which is a loan to a company by the investor who buys the bond), interest is paid during the life of the bond and the principal is paid back at maturity. In both cases,

the borrower receives the principal,

but pays back the principal *plus* the interest.

In a **simple discount loan,** however, the interest is deducted in advance from the amount of the loan and the *balance* is given to the borrower. The *full value* of the loan must be paid back at maturity. Thus,

the borrower receives the principal *less* the interest,

but pays back the principal.

The most common examples of simple discount loans are U.S. Treasury bills (T-bills), which are essentially short-term loans to the U.S. government by investors. T-bills are sold at a **discount** from their face value and the Treasury pays back the face value of the T-bill at maturity. The discount amount is the interest deducted in advance from the face value. The Treasury receives the face value less the discount, but pays back the full face value.

Example 8 **Finance** An investor bought a six-month $8000 treasury bill on February 28, 2013 that sold at a discount rate of .135%. What is the amount of the discount? What is the price of the T-bill? (Data from: www.treasurydirect.gov.)

Solution The discount rate on a T-bill is always a simple *annual* interest rate. Consequently, the discount (interest) is found with the simple interest formula, using $P = 8000$ (face value), $r = .00135$ (discount rate), and $t = .5$ (because 6 months is half a year):

$$\text{Discount} = Prt = 8000 * .00135 * .5 = \$5.40.$$

So the price of the T-bill is

$$\text{Face Value} - \text{Discount} = 8000 - 5.40 = \$7994.60.$$ ✓8

✓ **Checkpoint 8**

The maturity times and discount rates for $10,000 T-bills sold on March 7, 2013, are given. Find the discount amount and the price of each T-bill.

(a) one year; .15%

(b) six months; .12%

(c) three months; .11%

In a simple discount loan, such as a T-bill, the discount rate is not the actual interest rate the borrower pays. In Example 8, the discount rate .135% was applied to the face value of $8000, rather than the $7994.60 that the Treasury (the borrower) received.

Example 9 **Finance** Find the actual interest rate paid by the Treasury in Example 8.

Solution Use the formula for simple interest, $I = Prt$ with r as the unknown. Here, $P = 7994.60$ (the amount the Treasury received) and $I = 5.40$ (the discount amount). Since this is a six-month T-bill, $t = .5$, and we have

$$I = Prt$$
$$5.40 = 7994.60(r)(.5)$$
$$5.40 = 3997.3r \qquad \text{Multiply out right side.}$$
$$r = \frac{5.40}{3997.3} \approx .0013509. \qquad \text{Divide both sides by 3997.3.}$$

✓ **Checkpoint 9**

Find the actual interest rate paid by the Treasury for each T-bill in Checkpoint 8.

So the actual interest rate is .13509%. ✓9

5.1 Exercises

Unless stated otherwise, "interest" means simple interest, and "interest rate" and "discount rate" refer to annual rates. Assume 365 days in a year.

1. What factors determine the amount of interest earned on a fixed principal?

Find the interest on each of these loans. (See Example 1.)

2. $35,000 at 6% for 9 months

3. $2850 at 7% for 8 months

4. $1875 at 5.3% for 7 months

5. $3650 at 6.5% for 11 months

6. $5160 at 7.1% for 58 days

7. $2830 at 8.9% for 125 days

8. $8940 at 9%; loan made on May 7 and due September 19

9. $5328 at 8%; loan made on August 16 and due December 30

10. $7900 at 7%; loan made on July 7 and due October 25

Finance *For each of the given corporate bonds, whose interest rates are provided, find the semiannual interest payment and the total interest earned over the life of the bond. (See Example 2, Data from: www.finra.org.)*

11. $5000 IBM, 3-year bond; 1.25%

12. $9000 Barrick Gold Corp., 10-year bond; 3.85%

13. $12,500 Morgan Stanley, 10-year bond; 3.75%

14. $4500 Goldman Sachs, 3-year bond; 6.75%

15. $6500 Amazon.com Corp, 10-year bond; 2.5%

16. $10,000 Wells Fargo, 10-year bond; 3.45%

Find the future value of each of these loans. (See Example 3.)

17. $12,000 loan at 3.5% for 3 months

18. $3475 loan at 7.5% for 6 months

19. $6500 loan at 5.25% for 8 months

20. $24,500 loan at 9.6% for 10 months

21. What is meant by the *present value* of money?

22. In your own words, describe the *maturity value* of a loan.

Find the present value of each future amount. (See Examples 5 and 6.)

23. $15,000 for 9 months; money earns 6%

24. $48,000 for 8 months; money earns 5%

25. $15,402 for 120 days; money earns 6.3%

26. $29,764 for 310 days; money earns 7.2%

Finance *The given treasury bills were sold on April 4, 2013. Find (a) the price of the T-bill, and (b) the actual interest rate paid by the Treasury. (See Examples 8 and 9. Data from: www. treasurydirect.gov.)*

27. Three-month $20,000 T-bill with discount rate of .075%

28. One-month $12,750 T-bill with discount rate of .070%

29. Six-month $15,500 T-bill with discount rate of .105%

30. One-year $7000 T-bill with discount rate of .140%

Finance *Historically, treasury bills offered higher rates. On March 9, 2007 the discount rates were substantially higher than in April, 2013. For the following treasury bills bought in 2007, find (a) the price of the T-bill, and (b) the actual interest rate paid by the Treasury. (See Examples 8 and 9. Data from: www. treasury.gov.)*

31. Three-month $20,000 T-bill with discount rate of 4.96%

32. One-month $12,750 T-bill with discount rate of 5.13%

33. Six-month $15,500 T-bill with discount rate of 4.93%

34. Six-month $9000 T-bill with discount rate of 4.93%

Finance *Work the following applied problems.*

35. In March 1868, Winston Churchill's grandfather, L.W. Jerome, issued $1000 bonds (to pay for a road to a race track he owned in what is now the Bronx). The bonds carried a 7% annual interest rate payable semiannually. Mr. Jerome paid the interest until March 1874, at which time New York City assumed responsibility for the bonds (and the road they financed). (Data from: *New York Times,* February 13, 2009.)

    (a) The first of these bonds matured in March 2009. At that time, how much interest had New York City paid on this bond?

    (b) Another of these bonds will not mature until March 2147! At that time, how much interest will New York City have paid on it?

36. An accountant for a corporation forgot to pay the firm's income tax of $725,896.15 on time. The government charged a penalty of 9.8% interest for the 34 days the money was late. Find the total amount (tax and penalty) that was paid.

37. Mike Branson invested his summer earnings of $3000 in a savings account for college. The account pays 2.5% interest. How much will this amount to in 9 months?

38. To pay for textbooks, a student borrows $450 from a credit union at 6.5% simple interest. He will repay the loan in 38 days, when he expects to be paid for tutoring. How much interest will he pay?

39. An account invested in a money market fund grew from $67,081.20 to $67,359.39 in a month. What was the interest rate, to the nearest tenth?

40. A $100,000 certificate of deposit held for 60 days is worth $101,133.33. To the nearest tenth of a percent, what interest rate was earned?

41. Dave took out a $7500 loan at 7% and eventually repaid $7675 (principal and interest). What was the time period of the loan?

42. What is the time period of a $10,000 loan at 6.75%, in which the total amount of interest paid was $618.75?

43. Tuition of $1769 will be due when the spring term begins in 4 months. What amount should a student deposit today, at 3.25%, to have enough to pay the tuition?

44. A firm of accountants has ordered 7 new computers at a cost of $5104 each. The machines will not be delivered for 7 months. What amount could the firm deposit in an account paying 6.42% to have enough to pay for the machines?

45. John Sun Yee needs $6000 to pay for remodeling work on his house. A contractor agrees to do the work in 10 months. How much should Yee deposit at 3.6% to accumulate the $6000 at that time?

46. Lorie Reilly decides to go back to college. For transportation, she borrows money from her parents to buy a small car for $7200. She plans to repay the loan in 7 months. What amount can she deposit today at 5.25% to have enough to pay off the loan?

47. A six-month $4000 Treasury bill sold for $3930. What was the discount rate?

48. A three-month $7600 Treasury bill carries a discount of $80.75. What is the discount rate for this T-bill?

Finance *Work the next set of problems, in which you are to find the annual simple interest rate. Consider any fees, dividends, or profits as part of the total interest.*

49. A stock that sold for $22 at the beginning of the year was selling for $24 at the end of the year. If the stock paid a dividend of $.50 per share, what is the simple interest rate on an investment in this stock? (*Hint:* Consider the interest to be the increase in value plus the dividend.)

50. Jerry Ryan borrowed $8000 for nine months at an interest rate of 7%. The bank also charges a $100 processing fee. What is the actual interest rate for this loan?

51. You are due a tax refund of $760. Your tax preparer offers you a no-interest loan to be repaid by your refund check, which will arrive in four weeks. She charges a $60 fee for this service. What actual interest rate will you pay for this loan? (*Hint:* The time period of this loan is not 4/52, because a 365-day year is 52 weeks and 1 day. So use days in your computations.)

52. Your cousin is due a tax refund of $400 in six weeks. His tax preparer has an arrangement with a bank to get him the $400 now. The bank charges an administrative fee of $29 plus interest at 6.5%. What is the actual interest rate for this loan? (See the hint for Exercise 51.)

Finance   *Work these problems. (See Example 7.)*

53. A building contractor gives a $13,500 promissory note to a plumber who has loaned him $13,500. The note is due in nine months with interest at 9%. Three months after the note is signed, the plumber sells it to a bank. If the bank gets a 10% return on its investment, how much will the plumber receive? Will it be enough to pay a bill for $13,650?

54. Shalia Johnson owes $7200 to the Eastside Music Shop. She has agreed to pay the amount in seven months at an interest rate of 10%. Two months before the loan is due, the store needs $7550 to pay a wholesaler's bill. The bank will buy the note, provided that its return on the investment is 11%. How much will the store receive? Is it enough to pay the bill?

55. Let y_1 be the future value after t years of $100 invested at 8% annual simple interest. Let y_2 be the future value after t years of $200 invested at 3% annual simple interest.

(a) Think of y_1 and y_2 as functions of t and write the rules of these functions.

(b) Without graphing, describe the graphs of y_1 and y_2.

(c) Verify your answer to part (b) by graphing y_1 and y_2 in the first quadrant.

(d) What do the slopes and y-intercepts of the graphs represent (in terms of the investment situation that they describe)?

56. If $y = 16.25t + 250$ and y is the future value after t years of P dollars at interest rate r, what are P and r? (*Hint:* See Exercise 55.)

✓**Checkpoint Answers**

1. (a) $141.67   **(b)** $551.25

2. (a) $273.75; $16,425   **(b)** $675; $13,500

3. (a) $1023   **(b)** $9710.03   **(c)** $97,046.68

4. 8%

5. (a) $7075.47   **(b)** $86,829.27   **(c)** $160,893.96

6. $17,862.60

7. $22,011.43

8. (a) $15; $9985   **(b)** $6; $9994
   (c) $2.75; $9997.25

9. (a) About .15023%   **(b)** About .12007%
   (c) About .11003%

5.2 Compound Interest

With annual simple interest, you earn interest each year on your original investment. With annual **compound interest,** however, you earn interest both on your original investment *and* on any previously earned interest. To see how this process works, suppose you deposit $1000 at 5% annual interest. The following chart shows how your account would grow with both simple and compound interest:

| End of Year | SIMPLE INTEREST | | COMPOUND INTEREST | |
	Interest Earned	Balance	Interest Earned	Balance
	Original Investment: $1000		*Original Investment:* $1000	
1	1000(.05) = $50	$1050	1000(.05) = $50	$1050
2	1000(.05) = $50	$1100	1050(.05) = $52.50	$1102.50
3	1000(.05) = $50	$1150	1102.50(.05) = $55.13*	$1157.63

As the chart shows, simple interest is computed each year on the original investment, but compound interest is computed on the entire balance at the end of the preceding year. So simple interest always produces $50 per year in interest, whereas compound interest

---
*Rounded to the nearest cent.

✓ **Checkpoint 1**

Extend the chart in the text by finding the interest earned and the balance at the end of years 4 and 5 for **(a)** simple interest and **(b)** compound interest.

produces $50 interest in the first year and increasingly larger amounts in later years (because you earn interest on your interest). ✓₁

Example 1   If $7000 is deposited in an account that pays 4% interest compounded annually, how much money is in the account after nine years?

Solution   After one year, the account balance is

$$7000 + 4\% \text{ of } 7000 = 7000 + (.04)7000$$
$$= 7000(1 + .04) \qquad \text{Distributive property}$$
$$= 7000(1.04) = \$7280.$$

The initial balance has grown by a factor of 1.04. At the end of the second year, the balance is

$$7280 + 4\% \text{ of } 7280 = 7280 + (.04)7280$$
$$= 7280(1 + .04) \qquad \text{Distributive property}$$
$$= 7280(1.04) = 7571.20.$$

Once again, the balance at the beginning of the year has grown by a factor of 1.04. This is true in general: If the balance at the beginning of a year is P dollars, then the balance at the end of the year is

$$P + 4\% \text{ of } P = P + .04P$$
$$= P(1 + .04)$$
$$= P(1.04).$$

So the account balance grows like this:

Year 1	**Year 2**	**Year 3**

$$7000 \rightarrow 7000(1.04) \rightarrow \underbrace{[7000(1.04)](1.04)}_{7000(1.04)^2} \rightarrow \underbrace{[7000(1.04)(1.040)](1.04)}_{7000(1.04)^3} \rightarrow \cdots .$$

At the end of nine years, the balance is

$$7000(1.04)^9 = \$9963.18 \qquad \text{(rounded to the nearest penny)}.$$

The argument used in Example 1 applies in the general case and leads to this conclusion.

Compound Interest

If P dollars are invested at interest rate i per period, then the **compound amount** (future value) A after n compounding periods is

$$A = P(1 + i)^n.$$

In Example 1, for instance, we had $P = 7000, n = 9$, and $i = .04$ (so that $1 + i = 1 + .04 = 1.04$).

NOTE Compare this future value formula for compound interest with the one for simple interest from the previous section, using t as the number of years:

$$\text{Compound interest} \qquad A = P(1 + r)^t;$$
$$\text{Simple interest} \qquad A = P(1 + rt).$$

The important distinction between the two formulas is that, in the compound interest formula, the number of years, t, is an *exponent*, so that money grows much more rapidly when interest is compounded.

Example 2   Suppose $1000 is deposited for six years in an account paying 8.31% per year compounded annually.

(a) Find the compound amount.

Solution   In the formula above, $P = 1000$, $i = .0831$, and $n = 6$. The compound amount is

$$A = P(1 + i)^n$$
$$A = 1000(1.0831)^6$$
$$A = \$1614.40.$$

(b) Find the amount of interest earned.

Solution   Subtract the initial deposit from the compound amount:

$$\text{Amount of interest} = \$1614.40 - \$1000 = \$614.40. \quad \checkmark_2$$

✓ **Checkpoint 2**

Suppose $17,000 is deposited at 4% compounded annually for 11 years.

(a) Find the compound amount.

(b) Find the amount of interest earned.

TECHNOLOGY TIP
Spreadsheets are ideal for performing financial calculations. Figure 5.1 shows a Microsoft Excel spreadsheet with the formulas for compound and simple interest used to create columns B and C, respectively, when $1000 is invested at an annual rate of 10%. Notice how rapidly the compound amount increases compared with the maturity value with simple interest. For more details on the use of spreadsheets in the mathematics of finance, see the *Spreadsheet Manual* that is available with this text.

	A	B	C
1	period	compound	simple
2	1	1100	1100
3	2	1210	1200
4	3	1331	1300
5	4	1464.1	1400
6	5	1610.51	1500
7	6	1771.561	1600
8	7	1948.7171	1700
9	8	2143.58881	1800
10	9	2357.947691	1900
11	10	2593.74246	2000
12	11	2853.116706	2100
13	12	3138.428377	2200
14	13	3452.271214	2300
15	14	3797.498336	2400
16	15	4177.248169	2500
17	16	4594.972986	2600
18	17	5054.470285	2700
19	18	5559.917313	2800
20	19	6115.909045	2900
21	20	6727.499949	3000

Figure 5.1

Example 3   If a $16,000 investment grows to $50,000 in 18 years, what is the interest rate (assuming annual compounding)?

Solution   Use the compound interest formula, with $P = 16,000$, $A = 50,000$, and $n = 18$, and solve for i:

$$P(1 + i)^n = A$$
$$16,000(1 + i)^{18} = 50,000$$
$$(1 + i)^{18} = \frac{50,000}{16,000} = 3.125 \qquad \text{Divide both sides by 16,000.}$$
$$\sqrt[18]{(1 + i)^{18}} = \sqrt[18]{3.125} \qquad \text{Take 18th roots on both sides.}$$
$$1 + i = \sqrt[18]{3.125}$$
$$i = \sqrt[18]{3.125} - 1 \approx .06535. \qquad \text{Subtract 1 from both sides.}$$

So the interest rate is about 6.535%.

Interest can be compounded more than once a year. Common **compounding periods** include

semiannually (2 periods per year),

quarterly (4 periods per year),

monthly (12 periods per year), and

daily (usually 365 periods per year).

When the annual interest i is compounded m times per year, the interest rate per period is understood to be i/m.

Example 4   **Finance** In April 2013, www.bankrate.com advertised a one-year certificate of deposit (CD) for GE Capital Retail Bank at an interest rate of 1.05%. Find the value of the CD if $10,000 is invested for one year and interest is compounded according to the given periods.

(a) Annually

Solution Apply the formula $A = P(1 + i)^n$ with $P = 10,000$, $i = .0105$, and $n = 1$:

$$A = P(1 + i)^n = 10,000(1 + .0105)^1 = 10,000(1.0105) = \$10,105.$$

(b) Semiannually

Solution Use the same formula and value of P. Here interest is compounded twice a year, so the number of periods is $n = 2$ and the interest rate per period is $i = \dfrac{.0105}{2}$:

$$A = P(1 + i)^n = 10,000\left(1 + \frac{.0105}{2}\right)^2 = \$10,105.28.$$

(c) Quarterly

Solution Proceed as in part (b), but now interest is compounded 4 times a year, and so $n = 4$ and the interest rate per period is $i = \dfrac{.0105}{4}$:

$$A = P(1 + i)^n = 10,000\left(1 + \frac{.0105}{4}\right)^4 = \$10,105.41.$$

(d) Monthly

Solution Interest is compounded 12 times a year, so $n = 12$ and $i = \dfrac{.0105}{12}$:

$$A = P(1 + i)^n = 10,000\left(1 + \frac{.0105}{12}\right)^{12} = \$10,105.51.$$

(e) Daily

Solution Interest is compounded 365 times a year, so $n = 365$ and $i = \dfrac{.0105}{365}$:

$$A = P(1 + i)^n = 10,000\left(1 + \frac{.0105}{365}\right)^{365} = \$10,105.55.$$

Example 5   **Finance** The given CDs were advertised online by various banks in April 2013. Find the future value of each one. (Data from: cdrates.bankaholic.com.)

(a) Nationwide Bank: $100,000 for 5 years at 1.73% compounded daily.

Solution Use the compound interest formula with $P = 100,000$. Interest is compounded 365 times a year, so the interest rate per period is $i = \dfrac{.0173}{365}$. Since there are five years, the number of periods in 5 years is $n = 365(5) = 1825$. The future value is

$$A = P(1 + i)^n = 100,000\left(1 + \frac{.0173}{365}\right)^{1825} = \$109,034.91.$$

(b) California First National Bank: $5000 for 2 years at 1.06% compounded monthly.

Solution Use the compound interest formula with $P = 5000$. Interest is compounded 12 times a year, so the interest rate per period is $i = \dfrac{.0106}{12}$. Since there are two years, the number of periods in 2 years is $n = 12(2) = 24$. The future value is

$$A = P(1 + i)^n = 5000\left(1 + \frac{.0106}{12}\right)^{24} = \$5107.08. \ \boxed{\checkmark_3}$$

✓ **Checkpoint 3**

Find the future value for these CDs.

(a) National Republic Bank of Chicago: $1000 at 1.3% compounded monthly for 3 years.

(b) Discover Bank: $2500 at .8% compounded daily for 9 months (assume 30 days in each month).

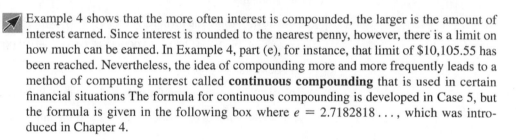 Example 4 shows that the more often interest is compounded, the larger is the amount of interest earned. Since interest is rounded to the nearest penny, however, there is a limit on how much can be earned. In Example 4, part (e), for instance, that limit of $10,105.55 has been reached. Nevertheless, the idea of compounding more and more frequently leads to a method of computing interest called **continuous compounding** that is used in certain financial situations The formula for continuous compounding is developed in Case 5, but the formula is given in the following box where $e = 2.7182818\ldots$, which was introduced in Chapter 4.

Continuous Compound Interest

The compound amount A for a deposit of P dollars at an interest rate r per year compounded continuously for t years is given by

$$A = Pe^{rt}.$$

Example 6 Suppose that $5000 is invested at an annual interest rate of 3.1% compounded continuously for 4 years. Find the compound amount.

Solution In the formula for continuous compounding, let $P = 5000, r = .031$, and $t = 4$. Then a calculator with an e^x key shows that

$$A = Pe^{rt} = 5000e^{.031(4)} = \$5660.08. \ \boxed{\checkmark_4}$$

✓ **Checkpoint 4**

Find the compound amount for $7500 invested at an annual interest rate of 2.07% compounded continuously for 3 years.

```
N=365
I%=1.05
PV=-10000
PMT=0
•FV=10105.55166
P/Y=365
C/Y=365
PMT:END BEGIN
```

Figure 5.2

TECHNOLOGY TIP TI-84+ and most Casios have a "TVM solver" for financial computations (in the TI APPS/financial menu or the Casio main menu); a similar one can be downloaded for TI-89. Figure 5.2 shows the solution of Example 4(e) on such a solver (FV means future value). The use of these solvers is explained in the next section. Most of the problems in this section can be solved just as quickly with an ordinary calculator.

Ordinary corporate or municipal bonds usually make semiannual simple interest payments. With a **zero-coupon bond,** however, there are no interest payments during the life of the bond. The investor receives a single payment when the bond matures, consisting of his original investment and the interest (compounded semiannually) that it has earned. Zero-coupon bonds are sold at a substantial discount from their face value, and the buyer receives the face value of the bond when it matures. The difference between the face value and the price of the bond is the interest earned.

Example 7   Doug Payne bought a 15-year zero-coupon bond paying 4.5% interest (compounded semiannually) for $12,824.50. What is the face value of the bond?

Solution   Use the compound interest formula with $P = 12,824.50$. Interest is paid twice a year, so the rate per period is $i = .045/2$, and the number of periods in 15 years is $n = 30$. The compound amount will be the face value:

$$A = P(1 + i)^n = 12,824.50(1 + .045/2)^{30} = 24,999.99618.$$

Rounding to the nearest cent, we see that the face value of the bond in $25,000.

Example 8   Suppose that the inflation rate is 3.5% (which means that the overall level of prices is rising 3.5% a year). How many years will it take for the overall level of prices to double?

Solution   We want to find the number of years it will take for $1 worth of goods or services to cost $2. Think of $1 as the present value and $2 as the future value, with an interest rate of 3.5%, compounded annually. Then the compound amount formula becomes

$$P(1 + i)^n = A$$
$$1(1 + .035)^n = 2,$$

which simplifies as

$$1.035^n = 2.$$

We must solve this equation for n. There are several ways to do this.

Graphical   Use a graphing calculator (with x in place of n) to find the intersection point of the graphs of $y_1 = 1.035^x$ and $y_2 = 2$. Figure 5.3 shows that the intersection point has (approximate) x-coordinate 20.14879. So it will take about 20.15 years for prices to double.

Algebraic   The same answer can be obtained by using natural logarithms, as in Section 4.4:

$$1.035^n = 2$$
$$\ln 1.035^n = \ln 2 \qquad \text{Take the logarithm of each side.}$$
$$n \ln 1.035 = \ln 2 \qquad \text{Power property of logarithms.}$$
$$n = \frac{\ln 2}{\ln 1.035} \qquad \text{Divide both sides by ln 1.035.}$$
$$n \approx 20.14879. \qquad \text{Use a calculator.} \boxed{6}$$

Effective Rate (APY)

If you invest $100 at 9%, compounded monthly, then your balance at the end of one year is

$$A = P(1 + i)^n = 100\left(1 + \frac{.09}{12}\right)^{12} = \$109.38.$$

You have earned $9.38 in interest, which is 9.38% of your original $100. In other words, $100 invested at 9.38% compounded *annually* will produce the same amount of interest

✓ Checkpoint 5

Find the face value of the zero coupon.

(a)   30-year bond at 6% sold for $2546

(b)   15-year bond at 5% sold for $16,686

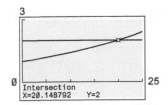

Figure 5.3

✓ Checkpoint 6

Using a calculator, find the number of years it will take for $500 to increase to $750 in an account paying 6% interest compounded semiannually.

(namely, $100 * .0938 = 9.38) as does 9% compounded monthly. In this situation, 9% is called the **nominal** or **stated rate**, while 9.38% is called the **effective rate** or **annual percentage yield (APY).**

In the discussion that follows, the nominal rate is denoted r and the APY (effective rate) is denoted r_E.

Effective Rate (r_E) or Annual Percentage Yield (APY)

The APY r_E is the annual compounding rate needed to produce the same amount of interest in one year, as the nominal rate does with more frequent compounding.

Example 9   **Finance**   In April 2013, Nationwide Bank offered its customers a 5-year $100,000 CD at 1.73% interest, compounded daily. Find the APY. (Data from: cdrates.bankaholic.com.)

Solution   The box given previously means that we must have the following:

$$\begin{matrix} \$100{,}000 \text{ at rate } r_E \\ \text{compounded annually} \end{matrix} = \begin{matrix} \$100{,}000 \text{ at } 1.73\%, \\ \text{compounded daily} \end{matrix}$$

$$100{,}000(1 + r_E)^1 = 100{,}000\left(1 + \frac{.0173}{365}\right)^{365} \qquad \text{Compound interest formula.}$$

$$(1 + r_E) = \left(1 + \frac{.0173}{365}\right)^{365} \qquad \text{Divide both sides by 100,000.}$$

$$r_E = \left(1 + \frac{.0173}{365}\right)^{365} - 1 \qquad \text{Subtract 1 from both sides.}$$

$$r_E \approx .0175.$$

So the APY is about 1.75%.

The argument in Example 9 can be carried out with 100,000 replaced by P, .0173 by r, and 365 by m. The result is the effective-rate formula.

Effective Rate (APY)

The effective rate (APY) corresponding to a stated rate of interest r compounded m times per year is

$$r_E = \left(1 + \frac{r}{m}\right)^m - 1.$$

Example 10   **Finance**   When interest rates are low (as they were when this text went to press), the interest rate and the APY are insignificantly different. To see when the difference is more pronounced, we will find the APY for each of the given money market checking accounts (with balances between $50,000 and $100,000), which were advertised in October 2008 when offered rates were higher.

(a) Imperial Capital Bank: 3.35% compounded monthly.

Solution   Use the effective-rate formula with $r = .0335$ and $m = 12$:

$$r_E = \left(1 + \frac{r}{m}\right)^m - 1 = \left(1 + \frac{.0335}{12}\right)^{12} - 1 = .034019.$$

So the APY is about 3.40%, a slight increase over the nominal rate of 3.35%.

(b) U.S. Bank: 2.33% compounded daily.

Solution Use the formula with $r = .0233$ and $m = 365$:

$$r_E = \left(1 + \frac{r}{m}\right)^m - 1 = \left(1 + \frac{.0233}{365}\right)^{365} - 1 = .023572.$$

The APY is about 2.36%. ✓₇

Example 11 Bank A is now lending money at 10% interest compounded annually. The rate at Bank B is 9.6% compounded monthly, and the rate at Bank C is 9.7% compounded quarterly. If you need to borrow money, at which bank will you pay the least interest?

Solution Compare the APYs:

Bank A: $\left(1 + \frac{.10}{1}\right)^1 - 1 = .10 = 10\%;$

Bank B: $\left(1 + \frac{.096}{12}\right)^{12} - 1 \approx .10034 = 10.034\%;$

Bank C: $\left(1 + \frac{.097}{4}\right)^4 - 1 \approx .10059 = 10.059\%.$

The lowest APY is at Bank A, which has the highest nominal rate. ✓₈

📄 **NOTE** Although you can find both the stated interest rate and the APY for most certificates of deposit and other interest-bearing accounts, most bank advertisements mention only the APY.

Present Value for Compound Interest

The formula for compound interest, $A = P(1 + i)^n$, has four variables: A, P, i, and n. Given the values of any three of these variables, the value of the fourth can be found. In particular, if A (the future amount), i, and n are known, then P can be found. Here, P is the amount that should be deposited today to produce A dollars in n periods.

Example 12 Keisha Jones must pay a lump sum of $6000 in 5 years. What amount deposited today at 6.2% compounded annually will amount to $6000 in 5 years?

Solution Here, $A = 6000$, $i = .062$, $n = 5$, and P is unknown. Substituting these values into the formula for the compound amount gives

$$6000 = P(1.062)^5$$

$$P = \frac{6000}{(1.062)^5} = 4441.49,$$

or $4441.49. If Jones leaves $4441.49 for 5 years in an account paying 6.2% compounded annually, she will have $6000 when she needs it. To check your work, use the compound interest formula with $P = \$4441.49$, $i = .062$, and $n = 5$. You should get $A = \$6000.00$. ✓₉

As Example 12 shows, $6000 in 5 years is (approximately) the same as $4441.49 today (if money can be deposited at 6.2% annual interest). An amount that can be deposited today to yield a given amount in the future is called the *present value* of the future amount. By solving $A = P(1 + i)^n$ for P, we get the following general formula for present value.

Present Value for Compound Interest

The **present value** of A dollars compounded at an interest rate i per period for n periods is

$$P = \frac{A}{(1 + i)^n}, \quad \text{or} \quad P = A(1 + i)^{-n}.$$

Example 13   A zero-coupon bond with face value $15,000 and a 6% interest rate (compounded semiannually) will mature in 9 years. What is a fair price to pay for the bond today?

Solution   Think of the bond as a 9-year investment paying 6%, compounded semiannually, whose future value is $15,000. Its present value (what it is worth today) would be a fair price. So use the present value formula with $A = 15{,}000$. Since interest is compounded twice a year, the interest rate per period is $i = .06/2 = .03$ and the number of periods in nine years is $n = 9(2) = 18$. Hence,

$$P = \frac{A}{(1 + i)^n} = \frac{15{,}000}{(1 + .03)^{18}} \approx 8810.919114.$$

So a fair price would be the present value of $8810.92. ☑10

✓**Checkpoint 10**

Find the fair price (present value) in Example 13 if the interest rate is 7.5%.

Example 14   **Economics**   The average annual inflation rate for the years 2010–2012 was 2.29%. How much did an item that sells for $1000 in early 2013 cost three years before? (Data from: inflationdata.com.)

Solution   Think of the price three years prior as the present value P and $1000 as the future value A. Then $i = .0229$, $n = 3$, and the present value is

$$P = \frac{A}{(1 + i)^n} = \frac{1000}{(1 + .0229)^3} = \$934.33.$$

So the item cost $934.33 three years prior. ☑11

✓**Checkpoint 11**

What did a $1000 item sell for 5 years prior if the annual inflation rate has been 3.2%?

Summary

At this point, it seems helpful to summarize the notation and the most important formulas for simple and compound interest. We use the following variables:

P = principal or present value;

A = future or maturity value;

r = annual (stated or nominal) interest rate;

t = number of years;

m = number of compounding periods per year;

i = interest rate per period;

n = total number of compounding periods;

r_E = effective rate (APY).

Simple Interest	Compound Interest	Continuous Compounding
$A = P(1 + rt)$	$A = P(1 + i)^n$	$A = Pe^{rt}$
$P = \dfrac{A}{1 + rt}$	$P = \dfrac{A}{(1 + i)^n} = A(1 + i)^{-n}$	$P = \dfrac{A}{e^{rt}}$
	$r_E = \left(1 + \dfrac{r}{m}\right)^m - 1$	

5.2 Exercises

Interest on the zero-coupon bonds here is compounded semiannually.

1. In the preceding summary what is the difference between *r* and *i*? between *t* and *n*?

2. Explain the difference between simple interest and compound interest.

3. What factors determine the amount of interest earned on a fixed principal?

4. In your own words, describe the *maturity value* of a loan.

5. What is meant by the *present value* of money?

6. If interest is compounded more than once per year, which rate is higher, the stated rate or the effective rate?

Find the compound amount and the interest earned for each of the following deposits. (See Examples 1, 2, 4, and 5.)

7. $1000 at 4% compounded annually for 6 years

8. $1000 at 6% compounded annually for 10 years

9. $470 at 8% compounded semiannually for 12 years

10. $15,000 at 4.6% compounded semiannually for 11 years

11. $6500 at 4.5% compounded quarterly for 8 years

12. $9100 at 6.1% compounded quarterly for 4 years

Finance *The following CDs were available on www.bankrate.com on April 13, 2013. Find the compound amount and the interest earned for each of the following. (See Example 5.)*

13. Virtual Bank: $10,000 at .9% compounded daily for 1 year

14. AloStar Bank of Commerce: $1000 at .85% compounded daily for 1 year

15. USAA: $5000 at .81% compounded monthly for 2 years

16. Centennial Bank: $20,000 at .45% compounded monthly for 2 years

17. E-LOAN: $100,000 at 1.52% compounded daily for 5 years

18. Third Federal Savings and Loans: $150,000 at 1.15% compounded quarterly for 5 years

Find the interest rate (with annual compounding) that makes the statement true. (See Example 3.)

19. $3000 grows to $3606 in 5 years

20. $2550 grows to $3905 in 11 years

21. $8500 grows to $12,161 in 7 years

22. $9000 grows to $17,118 in 16 years

Find the compound amount and the interest earned when the following investments have continuous compounding. (See Example 6.)

23. $20,000 at 3.5% for 5 years

24. $15,000 at 2.9% for 10 years

25. $30,000 at 1.8% for 3 years

26. $100,000 at 5.1% for 20 years

Find the face value (to the nearest dollar) of the zero-coupon bond. (See Example 7.)

27. 15-year bond at 5.2%; price $4630

28. 10-year bond at 4.1%; price $13,328

29. 20-year bond at 3.5%; price $9992

30. How do the nominal, or stated, interest rate and the effective interest rate (APY) differ?

Find the APY corresponding to the given nominal rates. (See Examples 9–11).

31. 4% compounded semiannually

32. 6% compounded quarterly

33. 5% compounded quarterly

34. 4.7% compounded semiannually

Find the present value of the given future amounts. (See Example 12.)

35. $12,000 at 5% compounded annually for 6 years

36. $8500 at 6% compounded annually for 9 years

37. $17,230 at 4% compounded quarterly for 10 years

38. $5240 at 6% compounded quarterly for 8 years

What price should you be willing to pay for each of these zero-coupon bonds? (See Example 13.)

39. 5-year $5000 bond; interest at 3.5%

40. 10-year $10,000 bond; interest at 4%

41. 15-year $20,000 bond; interest at 4.7%

42. 20-year $15,000 bond; interest at 5.3%

Finance *For Exercises 43 and 44, assume an annual inflation rate of 2.07% (the annual inflation rate of 2012 according to www.InflationData.com). Find the previous price of the following items. (See Example 14.)*

43. How much did an item that costs $5000 now cost 4 years prior?

44. How much did an item that costs $7500 now cost 5 years prior?

45. If the annual inflation rate is 3.6%, how much did an item that costs $500 now cost 2 years prior?

46. If the annual inflation rate is 1.18%, how much did an item that costs $1250 now cost 6 years prior?

47. If money can be invested at 8% compounded quarterly, which is larger, $1000 now or $1210 in 5 years? Use present value to decide.

48. If money can be invested at 6% compounded annually, which is larger, $10,000 now or $15,000 in 6 years? Use present value to decide.

Finance   *Work the following applied problems.*

49. A small business borrows $50,000 for expansion at 9% compounded monthly. The loan is due in 4 years. How much interest will the business pay?

50. A developer needs $80,000 to buy land. He is able to borrow the money at 10% per year compounded quarterly. How much will the interest amount to if he pays off the loan in 5 years?

51. Lora Reilly has inherited $10,000 from her uncle's estate. She will invest the money for 2 years. She is considering two investments: a money market fund that pays a guaranteed 5.8% interest compounded daily and a 2-year Treasury note at 6% annual interest. Which investment pays the most interest over the 2-year period?

52. Which of these 20-year zero-coupon bonds will be worth more at maturity: one that sells for $4510, with a 6.1% interest rate, or one that sells for $5809, with a 4.8% interest rate?

53. As the prize in a contest, you are offered $1000 now or $1210 in 5 years. If money can be invested at 6% compounded annually, which is larger?

54. Two partners agree to invest equal amounts in their business. One will contribute $10,000 immediately. The other plans to contribute an equivalent amount in 3 years, when she expects to acquire a large sum of money. How much should she contribute at that time to match her partner's investment now, assuming an interest rate of 6% compounded semiannually?

55. In the Capital Appreciation Fund, a mutual fund from T. Rowe Price, a $10,000 investment grew to $11,115 over the 3-year period 2010–2013. Find the annual interest rate, compounded yearly, that this investment earned.

56. In the Vanguard Information Technology Index Fund, a $10,000 investment grew to $16,904.75 over the 10-year period 2003–2013. Find the annual interest rate, compounded yearly, that this investment earned.

57. The Flagstar Bank in Michigan offered a 5-year certificate of deposit (CD) at 4.38% interest compounded quarterly in June 2005. On the same day on the Internet, Principal Bank offered a 5-year CD at 4.37% interest compounded monthly. Find the APY for each CD. Which bank paid a higher APY?

58. The Westfield Bank in Ohio offered the CD rates shown in the accompanying table in October 2008. The APY rates shown assume monthly compounding. Find the corresponding nominal rates to the nearest hundredth. (*Hint:* Solve the effective-rate equation for *r*.)

Term	6 mo	1 yr	2 yr	3 yr	5 yr
APY (%)	2.25	2.50	3.00	3.25	3.75

59. A company has agreed to pay $2.9 million in 5 years to settle a lawsuit. How much must it invest now in an account paying 5% interest compounded monthly to have that amount when it is due?

60. Bill Poole wants to have $20,000 available in 5 years for a down payment on a house. He has inherited $16,000. How much of the inheritance should he invest now to accumulate the $20,000 if he can get an interest rate of 5.5% compounded quarterly?

61. If inflation has been running at 3.75% per year and a new car costs $23,500 today, what would it have cost three years ago?

62. If inflation is 2.4% per year and a washing machine costs $345 today, what did a similar model cost five years ago?

Economics   *Use the approach in Example 8 to find the time it would take for the general level of prices in the economy to double at the average annual inflation rates in Exercises 63–66.*

63. 3%   **64.** 4%   **65.** 5%   **66.** 5.5%

67. The consumption of electricity has increased historically at 6% per year. If it continues to increase at this rate indefinitely, find the number of years before the electric utility companies will need to double their generating capacity.

68. Suppose a conservation campaign coupled with higher rates causes the demand for electricity to increase at only 2% per year, as it has recently. Find the number of years before the utility companies will need to double their generating capacity.

69. You decide to invest a $16,000 bonus in a money market fund that guarantees a 5.5% annual interest rate compounded monthly for 7 years. A one-time fee of $30 is charged to set up the account. In addition, there is an annual administrative charge of 1.25% of the balance in the account at the end of each year.

  (a) How much is in the account at the end of the first year?

  (b) How much is in the account at the end of the seventh year?

70. Joe Marusa decides to invest $12,000 in a money market fund that guarantees a 4.6% annual interest rate compounded daily for 6 years. A one-time fee of $25 is charged to set up the account. In addition, there is an annual administration charge of .9% of the balance in the account at the end of each year.

  (a) How much is in the account at the end of the first year?

  (b) How much is in the account at the end of the sixth year?

The following exercises are from professional examinations.

71. On January 1, 2002, Jack deposited $1000 into Bank *X* to earn interest at the rate of *j* per annum compounded semiannually. On January 1, 2007, he transferred his account to Bank *Y* to earn interest at the rate of *k* per annum compounded quarterly. On January 1, 2010, the balance at Bank *Y* was $1990.76. If Jack could have earned interest at the rate of *k* per annum compounded quarterly from January 1, 2002, through January 1, 2010, his balance would have been $2203.76. Which of the following represents the ratio *k*/*j*? (Deposit of Jack in Bank X from Course 140 Examination, Mathematics of Compound Interest. Copyright © Society of Actuaries. Reproduced by permission of Society of Actuaries.)

  (a) 1.25   **(b)** 1.30   **(c)** 1.35   **(d)** 1.40   **(e)** 1.45

72. On January 1, 2009, Tone Company exchanged equipment for a $200,000 non-interest-bearing note due on January 1, 2012. The prevailing rate of interest for a note of this type on January 1, 2009, was 10%. The present value of $1 at 10% for three periods is 0.75. What amount of interest revenue should be included in Tone's 2010 income statement? (Adapted from the Uniform CPA Examination, American Institute of Certified Public Accountants.)

  (a) $7500   **(b)** $15,000

  (c) $16,500   **(d)** $20,000

1. (a)

Year	Interest	Balance
4	$50	$1200
5	$50	$1250

(b)

Year	Interest	Balance
4	$57.88	$1215.51
5	$60.78	$1276.29

2. (a) $26,170.72 (b) $9170.72

3. (a) $1039.75 (b) $2514.84

4. $7980.52

5. (a) $15,000 (b) $35,000

6. About 7 years ($n = 6.86$)

7. (a) 12.68% (b) 8.24%

8. (a) 4.06% (b) 8.220%

9. (a) $4483.55 (b) $3725.53

10. $7732.24 **11.** $854.28

5.3 Annuities, Future Value, and Sinking Funds

So far in this chapter, only lump-sum deposits and payments have been discussed. Many financial situations, however, involve a sequence of payments at regular intervals, such as weekly deposits in a savings account or monthly payments on a mortgage or car loan. Such periodic payments are the subject of this section and the next.

The analysis of periodic payments will require an algebraic technique that we now develop. Suppose x is a real number. For reasons that will become clear later, we want to find the product

$$(x - 1)(1 + x + x^2 + x^3 + \cdots + x^{11}).$$

Using the distributive property to multiply this expression out, we see that all but two of the terms cancel:

$$x(1 + x + x^2 + x^3 + \cdots + x^{11}) - 1(1 + x + x^2 + x^3 + \cdots + x^{11})$$
$$= (x + x^2 + x^3 + \cdots + x^{11} + x^{12}) - 1 - x - x^2 - x^3 - \cdots - x^{11}$$
$$= x^{12} - 1.$$

Hence, $(x - 1)(1 + x + x^2 + x^3 + \cdots + x^{11}) = x^{12} - 1$. Dividing both sides by $x - 1$, we have

$$1 + x + x^2 + x^3 + \cdots + x^{11} = \frac{x^{12} - 1}{x - 1}.$$

The same argument, with any positive integer n in place of 12 and $n - 1$ in place of 11, produces the following result:

> If x is a real number and n is a positive integer, then
> $$1 + x + x^2 + x^3 + \cdots + x^{n-1} = \frac{x^n - 1}{x - 1}.$$

For example, when $x = 5$ and $n = 7$, we see that

$$1 + 5 + 5^2 + 5^3 + 5^4 + 5^5 + 5^6 = \frac{5^7 - 1}{5 - 1} = \frac{78,124}{4} = 19,531.$$

A calculator can easily add up the terms on the left side, but it is faster to use the formula (Figure 5.5).

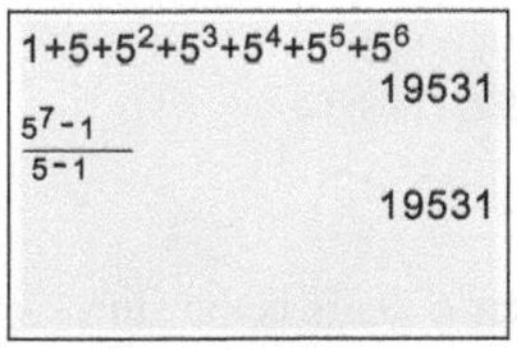

```
1+5+5²+5³+5⁴+5⁵+5⁶
                  19531
5⁷-1
5-1
                  19531
```

Figure 5.5

Ordinary Annuities

A sequence of equal payments made at equal periods of time is called an **annuity.** The time between payments is the **payment period,** and the time from the beginning of the first payment period to the end of the last period is called the **term of the annuity.** Annuities can be used to accumulate funds—for example, when you make regular deposits in a savings account. Or they can be used to pay out funds—as when you receive regular payments from a pension plan after you retire.

Annuities that pay out funds are considered in the next section. This section deals with annuities in which funds are accumulated by regular payments into an account or investment that earns compound interest. The **future value** of such an annuity is the final sum on deposit—that is, the total amount of all deposits and all interest earned by them.

We begin with **ordinary annuities**—ones where the payments are made at the *end* of each period and the frequency of payments is the same as the frequency of compounding the interest.

Example 1 $1500 is deposited at the end of each year for the next 6 years in an account paying 8% interest compounded annually. Find the future value of this annuity.

Solution Figure 5.6 shows the situation schematically.

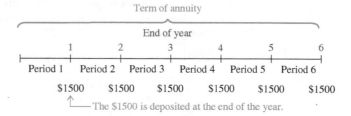

Figure 5.6

To find the future value of this annuity, look separately at each of the $1500 payments. The first $1500 is deposited at the end of period 1 and earns interest for the remaining 5 periods. From the formula in the box on page 233, the compound amount produced by this payment is

$$1500(1 + .08)^5 = 1500(1.08)^5.$$

The second $1500 payment is deposited at the end of period 2 and earns interest for the remaining 4 periods. So the compound amount produced by the second payment is

$$1500(1 + .08)^4 = 1500(1.08)^4.$$

Continue to compute the compound amount for each subsequent payment, as shown in Figure 5.7. Note that the last payment earns no interest.

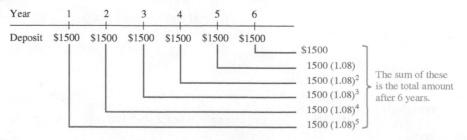

Figure 5.7

The last column of Figure 5.7 shows that the total amount after 6 years is the sum

$$1500 + 1500 \cdot 1.08 + 1500 \cdot 1.08^2 + 1500 \cdot 1.08^3 + 1500 \cdot 1.08^4 + 1500 \cdot 1.08^5$$
$$= 1500(1 + 1.08 + 1.08^2 + 1.08^3 + 1.08^4 + 1.08^5). \tag{1}$$

Now apply the algebraic fact in the box on page 243 to the expression in parentheses (with $x = 1.08$ and $n = 6$). It shows that the sum (the future value of the annuity) is

$$1500 \cdot \frac{1.08^6 - 1}{1.08 - 1} = \$11,003.89. \checkmark_1$$

✓ **Checkpoint 1**

Complete these steps for an annuity of $2000 at the end of each year for 3 years. Assume interest of 6% compounded annually.

(a) The first deposit of $2000 produces a total of _____.

(b) The second deposit becomes _____.

(c) No interest is earned on the third deposit, so the total in the account is _____.

Example 1 is the model for finding a formula for the future value of any annuity. Suppose that a payment of R dollars is deposited at the end of each period for n periods, at an interest rate of i per period. Then the future value of this annuity can be found by using the procedure in Example 1, with these replacements:

1500	.08	1.08	6	5
↓	↓	↓	↓	↓
R	i	$1 + i$	n	$n - 1$

The future value S in Example 1 — call it S — is the sum **(1)**, which now becomes

$$S = R[1 + (1 + i) + (1 + i)^2 + \cdots + (1 + i)^{n-2} + (1 + i)^{n-1}].$$

Apply the algebraic fact in the box on page 243 to the expression in brackets (with $x = 1 + i$). Then we have

$$S = R\left[\frac{(1 + i)^n - 1}{(1 + i) - 1}\right] = R\left[\frac{(1 + i)^n - 1}{i}\right].$$

The quantity in brackets in the right-hand part of the preceding equation is sometimes written $s_{\overline{n}|i}$ (read "s-angle-n at i"). So we can summarize as follows.[*]

Future Value of an Ordinary Annuity

The future value S of an ordinary annuity used to accumulate funds is given by

$$S = R\left[\frac{(1 + i)^n - 1}{i}\right], \quad \text{or} \quad S = R \cdot s_{\overline{n}|i},$$

where

R is the payment at the end of each period,

i is the interest rate per period, and

n is the number of periods.

TECHNOLOGY TIP Most computations with annuities can be done quickly with a spreadsheet program or a graphing calculator. On a calculator, use the TVM solver if there is one (see the Technology Tip on page 236); otherwise, use the programs in the Program Appendix.

Figure 5.8 shows how to do Example 1 on a TI-84+ TVM solver. First, enter the known quantities: N = number of payments, I% = annual interest rate, PV = present value, PMT = payment per period (entered as a negative amount), P/Y = number of payments per year, and C/Y = number of compoundings per year. At the bottom of the screen, set PMT: to "END" for ordinary annuities. Then put the cursor next to the unknown amount FV (future value), and press SOLVE.

Note: P/Y and C/Y should always be the same for problems in this text. If you use the solver for ordinary compound interest problems, set PMT = 0 and enter either PV or FV (whichever is known) as a negative amount.

```
N=6
I%=8
PV=0
PMT=-1500
•FV=11003.89356
P/Y=1
C/Y=1
PMT:END BEGIN
```

Figure 5.8

Example 2 A rookie player in the National Football League just signed his first 7-year contract. To prepare for his future, he deposits $150,000 at the end of each year for 7 years in an account paying 4.1% compounded annually. How much will he have on deposit after 7 years?

---

[*]We use S for the future value here instead of A, as in the compound interest formula, to help avoid confusing the two formulas.

Solution   His payments form an ordinary annuity with $R = 150{,}000, n = 7,$ and $i = .041.$ The future value of this annuity (by the previous formula) is

$$S = 150{,}000 \left[\frac{(1.041)^7 - 1}{.041} \right] = \$1{,}188{,}346.11.$$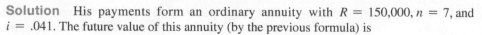

Example 3   Allyson, a college professor, contributed \$950 a month to the CREF stock fund (an investment vehicle available to many college and university employees). For the past 10 years this fund has returned 4.25%, compounded monthly.

(a) How much did Allyson earn over the course of the last 10 years?

Solution   Allyson's payments form an ordinary annuity, with monthly payment $R = 950.$ The interest per month is $i = \dfrac{.0425}{12},$ and the number of months in 10 years is $n = 10 * 12 = 120.$ The future value of this annuity is

$$S = R \left[\frac{(1 + i)^n - 1}{i} \right] = 950 \left[\frac{(1 + .0425/12)^{120} - 1}{.0425/12} \right] = \$141{,}746.90.$$

 (b)   As of April 14, 2013, the year to date return was 9.38%, compounded monthly. If this rate were to continue, and Allyson continues to contribute \$950 a month, how much would the account be worth at the end of the next 15 years?

Solution   Deal separately with the two parts of her account (the \$950 contributions in the future and the \$141,746.90 already in the account). The contributions form an ordinary annuity as in part (a). Now we have $R = 950, i = .0938/12,$ and $n = 12 * 15 = 180.$ So the future value is

$$S = R \left[\frac{(1 + i)^n - 1}{i} \right] = 950 \left[\frac{(1 + .0938/12)^{180} - 1}{.0938/12} \right] = \$372{,}068.65.$$

Meanwhile, the \$141,746.90 from the first 10 years is also earning interest at 9.38%, compounded monthly. By the compound amount formula (Section 5.2), the future value of this money is

$$141{,}746.90(1 + .0938/12)^{180} = \$575{,}691.85.$$

So the total amount in Allyson's account after 25 years is the sum

$$\$372{,}068.65 + \$575{,}691.85 = \$947{,}760.50.$$

Sinking Funds

A **sinking fund** is a fund set up to receive periodic payments. Corporations and municipalities use sinking funds to repay bond issues, to retire preferred stock, to provide for replacement of fixed assets, and for other purposes. If the payments are equal and are made at the end of regular periods, they form an ordinary annuity.

Example 4   A business sets up a sinking fund so that it will be able to pay off bonds it has issued when they mature. If it deposits \$12,000 at the end of each quarter in an account that earns 5.2% interest, compounded quarterly, how much will be in the sinking fund after 10 years?

Solution   The sinking fund is an annuity, with $R = 12{,}000, i = .052/4,$ and $n = 4(10) = 40.$ The future value is

$$S = R \left[\frac{(1 + i)^n - 1}{i} \right] = 12{,}000 \left[\frac{(1 + .052/4)^{40} - 1}{.052/4} \right] = \$624{,}369.81.$$

So there will be about \$624,370 in the sinking fund.

Example 5   A firm borrows $6 million to build a small factory. The bank requires it to set up a $200,000 sinking fund to replace the roof after 15 years. If the firm's deposits earn 6% interest, compounded annually, find the payment it should make at the end of each year into the sinking fund.

Solution   This situation is an annuity with future value $S = 200,000$, interest rate $i = .06$, and $n = 15$. Solve the future-value formula for R:

$$S = R\left[\frac{(1 + i)^n - 1}{i}\right]$$

$$200,000 = R\left[\frac{(1 + .06)^{15} - 1}{.06}\right] \qquad \text{Let } S = 200{,}000,\, i = .06,\, \text{and } n = 15.$$

$$200,000 = R[23.27597] \qquad \text{Compute the quantity in brackets.}$$

$$R = \frac{200,000}{23.27597} = \$8592.55. \qquad \text{Divide both sides by 23.27597.}$$

So the annual payment is about $8593. ✓₄

Checkpoint 4

Francisco Arce needs $8000 in 6 years so that he can go on an archaeological dig. He wants to deposit equal payments at the end of each quarter so that he will have enough to go on the dig. Find the amount of each payment if the bank pays

(a) 12% interest compounded quarterly;

(b) 8% interest compounded quarterly.

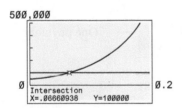

Figure 5.9

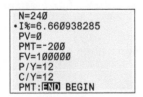

Figure 5.10

Checkpoint 5

Pete's Pizza deposits $5800 at the end of each quarter for 4 years.

(a) Find the final amount on deposit if the money earns 6.4% compounded quarterly.

(b) Pete wants to accumulate $110,000 in the 4-year period. What interest rate (to the nearest tenth) will be required?

Example 6   As an incentive for a valued employee to remain on the job, a company plans to offer her a $100,000 bonus, payable when she retires in 20 years. If the company deposits $200 a month in a sinking fund, what interest rate must it earn, with monthly compounding, in order to guarantee that the fund will be worth $100,000 in 20 years?

Solution   The sinking fund is an annuity with $R = 200$, $n = 12(20) = 240$, and future value $S = 100,000$. We must find the interest rate. If x is the annual interest rate in decimal form, then the interest rate per month is $i = x/12$. Inserting these values into the future-value formula, we have

$$R\left[\frac{(1 + i)^n - 1}{i}\right] = S$$

$$200\left[\frac{(1 + x/12)^{240} - 1}{x/12}\right] = 100,000.$$

This equation is hard to solve algebraically. You can get a rough approximation by using a calculator and trying different values for x. With a graphing calculator, you can get an accurate solution by graphing

$$y_1 = 200\left[\frac{(1 + x/12)^{240} - 1}{x/12}\right] \quad \text{and} \quad y_2 = 100,000$$

and finding the x-coordinate of the point where the graphs intersect. Figure 5.9 shows that the company needs an interest rate of about 6.661%. The same answer can be obtained on a TVM solver (Figure 5.10). ✓₅

Annuities Due

The formula developed previously is for *ordinary annuities*—annuities with payments at the *end* of each period. The results can be modified slightly to apply to **annuities due**—annuities where payments are made at the *beginning* of each period.

An example will illustrate how this is done. Consider an annuity due in which payments of $100 are made for 3 years, and an ordinary annuity in which payments of $100 are made for 4 years, both with 5% interest, compounded annually. Figure 5.11 computes the growth of each payment separately (as was done in Example 1).

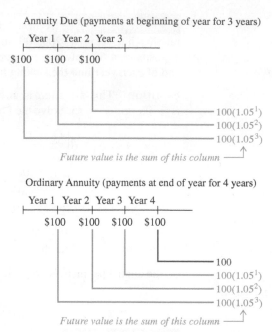

Figure 5.11

Figure 5.11 shows that the future values are the same, *except* for one $100 payment on the ordinary annuity (shown in red). So we can use the formula on page 245 to find the future value of the 4-year ordinary annuity and then subtract one $100 payment to get the future value of the 3-year annuity due:

Future value of   **=**   **Future value of**   **−**   **One payment**
3-year annuity due   **4-year ordinary annuity**

$$S = 100\left[\frac{1.05^4 - 1}{.05}\right] - 100 = \$331.01.$$

Essentially the same argument works in the general case.

Future Value of an Annuity Due

The future value S of an annuity due used to accumulate funds is given by

$$S = R\left[\frac{(1 + i)^{n+1} - 1}{i}\right] - R$$

$$S = \begin{array}{c}\text{Future value of}\\ \text{an ordinary annuity} - \text{One payment,}\\ \text{of } n + 1 \text{ payments}\end{array}$$

where

    R is the payment at the beginning of each period,

    i is the interest rate per period, and

    n is the number of periods.

Example 7   Payments of $500 are made at the beginning of each quarter for 7 years in an account paying 8% interest, compounded quarterly. Find the future value of this annuity due.

✓ Checkpoint 6

(a) Ms. Black deposits $800 at the beginning of each 6-month period for 5 years. Find the final amount if the account pays 6% compounded semiannually.

(b) Find the final amount if this account were an ordinary annuity.

Solution In 7 years, there are $n = 28$ quarterly periods. For an annuity due, add one period to get $n + 1 = 29$, and use the formula with $i = .08/4 = .02$:

$$S = R\left[\frac{(1 + i)^{n+1} - 1}{i}\right] - R = 500\left[\frac{(1 + .02)^{29} - 1}{.02}\right] - 500 = \$18,896.12.$$

After 7 years, the account balance will be $18,896.12. ✓ 6

Example 8 Jay Rechtien plans to have a fixed amount from his paycheck directly deposited into an account that pays 5.5% interest, compounded monthly. If he gets paid on the first day of the month and wants to accumulate $13,000 in the next three-and-a-half years, how much should he deposit each month?

Solution Jay's deposits form an annuity due whose future value is $S - 13,000$. The interest rate is $i = .055/12$. There are 42 months in three-and-a-half years. Since this is an annuity due, add one period, so that $n + 1 = 43$. Then solve the future-value formula for the payment R:

$$R\left[\frac{(1 + i)^{n+1} - 1}{i}\right] - R = S$$

$$R\left[\frac{(1 + .055/12)^{43} - 1}{.055/12}\right] - R = 13,000 \qquad \text{Let } i = .055/12, n = 43, \text{ and } S = 13,000.$$

$$R\left(\left[\frac{(1 + .055/12)^{43} - 1}{.055/12}\right] - 1\right) = 13,000 \qquad \text{Factor out } R \text{ on left side.}$$

$$R(46.4103) = 13,000 \qquad \text{Compute left side.}$$

$$R = \frac{13,000}{46.4103} = 280.110. \qquad \text{Divide both sides by 46.4103.}$$

Jay should have $280.11 deposited from each paycheck.

↗ TECHNOLOGY TIP

When a TVM solver is used for annuities due, the PMT: setting at the bottom of the screen should be "BEGIN". See Figure 5.12, which shows the solution of Example 8.

```
N=42
I%=5.5
PV=0
•PMT=-280.110136
FV=13000
P/Y=12
C/Y=12
PMT:END BEGIN
```

Figure 5.12

5.3 Exercises

Note: Unless stated otherwise, all payments are made at the end of the period.

Find each of these sums (to 4 decimal places).

1. $1 + 1.05 + 1.05^2 + 1.05^3 + \cdots + 1.05^{14}$

2. $1 + 1.046 + 1.046^2 + 1.046^3 + \cdots + 1.046^{21}$

Find the future value of the ordinary annuities with the given payments and interest rates. (See Examples 1, 2, 3(a), and 4.)

3. $R = \$12,000$, 6.2% interest compounded annually for 8 years

4. $R = \$20,000$, 4.5% interest compounded annually for 12 years

5. $R = \$865$, 6% interest compounded semiannually for 10 years

6. $R = \$7300$, 9% interest compounded semiannually for 6 years

7. $R = \$1200$, 8% interest compounded quarterly for 10 years

8. $R = \$20,000$, 6% interest compounded quarterly for 12 years

Find the final amount (rounded to the nearest dollar) in each of these retirement accounts, in which the rate of return on the

account and the regular contribution change over time. (See Example 3.)

9. $400 per month invested at 4%, compounded monthly, for 10 years; then $600 per month invested at 6%, compounded monthly, for 10 years.

10. $500 per month invested at 5%, compounded monthly, for 20 years; then $1000 per month invested at 8%, compounded monthly, for 20 years.

11. $1000 per quarter invested at 4.2%, compounded quarterly, for 10 years; then $1500 per quarter invested at 7.4%, compounded quarterly, for 15 years.

12. $1500 per quarter invested at 7.4%, compounded quarterly, for 15 years; then $1000 per quarter invested at 4.2%, compounded quarterly, for 10 years. (Compare with Exercise 11.)

Find the amount of each payment to be made into a sinking fund to accumulate the given amounts. Payments are made at the end of each period. (See Example 5.)

13. $11,000; money earns 5% compounded semiannually for 6 years

14. $65,000; money earns 6% compounded semiannually for $4\frac{1}{2}$ years

15. $50,000; money earns 8% compounded quarterly for $2\frac{1}{2}$ years

16. $25,000; money earns 9% compounded quarterly for $3\frac{1}{2}$ years

17. $6000; money earns 6% compounded monthly for 3 years

18. $9000; money earns 7% compounded monthly for $2\frac{1}{2}$ years

Find the interest rate needed for the sinking fund to reach the required amount. Assume that the compounding period is the same as the payment period. (See Example 6.)

19. $50,000 to be accumulated in 10 years; annual payments of $3940.

20. $100,000 to be accumulated in 15 years; quarterly payments of $1200.

21. $38,000 to be accumulated in 5 years; quarterly payments of $1675.

22. $77,000 to be accumulated in 20 years; monthly payments of $195.

23. What is meant by a sinking fund? List some reasons for establishing a sinking fund.

24. Explain the difference between an ordinary annuity and an annuity due.

Find the future value of each annuity due. (See Example 7.)

25. Payments of $500 for 10 years at 5% compounded annually

26. Payments of $1050 for 8 years at 3.5% compounded annually

27. Payments of $16,000 for 11 years at 4.7% compounded annually

28. Payments of $25,000 for 12 years at 6% compounded annually

29. Payments of $1000 for 9 years at 8% compounded semiannually

30. Payments of $750 for 15 years at 6% compounded semiannually

31. Payments of $100 for 7 years at 9% compounded quarterly

32. Payments of $1500 for 11 years at 7% compounded quarterly

Find the payment that should be used for the annuity due whose future value is given. Assume that the compounding period is the same as the payment period. (See Example 8.)

33. $8000; quarterly payments for 3 years; interest rate 4.4%

34. $12,000; annual payments for 6 years; interest rate 5.1%

35. $55,000; monthly payments for 12 years; interest rate 5.7%

36. $125,000; monthly payments for 9 years; interest rate 6%

Finance *Work the following applied problems.*

37. A typical pack-a-day smoker in Ohio spends about $170 per month on cigarettes. Suppose the smoker invests that amount at the end of each month in an investment fund that pays a return

of 5.3% compounded monthly. What would the account be worth after 40 years? (Data from: www.theawl.com.)

38. A typical pack-a-day smoker in Illinois spends about $307.50 per month on cigarettes. Suppose the smoker invests that amount at the end of each month in an investment fund that pays a return of 4.9% compounded monthly. What would the account be worth after 40 years? (Data from: www.theawl. com.)

39. The Vanguard Explorer Value fund had as of April 2013 a 10-year average return of 10.99%. (Data from: www.vanguard. com.)

   (a) If Becky Anderson deposited $800 a month in the fund for 10 years, find the final value of the amount of her investments. Assume monthly compounding.

   (b) If Becky had invested instead with the Vanguard Growth and Income fund, which had an average annual return of 7.77%, what would the final value of the amount of her investments be? Assume monthly compounding.

   (c) How much more did the Explorer Value fund generate than the Growth and Income fund?

40. The Janus Enterprise fund had as of April 2013 a 10-year average return of 12.54%. (Data from: www.janus.com.)

   (a) If Elaine Chuha deposited $625 a month in the fund for 8 years, find the final value of the amount of her investments. Assume monthly compounding.

   (b) If Elaine had invested instead with the Janus Twenty fund, which had an average annual return of 10.63%, what would the final value of the amount of her investments be? Assume monthly compounding.

   (c) How much more did the Janus Enterprise fund generate than the Janus Twenty fund?

41. Brian Feister, a 25-year-old professional, invests $200 a month in the T. Rowe Price Capital Opportunity fund, which has a 10-year average return of 8.75%. (Data from: www.troweprice.com.)

   (a) Brian wants to estimate what he will have for retirement when he is 60 years old if the rate stays constant. Assume monthly compounding.

   (b) If Brian makes no further deposits and makes no withdrawals after age 60, how much will he have for retirement at age 65?

42. Ian Morrison, a 30-year-old professional, invests $250 a month in the T. Rowe Price Equity Income fund, which has a 10-year average return of 9.04%. (Data from: www.troweprice.com.)

   (a) Ian wants to estimate what he will have for retirement when he is 65 years old if the rate stays constant. Assume monthly compounding.

   (b) If Ian makes no further deposits and makes no withdrawals after age 65, how much will he have for retirement at age 75? Assume monthly compounding.

43. A mother opened an investment account for her son on the day he was born, investing $1000. Each year on his birthday, she deposits another $1000, making the last deposit on his 18th birthday. If the account paid a return rate of 5.6% compounded annually, how much is in the account at the end of the day on the son's 18th birthday?

44. A grandmother opens an investment account for her only grand-daughter on the day she was born, investing $500. Each year on her birthday, she deposits another $500, making the last deposit on her 25th birthday. If the account paid a return rate of 6.2% compounded annually, how much is in the account at the end of the day on the granddaughter's 25th birthday?

45. Chuck Hickman deposits $10,000 at the beginning of each year for 12 years in an account paying 5% compounded annually. He then puts the total amount on deposit in another account paying 6% compounded semi-annually for another 9 years. Find the final amount on deposit after the entire 21-year period.

46. Suppose that the best rate that the company in Example 6 can find is 6.3%, compounded monthly (rather than the 6.661% it wants). Then the company must deposit more in the sinking fund each month. What monthly deposit will guarantee that the fund will be worth $100,000 in 20 years?

47. David Horwitz needs $10,000 in 8 years.

(a) What amount should he deposit at the end of each quarter at 5% compounded quarterly so that he will have his $10,000?

(b) Find Horwitz's quarterly deposit if the money is deposited at 5.8% compounded quarterly.

48. Harv's Meats knows that it must buy a new machine in 4 years. The machine costs $12,000. In order to accumulate enough money to pay for the machine, Harv decides to deposit a sum of money at the end of each 6 months in an account paying 6% compounded semiannually. How much should each payment be?

49. Barbara Margolius wants to buy a $24,000 car in 6 years. How much money must she deposit at the end of each quarter in an account paying 5% compounded quarterly so that she will have enough to pay for her car?

50. The Chinns agree to sell an antique vase to a local museum for $19,000. They want to defer the receipt of this money until they retire in 5 years (and are in a lower tax bracket). If the museum can earn 5.8%, compounded annually, find the amount of each annual payment it should make into a sinking fund so that it will have the necessary $19,000 in 5 years.

51. Diane Gray sells some land in Nevada. She will be paid a lump sum of $60,000 in 7 years. Until then, the buyer pays 8% simple interest quarterly.

(a) Find the amount of each quarterly interest payment.

(b) The buyer sets up a sinking fund so that enough money will be present to pay off the $60,000. The buyer wants to make semiannual payments into the sinking fund; the account pays 6% compounded semiannually. Find the amount of each payment into the fund.

52. Joe Seniw bought a rare stamp for his collection. He agreed to pay a lump sum of $4000 after 5 years. Until then, he pays 6% simple interest semiannually.

(a) Find the amount of each semiannual interest payment.

(b) Seniw sets up a sinking fund so that enough money will be present to pay off the $4000. He wants to make annual payments into the fund. The account pays 8% compounded annually. Find the amount of each payment.

53. To save for retirement, Karla Harby put $300 each month into an ordinary annuity for 20 years. Interest was compounded monthly. At the end of the 20 years, the annuity was worth $147,126. What annual interest rate did she receive?

54. Jennifer Wall made payments of $250 per month at the end of each month to purchase a piece of property. After 30 years, she owned the property, which she sold for $330,000. What annual interest rate would she need to earn on an ordinary annuity for a comparable rate of return?

55. When Joe and Sarah graduate from college, each expects to work a total of 45 years. Joe begins saving for retirement immediately. He plans to deposit $600 at the end of each quarter into an account paying 8.1% interest, compounded quarterly, for 10 years. He will then leave his balance in the account, earning the same interest rate, but make no further deposits for 35 years. Sarah plans to save nothing during the first 10 years and then begin depositing $600 at the end of each quarter in an account paying 8.1% interest, compounded quarterly, for 35 years.

(a) Without doing any calculations, predict which one will have the most in his or her retirement account after 45 years. Then test your prediction by answering the following questions (calculation required to the nearest dollar).

(b) How much will Joe contribute to his retirement account?

(c) How much will be in Joe's account after 45 years?

(d) How much will Sarah contribute to her retirement account?

(e) How much will be in Sarah's account after 45 years?

56. In a 1992 Virginia lottery, the jackpot was $27 million. An Australian investment firm tried to buy all possible combinations of numbers, which would have cost $7 million. In fact, the firm ran out of time and was unable to buy all combinations, but ended up with the only winning ticket anyway. The firm received the jackpot in 20 equal annual payments of $1.35 million. Assume these payments meet the conditions of an ordinary annuity. (Data from: *Washington Post*, March 10, 1992, p. A1.)

(a) Suppose the firm can invest money at 8% interest compounded annually. How many years would it take until the investors would be further ahead than if they had simply invested the $7 million at the same rate? (*Hint:* Experiment with different values of *n*, the number of years, or use a graphing calculator to plot the value of both investments as a function of the number of years.)

(b) How many years would it take in part (a) at an interest rate of 12%?

✓ **Checkpoint Answers**

1. **(a)** $2247.20   **(b)** $2120.00   **(c)** $6367.20

2. **(a)** $18,339.82   **(b)** $36,216.41

3. $872,354.36

4. **(a)** $232.38   **(b)** $262.97

5. **(a)** $104,812.44   **(b)** 8.9%

6. **(a)** $9446.24   **(b)** $9171.10

5.4 Annuities, Present Value, and Amortization

In the annuities studied previously, regular deposits were made into an interest-bearing account and the value of the annuity increased from 0 at the beginning to some larger amount at the end (the future value). Now we expand the discussion to include annuities that begin with an amount of money and make regular payments each period until the value of the annuity decreases to 0. Examples of such annuities are lottery jackpots, structured settlements imposed by a court in which the party at fault (or his or her insurance company) makes regular payments to the injured party, and trust funds that pay the recipients a fixed amount at regular intervals.

In order to develop the essential formula for dealing with "payout annuities," we need another useful algebraic fact. If x is a nonzero number and n is a positive integer, verify the following equality by multiplying out the right-hand side:[*]

$$x^{-1} + x^{-2} + x^{-3} + \cdots + x^{-(n-1)} + x^{-n} = x^{-n}(x^{n-1} + x^{n-2} + x^{n-3} + \cdots + x^{1} + 1).$$

Now use the sum formula in the box on page 243 to rewrite the expression in parentheses on the right-hand side:

$$x^{-1} + x^{-2} + x^{-3} + \cdots + x^{-(n-1)} + x^{-n} = x^{-n}\left(\frac{x^{n} - 1}{x - 1}\right)$$

$$= \frac{x^{-n}(x^{n} - 1)}{x - 1} = \frac{x^{0} - x^{-n}}{x - 1} = \frac{1 - x^{-n}}{x - 1}.$$

We have proved the following result:

If x is a nonzero real number and n is a positive integer, then

$$x^{-1} + x^{-2} + x^{-3} + \cdots + x^{-n} = \frac{1 - x^{-n}}{x - 1}.$$

Present Value

In Section 5.2, we saw that the present value of A dollars at interest rate i per period for n periods is the amount that must be deposited today (at the same interest rate) in order to produce A dollars in n periods. Similarly, the **present value of an annuity** is the amount that must be deposited today (at the same compound interest rate as the annuity) to provide all the payments for the term of the annuity. It does not matter whether the payments are invested to accumulate funds or are paid out to disperse funds; the amount needed to provide the payments is the same in either case. We begin with ordinary annuities.

Example 1   Your rich aunt has funded an annuity that will pay you $1500 at the end of each year for six years. If the interest rate is 8%, compounded annually, find the present value of this annuity.

Solution   Look separately at each payment you will receive. Then find the present value of each payment—the amount needed now in order to make the payment in the future. The sum of these present values will be the present value of the annuity, since it will provide all of the payments.

---

[*]Remember that powers of x are multiplied by *adding* exponents and that $x^{n}x^{-n} = x^{n-n} = x^{0} = 1$.

To find the first $1500 payment (due in one year), the present value of $1500 at 8% annual interest is needed now. According to the present-value formula for compound interest on page 240 (with $A = 1500$, $i = .08$, and $n = 1$), this present value is

$$\frac{1500}{1 + .08} = \frac{1500}{1.08} = 1500(1.08^{-1}) \approx \$1388.89.$$

This amount will grow to $1500 in one year.

For the second $1500 payment (due in two years), we need the present value of $1500 at 8% interest, compounded annually for two years. The present-value formula for compound interest (with $A = 1500$, $i = .08$, and $n = 2$) shows that this present value is

$$\frac{1500}{(1 + .08)^2} = \frac{1500}{1.08^2} = 1500(1.08^{-2}) \approx \$1286.01.$$

Less money is needed for the second payment because it will grow over two years instead of one.

A similar calculation shows that the third payment (due in three years) has present value $1500(1.08^{-3})$. Continue in this manner to find the present value of each of the remaining payments, as summarized in Figure 5.13.

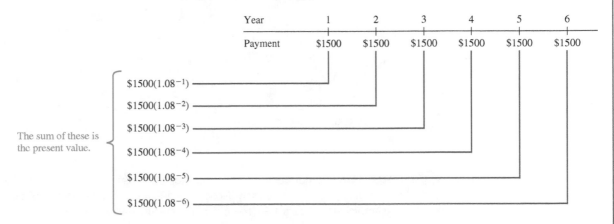

Figure 5.13

The left-hand column of Figure 5.13 shows that the present value is

$$1500 \cdot 1.08^{-1} + 1500 \cdot 1.08^{-2} + 1500 \cdot 1.08^{-3} + 1500 \cdot 1.08^{-4}$$
$$+ 1500 \cdot 1.08^{-5} + 1500 \cdot 1.08^{-6}$$
$$= 1500(1.08^{-1} + 1.08^{-2} + 1.08^{-3} + 1.08^{-4} + 1.08^{-5} + 1.08^{-6}). \qquad (1)$$

Now apply the algebraic fact in the box on page 252 to the expression in parentheses (with $x = 1.08$ and $n = 6$). It shows that the sum (the present value of the annuity) is

$$1500\left[\frac{1 - 1.08^{-6}}{1.08 - 1}\right] = 1500\left[\frac{1 - 1.08^{-6}}{.08}\right] = \$6934.32.$$

This amount will provide for all six payments and leave a zero balance at the end of six years (give or take a few cents due to rounding to the nearest penny at each step). ✓₁

Example 1 is the model for finding a formula for the future value of any ordinary annuity. Suppose that a payment of R dollars is made at the end of each period for n

✓ **Checkpoint 1**

Show that $6934.32 will provide all the payments in Example 1 as follows:

(a) Find the balance at the end of the first year after the interest has been added and the $1500 payment subtracted.

(b) Repeat part (a) to find the balances at the ends of years 2 through 6.

periods, at interest rate i per period. Then the present value of this annuity can be found by using the procedure in Example 1, with these replacements:

$$
\begin{array}{cccc}
1500 & .08 & 1.08 & 6 \\
\downarrow & \downarrow & \downarrow & \downarrow \\
R & i & 1+i & n
\end{array}
$$

The future value in Example 1 is the sum in equation **(1)**, which now becomes

$$P = R[(1 + i)^{-1} + (1 + i)^{-2} + (1 + i)^{-3} + \cdots + (1 + i)^{-n}].$$

Apply the algebraic fact in the box on page 252 to the expression in brackets (with $x = 1 + i$). Then we have

$$P = R\left[\frac{1 - (1 + i)^{-n}}{(1 + i) - 1}\right] = R\left[\frac{1 - (1 + i)^{-n}}{i}\right].$$

The quantity in brackets in the right-hand part of the preceding equation is sometimes written $a_{\overline{n}|i}$ (read "a-angle-n at i"). So we can summarize as follows.

Present Value of an Ordinary Annuity

The present value P of an ordinary annuity is given by

$$P = R\left[\frac{1 - (1 + i)^{-n}}{i}\right], \quad \text{or} \quad P = R \cdot a_{\overline{n}|i},$$

where

  R is the payment at the end of each period,

  i is the interest rate per period, and

  n is the number of periods.

 CAUTION Do not confuse the formula for the present value of an annuity with the one for the future value of an annuity. Notice the difference: The numerator of the fraction in the present-value formula is $1 - (1 + i)^{-n}$, but in the future-value formula, it is $(1 + i)^n - 1$.

 Example 2   Jim Riles was in an auto accident. He sued the person at fault and was awarded a structured settlement in which an insurance company will pay him $600 at the end of each month for the next seven years. How much money should the insurance company invest now at 4.7%, compounded monthly, to guarantee that all the payments can be made?

 Solution   The payments form an ordinary annuity. The amount needed to fund all the payments is the present value of the annuity. Apply the present-value formula with $R = 600, n = 7 \cdot 12 = 84$, and $i = .047/12$ (the interest rate per month). The insurance company should invest

$$P = R\left[\frac{1 - (1 + i)^{-n}}{i}\right] = 600\left[\frac{1 - (1 + .047/12)^{-84}}{.047/12}\right] = \$42,877.44. \; \boxed{2}$$

✓ Checkpoint 2

An insurance company offers to pay Jane Parks an ordinary annuity of $1200 per quarter for five years *or* the present value of the annuity now. If the interest rate is 6%, find the present value.

 Example 3   To supplement his pension in the early years of his retirement, Ralph Taylor plans to use $124,500 of his savings as an ordinary annuity that will make monthly payments to him for 20 years. If the interest rate is 5.2%, how much will each payment be?

Solution   The present value of the annuity is $P = \$124{,}500$, the monthly interest rate is $i = .052/12$, and $n = 12 \cdot 20 = 240$ (the number of months in 20 years). Solve the present-value formula for the monthly payment R:

$$P = R\left[\frac{1 - (1 + i)^{-n}}{i}\right]$$

$$124{,}500 = R\left[\frac{1 - (1 + .052/12)^{-240}}{.052/12}\right]$$

$$R = \frac{124{,}500}{\left[\dfrac{1 - (1 + .052/12)^{-240}}{.052/12}\right]} = \$835.46.$$

Taylor will receive \$835.46 a month (about \$10,026 per year) for 20 years. ✔₃

✓Checkpoint 3

Carl Dehne has \$80,000 in an account paying 4.8% interest, compounded monthly. He plans to use up all the money by making equal monthly withdrawals for 15 years. If the interest rate is 4.8%, find the amount of each withdrawal.

Example 4   Surinder Sinah and Maria Gonzalez are graduates of Kenyon College. They both agree to contribute to an endowment fund at the college. Sinah says he will give \$500 at the end of each year for 9 years. Gonzalez prefers to give a single donation today. How much should she give to equal the value of Sinah's gift, assuming that the endowment fund earns 7.5% interest, compounded annually?

Solution   Sinah's gift is an ordinary annuity with annual payments of \$500 for 9 years. Its *future* value at 7.5% annual compound interest is

$$S = R\left[\frac{(1 + i)^n - 1}{i}\right] = 500\left[\frac{(1 + .075)^9 - 1}{.075}\right] = 500\left[\frac{1.075^9 - 1}{.075}\right] = \$6114.92.$$

We claim that for Gonzalez to equal this contribution, she should today contribute an amount equal to the *present* value of this annuity, namely,

$$P = R\left[\frac{1 - (1 + i)^{-n}}{i}\right] = 500\left[\frac{1 - (1 + .075)^{-9}}{.075}\right] = 500\left[\frac{1 - 1.075^{-9}}{.075}\right] = \$3189.44.$$

To confirm this claim, suppose the present value $P = \$3189.44$ is deposited today at 7.5% interest, compounded annually for 9 years. According to the compound interest formula on page 233, P will grow to

$$3189.44(1 + .075)^9 = \$6114.92,$$

the future value of Sinah's annuity. So at the end of 9 years, Gonzalez and Sinah will have made identical gifts.

Example 4 illustrates the following alternative description of the present value of an "accumulation annuity."

> The present value of an annuity for accumulating funds is the single deposit that would have to be made today to produce the future value of the annuity (assuming the same interest rate and period of time.) ✔₄

✓Checkpoint 4

What lump sum deposited today would be equivalent to equal payments of

(a) \$650 at the end of each year for 9 years at 4% compounded annually?

(b) \$1000 at the end of each quarter for 4 years at 4% compounded quarterly?

Corporate bonds, which were introduced in Section 5.1, are routinely bought and sold in financial markets. In most cases, interest rates when a bond is sold differ from the interest rate paid by the bond (known as the **coupon rate**). In such cases, the price of a bond will not be its face value, but will instead be based on current interest rates. The next example shows how this is done.

Example 5   A 15-year \$10,000 bond with a 5% coupon rate was issued five years ago and is now being sold. If the current interest rate for similar bonds is 7%, what price should a purchaser be willing to pay for this bond?

Solution According to the simple interest formula (page 226), the interest paid by the bond each half-year is

$$I = Prt = 10{,}000 \cdot .05 \cdot \frac{1}{2} = \$250.$$

Think of the bond as a two-part investment: The first is an annuity that pays \$250 every six months for the next 10 years; the second is the \$10,000 face value of the bond, which will be paid when the bond matures, 10 years from now. The purchaser should be willing to pay the present value of each part of the investment, assuming 7% interest, compounded semiannually.[*] The interest rate per period is $i = .07/2$, and the number of six-month periods in 10 years is $n = 20$. So we have:

Present value of annuity

$$P = R\left[\frac{1 - (1 + i)^{-n}}{i}\right]$$

$$= 250\left[\frac{1 - (1 + .07/2)^{-20}}{.07/2}\right]$$

$$= \$3553.10$$

Present value of \$10,000 in 10 years

$$P = A(1 + i)^{-n}$$

$$= 10{,}000(1 + .07/2)^{-20}$$

$$= \$5025.66.$$

So the purchaser should be willing to pay the sum of these two present values:

$$\$3553.10 + \$5025.66 = \$8578.76. \quad \boxed{5}$$

✓ **Checkpoint 5**

Suppose the current interest rate for bonds is 4% instead of 7% when the bond in Example 5 is sold. What price should a purchaser be willing to pay for it?

📄 **NOTE** Example 5 and Checkpoint 5 illustrate the inverse relation between interest rates and bond prices: If interest rates rise, bond prices fall, and if interest rates fall, bond prices rise.

Loans and Amortization

If you take out a car loan or a home mortgage, you repay it by making regular payments to the bank. From the bank's point of view, your payments are an annuity that is paying it a fixed amount each month. The present value of this annuity is the amount you borrowed.

Example 6 **Finance** Chase Bank in April 2013 advertised a new car auto loan rate of 2.23% for a 48-month loan. Shelley Fasulko will buy a new car for \$25,000 with a down payment of \$4500. Find the amount of each payment. (Data from: www.chase.com.)

Solution After a \$4500 down payment, the loan amount is \$20,500. Use the present-value formula for an annuity, with $P = 20{,}500$, $n = 48$, and $i = .0223/12$ (the monthly interest rate). Then solve for payment R.

$$P = R\left[\frac{1 - (1 + i)^{-n}}{i}\right]$$

$$20{,}500 = R\left[\frac{1 - (1 + .0223/12)^{-48}}{.0223/12}\right]$$

$$R = \frac{20{,}500}{\left[\dfrac{1 - (1 + .0223/12)^{-48}}{.0223/12}\right]} \qquad \text{Solve for } R.$$

$$R = \$446.81 \quad \boxed{6}$$

✓ **Checkpoint 6**

Suzanne Bellini uses a Chase auto loan to purchase a used car priced at \$28,750 at an interest rate of 3.64% for a 60-month loan. What is the monthly payment?

A loan is **amortized** if both the principal and interest are paid by a sequence of equal periodic payments. The periodic payment needed to amortize a loan may be found, as in Example 6, by solving the present-value formula for R.

---

[*]The analysis here does not include any commissions or fees charged by the financial institution that handles the bond sale.

Amortization Payments

A loan of P dollars at interest rate i per period may be amortized in n equal periodic payments of R dollars made at the end of each period, where

$$R = \frac{P}{\left[\dfrac{1 - (1 + i)^{-n}}{i}\right]} = \frac{Pi}{1 - (1 + i)^{-n}}.$$

Example 7   **Finance**   In April 2013, the average rate for a 30-year fixed mortgage was 3.43%. Assume a down payment of 20% on a home purchase of $272,900. (Data from: Freddie Mac.)

(a) Find the monthly payment needed to amortize this loan.

Solution   The down payment is .20(272,900) = $54,580. Thus, the loan amount P is $272,900 − 54,580 = $218,320. We can now apply the formula in the preceding box, with $n = 12(30) = 360$ (the number of monthly payments in 30 years), and monthly interest rate $i = .0343/12.$[*]

$$R = \frac{Pi}{1 - (1 + i)^{-n}} = \frac{(218,320)(.0343/12)}{1 - (1 + .0343/12)^{-360}} = \$971.84$$

Monthly payments of $971.84 are required to amortize the loan.

(b) After 10 years, approximately how much is owed on the mortgage?

Solution   You may be tempted to say that after 10 years of payments on a 30-year mortgage, the balance will be reduced by a third. However, a significant portion of each payment goes to pay interest. So, much less than a third of the mortgage is paid off in the first 10 years, as we now see.

After 10 years (120 payments), the 240 remaining payments can be thought of as an annuity. The present value for this annuity is the (approximate) remaining balance on the mortgage. Hence, we use the present-value formula with $R = 971.84$, $i = .0343/12$, and $n = 240$:

$$P = 971.84\left[\frac{1 - (1 + .0343/12)^{-240}}{(.0343/12)}\right] = \$168,614.16.$$

So the remaining balance is about $168,614.16. The actual balance probably differs slightly from this figure because payments and interest amounts are rounded to the nearest penny.   ✓₇

✓ Checkpoint 7

Find the remaining balance after 20 years.

```
N=360
I%=3.43
PV=218320
•PMT=-971.8435089
FV=0
P/Y=12
C/Y=12
PMT:END BEGIN
```

Figure 5.14

TECHNOLOGY TIP   A TVM solver on a graphing calculator can find the present value of an annuity or the payment on a loan: Fill in the known information, put the cursor next to the unknown item (PV or PMT), and press SOLVE. Figure 5.14 shows the solution to Example 7(a) on a TVM solver. Alternatively, you can use the program in the Program Appendix.

Example 7(b) illustrates an important fact: Even though equal *payments* are made to amortize a loan, the loan *balance* does not decrease in equal steps. The method used to estimate the remaining balance in Example 7(b) works in the general case. If n payments

---

[*]Mortgage rates are quoted in terms of annual interest, but it is always understood that the monthly rate is $\frac{1}{12}$ of the annual interest rate and that interest is compounded monthly.

are needed to amortize a loan and x payments have been made, then the remaining payments form an annuity of $n - x$ payments. So we apply the present-value formula with $n - x$ in place of n to obtain this result.

> ## Remaining Balance
>
> If a loan can be amortized by n payments of R dollars each at an interest rate i per period, then the *approximate* remaining balance B after x payments is
>
> $$B = R\left[\frac{1 - (1 + i)^{-(n-x)}}{i}\right].$$

Amortization Schedules

The remaining-balance formula is a quick and convenient way to get a reasonable estimate of the remaining balance on a loan, but it is not accurate enough for a bank or business, which must keep its books exactly. To determine the exact remaining balance after each loan payment, financial institutions normally use an **amortization schedule,** which lists how much of each payment is interest, how much goes to reduce the balance, and how much is still owed after each payment.

Example 8 Beth Hill borrows $1000 for one year at 12% annual interest, compounded monthly.

(a) Find her monthly payment.

Solution Apply the amortization payment formula with $P = 1000, n = 12$, and monthly interest rate $i = .12/12 = .01$. Her payment is

$$R = \frac{Pi}{1 - (1 + i)^{-n}} = \frac{1000(.01)}{1 - (1 + .01)^{-12}} = \$88.85.$$

(b) After making five payments, Hill decides to pay off the remaining balance. Approximately how much must she pay?

Solution Apply the remaining-balance formula just given, with $R = 88.85, i = .01$, and $n - x = 12 - 5 = 7$. Her approximate remaining balance is

$$B = R\left[\frac{1 - (1 + i)^{-(n-x)}}{i}\right] = 88.85\left[\frac{1 - (1 + .01)^{-7}}{.01}\right] = \$597.80.$$

(c) Construct an amortization schedule for Hill's loan.

Solution An amortization schedule for the loan is shown in the table on the next page. It was obtained as follows: The annual interest rate is 12% compounded monthly, so the interest rate per month is $12\%/12 = 1\% = .01$. When the first payment is made, one month's interest, namely, $.01(1000) = \$10$, is owed. Subtracting this from the $88.85 payment leaves $78.85 to be applied to repayment. Hence, the principal at the end of the first payment period is $1000 - 78.85 = \$921.15$, as shown in the "payment 1" line of the table.

When payment 2 is made, one month's interest on the new balance of $921.15 is owed, namely, $.01(921.15) = \$9.21$. Continue as in the preceding paragraph to compute the entries in this line of the table. The remaining lines of the table are found in a similar fashion.

Payment Number	Amount of Payment	Interest for Period	Portion to Principal	Principal at End of Period
0	—	—	—	$1000.00
1	$88.85	$10.00	$78.85	921.15
2	88.85	9.21	79.64	841.51
3	88.85	8.42	80.43	761.08
4	88.85	7.61	81.24	679.84
5	88.85	6.80	82.05	597.79
6	88.85	5.98	82.87	514.92
7	88.85	5.15	83.70	431.22
8	88.85	4.31	84.54	346.68
9	88.85	3.47	85.38	261.30
10	88.85	2.61	86.24	175.06
11	88.85	1.75	87.10	87.96
12	88.84	.88	87.96	0

Note that Hill's remaining balance after five payments differs slightly from the estimate made in part (b).

The final payment in the amortization schedule in Example 8(c) differs from the other payments. It often happens that the last payment needed to amortize a loan must be adjusted to account for rounding earlier and to ensure that the final balance will be exactly 0.

 TECHNOLOGY TIP Most Casio graphing calculators can produce amortization schedules. For other calculators, use the amortization table program in the Program Appendix. Spreadsheets are another useful tool for creating amortization tables. Microsoft Excel (Microsoft Corporation Excel © 2013) has a built-in feature for calculating monthly payments. Figure 5.15 shows an Excel amortization table for Example 8. For more details, see the *Spreadsheet Manual,* also available with this text.

	A	B	C	D	E	F
1	Prnt#	Payment	Interest	Principal	End Principal	
2	0				1000	
3	1	88.85	10.00	78.85	921.15	
4	2	88.85	9.21	79.64	841.51	
5	3	88.85	8.42	80.43	761.08	
6	4	88.85	7.61	81.24	679.84	
7	5	88.85	6.80	82.05	597.79	
8	6	88.85	5.98	82.87	514.92	
9	7	88.85	5.15	83.70	431.22	
10	8	88.85	4.31	84.54	346.68	
11	9	88.85	3.47	85.38	261.30	
12	10	88.85	2.61	86.24	175.06	
13	11	88.85	1.75	87.10	87.96	
14	12	88.85	0.88	87.97	-0.01	

Figure 5.15

Annuities Due

We want to find the present value of an annuity due in which 6 payments of R dollars are made at the *beginning* of each period, with interest rate i per period, as shown schematically in Figure 5.16.

$$
\begin{array}{cccccc}
1 & 2 & 3 & 4 & 5 & 6 \\
|\!\!-\!\!|\!\!-\!\!|\!\!-\!\!|\!\!-\!\!|\!\!-\!\!|\!\!- \\
R & R & R & R & R & R
\end{array}
$$

Figure 5.16

The present value is the amount needed to fund all 6 payments. Since the first payment earns no interest, R dollars are needed to fund it. Now look at the last 5 payments by themselves in Figure 5.17.

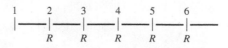

Figure 5.17

If you think of these 5 payments as being made at the end of each period, you see that they form an ordinary annuity. The money needed to fund them is the present value of this ordinary annuity. So the present value of the annuity due is given by

$$R + \begin{array}{c} \text{Present value of the ordinary} \\ \text{annuity of 5 payments} \end{array}$$

$$R + R\left[\frac{1 - (1 + i)^{-5}}{i}\right].$$

Replacing 6 by n and 5 by $n - 1$, and using the argument just given, produces the general result that follows.

Present Value of an Annuity Due

The present value P of an annuity due is given by

$$P = R + R\left[\frac{1 - (1 + i)^{-(n-1)}}{i}\right],$$

$$P = \begin{array}{c} \text{One} \\ \text{payment} \end{array} + \begin{array}{c} \text{Present value of} \\ \text{an ordinary annuity} \\ \text{of } n - 1 \text{ payments} \end{array}$$

where

 R is the payment at the beginning of each period,

 i is the interest rate per period, and

 n is the number of periods.

Example 9   **Finance**   The *Illinois Lottery Winner's Handbook* discusses the options of how to receive the winnings for a $12 million Lotto jackpot. One option is to take 26 annual payments of approximately $461,538.46, which is $12 million divided into 26 equal payments. The other option is to take a lump-sum payment (which is often called the "cash value"). If the Illinois lottery commission can earn 4.88% annual interest, how much is the cash value?

Solution   The yearly payments form a 26-payment annuity due. An equivalent amount now is the present value of this annuity. Apply the present-value formula with $R = 461,538.46$, $i = .0488$, and $n = 26$:

$$P = R + R\left[\frac{1 - (1 + i)^{-(n-1)}}{i}\right] = 461,538.46 + 461,538.46\left[\frac{1 - (1 + .0488)^{-25}}{.0488}\right]$$

$$= \$7,045,397.39.$$

The cash value is $7,045,397.39. ✓ 8

TECHNOLOGY TIP   Figure 5.18 shows the solution of Example 9 on a TVM solver. Since this is an annuity due, the PMT: setting at the bottom of the screen is "BEGIN".

✓ **Checkpoint 8**

What is the cash value for a Lotto jackpot of $25 million if the Illinois Lottery can earn 6.2% annual interest?

```
N=26
I%=4.88
•PV=7045397.393
PMT=-461538.46
FV=0
P/Y=1
C/Y=1
PMT:END BEGIN
```

Figure 5.18

5.4 Exercises

Unless noted otherwise, all payments and withdrawals are made at the end of the period.

1. Explain the difference between the present value of an annuity and the future value of an annuity.

Find the present value of each ordinary annuity. (See Examples 1, 2, and 4.)

2. Payments of $890 each year for 16 years at 6% compounded annually

3. Payments of $1400 each year for 8 years at 6% compounded annually

4. Payments of $10,000 semiannually for 15 years at 7.5% compounded semiannually

5. Payments of $50,000 quarterly for 10 years at 5% compounded quarterly

6. Payments of $15,806 quarterly for 3 years at 6.8% compounded quarterly

Find the amount necessary to fund the given withdrawals. (See Examples 1 and 2.)

7. Quarterly withdrawals of $650 for 5 years; interest rate is 4.9%, compounded quarterly.

8. Yearly withdrawals of $1200 for 14 years; interest rate is 5.6%, compounded annually.

9. Monthly withdrawals of $425 for 10 years; interest rate is 6.1%, compounded monthly.

10. Semiannual withdrawals of $3500 for 7 years; interest rate is 5.2%, compounded semiannually.

Find the payment made by the ordinary annuity with the given present value. (See Example 3.)

11. $90,000; monthly payments for 22 years; interest rate is 4.9%, compounded monthly.

12. $45,000; monthly payments for 11 years; interest rate is 5.3%, compounded monthly.

13. $275,000; quarterly payments for 18 years; interest rate is 6%, compounded quarterly.

14. $330,000; quarterly payments for 30 years; interest rate is 6.1% compounded quarterly.

Find the lump sum deposited today that will yield the same total amount as payments of $10,000 at the end of each year for 15 years at each of the given interest rates. (See Example 4 and the box following it.)

15. 3% compounded annually

16. 4% compounded annually

17. 6% compounded annually

18. What sum deposited today at 5% compounded annually for 8 years will provide the same amount as $1000 deposited at the end of each year for 8 years at 6% compounded annually?

19. What lump sum deposited today at 8% compounded quarterly for 10 years will yield the same final amount as deposits of $4000 at the end of each 6-month period for 10 years at 6% compounded semiannually?

Find the price a purchaser should be willing to pay for the given bond. Assume that the coupon interest is paid twice a year. (See Example 5.)

20. $20,000 bond with coupon rate 4.5% that matures in 8 years; current interest rate is 5.9%.

21. $15,000 bond with coupon rate 6% that matures in 4 years; current interest rate is 5%.

22. $25,000 bond with coupon rate 7% that matures in 10 years; current interest rate is 6%.

23. $10,000 bond with coupon rate 5.4% that matures in 12 years; current interest rate is 6.5%.

24. What does it mean to amortize a loan?

Find the payment necessary to amortize each of the given loans. (See Examples 6, 7(a), and 8(a).)

25. $2500; 8% compounded quarterly; 6 quarterly payments

26. $41,000; 9% compounded semiannually; 10 semiannual payments

27. $90,000; 7% compounded annually; 12 annual payments

28. $140,000; 12% compounded quarterly; 15 quarterly payments

29. $7400; 8.2% compounded semiannually; 18 semiannual payments

30. $5500; 9.5% compounded monthly; 24 monthly payments

Finance *In April 2013, the mortgage interest rates listed in Exercises 31–34 for the given companies were listed at www.hsh.com. Find the monthly payment necessary to amortize the given loans. (See Example 7(a).)*

31. $225,000 at 3.25% for 30 years from Amerisave

32. $330,000 at 3.125% for 20 years from Quicken Loans

33. $140,000 at 2.375% for 15 years from Discover Home Loans

34. $180,000 at 2.25% for 10 years from Roundpoint Mortgage Company

Finance *Find the monthly payment and estimate the remaining balance (to the nearest dollar). Assume interest is on the unpaid balance. The interest rates are from national averages from www.bankrate.com in April 2013. (See Examples 7 and 8.)*

35. Four-year new car loan for $26,799 at 3.13%; remaining balance after 2 years

36. Three-year used car loan for $15,875 at 2.96%; remaining balance after 1 year

37. Thirty-year mortgage for $210,000 at 3.54%; remaining balance after 12 years

38. Fifteen-year mortgage for $195,000 at 2.78%; remaining balance after 4.5 years

Use the amortization table in Example 8(c) to answer the questions in Exercises 39–42.

39. How much of the 5th payment is interest?

40. How much of the 10th payment is used to reduce the debt?

41. How much interest is paid in the first 5 months of the loan?

42. How much interest is paid in the last 5 months of the loan?

Find the cash value of the lottery jackpot (to the nearest dollar). Yearly jackpot payments begin immediately (26 for Mega Millions and 30 for Powerball). Assume the lottery can invest at the given interest rate. (See Example 9.)

43. Powerball: $57.6 million; 5.1% interest

44. Powerball: $207 million; 5.78% interest

45. Mega Millions: $41.6 million; 4.735% interest

46. Mega Millions: $23.4 million; 4.23% interest

Finance   *Work the following applied problems.*

47. An auto stereo dealer sells a stereo system for $600 down and monthly payments of $30 for the next 3 years. If the interest rate is 1.25% *per month* on the unpaid balance, find

(a) the cost of the stereo system;

(b) the total amount of interest paid.

48. John Kushida buys a used car costing $6000. He agrees to make payments at the end of each monthly period for 4 years. He pays 12% interest, compounded monthly.

(a) What is the amount of each payment?

(b) Find the total amount of interest Kushida will pay.

49. A speculator agrees to pay $15,000 for a parcel of land; this amount, with interest, will be paid over 4 years with semiannual payments at an interest rate of 10% compounded semiannually. Find the amount of each payment.

50. Alan Stasa buys a new car costing $26,750. What is the monthly payment if the interest rate is 4.2%, compounded monthly, and the loan is for 60 months? Find the total amount of interest Alan will pay.

Finance   *A student education loan has two repayment options. The standard plan repays the loan in 10 years with equal monthly payments. The extended plan allows from 12 to 30 years to repay the loan. A student borrows $35,000 at 7.43% compounded monthly.*

51. Find the monthly payment and total interest paid under the standard plan.

52. Find the monthly payment and total interest paid under the extended plan with 20 years to pay off the loan.

Finance   *Use the formula for the approximate remaining balance to work each problem. (See Examples 7(b) and 8(b).)*

53. When Teresa Flores opened her law office, she bought $14,000 worth of law books and $7200 worth of office furniture. She paid $1200 down and agreed to amortize the balance with semiannual payments for 5 years at 12% compounded semiannually.

(a) Find the amount of each payment.

(b) When her loan had been reduced below $5000, Flores received a large tax refund and decided to pay off the loan. How many payments were left at this time?

54. Kareem Adams buys a house for $285,000. He pays $60,000 down and takes out a mortgage at 6.9% on the balance. Find his monthly payment and the total amount of interest he will pay if the length of the mortgage is

(a) 15 years;

(b) 20 years;

(c) 25 years.

(d) When will half the 20-year loan be paid off?

55. Susan Carver will purchase a home for $257,000. She will use a down payment of 20% and finance the remaining portion at 3.9%, compounded monthly for 30 years.

(a) What will be the monthly payment?

(b) How much will remain on the loan after making payments for 5 years?

(c) How much interest will be paid on the total amount of the loan over the course of 30 years?

56. Mohsen Manouchehri will purchase a $230,000 home with a 20-year mortgage. If he makes a down payment of 20% and the interest rate is 3.3%, compounded monthly,

(a) what will the monthly payment be?

(b) how much will he owe after making payments for 8 years?

(c) how much in total interest will he pay over the course of the 20-year loan?

Work each problem.

57. Elizabeth Bernardi and her employer contribute $400 at the end of each month to her retirement account, which earns 7% interest, compounded monthly. When she retires after 45 years, she plans to make monthly withdrawals for 30 years. If her account earns 5% interest, compounded monthly, then when she retires, what is her maximum possible monthly withdrawal (without running out of money)?

58. Jim Milliken won a $15,000 prize. On March 1, he deposited it in an account earning 5.2% interest, compounded monthly. On March 1 one year later, he begins to withdraw the same amount at the beginning of each month for a year. Assuming that he uses up all the money in the account, find the amount of each monthly withdrawal.

59. Catherine Dohanyos plans to retire in 20 years. She will make 20 years of monthly contributions to her retirement account. One month after her last contribution, she will begin the first of 10 years of withdrawals. She wants to withdraw $2500 per month. How large must her monthly contributions be in order to accomplish her goal if the account earns interest of 7.1% compounded monthly for the duration of her contributions and the 120 months of withdrawals?

60. David Turner plans to retire in 25 years. He will make 25 years of monthly contributions to his retirement account. One month after his last contribution, he will begin the first of 10 years of withdrawals. He wants to withdraw $3000 per month. How large must his monthly contributions be in order to accomplish his goal if the account earns interest of 6.8% compounded monthly for the duration of his contributions and the 120 months of withdrawals?

61. William Blake plans to retire in 20 years. William will make 10 years (120 months) of equal monthly payments into his account. Ten years after his last contribution, he will begin the first of 120 monthly withdrawals of $3400 per month. Assume that the retirement account earns interest of 8.2% compounded monthly for the duration of his contributions, the 10 years in between his contributions and the beginning of his withdrawals, and the 10 years of withdrawals. How large must William's monthly contributions be in order to accomplish his goal?

62. Gil Stevens plans to retire in 25 years. He will make 15 years (180 months) of equal monthly payments into his account. Ten years after his last contribution, he will begin the first of 120 monthly withdrawals of $2900 per month. Assume that the retirement account earns interest of 5.4% compounded monthly for the duration of his contributions, the 10 years in between his

contributions and the beginning of his withdrawals, and the 10 years of withdrawals. How large must Gil's monthly contributions be in order to accomplish his goal?

Finance *In Exercises 63–66, prepare an amortization schedule showing the first four payments for each loan. (See Example 8(c).)*

63. An insurance firm pays $4000 for a new printer for its computer. It amortizes the loan for the printer in 4 annual payments at 8% compounded annually.

64. Large semitrailer trucks cost $72,000 each. Ace Trucking buys such a truck and agrees to pay for it by a loan that will be amortized with 9 semiannual payments at 6% compounded semiannually.

65. One retailer charges $1048 for a certain computer. A firm of tax accountants buys 8 of these computers. It makes a down payment of $1200 and agrees to amortize the balance with monthly payments at 12% compounded monthly for 4 years.

66. Joan Varozza plans to borrow $20,000 to stock her small boutique. She will repay the loan with semiannual payments for 5 years at 7% compounded semiannually.

✓ Checkpoint Answers

1. **(a)** $5989.07
   (b) $4968.20; $3865.66; $2674.91; $1388.90; $0.01

2. $20,602.37

3. $624.33

4. **(a)** $4832.97   **(b)** $14,717.87

5. $10,817.57

6. $524.82

7. $98,605.61

8. $13,023,058.46

CHAPTER 5 Summary and Review

Key Terms and Symbols

5.1 simple interest
principal
rate
time
future value (maturity value)
present value
discount and T-bills

5.2 compound interest
compound amount
compounding period
nominal rate (stated rate)
effective rate (APY)
present value

5.3 annuity
payment period

term of an annuity
ordinary annuity
future value of an ordinary annuity
sinking fund
annuity due
future value of an annuity due

5.4 present value of an ordinary annuity
amortization payments
remaining balance
amortization schedule
present value of an annuity due

Chapter 5 Key Concepts

A Strategy for Solving Finance Problems

We have presented a lot of new formulas in this chapter. By answering the following questions, you can decide which formula to use for a particular problem.

1. Is simple or compound interest involved?

    Simple interest is normally used for investments or loans of a year or less; compound interest is normally used in all other cases.

2. If simple interest is being used, what is being sought—interest amount, future value, present value, or discount?

3. If compound interest is being used, does it involve a lump sum (single payment) or an annuity (sequence of payments)?

    (a) For a lump sum,

       (i) is ordinary compound interest involved?

      (ii) what is being sought—present value, future value, number of periods, or effective rate (APY)?

    (b) For an annuity,

       (i) is it an ordinary annuity (payment at the end of each period) or an annuity due (payment at the beginning of each period)?

      (ii) what is being sought—present value, future value, or payment amount?

    Once you have answered these questions, choose the appropriate formula and work the problem. As a final step, consider whether the answer you get makes sense. For instance, the amount of interest or the payments in an annuity should be fairly small compared with the total future value.

Key Formulas

List of Variables

r is the annual interest rate.

m is the number of periods per year.

i is the interest rate per period. $i = \dfrac{r}{m}$

t is the number of years.

n is the number of periods. $n = tm$

P is the principal or present value.

A is the future value of a lump sum.

S is the future value of an annuity.

R is the periodic payment in an annuity.

B is the remaining balance on a loan.

Interest	Simple Interest	Compound Interest
Interest	$I = Prt$	$I = A - P$
Future value	$A = P(1 + rt)$	$A = P(1 + i)^n$
Present value	$P = \dfrac{A}{1 + rt}$	$P = \dfrac{A}{(1 + i)^n} = A(1 + i)^{-n}$
		Effective rate (or APY) $r_E = \left(1 + \dfrac{r}{m}\right)^m - 1$

Discount

If D is the **discount** on a T-bill with face value P at simple interest rate r for t years, then $D = Prt.$

Continuous Interest

If P dollars are deposited for t years at interest rate r per year, compounded continuously, the **compound amount (future value)** is $A = Pe^{rt}.$

The **present value** P of A dollars at interest rate r per year compounded continuously for t years is

$$P = \frac{A}{e^{rt}}.$$

Annuities

Ordinary annuity	Future value	$S = R\left[\dfrac{(1 + i)^n - 1}{i}\right] = R \cdot s_{\overline{n}\vert i}$	
	Present value	$P = R\left[\dfrac{1 - (1 + i)^{-n}}{i}\right] = R \cdot a_{\overline{n}\vert i}$	
Annuity due	Future value	$S = R\left[\dfrac{(1 + i)^{n+1} - 1}{i}\right] - R$	
	Present value	$P = R + R\left[\dfrac{1 - (1 + i)^{-(n-1)}}{i}\right]$	

Chapter 5 Review Exercises

Find the simple interest for the following loans.

1. $4902 at 6.5% for 11 months

2. $42,368 at 9.22% for 5 months

3. $3478 at 7.4% for 88 days

4. $2390 at 8.7% from May 3 to July 28

Find the semiannual (simple) interest payment and the total interest earned over the life of the bond.

5. $12,000 Merck Company 6-year bond at 4.75% annual interest

6. $20,000 General Electric 9-year bond at 5.25% annual interest

Find the maturity value for each simple interest loan.

7. $7750 at 6.8% for 4 months

8. $15,600 at 8.2% for 9 months

9. What is meant by the present value of an amount A?

Find the present value of the given future amounts; use simple interest.

10. $459.57 in 7 months; money earns 5.5%

11. $80,612 in 128 days; money earns 6.77%

12. A 9-month $7000 Treasury bill sells at a discount rate of 3.5%. Find the amount of the discount and the price of the T-bill.

13. A 6-month $10,000 T-bill sold at a 4% discount. Find the actual rate of interest paid by the Treasury.

14. For a given amount of money at a given interest rate for a given period greater than 1 year, does simple interest or compound interest produce more interest? Explain.

Find the compound amount and the amount of interest earned in each of the given scenarios.

15. $2800 at 6% compounded annually for 12 years

16. $57,809.34 at 4% compounded quarterly for 6 years

17. $12,903.45 at 6.37% compounded quarterly for 29 quarters

18. $4677.23 at 4.57% compounded monthly for 32 months

Find the amount of compound interest earned by each deposit.

19. $22,000 at 5.5%, compounded quarterly for 6 years

20. $2975 at 4.7%, compounded monthly for 4 years

Find the face value (to the nearest dollar) of the zero-coupon bond.

21. 5-year bond at 3.9%; price $12,366

22. 15-year bond at 5.2%; price $11,575

Find the APY corresponding to the given nominal rate.

23. 5% compounded semiannually

24. 6.5% compounded daily

Find the present value of the given amounts at the given interest rate.

25. $42,000 in 7 years; 12% compounded monthly

26. $17,650 in 4 years; 8% compounded quarterly

27. $1347.89 in 3.5 years; 6.2% compounded semiannually

28. $2388.90 in 44 months; 5.75% compounded monthly

Find the price that a purchaser should be willing to pay for these zero-coupon bonds.

29. 10-year $15,000 bond; interest at 4.4%

30. 25-year $30,000 bond; interest at 6.2%

31. What is meant by the future value of an annuity?

Find the future value of each annuity.

32. $1288 deposited at the end of each year for 14 years; money earns 7% compounded annually

33. $4000 deposited at the end of each quarter for 8 years; money earns 6% compounded quarterly

34. $233 deposited at the end of each month for 4 years; money earns 6% compounded monthly

35. $672 deposited at the beginning of each quarter for 7 years; money earns 5% compounded quarterly

36. $11,900 deposited at the beginning of each month for 13 months; money earns 7% compounded monthly

37. What is the purpose of a sinking fund?

Find the amount of each payment that must be made into a sinking fund to accumulate the given amounts. Assume payments are made at the end of each period.

38. $6500; money earns 5% compounded annually; 6 annual payments

39. $57,000; money earns 6% compounded semiannually for $8\frac{1}{2}$ years

40. $233,188; money earns 5.7% compounded quarterly for $7\frac{3}{4}$ years

41. $56,788; money earns 6.12% compounded monthly for $4\frac{1}{2}$ years

Find the present value of each ordinary annuity.

42. Payments of $850 annually for 4 years at 5% compounded annually

43. Payments of $1500 quarterly for 7 years at 8% compounded quarterly

44. Payments of $4210 semiannually for 8 years at 5.6% compounded semiannually

45. Payments of $877.34 monthly for 17 months at 6.4% compounded monthly

Find the amount necessary to fund the given withdrawals (which are made at the end of each period).

46. Quarterly withdrawals of $800 for 4 years with interest rate 4.6%, compounded quarterly

47. Monthly withdrawals of $1500 for 10 years with interest rate 5.8%, compounded monthly

48. Yearly withdrawals of $3000 for 15 years with interest rate 6.2%, compounded annually

Find the payment for the ordinary annuity with the given present value.

49. $150,000; monthly payments for 15 years, with interest rate 5.1%, compounded monthly

50. $25,000; quarterly payments for 8 years, with interest rate 4.9%, compounded quarterly

51. Find the lump-sum deposit today that will produce the same total amount as payments of $4200 at the end of each year for 12 years. The interest rate in both cases is 4.5%, compounded annually.

52. If the current interest rate is 6.5%, find the price (to the nearest dollar) that a purchaser should be willing to pay for a $24,000 bond with coupon rate 5% that matures in 6 years.

Find the amount of the payment necessary to amortize each of the given loans.

53. $32,000 at 8.4% compounded quarterly; 10 quarterly payments

54. $5607 at 7.6% compounded monthly; 32 monthly payments

Find the monthly house payments for the given mortgages.

55. $95,000 at 3.67% for 30 years

56. $167,000 at 2.91% for 15 years

57. Find the approximate remaining balance after 5 years of payments on the loan in Exercise 55.

58. Find the approximate remaining balance after 7.5 years of payments on the loan in Exercise 56.

Finance *According to www.studentaid.ed.gov, in 2013 the interest rate for a direct unsubsidized student loan was 6.8%. A portion of an amortization table is given here for a $15,000 direct unsubsidized student loan compounded monthly to be paid back in 10 years. Use the table to answer Exercises 59–62.*

Payment Number	Amount of Payment	Interest for Period	Portion to Principal	Principal at End of Period
0				15,000.00
1	172.62	85.00	87.62	14,912.38
2	172.62	84.50	88.12	14,824.26
3	172.62	84.00	88.62	14,735.64
4	172.62	83.50	89.12	14,646.52
5	172.62	83.00	89.62	14,556.90
6	172.62	82.49	90.13	14,466.77
7	172.62	81.98	90.64	14,376.13
8	172.62	81.46	91.16	14,284.97

59. How much of the seventh payment is interest?

60. How much of the fourth payment is used to reduce the debt?

61. How much interest is paid in the first 6 months of the loan?

62. How much has the debt been reduced at the end of the first 8 months?

Finance *Work the following applied problems.*

63. In February 2013, a Virginia family won a Powerball lottery prize of $217,000,000.

    (a) If they had chosen to receive the money in 30 yearly payments, beginning immediately, what would have been the amount of each payment?

    (b) The family chose the one-time lump-sum cash option. If the interest rate is 3.58%, approximately how much did they receive?

64. A firm of attorneys deposits $15,000 of profit-sharing money in an account at 6% compounded semiannually for $7\frac{1}{2}$ years. Find the amount of interest earned.

65. Tom, a graduate student, is considering investing $500 now, when he is 23, or waiting until he is 40 to invest $500. How much more money will he have at age 65 if he invests now, given that he can earn 5% interest compounded quarterly?

66. According to a financial Web site, on June 15, 2005, Frontenac Bank of Earth City, Missouri, paid 3.94% interest, compounded quarterly, on a 2-year CD, while E*TRADE Bank of Arlington, Virginia, paid 3.93% compounded daily. What was the effective rate for the two CDs, and which bank paid a higher effective rate? (Data from: www.bankrate.com.)

67. Chalon Bridges deposits semiannual payments of $3200, received in payment of a debt, in an ordinary annuity at 6.8% compounded semiannually. Find the final amount in the account and the interest earned at the end of 3.5 years.

68. Each year, a firm must set aside enough funds to provide employee retirement benefits of $52,000 in 20 years. If the firm can invest money at 7.5% compounded monthly, what amount must be invested at the end of each month for this purpose?

69. A benefactor wants to be able to leave a bequest to the college she attended. If she wants to make a donation of $2,000,000 in 10 years, how much each month does she need to place in an investment account that pays an interest rate of 5.5%, compounded monthly?

70. Suppose you have built up a pension with $12,000 annual payments by working 10 years for a company when you leave to accept a better job. The company gives you the option of collecting half the full pension when you reach age 55 or the full pension at age 65. Assume an interest rate of 8% compounded annually. By age 75, how much will each plan produce? Which plan would produce the larger amount?

71. In 3 years, Ms. Nguyen must pay a pledge of $7500 to her favorite charity. What lump sum can she deposit today at 10% compounded semiannually so that she will have enough to pay the pledge?

72. To finance the $15,000 cost of their kitchen remodeling, the Chews will make equal payments at the end of each month for 36 months. They will pay interest at the rate of 7.2% compounded monthly. Find the amount of each payment.

73. To expand her business, the owner of a small restaurant borrows $40,000. She will repay the money in equal payments at the end of each semiannual period for 8 years at 9% interest compounded semiannually. What payments must she make?

74. The Fix family bought a house for $210,000. They paid $42,000 down and took out a 30-year mortgage for the balance at 3.75%.

    (a) Find the monthly payment.

    (b) How much of the first payment is interest?

    After 15 years, the family sold their house for $255,000.

    (c) Estimate the current mortgage balance at the time of the sale.

(d) Find the amount of money they received from the sale after paying off the mortgage.

75. Over a 20-year period, the class A shares of the Davis New York Venture mutual fund increased in value at the rate of 11.2%, compounded monthly. If you had invested $250 at the end of each month in this fund, what would have the value of your account been at the end of those 20 years?

76. Dan Hook deposits $400 a month to a retirement account that has an interest rate of 3.1%, compounded monthly. After making 60 deposits, Dan changes his job and stops making payments for 3 years. After 3 years, he starts making deposits again, but now he deposits $525 per month. What will the value of the retirement account be after Dan makes his $525 monthly deposits for 5 years?

77. The proceeds of a $10,000 death benefit are left on deposit with an insurance company for 7 years at an annual effective interest rate of 5%.* The balance at the end of 7 years is paid to the beneficiary in 120 equal monthly payments of X, with the first payment made immediately. During the payout period, interest is credited at an annual effective interest rate of 3%. Which of the following is the correct value of X?

    (a) 117   (b) 118   (c) 129   (d) 135   (e) 158

78. Eileen Gianiodis wants to retire on $75,000 per year for her life expectancy of 20 years after she retires. She estimates that she will be able to earn an interest rate of 10.1%, compounded annually, throughout her lifetime. To reach her retirement goal, Eileen will make annual contributions to her account for the next 30 years. One year after making her last deposit, she will receive her first retirement check. How large must her yearly contributions be?

---

*The Proceeds of Death Benefit Left on Deposit with an Insurance Company from Course 140 Examination, Mathematics of Compound Interest. Copyright © Society of Actuaries. Reproduced by permission of Society of Actuaries.

Case Study 5 Continuous Compounding

Informally, you can think of *continuous compounding* as a process in which interest is compounded *very* frequently (for instance, every nanosecond). You will occasionally see an ad for a certificate of deposit in which interest is compounded continuously. That's pretty much a gimmick in most cases, because it produces only a few more cents than daily compounding. However, continuous compounding does play a serious role in certain financial situations, notably in the pricing of derivatives.* So let's see what is involved in continuous compounding.

As a general rule, the more often interest is compounded, the better off you are as an investor. (See Example 4 of Section

---

*Derivatives are complicated financial instruments. But investors have learned the hard way that they can sometimes cause serious problems—as was the case in the recession that began in 2008, which was blamed in part on the misuse of derivatives.

5.2.) But there is, alas, a limit on the amount of interest, no matter how often it is compounded. To see why this is so, suppose you have $1 to invest. The Exponential Bank offers to pay 100% annual interest, compounded n times per year and rounded to the nearest penny. Furthermore, you may pick any value for n that you want. Can you choose n so large that your $1 will grow to $5 in a year? We will test several values of n in the formula for the compound amount, with $P = 1$. In this case, the annual interest rate (in decimal form) is also 1. If there are n periods in the year, the interest rate per period is $i = 1/n$. So the amount that your dollar grows to is:

$$A = P(1 + i)^n = 1\left(1 + \frac{1}{n}\right)^n.$$

A computer gives the following results for various values of n:

Interest Is Compounded ...	n	$\left(1 + \dfrac{1}{n}\right)^n$
Annually	1	$\left(1 + \dfrac{1}{1}\right)^1 = 2$
Semiannually	2	$\left(1 + \dfrac{1}{2}\right)^2 = 2.25$
Quarterly	4	$\left(1 + \dfrac{1}{4}\right)^4 \approx 2.4414$
Monthly	12	$\left(1 + \dfrac{1}{12}\right)^{12} \approx 2.6130$
Daily	365	$\left(1 + \dfrac{1}{365}\right)^{365} \approx 2.71457$
Hourly	8760	$\left(1 + \dfrac{1}{8760}\right)^{8760} \approx 2.718127$
Every minute	525,600	$\left(1 + \dfrac{1}{525,600}\right)^{525,600} \approx 2.7182792$
Every second	31,536,000	$\left(1 + \dfrac{1}{31,536,000}\right)^{31,536,000} \approx 2.7182818$

Because interest is rounded to the nearest penny, the compound amount never exceeds $2.72, no matter how big n is. (A computer was used to develop the table, and the figures in it are accurate. If you try these computations with your calculator, however, your answers may not agree exactly with those in the table because of round-off error in the calculator.)

The preceding table suggests that as n takes larger and larger values, the corresponding values of $\left(1 + \dfrac{1}{n}\right)^n$ get closer and closer to a specific real number whose decimal expansion begins $2.71828 \cdots$. This is indeed the case, as is shown in calculus, and the number $2.71828 \cdots$ is denoted e. This fact is sometimes expressed by writing

$$\lim_{n \to \infty} \left(1 + \frac{1}{n}\right)^n = e,$$

which is read "the limit of $\left(1 + \dfrac{1}{n}\right)^n$ as n approaches infinity is e."

The preceding example is typical of what happens when interest is compounded n times per year, with larger and larger values of n. It can be shown that no matter what interest rate or principal is used, there is always an upper limit (involving the number e) on the compound amount, which is called the compound amount from continuous compounding.

Continuous Compounding

The compound amount A for a deposit of P dollars at an interest rate r per year compounded continuously for t years is given by

$$A = Pe^{rt}.$$

Most calculators have an e^x key for computing powers of e. See the Technology Tip on page 188 for details on using a calculator to evaluate e^x.

Example 1   Suppose $5000 is invested at an annual rate of 4% compounded continuously for 5 years. Find the compound amount.

Solution   In the formula for continuous compounding, let $P = 5000$, $r = .04$, and $t = 5$. Then a calculator with an e^x key shows that

$$A = 5000e^{(.04)5} = 5000e^{.2} \approx \$6107.01.$$

You can readily verify that daily compounding would have produced a compound amount about 6¢ less.

Exercises

1. Find the compound amount when $20,000 is invested at 6% compounded continuously for

   (a) 2 years;   (b) 10 years;   (c) 20 years.

2. (a) Find the compound amount when $2500 is invested at 5.5%, compounded monthly for two years.

   (b) Do part (a) when the interest rate is 5.5% compounded continuously.

3. Determine the compounded amount from a deposit of $25,000 when it is invested at 5% for 10 years and compounded in the following time periods:

   (a) annually   (b) quarterly   (c) monthly

   (d) daily   (e) continuously

4. Determine the compounded amount from a deposit of $250,000 when it is invested at 5% for 10 years and compounded in the following time periods:

   (a) annually   (b) quarterly   (c) monthly

   (d) daily   (e) continuously

5. It can be shown that if interest is compounded continuously at nominal rate r, then the effective rate r_E is $e^r - 1$. Find the effective rate of continuously compounded interest if the nominal rate is

   (a) 4.5%;   (b) 5.7%;   (c) 7.4%.

6. Suppose you win a court case and the defendant has up to 8 years to pay you $5000 in damages. Assume that the defendant will wait until the last possible minute to pay you.

   (a) If you can get an interest rate of 3.75% compounded continuously, what is the present value of the $5000? [*Hint:* Solve the continuous-compounding formula for P.]

   (b) If the defendant offers you $4000 immediately to settle his debt, should you take the deal?

Extended Projects

1. Investigate the interest rates for the subsidized and unsubsidized student loans. If you have taken out student loans or plan to take out student loans before graduating, calculate your own monthly payment and how much interest you will pay over the course of the repayment period. If you have not taken out, and you do not plan to take out a student loan, contact the financial aid office of your college and university to determine the median amount borrowed with student loans at your institution. Determine the monthly payment and how much interest is paid during repayment for the typical borrowing student.

2. Determine the best interest rate for a new car purchase for a 48-month loan at a bank near you. If you finance $25,999 with such a loan, determine the payment and the total interest paid over the course of the loan. Also, determine the best interest rate for a new car purchase for a 48-month loan at a credit union near you. Determine the monthly payment and total interest paid if the same auto loan is financed through the credit union. Is it true that the credit union would save you money?

Taken from *Finite Mathematics and Calculus with Applications*, Tenth Edition
by Margaret L. Lial, Raymond N. Greenwell, and Nathan P. Ritchey

7

Sets and Probability

The study of probability begins with counting. An exercise in Section 2 of this chapter counts trucks carrying different combinations of early, late, and extra late peaches from the orchard to canning facilities. You'll see trees in another context in Section 5, where we use branching tree diagrams to calculate conditional probabilities.

Our lives are bombarded by seemingly chance events — the chance of rain, the risk of an accident, the possibility the stock market increases, the likelihood of winning the lottery — all whose particular outcome may appear to be quite random. The field of probability attempts to quantify the likelihood of chance events and helps us to prepare for this uncertainty. In short, probability helps us to better understand the world in which we live. In this chapter and the next, we introduce the basic ideas of probability theory and give a sampling of some of its uses. Since the language of sets and set operations is used in the study of probability, we begin there.

7.1 Sets

APPLY IT In how many ways can two candidates win the 50 states plus the District of Columbia in a U.S. presidential election?
Using knowledge of sets, we will answer this question in Exercise 69.

Think of a **set** as a well-defined collection of objects in which it is possible to determine if a given object is included in the collection. A set of coins might include one of each type of coin now put out by the U.S. government. Another set might consist of all the students in your English class. By contrast, a collection of young adults does not constitute a set unless the designation "young adult" is clearly defined. For example, this set might be defined as those aged 18 to 29.

In mathematics, sets often consist of numbers. The set consisting of the numbers 3, 4, and 5 is written

$$\{3, 4, 5\},$$

with set braces, { }, enclosing the numbers belonging to the set. The numbers 3, 4, and 5 are called the **elements** or **members** of this set. To show that 4 is an element of the set $\{3, 4, 5\}$, we use the symbol $\in$ and write

$$4 \in \{3, 4, 5\},$$

read "4 is an element of the set containing 3, 4, and 5." Also, $5 \in \{3, 4, 5\}$.

To show that 8 is *not* an element of this set, place a slash through the symbol:

$$8 \notin \{3, 4, 5\}.$$

Sets often are named with capital letters, so that if

$$B = \{5, 6, 7\},$$

then, for example, $6 \in B$ and $10 \notin B$.

It is possible to have a set with no elements. Some examples are the set of counting numbers less than one, the set of foreign-born presidents of the United States, and the set of men more than 10 feet tall. A set with no elements is called the **empty set** (or **null set**) and is written $\varnothing$.

| CAUTION | Be careful to distinguish between the symbols 0, $\varnothing$, $\{0\}$, and $\{\varnothing\}$. The symbol 0 represents a *number*; $\varnothing$ represents a *set* with 0 elements; $\{0\}$ represents a set with one element, 0; and $\{\varnothing\}$ represents a set with one element, $\varnothing$. |

We use the symbol $n(A)$ to indicate the *number* of unique elements in a finite set A. For example, if $A = \{a, b, c, d, e\}$, then $n(A) = 5$. Using this notation, we can write the information in the previous Caution as $n(\varnothing) = 0$ and $n(\{0\}) = n(\{\varnothing\}) = 1$.

Two sets are *equal* if they contain the same elements. The sets $\{5, 6, 7\}$, $\{7, 6, 5\}$, and $\{6, 5, 7\}$ all contain exactly the same elements and are equal. In symbols,

$$\{5, 6, 7\} = \{7, 6, 5\} = \{6, 5, 7\}.$$

This means that the ordering of the elements in a set is unimportant. Note that each element of the set is listed only once. Sets that do not contain exactly the same elements are *not equal*. For example, the sets $\{5, 6, 7\}$ and $\{7, 8, 9\}$ do not contain exactly the same elements and, thus, are not equal. To indicate that these sets are not equal, we write

$$\{5, 6, 7\} \neq \{7, 8, 9\}.$$

Sometimes we are interested in a common property of the elements in a set, rather than a list of the elements. This common property can be expressed by using **set-builder notation**, for example,

$$\{x \,|\, x \text{ has property } P\}$$

(read "the set of all elements x such that x has property P") represents the set of all elements x having some stated property P.

EXAMPLE 1 Sets

Write the elements belonging to each set.

(a) $\{x \,|\, x \text{ is a natural number less than 5}\}$

SOLUTION The natural numbers less than 5 make up the set $\{1, 2, 3, 4\}$.

(b) $\{x \,|\, x \text{ is a state that borders Florida}\}$

SOLUTION The states that border Florida make up the set $\{\text{Alabama, Georgia}\}$.

TRY YOUR TURN 1

YOUR TURN 1 Write the elements belonging to the set. $\{x \,|\, x$ is a state whose name begins with the letter O$\}$.

The **universal set** for a particular discussion is a set that includes all the objects being discussed. In elementary school arithmetic, for instance, the set of whole numbers might be the universal set, while in a college algebra class the universal set might be the set of real numbers. The universal set will be specified when necessary, or it will be clearly understandable from the context of the problem.

Subsets
Sometimes every element of one set also belongs to another set. For example, if

$$A = \{3, 4, 5, 6\}$$

and

$$B = \{2, 3, 4, 5, 6, 7, 8\},$$

then every element of A is also an element of B. This is an example of the following definition.

Subset
Set A is a **subset** of set B (written $A \subseteq B$) if every element of A is also an element of B. Set A is a *proper subset* (written $A \subset B$) if $A \subseteq B$ and $A \neq B$.

To indicate that A is *not* a subset of B, we write $A \nsubseteq B$.

EXAMPLE 2 Sets

Decide whether the following statements are *true* or *false*.

(a) $\{3, 4, 5, 6\} = \{4, 6, 3, 5\}$

SOLUTION Both sets contain exactly the same elements, so the sets are equal and the given statement is true. (The fact that the elements are listed in a different order does not matter.)

YOUR TURN 2 Decide if the following statement is *true* or *false*. {2, 4, 6} ⊆ {6, 2, 4}

(b) {5, 6, 9, 12} ⊆ {5, 6, 7, 8, 9, 10, 11}

SOLUTION The first set is not a subset of the second because it contains an element, 12, that does not belong to the second set. Therefore, the statement is false.

TRY YOUR TURN 2

The empty set, ∅, by default, is a subset of every set A, since it is impossible to find an element of the empty set (it has no elements) that is not an element of the set A. Similarly, A is a subset of itself, since every element of A is also an element of the set A.

Subset Properties

For any set A,

$$\varnothing \subseteq A \quad \text{and} \quad A \subseteq A.$$

EXAMPLE 3 Subsets

List all possible subsets for each set.

(a) {7, 8}

SOLUTION There are 4 subsets of {7, 8}:

$$\varnothing, \quad \{7\}, \quad \{8\}, \quad \text{and} \quad \{7, 8\}.$$

(b) {a, b, c}

SOLUTION There are 8 subsets of {a, b, c}:

$$\varnothing, \quad \{a\}, \quad \{b\}, \quad \{c\}, \quad \{a, b\}, \quad \{a, c\}, \quad \{b, c\}, \quad \text{and} \quad \{a, b, c\}.$$

A good way to find the subsets of {7, 8} and the subsets of {a, b, c} in Example 3 is to use a **tree diagram**—a systematic way of listing all the subsets of a given set. Figure 1 shows tree diagrams for finding the subsets of {7, 8} and {a, b, c}.

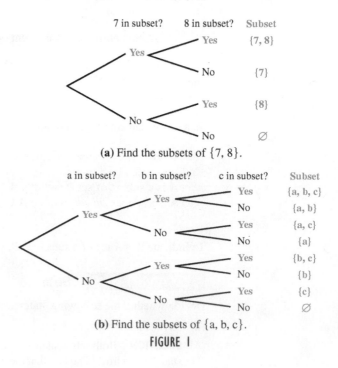

(a) Find the subsets of {7, 8}.

(b) Find the subsets of {a, b, c}.

FIGURE 1

As Figure 1 shows, there are two possibilities for each element (either it's in the subset or it's not), so a set with 2 elements has $2 \cdot 2 = 2^2 = 4$ subsets, and a set with 3 elements has $2^3 = 8$ subsets. This idea can be extended to a set with any finite number of elements, which leads to the following conclusion.

Number of Subsets

A set of k distinct elements has 2^k subsets.

In other words, if $n(A) = k$, then n(the set of all subsets of A) $= 2^k$.

EXAMPLE 4   Subsets

Find the number of subsets for each set.

(a) $\{3, 4, 5, 6, 7\}$

SOLUTION   This set has 5 elements; thus, it has 2^5 or 32 subsets.

(b) $\{x | x$ is a day of the week$\}$

SOLUTION   This set has 7 elements and therefore has $2^7 = 128$ subsets.

(c) $\varnothing$

SOLUTION   Since the empty set has 0 elements, it has $2^0 = 1$ subset—itself.

TRY YOUR TURN 3

YOUR TURN 3 Find the number of subsets for the set $\{x | x$ is a season of the year$\}$.

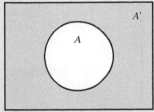

$A \subseteq B$

FIGURE 2

Figure 2 shows a set A that is a subset of set B. The rectangle and everything inside it represents the universal set, U. Such diagrams, called **Venn diagrams**—after the English logician John Venn (1834–1923), who invented them in 1876—are used to help illustrate relationships among sets. Venn diagrams are very similar to Euler diagrams, described in Section 6.6. Euler diagrams are used in logic to denote variables having a certain property or not, while Venn diagrams are used in the context of sets to denote something being an element of a set or not.

Set Operations
It is possible to form new sets by combining or manipulating one or more existing sets. Given a set A and a universal set U, the set of all elements of U that do *not* belong to A is called the *complement* of set A. For example, if set A is the set of all the female students in a class, and U is the set of all students in the class, then the complement of A would be the set of all students in the class who are not female (that is, who are male). The complement of set A is written A', read "A-prime."

Complement of a Set

Let A be any set, with U representing the universal set. Then the **complement** of A, colored pink in the figure, is

$$A' = \{x | x \notin A \text{ and } x \in U\}.$$

(Recall that the rectangle represents the universal set U.)

EXAMPLE 5 Set Operations

Let $U = \{1, 2, 3, 4, 5, 6, 7, 8, 9, 10, 11\}$, $A = \{1, 2, 4, 5, 7\}$, and $B = \{2, 4, 5, 7, 9, 11\}$. Find each set.

(a) A'

> **SOLUTION** Set A' contains the elements of U that are not in A.
>
> $$A' = \{3, 6, 8, 9, 10, 11\}$$

(b) $B' = \{1, 3, 6, 8, 10\}$

(c) $\varnothing' = U$ and $U' = \varnothing$

(d) $(A')' = A$

Given two sets A and B, the set of all elements belonging to *both* set A and set B is called the *intersection* of the two sets, written $A \cap B$. For example, the elements that belong to both set $A = \{1, 2, 4, 5, 7\}$ and set $B = \{2, 4, 5, 7, 9, 11\}$ are 2, 4, 5, and 7, so that

$$A \cap B = \{1, 2, 4, 5, 7\} \cap \{2, 4, 5, 7, 9, 11\} = \{2, 4, 5, 7\}.$$

Intersection of Two Sets

The **intersection** of sets A and B, shown in green in the figure, is

$$A \cap B = \{x \mid x \in A \text{ and } x \in B\}.$$

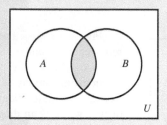

EXAMPLE 6 Set Operations

Let $A = \{3, 6, 9\}$, $B = \{2, 4, 6, 8\}$, and the universal set $U = \{0, 1, 2, \ldots, 10\}$. Find each set.

(a) $A \cap B$

> **SOLUTION**
>
> $$A \cap B = \{3, 6, 9\} \cap \{2, 4, 6, 8\} = \{6\}$$

(b) $A \cap B'$

> **SOLUTION**
>
> $$A \cap B' = \{3, 6, 9\} \cap \{0, 1, 3, 5, 7, 9, 10\} = \{3, 9\}$$

YOUR TURN 4 For the sets in Example 6, find $A' \cap B$.

TRY YOUR TURN 4

Two sets that have no elements in common are called *disjoint sets*. For example, there are no elements common to both $\{50, 51, 54\}$ and $\{52, 53, 55, 56\}$, so these two sets are disjoint, and

$$\{50, 51, 54\} \cap \{52, 53, 55, 56\} = \varnothing.$$

This result can be generalized as follows.

Disjoint Sets

For any sets A and B, if A and B are **disjoint sets**, then $A \cap B = \varnothing$.

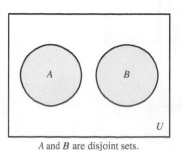

A and B are disjoint sets.

FIGURE 3

Figure 3 shows a pair of disjoint sets.

The set of all elements belonging to set A, to set B, or to both sets is called the *union* of the two sets, written $A \cup B$. For example,

$$\{1, 3, 5\} \cup \{3, 5, 7, 9\} = \{1, 3, 5, 7, 9\}.$$

Union of Two Sets

The **union** of sets A and B, shown in blue in the figure, is

$$A \cup B = \{x \mid x \in A \text{ or } x \in B \text{ (or both)}\}.$$

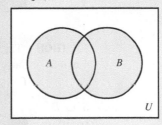

EXAMPLE 7   Union of Sets

Let $A = \{1, 3, 5, 7, 9, 11\}$, $B = \{3, 6, 9, 12\}$, $C = \{1, 2, 3, 4, 5\}$, and the universal set $U = \{0, 1, 2, \ldots, 12\}$. Find each set.

(a) $A \cup B$

SOLUTION Begin by listing the elements of the first set, $\{1, 3, 5, 7, 9, 11\}$. Then include any elements from the second set *that are not already listed*. Doing this gives

$$A \cup B = \{1, 3, 5, 7, 9, 11\} \cup \{3, 6, 9, 12\} = \{1, 3, 5, 7, 9, 11, 6, 12\}$$
$$= \{1, 3, 5, 6, 7, 9, 11, 12\}.$$

(b) $(A \cup B) \cap C'$

SOLUTION Begin with the expression in parentheses, which we calculated in part (a), and then intersect this with C'.

YOUR TURN 5 For the sets in Example 7, find $A \cup (B \cap C')$.

$$(A \cup B) \cap C' = \{1, 3, 5, 6, 7, 9, 11, 12\} \cap \{0, 6, 7, 8, 9, 10, 11, 12\}$$
$$= \{6, 7, 9, 11, 12\} \qquad \textbf{TRY YOUR TURN 5} \ \blacksquare$$

NOTE
1. As Example 7 shows, when forming sets, do not list the same element more than once. In our final answer, we listed the elements in numerical order to make it easier to see what elements are in the set, but the set is the same, regardless of the order of the elements.
2. As shown in the definitions, an element is in the *intersection* of sets A and B if it is in A *and* B. On the other hand, an element is in the *union* of sets A and B if it is in A *or* B (or both).
3. In mathematics, "A *or* B" implies A or B, or both. Since "or" includes the possibility of both, we will usually omit the words "or both".

EXAMPLE 8   Stocks

The following table gives the 52-week low and high prices, the closing price, and the change from the previous day for six stocks in the Standard & Poor's 100 on May 20, 2014. *Source: New York Stock Exchange*.

New York Stock Exchange				
Stock	Low	High	Close	Change
AT&T	31.74	37.17	35.22	−0.28
Coca-Cola	36.83	43.05	40.74	+0.16
Costco	107.38	126.12	114.62	−0.51
McDonald's	92.22	103.78	102.47	+0.94
Pepsico	77.01	87.68	85.89	+0.24
Walt Disney	60.41	83.65	82.12	+1.27

Let the universal set U consist of the six stocks listed in the table. Let A contain all stocks with a high price greater than $80, B all stocks with a closing price between $40 and $105, C all stocks with a positive price change, and D all stocks with a low price less than $40. Find the following.

(a) A'

SOLUTION Set A' contains all the listed stocks that are not in set A, or those with a high price less than or equal to $80, so

$$A' = \{AT\&T, Coca\text{-}Cola\}.$$

(b) $A \cap C$

SOLUTION The intersection of A and C will contain those stocks that are in both sets A and C, or those with a high price greater than $80 *and* a positive price change.

$$A \cap C = \{McDonald's, Pepsico, Walt Disney\}$$

(c) $B \cup D$

SOLUTION The union of B and D contains all stocks with a closing price between $40 and $105 *or* a low price less than $40.

$$B \cup D = \{AT\&T, Coca\text{-}Cola, McDonald's, Pepsico, Walt Disney\}$$

EXAMPLE 9 **Employment**

A department store classifies credit applicants by gender, marital status, and employment status. Let the universal set be the set of all applicants, M be the set of male applicants, S be the set of single applicants, and E be the set of employed applicants. Describe each set in words.

(a) $M \cap E$

SOLUTION The set $M \cap E$ includes all applicants who are both male *and* employed; that is, employed male applicants.

(b) $M' \cup S$

SOLUTION This set includes all applicants who are female (not male) *or* single. *All* female applicants and *all* single applicants are in this set.

(c) $M' \cap S'$

SOLUTION These applicants are female *and* married (not single); thus, $M' \cap S'$ is the set of all married female applicants.

(d) $M \cup E'$

SOLUTION $M \cup E'$ is the set of applicants that are male *or* unemployed. The set includes *all* male applicants and *all* unemployed applicants.

7.1 EXERCISES

In Exercises 1–10, write true or false for each statement.

1. $3 \in \{2, 5, 7, 9, 10\}$

2. $6 \in \{-2, 6, 9, 5\}$

3. $9 \notin \{2, 1, 5, 8\}$

4. $3 \notin \{7, 6, 5, 4\}$

5. $\{2, 5, 8, 9\} = \{2, 5, 9, 8\}$

6. $\{3, 7, 12, 14\} = \{3, 7, 12, 14, 0\}$

7. {all whole numbers greater than 7 and less than 10} $= \{8, 9\}$

8. $\{x \mid x$ is an odd integer; $6 \leq x \leq 18\} = \{7, 9, 11, 15, 17\}$

9. $0 \in \varnothing$

10. $\varnothing \in \{\varnothing\}$

Let $A = \{2, 4, 6, 10, 12\}$, $B = \{2, 4, 8, 10\}$, $C = \{4, 8, 12\}$, $D = \{2, 10\}$, $E = \{6\}$, and $U = \{2, 4, 6, 8, 10, 12, 14\}$. Insert $\subseteq$ or $\nsubseteq$ to make the statement true.

11. A ___ U

12. E ___ A

13. A ___ E

14. B ___ C

15. $\varnothing$ ___ A

16. $\{0, 2\}$ ___ D

17. D ___ B

18. A ___ C

19. Repeat Exercises 11–18 except insert $\subset$ or $\not\subset$ to make the statement true.

20. What is set-builder notation? Give an example.

Insert a number in each blank to make the statement true, using the sets for Exercises 11–18.

21. There are exactly ___ subsets of A.

22. There are exactly ___ subsets of B.

23. There are exactly ___ subsets of C.

24. There are exactly ___ subsets of D.

Insert ∩ or ∪ to make each statement true.

25. $\{5, 7, 9, 19\}$ ___ $\{7, 9, 11, 15\} = \{7, 9\}$

26. $\{8, 11, 15\}$ ___ $\{8, 11, 19, 20\} = \{8, 11\}$

27. $\{2, 1, 7\}$ ___ $\{1, 5, 9\} = \{1, 2, 5, 7, 9\}$

28. $\{6, 12, 14, 16\}$ ___ $\{6, 14, 19\} = \{6, 12, 14, 16, 19\}$

29. $\{3, 5, 9, 10\}$ ___ $\varnothing = \varnothing$

30. $\{3, 5, 9, 10\}$ ___ $\varnothing = \{3, 5, 9, 10\}$

31. $\{1, 2, 4\}$ ___ $\{1, 2, 4\} = \{1, 2, 4\}$

32. $\{0, 10\}$ ___ $\{10, 0\} = \{0, 10\}$

33. Describe the intersection and union of sets. How do they differ?

34. Is it possible for two nonempty sets to have the same intersection and union? If so, give an example.

Let $U = \{1, 2, 3, 4, 5, 6, 7, 8, 9\}$, $X = \{2, 4, 6, 8\}$, $Y = \{2, 3, 4, 5, 6\}$, and $Z = \{1, 2, 3, 8, 9\}$. List the members of each set, using set braces.

35. $X \cap Y$ **36.** $X \cup Y$

37. X' **38.** Y'

39. $X' \cap Y'$ **40.** $X' \cap Z$

41. $Y \cap (X \cup Z)$ **42.** $X' \cap (Y' \cup Z)$

43. $(X \cap Y') \cup (Z' \cap Y')$ **44.** $(X \cap Y) \cup (X' \cap Z)$

45. In Example 6, what set do you get when you calculate $(A \cap B) \cup (A \cap B')$?

46. Explain in words why $(A \cap B) \cup (A \cap B') = A$.

Let $U = \{$all students in this school$\}$, $M = \{$all students taking this course$\}$, $N = \{$all students taking accounting$\}$, and $P = \{$all students taking zoology$\}$. Describe each set in words.

47. M' **48.** $M \cup N$

49. $N \cap P$ **50.** $N' \cap P'$

51. Refer to the sets listed for Exercises 11–18. Which pairs of sets are disjoint?

52. Refer to the sets listed for Exercises 35–44. Which pairs are disjoint?

Refer to Example 8 in the text. Describe each set in Exercises 53–56 in words; then list the elements of each set.

53. B' **54.** $A \cap B$

55. $(A \cap B)'$ **56.** $(C \cup D)'$

57. Let $A = \{1, 2, 3, \{3\}, \{1, 4, 7\}\}$. Answer each of the following as *true* or *false*.

    (a) $1 \in A$ **(b)** $\{3\} \in A$ **(c)** $\{2\} \in A$

    (d) $4 \in A$ **(e)** $\{\{3\}\} \subset A$

    (f) $\{1, 4, 7\} \in A$ **(g)** $\{1, 4, 7\} \subseteq A$

58. Let $B = \{a, b, c, \{d\}, \{e, f\}\}$. Answer each of the following as *true* or *false*.

    (a) $a \in B$ **(b)** $\{b, c, d\} \subset B$ **(c)** $\{d\} \in B$

    (d) $\{d\} \subseteq B$ **(e)** $\{e, f\} \in B$

    (f) $\{a, \{e, f\}\} \subset B$ **(g)** $\{e, f\} \subset B$

APPLICATIONS

Business and Economics

Mutual Funds The tables below show five of the largest holdings of four major mutual funds on May 21, 2014. *Sources: fidelity.com, janus.com, vanguard.com, weitzinvestments.com.*

Vanguard 500	Fidelity New Millenium Fund
Apple	AIG
Berkshire Hathaway	Google
Google	Microsoft
Microsoft	Verizon
Wells Fargo	Wells Fargo

Janus Perkins Large Cap Value	Weitz Value Fund
AIG	Apache
Berkshire Hathaway	Berkshire Hathaway
Citigroup	DIRECTV
Pfizer	Texas Instruments
Wells Fargo	Wells Fargo

Let U be the smallest possible set that includes all the corporations listed, and V, F, J, and W be the set of top holdings for each mutual fund, respectively. Find each set:

59. $V \cap J$ **60.** $V \cap (F \cup W)$

61. $(J \cup F)'$ **62.** $J' \cap W'$

63. **Sales Calls** Suppose that Carolyn Gogolin has appointments with 9 potential customers. Carolyn will be ecstatic if all 9 of these potential customers decide to make a purchase from her. Of course, in sales there are no guarantees. How many different sets of customers may place an order with Carolyn? (*Hint:* Each set of customers is a subset of the original set of 9 customers.)

Life Sciences

Health The following table shows some symptoms of an overactive thyroid and an underactive thyroid. *Source: The Merck Manual of Diagnosis and Therapy.*

Underactive Thyroid	Overactive Thyroid
Sleepiness, s	Insomnia, i
Dry hands, d	Moist hands, m
Intolerance of cold, c	Intolerance of heat, h
Goiter, g	Goiter, g

Let U be the smallest possible set that includes all the symptoms listed, N be the set of symptoms for an underactive thyroid, and O be the set of symptoms for an overactive thyroid. Find each set.

64. O' **65.** N'

66. $N \cap O$ **67.** $N \cup O$

68. $N \cap O'$

Social Sciences

69. APPLY IT **Electoral College** U.S. presidential elections are decided by the Electoral College, in which each of the 50 states, plus the District of Columbia, gives all of its votes to a candidate.* Ignoring the number of votes each state has in the Electoral College, but including all possible combinations of states that could be won by either candidate, how many outcomes are possible in the Electoral College if there are two candidates? (*Hint:* The states that can be won by a candidate form a subset of all the states.)

General Interest

70. Musicians A concert featured a cellist, a flutist, a harpist, and a vocalist. Throughout the concert, different subsets of the four musicians performed together, with at least two musicians playing each piece. How many subsets of at least two are possible?

Television Cable Services The following table lists some of the most popular cable television networks. Use this information for Exercises 71–76. *Source: The World Almanac and Book of Facts 2014.*

Network	Subscribers (in millions)	Launch	Content
The Discovery Channel	99.1	1985	Nonfiction, nature, science
TNT	99.7	1988	Movies, sports, original programming
USA Network	99.0	1980	Sports, family entertainment
The Learning Channel (TLC)	98.5	1980	Original programming, family entertainment
TBS Superstation	99.7	1976	Movies, sports, original programming

*The exceptions are Maine and Nebraska, which allocate their electoral college votes according to the winner in each congressional district.

List the elements of the following sets. For exercises 74–76, describe each set in words.

71. F, the set of networks that were launched before 1985.

72. G, the set of networks that feature sports.

73. H, the set of networks that have more than 99.5 million viewers.

74. $F \cap H$ **75.** $G \cup H$ **76.** G'

77. Games In David Gale's game of Subset Takeaway, the object is for each player, at his or her turn, to pick a nonempty proper subset of a given set subject to the condition that no subset chosen earlier by either player can be a subset of the newly chosen set. The winner is the last person who can make a legal move. Consider the set $A = \{1, 2, 3\}$. Suppose Joe and Dorothy are playing the game and Dorothy goes first. If she chooses the proper subset $\{1\}$, then Joe cannot choose any subset that includes the element 1. Joe can, however, choose $\{2\}$ or $\{3\}$ or $\{2, 3\}$. Develop a strategy for Joe so that he can always win the game if Dorothy goes first. *Source: Scientific American.*

States In the following list of states, let $A = \{$states whose name contains the letter $e\}$, let $B = \{$states with a population of more than 4,000,000$\}$, and $C = \{$states with an area greater than 40,000 square miles$\}$. *Source: The World Almanac and Book of Facts 2014.*

State	Population (1000s)	Area (sq. mi.)
Alabama	4822	52,420
Alaska	731	665,384
Colorado	5187	104,094
Florida	19,318	65,758
Hawaii	1392	10,932
Indiana	6537	36,420
Kentucky	4380	40,408
Maine	1329	35,380
Nebraska	1856	77,348
New Jersey	8865	8723

78. (a) Describe in words the set $A \cup (B \cap C)'$.

  (b) List all elements in the set $A \cup (B \cap C)'$.

79. (a) Describe in words the set $(A \cup B)' \cap C$.

  (b) List all elements in the set $(A \cup B)' \cap C$.

YOUR TURN ANSWERS ▬▬

1. $\{$Ohio, Oklahoma, Oregon$\}$

2. True

3. $2^4 = 16$ subsets

4. $\{2, 4, 8\}$

5. $\{1, 3, 5, 6, 7, 9, 11, 12\}$

7.2 Applications of Venn Diagrams

APPLY IT   The responses to a survey of 100 households show that 76 have a DVD player, 21 have a Blu-ray player, and 12 have both. How many have neither a DVD player nor Blu-ray player?

In Example 3 we show how a Venn diagram can be used to sort out this information to answer the question.

Venn diagrams were used in the previous section to illustrate set union and intersection. The rectangular region of a Venn diagram represents the universal set U. Including only a single set A inside the universal set, as in Figure 4, divides U into two regions. Region 1 represents those elements of U outside set A (that is, the elements in A'), and region 2 represents those elements belonging to set A. (The numbering of these regions is arbitrary.)

The Venn diagram in Figure 5(a) shows two sets inside U. These two sets divide the universal set into four regions. As labeled in Figure 5(a), region 1 represents the set whose elements are outside both set A and set B. Region 2 shows the set whose elements belong to A and not to B. Region 3 represents the set whose elements belong to both A and B. Which set is represented by region 4? (Again, the labeling is arbitrary.)

Two other situations can arise when representing two sets by Venn diagrams. If it is known that $A \cap B = \emptyset$, then the Venn diagram is drawn as in Figure 5(b). If it is known that $A \subseteq B$, then the Venn diagram is drawn as in Figure 5(c). For the material presented throughout this chapter we will refer only to Venn diagrams like the one in Figure 5(a), and note that some of the regions of the Venn diagram may be equal to the empty (or null) set.

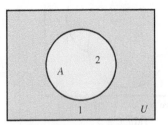

One set leads to 2 regions
(numbering is arbitrary).

FIGURE 4

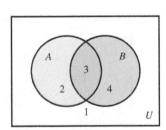 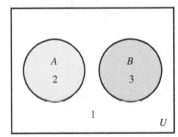 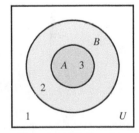

Two sets lead to 4 regions   Two sets lead to 3 regions   Two sets lead to 3 regions
(numbering is arbitrary).   (numbering is arbitrary).   (numbering is arbitrary).
    (a)   (b)   (c)

FIGURE 5

EXAMPLE 1   **Venn Diagrams**

Draw Venn diagrams similar to Figure 5(a) and shade the regions representing each set.

(a) $A' \cap B$

SOLUTION   Set A' contains all the elements outside set A. As labeled in Figure 5(a), A' is represented by regions 1 and 4. Set B is represented by regions 3 and 4. The intersection of sets A' and B, the set $A' \cap B$, is given by the region common to both sets. The result is the set represented by region 4, which is blue in Figure 6. When looking for the intersection, remember to choose the area that is in one region *and* the other region.

In addition to the fact that region 4 in Figure 6 is $A' \cap B$, notice that region 1 is $A' \cap B'$, region 2 is $A \cap B'$, and region 3 is $A \cap B$.

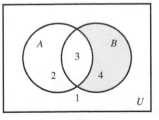

FIGURE 6

(b) $A' \cup B'$

SOLUTION Again, set A' is represented by regions 1 and 4, and set B' by regions 1 and 2. To find $A' \cup B'$, identify the region that represents the set of all elements in A', B', or both. The result, which is blue in Figure 7, includes regions 1, 2, and 4. When looking for the union, remember to choose the area that is in one region *or* the other region (or both).

YOUR TURN 1 Draw a Venn diagram and shade the region representing $A \cup B'$.

TRY YOUR TURN 1

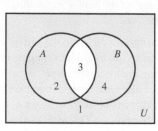

FIGURE 7

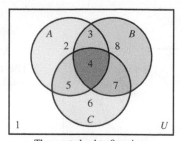

Three sets lead to 8 regions.

FIGURE 8

Venn diagrams also can be drawn with three sets inside U. These three sets divide the universal set into eight regions, which can be numbered (arbitrarily) as in Figure 8.

EXAMPLE 2 Venn Diagram

In a Venn diagram, shade the region that represents $A' \cup (B \cap C')$.

YOUR TURN 2 Draw a Venn diagram and shade the region representing $A' \cap (B \cup C)$.

SOLUTION First find $B \cap C'$. Set B is represented by regions 3, 4, 7, and 8, and set C' by regions 1, 2, 3, and 8. The overlap of these regions (regions 3 and 8) represents the set $B \cap C'$. Set A' is represented by regions 1, 6, 7, and 8. The union of the set represented by regions 3 and 8 and the set represented by regions 1, 6, 7, and 8 is the set represented by regions 1, 3, 6, 7, and 8, which are blue in Figure 9.

TRY YOUR TURN 2

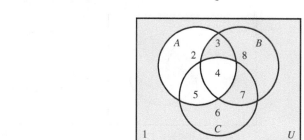

FIGURE 9

Applications Venn diagrams can be used to analyze many applications, as illustrated in the following examples.

EXAMPLE 3 Entertainment Technology

A researcher collecting data on 100 households finds that

    76 have a DVD player;

    21 have a Blu-ray player; and

    12 have both.

The researcher wants to answer the following questions.

(a) How many do not have a DVD player?

(b) How many have neither a DVD player nor a Blu-ray player?

(c) How many have a Blu-ray player but not a DVD player?

APPLY IT

SOLUTION A Venn diagram like the one in Figure 10 will help sort out this information. In Figure 10(a), we put the number 12 in the region common to both a DVD player and a Blu-ray player, because 12 households have both. Of the 21 with a Blu-ray player, $21 - 12 = 9$ have no DVD player, so in Figure 10(b) we put 9 in the region for a Blu-ray player but no DVD player. Similarly, $76 - 12 = 64$ households have a DVD player but not a Blu-ray player, so we put 64 in that region. Finally, the diagram shows that $100 - 64 - 12 - 9 = 15$ households have neither a DVD player nor a Blu-ray player. Now we can answer the questions:

(a) $15 + 9 = 24$ do not have a DVD player.

(b) 15 have neither.

(c) 9 have a Blu-ray player but not a DVD player.

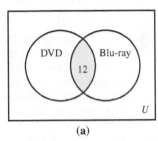 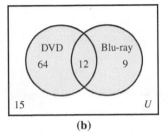

(a)   (b)

FIGURE 10

EXAMPLE 4 **Magazines**

A survey of 77 freshman business students at a large university produced the following results.

25 of the students read *Bloomberg Businessweek*;

19 read *The Wall Street Journal*;

27 do not read *Fortune*;

11 read *Bloomberg Businessweek* but not *The Wall Street Journal*;

11 read *The Wall Street Journal* and *Fortune*;

13 read *Bloomberg Businessweek* and *Fortune*;

9 read all three.

Use this information to answer the following questions.

(a) How many students read none of the publications?

(b) How many read only *Fortune*?

(c) How many read *Bloomberg Businessweek* and *The Wall Street Journal*, but not *Fortune*?

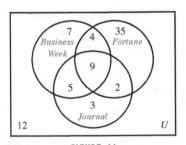

FIGURE 11

SOLUTION Since 9 students read all three publications, begin by placing 9 in the area that belongs to all three regions, as shown in Figure 11. Of the 13 students who read *Bloomberg Businessweek* and *Fortune*, 9 also read *The Wall Street Journal*. Therefore, only $13 - 9 = 4$ read just *Bloomberg Businessweek* and *Fortune*. Place the number 4 in the area of Figure 11 common only to *Bloomberg Businessweek* and *Fortune* readers.

In the same way, place $11 - 9 = 2$ in the region common only to *Fortune* and *The Wall Street Journal*. Of the 11 students who read *Bloomberg Businessweek* but not *The Wall Street Journal*, 4 read *Fortune*, so place $11 - 4 = 7$ in the region for those who read only *Bloomberg Businessweek*.

The data show that 25 students read *Bloomberg Businessweek*. However, $7 + 4 + 9 = 20$ readers have already been placed in the region representing *Bloomberg Businessweek*. The balance of this region will contain only $25 - 20 = 5$ students. These students read *Bloomberg Businessweek* and *The Wall Street Journal* but not *Fortune*. In the same way, $19 - (5 + 9 + 2) = 3$ students read only *The Wall Street Journal*.

YOUR TURN 3 One hundred students were asked which fast food restaurants they had visited in the past month. The results are as follows:

47 ate at McDonald's;

46 ate at Taco Bell;

44 ate at Wendy's;

17 ate at McDonald's and Taco Bell;

19 ate at Taco Bell and Wendy's;

22 ate at Wendy's and McDonald's;

13 ate at all three.

Determine how many ate only at Taco Bell.

Using the fact that 27 of the 77 students do not read *Fortune*, we know that 50 do read *Fortune*. We already have $4 + 9 + 2 = 15$ students in the region representing *Fortune*, leaving $50 - 15 = 35$ who read only *Fortune*.

A total of $7 + 4 + 35 + 5 + 9 + 2 + 3 = 65$ students are placed in the three circles in Figure 11. Since 77 students were surveyed, $77 - 65 = 12$ students read none of the three publications, and 12 is placed outside all three regions.

Now Figure 11 can be used to answer the questions asked above.

(a) There are 12 students who read none of the three publications.

(b) There are 35 students who read only *Fortune*.

(c) The overlap of the regions representing readers of *Bloomberg Businessweek* and *The Wall Street Journal* shows that 5 students read *Bloomberg Businessweek* and *The Wall Street Journal* but not *Fortune*. **TRY YOUR TURN 3**

| CAUTION | A common error in solving problems of this type is to make a circle represent one set and another circle represent its complement. In Example 4, with one circle representing those who read *Bloomberg Businessweek*, we did not draw another for those who do not read *Bloomberg Businessweek*. An additional circle is not only unnecessary (because those not in one set are automatically in the other) but very confusing, because the region outside or inside both circles must be empty. Similarly, if a problem involves men and women, do not draw one circle for men and another for women. Draw one circle; if you label it "women," for example, then men are automatically those outside the circle.

EXAMPLE 5 Utility Maintenance

Jeff Friedman is a section chief for an electric utility company. The employees in his section cut down trees, climb poles, and splice wire. Friedman reported the following information to the management of the utility.

"Of the 100 employees in my section,

45 can cut trees;

50 can climb poles;

57 can splice wire;

22 can climb poles but can't cut trees;

20 can climb poles and splice wire;

25 can cut trees and splice wire;

14 can cut trees and splice wire but can't climb poles;

 9 can't do any of the three (management trainees)."

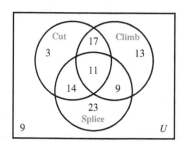

FIGURE 12

The data supplied by Friedman lead to the numbers shown in Figure 12. Add the numbers from all of the regions to get the total number of employees:

$$9 + 3 + 14 + 23 + 11 + 9 + 17 + 13 = 99.$$

Friedman claimed to have 100 employees, but his data indicated only 99. Management decided that Friedman didn't qualify as a section chief, and he was reassigned as a night-shift meter reader in Guam. (*Moral:* He should have taken this course.)

In all the examples above, we started with a piece of information specifying the relationship with all the categories. This is usually the best way to begin solving problems of this type.

As we saw in the previous section, we use the symbol $n(A)$ to indicate the *number* of elements in a finite set A. The following statement about the number of elements in the union of two sets will be used later in our study of probability.

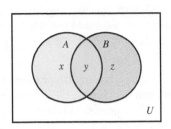

FIGURE 13

YOUR TURN 4 A group of students are sitting in the lounge. All are texting or listening to music or both. Eleven are listening to music and 15 are texting. Eight are doing both. How many students are in the lounge?

Union Rule for Sets

$$n(A \cup B) = n(A) + n(B) - n(A \cap B)$$

To prove this statement, let $x + y$ represent $n(A)$, y represent $n(A \cap B)$, and $y + z$ represent $n(B)$, as shown in Figure 13. Then

$$n(A \cup B) = x + y + z,$$
$$n(A) + n(B) - n(A \cap B) = (x + y) + (y + z) - y = x + y + z,$$

so
$$n(A \cup B) = n(A) + n(B) - n(A \cap B).$$

EXAMPLE 6 School Activities

A group of 10 students meet to plan a school function. All are majoring in accounting or economics or both. Five of the students are economics majors and 7 are majors in accounting. How many major in both subjects?

SOLUTION Let A represent the set of accounting majors and B represent the set of economics majors. Use the union rule, with $n(A) = 5, n(B) = 7$, and $n(A \cup B) = 10$. Find $n(A \cap B)$.

$$n(A \cup B) = n(A) + n(B) - n(A \cap B)$$
$$10 = 5 + 7 - n(A \cap B),$$

so
$$n(A \cap B) = 5 + 7 - 10 = 2. \qquad \text{TRY YOUR TURN 4} \blacksquare$$

When A and B are disjoint, then $n(A \cap B) = 0$, so the union rule simplifies to $n(A \cup B) = n(A) + n(B)$.

| **CAUTION** | The rule $n(A \cup B) = n(A) + n(B)$ is valid only when A and B are disjoint. When A and B are *not* disjoint, use the rule $n(A \cup B) = n(A) + n(B) - n(A \cap B)$. |

EXAMPLE 7 Endangered Species

The following table gives the number of threatened and endangered animal species in the world as of May, 2014. *Source: U.S. Fish and Wildlife Service.*

Endangered and Threatened Species			
	Endangered (*E*)	Threatened (*T*)	Totals
Amphibians and reptiles (*A*)	111	56	167
Arachnids and insects (*I*)	94	10	104
Birds (*B*)	291	33	324
Clams, crustaceans, corals and snails (*C*)	134	30	164
Fishes (*F*)	94	70	164
Mammals (*M*)	326	40	366
Totals	1050	239	1289

Using the letters given in the table to denote each set, find the number of species in each of the following sets.

(a) $E \cap B$

SOLUTION The set $E \cap B$ consists of all species that are endangered *and* are birds. From the table, we see that there are 291 such species.

(b) $E \cup B$

SOLUTION The set $E \cup B$ consists of all species that are endangered *or* are birds. We include all 1050 endangered species, plus the 33 bird species who are threatened but not endangered, for a total of 1083. Alternatively, we could use the formula $n(E \cup B) = n(E) + n(B) - n(E \cap B) = 1050 + 324 - 291 = 1083.$

(c) $(F \cup M) \cap T'$

SOLUTION Begin with the set $F \cup M$, which is all species that are fish or mammals. This consists of the four categories with 94, 70, 326, and 40 species. Of this set, take those that are *not* threatened, for a total of $94 + 326 = 420$ species. This is the number of species of fish and mammals in the table that are not threatened. ▬

EXAMPLE 8 Online Activities

Suppose that a group of 150 students have done at least one of these activities online: purchasing an item, banking, and watching a video. In addition,

90 students have made an online purchase;

50 students have banked online;

70 students have watched an online video;

15 students have made an online purchase and watched an online video;

12 have banked online and watched an online video; and

10 students have done all three.

How many students have made an online purchase and banked online?

SOLUTION Let P represent the set of students who have made a purchase online, B the set who have banked online, and V the set who have watched a video online. Since 10 students did all three activities, begin by placing 10 in the area that belongs to all three regions, as shown in Figure 14. Of the 15 students who belong in sets P and V, 10 also belong to set B. Thus, only $15 - 10 = 5$ students were in the area of Figure 14 common only to sets P and V. Likewise, there are $12 - 10 = 2$ students who belong to only sets B and V. Since there are already $5 + 10 + 2 = 17$ students in set V, there are $70 - 17 = 53$ students in only set V.

We cannot use the information about set P, since there are two regions in P for which we have no information. Similarly, we cannot use the information about set B. In such cases, we label a region with the variable x. Here we place x in the region common only to P and B, as shown in Figure 14.

Of the 90 students in set P, the number who are only in set P must be $90 - x - 10 - 5 = 75 - x$, and this expression is placed in the appropriate region in Figure 14. Similarly, the number who are in only set B is $50 - x - 10 - 2 = 38 - x$. Notice that because all 150 students participated in at least one activity, there are no elements in the region outside the three circles.

Now that the diagram is filled out, we can determine the value of x by recalling that the total number of students was 150. Thus,

$$(75 - x) + 5 + x + 10 + (38 - x) + 2 + 53 = 150.$$

Simplifying, we have $183 - x = 150$, implying that $x = 33$. The number of students who made an online purchase and banked online is

$$33 + 10 = 43.$$ ▬

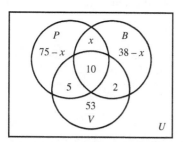

FIGURE 14

--- 7.2 WARM-UP EXERCISES ---

Let $U = \{1, 2, 3, 4, 5, 6, 7, 8, 9, 10\}, A = \{1, 3, 5, 7, 9\},$
$B = \{1, 2, 3, 4, 5\}$ and $C = \{1, 10\}$. List the members of each set.

W1. $(A \cap B)' \cup C$ *(Sec. 7.1)*   **W2.** $A \cap (B' \cup C)$ *(Sec. 7.1)*

7.2 EXERCISES

Sketch a Venn diagram like the one in the figure, and use shading to show each set.

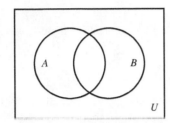

1. $B \cap A'$

2. $A \cup B'$

3. $A' \cup B$

4. $A' \cap B'$

5. $B' \cup (A' \cap B')$

6. $(A \cap B) \cup B'$

7. U'

8. $\varnothing'$

 9. Three sets divide the universal set into at most ____ regions.

10. What does the notation $n(A)$ represent?

Sketch a Venn diagram like the one shown, and use shading to show each set.

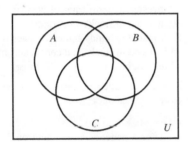

11. $(A \cap B) \cap C$

12. $(A \cap C') \cup B$

13. $A \cap (B \cup C')$

14. $A' \cap (B \cap C)$

15. $(A' \cap B') \cap C'$

16. $(A \cap B') \cap C$

17. $(A \cap B') \cup C'$

18. $A' \cap (B' \cup C)$

19. $(A \cup B') \cap C$

20. $A' \cup (B' \cap C')$

Use the union rule to answer the following questions.

21. If $n(A) = 5$, $n(B) = 12$, and $n(A \cap B) = 4$, what is $n(A \cup B)$?

22. If $n(A) = 15$, $n(B) = 30$, and $n(A \cup B) = 33$, what is $n(A \cap B)$?

23. Suppose $n(B) = 9$, $n(A \cap B) = 5$, and $n(A \cup B) = 22$. What is $n(A)$?

24. Suppose $n(A \cap B) = 5$, $n(A \cup B) = 38$, and $n(A) = 13$. What is $n(B)$?

Draw a Venn diagram and use the given information to fill in the number of elements for each region.

25. $n(U) = 41, n(A) = 16, n(A \cap B) = 12, n(B') = 20$

26. $n(A) = 28, n(B) = 12, n(A \cup B) = 32, n(A') = 19$

27. $n(A \cup B) = 24, n(A \cap B) = 6, n(A) = 11,$
$n(A' \cup B') = 25$

28. $n(A') = 31, n(B) = 25, n(A' \cup B') = 46, n(A \cap B) = 12$

29. $n(A) = 28, n(B) = 34, n(C) = 25, n(A \cap B) = 14,$
$n(B \cap C) = 15, n(A \cap C) = 11, n(A \cap B \cap C) = 9,$
$n(U) = 59$

30. $n(A) = 54, n(A \cap B) = 22, n(A \cup B) = 85,$
$n(A \cap B \cap C) = 4, n(A \cap C) = 15, n(B \cap C) = 16,$
$n(C) = 44, n(B') = 63$

31. $n(A \cap B) = 6, n(A \cap B \cap C) = 4, n(A \cap C) = 7,$
$n(B \cap C) = 4, n(A \cap C') = 11, n(B \cap C') = 8,$
$n(C) = 15, n(A' \cap B' \cap C') = 5$

32. $n(A) = 13, n(A \cap B \cap C) = 4, n(A \cap C) = 6,$
$n(A \cap B') = 6, n(B \cap C) = 6, n(B \cap C') = 11,$
$n(B \cup C) = 22, n(A' \cap B' \cap C') = 5$

In Exercises 33–36, show that the statement is true by drawing Venn diagrams and shading the regions representing the sets on each side of the equals sign.*

33. $(A \cup B)' = A' \cap B'$

34. $(A \cap B)' = A' \cup B'$

35. $A \cap (B \cup C) = (A \cap B) \cup (A \cap C)$

36. $A \cup (B \cap C) = (A \cup B) \cap (A \cup C)$

37. Use the union rule of sets to prove that $n(A \cup B \cup C) = n(A) + n(B) + n(C) - n(A \cap B) - n(A \cap C) - n(B \cap C) + n(A \cap B \cap C)$. (*Hint:* Write $A \cup B \cup C$ as $A \cup (B \cup C)$ and use the formula from Exercise 35.)

38. In Figure 8, let $U = \{$all humans who have ever lived$\}$, $A = \{$men$\}$, $B = \{$Americans$\}$, and $C = \{$politicians$\}$. For each of the eight regions in Figure 8, write the name of one person who belongs in that region. Many answers are possible.

39. Repeat Exercise 38, letting $U = \{$all countries of the world$\}$, $A = \{$countries in the Northern Hemisphere$\}$, $B = \{$countries with Spanish as the primary language$\}$, and $C = \{$countries bordering the Pacific Ocean$\}$. For each of the eight regions in Figure 8, write the name of one country that belongs in that region. Many answers are possible.

*The statements in Exercises 33 and 34 are known as De Morgan's Laws. They are named for the English mathematician Augustus De Morgan (1806–1871). They are analogous to De Morgan's Laws for logic seen in the previous chapter.

Business and Economics

Use Venn diagrams to answer the following questions.

40. Cooking Preferences Jeff Friedman, of Example 5 in the text, was again reassigned, this time to the home economics department of the electric utility. He interviewed 140 people in a suburban shopping center to discover some of their cooking habits. He obtained the following results:

> 58 use microwave ovens;
> 63 use electric ranges;
> 58 use gas ranges;
> 19 use microwave ovens and electric ranges;
> 17 use microwave ovens and gas ranges;
> 4 use both gas and electric ranges;
> 1 uses all three;
> 2 use none of the three.

Should he be reassigned one more time? Why or why not?

41. Harvesting Fruit Toward the middle of the harvesting season, peaches for canning come in three types, early, late, and extra late, depending on the expected date of ripening. During a certain week, the following data were recorded at a fruit delivery station:

> 34 trucks went out carrying early peaches;
> 61 carried late peaches;
> 50 carried extra late;
> 25 carried early and late;
> 30 carried late and extra late;
> 8 carried early and extra late;
> 6 carried all three;
> 9 carried only figs (no peaches at all).

(a) How many trucks carried only late variety peaches?

(b) How many carried only extra late?

(c) How many carried only one type of peach?

(d) How many trucks (in all) went out during the week?

42. Cola Consumption Market research showed that the adult residents of a certain small town in Georgia fit the following categories of cola consumption. (We assume here that no one drinks both regular cola and diet cola.)

Age	Drink Regular Cola (R)	Drink Diet Cola (D)	Drink No Cola (N)	Totals
21–25 (Y)	40	15	15	70
26–35 (M)	30	30	20	80
Over 35 (O)	10	50	10	70
Totals	80	95	45	220

Using the letters given in the table, find the number of people in each set.

(a) $Y \cap R$

(b) $M \cap D$

(c) $M \cup (D \cap Y)$

(d) $Y' \cap (D \cup N)$

(e) $O' \cup N$

(f) $M' \cap (R' \cap N')$

(g) Describe the set $M \cup (D \cap Y)$ in words.

43. Investment Habits The following table shows the results of a survey taken by a bank in a medium-sized town in Tennessee. The survey asked questions about the investment habits of bank customers. (We assume here that no one invests in more than one type of investment.)

Age	Stocks (S)	Bonds (B)	Savings Accounts (A)	Totals
18–29 (Y)	6	2	15	23
30–49 (M)	14	5	14	33
50 or over (O)	32	20	12	64
Totals	52	27	41	120

Using the letters given in the table, find the number of people in each set.

(a) $Y \cap B$

(b) $M \cup A$

(c) $Y \cap (S \cup B)$

(d) $O' \cup (S \cup A)$

(e) $(M' \cup O') \cap B$

(f) Describe the set $Y \cap (S \cup B)$ in words.

44. Investment Survey Most mathematics professors love to invest their hard-earned money. A recent survey of 150 math professors revealed that

> 111 invested in stocks;
> 98 invested in bonds;
> 100 invested in certificates of deposit;
> 80 invested in stocks and bonds;
> 83 invested in bonds and certificates of deposit;
> 85 invested in stocks and certificates of deposit;
> 9 did not invest in any of the three.

How many mathematics professors invested in stocks and bonds and certificates of deposit?

Life Sciences

45. Genetics After a genetics experiment on 50 pea plants, the number of plants having certain characteristics was tallied, with the following results.

> 22 were tall;
> 25 had green peas;
> 39 had smooth peas;
> 9 were tall and had green peas;
> 20 had green peas and smooth peas;
> 6 had all three characteristics;
> 4 had none of the characteristics.

(a) Find the number of plants that were tall and had smooth peas.

(b) How many plants were tall and had peas that were neither smooth nor green?

(c) How many plants were not tall but had peas that were smooth and green?

46. Blood Antigens Human blood can contain the A antigen, the B antigen, both the A and B antigens, or neither antigen. A third antigen, called the Rh antigen, is important in human reproduction, and again may or may not be present in an individual.

Blood is called type A-positive if the individual has the A and Rh but not the B antigen. A person having only the A and B antigens is said to have type AB-negative blood. A person having only the Rh antigen has type O-positive blood. Other blood types are defined in a similar manner. Identify the blood types of the individuals in regions (a)–(h) below.

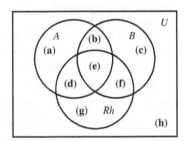

47. Blood Antigens   (Use the diagram from Exercise 46.) In a certain hospital, the following data were recorded.

   25 patients had the A antigen;
    8 had the A and not the B antigen;
   27 had the B antigen;
   22 had the B and Rh antigens;
   30 had the Rh antigen;
   12 had none of the antigens;
   16 had the A and Rh antigens;
   15 had all three antigens.

How many patients

(a) were represented?

(b) had exactly one antigen?

(c) had exactly two antigens?

(d) had O-positive blood?

(e) had AB-positive blood?

(f) had B-negative blood?

(g) had O-negative blood?

(h) had A-positive blood?

48. Mortality   The table lists the number of deaths in the United States during 2010 according to race and gender. Use this information and the letters given to find the number of people in each set. *Source: National Vital Statistics Reports.*

	White (W)	Black (B)	American Indian (I)	Asian or Pacific Islander (A)
Female (F)	1,063,235	141,157	7049	24,562
Male (M)	1,051,514	145,802	8516	26,600

(a) F

(b) $F \cap (I \cup A)$

(c) $M \cup B$

(d) $W' \cup I' \cup A'$

(e) In words, describe the set in part (b).

49. Hockey   The table lists the number of head and neck injuries for 319 ice hockey players wearing either a full shield or half shield in the Canadian Inter-University Athletics Union during one season. Using the letters given in the table, find the number of injuries in each set. *Source: JAMA.*

	Half Shield (H)	Full Shield (F)
Head and Face Injuries (A)	95	34
Concussions (B)	41	38
Neck Injuries (C)	9	7
Other Injuries (D)	202	150

(a) $A \cap F$

(b) $C \cap (H \cup F)$

(c) $D \cup F$

(d) $B' \cap C'$

50. Lyme Disease   Scientists have found a way to distinguish chronic-fatigue syndrome (CFS) from post-treatment Lyme disease by different proteins in a patient's spinal fluid. In a study of 4365 patients,

   1605 had the protein for normal patients, CFS, and post-treatment Lyme disease;
   1910 had the protein for CFS and Lyme;
    738 had the protein for CFS only;
   2783 had the protein for CFS;
   1771 had the normal protein as well as the one for Lyme;
   2768 had the protein for Lyme;
   2630 had the normal protein.

Source: Science News.

(a) How many had the protein for Lyme only?

(b) How many had the normal protein only?

(c) How many had none of the proteins?

Social Sciences

51. Military   The number of female military personnel in March 2013 is given in the following table. Use this information and the letters given to find the number of female military personnel in each set. *Source: Department of Defense.*

	Army (A)	Air Force (B)	Navy (C)	Marines (D)	Totals
Officers (O)	16,007	12,663	8893	1403	38,966
Enlisted (E)	55,016	48,924	47,195	12,907	164,042
Cadets & Midshipmen (M)	738	872	968	0	2578
Totals	71,761	62,459	57,056	14,310	205,586

(a) $A \cup B$

(b) $E \cup (C \cup D)$

(c) $O' \cap M'$

U.S. Population The projected U.S. population in 2020 (in millions) by age and race or ethnicity is given in the following table. Use this information in Exercises 52–57. *Source: U.S. Bureau of the Census.*

	Non-Hispanic White (A)	Hispanic (B)	Black (C)	Asian (D)	American Indian (E)
Under 45 (F)	110.6	37.6	30.2	13.1	2.2
45–64 (G)	55.3	10.3	9.9	4.3	0.6
65 and over (H)	41.4	4.7	5.0	2.2	0.3
Totals	207.3	52.6	45.1	19.6	3.1

Using the letters given in the table, find the number of people in each set.

52. $G \cup B$

53. $A \cap F$

54. $F \cap (B \cup H)$

55. $G \cup (C \cap H)$

56. $G' \cap (A' \cap C')$

57. $H \cup D$

Marital Status The following table gives the population breakdown (in millions) of the U.S. population in 2010 based on marital status and race or ethnic origin. *Source: U.S. Census Bureau.*

	White (W)	Black (B)	Hispanic (H)	Asian or Pacific Islander (A)
Never Married (N)	45.1	11.7	10.9	2.7
Married (M)	109.4	10.6	17.1	7.0
Widowed (I)	11.8	1.8	1.2	0.5
Divorced/Separated (D)	19.4	3.2	2.6	0.5

Find the number of people in each set. Describe each set in words.

58. $N \cap (B \cup H)$

59. $(M \cup I) \cap A$

60. $(D \cup W) \cap A'$

61. $M' \cap (B \cup A)$

General Interest

62. Native American Ceremonies At a pow-wow in Arizona, 75 Native American families from all over the Southwest came to participate in the ceremonies. A coordinator of the pow-wow took a survey and found that

15 families brought food, costumes, and crafts;
25 families brought food and crafts;
42 families brought food;
35 families brought crafts;
14 families brought crafts but not costumes;
10 families brought none of the three items;
18 families brought costumes but not crafts.

(a) How many families brought costumes and food?

(b) How many families brought costumes?

(c) How many families brought food, but not costumes?

(d) How many families did not bring crafts?

(e) How many families brought food or costumes?

63. Poultry Analysis A chicken farmer surveyed his flock with the following results. The farmer had

9 fat red roosters;
13 thin brown hens;
15 red roosters;
11 thin red chickens (hens and roosters);
17 red hens;
56 fat chickens (hens and roosters);
41 roosters;
48 hens.

Assume all chickens are thin or fat, red or brown, and hens (female) or roosters (male). How many chickens were

(a) in the flock?   **(b)** red?

(c) fat roosters?   **(d)** fat hens?

(e) thin and brown?   **(f)** red and fat?

YOUR TURN ANSWERS

1.
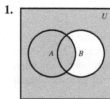

2.
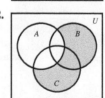

3. 23   **4.** 18

7.3 Introduction to Probability

What is the probability that a randomly selected person in the United States is Hispanic? That the person is Black?
After introducing probability, we will answer these questions in Exercise 58.

If you go to a supermarket and buy 5 pounds of peaches at 99 cents per pound, you can easily find the *exact* price of your purchase: $4.95. On the other hand, the produce manager of the market is faced with the problem of ordering peaches. The manager may have a good estimate of the number of pounds of peaches that will be sold during the day, but it is impossible to predict the *exact* amount. The number of pounds that customers will purchase during a day is *random*; The quantity cannot be predicted exactly. A great many problems that come up in applications of mathematics involve random phenomena—those for which exact prediction is impossible. The best that we can do is determine the *probability* of the possible outcomes.

Sample Spaces In probability, an **experiment** is an activity or occurrence with an observable result. Each repetition of an experiment is called a **trial**. The possible results of each trial are called **outcomes**. The set of all possible outcomes for an experiment is the **sample space** for that experiment. A sample space for the experiment of tossing a coin is made up of the outcomes heads (*h*) and tails (*t*). If *S* represents this sample space, then

$$S = \{h, t\}.$$

EXAMPLE 1 Sample Spaces

Give the sample space for each experiment.

(a) A spinner like the one in Figure 15 is spun.

> **SOLUTION** The three outcomes are 1, 2, or 3, so the sample space is
> $$S = \{1, 2, 3\}.$$

(b) For the purposes of a public opinion poll, respondents are classified as young, middle-aged, or senior, and as male or female.

> **SOLUTION** A sample space for this poll could be written as a set of ordered pairs:
> $$S = \{(\text{young, male}), (\text{young, female}), (\text{middle-aged, male}),$$
> $$(\text{middle-aged, female}), (\text{senior, male}), (\text{senior, female})\}.$$

(c) An experiment consists of studying the numbers of boys and girls in families with exactly 3 children. Let *b* represent *boy* and *g* represent *girl*.

> **SOLUTION** A three-child family can have 3 boys, written *bbb*, 3 girls, *ggg*, or various combinations, such as *bgg*. A sample space with four outcomes (not equally likely) is
> $$S_1 = \{3 \text{ boys}, 2 \text{ boys and } 1 \text{ girl}, 1 \text{ boy and } 2 \text{ girls}, 3 \text{ girls}\}.$$

Notice that a family with 3 boys or 3 girls can occur in just one way, but a family of 2 boys and 1 girl or 1 boy and 2 girls can occur in more than one way. If the *order* of the births is considered, so that *bgg* is different from *gbg* or *ggb*, for example, another sample space is

$$S_2 = \{bbb, bbg, bgb, gbb, bgg, gbg, ggb, ggg\}.$$

The second sample space, S_2, has equally likely outcomes if we assume that boys and girls are equally likely. This assumption, while not quite true, is approximately true, so we will use it throughout this book. The outcomes in S_1 are not equally likely, since there is more than one way to get a family with 2 boys and 1 girl (*bbg*, *bgb*, or *gbb*) or a family with 2 girls and 1 boy (*ggb*, *gbg*, or *bgg*), but only one way to get 3 boys (*bbb*) or 3 girls (*ggg*).   **TRY YOUR TURN 1**

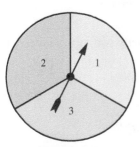

FIGURE 15

YOUR TURN 1 Two coins are tossed, and a head or a tail is recorded for each coin. Give a sample space where each outcome is equally likely.

| CAUTION | An experiment may have more than one sample space, as shown in Example 1(c). The most convenient sample spaces have equally likely outcomes, but it is not always possible to choose such a sample space.

Events

An **event** is a subset of a sample space. If the sample space for tossing a coin is $S = \{h, t\}$, then one event is $E = \{h\}$, which represents the outcome "heads."

An ordinary die is a cube whose six different faces show the following numbers of dots: 1, 2, 3, 4, 5, and 6. If the die is fair (not "loaded" to favor certain faces over others), then any one of the faces is equally likely to occur when the die is rolled. The sample space for the experiment of rolling a single fair die is $S = \{1, 2, 3, 4, 5, 6\}$. Some possible events are listed below.

The die shows an even number: $E_1 = \{2, 4, 6\}$.

The die shows a 1: $E_2 = \{1\}$.

The die shows a number less than 5: $E_3 = \{1, 2, 3, 4\}$.

The die shows a multiple of 3: $E_4 = \{3, 6\}$.

Using the notation introduced earlier in this chapter, notice that $n(S) = 6$, $n(E_1) = 3$, $n(E_2) = 1$, $n(E_3) = 4$, and $n(E_4) = 2$.

EXAMPLE 2 Events

For the sample space S_2 in Example 1(c), write the following events.

(a) Event H: the family has exactly two girls

SOLUTION Families with three children can have exactly two girls with either *bgg*, *gbg*, or *ggb*, so event H is

$$H = \{bgg, gbg, ggb\}.$$

(b) Event K: the three children are the same sex

SOLUTION Two outcomes satisfy this condition: all boys or all girls.

$$K = \{bbb, ggg\}$$

YOUR TURN 2 Two coins are tossed, and a head or a tail is recorded for each coin. Write the event E: the coins show exactly one head.

(c) Event J: the family has three girls

SOLUTION Only *ggg* satisfies this condition, so

$$J = \{ggg\}. \qquad \text{TRY YOUR TURN 2}$$

In Example 2(c), event J had only one possible outcome, *ggg*. Such an event, with only one possible outcome, is a **simple event**. If event E equals the sample space S, then E is called a **certain event**. If event $E = \varnothing$, then E is called an **impossible event**.

EXAMPLE 3 Events

Suppose a coin is flipped until both a head and a tail appear, or until the coin has been flipped four times, whichever comes first. Write each of the following events in set notation.

(a) The coin is flipped exactly three times.

SOLUTION This means that the first two flips of the coin did not include both a head and a tail, so they must both be heads or both be tails. Because the third flip is the last one, it must show the side of the coin not yet seen. Thus the event is

$$\{hht, tth\}.$$

(b) The coin is flipped at least three times.

SOLUTION In addition to the outcomes listed in part (a), there is also the possibility that the coin is flipped four times, which happens only when the first three flips are all heads or all tails. Thus the event is

$$\{hht, tth, hhhh, hhht, tttt, ttth\}.$$

(c) The coin is flipped at least two times.

SOLUTION This event consists of the entire sample space:

$$S = \{ht, th, hht, tth, hhhh, hhht, tttt, ttth\}.$$

This is an example of a certain event.

(d) The coin is flipped fewer than two times.

SOLUTION The coin cannot be flipped fewer than two times under the rules described, so the event is the empty set $\emptyset$. This is an example of an impossible event. ▬▬

Since events are sets, we can use set operations to find unions, intersections, and complements of events. A summary of the set operations for events is given below.

Set Operations for Events

Let E and F be events for a sample space S.

$E \cap F$ occurs when both E **and** F occur;

$E \cup F$ occurs when E **or** F **or both** occur;

E' occurs when E does **not** occur.

EXAMPLE 4   Minimum-Wage Workers

A study of workers earning the minimum wage grouped such workers into various categories, which can be interpreted as events when a worker is selected at random. Consider the following events:

E: worker is under 20;

F: worker is white;

G: worker is female.

Describe the following events in words. *Source: Economic Policy Institute.*

(a) E'

SOLUTION E' is the event that the worker is 20 or over.

(b) $F \cap G'$

SOLUTION $F \cap G'$ is the event that the worker is white and not a female, that is, the worker is a white male.

(c) $E \cup G$

SOLUTION $E \cup G$ is the event that the worker is under 20 or is female. Note that this event includes all workers under 20, both male and female, and all female workers of any age.   TRY YOUR TURN 3 ▬▬

YOUR TURN 3 In Example 4, describe the following event in words: $E' \cap F'$. ▬▬

Two events that cannot both occur at the same time, such as rolling an even number and an odd number with a single roll of a die, are called *mutually exclusive events*.

Mutually Exclusive Events
Events E and F are **mutually exclusive events** if $E \cap F = \emptyset$.

Any event E and its complement E' are mutually exclusive. By definition, mutually exclusive events are disjoint sets.

EXAMPLE 5 **Mutually Exclusive Events**

Let $S = \{1, 2, 3, 4, 5, 6\}$, the sample space for tossing a single die. Let $E = \{4, 5, 6\}$, and let $G = \{1, 2\}$. Then E and G are mutually exclusive events, since they have no outcomes in common: $E \cap G = \emptyset$. See Figure 16.

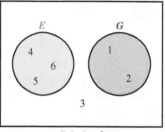

$E \cap G = \emptyset$
FIGURE 16

Probability For sample spaces with *equally likely* outcomes, the probability of an event is defined as follows.

Basic Probability Principle
Let S be a sample space of equally likely outcomes, and let event E be a subset of S. Then the **probability** that event E occurs is

$$P(E) = \frac{n(E)}{n(S)}.$$

By this definition, the probability of an event is a number that indicates the relative likelihood of the event.

CAUTION   The basic probability principle only applies when the outcomes are equally likely.

EXAMPLE 6 **Basic Probabilities**

Suppose a single fair die is rolled. Use the sample space $S = \{1, 2, 3, 4, 5, 6\}$ and give the probability of each event.

(a) E: the die shows an even number

SOLUTION   Here, $E = \{2, 4, 6\}$, a set with three elements. Since S contains six elements,

$$P(E) = \frac{3}{6} = \frac{1}{2}.$$

(b) F: the die shows a number less than 10

SOLUTION   Event F is a certain event, with

$$F = \{1, 2, 3, 4, 5, 6\},$$

so

$$P(F) = \frac{6}{6} = 1.$$

YOUR TURN 4 In Example 6, find the probability of event H: The die shows a number less than 5.

(c) G: the die shows an 8

SOLUTION   This event is impossible, so

$$P(G) = 0.$$

TRY YOUR TURN 4

A standard deck of 52 cards has four suits: hearts (♥), clubs (♣), diamonds (♦), and spades (♠), with 13 cards in each suit. The hearts and diamonds are red, and the spades and clubs are black. Each suit has an ace (A), a king (K), a queen (Q), a jack (J), and cards numbered from 2 to 10. The jack, queen, and king are called *face cards* and for many purposes can be thought of as having values 11, 12, and 13, respectively. The ace can be thought of as the low card (value 1) or the high card (value 14). See Figure 17. We will refer to this standard deck of cards often in our discussion of probability.

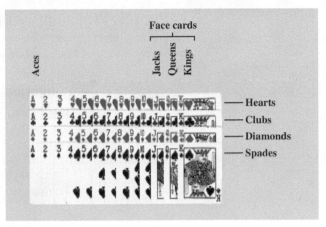

FIGURE 17

EXAMPLE 7   Playing Cards

If a single playing card is drawn at random from a standard 52-card deck, find the probability of each event.

(a) Drawing an ace

SOLUTION   There are 4 aces in the deck. The event "drawing an ace" is

$$\{\text{heart ace, diamond ace, club ace, spade ace}\}.$$

Therefore,

$$P(\text{ace}) = \frac{4}{52} = \frac{1}{13}.$$

(b) Drawing a face card

SOLUTION   Since there are 12 face cards (three in each of the four suits),

$$P(\text{face card}) = \frac{12}{52} = \frac{3}{13}.$$

(c) Drawing a spade

SOLUTION   The deck contains 13 spades, so

$$P(\text{spade}) = \frac{13}{52} = \frac{1}{4}.$$

(d) Drawing a spade or a heart

SOLUTION   Besides the 13 spades, the deck contains 13 hearts, so

$$P(\text{spade or heart}) = \frac{26}{52} = \frac{1}{2}.$$

YOUR TURN 5   Find the probability of drawing a jack or a king.

TRY YOUR TURN 5

In the preceding examples, the probability of each event was a number between 0 and 1. The same thing is true in general. Any event E is a subset of the sample space S, so $0 \leq n(E) \leq n(S)$. Since $P(E) = n(E)/n(S)$, it follows that $0 \leq P(E) \leq 1$. Note that a certain event has probability 1 and an impossible event has probability 0, as seen in Example 6.

For any event E, $\qquad 0 \leq P(E) \leq 1.$

Empirical Probability

In many real-life problems, it is not possible to establish exact probabilities for events. Instead, useful approximations are often found by drawing on past experience. The next example shows one approach to such **empirical probabilities**.

EXAMPLE 8 **Injuries**

The following table lists the estimated number of injuries in the United States associated with recreation equipment. *Source: National Safety Council.*

Recreation Equipment Injuries	
Equipment	**Number of Injuries**
Bicycles	515,871
Skateboards	143,682
Trampolines	107,345
Playground climbing equipment	77,845
Swings or swing sets	59,144

Find the probability that a randomly selected person whose injury is associated with recreation equipment was hurt on a trampoline.

SOLUTION We first find the total number of injuries. Verify that the amounts in the table sum to 903,887. The probability is then found by dividing the number of people injured on trampolines by the total number of people injured. Thus,

$$P(\text{Trampolines}) = \frac{107,345}{903,887} \approx 0.1188.$$

7.3 EXERCISES

1. What is meant by a "fair" coin or die?

2. What is the sample space for an experiment?

Write sample spaces for the experiments in Exercises 3–10.

3. A month of the year is chosen for a wedding.

4. A day in April is selected for a bicycle race.

5. A student is asked how many questions she answered correctly on a recent 80-question test.

6. A person is asked the number of hours (to the nearest hour) he watched television yesterday.

7. The management of an oil company must decide whether to go ahead with a new oil shale plant or to cancel it.

8. A record is kept each day for three days about whether a particular stock goes up or down.

9. A coin is tossed, and a die is rolled.

10. A box contains five balls, numbered 1, 2, 3, 4, and 5. A ball is drawn at random, the number on it recorded, and the ball replaced. The box is shaken, a second ball is drawn, and its number is recorded.

11. Define an event.

12. What is a simple event?

For the experiments in Exercises 13–18, write out the sample space S, choosing an S with equally likely outcomes, if possible. Then give the value of $n(S)$ and tell whether the outcomes in S are equally likely. Finally, write the indicated events in set notation.

13. A committee of 2 people is selected at random from 5 executives: Alam, Bartolini, Chinn, Dickson, and Ellsberg.

   (a) Chinn is on the committee.

   (b) Dickson and Ellsberg are not both on the committee.

   (c) Both Alam and Chinn are on the committee.

14. Five states are being considered as the location for three new high-energy physics laboratories: California (CA), Colorado (CO), New Jersey (NJ), New York (NY), and Utah (UT). Three states will be chosen at random. Write elements of the sample space in the form (CA, CO, NJ).

   (a) All three states border an ocean.

   (b) Exactly two of the three states border an ocean.

   (c) Exactly one of the three states is west of the Mississippi River.

15. Slips of paper marked with the numbers 1, 2, 3, 4, and 5 are placed in a box. After being mixed, two slips are drawn simultaneously.

   (a) Both slips are marked with even numbers.

   (b) One slip is marked with an odd number and the other is marked with an even number.

   (c) Both slips are marked with the same number.

16. An unprepared student takes a three-question, true/false quiz in which he guesses the answers to all three questions, so each answer is equally likely to be correct or wrong.

   (a) The student gets three answers wrong.

   (b) The student gets exactly two answers correct.

   (c) The student gets only the first answer correct.

17. A coin is flipped until two heads appear, up to a maximum of four flips. (If three tails are flipped, the coin is still tossed a fourth time to complete the experiment).

   (a) The coin is tossed four times.

   (b) Exactly two heads are tossed.

   (c) No heads are tossed.

18. One jar contains four balls, labeled 1, 2, 3, and 4. A second jar contains five balls, labeled 1, 2, 3, 4, and 5. An experiment consists of taking one ball from the first jar, and then taking a ball from the second jar.

   (a) The number on the first ball is even.

   (b) The number on the second ball is even.

   (c) The sum of the numbers on the two balls is 5.

   (d) The sum of the numbers on the two balls is 1.

A single fair die is rolled. Find the probabilities of each event.

19. Getting a 2

20. Getting an odd number

21. Getting a number less than 5

22. Getting a number greater than 2

23. Getting a 3 or a 4

24. Getting any number except 3

A card is drawn from a well-shuffled deck of 52 cards. Find the probability of drawing the following.

25. A 9

26. A black card

27. A black 9

28. A heart

29. The 9 of hearts

30. A face card

31. A 2 or a queen

32. A black 7 or a red 8

33. A red card or a 10

34. A spade or a king

A jar contains 3 white, 4 orange, 5 yellow, and 8 black marbles. If a marble is drawn at random, find the probability that it is the following.

35. White

36. Orange

37. Yellow

38. Black

39. Not black

40. Orange or yellow

Which of Exercises 41–48 are examples of empirical probability?

41. The probability of heads on 5 consecutive tosses of a coin

42. The probability that a freshman entering college will graduate with a degree

43. The probability that a person is allergic to penicillin

44. The probability of drawing an ace from a standard deck of 52 cards

45. The probability that a person will get lung cancer from smoking cigarettes

46. A weather forecast that predicts a 70% chance of rain tomorrow

47. A gambler's claim that on a roll of a fair die, $P(\text{even}) = 1/2$

48. A surgeon's prediction that a patient has a 90% chance of a full recovery

49. The student sitting next to you in class concludes that the probability of the ceiling falling down on both of you before class ends is 1/2, because there are two possible outcomes—the ceiling will fall or not fall. What is wrong with this reasoning?

50. The following puzzler was given on the *Car Talk* radio program.

   "Three different numbers are chosen at random, and one is written on each of three slips of paper. The slips are then placed face down on the table. The objective is to choose the slip upon which is written the largest number. Here are the rules: You can turn over any slip of paper and look at the amount written on it. If for any reason you think this is the largest, you're done; you keep it. Otherwise you discard it and turn over a second slip. Again, if you think this is the one with the biggest number, you keep that one and the game is over. If you don't, you discard that one too . . . . The chance of getting the highest number is one in three. Or is it? Is there a strategy by which you can improve the odds?" *Source: Car Talk*.

   The answer to the puzzler is that you can indeed improve the probability of getting the highest number by the following strategy. Pick one of the slips of paper, and after looking at the number, throw it away. Then pick a second slip; if it has a larger number than the first slip, stop. If not, pick the third slip. Find the probability of winning with this strategy.*

APPLICATIONS

Business and Economics

51. Survey of Workers The management of a firm wishes to check on the opinions of its assembly line workers. Before the workers are interviewed, they are divided into various categories. Define events E, F, and G as follows.

　　　E: worker is female
　　　F: worker has worked less than 5 years
　　　G: worker contributes to a voluntary retirement plan

Describe each event in words.

(a) E' 　　　　(b) $E \cap F$ 　　　　(c) $E \cup G'$

(d) F' 　　　　(e) $F \cup G$ 　　　　(f) $F' \cap G'$

52. Brand Choice A study considers consumers' choices between two brands, A and B, based on the proportion of unique features in each brand. Suppose that the number of features of brand A is a and of brand B is b, and that c is the number of common features. Show that

$$P(A) = \frac{a - c}{a + b - 2c} \quad \text{and} \quad P(B) = \frac{b - c}{a + b - 2c}.$$

Source: Marketing Science.

53. Investment Survey Exercise 44 of the previous section presented a survey of 150 mathematics professors. Use the information given in that exercise to find each probability.

(a) A randomly chosen professor invested in stocks and bonds and certificates of deposit.

(b) A randomly chosen professor invested in only bonds.

54. Labor Force The 2012 and the 2022 (projected) civilian labor forces by age are given in the following table. *Source: Bureau of Labor Statistics.*

Age (in years)	2012 (in millions)	2022 (in millions)
16 to 24	21.3	18.5
25 to 54	101.3	103.2
55 and over	32.4	41.8
Total	155.0	163.5

(a) In 2012, find the probability that a member of the civilian labor force is age 55 or older.

(b) In 2022, find the probability that a member of the civilian labor force is age 55 or over.

(c) What do these projections imply about the future civilian labor force?

Life Sciences

55. Medical Survey For a medical experiment, people are classified as to whether they smoke, have a family history of heart disease, or are overweight. Define events E, F, and G as follows.

　　　E: person smokes
　　　F: person has a family history of heart disease
　　　G: person is overweight

Describe each event in words.

(a) G' 　　　　(b) $F \cap G$ 　　　　(c) $E \cup G'$

56. Medical Survey Refer to Exercise 55. Describe each event in words.

(a) $E \cup F$ 　　　　(b) $E' \cap F$ 　　　　(c) $F' \cup G'$

57. Causes of Death There were 2,468,435 U.S. deaths in 2010. They are listed according to cause in the following table. If a randomly selected person died in 2010, use this information to find the following probabilities. *Source: Centers for Disease Control and Prevention.*

Cause	Number of Deaths
Heart disease	597,689
Cancer	574,743
Chronic lower respiratory disease	138,080
Cerebrovascular disease	129,476
Accidents	120,859
Alzheimer's disease	83,494
Diabetes mellitus	69,071
Influenza and pneumonia	50,097
All other causes	704,926

(a) The probability that the cause of death was heart disease

(b) The probability that the cause of death was cancer or heart disease

(c) The probability that the cause of death was not an accident and was not diabetes mellitus

Social Sciences

58. APPLY IT U.S. Population The projected U.S. population (in thousands) by race in 2020 and 2050 is given in the table. *Source: Bureau of the Census.*

Race	2020	2050
White	207,393	207,901
Hispanic	52,652	96,508
Black	41,538	53,555
Asian and Pacific Islander	18,557	32,432
Other	2602	3535

*This is a special case of the famous Googol problem. For more details, see "Recognizing the Maximum of a Sequence" by John P. Gilbert and Frederick Mosteller, *Journal of the American Statistical Association*, Vol. 61, No. 313, March 1966, pp. 35–73.

Find the probability that a randomly selected person in the given year is of the race specified.

(a) Hispanic in 2020

(b) Hispanic in 2050

(c) Black in 2020

(d) Black in 2050

59. Congressional Service The following table gives the number of years of service of senators in the 113th Congress of the United States of America. Find the probability that a randomly selected senator of the 113th Congress had served 20–29 years when Congress convened. *Source: Infoplease.com*.

Years of Service	Number of Senators
0–9	60
10–19	24
20–29	11
30–39	5

60. Civil War Estimates of the Union Army's strength and losses for the battle of Gettysburg are given in the following table, where *strength* is the number of soldiers immediately preceding the battle and *loss* indicates a soldier who was killed, wounded, captured, or missing. *Source: Regimental Strengths and Losses of Gettysburg*.

Unit	Strength	Loss
I Corps (Reynolds)	12,222	6059
II Corps (Hancock)	11,347	4369
III Corps (Sickles)	10,675	4211
V Corps (Sykes)	10,907	2187
VI Corps (Sedgwick)	13,596	242
XI Corps (Howard)	9188	3801
XII Corps (Slocum)	9788	1082
Cavalry (Pleasonton)	11,851	610
Artillery (Tyler)	2376	242
Total	91,950	22,803

(a) Find the probability that a randomly selected Union soldier was from the XI Corps.

(b) Find the probability that a soldier was lost in the battle.

(c) Find the probability that a I Corps soldier was lost in the battle.

(d) Which group had the highest probability of not being lost in the battle?

(e) Which group had the highest probability of loss?

(f) Explain why these probabilities vary.

61. Civil War Estimates of the Confederate Army's strength and losses for the battle of Gettysburg are given in the following table, where *strength* is the number of soldiers immediately preceding the battle and *loss* indicates a soldier who was killed, wounded, captured, or missing. *Source: Regimental Strengths and Losses at Gettysburg*.

Unit	Strength	Loss
I Corps (Longstreet)	20,706	7661
II Corps (Ewell)	20,666	6603
III Corps (Hill)	22,083	8007
Cavalry (Stuart)	6621	286
Total	70,076	22,557

(a) Find the probability that a randomly selected Confederate soldier was from the III Corps.

(b) Find the probability that a confederate soldier was lost in the battle.

(c) Find the probability that a I Corps soldier was lost in the battle.

(d) Which group had the highest probability of not being lost in the battle?

(e) Which group had the highest probability of loss?

General Interest

62. Native American Ceremonies Exercise 62 of the previous section presented a survey of families participating in a pow-wow in Arizona. Use the information given in that exercise to find each probability.

(a) A randomly chosen family brought costumes and food.

(b) A randomly chosen family brought crafts, but neither food nor costumes.

(c) A randomly chosen family brought food or costumes.

63. Poultry Analysis Exercise 63 of the previous section described a flock of chickens. See the information given in that exercise to find each of the following probabilities.

(a) A randomly chosen chicken was a fat red rooster.

(b) A randomly chosen chicken was a rooster.

(c) A randomly chosen chicken was red.

YOUR TURN ANSWERS

1. $S = \{HH, HT, TH, TT\}$ 2. $E = \{HT, TH\}$
3. $E' \cap F'$ is the event that the worker is 20 or over and is not white.
4. $P(H) = \dfrac{4}{6} = \dfrac{2}{3}$.
5. $P(\text{jack or a king}) = 8/52 = 2/13$.

7.4 Basic Concepts of Probability

What is the probability that a dollar of consumer debt is held by a finance company or credit union?

We will determine this probability in Example 8. But first we need to develop additional rules for calculating probability, beginning with the probability of a union of two events.

The Union Rule To determine the probability of the union of two events E and F in a sample space S, use the union rule for sets,

$$n(E \cup F) = n(E) + n(F) - n(E \cap F),$$

which was proved in Section 7.2. Assuming that the events in the sample space S are equally likely, divide both sides by $n(S)$, so that

$$\frac{n(E \cup F)}{n(S)} = \frac{n(E)}{n(S)} + \frac{n(F)}{n(S)} - \frac{n(E \cap F)}{n(S)}$$

$$P(E \cup F) = P(E) + P(F) - P(E \cap F).$$

Although our derivation is valid only for sample spaces with equally likely events, the result is valid for any events E and F from any sample space, and is called the **union rule for probability**.

> **Union Rule for Probability**
> For any events E and F from a sample space S,
>
> $$P(E \cup F) = P(E) + P(F) - P(E \cap F).$$

EXAMPLE 1 **Probabilities with Playing Cards**

If a single card is drawn from an ordinary deck of cards, find the probability that it will be a red or a face card.

SOLUTION Let R represent the event "red card" and F the event "face card." There are 26 red cards in the deck, so $P(R) = 26/52$. There are 12 face cards in the deck, so $P(F) = 12/52$. Since there are 6 red face cards in the deck, $P(R \cap F) = 6/52$. By the union rule, the probability of the card being red or a face card is

$$P(R \cup F) = P(R) + P(F) - P(R \cap F)$$

$$= \frac{26}{52} + \frac{12}{52} - \frac{6}{52} = \frac{32}{52} = \frac{8}{13}.$$ **TRY YOUR TURN 1**

YOUR TURN 1 In Example 1, find the probability of an ace or a club.

EXAMPLE 2 **Probabilities with Dice**

Suppose two fair dice are rolled. Find each probability.

(a) The first die shows a 2, or the sum of the results is 6 or 7.

SOLUTION The sample space for the throw of two dice is shown in Figure 18 on the next page, where 1-1 represents the event "the first die shows a 1 and the second die shows a 1," 1-2 represents "the first die shows a 1 and the second die shows a 2," and so on. Let A represent the event "the first die shows a 2," and B represent the event "the sum of the results is 6 or 7." These events are indicated in Figure 18. From the diagram, event A has 6 elements, B has 11 elements, the intersection of A and B has 2 elements, and the sample space has 36 elements. Thus,

$$P(A) = \frac{6}{36}, \quad P(B) = \frac{11}{36}, \quad \text{and} \quad P(A \cap B) = \frac{2}{36}.$$

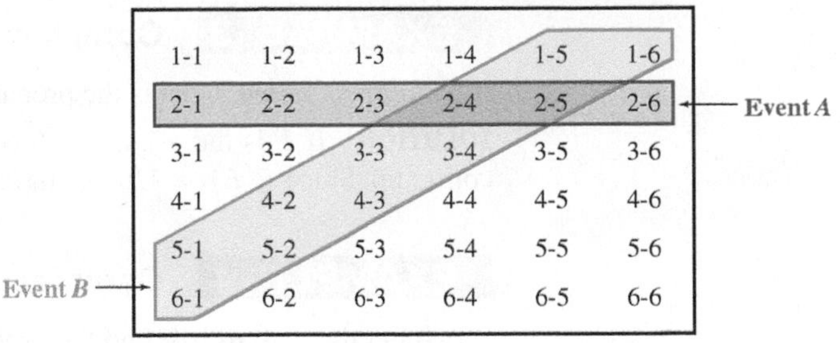

FIGURE 18

By the union rule,

$$P(A \cup B) = P(A) + P(B) - P(A \cap B)$$

$$P(A \cup B) = \frac{6}{36} + \frac{11}{36} - \frac{2}{36} = \frac{15}{36} = \frac{5}{12}.$$

(b) The sum of the results is 11, or the second die shows a 5.

SOLUTION $P(\text{sum is } 11) = 2/36$, $P(\text{second die shows a } 5) = 6/36$, and $P(\text{sum is } 11 \text{ and second die shows a } 5) = 1/36$, so

$$P(\text{sum is } 11 \text{ or second die shows a } 5) = \frac{2}{36} + \frac{6}{36} - \frac{1}{36} = \frac{7}{36}.$$

TRY YOUR TURN 2

YOUR TURN 2 In Example 2, find the probability that the sum is 8, or both die show the same number.

CAUTION You may wonder why we did not use $S = \{2, 3, 4, 5, \ldots, 12\}$ as the sample space in Example 2. Remember, we prefer to use a sample space with equally likely outcomes. The outcomes in set S above are not equally likely—a sum of 2 can occur in just one way, a sum of 3 in two ways, a sum of 4 in three ways, and so on, as shown in Figure 18.

If events E and F are mutually exclusive, then $E \cap F = \varnothing$ by definition; hence, $P(E \cap F) = 0$. In this case the union rule simplifies to $P(E \cup F) = P(E) + P(F)$.

CAUTION The rule $P(E \cup F) = P(E) + P(F)$ is valid only when E and F are mutually exclusive. When E and F are *not* mutually exclusive, use the rule $P(E \cup F) = P(E) + P(F) - P(E \cap F)$.

The Complement Rule

By the definition of E', for any event E from a sample space S,

$$E \cup E' = S \quad \text{and} \quad E \cap E' = \varnothing.$$

Since $E \cap E' = \varnothing$, events E and E' are mutually exclusive, so that

$$P(E \cup E') = P(E) + P(E').$$

However, $E \cup E' = S$, the sample space, and $P(S) = 1$. Thus

$$P(E \cup E') = P(E) + P(E') = 1.$$

Rearranging these terms gives the following useful rule for complements.

Complement Rule

$$P(E) = 1 - P(E') \quad \text{and} \quad P(E') = 1 - P(E).$$

EXAMPLE 3 Complement Rule

If a fair die is rolled, what is the probability that any number but 5 will come up?

SOLUTION If E is the event that 5 comes up, then E' is the event that any number but 5 comes up. Since $P(E) = 1/6$, we have $P(E') = 1 - 1/6 = 5/6$.

EXAMPLE 4 Complement Rule

If two fair dice are rolled, find the probability that the sum of the numbers rolled is greater than 3. Refer to Figure 18.

SOLUTION To calculate this probability directly, we must find the probabilities that the sum is 4, 5, 6, 7, 8, 9, 10, 11, or 12 and then add them. It is much simpler to first find the probability of the complement, the event that the sum is less than or equal to 3.

$$P(\text{sum} \le 3) = P(\text{sum is } 2) + P(\text{sum is } 3)$$
$$= \frac{1}{36} + \frac{2}{36}$$
$$= \frac{3}{36} = \frac{1}{12}$$

YOUR TURN 3 Find the probability that when two fair dice are rolled, the sum is less than 11.

Now use the fact that $P(E) = 1 - P(E')$ to get

$$P(\text{sum} > 3) = 1 - P(\text{sum} \le 3)$$
$$= 1 - \frac{1}{12} = \frac{11}{12}.$$

TRY YOUR TURN 3

Odds

Sometimes probability statements are given in terms of **odds**, a comparison of $P(E)$ with $P(E')$. For example, suppose $P(E) = 4/5$. Then $P(E') = 1 - 4/5 = 1/5$. These probabilities predict that E will occur 4 out of 5 times and E' will occur 1 out of 5 times. Then we say the *odds in favor* of E are 4 to 1.

> **Odds**
>
> The **odds in favor** of an event E are defined as the ratio of $P(E)$ to $P(E')$, or
>
> $$\frac{P(E)}{P(E')}, \text{ where } P(E') \ne 0.$$

EXAMPLE 5 Odds in Favor of Rain

Suppose the weather forecaster says that the probability of rain tomorrow is 1/3. Find the odds in favor of rain tomorrow.

SOLUTION Let E be the event "rain tomorrow." Then E' is the event "no rain tomorrow." Since $P(E) = 1/3$, $P(E') = 2/3$. By the definition of odds, the odds in favor of rain are

$$\frac{1/3}{2/3} = \frac{1}{2}, \quad \text{written} \quad 1 \text{ to } 2, \text{ or } 1{:}2.$$

YOUR TURN 4 If the probability of snow tomorrow is 3/10, find the odds in favor of snow tomorrow.

On the other hand, the odds that it will *not* rain, or the *odds against* rain, are

$$\frac{2/3}{1/3} = \frac{2}{1}, \quad \text{written} \quad 2 \text{ to } 1, \text{ or } 2{:}1.$$

TRY YOUR TURN 4

If the odds in favor of an event are, say, 3 to 5, then the probability of the event is 3/8, while the probability of the complement of the event is 5/8. (Odds of 3 to 5 indicate

3 outcomes in favor of the event out of a total of 8 possible outcomes.) This example suggests the following generalization.

If the odds favoring event E are m to n, then

$$P(E) = \frac{m}{m + n} \quad \text{and} \quad P(E') = \frac{n}{m + n}.$$

EXAMPLE 6   Package Delivery

The odds that a particular package will be delivered on time are 25 to 2.

(a) Find the probability that the package will be delivered on time.

SOLUTION   Odds of 25 to 2 show 25 favorable chances out of $25 + 2 = 27$ chances altogether:

$$P(\text{package will be delivered on time}) = \frac{25}{25 + 2} = \frac{25}{27}.$$

(b) Find the odds against the package being delivered on time.

SOLUTION   Using the complement rule, there is a 2/27 chance that the package will not be delivered on time. So the odds against the package being delivered on time are

$$\frac{P(\text{package will not be delivered on time})}{P(\text{package will be delivered on time})} = \frac{2/27}{25/27} = \frac{2}{25},$$

or 2:25.   **TRY YOUR TURN 5**

YOUR TURN 5   If the odds that a package will be delivered on time are 17 to 3, find the probability that the package will not be delivered on time.

EXAMPLE 7   Odds in Horse Racing

If the odds in favor of a particular horse's winning a race are 5 to 7, what is the probability that the horse will win the race?

SOLUTION   The odds indicate chances of 5 out of 12 $(5 + 7 = 12)$ that the horse will win, so

$$P(\text{winning}) = \frac{5}{12}.$$

YOUR TURN 6   If the odds against a particular horse winning a race are 7 to 3, what is the probability the horse will win the race?

Race tracks generally give odds *against* a horse winning. In this case, the track would give the odds as 7 to 5. Of course, race tracks, casinos, and other gambling establishments need to give odds that are more favorable to the house than those representing the actual probabilities, because they need to make a profit.   **TRY YOUR TURN 6**

Probability Distribution   A table listing each possible outcome of an experiment and its corresponding probability is called a **probability distribution**. The assignment of probabilities may be done in any reasonable way (on an empirical basis, as in the next example, or by theoretical reasoning, as in Section 7.3), provided that it satisfies the following conditions.

Properties of Probability

Let S be a sample space consisting of n distinct outcomes, $s_1, s_2, \ldots, s_n$. An acceptable probability assignment consists of assigning to each outcome s_i a number p_i (the probability of s_i) according to these rules.

1. The probability of each outcome is a number between 0 and 1, inclusive.

$$0 \leq p_1 \leq 1, \quad 0 \leq p_2 \leq 1, \ldots, \quad 0 \leq p_n \leq 1$$

2. The sum of the probabilities of all possible outcomes is 1.

$$p_1 + p_2 + p_3 + \cdots + p_n = 1$$

> **EXAMPLE 8** Consumer Credit

The following table lists the major holders of U.S. consumer credit (in billions of dollars) in 2012. *Source: The World Almanac and Book of Facts 2014.*

Consumer Credit	
Holder	Amount
Depository institutions	1218.6
Finance companies	680.7
Credit unions	243.6
Federal government	526.8
Nonfinancial business	48.5
Pools of securitized assets	49.9

(a) Construct a probability distribution for the probability that a dollar of consumer credit is held by each type of holder.

SOLUTION We first find the total amount of credit and then divide the amount held by each type of holder by the total. Verify that the amounts in the table sum to 2768.1. The probability that a dollar of consumer credit is held by a depository institution, for example, is $P(\text{depository institution}) = 1218.6/2768.1 \approx 0.4402$. Similarly, we could divide each amount by 2768.1, with the results (rounded to four decimal places) shown in the following table.

Consumer Credit	
Holder	Probability
Depository institutions	0.4402
Finance companies	0.2459
Credit unions	0.0880
Federal government	0.1903
Nonfinancial business	0.0175
Pools of securitized assets	0.0180

Verify that this distribution satisfies the conditions for probability. Each probability is between 0 and 1, so the first condition holds. The probabilities in this table sum to 0.9999. In theory, to satisfy the second condition, they should total 1.0000, but this does not always occur when the individual numbers are rounded.

(b) Find the probability that a dollar of consumer debt is held by a finance company or credit union.

APPLY IT

SOLUTION The categories in the table are mutually exclusive simple events. Thus, to find the probability that a dollar of consumer debt is held by a finance company or credit union, we use the union rule to calculate

$$P(\text{finance company or credit union}) = 0.2459 + 0.0880 = 0.3339.$$

We could get this same result by summing the amount held by finance companies and credit unions, and dividing the total by 2768.1.

Thus, about one-third of all consumer debt is held by finance companies and credit unions.

Probability distributions are discussed further in the next chapter.

EXAMPLE 9 Clothing

Susan is a college student who receives heavy sweaters from her aunt at the first sign of cold weather. Susan has determined that the probability that a sweater is the wrong size is 0.47, the probability that it is a loud color is 0.59, and the probability that it is both the wrong size and a loud color is 0.31.

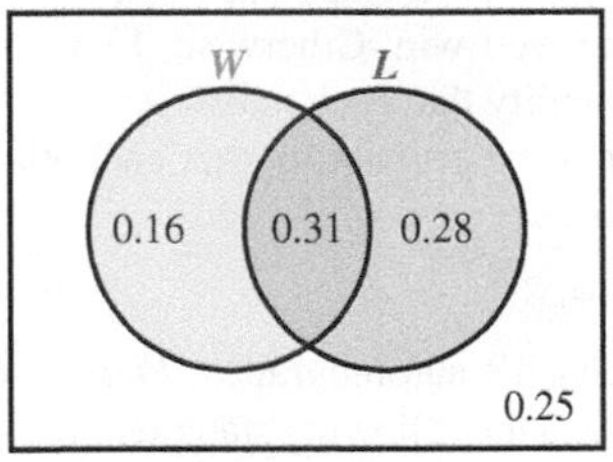

(a) Find the probability that the sweater is the correct size and not a loud color.

SOLUTION   Let W represent the event "wrong size," and L represent "loud color." Place the given information on a Venn diagram, starting with 0.31 in the intersection of the regions W and L (see Figure 19). As stated earlier, event W has probability 0.47. Since 0.31 has already been placed inside the intersection of W and L,

$$0.47 - 0.31 = 0.16$$

goes inside region W, but outside the intersection of W and L, that is, in the region $W \cap L'$. In the same way,

$$0.59 - 0.31 = 0.28$$

goes inside the region for L, and outside the overlap, that is, in the region $L \cap W'$.

Using regions W and L, the event we want is $W' \cap L'$. From the Venn diagram in Figure 19, the labeled regions have a total probability of

$$0.16 + 0.31 + 0.28 = 0.75.$$

Since the entire region of the Venn diagram must have probability 1, the region outside W and L, or $W' \cap L'$, has probability

$$1 - 0.75 = 0.25.$$

The probability is 0.25 that the sweater is the correct size and not a loud color.

(b) Find the probability that the sweater is the correct size or is not loud.

SOLUTION   The corresponding region, $W' \cup L'$, has probability

$$0.25 + 0.16 + 0.28 = 0.69.$$

Alternatively, we could write $W' \cup L' = (W \cap L)'$ using one of De Morgan's Laws. (See Exercises 33 and 34 in Section 7.2.) Then we can use the complement rule to get $P((W \cap L)') = 1 - P(W \cap L) = 1 - 0.31 = 0.69.$ ▬▬

FIGURE 19 (caption, left margin beneath Venn diagram)

7.4 WARM-UP EXERCISES

A card is drawn from a well-shuffled deck of 52 cards. Find the probabilities of the following.

W1. A heart or a queen   *(Sec. 7.3)*

W2. A black card or an ace   *(Sec. 7.3)*

7.4 EXERCISES

1. Define mutually exclusive events in your own words.

2. Explain the union rule for mutually exclusive events.

Decide whether the events in Exercises 3–8 are mutually exclusive.

3. Owning a dog and owning an MP3 player

4. Being a business major and being from Texas

5. Being retired and being 70 years old

6. Being a teenager and being 70 years old

7. Being one of the ten tallest people in the United States and being under 4 feet tall

8. Being male and being a nurse

Two dice are rolled. Find the probabilities of rolling the given sums.

9. (a) 2   **(b)** 4   **(c)** 5   **(d)** 6

10. (a) 8   **(b)** 9   **(c)** 10   **(d)** 13

11. (a) 9 or more   **(b)** Less than 7

  (c) Between 5 and 8 (exclusive)

12. (a) Not more than 5

  (b) Not less than 8

  (c) Between 3 and 7 (exclusive)

Two dice are rolled. Find the probabilities of the following events.

13. The first die is 3 or the sum is 8.

14. The second die is 5 or the sum is 10.

One card is drawn from an ordinary deck of 52 cards. Find the probabilities of drawing the following cards.

15. (a) A 9 or 10   **(b)** A red card or a 3

    (c) A 9 or a black 10   **(d)** A heart or a black card

    (e) A face card or a diamond

16. (a) Less than a 4 (count aces as ones)

    (b) A diamond or a 7   **(c)** A black card or an ace

    (d) A heart or a jack   **(e)** A red card or a face card

Kristina Karganova invites 13 relatives to a party: her mother, 2 aunts, 3 uncles, 2 brothers, 1 male cousin, and 4 female cousins. If the chances of any one guest arriving first are equally likely, find the probabilities that the first guest to arrive is as follows.

17. (a) A brother or an uncle

    (b) A brother or a cousin

    (c) A brother or her mother

18. (a) An uncle or a cousin

    (b) A male or a cousin

    (c) A female or a cousin

The numbers 1, 2, 3, 4, and 5 are written on slips of paper, and 2 slips are drawn at random one at a time without replacement. Find the probabilities in Exercises 19 and 20.

19. (a) The sum of the numbers is 9.

    (b) The sum of the numbers is 5 or less.

    (c) The first number is 2 or the sum is 6.

20. (a) Both numbers are even.

    (b) One of the numbers is even or greater than 3.

    (c) The sum is 5 or the second number is 2.

Use Venn diagrams to work Exercises 21 and 22.

21. Suppose $P(E) = 0.26$, $P(F) = 0.41$, and $P(E \cap F) = 0.16$. Find the following.

    (a) $P(E \cup F)$ **(b)** $P(E' \cap F)$

    (c) $P(E \cap F')$ **(d)** $P(E' \cup F')$

22. Let $P(Z) = 0.42$, $P(Y) = 0.35$, and $P(Z \cup Y) = 0.59$. Find each probability.

    (a) $P(Z' \cap Y')$ **(b)** $P(Z' \cup Y')$

    (c) $P(Z' \cup Y)$ **(d)** $P(Z \cap Y')$

23. Three unusual dice, A, B, and C, are constructed such that die A has the numbers 3, 3, 4, 4, 8, 8; die B has the numbers 1, 1, 5, 5, 9, 9; and die C has the numbers 2, 2, 6, 6, 7, 7.

    (a) If dice A and B are rolled, find the probability that B beats A, that is, the number that appears on die B is greater than the number that appears on die A.

    (b) If dice B and C are rolled, find the probability that C beats B.

    (c) If dice A and C are rolled, find the probability that A beats C.

    (d) Which die is better? Explain.

24. In the "Ask Marilyn" column of *Parade* magazine, a reader wrote about the following game: You and I each roll a die. If your die is higher than mine, you win. Otherwise, I win. The reader thought that the probability that each player wins is 1/2. Is this correct? If not, what is the probability that each player wins? *Source: Parade magazine*.

25. Define what is meant by odds.

26. On page 134 of Roger Staubach's autobiography, *First Down, Lifetime to Go*, Staubach makes the following statement regarding his experience in Vietnam:

    "Odds against a direct hit are very low but when your life is in danger, you don't worry too much about the odds."

    Is this wording consistent with our definition of odds, for and against? How could it have been said so as to be technically correct? *Source: First Down, Lifetime to Go*.

A single fair die is rolled. Find the odds in favor of getting the results in Exercises 27–30.

27. 3   **28.** 4, 5, or 6

29. 2, 3, 4, or 5   **30.** Some number less than 6

31. A marble is drawn from a box containing 3 yellow, 4 white, and 11 blue marbles. Find the odds in favor of drawing the following.

    (a) A yellow marble   **(b)** A blue marble

    (c) A white marble   **(d)** Not drawing a white marble

32. Two dice are rolled. Find the odds of rolling the following. (Refer to Figure 18.)

    (a) A sum of 3   **(b)** A sum of 7 or 11

    (c) A sum less than 5   **(d)** Not a sum of 6

33. What is a probability distribution?

34. What conditions must hold for a probability distribution to be acceptable?

An experiment is conducted for which the sample space is $S = \{s_1, s_2, s_3, s_4, s_5\}$. Which of the probability assignments in Exercises 35–40 are possible for this experiment? If an assignment is not possible, tell why.

35.

Outcomes	s_1	s_2	s_3	s_4	s_5
Probabilities	0.09	0.32	0.21	0.25	0.13

36.

Outcomes	s_1	s_2	s_3	s_4	s_5
Probabilities	0.92	0.03	0	0.02	0.03

37.

Outcomes	s_1	s_2	s_3	s_4	s_5
Probabilities	1/3	1/4	1/6	1/8	1/10

38.

Outcomes	s_1	s_2	s_3	s_4	s_5
Probabilities	1/5	1/3	1/4	1/5	1/10

39.

Outcomes	s_1	s_2	s_3	s_4	s_5
Probabilities	0.64	−0.08	0.30	0.12	0.02

40.

Outcomes	s_1	s_2	s_3	s_4	s_5
Probabilities	0.05	0.35	0.5	0.2	−0.3

One way to solve a probability problem is to repeat the experiment many times, keeping track of the results. Then the probability can be approximated using the basic definition of the probability of an event E: $P(E) = n(E)/n(S)$, where E occurs $n(E)$ times out of $n(S)$ trials of an experiment. This is called the Monte Carlo method of finding probabilities. If physically repeating the experiment is too tedious, it may be simulated using a random-number generator, available on most computers and scientific or graphing calculators. To simulate a coin toss or the roll of a die on the TI-84 Plus C, change the setting to display 0 digits, and enter `rand` or `rand*6+.5`, respectively. For a coin toss, interpret 0 as a head and 1 as a tail. In either case, the `ENTER` key can be pressed repeatedly to perform multiple simulations.

41. Suppose two dice are rolled. Use the Monte Carlo method with at least 50 repetitions to approximate the following probabilities. Compare with the results of Exercise 11.

(a) P(the sum is 9 or more)

(b) P(the sum is less than 7)

42. Suppose two dice are rolled. Use the Monte Carlo method with at least 50 repetitions to approximate the following probabilities. Compare with the results of Exercise 12.

(a) P(the sum is not more than 5)

(b) P(the sum is not less than 8)

43. Suppose three dice are rolled. Use the Monte Carlo method with at least 100 repetitions to approximate the following probabilities.

(a) P(the sum is 5 or less)

(b) P(neither a 1 nor a 6 is rolled)

44. Suppose a coin is tossed 5 times. Use the Monte Carlo method with at least 50 repetitions to approximate the following probabilities.

(a) P(exactly 4 heads)   (b) P(2 heads and 3 tails)

45. The following description of the classic "Linda problem" appeared in the *New Yorker*:

"In this experiment, subjects are told, 'Linda is thirty-one years old, single, outspoken, and very bright. She majored in philosophy. As a student, she was deeply concerned with issues of discrimination and social justice and also participated in antinuclear demonstrations.' They are then asked to rank the probability of several possible descriptions of Linda today. Two of them are 'bank teller' and 'bank teller and active in the feminist movement.'"

Many people rank the second event as more likely. Explain why this violates basic concepts of probability. *Source: New Yorker*.

46. You are given $P(A \cup B) = 0.7$ and $P(A \cup B') = 0.9$. Determine $P(A)$. Choose one of the following. *Source: Society of Actuaries.*

(a) 0.2   (b) 0.3   (c) 0.4   (d) 0.6   (e) 0.8

APPLICATIONS

Business and Economics

47. Defective Merchandise Suppose that 8% of a certain batch of calculators have a defective case, and that 11% have defective batteries. Also, 3% have both a defective case and defective batteries. A calculator is selected from the batch at random. Find the probability that the calculator has a good case and good batteries.

48. Profit The probability that a company will make a profit this year is 0.74.

(a) Find the probability that the company will not make a profit this year.

(b) Find the odds against the company making a profit.

49. Mobile Web Usage A survey asking mobile phone users how long they would wait for a page to load found the following results. *Source: Kissmetrics.*

Time (Seconds)	Percentage
< 1	3%
1–5	16%
6–10	30%
11–15	16%
16–20	15%
> 20	20%

Find the probabilities that a person would wait the following amounts.

(a) No more than 10 seconds

(b) At least 6 seconds

(c) Between 6 and 20 seconds

(d) Between 1 and 15 seconds

50. Employment The table shows the projected probabilities of a worker employed by different occupational groups in 2018. *Source: U.S. Department of Labor.*

Occupation	Probability
Management and business	0.1047
Professional	0.2182
Service	0.2024
Sales	0.1015
Office and administrative support	0.1560
Farming, fishing, forestry	0.0061
Construction	0.0531
Production	0.0585
Other	0.0995

If a worker in 2018 is selected at random, find the following.

(a) The probability that the worker is in sales or service

(b) The probability that the worker is not in construction

(c) The odds in favor of the worker being in production

51. Labor Force The following table gives the 2018 projected civilian labor force probability distribution by age and gender. *Source: U.S. Department of Labor.*

Age	Male	Female	Total
16–24	0.066	0.061	0.127
25–54	0.343	0.291	0.634
55 and over	0.122	0.117	0.239
Total	0.531	0.469	1.000

Find the probability that a randomly selected worker is the following.

(a) Female and 16 to 24 years old

(b) 16 to 54 years old

(c) Male or 25 to 54 years old

(d) Female or 16 to 24 years old

Life Sciences

52. Body Types A study on body types gave the following results: 45% were short; 25% were short and overweight; and 24% were not short and not overweight. Find the probabilities that a person is the following.

(a) Overweight

(b) Short, but not overweight

(c) Overweight, but not short

53. Color Blindness Color blindness is an inherited characteristic that is more common in males than in females. If M represents male and C represents red-green color blindness, we use the relative frequencies of the incidences of males and red-green color blindness as probabilities to get

$P(C) = 0.039, P(M \cap C) = 0.035, P(M \cup C) = 0.491.$

Find the following probabilities. *Source: Parsons' Diseases of the Eye.*

(a) $P(C')$

(b) $P(M)$

(c) $P(M')$

(d) $P(M' \cap C')$

(e) $P(C \cap M')$

(f) $P(C \cup M')$

54. Genetics Gregor Mendel, an Austrian monk, was the first to use probability in the study of genetics. In an effort to understand the mechanism of character transmittal from one generation to the next in plants, he counted the number of occurrences of various characteristics. Mendel found that the flower color in certain pea plants obeyed this scheme:

Pure red crossed with pure white produces red.

From its parents, the red offspring received genes for both red (R) and white (W), but in this case red is *dominant* and white *recessive*, so the offspring exhibits the color red. However, the offspring still carries both genes, and when two such offspring are crossed, several things can happen in the third generation.

The table below, which is called a *Punnett square*, shows the equally likely outcomes.

		Second Parent	
		R	W
First Parent	R	RR	RW
	W	WR	WW

Use the fact that red is dominant over white to find the following. Assume that there are an equal number of red and white genes in the population.

(a) P(a flower is red)

(b) P(a flower is white)

55. Genetics Mendel found no dominance in snapdragons, with one red gene and one white gene producing pink-flowered offspring. These second-generation pinks, however, still carry one red and one white gene, and when they are crossed, the next generation still yields the Punnett square from Exercise 54. Find each probability.

(a) P(red)   **(b)** P(pink)   **(c)** P(white)

(Mendel verified these probability ratios experimentally and did the same for many characteristics other than flower color. His work, published in 1866, was not recognized until 1890.)

56. Genetics In most animals and plants, it is very unusual for the number of main parts of the organism (such as arms, legs, toes, or flower petals) to vary from generation to generation. Some species, however, have *meristic variability,* in which the number of certain body parts varies from generation to generation. One researcher studied the front feet of certain guinea pigs and produced the following probabilities.

$$P(\text{only four toes, all perfect}) = 0.77$$
$$P(\text{one imperfect toe and four good ones}) = 0.13$$
$$P(\text{exactly five good toes}) = 0.10$$

Find the probability of each event. *Source: Genetics.*

(a) No more than four good toes

(b) Five toes, whether perfect or not

57. Doctor Visit The probability that a visit to a primary care physician's (PCP) office results in neither lab work nor referral to a specialist is 35%. Of those coming to a PCP's office, 30% are referred to specialists and 40% require lab work. Determine the probability that a visit to a PCP's office results in both lab work and referral to a specialist. Choose one of the following. (*Hint:* Use the union rule for probability.) *Source: Society of Actuaries.*

(a) 0.05   **(b)** 0.12   **(c)** 0.18

(d) 0.25   **(e)** 0.35

58. Shoulder Injuries Among a large group of patients recovering from shoulder injuries, it is found that 22% visit both a physical therapist and a chiropractor, whereas 12% visit neither of these. The probability that a patient visits a chiropractor exceeds by 0.14 the probability that a patient visits a physical therapist. Determine the probability that a randomly chosen member of this group visits a physical therapist. Choose one of the following. (*Hint:* Use the union rule for probability, and let $x = P$(patient visits a physical therapist).) *Source: Society of Actuaries.*

(a) 0.26   (b) 0.38   (c) 0.40

(d) 0.48   (e) 0.62

59. **Health Plan** An insurer offers a health plan to the employees of a large company. As part of this plan, the individual employees may choose exactly two of the supplementary coverages A, B, and C, or they may choose no supplementary coverage. The proportions of the company's employees that choose coverages A, B, and C are 1/4, 1/3, and 5/12, respectively. Determine the probability that a randomly chosen employee will choose no supplementary coverage. Choose one of the following. (*Hint:* Draw a Venn diagram with three sets, and let $x = P(A \cap B)$. Use the fact that 4 of the 8 regions in the Venn diagram have a probability of 0.) *Source: Society of Actuaries.*

(a) 0   (b) 47/144   (c) 1/2

(d) 97/144   (e) 7/9

Social Sciences

60. **Presidential Candidates** In 2002, *The New York Times* columnist William Safire gave the following odds against various prominent Democrats receiving their party's presidential nomination in 2004.

> Al Gore: 2 to 1
> Tom Daschle: 4 to 1
> John Kerry: 4 to 1
> Chris Dodd: 4 to 1
> Joe Lieberman: 5 to 1
> Joe Biden: 5 to 1
> Pat Leahy: 6 to 1
> Russell Feingold: 8 to 1
> John Edwards: 9 to 1
> Dick Gephardt: 15 to 1

John Allen Paulos observed that there is something wrong with those odds. Translate these odds into probabilities of winning the nomination, and then explain why these are not possible. *Sources: The New York Times and ABC News.*

61. **Earnings** The following data were gathered for 130 adult U.S. workers: 55 were women; 3 women earned more than $40,000; and 62 men earned $40,000 or less. Find the probability that an individual is

(a) a woman earning $40,000 or less;

(b) a man earning more than $40,000;

(c) a man or is earning more than $40,000;

(d) a woman or is earning $40,000 or less.

62. **Expenditures for Music** A survey of 100 people about their music expenditures gave the following information: 38 bought rock music; 20 were teenagers who bought rock music; and 26 were teenagers. Find the probabilities that a person is

(a) a teenager who buys nonrock music;

(b) someone who buys rock music or is a teenager;

(c) not a teenager;

(d) not a teenager, but a buyer of rock music.

63. **Refugees** In a refugee camp in southern Mexico, it was found that 90% of the refugees came to escape political oppression, 80% came to escape abject poverty, and 70% came to escape both. What is the probability that a refugee in the camp was not poor nor seeking political asylum?

64. **Community Activities** At the first meeting of a committee to plan a local Lunar New Year celebration, the persons attending are 3 Chinese men, 4 Chinese women, 3 Vietnamese women, 2 Vietnamese men, 4 Korean women, and 2 Korean men. A chairperson is selected at random. Find the probabilities that the chairperson is the following.

(a) Chinese

(b) Korean or a woman

(c) A man or Vietnamese

(d) Chinese or Vietnamese

(e) Korean and a woman

65. **Elections** If the odds that a given candidate will win an election are 3 to 2, what is the probability that the candidate will lose?

66. **Military** There were 205,586 female military personnel in March 2013 in various ranks and military branches, as listed in the table. *Source: Department of Defense.*

	Army (A)	Air Force (B)	Navy (C)	Marines (D)
Officers (O)	16,007	12,663	8893	1403
Enlisted (E)	55,016	48,924	47,195	12,907
Cadets & Midshipmen (M)	738	872	968	0

(a) Convert the numbers in the table to probabilities.

(b) Find the probability that a randomly selected woman is in the Army.

(c) Find the probability that a randomly selected woman is an officer in the Navy or Marine Corps.

(d) $P(A \cup B)$ (e) $P(E \cup (C \cup D))$

67. **Perceptions of Threat** Research has been carried out to measure the amount of intolerance that citizens of Russia have for left-wing Communists and right-wing Fascists, as indicated in the table below. Note that the numbers are given as percents and each row sums to 100 (except for rounding). *Source: Political Research Quarterly.*

	Russia				
	None at All	Don't Know	Not Very Much	Somewhat	Extremely
Left-Wing Communists	47.8	6.7	31.0	10.5	4.1
Right-Wing Fascists	3.0	3.2	7.1	27.1	59.5

(a) Find the probability that a randomly chosen citizen of Russia would be somewhat or extremely intolerant of right-wing Fascists.

(b) Find the probability that a randomly chosen citizen of Russia would be completely tolerant of left-wing Communists.

(c) Compare your answers to parts (a) and (b) and provide possible reasons for these numbers.

68. Perceptions of Threat Research has been carried out to measure the amount of intolerance that U.S. citizens have for left-wing Communists and right-wing Fascists, as indicated in the table. Note that the numbers are given as percents and each row sums to 100 (except for rounding). *Source: Political Research Quarterly.*

	United States				
	None at All	Don't Know	Not Very Much	Somewhat	Extremely
Left-Wing Communists	13.0	2.7	33.0	34.2	17.1
Right-Wing Fascists	10.1	3.3	20.7	43.1	22.9

(a) Find the probability that a randomly chosen U.S. citizen would have at least some intolerance of right-wing Fascists.

(b) Find the probability that a randomly chosen U.S. citizen would have at least some intolerance of left-wing Communists.

(c) Compare your answers to parts (a) and (b) and provide possible reasons for these numbers.

(d) Compare these answers to the answers to Exercise 67.

General Interest

69. Olympics In recent winter Olympics, each part of the women's figure skating program has 12 judges, but the scores of only 9 of the judges are randomly selected for the final results. As we will see in the next chapter, there are 220 possible ways for the 9 judges whose scores are counted to be selected. *The New York Times* examined those 220 possibilities for the short program in the 2006 Olympics, based on the published scores of the judges, and listed what the results would have been for each, as shown below. *Source: The New York Times.*

(a) The winner of the short program was Sasha Cohen. For a random combination of 9 judges, what is the probability of that outcome?

(b) The second place finisher in the short program was Irina Slutskaya. For a random combination of 9 judges, what is the probability of that outcome?

(c) The third place finisher in the short program was Shizuka Arakawa. For a random combination of 9 judges, what is the probability of that outcome? Do not include outcomes that include a tie.

Outcome	1. Slutskaya 2. Cohen 3. Arakawa	1. Slutskaya 2. Arakawa 3. Cohen	1. Slutskaya 2, 3. Arakawa and Cohen tied	1. Cohen 2. Slutskaya 3. Arakawa	1. Cohen 2. Arakawa 3. Slutskaya
Number of Possible Judging Combinations	92	33	3	67	25

70. Book of Odds The following table gives the probabilities that a particular event will occur. Convert each probability to the odds in favor of the event. *Source: The Book of Odds.*

Event	Probability for the Event
An NFL pass will be intercepted.	0.03
A U.S. president owned a dog during his term in office.	0.65
A woman owns a pair of high heels.	0.61
An adult smokes.	0.21
A flight is canceled.	0.02

71. Book of Odds The following table gives the odds that a particular event will occur. Convert each odd to the probability that the event will occur. *Source: The Book of Odds.*

Event	Odds for the Event
A Powerball entry will win the jackpot.	1 to 195,199,999
An adult will be struck by lightning during a year.	1 to 835,499
An adult will file for personal bankruptcy during a year.	1 to 157.6
A person collects stamps.	1 to 59.32

YOUR TURN ANSWERS

1. $16/52 = 4/13$

2. $10/36 = 5/18$

3. $33/36 = 11/12$

4. 3 to 7 or 3:7

5. 3/20

6. 3/10

7.5 Conditional Probability; Independent Events

APPLY IT What is the probability that a broker who uses research picks stocks that go up?

The manager for a brokerage firm has noticed that some of the firm's stockbrokers have selected stocks based on the firm's research, while other brokers tend to follow their own instincts. To see whether the research department performs better than the brokers' instincts, the manager surveyed 100 brokers, with results as shown in the following table.

Results of Stockbroker Survey			
	Picked Stocks That Went Up (A)	Didn't Pick Stocks That Went Up (A')	Totals
Used Research (B)	30	15	45
Didn't Use Research (B')	30	25	55
Totals	60	40	100

Letting A represent the event "picked stocks that went up," and letting B represent the event "used research," we can find the following probabilities.

$$P(A) = \frac{60}{100} = 0.6 \qquad P(A') = \frac{40}{100} = 0.4$$

$$P(B) = \frac{45}{100} = 0.45 \qquad P(B') = \frac{55}{100} = 0.55$$

APPLY IT   To answer the question asked at the beginning of this section, suppose we want to find the probability that a broker using research will pick stocks that go up. From the table, of the 45 brokers who use research, 30 picked stocks that went up, with

$$P(\text{broker who uses research picks stocks that go up}) = \frac{30}{45} \approx 0.6667.$$

This is a different number than the probability that a broker picks stocks that go up, 0.6, since we have additional information (the broker uses research) that has *reduced the sample space*. In other words, we found the probability that a broker picks stocks that go up, A, given the additional information that the broker uses research, B. This is called the *conditional probability* of event A, given that event B has occurred. It is written $P(A|B)$ and read as "the probability of A given B." In this example,

$$P(A|B) = \frac{30}{45}.$$

To generalize this result, assume that E and F are two events for a particular experiment and that all events in the sample space S are equally likely. We want to find $P(E|F)$, the probability that E occurs given F has occurred. Since we assume that F has occurred, reduce the sample space to F: Look only at the elements inside F. See Figure 20. Of those $n(F)$ elements, there are $n(E \cap F)$ elements where E also occurs. This makes

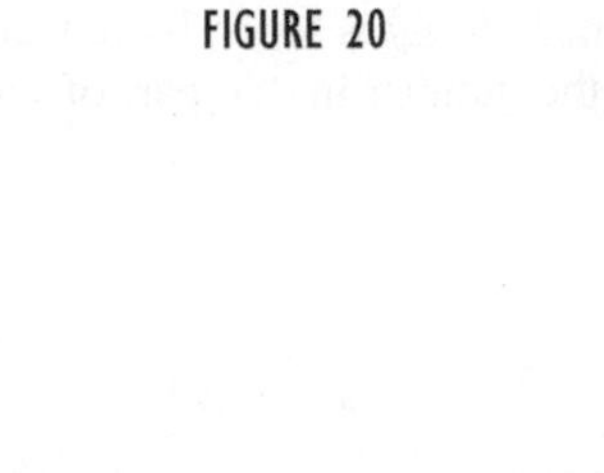

$$P(E|F) = \frac{n(E \cap F)}{n(F)}.$$

This equation can also be written as the quotient of two probabilities. Divide numerator and denominator by $n(S)$ to get

$$P(E|F) = \frac{n(E \cap F)/n(S)}{n(F)/n(S)} = \frac{P(E \cap F)}{P(F)}.$$

Event F has a total of $n(F)$ elements.

FIGURE 20

This last result motivates the definition of conditional probability.

Conditional Probability

The **conditional probability** of event E given event F, written $P(E|F)$, is

$$P(E|F) = \frac{P(E \cap F)}{P(F)}, \quad \text{where } P(F) \neq 0.$$

Although the definition of conditional probability was motivated by an example with equally likely outcomes, it is valid in all cases. However, for *equally likely outcomes*, conditional probability can be found by directly applying the definition, or by first reducing the sample space to event F, and then finding the number of outcomes in F that are also in event E. Thus,

$$P(E|F) = \frac{n(E \cap F)}{n(F)}.$$

In the preceding example, the conditional probability could have also been found using the definition of conditional probability:

$$P(A|B) = \frac{P(A \cap B)}{P(B)} = \frac{30/100}{45/100} = \frac{30}{45} = \frac{2}{3}.$$

EXAMPLE 1   Stocks

Use the information given in the chart at the beginning of this section to find the following probabilities.

(a) $P(B|A)$

SOLUTION   This represents the probability that the broker used research, given that the broker picked stocks that went up. Reduce the sample space to A. Then find $n(A \cap B)$ and $n(A)$.

$$P(B|A) = \frac{P(B \cap A)}{P(A)} = \frac{n(A \cap B)}{n(A)} = \frac{30}{60} = \frac{1}{2}$$

If a broker picked stocks that went up, then the probability is 1/2 that the broker used research.

(b) $P(A'|B)$

SOLUTION   In words, this is the probability that a broker picks stocks that do not go up, even though he used research.

$$P(A'|B) = \frac{n(A' \cap B)}{n(B)} = \frac{15}{45} = \frac{1}{3}$$

(c) $P(B'|A')$

SOLUTION   Here, we want the probability that a broker who picked stocks that did not go up did not use research.

$$P(B'|A') = \frac{n(B' \cap A')}{n(A')} = \frac{25}{40} = \frac{5}{8} \quad \text{TRY YOUR TURN 1}$$

Venn diagrams are useful for illustrating problems in conditional probability. A Venn diagram for Example 1, in which the probabilities are used to indicate the number in the set defined by each region, is shown in Figure 21. In the diagram, $P(B|A)$ is found by reducing the sample space to just set A. Then $P(B|A)$ is the ratio of the number in that part of set B that is also in A to the number in set A, or $0.3/0.6 = 0.5$.

YOUR TURN 1   In Example 1, find $P(A|B')$.

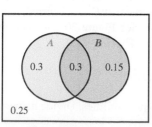

$$P(A) = 0.3 + 0.3 = 0.6$$

FIGURE 21

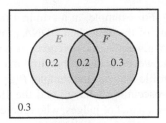

FIGURE 22

YOUR TURN 2 Given $P(E) = 0.56$, $P(F) = 0.64$, and $P(E \cup F) = 0.80$, find $P(E \mid F)$.

EXAMPLE 2   **Conditional Probabilities**

Given $P(E) = 0.4$, $P(F) = 0.5$, and $P(E \cup F) = 0.7$, find $P(E|F)$.

SOLUTION   Find $P(E \cap F)$ first. By the union rule,

$$P(E \cup F) = P(E) + P(F) - P(E \cap F)$$
$$0.7 = 0.4 + 0.5 - P(E \cap F)$$
$$P(E \cap F) = 0.2.$$

$P(E|F)$ is the ratio of the probability of that part of E that is in F to the probability of F, or

$$P(E|F) = \frac{P(E \cap F)}{P(F)} = \frac{0.2}{0.5} = \frac{2}{5}. \quad \text{TRY YOUR TURN 2} \ \blacksquare$$

The Venn diagram in Figure 22 illustrates Example 2.

EXAMPLE 3   **Tossing Coins**

Two fair coins were tossed, and it is known that at least one was a head. Find the probability that both were heads.

SOLUTION   At first glance, the answer may appear to be 1/2, but this is not the case. The sample space has four equally likely outcomes, $S = \{hh, ht, th, tt\}$. Because of the condition that at least one coin was a head, the sample space is reduced to $\{hh, ht, th\}$. Since only one outcome in this reduced sample space is 2 heads,

$$P(2 \text{ heads} \mid \text{at least 1 head}) = \frac{1}{3}.$$

Alternatively, we could use the conditional probability definition. Define two events:

$$E_1 = \text{at least 1 head} = \{hh, ht, th\}$$

and

$$E_2 = 2 \text{ heads} = \{hh\}.$$

YOUR TURN 3 In Example 3, find the probability of exactly one head, given that there is at least one tail.

Since there are four equally likely outcomes, $P(E_1) = 3/4$ and $P(E_1 \cap E_2) = 1/4$. Therefore,

$$P(E_2|E_1) = \frac{P(E_2 \cap E_1)}{P(E_1)} = \frac{1/4}{3/4} = \frac{1}{3}. \quad \text{TRY YOUR TURN 3} \ \blacksquare$$

EXAMPLE 4   **Playing Cards**

Two cards are drawn from a standard deck, one after another without replacement. Find the probability that the second card is red, given that the first card is red.

SOLUTION   According to the conditional probability formula,

$$P(\text{second card is red} \mid \text{first card is red})$$
$$= \frac{P(\text{second card is red and the first card is red})}{P(\text{first card is red})}.$$

We will soon see how to compute probabilities such as the one in the numerator. But there is a much simpler way to calculate this conditional probability. We only need to observe that with one red card gone, there are 51 cards left, 25 of which are red, so

$$P(\text{second card is red}|\text{first card is red}) = \frac{25}{51}. \quad \blacksquare$$

It is important not to confuse $P(A \mid B)$ with $P(B \mid A)$. For example, in a criminal trial, a prosecutor may point out to the jury that the probability of the defendant's DNA profile matching that of a sample taken at the scene of the crime, given that the defendant is innocent, $P(D \mid I)$, is very small. What the jury must decide, however, is the probability that the defendant is innocent, given that the defendant's DNA profile matches the sample, $P(I \mid D)$. Confusing the two is an error sometimes called "the prosecutor's fallacy," and the 1990 conviction of a rape suspect in England was overturned by a panel of judges, who ordered a retrial, because the fallacy made the original trial unfair. *Source: New Scientist.*

In the next section, we will see how to compute $P(A \mid B)$ when we know $P(B \mid A)$.

Product Rule
If $P(E) \neq 0$ and $P(F) \neq 0$, then the definition of conditional probability shows that

$$P(E \mid F) = \frac{P(E \cap F)}{P(F)} \quad \text{and} \quad P(F \mid E) = \frac{P(F \cap E)}{P(E)}.$$

Using the fact that $P(E \cap F) = P(F \cap E)$, and solving each of these equations for $P(E \cap F)$, we obtain the following rule.

Product Rule of Probability
If E and F are events, then $P(E \cap F)$ may be found by either of these formulas.

$$P(E \cap F) = P(F) \cdot P(E \mid F) \quad \text{or} \quad P(E \cap F) = P(E) \cdot P(F \mid E)$$

The product rule gives a method for finding the probability that events E and F both occur, as illustrated by the next few examples.

EXAMPLE 5 Business Majors

In a class with 2/5 women and 3/5 men, 25% of the women are business majors. Find the probability that a student chosen from the class at random is a female business major.

SOLUTION Let B and W represent the events "business major" and "woman," respectively. We want to find $P(B \cap W)$. By the product rule,

$$P(B \cap W) = P(W) \cdot P(B \mid W).$$

Using the given information, $P(W) = 2/5 = 0.4$ and $P(B \mid W) = 0.25$. Thus,

$$P(B \cap W) = 0.4(0.25) = 0.10. \quad \textbf{TRY YOUR TURN 4}$$

YOUR TURN 4 At a local college, 4/5 of the students live on campus. Of those who live on campus, 25% have cars on campus. Find the probability that a student lives on campus and has a car.

The next examples show how a tree diagram is used with the product rule to find the probability of a sequence of events.

EXAMPLE 6 Advertising

A company needs to hire a new director of advertising. It has decided to try to hire either person A or B, who are assistant advertising directors for its major competitor. To decide between A and B, the company does research on the campaigns managed by either A or B (no campaign is managed by both) and finds that A is in charge of twice as many advertising campaigns as B. Also, A's campaigns have satisfactory results 3 out of 4 times, while B's campaigns have satisfactory results only 2 out of 5 times. Suppose one of the competitor's advertising campaigns (managed by A or B) is selected randomly.

We can represent this situation using a tree diagram as follows. Let A denote the event "Person A manages the job" and B the event "person B manages the job." Notice that A and

B are complementary events. Since A does twice as many jobs as B, we have $P(A) = 2/3$ and $P(B) = 1/3$, as noted on the first-stage branches of the tree in Figure 23.

Let S be the event "satisfactory results" and U the event "unsatisfactory results." When A manages the job, the probability of satisfactory results is 3/4 and of unsatisfactory results 1/4 as noted on the second-stage branches. Similarly, the probabilities when B manages the job are noted on the remaining second-stage branches. The composite branches labeled 1 to 4 represent the four mutually exclusive possibilities for the managing and outcome of the selected campaign.

(a) Find the probability that A is in charge of the selected campaign and that it produces satisfactory results.

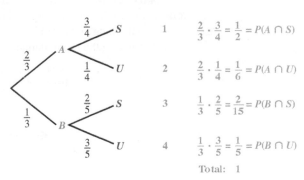

Executive **Campaign** Branch Probability

Branch 1: $\frac{2}{3} \cdot \frac{3}{4} = \frac{1}{2} = P(A \cap S)$

Branch 2: $\frac{2}{3} \cdot \frac{1}{4} = \frac{1}{6} = P(A \cap U)$

Branch 3: $\frac{1}{3} \cdot \frac{2}{5} = \frac{2}{15} = P(B \cap S)$

Branch 4: $\frac{1}{3} \cdot \frac{3}{5} = \frac{1}{5} = P(B \cap U)$

Total: 1

FIGURE 23

SOLUTION We are asked to find $P(A \cap S)$. We know that when A does the job, the probability of success is 3/4, that is, $P(S|A) = 3/4$. Hence, by the product rule,

$$P(A \cap S) = P(A) \cdot P(S|A) = \frac{2}{3} \cdot \frac{3}{4} = \frac{1}{2}.$$

The event $A \cap S$ is represented by branch 1 of the tree, and, as we have just seen, its probability is the product of the probabilities of the pieces that make up that branch.

(b) Find the probability that B runs the campaign and that it produces satisfactory results.

SOLUTION We must find $P(B \cap S)$. The event is represented by branch 3 of the tree, and, as before, its probability is the product of the probabilities of the pieces of that branch:

$$P(B \cap S) = P(B) \cdot P(S|B) = \frac{1}{3} \cdot \frac{2}{5} = \frac{2}{15}.$$

(c) What is the probability that the selected campaign is satisfactory?

SOLUTION The event S is the union of the mutually exclusive events $A \cap S$ and $B \cap S$, which are represented by branches 1 and 3 of the diagram. By the union rule,

$$P(S) = P(A \cap S) + P(B \cap S) = \frac{1}{2} + \frac{2}{15} = \frac{19}{30}.$$

Thus, the probability of an event that appears on several branches is the sum of the probabilities of each of these branches.

(d) What is the probability that the selected campaign is unsatisfactory?

SOLUTION $P(U)$ can be read from branches 2 and 4 of the tree.

$$P(U) = \frac{1}{6} + \frac{1}{5} = \frac{11}{30}$$

Alternatively, since U is the complement of S,

$$P(U) = 1 - P(S) = 1 - \frac{19}{30} = \frac{11}{30}. \quad \text{TRY YOUR TURN 5} \ \blacksquare$$

YOUR TURN 5 In Example 6, what is the probability that A is in charge of the selected campaign and that it produces unsatisfactory results?

EXAMPLE 7 **Environmental Inspections**

The Environmental Protection Agency is considering inspecting 6 plants for environmental compliance: 3 in Chicago, 2 in Los Angeles, and 1 in New York. Due to a lack of inspectors, they decide to inspect two plants selected at random, one this month and one next month, with each plant equally likely to be selected, but no plant selected twice. What is the probability that 1 Chicago plant and 1 Los Angeles plant are selected?

SOLUTION A tree diagram showing the various possible outcomes is given in Figure 24. In this diagram, the events of inspecting a plant in Chicago, Los Angeles, and New York are represented by C, LA, and NY, respectively. For the first inspection, $P(\text{C first}) = 3/6 = 1/2$ because 3 of the 6 plants are in Chicago, and all plants are equally likely to be selected. Likewise, $P(\text{LA first}) = 1/3$ and $P(\text{NY first}) = 1/6$.

For the second inspection, we first note that one plant has been inspected and, therefore, removed from the list, leaving 5 plants. For example, $P(\text{LA second} \mid \text{C first}) = 2/5$, since 2 of the 5 remaining plants are in Los Angeles. The remaining second inspection probabilities are calculated in the same manner.

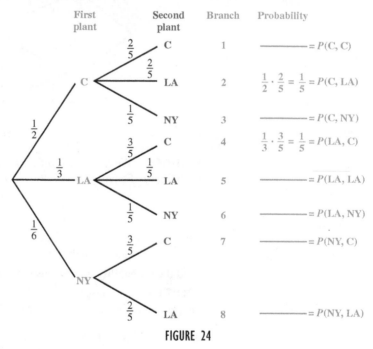

FIGURE 24

We want to find the probability of selecting exactly 1 Chicago plant and 1 Los Angeles plant. This event can occur in two ways: inspecting Chicago this month and Los Angeles next month (branch 2 of the tree diagram), or inspecting Los Angeles this month and Chicago next month (branch 4). For branch 2,

$$P(\text{C first}) \cdot P(\text{LA second} \mid \text{C first}) = \frac{1}{2} \cdot \frac{2}{5} = \frac{1}{5}.$$

For branch 4, where Los Angeles is inspected first,

$$P(\text{LA first}) \cdot P(\text{C second} \mid \text{LA first}) = \frac{1}{3} \cdot \frac{3}{5} = \frac{1}{5}.$$

Since the two events are mutually exclusive, the final probability is the sum of these two probabilities.

$$
\begin{aligned}
P(1\ \text{C},\ 1\ \text{LA}) &= P(\text{C first}) \cdot P(\text{LA second} \mid \text{C first}) \\
&\quad + P(\text{LA first}) \cdot P(\text{C second} \mid \text{LA first}) \\
&= \frac{2}{5}
\end{aligned}
$$

YOUR TURN 6 In Example 7, what is the probability that 1 New York plant and 1 Chicago plant are selected?

TRY YOUR TURN 6

FOR REVIEW

You may wish to refer to the picture of a deck of cards shown in Figure 17 (Section 7.3) and the description accompanying it.

The product rule is often used with *stochastic processes*, which are mathematical models that evolve over time in a probabilistic manner. For example, selecting factories at random for inspection is such a process, in which the probabilities change with each successive selection.

EXAMPLE 8   Playing Cards

Two cards are drawn from a standard deck, one after another without replacement.

(a) Find the probability that the first card is a heart and the second card is red.

SOLUTION   Start with the tree diagram in Figure 25. On the first draw, since there are 13 hearts among the 52 cards, the probability of drawing a heart is $13/52 = 1/4$. On the second draw, since a (red) heart has been drawn already, there are 25 red cards in the remaining 51 cards. Thus, the probability of drawing a red card on the second draw, given that the first is a heart, is $25/51$. By the product rule of probability,

$$P(\text{heart first and red second})$$
$$= P(\text{heart first}) \cdot P(\text{red second} \mid \text{heart first})$$
$$= \frac{1}{4} \cdot \frac{25}{51} = \frac{25}{204} \approx 0.123.$$

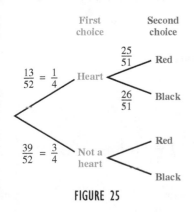

FIGURE 25

(b) Find the probability that the second card is red.

SOLUTION   To solve this, we need to fill out the bottom branch of the tree diagram in Figure 25. Unfortunately, if the first card is not a heart, it is not clear how to find the probability that the second card is red, because it depends upon whether the first card is red or black. One way to solve this problem would be to divide the bottom branch into two separate branches: diamond and black card (club or spade).

There is a simpler way, however, since we don't care whether or not the first card is a heart, as we did in part (a). Instead, we'll consider whether the first card is red or black and then do the same for the second card. The result, with the corresponding probabilities, is in Figure 26. The probability that the second card is red is found by multiplying the probabilities along the two branches and adding.

$$P(\text{red second}) = \frac{1}{2} \cdot \frac{25}{51} + \frac{1}{2} \cdot \frac{26}{51}$$
$$= \frac{1}{2}$$

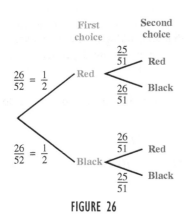

FIGURE 26

The probability is $1/2$, exactly the same as the probability that any card is red. If we know nothing about the first card, there is no reason for the probability of the second card to be anything other than $1/2$.

Independent Events   Suppose, in Example 8(a), that we draw the two cards *with* replacement rather than without replacement (that is, we put the first card back before drawing the second card). If the first card is a heart, then the probability of drawing a red card on the second draw is $26/52$, rather than $25/51$, because there are still 52 cards in the deck, 26 of them red. In this case, $P(\text{red second} \mid \text{heart first})$ is the same as $P(\text{red second})$. The value of the second card is not affected by the value of the first card. We say that the event that the second card is red is *independent* of the event that the first card is a heart, since the knowledge of the first card does not influence what happens to the second card. On the other hand, when we draw without replacement, the events that the first card is a heart and that the second card is red are *dependent* events. The fact that the first card is a heart means there is one less red card in the deck, influencing the probability that the second card is red.

As another example, consider tossing a fair coin twice. If the first toss shows heads, the probability that the next toss is heads is still $1/2$. Coin tosses are independent events, since the outcome of one toss does not influence the outcome of the next toss. Similarly, rolls of a fair die are independent events.

On the other hand, the events "the milk is old" and "the milk is sour" are dependent events; if the milk is old, there is an increased chance that it is sour. Also, in the example at the beginning of this section, the events A (broker picked stocks that went up) and B (broker used research) are dependent events, because information about the use of research affected the probability of picking stocks that go up. That is, $P(A|B)$ is different from $P(A)$.

If events E and F are independent, then the knowledge that E has occurred gives no (probability) information about the occurrence or nonoccurrence of event F. That is, $P(F)$ is exactly the same as $P(F|E)$, or

$$P(F|E) = P(F).$$

This, in fact, is the formal definition of independent events.

Independent Events

Events E and F are **independent events** if

$$P(F|E) = P(F) \quad \text{or} \quad P(E|F) = P(E).$$

If the events are not independent, they are **dependent events**.

Notice that the mathematical definition of independence does not always correspond to the intuitive definition of independence. For example, you may think that whether you like a movie and your friend likes a movie are independent, since it is possible that you like the movie and your friend doesn't, or vice versa. In fact, if your taste in movies is similar to your friend's, the fact that you like the movie might increase the probability that your friend likes the movie. If your tastes are very different, it is possible that your liking the movie makes it less likely that your friend likes it. In either of these cases, the events are dependent. Only if your liking the movie tells nothing about whether your friend will like it are the events independent.

When E and F are independent events, then $P(F|E) = P(F)$ and the product rule becomes

$$P(E \cap F) = P(E) \cdot P(F|E) = P(E) \cdot P(F).$$

Conversely, if this equation holds, then it follows that $P(F) = P(F|E)$. Consequently, we have this useful fact:

Product Rule for Independent Events

Events E and F are independent events if and only if

$$P(E \cap F) = P(E) \cdot P(F).$$

EXAMPLE 9 Calculator

A calculator requires a keystroke assembly and a logic circuit. Assume that 99% of the keystroke assemblies are satisfactory and 97% of the logic circuits are satisfactory. Find the probability that a finished calculator will be satisfactory.

SOLUTION If the failure of a keystroke assembly and the failure of a logic circuit are independent events, then

$P(\text{satisfactory calculator})$

$= P(\text{satisfactory keystroke assembly}) \cdot P(\text{satisfactory logic circuit})$

$= (0.99)(0.97) \approx 0.96.$

YOUR TURN 7 The probability that you roll a five on a single die is 1/6. Find the probability you roll two five's in a row.

(The probability of a defective calculator is $1 - 0.96 = 0.04$.)   TRY YOUR TURN 7

CAUTION	It is common for students to confuse the ideas of *mutually exclusive* events and *independent* events. Events E and F are mutually exclusive if $E \cap F = \varnothing$. For example, if a family has exactly one child, the only possible outcomes are $B = \{\text{boy}\}$ and $G = \{\text{girl}\}$. These two events are mutually exclusive. The events are *not* independent, however, since $P(G|B) = 0$ (if a family with only one child has a boy, the probability it has a girl is then 0). Since $P(G|B) \neq P(G)$, the events are not independent.

Of all the families with exactly two children, the events $G_1 = \{\text{first child is a girl}\}$ and $G_2 = \{\text{second child is a girl}\}$ are independent, since $P(G_2|G_1)$ equals $P(G_2)$. However, G_1 and G_2 are not mutually exclusive, since $G_1 \cap G_2 = \{\text{both children are girls}\} \neq \varnothing$.

To show that two events E and F are independent, show that $P(F|E) = P(F)$ or that $P(E|F) = P(E)$ or that $P(E \cap F) = P(E) \cdot P(F)$. Another way is to observe that knowledge of one outcome does not influence the probability of the other outcome, as we did for coin tosses.

NOTE   In some cases, it may not be apparent from the physical description of the problem whether two events are independent or not. For example, it is not obvious whether the event that a baseball player gets a hit tomorrow is independent of the event that he got a hit today. In such cases, it is necessary to calculate whether $P(F|E) = P(F)$ or, equivalently, whether $P(E \cap F) = P(E) \cdot P(F)$.

EXAMPLE 10   Snow in Manhattan

On a typical January day in Manhattan the probability of snow is 0.10, the probability of a traffic jam is 0.80, and the probability of snow or a traffic jam (or both) is 0.82. Are the event "it snows" and the event "a traffic jam occurs" independent?

YOUR TURN 8 The probability that you do your math homework is 0.8, the probability that you do your history assignment is 0.7, and the probability of you doing your math homework or your history assignment is 0.9. Are the events "do your math homework" and "do your history assignment" independent?

SOLUTION   Let S represent the event "it snows" and T represent the event "a traffic jam occurs." We must determine whether

$$P(T|S) = P(T) \quad \text{or} \quad P(S|T) = P(S).$$

We know $P(S) = 0.10$, $P(T) = 0.8$, and $P(S \cup T) = 0.82$. We can use the union rule (or a Venn diagram) to find $P(S \cap T) = 0.08$, $P(T|S) = 0.8$, and $P(S|T) = 0.1$. Since

$$P(T|S) = P(T) = 0.8 \quad \text{and} \quad P(S|T) = P(S) = 0.1,$$

the events "it snows" and "a traffic jam occurs" are independent.   **TRY YOUR TURN 8**

Although we showed $P(T|S) = P(T)$ and $P(S|T) = P(S)$ in Example 10, only one of these results is needed to establish independence. It is also important to note that independence of events does not necessarily follow intuition; it is established from the mathematical definition of independence.

7.5 WARM-UP EXERCISES

Two dice are rolled. Find the probabilities of the following.

W1. The first die is 5 or the sum is 9.   *(Sec. 7.4)*

W2. The second die is 6 or the sum is 11.   *(Sec. 7.4)*

7.5 EXERCISES

If a single fair die is rolled, find the probabilities of the following results.

1. A 2, given that the number rolled was odd

2. A 4, given that the number rolled was even

3. An even number, given that the number rolled was 6

4. An odd number, given that the number rolled was 6

If two fair dice are rolled, find the probabilities of the following results.

5. A sum of 8, given that the sum is greater than 7

6. A sum of 6, given that the roll was a "double" (two identical numbers)

7. A double, given that the sum was 9

8. A double, given that the sum was 8

If two cards are drawn without replacement from an ordinary deck, find the probabilities of the following results.

9. The second is a heart, given that the first is a heart.

10. The second is black, given that the first is a spade.

11. The second is a face card, given that the first is a jack.

12. The second is an ace, given that the first is not an ace.

13. A jack and a 10 are drawn.

14. An ace and a 4 are drawn.

15. Two black cards are drawn.

16. Two hearts are drawn.

17. In your own words, explain how to find the conditional probability $P(E|F)$.

18. In your own words, define independent events.

Decide whether the following pairs of events are dependent or independent.

19. A red die and a green die are rolled. A is the event that the red die comes up even, and B is the event that the green die comes up even.

20. C is the event that it rains more than 10 days in Chicago next June, and D is the event that it rains more than 15 days.

21. E is the event that a resident of Texas lives in Dallas, and F is the event that a resident of Texas lives in either Dallas or Houston.

22. A coin is flipped. G is the event that today is Tuesday, and H is the event that the coin comes up heads.

In the previous section, we described an experiment in which the numbers 1, 2, 3, 4, and 5 are written on slips of paper, and 2 slips are drawn at random one at a time without replacement. Find each probability in Exercises 23 and 24.

23. The probability that the first number is 3, given the following.

   (a) The sum is 7.   (b) The sum is 8.

24. The probability that the sum is 8, given the following.

   (a) The first number is 5.   (b) The first number is 4.

25. Suppose two dice are rolled. Let A be the event that the sum of the two dice is 7. Find an event B related to numbers on the dice such that A and B are

   (a) independent;   (b) dependent.

26. Your friend asks you to explain how the product rule for independent events differs from the product rule for dependent events. How would you respond?

27. Another friend asks you to explain how to tell whether two events are dependent or independent. How would you reply? (Use your own words.)

28. A student reasons that the probability in Example 3 of both coins being heads is just the probability that the other coin is a head, that is, 1/2. Explain why this reasoning is wrong.

29. Let A and B be independent events with $P(A) = \frac{1}{4}$ and $P(B) = \frac{1}{5}$. Find $P(A \cap B)$ and $P(A \cup B)$.

30. If A and B are events such that $P(A) = 0.5$ and $P(A \cup B) = 0.7$, find $P(B)$ when

   (a) A and B are mutually exclusive;

   (b) A and B are independent.

31. The following problem, submitted by Daniel Hahn of Blairstown, Iowa, appeared in the "Ask Marilyn" column of *Parade* magazine.

   "You discover two booths at a carnival. Each is tended by an honest man with a pair of covered coin shakers. In each shaker is a single coin, and you are allowed to bet upon the chance that both coins in that booth's shakers are heads after the man in the booth shakes them, does an inspection, and can tell you that at least one of the shakers contains a head. The difference is that the man in the first booth always looks inside both of his shakers, whereas the man in the second booth looks inside only one of the shakers. Where will you stand the best chance?" *Source: Parade magazine.*

32. The following question was posed in *Chance News* by Craig Fox and Yoval Rotenstrich. You are playing a game in which a fair coin is flipped and a fair die is rolled. You win a prize if both the coin comes up heads and a 6 is rolled on the die. Now suppose the coin is tossed and the die is rolled, but you are not allowed to see either result. You are told, however, that either the head or the 6 occurred. You are then offered the chance to cancel the game and play a new game in which a die is rolled (there is no coin), and you win a prize if a 6 is rolled. *Source: Chance News.*

   (a) Is it to your advantage to switch to the new game, or to stick with the original game? Answer this question by calculating your probability of winning in each case.

   (b) Many people erroneously think that it's better to stick with the original game. Discuss why this answer might seem intuitive, but why it is wrong.

33. Suppose a male defendant in a court trial has a mustache, beard, tattoo, and an earring. Suppose, also, that an eyewitness has identified the perpetrator as someone with these characteristics. If the respective probabilities for the male population in this region are 0.35, 0.30, 0.10, and 0.05, is it fair to multiply these probabilities together to conclude that the probability that a person having these characteristics is 0.000525, or 21 in 40,000, and thus decide that the defendant must be guilty?

34. In a two-child family, if we assume that the probabilities of a male child and a female child are each 0.5, are the events *all children are the same sex* and *at most one male* independent? Are they independent for a three-child family?

35. Laura Johnson, a game show contestant, could win one of two prizes: a shiny new Porsche or a shiny new penny. Laura is given two boxes of marbles. The first box has 50 pink marbles in it and the second box has 50 blue marbles in it. The game show host will pick someone from the audience to be blindfolded and then draw a marble from one of the two boxes. If a pink marble is drawn, she wins the Porsche. Otherwise, Laura wins the penny. Can Laura increase her chances of winning by redistributing some of the marbles from one box to the other? Explain. *Source: Car Talk.*

APPLICATIONS

Business and Economics

Banking The Midtown Bank has found that most customers at the tellers' windows either cash a check or make a deposit. The following table indicates the transactions for one teller for one day.

	Cash Check	No Check	Totals
Make Deposit	60	20	80
No Deposit	30	10	40
Totals	90	30	120

Letting *C* represent "cashing a check" and *D* represent "making a deposit," express each probability in words and find its value.

36. $P(C \mid D)$ 37. $P(D' \mid C)$ 38. $P(C' \mid D')$

39. $P(C' \mid D)$ 40. $P[(C \cap D)']$

41. **Airline Delays** During March 2014, the major U.S. airline with the fewest delays was Delta, for which 84.32% of their flights arrived on time. Assume that the event that a given flight arrives on time is independent of the event that another flight arrives on time. *Source: U.S. Department of Transportation.*

   (a) Jessica Cipperly plans to take four separate flights for her publisher next month on Delta. Assuming that the airline has the same on-time performance as in March 2014, what is the probability that all four flights arrive on time?

   (b) Discuss how realistic it is to assume that the on-time arrivals of the different flights are independent.

42. **Backup Computers** Corporations where a computer is essential to day-to-day operations, such as banks, often have a second backup computer in case the main computer fails. Suppose there is a 0.003 chance that the main computer will fail in a given time period and a 0.005 chance that the backup computer will fail while the main computer is being repaired. Assume these failures represent independent events, and find the fraction of the time that the corporation can assume it will have computer service. How realistic is our assumption of independence?

43. **ATM Transactions** Among users of automated teller machines (ATMs), 92% use ATMs to withdraw cash, and 32% use them to check their account balance. Suppose that 96% use ATMs to either withdraw cash or check their account balance (or both). Given a woman who uses an ATM to check her account balance, what is the probability that she also uses an ATM to get cash? *Source: Chicago Tribune.*

Quality Control A bicycle factory runs two assembly lines, A and B. If 95% of line A's products pass inspection, while only 85% of line B's products pass inspection, and 60% of the factory's bikes come off assembly line A (the rest off B), find the probabilities that one of the factory's bikes did not pass inspection and came off the following.

44. Assembly line A   45. Assembly line B

46. Find the probability that one of the factory's bikes did not pass inspection.

Life Sciences

47. **Genetics** Both of a certain pea plant's parents had a gene for red and a gene for white flowers. (See Exercise 54 in Section 7.4.) If the offspring has red flowers, find the probability that it combined a gene for red and a gene for white (rather than 2 for red).

48. **Medical Experiment** A medical experiment showed that the probability that a new medicine is effective is 0.75, the probability that a patient will have a certain side effect is 0.4, and the probability that both events occur is 0.3. Decide whether these events are dependent or independent.

Genetics Assuming that boy and girl babies are equally likely, fill in the remaining probabilities on the tree diagram below and use that information to find the probability that a family with three children has all girls, given the following.

49. The first is a girl.   50. The third is a girl.

51. The second is a girl.   52. At least 2 are girls.

53. At least 1 is a girl.

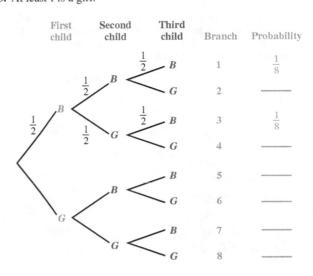

Color Blindness The following table shows frequencies for red-green color blindness, where *M* represents "person is male" and *C* represents "person is color-blind." Use this table to find the following probabilities. (See Exercise 53, Section 7.4.)

	M	*M′*	Totals
C	0.035	0.004	0.039
C'	0.452	0.509	0.961
Totals	0.487	0.513	1.000

54. $P(M)$

55. $P(C)$

56. $P(M \cap C)$

57. $P(M \cup C)$

58. $P(M|C)$

59. $P(C|M)$

60. $P(M'|C)$

61. Are the events *C* and *M*, described above, dependent? What does this mean?

62. Color Blindness A scientist wishes to determine whether there is a relationship between color blindness (*C*) and deafness (*D*).

 (a) Suppose the scientist found the probabilities listed in the table. What should the findings be? (See Exercises 54–61.)

 (b) Explain what your answer tells us about color blindness and deafness.

	D	*D′*	Totals
C	0.0008	0.0392	0.0400
C'	0.0192	0.9408	0.9600
Totals	0.0200	0.9800	1.0000

63. Overweight According to a recent report, 68.3% of men and 64.1% of women in the United States were overweight. Given that 49.3% of Americans are men and 50.7% are women, find the probability that a randomly selected American fits the following description. *Source: JAMA.*

 (a) An overweight man
 (b) Overweight
 (c) Are the events "male" and "overweight" independent?

Hockey The table below lists the number of head and neck injuries for 319 ice hockey players' exposures wearing either a full shield or half shield in the Canadian Inter-University Athletics Union. For a randomly selected injury, find each probability. *Source: JAMA.*

64. $P(A)$

65. $P(C|F)$

66. $P(A|H)$

67. $P(B'|H')$

	Half Shield (*H*)	Full Shield (*F*)	Totals
Head and Face Injuries (*A*)	95	34	129
Concussions (*B*)	41	38	79
Neck Injuries (*C*)	9	7	16
Other Injuries (*D*)	202	150	352
Totals	347	229	576

68. Are the events *A* and *H* independent events?*

69. Blood Pressure A doctor is studying the relationship between blood pressure and heartbeat abnormalities in her patients. She tests a random sample of her patients and notes their blood pressures (high, low, or normal) and their heartbeats (regular or irregular). She finds that:

 (i) 14% have high blood pressure.

 (ii) 22% have low blood pressure.

 (iii) 15% have an irregular heartbeat.

 (iv) Of those with an irregular heartbeat, one-third have high blood pressure.

 (v) Of those with normal blood pressure, one-eighth have an irregular heartbeat.

What portion of the patients selected have a regular heartbeat and low blood pressure? Choose one of the following. (*Hint:* Make a table similar to the one for Exercises 54–61.) *Source: Society of Actuaries.*

 (a) 2%   (b) 5%   (c) 8%   (d) 9%   (e) 20%

70. Breast Cancer To explain why the chance of a woman getting breast cancer in the next year goes up each year, while the chance of a woman getting breast cancer in her lifetime goes down, Ruma Falk made the following analogy. Suppose you are looking for a letter that you may have lost. You have 8 drawers in your desk. There is a probability of 0.1 that the letter is in any one of the 8 drawers and a probability of 0.2 that the letter is not in any of the drawers. *Source: Chance News.*

 (a) What is the probability that the letter is in drawer 1?

 (b) Given that the letter is not in drawer 1, what is the probability that the letter is in drawer 2?

 (c) Given that the letter is not in drawer 1 or 2, what is the probability that the letter is in drawer 3?

 (d) Given that the letter is not in drawers 1–7, what is the probability that the letter is in drawer 8?

 (e) Based on your answers to parts (a)–(d), what is happening to the probability that the letter is in the next drawer?

 (f) What is the probability that the letter is in some drawer?

 (g) Given that the letter is not in drawer 1, what is the probability that the letter is in some drawer?

 (h) Given that the letter is not in drawer 1 or 2, what is the probability that the letter is in some drawer?

 (i) Given that the letter is not in drawers 1–7, what is the probability that the letter is in some drawer?

 (j) Based on your answers to parts (f)–(i), what is happening to the probability that the letter is in some drawer?

71. Twins A 1920 study of 17,798 pairs of twins found that 5844 consisted of two males, 5612 consisted of two females, and 6342 consisted of a male and a female. Of course, all of the

*We are assuming here and in other exercises that the events consist entirely of the numbers given in the table. If the numbers are interpreted as a sample of all people fitting the description of the events, then testing for independence is more complicated, requiring a technique from statistics known as a *contingency table.*

mixed-gender pairs were not identical twins. The same-gender pairs may or may not have been identical twins. The goal here is to use the data to estimate p, the probability that a pair of twins is identical.

(a) Use the data to find the proportion of twins who were male.

(b) Denoting your answer from part (a) by $P(B)$, show that the probability that a pair of twins consists of two males is

$$pP(B) + (1 - p)(P(B))^2.$$

(*Hint:* Draw a tree diagram. The first set of branches should be identical and not identical. Then note that if one member of a pair of identical twins is male, the other must also be male.)

(c) Using your answers from parts (a) and (b), plus the fact that 5844 of the 17,798 twin pairs consisted of two males, find an estimate for the value of p.

(d) Find an expression, similar to the one in part (b), for the probability that a pair of twins is female.

(e) Using your answers from parts (a) and (d), plus the fact that 5612 of the 17,798 twin pairs were female, find an estimate for the value of p.

(f) Find an expression, similar to those in parts (b) and (d), for the probability that a pair of twins consists of one male and one female.

(g) Using your answers from parts (a) and (f), plus the fact that 6342 of the 17,798 twin pairs consisted of one male and one female, find an estimate for the value of p.

Social Sciences

72. Working Women A survey has shown that 52% of the women in a certain community work outside the home. Of these women, 64% are married, while 86% of the women who do not work outside the home are married. Find the probabilities that a woman in that community can be categorized as follows.

(a) Married

(b) A single woman working outside the home

(c) Are the events that a woman is married and that she works outside the home independent? Explain.

73. Cigarette Smokers The following table gives a recent estimate (in millions) of the smoking status among persons 25 years of age and over and their highest level of education. *Source: National Health Interview Survey.*

Education	Current Smoker	Former Smoker	Non-Smoker	Total
Less than a high school diploma	7.90	6.66	14.12	28.68
High school diploma or GED	14.38	13.09	25.70	53.17
Some college	12.41	13.55	28.65	54.61
Bachelor's degree or higher	4.97	12.87	38.34	56.18
Total	39.66	46.17	106.81	192.64

(a) Find the probability that a person is a current smoker.

(b) Find the probability that a person has less than a high school diploma.

(c) Find the probability that a person is a current smoker and has less than a high school diploma.

(d) Find the probability that a person is a current smoker, given that the person has less than a high school diploma.

(e) Are the events "current smoker" and "less than a high school diploma" independent events?

Physical Sciences

74. Rain Forecasts In a letter to the journal *Nature*, Robert A. J. Matthews gives the following table of outcomes of forecast and weather over 1000 1-hour walks, based on the United Kingdom's Meteorological office's 83% accuracy in 24-hour forecasts. *Source: Nature.*

	Rain	No Rain	Totals
Forecast of Rain	66	156	222
Forecast of No Rain	14	764	778
Totals	80	920	1000

(a) Verify that the probability that the forecast called for rain, given that there was rain, is indeed 83%. Also verify that the probability that the forecast called for no rain, given that there was no rain, is also 83%.

(b) Calculate the probability that there was rain, given that the forecast called for rain.

(c) Calculate the probability that there was no rain, given that the forecast called for no rain.

(d) Observe that your answer to part (c) is higher than 83% and that your answer to part (b) is much lower. Discuss which figure best describes the accuracy of the weather forecast in recommending whether or not you should carry an umbrella.

75. Earthquakes There are seven geologic faults (and possibly more) capable of generating a magnitude 6.7 earthquake in the region around San Francisco. Their probabilities of rupturing by the year 2032 are 27%, 21%, 11%, 10%, 4%, 3%, and 3%. *Source: Science News.*

(a) Calculate the probability that at least one of these faults erupts by the year 2032, assuming that these are independent events.

(b) Scientists forecast a 62% chance of an earthquake with magnitude at least 6.7 in the region around San Francisco by the year 2032. Compare this with your answer from part (a). Consider the realism of the assumption of independence. Also consider the role of roundoff. For example, the probability of 10% for one of the faults is presumably rounded to the nearest percent, with the actual probability between 9.5% and 10.5%.

76. Reliability The probability that a key component of a space rocket will fail is 0.03.

(a) How many such components must be used as backups to ensure that the probability of at least one of the components working is 0.999999 or more?

(b) Is it reasonable to assume independence here?

General Interest

77. Titanic The table at the bottom of the page lists the number of passengers who were on the *Titanic* and the number of passengers who survived, according to class of ticket. Use this information to determine the following (round answers to four decimal places). *Source: The Mathematics Teacher.*

(a) What is the probability that a randomly selected passenger was second class?

(b) What is the overall probability of surviving?

(c) What is the probability of a first-class passenger surviving?

(d) What is the probability of a child who was also in the third class surviving?

(e) Given that the survivor is from first class, what is the probability that she was a woman?

(f) Given that a man has survived, what is the probability that he was in third class?

(g) Are the events third-class survival and man survival independent events? What does this imply?

78. Real Estate A real estate agent trying to sell you an attractive beachfront house claims that it will not collapse unless it is subjected simultaneously to extremely high winds and extremely high waves. According to weather service records, there is a 0.001 probability of extremely high winds, and the same for extremely high waves. The real estate agent claims, therefore, that the probability of both occurring is $(0.001)(0.001) = 0.000001$. What is wrong with the agent's reasoning?

79. Age and Loans Suppose 20% of the population are 65 or over, 26% of those 65 or over have loans, and 53% of those under 65 have loans. Find the probabilities that a person fits into the following categories.

(a) 65 or over and has a loan

(b) Has a loan

(c) Are the events that a person is 65 or over and that the person has a loan independent? Explain.

80. Women Joggers In a certain area, 15% of the population are joggers and 40% of the joggers are women. If 55% of those who do not jog are women, find the probabilities that an individual from that community fits the following descriptions.

(a) A woman jogger

(b) A man who is not a jogger

(c) A woman

(d) Are the events that a person is a woman and a person is a jogger independent? Explain.

81. Diet Soft Drinks Two-thirds of the population are on a diet at least occasionally. Of this group, 4/5 drink diet soft drinks, while 1/2 of the rest of the (nondieting) population drink diet soft drinks. Find the probabilities that a person fits into the following categories.

(a) Drinks diet soft drinks

(b) Diets, but does not drink diet soft drinks

82. Driver's License Test The Motor Vehicle Department has found that the probability of a person passing the test for a driver's license on the first try is 0.75. The probability that an individual who fails on the first test will pass on the second try is 0.80, and the probability that an individual who fails the first and second tests will pass the third time is 0.70. Find the probabilities that an individual will do the following.

(a) Fail both the first and second tests

(b) Fail three times in a row

(c) Require at least two tries

83. Ballooning A pair of mathematicians in a hot air balloon were told that there are four independent burners, any one of which is sufficient to keep the balloon aloft. If the probability of any one burner failing during a flight is 0.001, what is the probability that the balloon will crash due to all four burners failing?

84. Speeding Tickets A smooth-talking young man has a 1/3 probability of talking a policeman out of giving him a speeding ticket. The probability that he is stopped for speeding during a given weekend is 1/2. Find the probabilities of the events in parts (a) and (b).

(a) He will receive no speeding tickets on a given weekend.

(b) He will receive no speeding tickets on 3 consecutive weekends.

(c) We have assumed that what happens on the second or third weekend is the same as what happened on the first weekend. Is this realistic? Will driving habits remain the same after getting a ticket?

	Children		Women		Men		Totals	
	On	Survived	On	Survived	On	Survived	On	Survived
First Class	6	6	144	140	175	57	325	203
Second Class	24	24	93	80	168	14	285	118
Third Class	79	27	165	76	462	75	706	178
Totals	109	57	402	296	805	146	1316	499

85. **Luxury Cars** In one area, 4% of the population drive luxury cars. However, 17% of the CPAs drive luxury cars. Are the events "person drives a luxury car" and "person is a CPA" independent?

86. **Studying** A teacher has found that the probability that a student studies for a test is 0.60, the probability that a student gets a good grade on a test is 0.70, and the probability that both occur is 0.52.

(a) Are these events independent?

(b) Given that a student studies, find the probability that the student gets a good grade.

(c) Given that a student gets a good grade, find the probability that the student studied.

87. **Basketball** A basketball player is fouled and now faces a one-and-one free throw situation. She shoots the first free throw. If she misses it, she scores 0 points. If she makes the first free throw, she gets to shoot a second free throw. If she misses the second free throw, she scores only one point for the first shot. If she makes the second free throw, she scores two points (one for each made shot). *Source: The Mathematics Teacher.*

(a) If her free-throwing percentage for this season is 60%, calculate the probability that she scores 0 points, 1 point, or 2 points.

(b) Determine the free-throwing percentage necessary for the probability of scoring 0 points to be the same as the probability of scoring 2 points.* (*Hint:* Let p be the free-throwing percentage, and then solve $p^2 = 1 - p$ for p. Use only the positive value of p.)

88. **Basketball** The same player from Exercise 87 is now shooting two free throws (that is, she gets to shoot a second free throw whether she makes or misses the first shot.) Assume her free-throwing percentage is still 60%. Find the probability she scores 0 points, 1 point, or 2 points. *Source: The Mathematics Teacher.*

89. **Football** A football coach whose team is 14 points behind needs two touchdowns to win. Each touchdown is worth 6 points. After a touchdown, the coach can choose either a 1-point kick, which is almost certain to succeed, or a 2-point conversion, which is roughly half as likely to succeed. After the first touchdown, the coach must decide whether to go for 1 or 2 points. If the 2-point conversion is successful, the almost certain 1-point kick after the second touchdown will win the game. If the 2-point conversion fails, the team can try another 2-point conversion after the second touchdown to tie. Some coaches, however, prefer to go for the almost certain 1-point kick after the first touchdown, hoping that the momentum will help them get a 2-point conversion after the second touchdown and win the game. They fear that an unsuccessful 2-point conversion after the first touchdown will discourage the team, which can then at best tie. *Source: The Mathematics Teacher.*

(a) Draw a tree diagram for the 1-point kick after the first touchdown and the 2-point conversion after the second touchdown. Letting the probability of success for the 1-point kick and the 2-point conversion be k and r, respectively, show that

$$P(\text{win}) = kr,$$
$$P(\text{tie}) = r(1 - k), \quad \text{and}$$
$$P(\text{lose}) = 1 - r.$$

(b) Consider the case of trying for a 2-point conversion after the first touchdown. If it succeeds, try a 1-point kick after the second touchdown. If the 2-point conversion fails, try another one after the second touchdown. Draw a tree diagram and use it to show that

$$P(\text{win}) = kr,$$
$$P(\text{tie}) = r(2 - k - r), \quad \text{and}$$
$$P(\text{lose}) = (1 - r)^2.$$

(c) What can you say about the probability of winning under each strategy?

(d) Given that $r < 1$, which strategy has a smaller probability of losing? What does this tell you about the value of the two strategies?

90. **NCAA** Large money prizes are offered each year to anyone who can correctly pick the outcome of all 63 games in the NCAA's men's college basketball tournament. The probability of correctly doing so has been estimated as between one in 150 million and one in nine million trillion. *Source: The Numbers Guy.*

(a) Suppose you choose the winner of each game by flipping a fair coin. What is the probability of getting all 63 games correct?

(b) Explain why someone who knows something about basketball should have a higher probability of getting all 63 games correct than the answer to part (a).

(c) What probability of predicting the outcome of a game would be necessary to predict all 63 games correctly with a probability of one in 150 million? Assume that the probability of getting each game correct is constant.

* The solution is the reciprocal of the number $\frac{1 + \sqrt{5}}{2}$, known as the golden ratio or the divine proportion. This number has great significance in architecture, science, and mathematics.

YOUR TURN ANSWERS

1. 30/55 = 6/11	**2.** 0.625
3. 2/3	**4.** 1/5
5. 1/6	**6.** 1/5
7. 1/36	**8.** No

7.6 Bayes' Theorem

APPLY IT What is the probability that a particular defective item was produced by a new machine operator?

This question will be answered in Example 2 using Bayes' theorem, discussed in this section.

Suppose the probability that an applicant is hired, *given the applicant is qualified*, is known. The manager might also be interested in the probability that the applicant is qualified, *given the applicant was hired*. More generally, if $P(E|F)$ is known for two events E and F, then $P(F|E)$ can be found using a tree diagram. Since $P(E|F)$ is known, the first outcome is either F or F'. Then for each of these outcomes, either E or E' occurs, as shown in Figure 27.

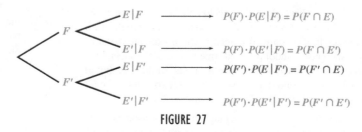

FIGURE 27

The four cases have the probabilities shown on the right. Notice $P(E \cap F)$ is the first case and $P(E)$ is the sum of the first and third cases in the tree diagram. By the definition of conditional probability,

$$P(F|E) = \frac{P(F \cap E)}{P(E)} = \frac{P(F) \cdot P(E|F)}{P(F) \cdot P(E|F) + P(F') \cdot P(E|F')}.$$

This result is a special case of Bayes' theorem, which is generalized later in this section.

Bayes' Theorem (Special Case)

$$P(F|E) = \frac{P(F) \cdot P(E|F)}{P(F) \cdot P(E|F) + P(F') \cdot P(E|F')}$$

EXAMPLE 1 Worker Errors

For a fixed length of time, the probability of a worker error on a certain production line is 0.1, the probability that an accident will occur when there is a worker error is 0.3, and the probability that an accident will occur when there is no worker error is 0.2. Find the probability of a worker error if there is an accident.

SOLUTION Let E represent the event of an accident, and let F represent the event of worker error. From the information given,

$$P(F) = 0.1, \qquad P(E|F) = 0.3, \qquad \text{and} \qquad P(E|F') = 0.2.$$

These probabilities are shown on the tree diagram in Figure 28 on the next page.

Find $P(F|E)$ by dividing the probability that both E and F occur, given by branch 1, by the probability that E occurs, given by the sum of branches 1 and 3.

$$P(F|E) = \frac{P(F) \cdot P(E|F)}{P(F) \cdot P(E|F) + P(F') \cdot P(E|F')}$$

$$= \frac{(0.1)(0.3)}{(0.1)(0.3) + (0.9)(0.2)} = \frac{0.03}{0.21} = \frac{1}{7} \approx 0.1429$$

YOUR TURN 1 The probability that a student will pass a math exam is 0.8 if he or she attends the review session and 0.65 if he or she does not attend the review session. Sixty percent of the students attend the review session. What is the probability that, given a student passed, the student attended the review session?

TRY YOUR TURN 1

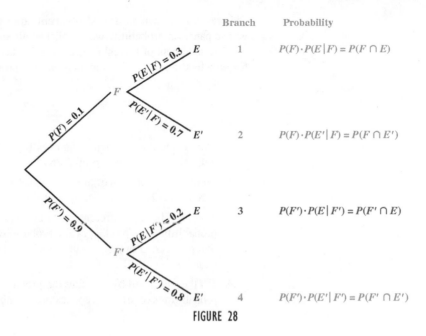

	Branch	Probability

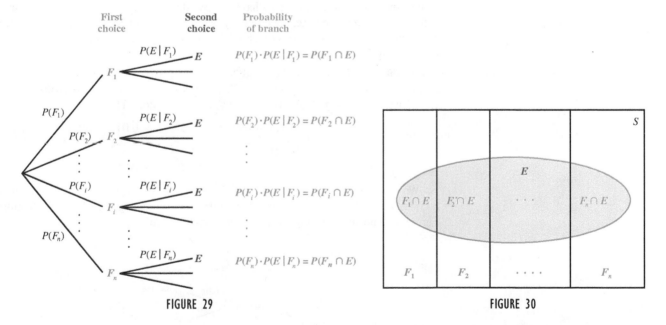

FIGURE 28

The special case of Bayes' theorem can be generalized to more than two events with the tree diagram in Figure 29. This diagram shows the paths that can produce an event E. We assume that the events $F_1, F_2, \ldots, F_n$ are mutually exclusive events (that is, disjoint events) whose union is the sample space, and that E is an event that has occurred. See Figure 30.

FIGURE 29

FIGURE 30

The probability $P(F_i \mid E)$, where $1 \le i \le n$, can be found by dividing the probability for the branch containing $P(E \mid F_i)$ by the sum of the probabilities of all the branches producing event E.

Bayes' Theorem

$$P(F_i \mid E) = \frac{P(F_i) \cdot P(E \mid F_i)}{P(F_1) \cdot P(E \mid F_1) + P(F_2) \cdot P(E \mid F_2) + \cdots + P(F_n) \cdot P(E \mid F_n)}$$

This result is known as **Bayes' theorem**, after the Reverend Thomas Bayes (1702–1761), whose paper on probability was published about three years after his death.

The statement of Bayes' theorem can be daunting. Actually, it is easier to remember the formula by thinking of the tree diagram that produced it. Use the following steps.

Using Bayes' Theorem

1. Start a tree diagram with branches representing $F_1, F_2, \ldots, F_n$. Label each branch with its corresponding probability.

2. From the end of each of these branches, draw a branch for event E. Label this branch with the probability of reaching it, $P(E|F_i)$.

3. You now have n different paths that result in event E. Next to each path, put its probability—the product of the probabilities that the first branch occurs, $P(F_i)$, and that the second branch occurs, $P(E|F_i)$; that is, the product $P(F_i) \cdot P(E|F_i)$, which equals $P(F_i \cap E)$.

4. $P(F_i|E)$ is found by dividing the probability of the branch for F_i by the sum of the probabilities of all the branches producing event E.

EXAMPLE 2   Machine Operators

Based on past experience, a company knows that an experienced machine operator (one or more years of experience) will produce a defective item 1% of the time. Operators with some experience (up to one year) have a 2.5% defect rate, and new operators have a 6% defect rate. At any one time, the company has 60% experienced operators, 30% with some experience, and 10% new operators. Find the probability that a particular defective item was produced by a new operator.

APPLY IT

SOLUTION   Let E represent the event "item is defective," F_1 represent "item was made by an experienced operator," F_2 represent "item was made by an operator with some experience," and F_3 represent "item was made by a new operator." Then

$$P(F_1) = 0.60 \qquad P(E|F_1) = 0.01$$
$$P(F_2) = 0.30 \qquad P(E|F_2) = 0.025$$
$$P(F_3) = 0.10 \qquad P(E|F_3) = 0.06.$$

We need to find $P(F_3|E)$, the probability that an item was produced by a new operator, given that it is defective. First, draw a tree diagram using the given information, as in Figure 31. The steps leading to event E are shown in red.

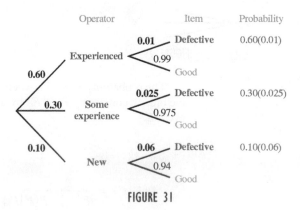

FIGURE 31

YOUR TURN 2 The English department at a small college has found that 12% of freshmen test into English I, 68% test into English II, and 20% test into English III. Eighty percent of students in English I will seek help from the writing center, 40% of those in English II, and 11% of those in English III. Given that a student received help from the writing center, find the probability that the student is in English I.

Find $P(F_3 | E)$ with the bottom branch of the tree in Figure 31: Divide the probability for this branch by the sum of the probabilities of all the branches leading to E, or

$$P(F_3 | E) = \frac{0.10(0.06)}{0.60(0.01) + 0.30(0.025) + 0.10(0.06)} = \frac{0.006}{0.0195} = \frac{4}{13} \approx 0.3077.$$

In a similar way, the probability that the defective item was produced by an operator with some experience is

$$P(F_2 | E) = \frac{0.30(0.025)}{0.60(0.01) + 0.30(0.025) + 0.10(0.06)} = \frac{0.0075}{0.0195} = \frac{5}{13} \approx 0.3846.$$

Finally, the probability that the defective item was produced by an experienced operator is $P(F_1 | E) = 4/13 \approx 0.3077$. Check that $P(F_1 | E) + P(F_2 | E) + P(F_3 | E) = 1$ (that is, the defective item was made by *someone*). **TRY YOUR TURN 2**

EXAMPLE 3 Manufacturing

A manufacturer buys items from six different suppliers. The fraction of the total number of items obtained from each supplier, along with the probability that an item purchased from that supplier is defective, is shown in the following table.

	Manufacturing Supplies	
Supplier	Fraction of Total Supplied	Probability of Defect
1	0.05	0.04
2	0.12	0.02
3	0.16	0.07
4	0.23	0.01
5	0.35	0.03
6	0.09	0.05

Find the probability that a defective item came from supplier 5.

SOLUTION Let F_1 be the event that an item came from supplier 1, with F_2, F_3, F_4, F_5, and F_6 defined in a similar manner. Let E be the event that an item is defective. We want to find $P(F_5 | E)$. Use the probabilities in the table above to prepare a tree diagram, or work with the rows of the table to get

$$P(F_5 | E) = \frac{(0.35)(0.03)}{(0.05)(0.04) + (0.12)(0.02) + (0.16)(0.07) + (0.23)(0.01) + (0.35)(0.03) + (0.09)(0.05)}$$

$$= \frac{0.0105}{0.0329} \approx 0.319.$$

There is about a 32% chance that a defective item came from supplier 5. Even though supplier 5 has only 3% defectives, his probability of being "guilty" is relatively high, about 32%, because of the large fraction supplied by 5.

CAUTION Notice that the 0.04 in the upper right of the previous table represents the probability of a defective item *given* that the item came from supplier 1. In contrast, the probability of 0.035 in the table for Exercises 54–61 of the previous section represents the probability that a person is color-blind *and* male. The tables in this section represent probability in a different way than those of the previous section. Tables that you encounter outside of this course might represent probability in either way. You can usually tell what is intended by the context, but be careful!

⊞ **TECHNOLOGY NOTE** The calculations in the previous example can be easily performed using Excel. Put the fraction of total supplied in column A and the probability of defect in column B. In cell C1, put "=A1*B1". Copy this formula and paste it into cells C2 through C6. In cell C7, put "=SUM(C1:C6)". Finally, in any cell, put "=C5/C7".

7.6 WARM-UP EXERCISES

Suppose 1/3 of the marbles in jar A are red, and the rest are yellow. Of the marbles in jar B, 1/5 are red and the rest are yellow. Jar A is selected with probability 3/4 and jar B with probability 1/4. A jar is selected, and a marble is then picked from that jar. Find the probabilities of the following.

W1. The marble is from jar A and is yellow. *(Sec. 7.5)*

W2. The marble is red. *(Sec. 7.5)*

7.6 EXERCISES

For two events M and N, $P(M) = 0.4$, $P(N|M) = 0.3$, and $P(N|M') = 0.4$. Find the following.

1. $P(M|N)$

2. $P(M'|N)$

For mutually exclusive events R_1, R_2, and R_3, we have $P(R_1) = 0.15$, $P(R_2) = 0.55$, and $P(R_3) = 0.30$. Also, $P(Q|R_1) = 0.40$, $P(Q|R_2) = 0.20$, and $P(Q|R_3) = 0.70$. Find the following.

3. $P(R_1|Q)$

4. $P(R_2|Q)$

5. $P(R_3|Q)$

6. $P(R_1'|Q)$

Suppose you have three jars with the following contents: 2 black balls and 1 white ball in the first, 1 black ball and 2 white balls in the second, and 1 black ball and 1 white ball in the third. One jar is to be selected, and then 1 ball is to be drawn from the selected jar. If the probabilities of selecting the first, second, or third jar are 1/2, 1/3, and 1/6, respectively, find the probabilities that if a white ball is drawn, it came from the following jars.

7. The second jar

8. The third jar

APPLICATIONS

Business and Economics

9. Employment Test A manufacturing firm finds that 70% of its new hires turn out to be good workers and 30% become poor workers. All current workers are given a reasoning test. Of the good workers, 85% pass it; 35% of the poor workers pass it. Assume that these figures will hold true in the future. If the company makes the test part of its hiring procedure and only hires people who meet the previous requirements and pass the test, what percent of the new hires will turn out to be good workers?

Job Qualifications Of all the people applying for a certain job, 75% are qualified and 25% are not. The personnel manager claims that she approves qualified people 85% of the time; she approves an unqualified person 20% of the time. Find each probability.

10. A person is qualified if he or she was approved by the manager.

11. A person is unqualified if he or she was approved by the manager.

Quality Control A building contractor buys 70% of his cement from supplier A and 30% from supplier B. A total of 90% of the bags from A arrive undamaged, while 95% of the bags from B arrive undamaged. Give the probabilities that a damaged bag is from the following sources.

12. Supplier A

13. Supplier B

Appliance Reliability Companies A, B, and C produce 15%, 40%, and 45%, respectively, of the major appliances sold in a certain area. In that area, 1% of the company A appliances, $1\frac{1}{2}$% of the company B appliances, and 2% of the company C appliances need service within the first year. Suppose a defective appliance is chosen at random; find the probabilities that it was manufactured by the following companies.

14. Company A

15. Company B

Television Advertising On a given weekend in the fall, a tire company can buy television advertising time for a college football game, a baseball game, or a professional football game. If the company sponsors the college football game, there is a 70% chance of a high rating, a 50% chance if they sponsor a baseball game, and a 60% chance if they sponsor a professional football game. The probabilities of the company sponsoring these various games are 0.5, 0.2, and 0.3, respectively. Suppose the company does get a high rating; find the probabilities that it sponsored the following.

16. A college football game

17. A professional football game

18. Auto Insurance An auto insurance company insures drivers of all ages. An actuary compiled the following statistics on the company's insured drivers:

Age of Driver	Probability Of Accident	Portion of Company's Insured Drivers
16–20	0.06	0.08
21–30	0.03	0.15
31–65	0.02	0.49
66–99	0.04	0.28

A randomly selected driver that the company insures has an accident. Calculate the probability that the driver was age 16–20. Choose one of the following. *Source: Society of Actuaries*.

(a) 0.13   (b) 0.16   (c) 0.19   (d) 0.23   (e) 0.40

19. **Life Insurance** An insurance company issues life insurance policies in three separate categories: standard, preferred, and ultra-preferred. Of the company's policyholders, 50% are standard, 40% are preferred, and 10% are ultra-preferred. Each standard policyholder has probability 0.010 of dying in the next year, each preferred policyholder has probability 0.005 of dying in the next year, and each ultra-preferred policyholder has probability 0.001 of dying in the next year. A policyholder dies in the next year. What is the probability that the deceased policyholder was ultra-preferred? Choose one of the following. *Source: Society of Actuaries*.

(a) 0.0001   (b) 0.0010   (c) 0.0071   (d) 0.0141   (e) 0.2817

20. **Automobile Collisions** An actuary studied the likelihood that different types of drivers would be involved in at least one collision during any one-year period. The results of the study are presented below.

Type of Driver	Percentage of All Drivers	Probability of at Least One Collision
Teen	8%	0.15
Young Adult	16%	0.08
Midlife	45%	0.04
Senior	31%	0.05
Total	100%	

Given that a driver has been involved in at least one collision in the past year, what is the probability that the driver is a young adult driver? Choose one of the following. *Source: Society of Actuaries*.

(a) 0.06   (b) 0.16   (c) 0.19   (d) 0.22   (e) 0.25

21. **Shipping Errors** The following information pertains to three shipping terminals operated by Krag Corp. *Source: CPA Examination*.

Terminal	Percentage of Cargo Handled	Percentage of Error
Land	50	2
Air	40	4
Sea	10	14

Krag's internal auditor randomly selects one set of shipping documents, ascertaining that the set selected contains an error. Which of the following gives the probability that the error occurred in the Land Terminal?

(a) 0.02   (b) 0.10   (c) 0.25   (d) 0.50

22. **Mortgage Defaults** A bank finds that the relationship between mortgage defaults and the size of the down payment is given by the following table.

Down Payment	Number of Mortgages with This Down Payment	Probability of Default
5%	1260	0.06
10%	700	0.04
20%	560	0.02
25%	280	0.01

(a) If a default occurs, what is the probability that it is on a mortgage with a 5% down payment?

(b) What is the probability that a mortgage that is paid to maturity has a 10% down payment?

Life Sciences

23. **Colorectal Cancer** Researchers found that only one out of 24 physicians could give the correct answer to the following problem: "The probability of colorectal cancer can be given as 0.3%. If a person has colorectal cancer, the probability that the hemoccult test is positive is 50%. If a person does not have colorectal cancer, the probability that he still tests positive is 3%. What is the probability that a person who tests positive actually has colorectal cancer?" What is the correct answer? *Source: Science*.

24. **Hepatitis Blood Test** The probability that a person with certain symptoms has hepatitis is 0.8. The blood test used to confirm this diagnosis gives positive results for 90% of people with the disease and 5% of those without the disease. What is the probability that an individual who has the symptoms and who reacts positively to the test actually has hepatitis?

25. **Sensitivity and Specificity** The **sensitivity** of a medical test is defined as the probability that a test will be positive given that a person has a disease, written $P(T^+ | D^+)$. The **specificity** of a test is defined as the probability that a test will be negative given that the person does not have the disease, written $P(T^- | D^-)$. For example, the sensitivity and specificity for breast cancer during a mammography exam are approximately 79.6% and 90.2%, respectively. *Source: National Cancer Institute*.

(a) It is estimated that 0.5% of U.S. women under the age 40 have breast cancer. Find the probability that a woman under 40 who tests positive during a mammography exam actually has breast cancer.

(b) Given that a woman under 40 tests negative during a mammography exam, find the probability that she does not have breast cancer.

(c) According to the National Cancer Institute, failure to diagnose breast cancer is the most common cause of medical malpractice litigation. Given a woman under 40 tests negative for breast cancer, find the probability that she does have breast cancer.

(d) It is estimated that 1.5% of U.S. women over the age of 50 have breast cancer. Find the probability that a woman over 50 who tests positive actually has breast cancer.

26. Test for HIV Clinical studies have demonstrated that rapid HIV tests have a sensitivity (probability that a test will be positive given that a person has the disease) of approximately 99.9% and a specificity (probability that a test will be negative given that the person does not have the disease) of approximately 99.8%. *Source: Centers for Disease Control and Prevention*

(a) In some HIV clinics, the prevalence of HIV was high, about 5%. Find the probability a person actually has HIV, given that the test came back positive from one of these clinics.

(b) In other clinics, like a family planning clinic, the prevalence of HIV was low, about 0.1%. Find the probability that a person actually has HIV, given that the test came back positive from one of these clinics.

(c) The answers in parts (a) and (b) are significantly different. Explain why.

27. Smokers A health study tracked a group of persons for five years. At the beginning of the study, 20% were classified as heavy smokers, 30% as light smokers, and 50% as non-smokers. Results of the study showed that light smokers were twice as likely as nonsmokers to die during the five-year study but only half as likely as heavy smokers. A randomly selected participant from the study died over the five-year period. Calculate the probability that the participant was a heavy smoker. Choose one of the following. (*Hint:* Let $x = P$(a nonsmoker dies).) *Source: Society of Actuaries.*

(a) 0.20　　(b) 0.25　　(c) 0.35　　(d) 0.42　　(e) 0.57

28. Emergency Room Upon arrival at a hospital's emergency room, patients are categorized according to their condition as critical, serious, or stable. In the past year:

(i) 10% of the emergency room patients were critical;

(ii) 30% of the emergency room patients were serious;

(iii) the rest of the emergency room patients were stable;

(iv) 40% of the critical patients died;

(v) 10% of the serious patients died; and

(vi) 1% of the stable patients died.

Given that a patient survived, what is the probability that the patient was categorized as serious upon arrival? Choose one of the following. *Source: Society of Actuaries.*

(a) 0.06　　(b) 0.29　　(c) 0.30　　(d) 0.39　　(e) 0.64

29. Blood Test A blood test indicates the presence of a particular disease 95% of the time when the disease is actually present. The same test indicates the presence of the disease 0.5% of the time when the disease is not present. One percent of the population actually has the disease. Calculate the probability that a person has the disease, given that the test indicates the presence of the disease. Choose one of the following. *Source: Society of Actuaries.*

(a) 0.324　　(b) 0.657　　(c) 0.945　　(d) 0.950　　(e) 0.995

30. Circulation The probability that a randomly chosen male has a circulation problem is 0.25. Males who have a circulation problem are twice as likely to be smokers as those who do not have a circulation problem. What is the conditional probability that a male has a circulation problem, given that he is a smoker? Choose one of the following. *Source: Society of Actuaries.*

(a) 1/4　　(b) 1/3　　(c) 2/5　　(d) 1/2　　(e) 2/3

Social Sciences

31. Alcohol Abstinence The Harvard School of Public Health completed a study on alcohol consumption on college campuses. They concluded that 20.7% of women attending all-women colleges abstained from alcohol, compared to 18.6% of women attending coeducational colleges. Approximately 4.7% of women college students attend all-women schools. *Source: Harvard School of Public Health.*

(a) What is the probability that a randomly selected female student abstains from alcohol?

(b) If a randomly selected female student abstains from alcohol, what is the probability she attends a coeducational college?

32. Murder During the murder trial of O. J. Simpson, Alan Dershowitz, an advisor to the defense team, stated on television that only about 0.1% of men who batter their wives actually murder them. Statistician I. J. Good observed that even if, given that a husband is a batterer, the probability he is guilty of murdering his wife is 0.001, what we really want to know is the probability that the husband is guilty, given that the wife was murdered. Good estimates the probability of a battered wife being murdered, given that her husband is not guilty, as 0.001. The probability that she is murdered if her husband is guilty is 1, of course. Using these numbers and Dershowitz's 0.001 probability of the husband being guilty, find the probability that the husband is guilty, given that the wife was murdered. *Source: Nature.*

Children's Economic Situation The following table gives the proportion of children in the United States in 2012 who are living in a family in each income group, as well as the proportion who are living with two married parents in each income group. *Source: U.S. Census Bureau.*

Family Income	Proportion of Population	Proportion with two Married Parents
Under $15,000	0.132	0.187
$15,000–$29,999	0.147	0.385
$30,000–$49,999	0.177	0.576
$50,000–$74,999	0.171	0.727
$75,000–$99,999	0.124	0.854
$100,000 and over	0.249	0.916

33. Find the probability that a child living with two married parents lives in a family with an income of $100,000 or over.

34. Find the probability that a child not living with two married parents lives in a family with an income of $100,000 or over.

35. Find the probability that a child living with two married parents lives in a family with an income under $15,000.

36. **Seat Belt Effectiveness**   A federal study showed that 63.8% of occupants involved in a fatal car crash wore seat belts. Of those in a fatal crash who wore seat belts, 2% were ejected from the vehicle. For those not wearing seat belts, 36% were ejected from the vehicle. *Source: National Highway Traffic Safety Administration.*

  (a) Find the probability that a randomly selected person in a fatal car crash who was ejected from the vehicle was wearing a seat belt.

  (b) Find the probability that a randomly selected person in a fatal car crash who was not ejected from the vehicle was not wearing a seat belt.

Smokers by Age Group   **The following table gives the proportion of U.S. adults in each age group in 2012, as well as the proportion in each group who smoke.** *Source: Centers for Disease Control and Prevention.*

Age	Proportion of Population	Proportion that Smoke
18–24 years	0.131	0.173
25–44 years	0.345	0.216
45–64 years	0.345	0.195
65 years and over	0.180	0.089

37. Find the probability that a randomly selected adult who smokes is between 18 and 24 years of age (inclusive).

38. Find the probability that a randomly selected adult who does not smoke is between 45 and 64 years of age (inclusive).

General Interest

39. **Terrorists**   John Allen Paulos has pointed out a problem with massive, untargeted wiretaps. To illustrate the problem, he supposes that one out of every million Americans has terrorist ties.

Furthermore, he supposes that the terrorist profile is 99% accurate, so that if a person has terrorist ties, the profile will pick them up 99% of the time, and if the person does not have terrorist ties, the profile will accidentally pick them up only 1% of the time. Given that the profile has picked up a person, what is the probability that the person actually has terrorist ties? Discuss how your answer affects your opinion on domestic wiretapping. *Source: Who's Counting.*

40. **Three Prisoners**   The famous "problem of three prisoners" is as follows.

Three men, A, B, and C, were in jail. A knew that one of them was to be set free and the other two were to be executed. But he didn't know who was the one to be spared. To the jailer who did know, A said, "Since two out of the three will be executed, it is certain that either B or C will be, at least. You will give me no information about my own chances if you give me the name of one man, B or C, who is going to be executed." Accepting this argument after some thinking, the jailer said "B will be executed." Thereupon A felt happier because now either he or C would go free, so his chance had increased from 1/3 to 1/2. *Source: Cognition.*

  (a) Assume that initially each of the prisoners is equally likely to be set free. Assume also that if both B and C are to be executed, the jailer is equally likely to name either B or C. Show that A is wrong, and that his probability of being freed, given that the jailer says B will be executed, is still 1/3.

  (b) Now assume that initially the probabilities of A, B, and C being freed are 1/4, 1/4, and 1/2, respectively. As in part (a), assume also that if both B and C are to be executed, the jailer is equally likely to name either B or C. Now show that A's probability of being freed, given that the jailer says B will be executed, actually drops to 1/5. Discuss the reasonableness of this answer, and why this result might violate someone's intuition.

YOUR TURN ANSWERS ▬▬▬
1. 0.6486
2. 0.2462

CHAPTER REVIEW

SUMMARY

We began this chapter by introducing sets, which are collections of objects. We introduced the following set operations:

  • complement (A' is the set of elements not in A),

  • intersection ($A \cap B$ is the set of elements belonging to both set A and set B), and

  • union ($A \cup B$ is the set of elements belonging to either set A or set B or both).

We used tree diagrams and Venn diagrams to define and study concepts in set operations as well as in probability. We introduced the following terms:

  • experiment (an activity or occurrence with an observable result),

  • trial (a repetition of an experiment),

  • outcome (a result of a trial),

- sample space (the set of all possible outcomes for an experiment), and
- event (a subset of a sample space).

We investigated how to compute various probabilities and we explored some of the properties of probability. In particular, we studied the following concepts:

- empirical probability (based on how frequently an event actually occurred),
- conditional probability (in which some other event is assumed to have occurred),

- odds (an alternative way of expressing probability),
- independent events (in which the occurrence of one event does not affect the probability of another), and
- Bayes' theorem (used to calculate certain types of conditional probability).

Throughout the chapter, many applications of probability were introduced and analyzed. In the next two chapters, we will employ these techniques to further our study into the fields of probability and statistics.

Sets Summary

Number of Subsets A set of k distinct elements has 2^k subsets.

Disjoint Sets If sets A and B are disjoint, then

$$A \cap B = \varnothing \quad \text{and} \quad n(A \cap B) = 0.$$

Union Rule for Sets For any sets A and B,

$$n(A \cup B) = n(A) + n(B) - n(A \cap B).$$

Probability Summary

Basic Probability Principle Let S be a sample space of equally likely outcomes, and let event E be a subset of S. Then the probability that event E occurs is

$$P(E) = \frac{n(E)}{n(S)}.$$

Mutually Exclusive Events If E and F are mutually exclusive events,

$$E \cap F = \varnothing \quad \text{and} \quad P(E \cap F) = 0.$$

Union Rule For any events E and F from a sample space S,

$$P(E \cup F) = P(E) + P(F) - P(E \cap F).$$

Complement Rule $P(E) = 1 - P(E') \quad \text{and} \quad P(E') = 1 - P(E)$

Odds The odds in favor of event E are $\dfrac{P(E)}{P(E')}$, where $P(E') \neq 0$.

If the odds favoring event E are m to n, then

$$P(E) = \frac{m}{m + n} \quad \text{and} \quad P(E') = \frac{n}{m + n}.$$

Properties of Probability **1.** For any event E in sample space S, $0 \leq P(E) \leq 1$.

2. The sum of the probabilities of all possible distinct outcomes is 1.

Conditional Probability The conditional probability of event E, given that event F has occurred, is

$$P(E|F) = \frac{P(E \cap F)}{P(F)}, \quad \text{where } P(F) \neq 0.$$

For equally likely outcomes, conditional probability is found by reducing the sample space to event F; then

$$P(E|F) = \frac{n(E \cap F)}{n(F)}.$$

Product Rule of Probability   If E and F are events, then $P(E \cap F)$ may be found by either of these formulas.

$$P(E \cap F) = P(F) \cdot P(E|F) \quad \text{or} \quad P(E \cap F) = P(E) \cdot P(F|E)$$

Independent Events   If E and F are independent events,

$$P(E|F) = P(E), \quad P(F|E) = P(F), \quad \text{and} \quad P(E \cap F) = P(E) \cdot P(F).$$

Bayes' Theorem $P(F_i|E) = \dfrac{P(F_i) \cdot P(E|F_i)}{P(F_1) \cdot P(E|F_1) + P(F_2) \cdot P(E|F_2) + \cdots + P(F_n) \cdot P(E|F_n)}$

KEY TERMS

7.1
set
element (member)
empty set (or null set)
set-builder notation
universal set
subset
tree diagram
Venn diagram
complement
intersection

disjoint sets
union

7.2
union rule for sets

7.3
experiment
trial
outcome
sample space
event

simple event
certain event
impossible event
mutually exclusive events
probability
empirical probability

7.4
union rule for probability
odds
probability distribution

7.5
conditional probability
product rule
independent events
dependent events

7.6
Bayes' theorem
sensitivity
specificity

REVIEW EXERCISES

CONCEPT CHECK

Determine whether each of the following statements is true or false, and explain why.

1. A set is a subset of itself.

2. A set has more subsets than it has elements.

3. The union of two sets always has more elements than either set.

4. The intersection of two sets always has fewer elements than either set.

5. The number of elements in the union of two sets can be found by adding the number of elements in each set.

6. The probability of an event is always at least 0 and no larger than 1.

7. The probability of the union of two events can be found by adding the probability of each event.

8. The probability of drawing the Queen of Hearts from a deck of cards is an example of empirical probability.

9. If two events are mutually exclusive, then they are independent.

10. The probability of two independent events can be found by multiplying the probabilities of each event.

11. The probability of an event E given an event F is the same as the probability of F given E.

12. Bayes' theorem can be useful for calculating conditional probability.

PRACTICE AND EXPLORATIONS

Write true or false for each statement.

13. $9 \in \{8, 4, -3, -9, 6\}$

14. $4 \notin \{3, 9, 7\}$

15. $2 \notin \{0, 1, 2, 3, 4\}$

16. $0 \in \{0, 1, 2, 3, 4\}$

17. $\{3, 4, 5\} \subseteq \{2, 3, 4, 5, 6\}$

18. $\{1, 2, 5, 8\} \subseteq \{1, 2, 5, 10, 11\}$

19. $\{3, 6, 9, 10\} \subseteq \{3, 9, 11, 13\}$

20. $\varnothing \subseteq \{1\}$

21. $\{2, 8\} \not\subseteq \{2, 4, 6, 8\}$

22. $0 \subseteq \varnothing$

In Exercises 23–32, let $U = \{a, b, c, d, e, f, g, h\}$, $K = \{c, d, e, f, h\}$, and $R = \{a, c, d, g\}$. Find the following.

23. The number of subsets of K

24. The number of subsets of R

25. K'

26. R'

27. $K \cap R$

28. $K \cup R$

29. $(K \cap R)'$

30. $(K \cup R)'$

31. $\varnothing'$

32. U'

In Exercises 33–38, let

$U = \{$all employees of the K. O. Brown Company$\}$;

$A = \{$employees in the accounting department$\}$;

$B = \{$employees in the sales department$\}$;

$C = \{$female employees$\}$;

$D = \{$employees with an MBA degree$\}$.

Describe each set in words.

33. $A \cap C$ **34.** $B \cap D$ **35.** $A \cup D$

36. $A' \cap D$ **37.** $B' \cap C'$ **38.** $(B \cup C)'$

Draw a Venn diagram and shade each set.

39. $A \cup B'$ **40.** $A' \cap B$

41. $(A \cap B) \cup C$ **42.** $(A \cup B)' \cap C$

Write the sample space S for each experiment, choosing an S with equally likely outcomes, if possible.

43. Rolling a die

44. Drawing a card from a deck containing only the 13 spades

45. Measuring the weight of a person to the nearest half pound (the scale will not measure more than 300 lb)

46. Tossing a coin 4 times

A jar contains 5 balls labeled 3, 5, 7, 9, and 11, respectively, while a second jar contains 4 red and 2 green balls. An experiment consists of pulling 1 ball from each jar, in turn. In Exercises 47–50, write each set using set notation.

47. The sample space

48. The number on the first ball is greater than 5.

49. The second ball is green.

50. Are the outcomes in the sample space in Exercise 47 equally likely?

In Exercises 51–58, find the probability of each event when a single card is drawn from an ordinary deck.

51. A heart   **52.** A red queen

53. A face card or a heart

54. Black or a face card

55. Red, given that it is a queen

56. A jack, given that it is a face card

57. A face card, given that it is a king

58. A king, given that it is not a face card

59. Describe what is meant by disjoint sets.

60. Describe what is meant by mutually exclusive events.

61. How are disjoint sets and mutually exclusive events related?

62. Define independent events.

63. Are independent events always mutually exclusive? Are they ever mutually exclusive?

64. An uproar has raged since September 1990 over the answer to a puzzle published in *Parade* magazine, a supplement of the Sunday newspaper. In the "Ask Marilyn" column, Marilyn vos Savant answered the following question:

"Suppose you're on a game show, and you're given the choice of three doors. Behind one door is a car; behind the others, goats. You pick a door, say number 1, and the host, who knows what's behind the other doors, opens another door, say number 3, which has a goat. He then says to you, 'Do you want to pick door number 2?' Is it to your advantage to take the switch?"

Ms. vos Savant estimates that she has since received some 10,000 letters; most of them, including many from mathematicians and statisticians, disagreed with her answer. Her answer has been debated by both professionals and amateurs and tested in classes at all levels from grade school to graduate school. But by performing the experiment repeatedly, it can be shown that vos Savant's answer was correct. Find the probabilities of getting the car if you switch or do not switch, and then answer the question yourself. (*Hint:* Consider the sample space.) *Source: Parade magazine.*

Find the odds in favor of a card drawn from an ordinary deck being the following.

65. A club   **66.** A black jack

67. A red face card or a queen

68. An ace or a club

Find the probabilities of getting the following sums when two fair dice are rolled.

69. 8   **70.** 0

71. At least 10   **72.** No more than 5

73. An odd number greater than 8

74. 12, given that the sum is greater than 10

75. 7, given that at least one die shows a 4

76. At least 9, given that at least one die shows a 5

77. Suppose $P(E) = 0.51$, $P(F) = 0.37$, and $P(E \cap F) = 0.22$. Find the following.

(a) $P(E \cup F)$ (b) $P(E \cap F')$

(c) $P(E' \cup F)$ (d) $P(E' \cap F')$

78. An urn contains 10 balls: 4 red and 6 blue. A second urn contains 16 red balls and an unknown number of blue balls. A single ball is drawn from each urn. The probability that both balls are the same color is 0.44. Calculate the number of blue balls in the second urn. Choose one of the following. *Source: Society of Actuaries.*

(a) 4   (b) 20   (c) 24   (d) 44   (e) 64

79. Box A contains 5 red balls and 1 black ball; box B contains 2 red balls and 3 black balls. A box is chosen, and a ball is selected from it. The probability of choosing box A is 3/8. If the selected ball is black, what is the probability that it came from box A?

80. Find the probability that the ball in Exercise 79 came from box B, given that it is red.

⊕ Let E and F be two events with $P(E) = 0.2$, $P(F) = 0.3$, and $P(E \cap F) = 0.05$. Calculate each of the following. *Source: Mike Cohen.*

81. $P(E \cup F)$ **82.** $P(E' \cap F')$ **83.** $P(E' \cap F)$

84. $P(E' \cup F')$ **85.** $P(E \cap F')$ **86.** $P(E|F)$

87. $P(F|E)$ **88.** $P(E'|F')$ **89.** $P(F'|E)$

90. $P(E'|E)$ **91.** $P(E|E \cap F)$ **92.** $P(E|E \cup F)$

93. Are events E and F independent? Explain.

94. Explain why the answer to Exercise 90 must be 0.

95. Explain why the answer to Exercise 91 must be 1.

APPLICATIONS

Business and Economics

96. Workplace Drug Testing   In the "Ask Marilyn" column of *Parade* magazine, a reader wrote:

"I manage a drug-testing program for an organization with 400 employees. Every three months, a random-number generator selects 100 names for testing. Afterward, these names go back into the selection pool. Obviously, the probability of an employee being chosen in one quarter is 25 percent. But what's the likelihood of being chosen over the course of a year?" *Source: Parade magazine.*

(a) Marilyn originally interpreted the question as, "What is the probability of being selected in any specific quarter in the year?" What is the answer to that question?

(b) Another reader wrote to point out that Marilyn answered a different question. What is the correct answer to the question that the reader asked?

Appliance Repairs   Of the appliance repair shops listed in the phone book, 80% are competent and 20% are not. A competent shop can repair an appliance correctly 95% of the time; an incompetent shop can repair an appliance correctly 55% of the time. Suppose an appliance was repaired correctly. Find the probabilities that it was repaired by the following.

97. A competent shop   **98.** An incompetent shop

Suppose an appliance was repaired incorrectly. Find the probabilities that it was repaired by the following.

99. A competent shop   **100.** An incompetent shop

101. Find the probability that an appliance brought to a shop chosen at random is repaired correctly.

102. Are the events that a repair shop is competent and that the repair is done correctly independent? Explain.

103. Sales   A company sells printers and copiers. Let E be the event "a customer buys a printer," and let F be the event "a customer buys a copier." Write the following using $\cap, \cup,$ or $'$ as necessary.

(a) A customer buys neither machine.

(b) A customer buys at least one of the machines.

104. Defective Items   A sample shipment of five hair dryers is chosen at random. The probability of exactly 0, 1, 2, 3, 4, or 5 hair dryers being defective is given in the following table.

Number Defective	0	1	2	3	4	5
Probability	0.34	0.26	0.18	0.12	0.07	0.03

Find the probabilities that the following numbers of hair dryers are defective.

(a) No more than 3   **(b)** At least 3

105. Defective Items   A manufacturer buys items from four different suppliers. The fraction of the total number of items that is obtained from each supplier, along with the probability that an item purchased from that supplier is defective, is shown in the table.

Supplier	Fraction of Total Supplied	Probability of Defective
1	0.17	0.01
2	0.39	0.02
3	0.35	0.05
4	0.09	0.03

(a) Find the probability that a randomly selected item is defective.

(b) Find the probability that a defective item came from supplier 4.

(c) Find the probability that a defective item came from supplier 2.

(d) Are the events that an item came from supplier 4 and that the item is defective independent? Explain.

106. Car Buyers   The table shows the results of a survey of buyers of a certain model of car.

Car Type	Satisfied	Not Satisfied	Totals
New	300	100	
Used	450		600
Totals		250	

(a) Complete the table.

(b) How many buyers were surveyed?

(c) How many bought a new car and were satisfied?

(d) How many were not satisfied?

(e) How many bought used cars?

(f) How many of those who were not satisfied had purchased a used car?

(g) Rewrite the event stated in part (f) using the expression "given that."

(h) Find the probability of the outcome in parts (f) and (g).

(i) Find the probability that a used-car buyer is not satisfied.

(j) You should have different answers in parts (h) and (i). Explain why.

(k) Are the events that a car is new and that the customer is satisfied independent? Explain.

107. Auto Insurance An insurance company examines its pool of auto insurance customers and gathers the following information:

(i) All customers insure at least one car.

(ii) 70% of the customers insure more than one car.

(iii) 20% of the customers insure a sports car.

(iv) Of those customers who insure more than one car, 15% insure a sports car.

Calculate the probability that a randomly selected customer insures exactly one car and that car is not a sports car. Choose one of the following. (*Hint:* Draw a tree diagram, and let x be the probability that a customer who insures exactly one car insures a sports car.) *Source: Society of Actuaries.*

(a) 0.13　(b) 0.21　(c) 0.24　(d) 0.25　(e) 0.30

108. Auto Insurance An auto insurance company has 10,000 policyholders. Each policyholder is classified as:

(i) young or old;

(ii) male or female; and

(iii) married or single.

Of these policyholders, 3000 are young, 4600 are male, and 7000 are married. The policyholders can also be classified as 1320 young males, 3010 married males, and 1400 young married persons. Finally, 600 of the policyholders are young married males. How many of the company's policyholders are young, female, and single? Choose one of the following. *Source: Society of Actuaries.*

(a) 280　(b) 423　(c) 486　(d) 880　(e) 896

109. Auto Insurance An actuary studying the insurance preferences of automobile owners makes the following conclusions:

(i) An automobile owner is twice as likely to purchase collision coverage as disability coverage.

(ii) The event that an automobile owner purchases collision coverage is independent of the event that he or she purchases disability coverage.

(iii) The probability that an automobile owner purchases both collision and disability coverages is 0.15.

What is the probability that an automobile owner purchases neither collision nor disability coverage? Choose one of the following. *Source: Society of Actuaries.*

(a) 0.18　(b) 0.33　(c) 0.48　(d) 0.67　(e) 0.82

110. Insurance An insurance company estimates that 40% of policyholders who have only an auto policy will renew next year and 60% of policyholders who have only a homeowners policy will renew next year. The company estimates that 80% of policyholders who have both an auto and a homeowners policy will renew at least one of these policies next year. Company records show that 65% of policyholders have an auto policy, 50% of policyholders have a homeowners policy, and 15% of policyholders have both an auto and a homeowners policy. Using the company's estimates, calculate the percentage of policyholders that will renew at least one policy next year. Choose one of the following. *Source: Society of Actuaries.*

(a) 20　(b) 29　(c) 41　(d) 53　(e) 70

Life Sciences

111. Sickle Cell Anemia The table shows the four possible (equally likely) combinations when both parents are carriers of the sickle cell anemia trait. Each carrier parent has normal cells (N) and trait cells (T).

		Second Parent	
		N_2	T_2
First Parent	N_1		$N_1 T_2$
	T_1		

(a) Complete the table.

(b) If the disease occurs only when two trait cells combine, find the probability that a child born to these parents will have sickle cell anemia.

(c) The child will carry the trait but not have the disease if a normal cell combines with a trait cell. Find this probability.

(d) Find the probability that the child is neither a carrier nor has the disease.

112. Blood Antigens In Exercise 46 of Section 7.2, we described the eight types of human blood. The percentage of the population having each type is as follows:

O^+: 38%;　O^-: 8%;　A^+: 32%;　A^-: 7%;
B^+: 9%;　B^-: 2%;　AB^+: 3%;　AB^-: 1%.

When a person receives a blood transfusion, it is important that the blood be compatible, which means that it introduces no new antigens into the recipient's blood. The following diagram helps illustrate what blood types are compatible.

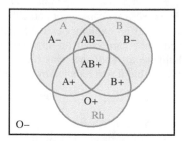

The universal blood type is O^-, since it has none of the additional antigens. The circles labeled A, B, and Rh contain blood types with the A antigen, B antigen, and Rh antigen, respectively. A person with O^- blood can be transfused only with O^- blood, because any other type would introduce a new antigen. Thus the probability that blood from a random donor is compatible is just 8%. A person with AB^+ blood already has all antigens, so the probability that blood from a random donor is compatible is 100%. Find the probability that blood from a random donor is compatible with a person with each blood type. *Source: The Mathematics Teacher.*

(a) O^+　　(b) A^+　　(c) B^+

(d) A^-　　(e) B^-　　(f) AB^-

113. Risk Factors An actuary is studying the prevalence of three health risk factors, denoted by A, B, and C, within a population of women. For each of the three factors, the probability is 0.1 that a woman in the population has only this risk factor (and no others). For any two of the three factors, the probability is 0.12 that she has exactly these two risk factors (but not the other). The probability that a woman has all three risk factors, given that she has A and B, is 1/3. What is the probability that a woman has none of the three risk factors, given that she does not have risk factor A? Choose one of the following. *Source: Society of Actuaries*.

(a) 0.280 **(b)** 0.311 **(c)** 0.467 **(d)** 0.484 **(e)** 0.700

Social Sciences

114. Elections In the 2012 presidential election, over 126 million people voted, of which 46% were male and 54% were female. Of the male voters, 45% voted for Barack Obama and 52% voted for Mitt Romney. Of the female voters, 55% voted for Obama and 44% voted for Romney. *Source: Huffington Post*.

(a) Find the percentage of voters who voted for Obama.

(b) Find the probability that a randomly selected voter for Obama was male.

(c) Find the probability that a randomly selected voter for Obama was female.

115. Television Viewing Habits A telephone survey of television viewers revealed the following information:

> 20 watch situation comedies;
> 19 watch reality shows;
> 27 watch movies;
> 19 watch movies but not reality shows;
> 15 watch situation comedies but not reality shows;
> 10 watch both situation comedies and movies;
> 3 watch all three;
> 7 watch none of these.

(a) How many viewers were interviewed?

(b) How many viewers watch comedies and movies but not reality shows?

(c) How many viewers watch only movies?

(d) How many viewers do not watch movies?

116. Randomized Response Method for Getting Honest Answers to Sensitive Questions There are many personal questions that most people would rather not answer. In fact, when a person is asked such a question, a common response is to provide a false answer. In 1965, Stanley Warner developed a method to ensure that the identity of an individual who answers a question remains anonymous, thus ensuring an honest answer to the question. For this method, instead of one sensitive question being asked to a person, there are two questions, one sensitive and one non-sensitive, and which question the person answers depends on a randomized procedure. The interviewer, who doesn't know which question a person is answering, simply records the answer given as either "Yes" or "No." In this way, there is no way of knowing to which question the person answered "Yes" or "No." Then, using conditional probability, we can estimate the percentage of people who answer "Yes" to the sensitive question. For example, suppose that the two questions are

> *A*: Does your birth year end in an odd digit? (Nonsensitive)
> *B*: Have you ever intentionally cheated on an examination? (Sensitive)

We already know that $P(\text{"Yes"} \mid \text{Question } A) = 1/2$, since half the years are even and half are odd. The answer we seek is $P(\text{"Yes"} \mid \text{Question } B)$. In this experiment, a student is asked to flip a coin and answer question A if the coin comes up heads and otherwise answer question B. Note that the interviewer does not know the outcome of the coin flip or which question is being answered. The percentage of students answering "Yes" is used to approximate $P(\text{"Yes"})$, which is then used to estimate the percentage of students who have cheated on an examination. *Source: Journal of the American Statistical Association*.

(a) Use the fact that the event "Yes" is the union of the event "Yes and Question *A*" with the event "Yes and Question *B*" to prove that

$$P(\text{"Yes"} \mid \text{Question } B)$$
$$= \frac{P(\text{"Yes"}) - P(\text{"Yes"} \mid \text{Question } A) \cdot P(\text{Question } A)}{P(\text{Question } B)}.$$

(b) If this technique is tried on 100 subjects and 60 answered "Yes," what is the approximated probability that a person randomly selected from the group has intentionally cheated on an examination?

117. Police Lineup To illustrate the difficulties with eyewitness identifications from police lineups, John Allen Paulos considers a "lineup" of three pennies, in which we know that two are fair (innocent) and the third (the culprit) has a 75% probability of landing heads. The probability of picking the culprit by chance is, of course, 1/3. Suppose we observe three heads in a row on one of the pennies. If we then guess that this penny is the culprit, what is the probability that we're right? *Source: Who's Counting*.

118. SIDS On July 15, 2005, a panel in England ruled that Roy Meadow, a renowned expert on child abuse and co-founder of London's Royal College of Paediatrics and Child Health, should be erased from the register of physicians in Britain for his faulty statistics at the trial of Sally Clark, who was convicted of murdering her first two babies. Meadow testified at the trial that the probability of a baby dying of sudden death syndrome (SIDS) is 1/8543. He then calculated that the probability of two babies in a family dying of SIDS is $(1/8543)^2 \approx 1/73,000,000$. With such a small probability of both babies dying of SIDS, he concluded that the babies were instead murdered. What assumption did Meadow make in doing this calculation? Discuss reasons why this assumption may be invalid. (*Note:* Clark spent three years in prison before her conviction was reversed.) *Source: Science*.

Physical Sciences

119. Earthquake It has been reported that government scientists have predicted that the odds for a major earthquake occurring in the San Francisco Bay area during the next 30 years are 9 to 1. What is the probability that a major earthquake will occur during the next 30 years in San Francisco? *Source: The San Francisco Chronicle*.

General Interest

120. Making a First Down A first down is desirable in football—it guarantees four more plays by the team making it, assuming no score or turnover occurs in the plays. After getting a first down, a team can get another by advancing the ball at least 10 yards. During the four plays given by a first down, a team's position will be indicated by a phrase such as "third and 4," which means that the team has already had two of its four plays, and that 4 more yards are needed to get 10 yards necessary for another first down. An article in a management journal offers the following results for 189 games for a particular National Football League season. "Trials" represents the number of times a team tried to make a first down, given that it was currently playing either a third or a fourth down. Here, n represents the number of yards still needed for a first down. *Source: Management Science.*

n	Trials	Successes	Probability of Making First Down with n Yards to Go
1	543	388	
2	327	186	
3	356	146	
4	302	97	
5	336	91	

(a) Complete the table.

(b) Why is the sum of the answers in the table not equal to 1?

121. States Of the 50 United States, the following is true:

24 are west of the Mississippi River (western states);*

22 had populations less than 3.6 million in the 2010 census (small states);

26 begin with the letters A through M (early states);

9 are large late (beginning with the letters N through Z) eastern states;

14 are small western states;

11 are small early states;

7 are small early western states.

(a) How many western states had populations more than 3.6 million in the 2010 census and begin with the letters N through Z?

(b) How many states east of the Mississippi had populations more than 3.6 million in the 2010 census?

122. Music Country-western songs often emphasize three basic themes: love, prison, and trucks. A survey of the local country-western radio station produced the following data:

12 songs were about a truckdriver who was in love while in prison;

13 were about a prisoner in love;

28 were about a person in love;

18 were about a truckdriver in love;

33 were about people not in prison;

18 were about prisoners;

15 were about truckdrivers who were in prison;

16 were about truckdrivers who were not in prison.

*We count here states such as Minnesota, which has more than half of its area to the west of the Mississippi.

(a) How many songs were surveyed?

Find the number of songs about

(b) truckdrivers;

(c) prisoners who are neither truckdrivers nor in love;

(d) prisoners who are in love but are not truckdrivers;

(e) prisoners who are not truckdrivers;

(f) people not in love.

123. Gambling The following puzzle was featured on the Puzzler part of the radio program *Car Talk* on February 23, 2002. A con man puts three cards in a bag; one card is green on both sides, one is red on both sides, and the third is green on one side and red on the other. He lets you pick one card out of the bag and put it on a table, so you can see that a red side is face up, but neither of you can see the other side. He offers to bet you even money that the other side is also red. In other words, if you bet $1, you lose if the other side is red but get back $2 if the other side is green. Is this a good bet? What is the probability that the other side is red? *Source: Car Talk.*

124. Missiles In his novel *Debt of Honor*, Tom Clancy writes the following:

"There were ten target points—missile silos, the intelligence data said, and it pleased the Colonel [Zacharias] to be eliminating the hateful things, even though the price of that was the lives of other men. There were only three of them [bombers], and his bomber, like the others, carried only eight weapons [smart bombs]. The total number of weapons carried for the mission was only twenty-four, with two designated for each silo, and Zacharias's last four for the last target. Two bombs each. Every bomb had a 95% probability of hitting within four meters of the aim point, pretty good numbers really, except that this sort of mission had precisely no margin for error. Even the paper probability was less than half a percent chance of a double miss, but that number times ten targets meant a 5% chance that [at least] one missile would survive, and that could not be tolerated." *Source: Debt of Honor.*

Determine whether the calculations in this quote are correct by the following steps.

(a) Given that each bomb had a 95% probability of hitting the missile silo on which it was dropped, and that two bombs were dropped on each silo, what is the probability of a double miss?

(b) What is the probability that a specific silo was destroyed (that is, that at least one bomb of the two bombs struck the silo)?

(c) What is the probability that all ten silos were destroyed?

(d) What is the probability that at least one silo survived? Does this agree with the quote?

(e) What assumptions need to be made for the calculations in parts (a) through (d) to be valid? Discuss whether these assumptions seem reasonable.

125. Viewing Habits   A survey of a group's viewing habits over the last year revealed the following information:

(i) 28% watched gymnastics;

(ii) 29% watched baseball;

(iii) 19% watched soccer;

(iv) 14% watched gymnastics and baseball;

(v) 12% watched baseball and soccer;

(vi) 10% watched gymnastics and soccer;

(vii) 8% watched all three sports.

Calculate the percentage of the group that watched none of the three sports during the last year. Choose one of the following. *Source: Society of Actuaries.*

(a) 24   (b) 36   (c) 41

(d) 52   (e) 60

EXTENDED APPLICATION

MEDICAL DIAGNOSIS

When a patient exhibits symptoms that may, or may not, indicate one of many possible diseases, an understanding of probability can be useful. Data giving the probability that someone with a particular disease will exhibit certain symptoms are readily available. What the medical team wants to know, however, is the probability that the patient has the disease, given the presence of these specific symptoms. This is a classic situation for Bayes' Theorem: We know $P(A|B)$, but what we really want to know is $P(B|A)$.

People suffering from hypothyroidism (underactive thyroid) can experience tiredness, inability to tolerate cold, and weight gain. By contrast, hyperthyroidism, or overactive thyroid, can speed up virtually every function of the body.

The table at the bottom of the page contains data from a study of 879 people. These included 314 with normal thyroids, 268 with some thyroid abnormality but who were otherwise euthyroid (normal thyroid), 123 who were hypothyroid, and 174 who were hyperthyroid. The original data listed 21 symptoms, but for simplicity we have listed only the first five, with the proportion of patients in each group exhibiting each symptom.

These numbers tell us, for example, that a hypothyroid person has a 0.06 probability of exhibiting a recent onset of nervousness. The figures for a euthyroid or a hyperthyroid person are 0.37 and 0.92, respectively. If we denote

T_1 = patient is hypothyroid,

T_2 = patient is euthyroid, and

T_3 = patient is hyperthyroid,

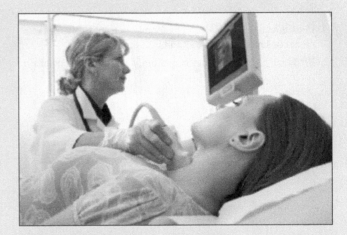

then we could write this information as $P(N|T_1) = 0.06$, $P(N|T_2) = 0.37$, and $P(N|T_3) = 0.92$. It is known that for the general population, $P(T_1) = 0.15$, $P(T_2) = 0.65$, and $P(T_3) = 0.20$.

The study's authors assumed the symptoms to be independent. For example, if a patient is euthyroid, they calculated the probability that the patient had a recent onset of both nervousness and heat sensitivity as

$$P(N \cap H|T_2) = P(N|T_2)P(H|T_2) = (0.37)(0.17) = 0.06,$$

or 6%. (Following the researchers' practice in most of their calculations, we will round all probabilities to the hundredth place. Higher precision is not justified because some of the original probabilities were known only to the hundredth place.)

Symptom	Hypothyroid	Euthyroid	Hyperthyroid
Recent onset of nervousness (N)	0.06	0.37	0.92
Recent onset of heat sensitivity (H)	0.00	0.17	0.74
Recent onset of increased sweating (S)	0.13	0.25	0.68
Recent onset of increased appetite (A)	0.03	0.10	0.61
Recent onset of weight loss (W)	0.13	0.45	0.84

Suppose a patient has a recent onset of nervousness, and the medical team wants to know the probability of hyperthyroidism. We know that $P(N|T_3) = 0.92$, but the medical team wants to know $P(T_3|N)$. For the general population, $P(T_3) = 0.20$, but we would expect the probability to be higher for someone with a symptom. The question is how much higher. Using Bayes' Theorem,

$$P(T_3|N) = \frac{P(N|T_3)P(T_3)}{P(N|T_1)P(T_1) + P(N|T_2)P(T_2) + P(N|T_3)P(T_3)}$$

$$= \frac{(0.92)(0.20)}{(0.06)(0.15) + (0.37)(0.65) + (0.92)(0.20)}$$

$$\approx 0.42.$$

There is a 42% chance that a patient with a recent onset of nervousness is hyperthyroid. *Source: JAMA*.

EXERCISES

1. Find the probability that a randomly selected patient has a recent onset of nervousness and is euthyroid.

2. Find the probability that a randomly selected patient has a recent onset of heat sensitivity.

3. Find the probability that a patient with a recent onset of heat sensitivity is hyperthyroid.

4. Find the probability that a patient with a recent onset of weight loss is hypothyroid.

5. Put the probabilities in the table into a spreadsheet. Then create additional cells in the spreadsheet that will calculate the probability of hypothyroid, euthyroid, or hyperthyroid given any of the five symptoms. (*Hint:* To copy and paste the formula from one cell into another, you may want to use notation such as A$1, which allows the column to change but keeps the row fixed at row 1, or A1, which keeps the row and column fixed.)

DIRECTIONS FOR GROUP PROJECT

Find an article on medical decision making from a medical journal and develop a doctor-patient scenario for that particular decision. Then create a role-playing activity in which the physician and medical team present the various options and the mathematics associated with making such a decision to a patient. Make sure to present the mathematics in a manner that the average patient might understand. (Hint: Many leading medical journals include articles on decision making in medical settings; one such journal is Medical Decision Making.*)*

8

Counting Principles; Further Probability Topics

If you have 31 ice cream flavors available, how many different three-scoop cones can you make? The answer, which is surprisingly large, involves counting permutations or combinations, the subject of the first two sections in this chapter. The counting formulas we will develop have important applications in probability theory.

I f we flip two coins and record heads or tails for each coin, we can list the four possible outcomes in the sample space as $S = \{hh, ht, th, tt\}$. But what if we flip 10 coins? As we shall see, there are over 1000 possible outcomes, which makes a list of the sample space impractical. Fortunately, there are methods for counting the outcomes in a set without actually listing them. We introduce these methods in the first two sections, and then we use this approach in the third section to find probabilities. In the fourth section, we introduce binomial experiments, which consist of repeated independent trials with only two possible outcomes, and develop a formula for binomial probabilities. The final section continues the discussion of probability distributions that we began in Chapter 7.

8.1 The Multiplication Principle; Permutations

APPLY IT   In how many ways can seven panelists be seated in a row of seven chairs? *Before we answer this question in Example 8, we will begin with a simpler example.*

Suppose a breakfast consists of one pastry, for which you can choose a bagel, a muffin, or a donut, and one beverage, for which you can choose coffee or juice. How many different breakfasts can you have? For each of the 3 pastries there are 2 different beverages, or a total of $3 \cdot 2 = 6$ different breakfasts, as shown in Figure 1. This example illustrates a general principle of counting, called the **multiplication principle**.

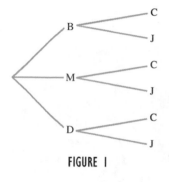

FIGURE 1

> **Multiplication Principle**
>
> Suppose n choices must be made, with
>
> $$m_1 \text{ ways to make choice 1,}$$
> $$m_2 \text{ ways to make choice 2,}$$
>
> and so on, with
>
> $$m_n \text{ ways to make choice } n.$$
>
> Then there are
>
> $$m_1 \cdot m_2 \cdot \cdots \cdot m_n$$
>
> different ways to make the entire sequence of choices.

EXAMPLE 1   Combination Lock

A certain combination lock can be set to open to any 3-letter sequence.

(a) How many sequences are possible?

SOLUTION   Since there are 26 letters in the alphabet, there are 26 choices for each of the 3 letters. By the multiplication principle, there are $26 \cdot 26 \cdot 26 = 17{,}576$ different sequences.

(b) How many sequences are possible if no letter is repeated?

SOLUTION   There are 26 choices for the first letter. It cannot be used again, so there are 25 choices for the second letter and then 24 choices for the third letter. Consequently, the number of such sequences is $26 \cdot 25 \cdot 24 = 15{,}600$.   **TRY YOUR TURN 1**

YOUR TURN 1   A combination lock can be set to open to any 4-digit sequence. How many sequences are possible? How many sequences are possible if no digit is repeated?

EXAMPLE 2   Morse Code

Morse code uses a sequence of dots and dashes to represent letters and words. How many sequences are possible with at most 3 symbols?

SOLUTION   "At most 3" means "1 or 2 or 3" here. Each symbol may be either a dot or a dash. Thus the following number of sequences are possible in each case.

Morse Code	
Number of Symbols	Number of Sequences
1	2
2	$2 \cdot 2 = 4$
3	$2 \cdot 2 \cdot 2 = 8$

Altogether, $2 + 4 + 8 = 14$ different sequences are possible.

EXAMPLE 3   I Ching

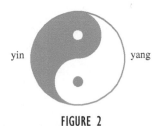

yin   yang

FIGURE 2

An ancient Chinese philosophical work known as the *I Ching (Book of Changes)* is often used as an oracle from which people can seek and obtain advice. The philosophy describes the duality of the universe in terms of two primary forces: *yin* (passive, dark, receptive) and *yang* (active, light, creative). Figure 2 shows the traditional symbol for yin and yang. The yin energy can also be represented by a broken line (– –) and the yang by a solid line (—). These lines are written on top of one another in groups of three, known as *trigrams*. For example, the trigram $\equiv\equiv$ is called *Tui*, the Joyous, and has the image of a lake.

(a)   How many trigrams are there altogether?

SOLUTION   Think of choosing between the 2 types of lines for each of the 3 positions in the trigram. There will be 2 choices for each position, so there are $2 \cdot 2 \cdot 2 = 8$ different trigrams.

(b)   The trigrams are grouped together, one on top of the other, in pairs known as *hexagrams*. Each hexagram represents one aspect of the *I Ching* philosophy. How many hexagrams are there?

SOLUTION   For each position in the hexagram there are 8 possible trigrams, giving $8 \cdot 8 = 64$ hexagrams.

EXAMPLE 4   Books

A teacher has 5 different books that he wishes to arrange side by side. How many different arrangements are possible?

YOUR TURN 2   A teacher is lining up 8 students for a spelling bee. How many different line-ups are possible?

SOLUTION   Five choices will be made, one for each space that will hold a book. Any of the 5 books could be chosen for the first space. There are 4 choices for the second space, since 1 book has already been placed in the first space; there are 3 choices for the third space, and so on. By the multiplication principle, the number of different possible arrangements is $5 \cdot 4 \cdot 3 \cdot 2 \cdot 1 = 120$.   **TRY YOUR TURN 2**

FOR REVIEW

The natural numbers, also referred to as the positive integers, are the numbers 1, 2, 3, 4, etc.

The use of the multiplication principle often leads to products such as $5 \cdot 4 \cdot 3 \cdot 2 \cdot 1$, the product of all the natural numbers from 5 down to 1. If n is a natural number, the symbol $n!$ (read "*n factorial*") denotes the product of all the natural numbers from n down to 1. If $n = 1$, this formula is understood to give $1! = 1$.

Factorial Notation

For any natural number n,

$$n! = n(n-1)(n-2)\cdots(3)(2)(1).$$

Also, by definition,

$$0! = 1.$$

With this symbol, the product $5 \cdot 4 \cdot 3 \cdot 2 \cdot 1$ can be written as 5!. Also, $3! = 3 \cdot 2 \cdot 1 = 6$. The definition of $n!$ could be used to show that $n[(n-1)]! = n!$ for all natural numbers $n \geq 2$. It is helpful if this result also holds for $n = 1$. This can happen only if 0! equals 1, as defined above.

As n gets large, $n!$ grows very quickly. For example, $5! = 120$, while $10! = 3,628,800$. Most calculators can be used to determine $n!$ for small values of n. A calculator with a 10-digit display and scientific notation capability will usually give the exact value of $n!$ for $n \leq 13$, and approximate values of $n!$ for $14 \leq n \leq 69$. The value of 70! is approximately 1.198×10^{100}, which is too large for most calculators. To get a sense of how large 70! is, suppose a computer counted the numbers from 1 to 70! at a rate of 1 billion numbers per second. If the computer started when the universe began, by now it would have calculated only a tiny fraction of the total.

TECHNOLOGY NOTE

On many graphing calculators, the factorial of a number is accessible through a menu. On the TI-84 Plus C, for example, this menu is found by pressing the MATH key, selecting PROB (for probability), and then selecting the !.

YOUR TURN 3 A teacher wishes to place 5 out of 8 different books on her shelf. How many arrangements of 5 books are possible?

EXAMPLE 5 Books

Suppose the teacher in Example 4 wishes to place only 3 of the 5 books on his desk. How many arrangements of 3 books are possible?

SOLUTION The teacher again has 5 ways to fill the first space, 4 ways to fill the second space, and 3 ways to fill the third. Since he wants to use only 3 books, only 3 spaces can be filled (3 events) instead of 5, for $5 \cdot 4 \cdot 3 = 60$ arrangements. **TRY YOUR TURN 3**

Permutations
The answer 60 in Example 5 is called the number of *permutations* of 5 things taken 3 at a time. A **permutation** of r (where $r \geq 1$) elements from a set of n elements is any specific ordering or arrangement, *without repetition*, of the r elements. Each rearrangement of the r elements is a different permutation. The number of permutations of n things taken r at a time (with $r \leq n$) is written $P(n, r)$.* Based on the work in Example 5,

$$P(5, 3) = 5 \cdot 4 \cdot 3 = 60.$$

Factorial notation can be used to express this product as follows.

$$5 \cdot 4 \cdot 3 = 5 \cdot 4 \cdot 3 \cdot \frac{2 \cdot 1}{2 \cdot 1} = \frac{5 \cdot 4 \cdot 3 \cdot 2 \cdot 1}{2 \cdot 1} = \frac{5!}{2!} = \frac{5!}{(5-3)!}$$

This example illustrates the general rule of permutations, which can be stated as follows.

Permutations

If $P(n, r)$ (where $r \leq n$) is the number of permutations of n elements taken r at a time, then

$$P(n, r) = \frac{n!}{(n-r)!}.$$

*An alternate notation for $P(n, r)$ is $_nP_r$.

CAUTION	The letter P here represents *permutations*, not *probability*. In probability notation, the quantity in parentheses describes an *event*. In permutations notation, the quantity in parentheses always comprises *two numbers*.

The proof of the permutations rule follows the discussion in Example 5. There are n ways to choose the first of the r elements, $n - 1$ ways to choose the second, and $n - r + 1$ ways to choose the rth element, so that

$$P(n, r) = n(n - 1)(n - 2) \cdots (n - r + 1).$$

Now multiply on the right by $(n - r)!/(n - r)!$.

$$P(n, r) = n(n - 1)(n - 2) \cdots (n - r + 1) \cdot \frac{(n - r)!}{(n - r)!}$$

$$= \frac{n(n - 1)(n - 2) \cdots (n - r + 1)(n - r)!}{(n - r)!}$$

$$= \frac{n!}{(n - r)!}$$

Because we defined 0! equal to 1, the formula for permutations gives the special case

$$P(n, n) = \frac{n!}{(n - n)!} = \frac{n!}{0!} = \frac{n!}{1} = n!.$$

This result also follows from the multiplication principle, because $P(n, n)$ gives the number of permutations of n objects, and there are n choices for the first object, $n - 1$ for the second, and so on, down to just 1 choice for the last object. Example 4 illustrated this idea.

$P(n, n)$
The number of permutations of a set with n elements is $n!$; that is $P(n, n) = n!$.

EXAMPLE 6	**Permutations of Letters**

Find the following.

(a) The number of permutations of the letters A, B, and C.

　　SOLUTION　By the formula $P(n, n) = n!$, with $n = 3$,

$$P(3, 3) = 3! = 3 \cdot 2 \cdot 1 = 6.$$

The 6 *permutations* (or *arrangements*) are ABC, ACB, BAC, BCA, CAB, CBA.

(b) The number of permutations if just 2 of the letters A, B, and C are to be used

　　SOLUTION　Find $P(3, 2)$.

$$P(3, 2) = \frac{3!}{(3 - 2)!} = \frac{3!}{1!} = 3! = 6$$

This result is exactly the same answer as in part (a). This is because, in the case of $P(3, 3)$, after the first 2 choices are made, the third is already determined, as shown in the table below.

YOUR TURN 4　Find the number of permutations of the letters L, M, N, O, P, and Q, if just three of the letters are to be used.

Permutations of Three Letters					
First Two Letters	AB	AC	BA	BC	CA	CB
Third Letter	C	B	C	A	B	A

TRY YOUR TURN 4

To find $P(n, r)$, we can use either the permutations formula or direct application of the multiplication principle, as the following example shows.

EXAMPLE 7 Politics

In a recent election, eight candidates sought the Republican nomination for president. In how many ways could voters rank their first, second, and third choices?

SOLUTION

Method 1
Calculating by Hand

This is the same as finding the number of permutations of 8 elements taken 3 at a time. Since there are 3 choices to be made, the multiplication principle gives $P(8, 3) = 8 \cdot 7 \cdot 6 = 336$. Alternatively, use the permutations formula to get

$$P(8, 3) = \frac{8!}{(8-3)!} = \frac{8!}{5!} = \frac{8 \cdot 7 \cdot 6 \cdot 5 \cdot 4 \cdot 3 \cdot 2 \cdot 1}{5 \cdot 4 \cdot 3 \cdot 2 \cdot 1} = 8 \cdot 7 \cdot 6 = 336.$$

Method 2
Graphing Calculator

Graphing calculators have the capacity to compute permutations. For example, on a TI-84 Plus C, $P(8, 3)$ can be calculated by inputting 8 followed by `nPr` (found in the `MATH-PROB` menu), and a 3 yielding 336, as shown in Figure 3.

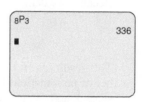

```
8P3
          336
■
```

FIGURE 3

Method 3
Spreadsheet

Spreadsheets can also compute permutations. For example, in Microsoft Excel, $P(8, 3)$ can be calculated by inputting 8 and 3 in cells, say, A1 and B1, and then typing "`=FACT(A1)/ FACT(A1-B1)`" in cell C1 or, for that matter, any other cell.

CAUTION When calculating the number of permutations with the formula, do not try to cancel unlike factorials. For example,

$$\frac{8!}{4!} \neq 2! = 2 \cdot 1 = 2.$$

$$\frac{8!}{4!} = \frac{8 \cdot 7 \cdot 6 \cdot 5 \cdot 4 \cdot 3 \cdot 2 \cdot 1}{4 \cdot 3 \cdot 2 \cdot 1} = 8 \cdot 7 \cdot 6 \cdot 5 = 1680.$$

Always write out the factors first, then cancel where appropriate.

EXAMPLE 8 Television Panel

A televised talk show will include 4 women and 3 men as panelists.

(a) In how many ways can the panelists be seated in a row of 7 chairs?

SOLUTION Find $P(7, 7)$, the total number of ways to seat 7 panelists in 7 chairs.

$$P(7, 7) = 7! = 7 \cdot 6 \cdot 5 \cdot 4 \cdot 3 \cdot 2 \cdot 1 = 5040$$

There are 5040 ways to seat the 7 panelists.

(b) In how many ways can the panelists be seated if the men and women are to be alternated?

SOLUTION Use the multiplication principle. In order to alternate men and women, a woman must be seated in the first chair (since there are 4 women and only 3 men), any of the men next, and so on. Thus there are 4 ways to fill the first seat, 3 ways to fill the second seat, 3 ways to fill the third seat (with any of the 3 remaining women), and so on. This gives

$$\underset{W_1}{4} \cdot \underset{M_1}{3} \cdot \underset{W_2}{3} \cdot \underset{M_2}{2} \cdot \underset{W_3}{2} \cdot \underset{M_3}{1} \cdot \underset{W_4}{1} = 144$$

ways to seat the panelists.

(c) In how many ways can the panelists be seated if the men must sit together, and the women must also sit together?

SOLUTION Use the multiplication principle. We first must decide how to arrange the two groups (men and women). There are 2! ways of doing this. Next, there are 4! ways of arranging the women and 3! ways of arranging the men, for a total of

$$2!\, 4!\, 3! = 2 \cdot 24 \cdot 6 = 288$$

ways.

YOUR TURN 5 Two freshmen, 2 sophomores, 2 juniors, and 3 seniors are on a panel. In how many ways can the panelists be seated if each class must sit together?

(d) In how many ways can one woman and one man from the panel be selected?

SOLUTION There are 4 ways to pick the woman and 3 ways to pick the man, for a total of

$$4 \cdot 3 = 12$$

ways.   **TRY YOUR TURN 5**

If the n objects in a permutation are not all distinguishable—that is, if there are n_1 of type 1, n_2 of type 2, and so on for r different types, then the number of **distinguishable permutations** is

$$\frac{n!}{n_1!\, n_2! \cdots n_r!}.$$

For example, suppose we want to find the number of permutations of the numbers 1, 1, 4, 4, 4. We cannot distinguish between the two 1's or among the three 4's, so using 5! would give too many distinguishable arrangements. Since the two 1's are indistinguishable and account for 2! of the permutations, we divide 5! by 2!. Similarly, we also divide by 3! to account for the three indistinguishable 4's. This gives

$$\frac{5!}{2!\, 3!} = 10$$

permutations.

EXAMPLE 9 Mississippi

In how many ways can the letters in the word *Mississippi* be arranged?

SOLUTION This word contains 1 m, 4 i's, 4 s's, and 2 p's. To use the formula, let $n = 11$, $n_1 = 1$, $n_2 = 4$, $n_3 = 4$, and $n_4 = 2$ to get

YOUR TURN 6 In how many ways can the letters in the word *Tennessee* be arranged?

$$\frac{11!}{1!\, 4!\, 4!\, 2!} = 34,650$$

arrangements.   **TRY YOUR TURN 6**

EXAMPLE 10 Yogurt

NOTE
If Example 9 had asked for the number of ways that the letters in a word with 11 *different* letters could be arranged, the answer would be 11! = 39,916,800.

A student buys 3 cherry yogurts, 2 raspberry yogurts, and 2 blueberry yogurts. She puts them in her dormitory refrigerator to eat one a day for the next week. Assuming yogurts of the same flavor are indistinguishable, in how many ways can she select yogurts to eat for the next week?

YOUR TURN 7 A student has 4 pairs of identical blue socks, 5 pairs of identical brown socks, 3 pairs of identical black socks, and 2 pairs of identical white socks. In how many ways can he select socks to wear for the next two weeks?

SOLUTION This problem is again one of distinguishable permutations. The 7 yogurts can be selected in 7! ways, but since the 3 cherry, 2 raspberry, and 2 blueberry yogurts are indistinguishable, the total number of distinguishable orders in which the yogurts can be selected is

$$\frac{7!}{3!\,2!\,2!} = 210.$$

TRY YOUR TURN 7 ▬

8.1 EXERCISES

In Exercises 1–12, evaluate the factorial or permutation.

1. 6!   **2.** 7!

3. 15!   **4.** 16!

5. $P(13, 2)$ **6.** $P(12, 3)$

7. $P(38, 17)$ **8.** $P(33, 19)$

9. $P(n, 0)$ **10.** $P(n, n)$

11. $P(n, 1)$ **12.** $P(n, n - 1)$

13. How many different types of homes are available if a builder offers a choice of 6 basic plans, 3 roof styles, and 2 exterior finishes?

14. A menu offers a choice of 3 salads, 8 main dishes, and 7 desserts. How many different meals consisting of one salad, one main dish, and one dessert are possible?

15. A couple has narrowed down the choice of a name for their new baby to 4 first names and 5 middle names. How many different first- and middle-name arrangements are possible?

16. In a club with 16 members, how many ways can a slate of 3 officers consisting of president, vice-president, and secretary/treasurer be chosen?

17. Define *permutation* in your own words.

18. Explain the difference between *distinguishable* and *indistinguishable* permutations.

19. In Example 6, there are six 3-letter permutations of the letters A, B, and C. How many 3-letter subsets (unordered groups of letters) are there?

20. In Example 6, how many unordered 2-letter subsets of the letters A, B, and C are there?

21. Find the number of distinguishable permutations of the letters in each word.

  (a) initial   **(b)** little   **(c)** decreed

22. A printer has 5 A's, 4 B's, 2 C's, and 2 D's. How many different "words" are possible that use all these letters? (A "word" does not have to have any meaning here.)

23. Kelly Clark has different books to arrange on a shelf: 4 blue, 3 green, and 2 red.

  (a) In how many ways can the books be arranged on a shelf?

  (b) If books of the same color are to be grouped together, how many arrangements are possible?

(c) In how many distinguishable ways can the books be arranged if books of the same color are identical but need not be grouped together?

(d) In how many ways can you select 3 books, one of each color, if the order in which the books are selected does not matter?

(e) In how many ways can you select 3 books, one of each color, if the order in which the books are selected matters?

24. A child has a set of differently shaped plastic objects. There are 3 pyramids, 4 cubes, and 7 spheres.

  (a) In how many ways can she arrange the objects in a row if each is a different color?

  (b) How many arrangements are possible if objects of the same shape must be grouped together and each object is a different color?

  (c) In how many distinguishable ways can the objects be arranged in a row if objects of the same shape are also the same color (and thus indistinguishable) but need not be grouped together?

  (d) In how many ways can you select 3 objects, one of each shape, if the order in which the objects are selected does not matter and each object is a different color?

  (e) In how many ways can you select 3 objects, one of each shape, if the order in which the objects are selected matters and each object is a different color?

25. If you already knew the value of 9!, how could you find the value of 10! quickly?

26. Given that 450! is approximately equal to $1.7333687 \times 10^{1000}$ (to 8 digits of accuracy), find 451! to 7 digits of accuracy.

27. When calculating $n!$, the number of ending zeros in the answer can be determined prior to calculating the actual number by finding the number of times 5 can be factored from $n!$. For example, 7! has only one 5 occurring in its calculation, and so there is only one ending zero in 5040. The number 10! has two 5's (one from the 5 and one from the 10) and so there must be two ending zeros in the answer 3,628,800. Use this idea to determine the number of zeros that occur in the following factorials, and then explain why this works.

  (a) 13!   **(b)** 27!   **(c)** 75!

28. Because of the view screen, calculators show only a fixed number of digits, often 10 digits. Thus, an approximation of a number will be shown by including only the 10 largest place values of the number. Using the ideas from the previous exercise, determine if the following numbers are correct or if they are incorrect by checking if they have the correct number of ending zeros. (*Note:* Just because a number has the correct number of zeros does not imply that it is correct.)

(a) $12! = 479,001,610$

(b) $23! = 25,852,016,740,000,000,000,000$

(c) $15! = 1,307,643,680,000$

(d) $14! = 87,178,291,200$

29. Some students find it puzzling that $0! = 1$, and think that $0!$ should equal 0. If this were true, what would be the value of $P(4, 4)$ using the permutations formula?

APPLICATIONS

Business and Economics

30. Messenger Bags Timbuk2 sells custom messenger bags in 4 sizes. For each size, there are 53 color/fabric combinations. Any of these 53 can be chosen for the left, center, and right panel. In addition, there are 18 choices of binding color, 27 choices of logo color, 12 choices of liner color, and 48 choices of strap pad color. There are 3 choices for the interior style. The bag can be right- or left-handed. It can be ordered with or without a grab strap, a chiller insert, a camera insert, and a water-bottle pocket. How many different Timbuk2 bags are possible? *Source: Timbuk2.com.*

31. Marketing In a recent marketing campaign, Olive Garden Italian Restaurant® offered a "Never-Ending Pasta Bowl." The customer could order an array of pasta dishes, selecting from 7 types of pasta and 6 types of sauce, including 2 with meat.

(a) If the customer selects one pasta type and one sauce type, how many different "pasta bowls" can a customer order?

(b) How many different "pasta bowls" can a customer order without meat?

32. Investments Kristen Elmore's financial advisor has given her a list of 9 potential investments and has asked her to select and rank her favorite five. In how many different ways can she do this?

33. Scheduling A local television station has eleven slots for commercials during a special broadcast. Six restaurants and 5 stores have bought slots for the broadcast.

(a) In how many ways can the commercials be arranged?

(b) In how many ways can the commercials be arranged so that the restaurants are grouped together and the stores are grouped together?

(c) In how many ways can the commercials be arranged so that the restaurant and store commercials are alternating?

Life Sciences

34. Drug Sequencing Twelve drugs have been found to be effective in the treatment of a disease. It is believed that the sequence in which the drugs are administered is important in the effectiveness of the treatment. In how many different sequences can 5 of the 12 drugs be administered?

35. Insect Classification A biologist is attempting to classify 52,000 species of insects by assigning 3 initials to each species. Is it possible to classify all the species in this way? If not, how many initials should be used?

36. Science Conference At an annual college science conference, student presentations are scheduled one after another in the afternoon session. This year, 5 students are presenting in biology, 5 students are presenting in chemistry, and 2 students are presenting in physics.

(a) In how many ways can the presentations be scheduled?

(b) In how many ways can the presentations be scheduled so that each subject is grouped together?

(c) In how many ways can the presentations be scheduled if the conference must begin and end with a physics presentation?

Social Sciences

37. Social Science Experiment In an experiment on social interaction, 6 people will sit in 6 seats in a row. In how many ways can this be done?

38. Election Ballots In an election with 3 candidates for one office and 6 candidates for another office, how many different ballots may be printed?

General Interest

39. Baseball Teams A baseball team has 19 players. How many 9-player batting orders are possible?

40. Union Elections A chapter of union Local 715 has 35 members. In how many different ways can the chapter select a president, a vice-president, a treasurer, and a secretary?

41. Programming Music A concert to raise money for an economics prize is to consist of 5 works: 2 overtures, 2 sonatas, and a piano concerto.

(a) In how many ways can the program be arranged?

(b) In how many ways can the program be arranged if an overture must come first?

42. Programming Music A zydeco band from Louisiana will play 5 traditional and 3 original Cajun compositions at a concert. In how many ways can they arrange the program if

(a) they begin with a traditional piece?

(b) an original piece will be played last?

43. Radio Station Call Letters How many different 4-letter radio station call letters can be made if

(a) the first letter must be K or W and no letter may be repeated?

(b) repeats are allowed, but the first letter is K or W?

(c) the first letter is K or W, there are no repeats, and the last letter is R?

44. Telephone Numbers How many 7-digit telephone numbers are possible if the first digit cannot be zero and

(a) only odd digits may be used?

(b) the telephone number must be a multiple of 10 (that is, it must end in zero)?

(c) the telephone number must be a multiple of 100?

(d) the first 3 digits are 481?

(e) no repetitions are allowed?

Telephone Area Codes Several years ago, the United States began running out of telephone numbers. Telephone companies introduced new area codes as numbers were used up, and eventually almost all area codes were used up.

45. (a) Until recently, all area codes had a 0 or 1 as the middle digit, and the first digit could not be 0 or 1. How many area codes are there with this arrangement? How many telephone numbers does the current 7-digit sequence permit per area code? (The 3-digit sequence that follows the area code cannot start with 0 or 1. Assume there are no other restrictions.)

(b) The actual number of area codes under the previous system was 152. Explain the discrepancy between this number and your answer to part (a).

(c) The shortage of area codes was avoided by removing the restriction on the second digit. (This resulted in problems for some older equipment, which used the second digit to determine that a long-distance call was being made.) How many area codes are available under the new system?

46. **IP Addresses** Every computer or other device connected to the Internet has an IP address, which until recently consisted of 32 binary digits, known as bits, each of which can be 0 or 1. As all the available IP addresses were becoming used up, a new system was devised with 128 bits. How many IP addresses were available under the older system, and how many are available with the new system? *Source: The New York Times.*

47. **License Plates** For many years, the state of California used 3 letters followed by 3 digits on its automobile license plates.

(a) How many different license plates are possible with this arrangement?

(b) When the state ran out of new numbers, the order was reversed to 3 digits followed by 3 letters. How many new license plate numbers were then possible?

(c) By 1980, the numbers described in part (b) were also used up. The state then issued plates with 1 digit followed by 3 letters and then 3 digits. How many new license plate numbers will this provide?

48. **Social Security Numbers** A social security number has 9 digits. How many social security numbers are there? The U.S. population in 2014 was about 318 million. Is it possible for every U.S. resident to have a unique social security number? (Assume no restrictions.)

49. **Postal Zip Codes** The U.S. Postal Service currently uses 5-digit zip codes in most areas. How many zip codes are possible if there are no restrictions on the digits used? How many would be possible if the first number could not be 0?

50. **Postal Zip Codes** The U.S. Postal Service is encouraging the use of 9-digit zip codes in some areas, adding 4 digits after the usual 5-digit code. How many such zip codes are possible with no restrictions?

51. **Games** The game of Sets uses a special deck of cards. Each card has either one, two, or three identical shapes, all of the same color and style. There are three possible shapes: squiggle,

diamond, and oval. There are three possible colors: green, purple, and red. There are three possible styles: solid, shaded, or outline. The deck consists of all possible combinations of shape, color, style, and number of shapes. How many cards are in the deck? *Source: Sets.*

52. **Games** In the game of Scattergories, the players take 12 turns. In each turn, a 20-sided die is rolled; each side has a letter. The players must then fill in 12 categories (e.g., vegetable, city, etc.) with a word beginning with the letter rolled. Considering that a game consists of 12 rolls of the 20-sided die, and that rolling the same side more than once is allowed, how many possible games are there? *Source: Milton Bradley.*

53. **Games** The game of Twenty Questions consists of asking 20 questions to determine a person, place, or thing that the other person is thinking of. The first question, which is always "Is it an animal, vegetable, or mineral?" has three possible answers. All the other questions must be answered "Yes" or "No." How many possible objects can be distinguished in this game, assuming that all 20 questions are asked? Are 20 questions enough?

54. **Traveling Salesman** In the famous Traveling Salesman Problem, a salesman starts in any one of a set of cities, visits every city in the set once, and returns to the starting city. He would like to complete this circuit with the shortest possible distance.

(a) Suppose the salesman has 10 cities to visit. Given that it does not matter what city he starts in, how many different circuits can he take?

(b) The salesman decides to check all the different paths in part (a) to see which is shortest, but realizes that a circuit has the same distance whichever direction it is traveled. How many different circuits must he check?

(c) Suppose the salesman has 70 cities to visit. Would it be feasible to have a computer check all the different circuits? Explain your reasoning.

55. **Circular Permutations** Circular permutations arise in applications involving arrangements around a closed loop, as in the previous exercise. Here are two examples.

(a) A ferris wheel has 20 seats. How many ways can 20 students arrange themselves on the ferris wheel if each student takes a different seat? We consider two arrangements to be identical if they differ only by rotations of the wheel.

(b) A necklace is to be strung with 15 beads, each of a different color. In how many ways can the beads be arranged? We consider two arrangements to be identical if they differ only by rotations of the necklace or by flipping the necklace over. (*Hint:* If every arrangement is counted twice, the correct number of arrangements can be found by dividing by 2.)

YOUR TURN ANSWERS

1. 10,000; 5040	**2.** 40,320	**3.** 6720	**4.** 120
5. 1152	**6.** 3780	**7.** 2,522,520	

8.2 Combinations

APPLY IT   In how many ways can a manager select 4 employees for promotion from 12 eligible employees?
As we shall see in Example 5, permutations alone cannot be used to answer this question, but combinations will provide the answer.

In the previous section, we saw that there are 60 ways that a teacher can arrange 3 of 5 different books on his desk. That is, there are 60 permutations of 5 books taken 3 at a time. Suppose now that the teacher does not wish to arrange the books on his desk but rather wishes to choose, without regard to order, any 3 of the 5 books for a book sale to raise money for his school. In how many ways can this be done?

At first glance, we might say 60 again, but this is incorrect. The number 60 counts all possible *arrangements* of 3 books chosen from 5. The following 6 arrangements, however, would all lead to the same set of 3 books being given to the book sale.

mystery-biography-textbook	biography-textbook-mystery
mystery-textbook-biography	textbook-biography-mystery
biography-mystery-textbook	textbook-mystery-biography

The list shows 6 different *arrangements* of 3 books, but only one *subset* of 3 books. A subset of items listed *without regard to order* is called a **combination**. The number of combinations of 5 things taken 3 at a time is written $C(5, 3)$.* Since they are subsets, combinations are *not ordered*.

To evaluate $C(5, 3)$, start with the $5 \cdot 4 \cdot 3$ *permutations* of 5 things taken 3 at a time. Since combinations are not ordered, find the number of combinations by dividing the number of permutations by the number of ways each group of 3 can be ordered; that is, divide by 3!.

$$C(5, 3) = \frac{5 \cdot 4 \cdot 3}{3!} = \frac{5 \cdot 4 \cdot 3}{3 \cdot 2 \cdot 1} = 10$$

There are 10 ways that the teacher can choose 3 books for the book sale.

Generalizing this discussion gives the following formula for the number of combinations of n elements taken r at a time:

$$C(n, r) = \frac{P(n, r)}{r!}.$$

Another version of this formula is found as follows.

$$C(n, r) = \frac{P(n, r)}{r!}$$

$$= \frac{n!}{(n - r)!} \cdot \frac{1}{r!} \qquad P(n, r) = \frac{n!}{(n - r)!}.$$

$$= \frac{n!}{(n - r)! \, r!}$$

*Other common notations for $C(n, r)$ are $_nC_r$, C_r^n, and $\binom{n}{r}$.

The previous steps lead to the following result.

> ## Combinations
>
> If $C(n, r)$, denotes the number of combinations of n elements taken r at a time, where $r \leq n$, then
>
> $$C(n, r) = \frac{n!}{(n - r)! \, r!}.$$

EXAMPLE 1 Committees

How many committees of 3 people can be formed from a group of 8 people?

SOLUTION

Method 1
Calculating by Hand

A committee is an unordered group, so use the combinations formula for $C(8, 3)$.

$$C(8, 3) = \frac{8!}{5!3!} = \frac{8 \cdot 7 \cdot 6 \cdot 5 \cdot 4 \cdot 3 \cdot 2 \cdot 1}{5 \cdot 4 \cdot 3 \cdot 2 \cdot 1 \cdot 3 \cdot 2 \cdot 1} = \frac{8 \cdot 7 \cdot 6}{3 \cdot 2 \cdot 1} = 56$$

Method 2
Graphing Calculator

Graphing calculators have the capacity to compute combinations. For example, on a TI-84 Plus C, $C(8, 3)$ can be calculated by inputting 8 followed by nCr (found in the MATH-PROB menu) and a 3 yielding 56, as shown in Figure 4.

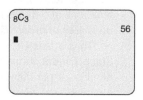

FIGURE 4

Method 3
Spreadsheet

Spreadsheets can also compute combinations. For example, in Microsoft Excel, $C(8, 3)$ can be calculated by inputting 8 and 3 in cells, say, A1 and B1, and then typing "=FACT(A1)/(FACT(A1-B1)*FACT(B1))" in cell C1 or, for that matter, any other cell. The command "=MULTINOMIAL(5,3)" also gives this answer.

YOUR TURN 1 How many committees of 4 people can be formed from a group of 10 people?

TRY YOUR TURN 1

Example 1 shows an alternative way to compute $C(n, r)$. Take r or $n - r$, whichever is smaller. Write the factorial of this number in the denominator. In the numerator, write out a sufficient number of factors of $n!$ so there is one factor in the numerator for each factor in the denominator. For example, to calculate $C(8, 3)$ or $C(8, 5)$ write

$$\frac{8 \cdot 7 \cdot 6}{3 \cdot 2 \cdot 1} = 56.$$

The factors that are omitted (written in color in Example 1) cancel out of the numerator and denominator, so need not be included.

Notice from the previous discussion that $C(8, 3) = C(8, 5)$. (See Exercise 25 for a generalization of this idea.) One interpretation of this fact is that the number of ways to form a committee of 3 people chosen from a group of 8 is the same as the number of ways to choose the 5 people who are not on the committee.

Notice that this is *not* true with permutations: $P(8, 3) \neq P(8, 5)$.

EXAMPLE 2 Lawyers

Three lawyers are to be selected from a group of 30 to work on a special project.

(a) In how many different ways can the lawyers be selected?

SOLUTION Here we wish to know the number of 3-element combinations that can be formed from a set of 30 elements. (We want combinations, not permutations, since order within the group of 3 doesn't matter.)

$$C(30, 3) = \frac{30!}{27!3!} = \frac{30 \cdot 29 \cdot 28 \cdot 27!}{27! \cdot 3 \cdot 2 \cdot 1} \qquad 30! = 30 \cdot 29 \cdot 28 \cdot 27!$$
$$= \frac{30 \cdot 29 \cdot 28}{3 \cdot 2 \cdot 1}$$
$$= 4060$$

There are 4060 ways to select the project group.

(b) In how many ways can the group of 3 be selected if a certain lawyer must work on the project?

SOLUTION Since 1 lawyer already has been selected for the project, the problem is reduced to selecting 2 more from the remaining 29 lawyers.

$$C(29, 2) = \frac{29!}{27! \, 2!} = \frac{29 \cdot 28 \cdot 27!}{27! \cdot 2 \cdot 1} = \frac{29 \cdot 28}{2 \cdot 1} = 29 \cdot 14 = 406$$

In this case, the project group can be selected in 406 ways.

(c) In how many ways can a nonempty group of at most 3 lawyers be selected from these 30 lawyers?

SOLUTION Here, by "at most 3" we mean "1 or 2 or 3." (The number 0 is excluded because the group is nonempty.) Find the number of ways for each case.

Case		Number of Ways
1	$C(30, 1) =$	$\dfrac{30!}{29! \, 1!} = \dfrac{30 \cdot 29!}{29! \, (1)} = 30$
2	$C(30, 2) =$	$\dfrac{30!}{28! \, 2!} = \dfrac{30 \cdot 29 \cdot 28!}{28! \cdot 2 \cdot 1} - 435$
3	$C(30, 3) =$	$\dfrac{30!}{27! \, 3!} = \dfrac{30 \cdot 29 \cdot 28 \cdot 27!}{27! \cdot 3 \cdot 2 \cdot 1} = 4060$

YOUR TURN 2 From a class of 15 students, a group of 3 or 4 students will be selected to work on a special project. In how many ways can a group of 3 or 4 students be selected?

The total number of ways to select at most 3 lawyers will be the sum

$$30 + 435 + 4060 = 4525. \qquad \textbf{TRY YOUR TURN 2}$$

EXAMPLE 3 Sales

A salesman has 10 accounts in a certain city.

(a) In how many ways can he select 3 accounts to call on?

SOLUTION Within a selection of 3 accounts, the arrangement of the calls is not important, so there are

$$C(10, 3) = \frac{10!}{7! \, 3!} = \frac{10 \cdot 9 \cdot 8}{3 \cdot 2 \cdot 1} = 120$$

ways he can make a selection of 3 accounts.

(b) In how many ways can he select at least 8 of the 10 accounts to use in preparing a report?

SOLUTION "At least 8" means "8 or more," which is "8 or 9 or 10." First find the number of ways to choose in each case.

Case	Number of Ways
8	$C(10, 8) = \dfrac{10!}{2!\,8!} = \dfrac{10 \cdot 9}{2 \cdot 1} = 45$
9	$C(10, 9) = \dfrac{10!}{1!\,9!} = \dfrac{10}{1} = 10$
10	$C(10, 10) = \dfrac{10!}{0!\,10!} = 1$

He can select at least 8 of the 10 accounts in $45 + 10 + 1 = 56$ ways.

CAUTION When we are making a first decision *and* a second decision, we *multiply* to find the total number of ways. When we are making a decision in which the first choice *or* the second choice are valid choices, we *add* to find the total number of ways.

The formulas for permutations and combinations given in this section and in the previous section will be very useful in solving probability problems in the next section. Any difficulty in using these formulas usually comes from being unable to differentiate between them. Both permutations and combinations give the number of ways to choose r objects from a set of n objects. The differences between permutations and combinations are outlined in the following table.

Permutations	Combinations
Different orderings or arrangements of the r objects are different permutations.	Each choice or subset of r objects gives one combination. Order within the group of r objects does not matter.
$P(n, r) = \dfrac{n!}{(n - r)!}$	$C(n, r) = \dfrac{n!}{(n - r)!\,r!}$
Clue words: arrangement, schedule, order	Clue words: group, committee, set, sample
Order matters!	Order does not matter!

In the next examples, concentrate on recognizing which formula should be applied.

EXAMPLE 4 **Permutations and Combinations**

For each problem, tell whether permutations or combinations should be used to solve the problem.

(a) How many 4-digit code numbers are possible if no digits are repeated?

SOLUTION Since changing the order of the 4 digits results in a different code, use permutations.

(b) A sample of 3 light bulbs is randomly selected from a batch of 15. How many different samples are possible?

SOLUTION The order in which the 3 light bulbs are selected is not important. The sample is unchanged if the items are rearranged, so combinations should be used.

(c) In a baseball conference with 8 teams, how many games must be played so that each team plays every other team exactly once?

SOLUTION Selection of 2 teams for a game is an *unordered* subset of 2 from the set of 8 teams. Use combinations again.

(d) In how many ways can 4 patients be assigned to 6 different hospital rooms so that each patient has a private room?

SOLUTION The room assignments are an *ordered* selection of 4 rooms from the 6 rooms. Exchanging the rooms of any 2 patients within a selection of 4 rooms gives a different assignment, so permutations should be used. **TRY YOUR TURN 3**

YOUR TURN 3 Solve the problems in Example 4.

APPLY IT

EXAMPLE 5 Promotions

A manager must select 4 employees for promotion; 12 employees are eligible.

(a) In how many ways can the 4 be chosen?

SOLUTION Since there is no reason to differentiate among the 4 who are selected, use combinations.

$$C(12, 4) = \frac{12!}{8! \, 4!} = 495$$

YOUR TURN 4 In how many ways can a committee of 3 be chosen from a group of 20 students? In how many ways can three officers (president, treasurer, and secretary) be selected from a group of 20 students?

(b) In how many ways can 4 employees be chosen (from 12) to be placed in 4 different jobs?

SOLUTION In this case, once a group of 4 is selected, they can be assigned in many different ways (or arrangements) to the 4 jobs. Therefore, this problem requires permutations.

$$P(12, 4) = \frac{12!}{8!} = 11,880$$

TRY YOUR TURN 4

FOR REVIEW

Example 6 involves a standard deck of 52 playing cards, as shown in Figure 17 in Chapter 7. Recall the discussion that accompanies the photograph.

EXAMPLE 6 Playing Cards

Five cards are dealt from a standard 52-card deck.

(a) How many such hands have only face cards?

SOLUTION The face cards are the king, queen, and jack of each suit. Since there are 4 suits, there are 12 face cards. The arrangement of the 5 cards is not important, so use combinations to get

$$C(12, 5) = \frac{12!}{7! \, 5!} = 792.$$

(b) How many such hands have a full house of aces and eights (3 aces and 2 eights)?

SOLUTION The arrangement of the 3 aces or the 2 eights does not matter, so we use combinations. There are $C(4, 3)$ ways to get 3 aces from the four aces in the deck, and $C(4, 2)$ ways to get 2 eights. By the multiplication principle we get

$$C(4, 3) \cdot C(4, 2) = 4 \cdot 6 = 24.$$

(c) How many such hands have exactly 2 hearts?

SOLUTION There are 13 hearts in the deck, so the 2 hearts will be selected from those 13 cards. The other 3 cards must come from the remaining 39 cards that are not hearts. Use combinations and the multiplication principle to get

$$C(13, 2) \cdot C(39, 3) = 78 \cdot 9139 = 712,842.$$

Notice that the two numbers in red in the combinations add up to 52, the total number of cards, and the two numbers in blue add up to 5, the number of cards in a hand.

(d) How many such hands have cards of a single suit?

YOUR TURN 5 How many five card hands have exactly 2 aces?

SOLUTION Since the arrangement of the 5 cards is not important, use combinations. The total number of ways that 5 cards of a particular suit of 13 cards can occur is $C(13, 5)$. There are four different suits, so the multiplication principle gives

$$4 \cdot C(13, 5) = 4 \cdot 1287 = 5148$$

ways to deal 5 cards of the same suit.

TRY YOUR TURN 5

As Example 6 shows, often both combinations and the multiplication principle must be used in the same problem.

EXAMPLE 7 Soup

To illustrate the differences between permutations and combinations in another way, suppose 2 cans of soup are to be selected from 4 cans on a shelf: noodle (N), bean (B), mushroom (M), and tomato (T). As shown in Figure 5(a), there are 12 ways to select 2 cans from the 4 cans if the order matters (if noodle first and bean second is considered different from bean, then noodle, for example). On the other hand, if order is unimportant, then there are 6 ways to choose 2 cans of soup from the 4, as illustrated in Figure 5(b).

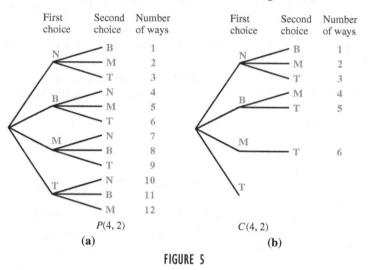

FIGURE 5

CAUTION It should be stressed that not all counting problems lend themselves to either permutations or combinations. When a tree diagram or the multiplication principle can be used directly, it's often best to use it.

8.2 WARM-UP EXERCISES

W1. How many three-digit numbers can be formed using only odd digits if no repetitions are allowed? *(Sec. 8.1)*

W2. How many distinguishable permutations of the letters in the word "bananas" are there? *(Sec. 8.1)*

8.2 EXERCISES

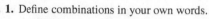 **1.** Define combinations in your own words.

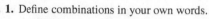 **2.** Explain the difference between a permutation and a combination.

Evaluate each combination.

3. $C(8, 3)$

4. $C(12, 5)$

5. $C(44, 20)$

6. $C(40, 18)$

7. $C(n, 0)$

8. $C(n, n)$

9. $C(n, 1)$

10. $C(n, n - 1)$

11. In how many ways can a hand of 6 clubs be chosen from an ordinary deck?

12. In how many ways can a hand of 6 red cards be chosen from an ordinary deck?

13. Five cards are marked with the numbers 1, 2, 3, 4, and 5, then shuffled, and 2 cards are drawn.

    (a) How many different 2-card combinations are possible?

    (b) How many 2-card hands contain a number less than 3?

14. An economics club has 31 members.

    (a) If a committee of 4 is to be selected, in how many ways can the selection be made?

    (b) In how many ways can a committee of at least 1 and at most 3 be selected?

15. Use a tree diagram for the following.

    (a) Find the number of ways 2 letters can be chosen from the set {L, M, N} if order is important and repetition is allowed.

    (b) Reconsider part (a) if no repeats are allowed.

    (c) Find the number of combinations of 3 elements taken 2 at a time. Does this answer differ from part (a) or (b)?

16. Repeat Exercise 15 using the set {L, M, N, P}.

In Exercises 17–24, decide whether each exercise involves permutations or combinations, and then solve the problem.

17. In a club with 9 male and 11 female members, how many 5-member committees can be chosen that have

    (a) all men?   (b) all women?

    (c) 3 men and 2 women?

18. In Exercise 17, how many committees can be selected that have

    (a) at least 4 women?   (b) no more than 2 men?

19. In a game of musical chairs, 12 children will sit in 11 chairs arranged in a row (one will be left out). In how many ways can this happen, if we count rearrangements of the children in the chairs as different outcomes?

20. A group of 3 students is to be selected from a group of 14 students to take part in a class in cell biology.

    (a) In how many ways can this be done?

    (b) In how many ways can the group who will not take part be chosen?

21. Marbles are being drawn without replacement from a bag containing 16 marbles.

    (a) How many samples of 2 marbles can be drawn?

    (b) How many samples of 4 marbles can be drawn?

    (c) If the bag contains 3 yellow, 4 white, and 9 blue marbles, how many samples of 2 marbles can be drawn in which both marbles are blue?

22. There are 7 rotten apples in a crate of 26 apples.

    (a) How many samples of 3 apples can be drawn from the crate?

    (b) How many samples of 3 could be drawn in which all 3 are rotten?

    (c) How many samples of 3 could be drawn in which there are two good apples and one rotten one?

23. A bag contains 5 black, 1 red, and 3 yellow jelly beans; you take 3 at random. How many samples are possible in which the jelly beans are

    (a) all black?   (b) all red?

    (c) all yellow?   (d) 2 black and 1 red?

    (e) 2 black and 1 yellow?   (f) 2 yellow and 1 black?

    (g) 2 red and 1 yellow?

24. In how many ways can 5 out of 9 plants be arranged in a row on a windowsill?

25. Show that $C(n, r) = C(n, n - r)$.

26. (a) Calculate how many numbers between 100 and 999 contain exactly one 5 by subtracting the number that contain no 5's, two 5's, or three 5's from the total.

    (b) Calculate the answer to part (a) directly by creating a tree diagram and considering whether the first digit is a 5 or not, then the second digit, and then the third.

27. The following problem was posed on National Public Radio's *Weekend Edition*: In how many points can 6 circles intersect? *Source: National Public Radio.*

    (a) Find the answer for 6 circles.

    (b) Find the general answer for *n* circles.

28. How many different dominoes can be formed from the numbers 0 . . . 6? (*Hint:* A domino may have the same number of dots on both halves of it, or it may have a different number of dots on each half.)

APPLICATIONS

Business and Economics

29. **Work Assignments** From a group of 8 newly hired office assistants, 3 are selected. Each of these 3 assistants will be assigned to a different manager. In how many ways can they be selected and assigned?

30. **Assembly Line Sampling** Five items are to be randomly selected from the first 50 items on an assembly line to determine the defect rate. How many different samples of 5 items can be chosen?

31. **Sales Schedules** A salesperson has the names of 6 prospects.

    (a) In how many ways can she arrange her schedule if she calls on all 6?

    (b) In how many ways can she arrange her schedule if she can call on only 4 of the 6?

32. **Worker Grievances** A group of 9 workers decides to send a delegation of 3 to their supervisor to discuss their grievances.

    (a) How many delegations are possible?

    (b) If it is decided that a particular worker must be in the delegation, how many different delegations are possible?

    (c) If there are 4 women and 5 men in the group, how many delegations would include at least 1 woman?

33. Hamburger Variety Hamburger Hut sells regular hamburgers as well as a larger burger. Either type can include cheese, relish, lettuce, tomato, mustard, or catsup.

(a) How many different hamburgers can be ordered with exactly three extras?

(b) How many different regular hamburgers can be ordered with exactly three extras?

(c) How many different regular hamburgers can be ordered with at least five extras?

34. Ice Cream Flavors Baskin-Robbins advertises that it has 31 flavors of ice cream.

(a) How many different double-scoop cones can be made? Assume that the order of the scoops matters.

(b) How many different triple-scoop cones can be made?

(c) How many different double-scoop cones can be made if order doesn't matter?

(d) How many different triple-scoop cones can be made if order doesn't matter?

Life Sciences

35. Research Participants From a group of 16 smokers and 22 nonsmokers, a researcher wants to randomly select 8 smokers and 8 nonsmokers for a study. In how many ways can the study group be selected?

36. Plant Hardiness In an experiment on plant hardiness, a researcher gathers 6 wheat plants, 3 barley plants, and 2 rye plants. She wishes to select 4 plants at random.

(a) In how many ways can this be done?

(b) In how many ways can this be done if exactly 2 wheat plants must be included?

Social Sciences

37. Legislative Committee A legislative committee consists of 5 Democrats and 4 Republicans. A delegation of 3 is to be selected to visit a small Pacific island republic.

(a) How many different delegations are possible?

(b) How many delegations would have all Democrats?

(c) How many delegations would have 2 Democrats and 1 Republican?

(d) How many delegations would include at least 1 Republican?

38. Political Committee From 10 names on a ballot, 4 will be elected to a political party committee. In how many ways can the committee of 4 be formed if each person will have a different responsibility, and different assignments of responsibility are considered different committees?

39. Judges When Paul Martinek, publisher of *Lawyers Weekly USA*, was a guest on the television news program *The O'Reilly Factor*, he discussed a decision by a three-judge panel, chosen at random from judges in the Ninth Circuit in California. The judges had ruled that the mandatory recitation of the Pledge of Allegiance is unconstitutional because of the phrase "under God." According to Martinek, "Because there are 45 judges in the Ninth Circuit, there are 3000 different combinations of three-judge panels." Is this true? If not, what is the correct number? *Source: The Mathematics Teacher.*

General Interest

40. Bridge How many different 13-card bridge hands can be selected from an ordinary deck?

41. Poker Five cards are chosen from an ordinary deck to form a hand in poker. In how many ways is it possible to get the following results?

(a) 4 queens   (b) No face card

(c) Exactly 2 face cards   (d) At least 2 face cards

(e) 1 heart, 2 diamonds, and 2 clubs

42. Poker In poker, a flush consists of 5 cards with the same suit, such as 5 diamonds.

(a) Find the number of ways of getting a flush consisting of cards with values from 5 to 10 by listing all the possibilities.

(b) Find the number of ways of getting a flush consisting of cards with values from 5 to 10 by using combinations.

43. Baseball If a baseball coach has 5 good hitters and 4 poor hitters on the bench and chooses 3 players at random, in how many ways can he choose at least 2 good hitters?

44. Softball The coach of the Morton Valley Softball Team has 6 good hitters and 8 poor hitters. He chooses 3 hitters at random.

(a) In how many ways can he choose 2 good hitters and 1 poor hitter?

(b) In how many ways can he choose 3 good hitters?

(c) In how many ways can he choose at least 2 good hitters?

45. Flower Selection Five orchids from a collection of 20 are to be selected for a flower show.

(a) In how many ways can this be done?

(b) In how many ways can the 5 be selected if 2 special plants from the 20 must be included?

46. Lottery A state lottery game requires that you pick 6 different numbers from 1 to 99. If you pick all 6 winning numbers, you win the jackpot.

(a) How many ways are there to choose 6 numbers if order is not important?

(b) How many ways are there to choose 6 numbers if order matters?

47. Lottery In Exercise 46, if you pick 5 of the 6 numbers correctly, you win $250,000. In how many ways can you pick exactly 5 of the 6 winning numbers without regard to order?

48. Committees Suppose that out of 19 members of a club, two committees are to be formed. A nominating committee is to consist of 7 members, and a public relations committee is to consist of 5 members. No one can be on both committees.

(a) Calculate the number of ways that the two committees can be formed, assuming that the nominating committee is formed first.

(b) Calculate the number of ways that the two committees can be formed, assuming that the public relations committee is formed first. Verify that this answer is the same as that of part (a).

(c) Suppose the 7 members of the nominating committee wear red T-shirts, the 5 members of the public relations committee wear yellow T-shirts, and the remaining members of the club wear white T-shirts. A photographer lines up the members of the club to take a picture, but the picture is so blurry that people wearing the same color T-shirt are indistinguishable. In how many distinguishable ways can the club members line up? Explain why this answer is the same as the answers to parts (a) and (b).

49. **Committee** A small department of 5 people decides to form a hiring committee. The only restriction on the size of the committee is that it must have at least 2 members.

   (a) Calculate the number of different committees possible by adding up the number of committees of different sizes.

   (b) Calculate the number of different committees possible by taking the total number of subsets of the 5 members and subtracting the number of committees that are invalid because they have too few members.

50. **License Plates** Officials from a particular state are considering a new type of license plate consisting of three letters followed by three numbers. If the letters cannot be repeated and must be in alphabetical order, calculate the number of possible distinct license plates.

51. **Passwords** A certain website requires users to log on using a security password.

   (a) If passwords must consist of six letters, followed by a single digit, determine the total number of possible distinct passwords.

   (b) If passwords must consist of six non-repetitive letters, followed by a single digit, determine the total number of possible distinct passwords.

52. **Pizza Varieties** A television commercial for Little Caesars pizza announced that with the purchase of two pizzas, one could receive free any combination of up to five toppings on each pizza. The commercial shows a young child waiting in line at Little Caesars who calculates that there are 1,048,576 possibilities for the toppings on the two pizzas. *Source: The Mathematics Teacher.*

   (a) Verify the child's calculation. Use the fact that Little Caesars has 11 toppings to choose from. Assume that the order of the two pizzas matters; that is, if the first pizza has combination 1 and the second pizza has combination 2, that is different from combination 2 on the first pizza and combination 1 on the second.

   (b) In a letter to *The Mathematics Teacher*, Joseph F. Heiser argued that the two combinations described in part (a) should be counted as the same, so the child has actually overcounted. Give the number of possibilities if the order of the two pizzas doesn't matter.

53. **Pizza** In an ad for Pizza Hut, Jessica Simpson explains to the Muppets that there are more than 6 million possibilities for their 4forAll Pizza. Griffin Weber and Glenn Weber wrote an article explaining that the number of possibilities is far more than 6 million. *Source: The College Mathematics Journal.*

   (a) Each pizza can have up to 3 toppings, out of 17 possible choices, or can be one of four specialty pizzas. Calculate the number of different pizzas possible.

   (b) Out of the total possible pizzas calculated in part (a), a 4forAll Pizza consists of four pizzas in a box. Keeping in mind that the four pizzas could all be different, or there could be two or three different pizzas in the box, or all four pizzas could be the same, calculate the total number of 4forAll Pizzas possible.

   (c) The article considers another way of counting the number in part (b). Suppose that only 8 pizzas were available, and they were listed in a row with lines separating each type, as in the following diagram:

   $$A \mid B \mid C \mid D \mid E \mid F \mid G \mid H.$$

   A person orders 4 pizzas by placing 4 X's in the desired places on the diagram, after which the letters can be ignored. For example, an order for 2 of A, 1 of C, and 1 of G would look like the following diagram.

   $$XX \mid \mid X \mid \mid \mid \mid X \mid$$

   The number of ways this can be done is then the number of ways of arranging 11 objects, 4 of which are X and the other 7 of which are vertical lines, or

   $$C(11, 4) = 330.$$

   Use similar reasoning to verify the answer to part (b).

54. **Cereal** The Post Corporation once introduced the cereal, *Create a Crunch*™, in which the consumers could combine ingredients to create their own unique cereal. Each box contained 8 packets of food goods. There were four types of cereal: Frosted Alpha Bits®, Cocoa Pebbles®, Fruity Pebbles®, and Honey Comb®. Also included in the box were four "Add-Ins": granola, blue rice cereal, marshmallows, and sprinkles.

   (a) What is the total number of breakfasts that could be made if a breakfast is defined as any one or more cereals or add-ins?

   (b) If Sarah Taylor chose to mix one type of cereal with one add-in, how many different breakfasts could she make?

   (c) If Kristen Schmitt chose to mix two types of cereal with three add-ins, how many different breakfasts could she make?

   (d) If Matthew Piscicuto chose to mix at least one type of cereal with at least one type of add-in, how many breakfasts could he make?

   (e) If Heather Murray's favorite cereal is Fruity Pebbles®, how many different cereals could she make if each of her mixtures must include this cereal?

55. **Appetizers** Applebee's restaurant recently advertised "Ultimate Trios," where the customer was able to pick any three trio-sized appetizers from a list of nine options. The ad claimed that there were over 200 combinations.

   (a) If each customer's selection must be a different item, how many meal combinations are possible?

   (b) If each customer can select the same item two or even three times in each trio, how many different trios are possible?

   (c) Using the answers to parts (a) and (b), discuss that restaurant's claim.

(d) Two of the trio items, the Buffalo chicken wings and the boneless Buffalo wings, each have five different sauce options. This implies that there are actually 17 different trio choices that are available to a customer. In this scenario, how many different trio meal combinations are possible? (Assume that each of the three selected items is different.)

(e) How many different trios are possible if 2 of the items are different flavored boneless Buffalo wings? (Assume that the third item is not a boneless Buffalo wing.)

56. Football Writer Gregg Easterbrook, discussing ESPN's unsuccessful attempt to predict the winners for the six National Football League (NFL) divisions and the six wild-card slots, claimed that there were 180 different ways to make this forecast. Reader Milton Eisner wrote in to tell him that the actual number is much larger. To make the calculation, note that at the time the NFL consisted of two conferences, each of which consisted of three divisions. Five of the divisions had five teams, while the other had six. There was one winner from each of the six divisions, plus three wild-card slots from each of the two conferences. How many ways could the six division winners and six wild-card slots have been chosen? *Source: Slate Magazine.*

57. Music In the opera *Amahl and the Night Visitors*, the shepherds sing a chorus involving 18 different names, a challenge for singers trying to remember the names in the correct order. (Two of the three authors of this textbook have sung this chorus in public.)

(a) In how many ways can the names be arranged?

(b) Not all the arrangements of names in part (a) could be sung, because 10 of the names have 3 syllables, 4 have 2 syllables, and 4 have 4 syllables. Of the 6 lines in the chorus, 4 lines consist of a 3-syllable name repeated, followed by a 2-syllable and then a 4-syllable name (e.g., Emily, Emily, Michael, Bartholomew), and 2 lines consist of a 3-syllable name repeated, followed by two more 3-syllable names (e.g., Josephine, Josephine, Angela, Jeremy). No names are repeated except where we've indicated. (If you think this is confusing, you should try memorizing the chorus.) How many arrangements of the names could fit this pattern?

58. Olympics In a recent Winter Olympics, there were 12 judges for each part of the women's figure skating program, but the scores of only 9 of the judges were randomly selected for the final results. *Source: The New York Times.*

(a) In how many ways can the 9 judges whose scores are counted be selected?

(b) Women's figure skating consists of a short program and a long program, with different judges for each part. How many different sets of judges' scores are possible for the entire event?

YOUR TURN ANSWERS
1. 210   **2.** 1820   **3.** (a) 5040 (b) 455 (c) 28 (d) 360
4. 1140; 6840   **5.** 103,776

8.3 Probability Applications of Counting Principles

APPLY IT   If 3 engines are tested from a shipping container packed with 12 diesel engines, 2 of which are defective, what is the probability that at least 1 of the defective engines will be found (in which case the container will not be shipped)?

This problem, which is solved in Example 3, could theoretically be solved with a tree diagram, but it would require a tree with a large number of branches. Many of the probability problems involving *dependent* events that were solved earlier by using tree diagrams can also be solved by using permutations or combinations. Permutations and combinations are especially helpful when the numbers involved are large.

To compare the method of using permutations or combinations with the method of tree diagrams used in Section 7.5, the first example repeats Example 7 from that section.

EXAMPLE 1   Environmental Inspections

The Environmental Protection Agency is considering inspecting 6 plants for environmental compliance: 3 in Chicago, 2 in Los Angeles, and 1 in New York. Due to a lack of inspectors, they decide to inspect 2 plants selected at random, 1 this month and 1 next month, with each plant equally likely to be selected, but no plant is selected twice. What is the probability that 1 Chicago plant and 1 Los Angeles plant are selected?

SOLUTION

Method 1
Multiplication Principle

To find the probability, we use the probability fraction, $P(E) = n(E)/n(S)$, where E is the event that 1 Chicago plant and 1 Los Angeles plant is selected and S is the sample space. We will use the multiplication principle, since the plants are selected one at a time, and the first is inspected this month while the second is inspected next month.

To calculate the numerator, we find the number of elements in E. There are two ways to select a Chicago plant and a Los Angeles plant: Chicago first and Los Angeles second, or Los Angeles first and Chicago second. The Chicago plant can be selected from the 3 Chicago plants in $C(3, 1)$ ways, and the Los Angeles plant can be selected from the 2 Los Angeles plants in $C(2, 1)$ ways. Using the multiplication principle, we can select a Chicago plant then a Los Angeles plant in $C(3, 1) \cdot C(2, 1)$ ways, and a Los Angeles plant then a Chicago plant in $C(2, 1) \cdot C(3, 1)$ ways. By the union rule, we can select one Chicago plant and one Los Angeles plant in

$$C(3, 1) \cdot C(2, 1) + C(2, 1) \cdot C(3, 1) \text{ ways,}$$

giving the numerator of the probability fraction.

For the denominator, we calculate the number of elements in the sample space. There are 6 ways to select the first plant and 5 ways to select the second, for a total of $6 \cdot 5$ ways. The required probability is

$$P(1 \text{ C and } 1 \text{ LA}) = \frac{C(3, 1) \cdot C(2, 1) + C(2, 1) \cdot C(3, 1)}{6 \cdot 5}$$

$$= \frac{3 \cdot 2 + 2 \cdot 3}{6 \cdot 5} = \frac{12}{30} = \frac{2}{5}.$$

This agrees with the answer found in Example 7 of Section 7.5.

FOR REVIEW

The use of combinations to solve probability problems depends on the basic probability principle introduced in Section 7.3 and repeated here:
Let S be a sample space with equally likely outcomes, and let event E be a subset of S. Then the probability that event E occurs, written $P(E)$, is

$$P(E) = \frac{n(E)}{n(S)},$$

where $n(E)$ and $n(S)$ represent the number of elements in sets E and S.

Method 2
Combinations

This example can be solved more simply by observing that the probability that 1 Chicago plant and 1 Los Angeles plant are selected should not depend upon the order in which the plants are selected, so we may use combinations. The numerator is simply the number of ways of selecting 1 Chicago plant out of 3 Chicago plants and 1 Los Angeles plant out of 2 Los Angeles plants. The denominator is just the number of ways of selecting 2 plants out of 6. Then

$$P(1 \text{ C and } 1 \text{ LA}) = \frac{C(3, 1) \cdot C(2, 1)}{C(6, 2)} = \frac{6}{15} = \frac{2}{5}.$$

This helps explain why combinations tend to be used more often than permutations in probability. Even if order matters in the original problem, it is sometimes possible to ignore order and use combinations. Be careful to do this only when the final result does not depend on the order of events. Order often does matter. (If you don't believe this, try getting dressed tomorrow morning and then taking your shower.)

Method 3
Tree Diagram

In Section 7.5, we found this probability using the tree diagram shown in Figure 6 on the next page. Two of the branches correspond to drawing 1 Chicago plant and 1 Los Angeles plant. The probability for each branch is calculated by multiplying the probabilities along the branch, as we did in the previous chapter. The resulting probabilities for the two branches are then added, giving the result

$$P(1 \text{ C and } 1 \text{ LA}) = \frac{3}{6} \cdot \frac{2}{5} + \frac{2}{6} \cdot \frac{3}{5} = \frac{2}{5}.$$

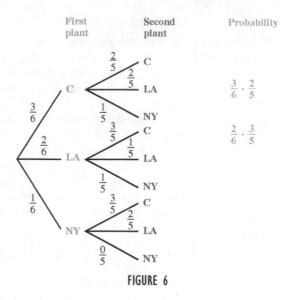

First plant   Second plant   Probability

FIGURE 6

YOUR TURN 1 In Example 1, what is the probability that 1 New York plant and 1 Chicago plant are selected?

TRY YOUR TURN 1

CAUTION The problems in the first two sections of this chapter asked how many ways a certain operation can be done. The problems in this section ask what is the probability that a certain event occurs; the solution involves answering questions about how many ways the event and the operation can be done.

- If a problem asks how many ways something can be done, the answer must be a nonnegative integer.
- If a problem asks for a probability, the answer must be a number between 0 and 1.

EXAMPLE 2 Nursing

From a group of 22 nurses, 4 are to be selected to present a list of grievances to management.

(a) In how many ways can this be done?

SOLUTION Four nurses from a group of 22 can be selected in $C(22, 4)$ ways. (Use combinations, since the group of 4 is an unordered set.)

$$C(22, 4) = \frac{22!}{18!\, 4!} = \frac{(22)(21)(20)(19)}{(4)(3)(2)(1)} = 7315$$

There are 7315 ways to choose 4 people from 22.

(b) One of the nurses is Erica Eastep. Find the probability that Erica will be among the 4 selected.

SOLUTION The probability that Erica will be selected is given by $n(E)/n(S)$, where E is the event that the chosen group includes Erica, and S is the sample space for the experiment of choosing a group of 4. There is only $C(1, 1) = 1$ way to choose Erica. The number of ways that the other 3 nurses can be chosen from the remaining 21 nurses is

$$C(21, 3) = \frac{21!}{18!\, 3!} = 1330.$$

The probability that Erica will be one of the 4 chosen is

$$P(\text{Erica is chosen}) = \frac{n(E)}{n(S)} = \frac{C(1, 1) \cdot C(21, 3)}{C(22, 4)} = \frac{1330}{7315} \approx 0.1818.$$

YOUR TURN 2 If 8 of the 22 nurses are men in Example 2, what is the probability that exactly 2 men are among the 4 nurses selected?

Notice that the two numbers in red in the numerator, 1 and 21, add up to the number in red in the denominator, 22. This indicates that the 22 nurses have been split into two groups, one of size 1 (Erica) and the other of size 21 (the other nurses). Similarly, the green numbers indicate that the 4 nurses chosen consist of two groups of size 1 (Erica) and size 3 (the other nurses chosen).

(c) Find the probability that Erica will not be selected.

> **SOLUTION** The probability that Erica will not be chosen is $1 - 0.1818 = 0.8182$.
>
> **TRY YOUR TURN 2**

EXAMPLE 3   Diesel Engines

When shipping diesel engines abroad, it is common to pack 12 engines in one container. Suppose that a company has received complaints from its customers that many of the engines arrive in nonworking condition. To help solve this problem, the company decides to make a spot check of containers after loading. The company will test 3 engines from a container at random; if any of the 3 are nonworking, the container will not be shipped until each engine in it is checked. Suppose a given container has 2 nonworking engines. Find the probability that the container will not be shipped.

APPLY IT

SOLUTION The container will not be shipped if the sample of 3 engines contains 1 or 2 defective engines. If $P(1 \text{ defective})$ represents the probability of exactly 1 defective engine in the sample, then

$$P(\text{not shipping}) = P(1 \text{ defective}) + P(2 \text{ defective}).$$

There are $C(12, 3)$ ways to choose the 3 engines for testing:

$$C(12, 3) = \frac{12!}{9! \, 3!} = 220.$$

There are $C(2, 1)$ ways of choosing 1 defective engine from the 2 in the container, and for each of these ways, there are $C(10, 2)$ ways of choosing 2 good engines from among the 10 in the container. By the multiplication principle, there are

$$C(2, 1) \cdot C(10, 2) = \frac{2!}{1! \, 1!} \cdot \frac{10!}{8! \, 2!} = 2 \cdot 45 = 90$$

ways of choosing a sample of 3 engines containing 1 defective engine with

$$P(1 \text{ defective}) = \frac{90}{220} = \frac{9}{22}.$$

There are $C(2, 2)$ ways of choosing 2 defective engines from the 2 defective engines in the container, and $C(10, 1)$ ways of choosing 1 good engine from among the 10 good engines, for

$$C(2, 2) \cdot C(10, 1) = 1 \cdot 10 = 10$$

ways of choosing a sample of 3 engines containing 2 defective engines. Finally,

$$P(2 \text{ defective}) = \frac{10}{220} = \frac{1}{22}$$

and

$$P(\text{not shipping}) = P(1 \text{ defective}) + P(2 \text{ defective})$$

$$= \frac{9}{22} + \frac{1}{22} = \frac{10}{22} \approx 0.4545.$$

YOUR TURN 3 Suppose the container in Example 3 has 4 nonworking engines. Find the probability that the container will not be shipped.

Notice that the probability is $1 - 0.4545 = 0.5455$ that the container will be shipped, even though it has 2 defective engines. The management must decide whether this probability is acceptable; if not, it may be necessary to test more than 3 engines from a container.

TRY YOUR TURN 3

FOR REVIEW

Recall from Section 7.4 that if E and E' are complements, then $P(E') = 1 - P(E)$. In Example 3, the event "0 defective in the sample" is the complement of the event "1 or 2 defective in the sample," since there are only 0 or 1 or 2 defective engines possible in the sample of 3 engines.

Observe that in Example 3, the complement of finding 1 or 2 defective engines is finding 0 defective engines. Then instead of finding the sum $P(1 \text{ defective}) + P(2 \text{ defective})$, the result in Example 3 could be found as $1 - P(0 \text{ defective})$.

$$P(\text{not shipping}) = 1 - P(0 \text{ defective in sample})$$

$$= 1 - \frac{C(2, 0) \cdot C(10, 3)}{C(12, 3)}$$

$$= 1 - \frac{1(120)}{220}$$

$$= 1 - \frac{120}{220} = \frac{100}{220} \approx 0.4545$$

EXAMPLE 4   Poker

In a common form of the card game *poker*, a hand of 5 cards is dealt to each player from a deck of 52 cards. There are a total of

$$C(52, 5) = \frac{52!}{47! \, 5!} = 2{,}598{,}960$$

such hands possible. Find the probability of getting each of the following hands.

(a) A hand containing only hearts, called a *heart flush*

SOLUTION   There are 13 hearts in a deck, with

$$C(13, 5) = \frac{13!}{8! \, 5!} = \frac{(13)(12)(11)(10)(9)}{(5)(4)(3)(2)(1)} = 1287$$

different hands containing only hearts. The probability of a heart flush is

$$P(\text{heart flush}) = \frac{C(13, 5) \cdot C(39, 0)}{C(52, 5)} = \frac{1287}{2{,}598{,}960} \approx 0.0004952.$$

You don't really need the $C(39, 0)$, since this just equals 1, but it might help to remind you that you are choosing none of the 39 cards that remain after the hearts are removed.

(b) A flush of any suit (5 cards of the same suit)

SOLUTION   There are 4 suits in a deck, so

$$P(\text{flush}) = 4 \cdot P(\text{heart flush}) = 4 \cdot 0.0004952 \approx 0.001981.$$

(c) A full house of aces and eights (3 aces and 2 eights)

SOLUTION   There are $C(4, 3)$ ways to choose 3 aces from among the 4 in the deck, and $C(4, 2)$ ways to choose 2 eights.

$$P(3 \text{ aces}, 2 \text{ eights}) = \frac{C(4, 3) \cdot C(4, 2) \cdot C(44, 0)}{C(52, 5)} = \frac{4 \cdot 6 \cdot 1}{2{,}598{,}960} \approx 0.000009234$$

(d) Any full house (3 cards of one value, 2 of another)

SOLUTION

Method 1
Standard Procedure

The 13 values in a deck give 13 choices for the first value. As in part (c), there are $C(4, 3)$ ways to choose the 3 cards from among the 4 cards that have that value. This leaves 12 choices for the second value (order *is* important here, since a full house of 3 aces and 2 eights is not the same as a full house of 3 eights and 2 aces). From the 4 cards that have the second value, there are $C(4, 2)$ ways to choose 2. The probability of any full house is then

$$P(\text{full house}) = \frac{13 \cdot C(4, 3) \cdot 12 \cdot C(4, 2)}{2{,}598{,}960} \approx 0.001441.$$

Method 2
Alternative Procedure

As an alternative way of counting the numerator, first count the number of different values in the hand.* Since there are 13 values from which to choose, and we need 2 different values (one for the set of 3 cards and one for the set of 2), there are $C(13, 2)$ ways to choose the values. Next, of the two values chosen, select the value for which there are 3 cards, which can be done $C(2, 1)$ ways. This automatically determines that the other value is the one for which there are 2 cards. Next, choose the suits for each value. For the value with 3 cards, there are $C(4, 3)$ values of the suits, and for the value with 2 cards, there are $C(4, 2)$ values. Putting this all together,

YOUR TURN 4 In Example 4, what is the probability of a hand containing two pairs, one of aces and the other of kings? (This hand contains 2 aces, 2 kings, and a fifth card that is neither an ace nor a king.)

$$P(\text{full house}) = \frac{C(13, 2) \cdot C(2, 1) \cdot C(4, 3) \cdot C(4, 2)}{2,598,960} \approx 0.001441.$$

TRY YOUR TURN 4 ▰

EXAMPLE 5 Letters

Each of the letters w, y, o, m, i, n, and g is placed on a separate slip of paper. A slip is pulled out, and its letter is recorded in the order in which the slip was drawn. This is done four times.

(a) If the slip is not replaced after the letter is recorded, find the probability that the word "wing" is formed.

SOLUTION The sample space contains all possible arrangements of the seven letters, taken four at a time. Since order matters, use *permutations* to find the number of arrangements in the sample space.

$$P(7, 4) = \frac{7!}{3!} = 7 \cdot 6 \cdot 5 \cdot 4 = 840$$

Since there is only one way that the word "wing" can be formed, the required probability is $1/840 \approx 0.001190$.

YOUR TURN 5 Find the probability that the word "now" is formed if 3 slips are chosen without replacement in Example 5. Find the probability that the word "now" is formed if 3 slips are chosen with replacement.

(b) If the slip is replaced after the letter is recorded, find the probability that the word "wing" is formed.

SOLUTION Since the letters can be repeated, there are 7 possible outcomes for each draw of the slip. To calculate the number of arrangements in the sample space, use the *multiplication principle*. The number of arrangements in the sample space is $7^4 = 2401$, and the required probability is $1/2401 \approx 0.0004165$.   **TRY YOUR TURN 5** ▰

EXAMPLE 6 Birthdays

Suppose a group of n people is in a room. Find the probability that at least 2 of the people have the same birthday.

SOLUTION "Same birthday" refers to the month and the day, not necessarily the same year. Also, ignore leap years, and assume that each day in the year is equally likely as a birthday. To see how to proceed, we first look at the case in which $n = 5$ and find the probability that *no 2 people* from among 5 people have the same birthday. There are 365 different birthdays possible for the first of the 5 people, 364 for the second (so that the people have different birthdays), 363 for the third, and so on. The number of ways the 5 people can have different birthdays is thus the number of permutations of 365 days taken 5 at a time or

$$P(365, 5) = 365 \cdot 364 \cdot 363 \cdot 362 \cdot 361.$$

The number of ways that 5 people can have the same birthday or different birthdays is

$$365 \cdot 365 \cdot 365 \cdot 365 \cdot 365 = (365)^5.$$

*We learned this approach from Professor Peter Grassi of Hofstra University.

Finally, the *probability* that none of the 5 people have the same birthday is

$$\frac{P(365, 5)}{365^5} = \frac{365 \cdot 364 \cdot 363 \cdot 362 \cdot 361}{365 \cdot 365 \cdot 365 \cdot 365 \cdot 365} \approx 0.9729.$$

The probability that at least 2 of the 5 people *do* have the same birthday is $1 - 0.9729 = 0.0271$.

Now this result can be extended to more than 5 people. Generalizing, the probability that no 2 people among n people have the same birthday is

$$\frac{P(365, n)}{365^n}.$$

The probability that at least 2 of the n people *do* have the same birthday is

$$1 - \frac{P(365, n)}{365^n}.$$

The following table shows this probability for various values of n.

Number of People, n	Probability That Two Have the Same Birthday
5	0.0271
10	0.1169
15	0.2529
20	0.4114
22	0.4757
23	0.5073
25	0.5687
30	0.7063
35	0.8144
40	0.8912
50	0.9704
366	1

The probability that 2 people among 23 have the same birthday is 0.5073, a little more than half. Many people are surprised at this result; it seems that a larger number of people should be required.

TECHNOLOGY NOTE

Using a graphing calculator, we can graph the probability formula in the previous example as a function of n, but care must be taken that the graphing calculator evaluates the function at integer points. Figure 7 was produced on a TI-84 Plus C by letting $Y_1 = 1 - (365 \text{ nPr } X)/365 \wedge X$ on $0 \le x \le 44$. (This domain ensures integer values for x.) Notice that the graph does not extend past $x = 39$. This is because $P(365, n)$ and 365^n are too large for the calculator when $n \ge 40$.

An alternative way of doing the calculations that does not run into such large numbers is based on the concept of conditional probability. The probability that the first person's birthday does not match any so far is 365/365. The probability that the second person's birthday does not match the first's is 364/365. The probability that the third person's birthday does not match the first's or the second's is 363/365. By the product rule of probability, the probability that none of the first 3 people have matching birthdays is

$$\frac{365}{365} \cdot \frac{364}{365} \cdot \frac{363}{365}.$$

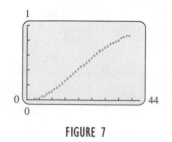

FIGURE 7

Similarly, the probability that no two people in a group of 40 have the same birthday is

$$\frac{365}{365} \cdot \frac{364}{365} \cdot \frac{363}{365} \cdot \cdots \cdot \frac{326}{365}.$$

This probability can be calculated (and then subtracted from 1 to get the probability we seek) without overflowing the calculator by multiplying each fraction times the next, rather then trying to compute the entire numerator and the entire denominator. The calculations are somewhat tedious to do by hand but can be programmed on a graphing calculator or computer.

As we saw in Examples 1 and 4(d), probability can sometimes be calculated in more than one way. We now look at one more example of this.

EXAMPLE 7   Fruit

Ray and Nate are arranging a row of fruit at random on a table. They have 5 apples, 6 oranges, and 7 lemons. What is the probability that all fruit of the same kind are together?

SOLUTION

**Method 1
Distinguishable Permutations**

Ray can't tell individual pieces of fruit of the same kind apart. All apples look the same to him, as do all oranges and all lemons. So in the denominator of the probability, he calculates the number of distinguishable ways to arrange the 18 pieces of fruit, given that all apples are indistinguishable, as are all oranges and all lemons.

$$\frac{18!}{5!\, 6!\, 7!} = 14,702,688$$

As for the numerator, the only choice is how to arrange the 3 kinds of fruit, for which there are $3! = 6$ ways. Thus

$$P(\text{all fruit of the same kind are together}) = \frac{6}{14,702,688} \approx 4.081 \times 10^{-7}.$$

**Method 2
Permutations**

Nate has better eyesight than Ray and can tell the individual pieces of fruit apart. So in the denominator of the probability, he calculates the number of ways to arrange the 18 pieces of fruit, which is

$$18! \approx 6.4024 \times 10^{15}.$$

For the numerator, he first must choose how to arrange the 3 kinds of fruit, for which there are 3! ways. Then there are 5! ways to arrange the apples, 6! ways to arrange the oranges, and 7! ways to arrange the lemons, for a total number of possibilities of

$$3!\, 5!\, 6!\, 7! = 2,612,736,000.$$

Therefore,

YOUR TURN 6 If Ray and Nate arrange 2 kiwis, 3 apricots, 4 pineapples, and 5 coconuts in a row at random, what is the probability that all fruit of the same kind are together?

$$P(\text{all fruit of the same kind are together}) = \frac{2,612,736,000}{6.4024 \times 10^{15}} \approx 4.081 \times 10^{-7}.$$

The results for Method 1 and Method 2 are the same. The probability does not depend on whether a person can distinguish individual pieces of the same kind of fruit.

TRY YOUR TURN 6

W1. How many ways is it possible to select 6 cards from an ordinary deck if all cards must be from the same suit? (*Sec. 8.2*)

W2. If the Senate has 59 Democrats and 41 Republicans, how many ways can a committee be chosen with 3 of each? (*Sec. 8.2*)

8.3 EXERCISES

A basket contains 7 red apples and 4 yellow apples. A sample of 3 apples is drawn. Find the probabilities that the sample contains the following.

1. All red apples

2. All yellow apples

3. 2 yellow and 1 red apple

4. More red than yellow apples

In a club with 9 male and 11 female members, a 5-member committee will be randomly chosen. Find the probability that the committee contains the following.

5. All men

6. All women

7. 3 men and 2 women

8. 2 men and 3 women

9. At least 4 women

10. No more than 2 men

Two cards are drawn at random from an ordinary deck of 52 cards.

11. How many 2-card hands are possible?

Find the probability that the 2-card hand described above contains the following.

12. 2 aces

13. At least 1 ace

14. All spades

15. 2 cards of the same suit

16. Only face cards

17. No face cards

18. No card higher than 8 (count ace as 1)

Twenty-six slips of paper are each marked with a different letter of the alphabet and placed in a basket. A slip is pulled out, its letter recorded (in the order in which the slip was drawn), and the slip is replaced. This is done 5 times. Find the probabilities that the following "words" are formed.

19. Chuck

20. A word that starts with "p"

21. A word with no repetition of letters

22. A word that contains no "*x*," "*y*," or "*z*"

23. Discuss the relative merits of using tree diagrams versus combinations to solve probability problems. When would each approach be most appropriate?

24. Several examples in this section used the rule $P(E') = 1 - P(E)$. Explain the advantage (especially in Example 6) of using this rule.

For Exercises 25–28, refer to Example 6 in this section.

25. A total of 43 men have served as president through 2010.* Set up the probability that, if 43 men were selected at random, at least 2 have the same birthday.[†]

26. Set up the probability that at least 2 of the 100 U.S. senators have the same birthday.

27. What is the probability that at least 2 of the 435 members of the House of Representatives have the same birthday?

28. Argue that the probability that in a group of *n* people *exactly one pair* have the same birthday is

$$C(n, 2) \cdot \frac{P(365, n-1)}{365^n}.$$

29. After studying all night for a final exam, a bleary-eyed student randomly grabs 2 socks from a drawer containing 9 black, 6 brown, and 2 blue socks, all mixed together. What is the probability that she grabs a matched pair?

30. Three crows, 4 blue jays, and 5 starlings sit in a random order on a section of telephone wire. Find the probability that birds of a feather flock together, that is, that all birds of the same type are sitting together.

31. If the letters l, i, t, t, l, and e are chosen at random, what is the probability that they spell the word "little"?

32. If the letters M, i, s, s, i, s, s, i, p, p, and i are chosen at random, what is the probability that they spell the word "Mississippi"?

33. An elevator has 4 passengers and stops at 7 floors. It is equally likely that a person will get off at any one of the 7 floors. Find the probability that at least 2 passengers leave at the same floor. (*Hint:* Compare this with the birthday problem.)

34. On National Public Radio, the *Weekend Edition* program posed the following probability problem: Given a certain number of balls, of which some are blue, pick 5 at random. The probability that all 5 are blue is 1/2. Determine the original number of balls and decide how many were blue. *Source: Weekend Edition.*

*Although Obama is the 44th president, the 22nd and 24th presidents were the same man: Grover Cleveland.

[†]In fact, James Polk and Warren Harding were both born on November 2.

35. A reader wrote to the "Ask Marilyn" column in *Parade* magazine,

"You have six envelopes to pick from. Two-thirds (that is, four) are empty. One-third (that is, two) contain a $100 bill. You're told to choose 2 envelopes at random. Which is more likely: (1) that you'll get at least one $100 bill, or (2) that you'll get no $100 bill at all?"

Find the two probabilities. *Source: Parade magazine.*

APPLICATIONS

Business and Economics
Quality Control   A shipment of 11 printers contains 2 that are defective. Find the probability that a sample of the following sizes, drawn from the 11, will not contain a defective printer.

36. 1   **37.** 2   **38.** 3   **39.** 4

Refer to Example 3. The managers feel that the probability of 0.5455 that a container will be shipped even though it contains 2 defective engines is too high. They decide to increase the sample size chosen. Find the probabilities that a container will be shipped even though it contains 2 defective engines, if the sample size is increased to the following.

40. 4   **41.** 5

42. Sales Presentations   Melanie Banfield and Boyd Shepherd are among 9 representatives making presentations at the annual sales meeting. The presentations are randomly ordered. Find the probability that Melanie is the first presenter and Boyd is the last presenter.

43. Sales Schedule   Dan LaChapelle has the name of 6 prospects, including a customer in Scottsdale. He randomly arranges his schedule to call on only 4 of the 6 prospects. Find the probability that the customer from Scottsdale is not called upon.

Social Sciences
44. Election Ballots   Five names are put on a ballot in a randomly selected order. What is the probability that they are not in alphabetical order?

45. Native American Council   At the first meeting of a committee to plan a Northern California pow-wow, there were 3 women and 3 men from the Miwok tribe, 3 women and 2 men from the Hoopa tribe, and 4 women and 5 men from the Pomo tribe. If the ceremony subcouncil consists of 5 people and is randomly selected, find the probabilities that the subcouncil contains the following:

(a) 3 men and 2 women;

(b) exactly 3 Miwoks and 2 Pomos;

(c) 2 Miwoks, 2 Hoopas, and a Pomo;

(d) 2 Miwoks, 2 Hoopas, and 2 Pomos;

(e) more women than men;

(f) exactly 3 Hoopas;

(g) at least 2 Pomos.

46. Education   A school in Bangkok requires that students take an entrance examination. After the examination, there is a drawing in which 5 students are randomly selected from each group of 40 for automatic acceptance into the school, regardless of their performance on the examination. The drawing consists of placing 35 red and 5 green pieces of paper into a box. Each student picks a piece of paper from the box and then does not return the piece of paper to the box. The 5 lucky students who pick the green pieces are automatically accepted into the school. *Source: The Mathematics Teacher.*

(a) What is the probability that the first person wins automatic acceptance?

(b) What is the probability that the last person wins automatic acceptance?

(c) If the students are chosen by the order of their seating, does this give the student who goes first a better chance of winning than the second, third, . . . person? (*Hint:* Imagine that the 40 pieces of paper have been mixed up and laid in a row so that the first student picks the first piece of paper, the second student picks the second piece of paper, and so on.)

47. Education   At a conference promoting excellence in education for African Americans in Detroit, special-edition books were selected to be given away in contests. There were 9 books written by Langston Hughes, 5 books by James Baldwin, and 7 books by Toni Morrison. The judge of one contest selected 6 books at random for prizes. Find the probabilities that the selection consisted of the following.

(a) 3 Hughes and 3 Morrison books

(b) Exactly 4 Baldwin books

(c) 2 Hughes, 3 Baldwin, and 1 Morrison book

(d) At least 4 Hughes books

(e) Exactly 4 books written by males (Morrison is female)

(f) No more than 2 books written by Baldwin

General Interest
Poker   Find the probabilities of the following hands at poker. Assume aces are either high or low.

48. Royal flush (5 highest cards of a single suit)

49. Straight flush (5 in a row in a single suit, but not a royal flush)

50. Four of a kind (4 cards of the same value)

51. Straight (5 cards in a row, not all of the same suit), with ace either high or low

52. Three of a kind (3 cards of one value, with the other cards of two different values)

53. Two pairs (2 cards of one value, 2 of another value, and 1 of a third value)

54. One pair (2 cards of one value, with the other cards of three different values)

Bridge   A bridge hand is made up of 13 cards from a deck of 52. Find the probabilities that a hand chosen at random contains the following.

55. Only hearts

56. At least 3 aces

57. Exactly 2 aces and exactly 2 kings

58. 6 of one suit, 4 of another, and 3 of another

Texas Hold'Em In a version of poker called Texas Hold'Em, each player has 2 cards, and by the end of the round an additional 5 cards are on the table, shared by all the players. (For more about poker hands, see Example 4 and Exercises 48–54.) Each player's hand consists of the best 5 cards out of the 7 cards available to that player. For example, if a player holds 2 kings, and on the table there is one king and 4 cards with 4 other values, then the player has three of a kind. It's possible that the player has an even better hand. Perhaps five of the seven cards are of the same suit, making a flush, or the other 4 cards are queen, jack, 10, and 9, so the player has a straight. For Exercises 59–64, calculate the probability of each hand in Texas Hold'Em, but for simplicity, ignore the possibility that the cards might form an even better hand.

59. One pair (2 cards of one value, with the other cards of five different values)

60. Two pairs (2 cards of one value, 2 of another, with the other cards of three different values)

61. Three of a kind (3 cards of one value, with the other cards of four different values)

62. Four of a kind (4 cards of one value, with the other cards of three different values)

63. Flush (at least 5 cards of the same suit)

64. Full house (3 cards of one value and two of another. Careful: The two unused cards could be a pair of another value or two different cards of other values. Also, the 7 cards could consist of 3 cards of one value, 3 of second value, and one card of a third value. We won't consider the case of 3 cards of one value and 4 of another, because even though this forms a full house, it also forms four of a kind, which is better.)

65. Suppose you are playing Texas Hold'Em and you've just received your two cards. You observe that they are both hearts. You get excited, because if at least 3 of the 5 cards that are on the table are hearts, you'll have a flush, which means that you'll likely win the round. Given that your two cards are hearts, and you know nothing of any other cards, what is the probability that you'll have a flush by the time all 5 cards are on the table?

66. **Lottery** In the previous section, we found the number of ways to pick 6 different numbers from 1 to 99 in a state lottery. Assuming order is unimportant, what is the probability of picking all 6 numbers correctly to win the big prize?

67. **Lottery** In Exercise 66, what is the probability of picking exactly 5 of the 6 numbers correctly?

68. **Lottery** An article in *The New York Times* discussing the odds of winning the lottery stated,

"And who cares if a game-theory professor once calculated the odds of winning as equal to a poker player's chance of drawing four royal flushes in a row, all in spades—then getting up from the card table and meeting four strangers, all with the same birthday?"

Calculate this probability. Does this probability seem comparable to the odds of winning the lottery? (Ignore February 29 as a birthday, and assume that all four strangers have the same birthday as each other, not necessarily the same as the poker player.) *Source: The New York Times Magazine.*

69. **Lottery** A reader wrote to the "Ask Marilyn" column in *Parade* magazine, "A dozen glazed doughnuts are riding on the answer to this question: Are the odds of winning in a lotto drawing higher when picking 6 numbers out of 49 or when picking 5 numbers out of 52?" Calculate each probability to answer the question. *Source: Parade magazine.*

70. **Lottery** On May 18, 2013, the Powerball Lottery had a jackpot of $590.5 million, which was a record at the time. To enter the lottery, 5 numbers are picked between 1 and 55, plus a bonus number between 1 and 42. All 6 numbers must be correct to win the jackpot.

(a) What is the probability of winning the jackpot with a single ticket?

(b) In an article for the *Minneapolis Star Tribune*, mathematician Douglas Arnold was quoted as saying, "If you were to select a group of Powerball numbers every minute for 138 years, you would have about a 50 percent chance of picking the winning Powerball ticket." Calculate the actual probability, using an estimate of 365.25 for the number of days in the year. (Arnold later told *Chance News* that this was an "off-the-top-of-my-head calculation" made when a reporter called.) *Sources: Minneapolis Star Tribune and Chance News.*

71. **Canadian Lottery** In June 2004, Canada introduced a change in its lottery that violated the usual convention that the smaller the probability of an event, the bigger the prize. In this lottery, participants have to guess six numbers from 1 to 49. Six numbers between 1 and 49 are then drawn at random, plus a seventh "bonus number." *Source: Chance.*

(a) A fifth prize of $10 goes to those who correctly guess exactly three of the six numbers, but do not guess the bonus number. Find the probability of winning fifth prize.

(b) A sixth prize of $5 goes to those who correctly guess exactly two of the six numbers plus the bonus number. Find the probability of winning sixth prize, and compare this with the probability of winning fifth prize.

72. **Barbie** A controversy arose in 1992 over the Teen Talk Barbie doll, each of which was programmed with four sayings randomly picked from a set of 270 sayings. The controversy was over the saying, "Math class is tough," which some felt gave a negative message toward girls doing well in math. In an interview with *Science*, a spokeswoman for Mattel, the makers of Barbie, said that "There's a less than 1% chance you're going to get a doll that says math class is tough." Is this figure correct? If not, give the correct figure. *Source: Science.*

73. **Football** During the 1988 college football season, the Big Eight Conference ended the season in a "perfect progression," as shown in the following table. *Source: The American Statistician.*

Won	Lost	Team
7	0	Nebraska (NU)
6	1	Oklahoma (OU)
5	2	Oklahoma State (OSU)
4	3	Colorado (CU)
3	4	Iowa State (ISU)
2	5	Missouri (MU)
1	6	Kansas (KU)
0	7	Kansas State (KSU)

Someone wondered what the probability of such an outcome might be.

(a) How many games do the 8 teams play?

(b) Assuming no ties, how many different outcomes are there for all the games together?

(c) In how many ways could the 8 teams end in a perfect progression?

(d) Assuming that each team had an equally likely probability of winning each game, find the probability of a perfect progression with 8 teams.

(e) Find a general expression for the probability of a perfect progression in an n-team league with the same assumptions.

74. Unluckiest Fan During the 2009 season, the Washington Nationals baseball team won 59 games and lost 103 games. Season ticket holder Stephen Krupin reported in an interview that he watched the team lose all 19 games that he attended that season. The interviewer speculated that this must be a record for bad luck. *Source:* **NPR**.

(a) Based on the full 2009 season record, calculate the probability that a person would attend 19 Washington Nationals games and the Nationals would lose all 19 games.

(b) However, Mr. Krupin only attended home games. The Nationals had 33 wins and 48 losses at home in 2009. Calculate the probability that a person would attend 19 Washington Nationals home games and the Nationals would lose all 19 games.

75. Bingo Bingo has become popular in the United States, and it is an efficient way for many organizations to raise money. The bingo card has 5 rows and 5 columns of numbers from 1 to 75, with the center given as a free cell. Balls showing one of the 75 numbers are picked at random from a container. If the drawn number appears on a player's card, then the player covers the number. In general, the winner is the person who first has a card with an entire row, column, or diagonal covered. *Source: Mathematics Teacher*.

(a) Find the probability that a person will win bingo after just four numbers are called.

(b) An L occurs when the first column and the bottom row are both covered. Find the probability that an L will occur in the fewest number of calls.

(c) An X-out occurs when both diagonals are covered. Find the probability that an X-out occurs in the fewest number of calls.

(d) If bingo cards are constructed so that column one has 5 of the numbers from 1 to 15, column two has 5 of the numbers from 16 to 30, column three has 4 of the numbers from 31 to 45, column four has 5 of the numbers from 46 to 60, and column five has 5 of the numbers from 61 to 75, how many different bingo cards could be constructed? (*Hint:* Order matters!)

76. Suppose a box contains 3 red and 3 blue balls. A ball is selected at random and removed, without observing its color. The box now contains either 3 red and 2 blue balls or 2 red and 3 blue balls. *Source: 40 Puzzles and Problems in Probability and Mathematical Statistics*.

(a) Nate removes a ball at random from the box, observes its color, and puts the ball back. He performs this experiment a total of 6 times, and each time the ball is blue. What is the probability that a red ball was initially removed from the box? (*Hint:* Use Bayes' Theorem.)

(b) Ray removes a ball at random from the box, observes its color, and puts the ball back. He performs this experiment a total of 80 times. Out of these, the ball was blue 44 times and red 36 times. What is the probability that a red ball was initially removed from the box?

(c) Many people intuitively think that Nate's experiment gives more convincing evidence than Ray's experiment that a red ball was removed. Explain why this is wrong.

YOUR TURN ANSWERS
1. 1/5 **2.** 0.3483 **3.** 0.7455
4. 0.0006095 **5.** 1/210; 1/343 **6.** 9.514×10^{-6}

8.4 Binomial Probability

APPLY IT What is the probability that 3 out of 6 randomly selected college students attend more than one institution during their college career? *We will calculate this probability in Example 2.*

The question above involves an experiment that is repeated 6 times. Many probability problems are concerned with experiments in which an event is repeated many times. Other examples include finding the probability of getting 7 heads in 8 tosses of a coin, of hitting a target 6 times out of 6, and of finding 1 defective item in a sample of 15 items. Probability problems of this kind are called **Bernoulli trials** problems, or **Bernoulli processes**, named after the Swiss mathematician Jakob Bernoulli (1654–1705), who is well known for his work in probability theory. In each case, some outcome is designated a success and any other outcome is considered a failure. This labeling is arbitrary and does not necessarily have anything to do with real success or failure. Thus, if the probability of a success in a single trial is p, the probability of failure will be $1 - p$. A Bernoulli trials problem, or **binomial experiment**, must satisfy the following conditions.

Binomial Experiment

1. The same experiment is repeated a fixed number of times.
2. There are only two possible outcomes, success and failure.
3. The repeated trials are independent, so that the probability of success remains the same for each trial.

EXAMPLE 1   Sleep

The chance that an American falls asleep with the TV on at least three nights a week is 1/4. Suppose a researcher selects 5 Americans at random and is interested in the probability that all 5 are "TV sleepers." *Source: Harper's Magazine.*

SOLUTION   Here the experiment, selecting a person, is repeated 5 times. If selecting a TV sleeper is labeled a success, then getting a "non-TV sleeper" is labeled a failure. The 5 trials are almost independent. There is a very slight dependence; if, for example, the first person selected is a TV sleeper, then there is one less TV sleeper to choose from when we select the next person (assuming we never select the same person twice). When selecting a small sample out of a large population, however, the probability changes negligibly, so researchers consider such trials to be independent. Thus, the probability that all 5 in our sample are sleepers is

$$\frac{1}{4} \cdot \frac{1}{4} \cdot \frac{1}{4} \cdot \frac{1}{4} \cdot \frac{1}{4} = \left(\frac{1}{4}\right)^5 \approx 0.0009766.$$

FOR REVIEW

Recall that if A and B are independent events,

$$P(A \text{ and } B) = P(A)P(B).$$

Now suppose the problem in Example 1 is changed to that of finding the probability that exactly 4 of the 5 people in the sample are TV sleepers. This outcome can occur in more than one way, as shown below, where s represents a success (a TV sleeper) and f represents a failure (a non-TV sleeper).

outcome 1:	s	s	s	s	f
outcome 2:	s	s	s	f	s
outcome 3:	s	s	f	s	s
outcome 4:	s	f	s	s	s
outcome 5:	f	s	s	s	s

Keep in mind that since the probability of success is 1/4, the probability of failure is $1 - 1/4 = 3/4$. The probability, then, of each of these 5 outcomes is

$$\left(\frac{1}{4}\right)^4 \left(\frac{3}{4}\right).$$

Since the 5 outcomes represent mutually exclusive events, add the 5 identical probabilities, which is equivalent to multiplying the above probability by 5. The result is

$$P(4 \text{ of the 5 people are TV sleepers}) = 5\left(\frac{1}{4}\right)^4 \left(\frac{3}{4}\right) = \frac{15}{4^5} \approx 0.01465.$$

In the same way, we can compute the probability of selecting 3 TV sleepers in our sample of 5. The probability of any one way of achieving 3 successes and 2 failures will be

$$\left(\frac{1}{4}\right)^3 \left(\frac{3}{4}\right)^2.$$

Rather than list all the ways of achieving 3 successes out of 5 trials, we will count this number using combinations. The number of ways to select 3 elements out of a set of 5 is $C(5, 3) = 5!/(2! \, 3!) = 10$, giving

$$P(3 \text{ of the 5 people are TV sleepers}) = 10\left(\frac{1}{4}\right)^3\left(\frac{3}{4}\right)^2 = \frac{90}{4^5} \approx 0.08789.$$

A similar argument works in the general case.

Binomial Probability

If p is the probability of success in a single trial of a binomial experiment, the probability of x successes and $n - x$ failures in n independent repeated trials of the experiment, known as **binomial probability**, is

$$P(x \text{ successes in } n \text{ trials}) = C(n, x) \cdot p^x \cdot (1 - p)^{n-x}.$$

EXAMPLE 2 College Students

A recent survey found that 59% of college students attend more than one institution during their college career. Suppose a sample of 6 students is chosen. Assuming that each student's college attendance pattern is independent of the others, find the probability of each of the following. *Source: The New York Times*.

(a) Exactly 3 of the 6 students attend more than one institution.

APPLY IT

SOLUTION Think of the 6 students chosen as 6 independent trials. A success occurs if the student attends more than one institution. Then this is a binomial experiment with $n = 6$ and $p = P$ (attend more than one institution) $= 0.59$. To find the probability that exactly 3 students attend more than one institution, let $x = 3$ and use the binomial probability formula.

$$
\begin{aligned}
P(\text{exactly 3 of 6 students}) &= C(6, 3)(0.59)^3(1 - 0.59)^{6-3} \\
&= 20(0.59)^3(0.41)^3 \\
&= 20(0.2054)(0.06892) \\
&\approx 0.2831
\end{aligned}
$$

(b) None of the 6 students attend more than one institution.

YOUR TURN 1 Find the probability that exactly 2 of the 6 students in Example 2 attend more than 1 institution.

SOLUTION Let $x = 0$.

$$
\begin{aligned}
P(\text{exactly 0 of 6 students}) &= C(6, 0)(0.59)^0(1 - 0.59)^6 \\
&= 1(1)(0.41)^6 \approx 0.00475
\end{aligned}
$$

TRY YOUR TURN 1

EXAMPLE 3 Checkout Scanners

The Federal Trade Commission (FTC) monitors pricing accuracy to ensure that consumers are charged the correct price at the checkout. According to the FTC, 29% of stores that use checkout scanners do not accurately charge customers. *Source: Federal Trade Commission*.

(a) If you shop at 3 stores that use checkout scanners, what is the probability that you will be incorrectly charged in at least one store?

SOLUTION We can treat this as a binomial experiment, letting $n = 3$ and $p = 0.29$. We need to find the probability of "at least 1" incorrect charge, which means 1 or 2 or 3 incorrect charges. To make our calculation simpler, we will use the complement.

We will find the probability of being charged incorrectly in none of the 3 stores, that is, $P(0$ incorrect charges$)$, and then find $1 - P(0$ incorrect charges$)$.

$$P(0 \text{ incorrect charges}) = C(3, 0)(0.29)^0(0.71)^3$$
$$= 1(1)(0.357911) \approx 0.3579$$
$$P(\text{at least one}) = 1 - P(0 \text{ incorrect charges})$$
$$\approx 1 - 0.3579 = 0.6421$$

(b) If you shop at 3 stores that use checkout scanners, what is the probability that you will be incorrectly charged in at most one store?

SOLUTION "At most one" means 0 or 1, so

$$P(0 \text{ or } 1) = P(0) + P(1)$$
$$= C(3, 0)(0.29)^0(0.71)^3 + C(3, 1)(0.29)^1(0.71)^2$$
$$= 1(1)(0.357911) + 3(0.29)(0.5041) \approx 0.7965.$$

TRY YOUR TURN 2

> **YOUR TURN 2** In Example 3, if you shop at 4 stores that use checkout scanners, find the probability that you will be charged incorrectly in at least one store.

The triangular array of numbers shown below is called **Pascal's triangle** in honor of the French mathematician Blaise Pascal (1623–1662), who was one of the first to use it extensively. The triangle was known long before Pascal's time and appears in Chinese and Islamic manuscripts from the eleventh century.

Pascal's Triangle

```
                    1
                 1     1
              1     2     1
           1     3     3     1
        1     4     6     4     1
     1     5    10    10     5     1
     ⋮     ⋮     ⋮     ⋮     ⋮
```

The array provides a quick way to find binomial probabilities. The nth row of the triangle, where $n = 0, 1, 2, 3, \ldots$, gives the coefficients $C(n, r)$ for $r = 0, 1, 2, 3, \ldots, n$. For example, for $n = 4$, $1 = C(4, 0)$, $4 = C(4, 1)$, $6 = C(4, 2)$, and so on. Each number in the triangle is the sum of the two numbers directly above it. For example, in the row for $n = 4$, 1 is the sum of 1, the only number above it, 4 is the sum of 1 and 3, 6 is the sum of 3 and 3, and so on. Adding in this way gives the sixth row:

$$1 \quad 6 \quad 15 \quad 20 \quad 15 \quad 6 \quad 1.$$

Notice that Pascal's triangle tells us, for example, that $C(4, 1) + C(4, 2) = C(5, 2)$ (that is, $4 + 6 = 10$). Using the combinations formula, it can be shown that, in general, $C(n, r) + C(n, r + 1) = C(n + 1, r + 1)$. This is left as an exercise.

EXAMPLE 4 Pascal's Triangle

Use Pascal's triangle to find the probability in Example 3 that if you shop at 6 stores that use checkout scanners, at least 3 will charge you incorrectly

SOLUTION The probability of success is 0.29. Since at least 3 means 3, 4, 5, or 6,

$$P(\text{at least 3}) = P(3) + P(4) + P(5) + P(6)$$
$$= C(6, 3)(0.29)^3(0.71)^3 + C(6, 4)(0.29)^4(0.71)^2$$
$$+ C(6, 5)(0.29)^5(0.71)^1 + C(6, 6)(0.29)^6(0.71)^0.$$

Use the sixth row of Pascal's triangle for the combinations to get

$$P(\text{at least } 3) = 20(0.29)^3(0.71)^3 + 15(0.29)^4(0.71)^2$$
$$+ 6(0.29)^5(0.71)^1 + 1(0.29)^6(0.71)^0$$
$$= 0.1746 + 0.0535 + 0.0087 + 0.0006$$
$$= 0.2374.$$

YOUR TURN 3 In Example 3, find the probability that if you shop at 6 stores with checkout scanners, at most 3 stores will charge you incorrectly.

TRY YOUR TURN 3

EXAMPLE 5   Independent Jury

If each member of a 9-person jury acts independently of each other and makes the correct determination of guilt or innocence with probability 0.65, find the probability that the majority of jurors will reach a correct verdict. *Source: Frontiers in Economics.*

SOLUTION

Method 1
Calculating by Hand

Since the jurors in this particular situation act independently, we can treat this as a binomial experiment. Thus, the probability that the majority of the jurors will reach the correct verdict is given by

$$P(\text{at least } 5) = C(9, 5)(0.65)^5(0.35)^4 + C(9, 6)(0.65)^6(0.35)^3$$
$$+ C(9, 7)(0.65)^7(0.35)^2 + C(9, 8)(0.65)^8(0.35)^1 + C(9, 9)(0.65)^9$$
$$= 0.2194 + 0.2716 + 0.2162 + 0.1004 + 0.0207$$
$$= 0.8283.$$

 Method 2
Graphing Calculator

Some graphing calculators provide binomial probabilities. On a TI-84 Plus, for example, the command `binompdf(9,.65,5)`, found in the DISTR menu, gives 0.219386301, which is the probability that $x = 5$. (On a TI-84 Plus C, after DISTR-binompdf, put 9 after `trials`, .65 after p, and 5 after x value. Then, when the cursor is on Paste, press ENTER.) Alternatively, the command `binomcdf(9,.65,4)` gives 0.1717192855 as the probability that 4 or fewer jurors will make the correct decision. Subtract 0.1717192855 from 1 to get 0.8282807145 as the probability that the majority of the jurors will make the correct decision. This value rounds to 0.8283, which is in agreement with Method 1. Often, graphing calculators are more accurate than calculations by hand due to the accumulation of rounding errors when doing successive calculations by hand.

Method 3
Spreadsheet

Some spreadsheets also provide binomial probabilities. In Microsoft Excel, for example, the command "=BINOMDIST(5,9,.65,0)" gives 0.219386301, which is the probability that $x = 5$. Alternatively, the command "=BINOMDIST(4,9,.65,1)" gives 0.171719286 as the probability that 4 or fewer jurors will make the correct decision. Subtract 0.171719286 from 1 to get 0.828280714 as the probability that the majority of the jurors will make the correct decision. This value agrees with the value found in Methods 1 and 2.

8.4 WARM-UP EXERCISES

W1. How many ways can a committee of 10 senators be formed out of 100 senators? *(Sec. 8.2)*

W2. How many ways can a sample of 8 items be chosen from a batch of 32? *(Sec. 8.2)*

8.4 EXERCISES

Suppose that a family has 5 children. Also, suppose that the probability of having a girl is 1/2. Find the probabilities that the family has the following children.

1. Exactly 2 girls and 3 boys

2. Exactly 3 girls and 2 boys

3. No girls

4. No boys

5. At least 4 girls

6. At least 3 boys

7. No more than 3 boys

8. No more than 4 girls

A die is rolled 12 times. Find the probabilities of rolling the following.

9. Exactly 12 ones

10. Exactly 6 ones

11. Exactly 1 one

12. Exactly 2 ones

13. No more than 3 ones

14. No more than 1 one

15. How do you identify a probability problem that involves a binomial experiment?

16. How is Pascal's triangle used to find probabilities?

17. Using the definition of combination in Section 8.2, prove that

$$C(n, r) + C(n, r + 1) = C(n + 1, r + 1).$$

(This is the formula underlying Pascal's triangle.)

In Exercises 18 and 19, argue that the use of binomial probabilities is not applicable and, thus, the probabilities that are computed are not correct.

18. In England, a woman was found guilty of smothering her two infant children. Much of the Crown's case against the lady was based on the testimony from a pediatrician who indicated that the chances of two crib deaths occurring in both siblings was only about 1 in 73 million. This number was calculated by assuming that the probability of a single crib death is 1 in 8543 and the probability of two crib deaths is 1 in 8543^2 (i.e., binomial). (See Chapter 7 Review Exercise 118.) *Source: Science.*

19. A contemporary radio station in Boston has a contest in which a caller is asked his or her date of birth. If the caller's date of birth, including the day, month, and year of birth, matches a predetermined date, the caller wins $1 million. Assuming that there were 36,525 days in the 20th century and the contest was run 51 times on consecutive days, the probability that the grand prize will be won is

$$1 - \left(1 - \frac{1}{36,525}\right)^{51} \approx 0.0014.$$

Source: Chance News.

APPLICATIONS

Business and Economics

Management The survey discussed in Example 3 also found that customers are charged incorrectly for 1 out of every 30 items, on average. Suppose a customer purchases 15 items. Find the following probabilities.

20. A customer is charged incorrectly on 3 items.

21. A customer is not charged incorrectly for any item.

22. A customer is charged incorrectly on at least one item.

23. A customer is charged incorrectly on at least 2 items.

24. A customer is charged incorrectly on at most 2 items.

Credit Cards A survey of consumer finance found that 25.4% of credit-card-holding families hardly ever pay off the balance. Suppose a random sample of 20 credit-card-holding families is taken. Find the probabilities of each of the following results. *Source: Statistical Abstract of the United States.*

25. Exactly 6 families hardly ever pay off the balance.

26. Exactly 9 families hardly ever pay off the balance.

27. At least 4 families hardly ever pay off the balance.

28. At most 5 families hardly ever pay off the balance.

Quality Control A factory tests a random sample of 20 transistors for defects. The probability that a particular transistor will be defective has been established by past experience as 0.05.

29. What is the probability that there are no defective transistors in the sample?

30. What is the probability that the number of defective transistors in the sample is at most 2?

31. **Quality Control** The probability that a certain machine turns out a defective item is 0.05. Find the probabilities that in a run of 75 items, the following results are obtained.

    (a) Exactly 5 defective items

    (b) No defective items

    (c) At least 1 defective item

32. **Survey Results** A company is taking a survey to find out whether people like its product. Its last survey indicated that 70% of the population like the product. Based on that, in a sample of 58 people, find the probabilities of the following.

    (a) All 58 like the product.

    (b) From 28 to 30 (inclusive) like the product.

33. **Pecans** Pecan producers blow air through the pecans so that the lighter ones are blown out. The lighter-weight pecans are generally bad and the heavier ones tend to be better. These "blow outs" and "good nuts" are often sold to tourists along the highway. Suppose 60% of the "blow outs" are good, and 80% of the "good nuts" are good. *Source: Irvin R. Hentzel.*

(a) What is the probability that if you crack and check 20 "good nuts" you will find 8 bad ones?

(b) What is the probability that if you crack and check 20 "blow outs" you will find 8 bad ones?

(c) If we assume that 70% of the roadside stands sell "good nuts," and that out of 20 nuts we find 8 that are bad, what is the probability that the nuts are "blow outs"?

34. Hurricane Insurance A company prices its hurricane insurance using the following assumptions:

  (i) In any calendar year, there can be at most one hurricane.

 (ii) In any calendar year, the probability of a hurricane is 0.05.

(iii) The number of hurricanes in any calendar year is independent of the number of hurricanes in any other calendar year.

Using the company's assumptions, calculate the probability that there are fewer than 3 hurricanes in a 20-year period. Choose one of the following. *Source: Society of Actuaries.*

  (a) 0.06   **(b)** 0.19   **(c)** 0.38   **(d)** 0.62   **(e)** 0.92

Life Sciences

Breast Cancer A recent study found that 85% of breast-cancer cases are detectable by mammogram. Suppose a random sample of 15 women with breast cancer are given mammograms. Find the probability of each of the following results, assuming that detection in the cases is independent. *Source: Harper's Index.*

35. All of the cases are detectable.

36. None of the cases are detectable.

37. Not all cases are detectable.

38. More than half of the cases are detectable.

Births of Twins The probability that a birth will result in twins is 0.012. Assuming independence (perhaps not a valid assumption), what are the probabilities that out of 100 births in a hospital, there will be the following numbers of sets of twins?

39. Exactly 2 sets of twins

40. At most 2 sets of twins

41. Births In 2012, the University of Minnesota Medical Center had a string of 19 births, all of whom were boys. *Source: CBS Minnesota.*

(a) Assuming boy and girl births are equally likely, what is the probability of 19 births in a row being boys?

(b) There are about 4 million births per year in the United States and about 5700 hospitals. For the sake of simplicity, suppose the births over a ten-year period were evenly distributed over all the hospitals, and suppose each of those hospitals divided their births into strings of 19 consecutive births. What is the probability, in any one of those hospitals, of having a string of all boys?

(c) Based on your answer to part (b), what is the probability that at least one of those 5700 hospitals would have a string of all boys?

(d) Explain why the actual probability of a hospital seeing a string of 19 boy births somewhere in the United States over a 10-year period is higher than the value calculated in part (c).

42. Births In Clay County, North Carolina, 54 out of 84 births in 2012, or about 64%, were male, while in Macon County, 201 out of 346 births, or about 58%, were male. *Source: North Carolina State Center for Health Statistics.*

(a) Which of these two events seems less likely to you? Now compute the probability of at least 54 out of 84 births being male, and at least 201 out of 346 births being male, assuming male and female births are equally likely. Does this surprise you?

(b) Explain why the Macon County births are more unusual, even though the Clay County births have a higher percentage of males.

(c) Explain why, in part (a), we calculated the probability of at least 54 births out of 84 being male, rather than the probability that exactly 54 births out of 84 are male.

43. Color Blindness The probability that a male will be color-blind is 0.042. Find the probabilities that in a group of 53 men, the following will be true.

(a) Exactly 5 are color-blind.

(b) No more than 5 are color-blind.

(c) At least 1 is color-blind.

44. Pharmacology In placebo-controlled trials of Pravachol®, a drug that is prescribed to lower cholesterol, 7.3% of the patients who were taking the drug experienced nausea/vomiting, whereas 7.1% of the patients who were taking the placebo experienced nausea/vomiting. *Source: Bristol-Myers Squibb Company.*

(a) If 100 patients who are taking Pravachol® are selected, what is the probability that 10 or more will experience nausea/vomiting?

(b) If a second group of 100 patients receives a placebo, what is the probability that 10 or more will experience nausea/vomiting?

(c) Since 7.3% is larger than 7.1%, do you believe that the Pravachol® causes more people to experience nausea/vomiting than a placebo? Explain.

45. Genetic Fingerprinting The use of DNA has become an integral part of many court cases. When DNA is extracted from cells and body fluids, genetic information is represented by bands of information, which look similar to a bar code at a grocery store. It is generally accepted that in unrelated people, the probability of a particular band matching is 1 in 4. *Source: University of Exeter.*

(a) If 5 bands are compared in unrelated people, what is the probability that all 5 of the bands match? (Express your answer in terms of "1 chance in ?".)

(b) If 20 bands are compared in unrelated people, what is the probability that all 20 of the bands match? (Express your answer in terms of "1 chance in ?".)

(c) If 20 bands are compared in unrelated people, what is the probability that 16 or more bands match? (Express your answer in terms of "1 chance in ?".)

(d) If you were deciding paternity and there were 16 matches out of 20 bands compared, would you believe that the person being tested was the father? Explain.

46. Salmonella According to *The Salt Lake Tribune*, the Coffee Garden in Salt Lake City ran into trouble because of their four-egg quiche:

"A Salt Lake County Health Department inspector paid a visit recently and pointed out that research by the Food and Drug Administration indicates that one in four eggs carries *Salmonella* bacterium, so restaurants should never use more than three eggs when preparing quiche.

The manager on duty wondered aloud if simply throwing out three eggs from each dozen and using the remaining nine in four-egg quiches would serve the same purpose.

The inspector wasn't sure, but she said she would research it." *Source: The Salt Lake Tribune*.

(a) Assuming that one in four eggs carries *Salmonella*, and that the event that any one egg is infected is independent of whether any other egg is infected, find the probability that at least one of the eggs in a four-egg quiche carries *Salmonella*.

(b) Repeat part (a) for a three-egg quiche.

(c) Discuss whether the assumption of independence is justified.

(d) Discuss whether the inspector's reasoning makes sense.

47. Herbal Remedies According to Dr. Peter A.G.M. De Smet of the Netherlands, "If an herb caused an adverse reaction in 1 in 1,000 users, a traditional healer would have to treat 4,800 patients with that herb (i.e., one new patient every single working day for more than 18 years) to have a 95 percent chance of observing the reaction in more than one user." Verify this calculation by finding the probability of observing more than one reaction in 4800 patients, given that 1 in 1000 has a reaction. *Source: The New England Journal of Medicine*.

48. Vaccines A hospital receives 1/5 of its flu vaccine shipments from Company X and the remainder of its shipments from other companies. Each shipment contains a very large number of vaccine vials. For Company X's shipments, 10% of the vials are ineffective. For every other company, 2% of the vials are ineffective. The hospital tests 30 randomly selected vials from a shipment and finds that one vial is ineffective. What is the probability that this shipment came from Company X? Choose one of the following. (*Hint:* Find the probability that one out of 30 vials is ineffective, given that the shipment came from Company X and that the shipment came from other companies. Then use Bayes' theorem.) *Source: Society of Actuaries*.

(a) 0.10   (b) 0.14   (c) 0.37   (d) 0.63   (e) 0.86

49. Health Study A study is being conducted in which the health of two independent groups of ten policyholders is being monitored over a one-year period of time. Individual participants in the study drop out before the end of the study with probability 0.2 (independently of the other participants). What is the probability that at least 9 participants complete the study in one of the two groups, but not in both groups? Choose one of the following. *Source: Society of Actuaries*.

(a) 0.096   (b) 0.192   (c) 0.235   (d) 0.376   (e) 0.469

Social Sciences

50. Women Working A recent study found that 60% of working mothers would prefer to work part-time if money were not a concern. Find the probability that if 10 working mothers are

selected at random, at least 3 of them would prefer to work part-time. *Source: Pew Research Center*.

Volunteering A recent survey found that 83% of first-year college students were involved in volunteer work at least occasionally. Suppose a random sample of 12 college students is taken. Find the probabilities of each of the following results. *Source: The New York Times*.

51. Exactly 7 students volunteered at least occasionally.

52. Exactly 9 students volunteered at least occasionally.

53. At least 9 students volunteered at least occasionally.

54. At most 9 students volunteered at least occasionally.

55. Minority Enrollment According to the U.S. Department of Education, 32.2% of all students enrolled in degree-granting institutions (those that grant associate's or higher degrees) belong to minorities. Find the probabilities of the following results in a random sample of 10 students enrolled in degree-granting institutions. *Source: National Center for Education Statistics*.

(a) Exactly 2 belong to a minority.

(b) Three or fewer belong to a minority.

(c) Exactly 5 do not belong to a minority.

(d) Six or more do not belong to a minority.

56. Cheating According to a poll conducted by *U.S. News and World Report*, 84% of college students believe they need to cheat to get ahead in the world today. *Source: U.S. News and World Report*.

(a) Do the results of this poll indicate that 84% of all college students cheat? Explain.

(b) If this result is accurate and 100 college students are asked if they believe that cheating is necessary to get ahead in the world, what is the probability that 90 or more of the students will answer affirmatively to the question?

57. Education A study by Cleveland Clinic tracked a cohort of very-low-birth-weight infants for twenty years. The results of the study indicated that 74% of the very-low-birth-weight babies graduated from high school during this time period. The study also reported that 83% of the comparison group of normal-birth-weight babies graduated from high school during the same period. *Source: The New England Journal of Medicine*.

(a) If 40 very-low-birth-weight babies were tracked through high school, what is the probability that at least 30 will graduate from high school by age 20?

(b) If 40 babies from the comparison group were tracked through high school, what is the probability that at least 30 will graduate from high school by age 20?

58. War Dead A newspaper article questioned whether soldiers and marines from some states bear greater risks in Afghanistan and Iraq than those from others. Out of 644,066 troops deployed as of the time of the article, 1174 had been killed, for a probability of being killed of $p = 1174/644{,}066$. Assume the deaths are independent.* *Source: Valley News*.

(a) Vermont had 9 deaths out of 1613 troops deployed. Find the probability of at least this many deaths.

*For further statistical analysis, see www.dartmouth.edu/~chance/ForWiki/GregComments.pdf.

(b) Massachusetts had 28 deaths out of 7146 troops deployed. Find the probability of at least this many deaths.

(c) Florida had 54 deaths out of 62,572 troops deployed. Find the probability of at most this many deaths.

(d) Discuss why the assumption of independence may be questionable.

59. Sports In many sports championships, such as the World Series in baseball and the Stanley Cup final series in hockey, the winner is the first team to win four games. For this exercise, assume that each game is independent of the others, with a constant probability p that one specified team (say, the National League team) wins.

(a) Find the probability that the series lasts for four, five, six, and seven games when $p = 0.5$. (*Hint:* Suppose the National League wins the series, so they must win the last game. Consider how the previous games might come out. Then consider the probability that the American League wins.)

(b) Morrison and Schmittlein have found that the Stanley Cup finals can be described by letting $p = 0.73$ be the probability that the better team wins each game. Find the probability that the series lasts for four, five, six, and seven games. *Source: Chance.*

(c) Some have argued that the assumption of independence does not apply. Discuss this issue. *Source: Mathematics Magazine.*

YOUR TURN ANSWERS

1. 0.1475   **2.** 0.7459   **3.** 0.9372

8.5 Probability Distributions; Expected Value

APPLY IT What is the expected payback for someone who buys one ticket in a raffle?

In Example 4, we will calculate the expected payback or expected value of this raffle.

We shall see that the *expected value* of a probability distribution is a type of average. Probability distributions were introduced briefly in Chapter 7 on Sets and Probability. Now we take a more complete look at probability distributions. A probability distribution depends on the idea of a *random variable*, so we begin with that.

Random Variables When researchers carry out an experiment it is necessary to quantify the possible outcomes of the experiment. This process will enable the researcher to recognize individual outcomes and analyze the data. The most common way to keep track of the individual outcomes of the experiment is to assign a numerical value to each of the different possible outcomes of the experiment. For example, if a coin is tossed 2 times, the possible outcomes are: *hh, ht, th,* and *tt.* For each of these possible outcomes, we could record the number of heads. Then the outcome, which we will label x, is one of the numbers 0, 1, or 2. Of course, we could have used other numbers, like 00, 01, 10, and 11, to indicate these same outcomes, but the values of 0, 1, and 2 are simpler and provide an immediate description of the exact outcome of the experiment. Notice that using this random variable also gives us a way to readily know how many tails occurred in the experiment. Thus, in some sense, the values of x are random, so x is called a **random variable**.

Random Variable

A **random variable** is a function that assigns a real number to each outcome of an experiment.

Probability Distribution

A table that lists the possible values of a random variable, together with the corresponding probabilities, is called a **probability distribution**. The sum of the probabilities in a probability distribution must always equal 1. (The sum in some distributions may vary slightly from 1 because of rounding.)

EXAMPLE 1 Computer Monitors

A shipment of 12 computer monitors contains 3 broken monitors. A shipping manager checks a sample of four monitors to see if any are broken. Give the probability distribution for the number of broken monitors that the shipping manager finds.

SOLUTION Let x represent the random variable "number of broken monitors found by the manager." Since there are 3 broken monitors, the possible values of x are 0, 1, 2, and 3. We can calculate the probability of each x using the methods of Section 8.3. There are 3 broken monitors, and 9 unbroken monitors, so the number of ways of choosing 0 broken monitors (which implies 4 unbroken monitors) is $C(3, 0) \cdot C(9, 4)$. The number of ways of choosing a sample of 4 monitors is $C(12, 4)$. Therefore, the probability of choosing 0 broken monitors is

$$P(0) = \frac{C(3, 0) \cdot C(9, 4)}{C(12, 4)} = \frac{1\left(\dfrac{9 \cdot 8 \cdot 7 \cdot 6}{4 \cdot 3 \cdot 2 \cdot 1}\right)}{\left(\dfrac{12 \cdot 11 \cdot 10 \cdot 9}{4 \cdot 3 \cdot 2 \cdot 1}\right)} = \frac{126}{495} = \frac{14}{55}.$$

Similarly, the probability of choosing 1 broken monitor is

$$P(1) = \frac{C(3, 1) \cdot C(9, 3)}{C(12, 4)} = \frac{3 \cdot 84}{495} = \frac{252}{495} = \frac{28}{55}.$$

The probability of choosing 2 broken monitors is

$$P(2) = \frac{C(3, 2) \cdot C(9, 2)}{C(12, 4)} = \frac{3 \cdot 36}{495} = \frac{108}{495} = \frac{12}{55}.$$

The probability of choosing 3 broken monitors is

$$P(3) = \frac{C(3, 3) \cdot C(9, 1)}{C(12, 4)} = \frac{1 \cdot 9}{495} = \frac{9}{495} = \frac{1}{55}.$$

The results can be put in a table, called a probability distribution.

YOUR TURN 1 Suppose the inspector in Example 1 chose only two monitors to inspect. Find the probability distribution for the number of broken monitors.

Probability Distribution of Broken Monitors in Sample			
x	0	1	2	3
$P(x)$	14/55	28/55	12/55	1/55

TRY YOUR TURN 1

Instead of writing the probability distribution as a table, we could write the same information as a set of ordered pairs:

$$\{(0, 14/55), (1, 28/55), (2, 12/55), (3, 1/55)\}.$$

There is just one probability for each value of the random variable. Thus, a probability distribution defines a function, called a **probability distribution function**, or simply a **probability function**. We shall use the terms "probability distribution" and "probability function" interchangeably.

The information in a probability distribution is often displayed graphically as a special kind of bar graph called a **histogram**. The bars of a histogram all have the same width, usually 1. (The widths might be different from 1 when the values of the random variable are not consecutive integers.) The heights of the bars are determined by the probabilities. A histogram for the data in Example 1 is given in Figure 8. A histogram shows important

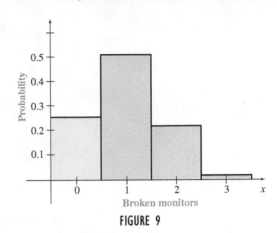

FIGURE 8   FIGURE 9

characteristics of a distribution that may not be readily apparent in tabular form, such as the relative sizes of the probabilities and any symmetry in the distribution.

The area of the bar above $x = 0$ in Figure 8 is the product of 1 and 14/55, or $1 \cdot 14/55 = 14/55$. Since each bar has a width of 1, its area is equal to the probability that corresponds to that value of x. The probability that a particular value will occur is thus given by the area of the appropriate bar of the graph. For example, the probability that one or more monitors is broken is the sum of the areas for $x = 1$, $x = 2$, and $x = 3$. This area, shown in pink in Figure 9, corresponds to 41/55 of the total area, since

$$P(x \geq 1) = P(x = 1) + P(x = 2) + P(x = 3)$$
$$= 28/55 + 12/55 + 1/55 = 41/55.$$

EXAMPLE 2   Probability Distributions

(a) Give the probability distribution for the number of heads showing when two coins are tossed.

SOLUTION   Let x represent the random variable "number of heads." Then x can take on the values 0, 1, or 2. Now find the probability of each outcome. To find the probability of 0, 1, or 2 heads, we can either use binomial probability, or notice that there are 4 outcomes in the sample space: $\{hh, ht, th, tt\}$. The results are shown in the table with Figure 10.

Probability Distribution of Heads		
x	0	1	2
$P(x)$	1/4	1/2	1/4

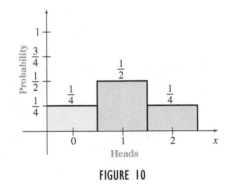

FIGURE 10

YOUR TURN 2 Find the probability distribution and draw a histogram for the number of tails showing when three coins are tossed.

(b) Draw a histogram for the distribution in the table. Find the probability that at least one coin comes up heads.

SOLUTION   The histogram is shown in Figure 10. The portion in pink represents

$$P(x \geq 1) = P(x = 1) + P(x = 2)$$
$$= \frac{3}{4}.$$

TRY YOUR TURN 2

Expected Value   In working with probability distributions, it is useful to have a concept of the typical or average value that the random variable takes on. In Example 2, for instance, it seems reasonable that, on the average, one head shows when two coins are tossed. This does not tell what will happen the next time we toss two coins; we may get two heads, or we may get none. If we tossed two coins many times, however, we would expect that, in the long run, we would average about one head for each toss of two coins.

A way to solve such problems in general is to imagine flipping two coins 4 times. Based on the probability distribution in Example 2, we would expect that 1 of the 4 times we would get 0 heads, 2 of the 4 times we would get 1 head, and 1 of the 4 times we would get 2 heads. The total number of heads we would get, then, is

$$0 \cdot 1 + 1 \cdot 2 + 2 \cdot 1 = 4.$$

The expected numbers of heads per toss is found by dividing the total number of heads by the total number of tosses, or

$$\frac{0 \cdot 1 + 1 \cdot 2 + 2 \cdot 1}{4} = 0 \cdot \frac{1}{4} + 1 \cdot \frac{1}{2} + 2 \cdot \frac{1}{4} = 1.$$

Notice that the expected number of heads turns out to be the sum of the three values of the random variable x multiplied by their corresponding probabilities. We can use this idea to define the *expected value* of a random variable as follows.

Expected Value

Suppose the random variable x can take on the n values $x_1, x_2, x_3, \ldots, x_n$. Also, suppose the probabilities that these values occur are, respectively, $p_1, p_2, p_3, \ldots, p_n$. Then the **expected value** of the random variable is

$$E(x) = x_1 p_1 + x_2 p_2 + x_3 p_3 + \cdots + x_n p_n.$$

EXAMPLE 3   **Computer Monitors**

In Example 1, find the expected number of broken monitors that the shipping manager finds.

SOLUTION   Using the values in the first table in this section and the definition of expected value, we find that

$$E(x) = 0 \cdot \frac{14}{55} + 1 \cdot \frac{28}{55} + 2 \cdot \frac{12}{55} + 3 \cdot \frac{1}{55} = 1.$$

On average, the shipping manager will find 1 broken monitor in the sample of 4. On reflection, this seems natural; 3 of the 12 monitors, or 1/4 of the total, are broken. We should expect, then, that 1/4 of the sample of 4 monitors are broken.   ▬

Physically, the expected value of a probability distribution represents a balance point. If we think of the histogram in Figure 8 as a series of weights with magnitudes represented by the heights of the bars, then the system would balance if supported at the point corresponding to the expected value.

EXAMPLE 4   **Symphony Orchestra**

Suppose a local symphony decides to raise money by raffling an HD television worth $400, a dinner for two worth $80, and 2 CDs worth $20 each. A total of 2000 tickets are sold at $1 each. Find the expected payback for a person who buys one ticket in the raffle.

APPLY IT
Method 1
Direct Calculation

SOLUTION

Here the random variable represents the possible amounts of payback, where payback equals the amount won minus the cost of the ticket. The payback of the person winning the television is $400 (amount won) − $1 (cost of ticket) = $399. The payback for each losing ticket is $0 − $1 = −$1.

The paybacks of the various prizes, as well as their respective probabilities, are shown in the table below. The probability of winning $19 is 2/2000 because there are 2 prizes worth $20. We have not reduced the fractions in order to keep all the denominators equal. Because there are 4 winning tickets, there are 1996 losing tickets, so the probability of winning −$1 is 1996/2000.

Probability Distribution of Prize Winnings			
x	$399	$79	$19	−$1
$P(x)$	1/2000	1/2000	2/2000	1996/2000

The expected payback for a person buying one ticket is

$$399\left(\frac{1}{2000}\right) + 79\left(\frac{1}{2000}\right) + 19\left(\frac{2}{2000}\right) + (-1)\left(\frac{1996}{2000}\right) = -\frac{1480}{2000}$$
$$= -0.74.$$

On average, a person buying one ticket in the raffle will lose $0.74, or 74¢.

It is not possible to lose 74¢ in this raffle: Either you lose $1, or you win a prize worth $400, $80, or $20, minus the $1 you pay to play. But if you bought tickets in many such raffles over a long period of time, you would lose 74¢ per ticket on average. It is important to note that the expected value of a random variable may be a number that can never occur in any one trial of the experiment.

Method 2
Alternate Procedure

An alternative way to compute expected value in this and other examples is to calculate the expected amount won and then subtract the cost of the ticket afterward. The amount won is either $400 (with probability 1/2000), $80 (with probability 1/2000), $20 (with probability 2/2000), or $0 (with probability 1996/2000). The expected payback for a person buying one ticket is then

YOUR TURN 3 Suppose that there is a $5 raffle with prizes worth $1000, $500, and $250. Suppose 1000 tickets are sold and you purchase a ticket. Find your expected payback for this raffle.

$$400\left(\frac{1}{2000}\right) + 80\left(\frac{1}{2000}\right) + 20\left(\frac{2}{2000}\right) + 0\left(\frac{1996}{2000}\right) - 1 = -\frac{1480}{2000}$$
$$= -0.74.$$

TRY YOUR TURN 3

EXAMPLE 5   Friendly Wager

Each day Donna and Mary toss a coin to see who buys coffee ($1.20 a cup). One tosses and the other calls the outcome. If the person who calls the outcome is correct, the other buys the coffee; otherwise the caller pays. Find Donna's expected payback.

SOLUTION   Assume that an honest coin is used, that Mary tosses the coin, and that Donna calls the outcome. The possible results and corresponding probabilities are shown below.

	Possible Results			
Result of Toss	Heads	Heads	Tails	Tails
Call	Heads	Tails	Heads	Tails
Caller Wins?	Yes	No	No	Yes
Probability	1/4	1/4	1/4	1/4

Donna wins a $1.20 cup of coffee whenever the results and calls match, and she loses a $1.20 cup when there is no match. Her expected payback is

$$(1.20)\left(\frac{1}{4}\right) + (-1.20)\left(\frac{1}{4}\right) + (-1.20)\left(\frac{1}{4}\right) + (1.20)\left(\frac{1}{4}\right) = 0.$$

This implies that, over the long run, Donna neither wins nor loses.

A game with an expected value of 0 (such as the one in Example 5) is called a **fair game**. Casinos do not offer fair games. If they did, they would win (on average) $0, and have a hard time paying the help! Casino games have expected winnings for the house that vary from 1.5 cents per dollar to 60 cents per dollar. Exercises 47–52 at the end of the section ask you to find the expected payback for certain games of chance.

The idea of expected value can be very useful in decision making, as shown by the next example.

EXAMPLE 6   Life Insurance

At age 50, you receive a letter from Mutual of Mauritania Insurance Company. According to the letter, you must tell the company immediately which of the following two options you will choose: take $20,000 at age 60 (if you are alive, $0 otherwise) or $30,000 at age 70 (again, if you are alive, $0 otherwise). Based *only* on the idea of expected value, which should you choose?

SOLUTION   Life insurance companies have constructed elaborate tables showing the probability of a person living a given number of years into the future. From a recent such table, the probability of living from age 50 to 60 is 0.88, while the probability of living from age 50 to 70 is 0.64. The expected values of the two options are given below.

$$\text{First option: } (20{,}000)(0.88) + (0)(0.12) = 17{,}600$$
$$\text{Second option: } (30{,}000)(0.64) + (0)(0.36) = 19{,}200$$

Based strictly on expected values, choose the second option.

EXAMPLE 7   Bachelor's Degrees

According to the National Center for Education Statistics, 79.4% of those earning bachelor's degrees in education in the United States in 2011–2012 were female. Suppose 5 holders of bachelor's degrees in education from 2011 to 2012 are picked at random. *Source: National Center for Education Statistics.*

(a) Find the probability distribution for the number that are female.

SOLUTION   We first note that each of the 5 people in the sample is either female (with probability 0.794) or male (with probability 0.206). As in the previous section, we may assume that the probability for each member of the sample is independent of that of any other. Such a situation is described by binomial probability with $n = 5$ and $p = 0.794$, for which we use the binomial probability formula

$$P(x \text{ successes in } n \text{ trials}) = C(n, x) \cdot p^x \cdot (1 - p)^{n-x},$$

where x is the number of females in the sample. For example, the probability of 0 females is

$$P(x = 0) = C(5, 0)(0.794)^0(0.206)^5 \approx 0.0004.$$

Similarly, we could calculate the probability that x is any value from 0 to 5, resulting in the probability distribution below (with all probabilities rounded to four places).

Probability Distribution of Female Education Graduate					
x	0	1	2	3	4	5
$P(x)$	0.0004	0.0071	0.0551	0.2124	0.4094	0.3156

YOUR TURN 4 In the same survey quoted in Example 7, 80.9% of those earning bachelor's degrees in engineering were male. Suppose 5 holders of bachelor's degrees in engineering were picked at random, find the expected number of male engineers.

(b) Find the expected number of females in the sample of 5 people.

SOLUTION   Using the formula for expected value, we have

$$E(x) = 0(0.0004) + 1(0.0071) + 2(0.0551) + 3(0.2124)$$
$$+ 4(0.4094) + 5(0.3156) = 3.9701.$$

On average, 3.970 of the people in the sample of 5 will be female.

TRY YOUR TURN 4

There is another way to get the answer in part (b) of the previous example. Because 79.4% of those earning bachelor's degrees in education in the United States in 2011–2012 are female, it is reasonable to expect 79.4% of our sample to be female. Thus, 79.4% of 5 is $5(0.794) = 3.970$. Notice that what we have done is to multiply n by p. It can be shown that this method always gives the expected value for binomial probability.

Expected Value for Binomial Probability
For binomial probability, $E(x) = np$. In other words, the expected number of successes is the number of trials times the probability of success in each trial.

EXAMPLE 8   **Female Children**

Suppose a family has 3 children.

(a) Find the probability distribution for the number of girls.

SOLUTION   Assuming girls and boys are equally likely, the probability distribution is binomial with $n = 3$ and $p = 1/2$. Letting x be the number of girls in the formula for binomial probability, we find, for example,

$$P(x = 0) = C(3, 0)\left(\frac{1}{2}\right)^0\left(\frac{1}{2}\right)^3 = \frac{1}{8}.$$

The other values are found similarly, and the results are shown in the following table.

Probability Distribution of Number of Girls			
x	0	1	2	3
$P(x)$	1/8	3/8	3/8	1/8

We can verify this by noticing that in the sample space S of all 3-child families, there are eight equally likely outcomes: $S = \{ggg, ggb, gbg, gbb, bgg, bgb, bbg, bbb\}$. One of the outcomes has 0 girls, three have 1 girl, three have 2 girls, and one has 3 girls.

(b) Find the expected number of girls in a 3-child family using the distribution from part (a).

SOLUTION   Using the formula for expected value, we have

$$\text{Expected number of girls} = 0\left(\frac{1}{8}\right) + 1\left(\frac{3}{8}\right) + 2\left(\frac{3}{8}\right) + 3\left(\frac{1}{8}\right)$$
$$= \frac{12}{8} = 1.5.$$

On average, a 3-child family will have 1.5 girls. This result agrees with our intuition that, on average, half the children born will be girls.

(c) Find the expected number of girls in a 3-child family using the formula for expected value for binomial probability.

SOLUTION Using the formula $E(x) = np$ with $n = 3$ and $p = 1/2$, we have

YOUR TURN 5 Find the expected number of girls in a family of a dozen children.

$$\text{Expected number of girls} = 3\left(\frac{1}{2}\right) = 1.5.$$

This agrees with our answer from part (b), as it must.   **TRY YOUR TURN 5**

8.5 WARM-UP EXERCISES

W1. A die is rolled 5 times. Find the probability of getting exactly 0, 1, 2, 3, 4, and 5 sixes.   *(Sec. 8.4)*

W2. Four cards are drawn one at a time, with replacement, from an ordinary deck. Find the probability of getting exactly 0, 1, 2, 3, and 4 spades.   *(Sec. 8.4)*

8.5 EXERCISES

For each experiment described below, let *x* determine a random variable, and use your knowledge of probability to prepare a probability distribution.

1. Four coins are tossed, and the number of heads is noted.

2. Two dice are rolled, and the total number of points is recorded.

3. Three cards are drawn from a deck. The number of aces is counted.

4. Two balls are drawn from a bag in which there are 4 white balls and 2 black balls. The number of black balls is counted.

Draw a histogram for the following, and shade the region that gives the indicated probability.

5. Exercise 1; $P(x \le 2)$

6. Exercise 2; $P(x \ge 11)$

7. Exercise 3; $P(\text{at least one ace})$

8. Exercise 4; $P(\text{at least one black ball})$

Find the expected value for each random variable.

9.
x	2	3	4	5
$P(x)$	0.1	0.4	0.3	0.2

10.
y	4	6	8	10
$P(y)$	0.4	0.4	0.05	0.15

11.
z	9	12	15	18	21
$P(z)$	0.14	0.22	0.38	0.19	0.07

12.
x	30	32	36	38	44
$P(x)$	0.31	0.29	0.26	0.09	0.05

Find the expected value for the random variable *x* having the probability function shown in each graph.

13.

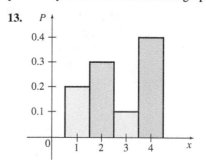

14.

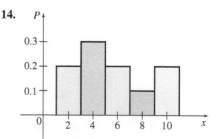

15.

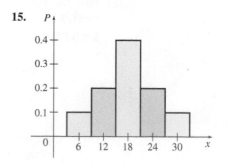

16.

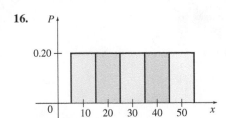

17. For the game in Example 5, find Mary's expected payback. Is it a fair game?

18. Suppose one day Mary brings a 2-headed coin and uses it to toss for the coffee. Since Mary tosses, Donna calls.

(a) Is this still a fair game?

(b) What is Donna's expected payback if she calls heads?

(c) What is Donna's expected payback if she calls tails?

Solve each exercise. Many of these exercises require the use of combinations.

19. Suppose 3 marbles are drawn without replacement from a bag containing 3 yellow and 4 white marbles.

(a) Draw a histogram for the number of yellow marbles in the sample.

(b) What is the expected number of yellow marbles in the sample?

20. Suppose 5 apples in a barrel of 25 apples are known to be rotten.

(a) Draw a histogram for the number of rotten apples in a sample of 2 apples.

(b) What is the expected number of rotten apples in a sample of 2 apples?

21. Suppose a die is rolled 4 times.

(a) Find the probability distribution for the number of times 1 is rolled.

(b) What is the expected number of times 1 is rolled?

22. A delegation of 3 is selected from a city council made up of 5 liberals and 6 conservatives.

(a) What is the expected number of liberals in the delegation?

(b) What is the expected number of conservatives in the delegation?

23. From a group of 3 women and 5 men, a delegation of 2 is selected. Find the expected number of women in the delegation.

24. In a club with 20 senior and 10 junior members, what is the expected number of junior members on a 4-member committee?

25. If 2 cards are drawn at one time from a deck of 52 cards, what is the expected number of diamonds?

26. Suppose someone offers to pay you $5 if you draw 2 diamonds in the game in Exercise 25. He says that you should pay 50 cents for the chance to play. Is this a fair game?

27. Your friend missed class the day probability distributions were discussed. How would you explain probability distribution to him?

28. Explain what expected value means in your own words.

29. Four slips of paper numbered 2, 3, 4, and 5 are in a hat. You draw a slip, note the result, and then draw a second slip and note the result (without replacing the first).

(a) Find the probability distribution for the sum of the two slips.

(b) Draw a histogram for the probability distribution in part (a).

(c) Find the odds that the sum is even.

(d) Find the expected value of the sum.

APPLICATIONS

Business and Economics

30. **Complaints** A local used-car dealer gets complaints about his cars as shown in the table below. Find the expected number of complaints per day.

Number of Complaints per Day	0	1	2	3	4	5	6
Probability	0.02	0.06	0.16	0.25	0.32	0.13	0.06

31. **Payout on Insurance Policies** An insurance company has written 100 policies for $100,000, 500 policies for $50,000, and 1000 policies for $10,000 for people of age 20. If experience shows that the probability that a person will die at age 20 is 0.0012, how much can the company expect to pay out during the year the policies were written?

32. **Device Failure** An insurance policy on an electrical device pays a benefit of $4000 if the device fails during the first year. The amount of the benefit decreases by $1000 each successive year until it reaches 0. If the device has not failed by the beginning of any given year, the probability of failure during that year is 0.4. What is the expected benefit under this policy? Choose one of the following. *Source: Society of Actuaries.*

(a) $2234 (b) $2400 (c) $2500 (d) $2667 (e) $2694

33. **Pecans** Refer to Exercise 33 in Section 8.4. Suppose that 60% of the pecan "blow outs" are good, and 80% of the "good nuts" are good.

(a) If you purchase 50 pecans, what is the expected number of good nuts you will find if you purchase "blow outs"?

(b) If you purchase 50 pecans, what is the expected number of bad nuts you will find if you have purchased "good nuts"?

34. **Rating Sales Accounts** Levi Strauss and Company uses expected value to help its salespeople rate their accounts. For each account, a salesperson estimates potential additional volume and the probability of getting it. The product of these figures gives the expected value of the potential, which is added to the existing volume. The totals are then classified as A, B, or C, as follows: $40,000 or below, class C; from $40,000 up to and including $55,000, class B; above $55,000, class A. Complete the table on the next page for one salesperson. *Source: James McDonald.*

Account Number	Existing Volume	Potential Additional Volume	Probability of Getting It	Expected Value of Potential	Existing Volume + Expected Value of Potential	Class
1	$15,000	$10,000	0.25	$2500	$17,500	C
2	$40,000	$0	—	—	$40,000	C
3	$20,000	$10,000	0.20			
4	$50,000	$10,000	0.10			
5	$5000	$50,000	0.50			
6	$0	$100,000	0.60			
7	$30,000	$20,000	0.80			

35. Tour Bus A tour operator has a bus that can accommodate 20 tourists. The operator knows that tourists may not show up, so he sells 21 tickets. The probability that an individual tourist will not show up is 0.02, independent of all other tourists. Each ticket costs $50, and is non-refundable if a tourist fails to show up. If a tourist shows up and a seat is not available, the tour operator has to pay $100 (ticket cost + $50 penalty) to the tourist. What is the expected revenue of the tour operator? Choose one of the following. *Source: Society of Actuaries.*

(a) $935 (b) $950 (c) $967 (d) $976 (e) $985

Life Sciences

36. Animal Offspring In a certain animal species, the probability that a healthy adult female will have no offspring in a given year is 0.29, while the probabilities of 1, 2, 3, or 4 offspring are, respectively, 0.23, 0.18, 0.16, and 0.14. Find the expected number of offspring.

37. Ear Infections Otitis media, or middle ear infection, is initially treated with an antibiotic. Researchers have compared two antibiotics, amoxicillin and cefaclor, for their cost effectiveness. Amoxicillin is inexpensive, safe, and effective. Cefaclor is also safe. However, it is considerably more expensive and it is generally more effective. Use the tree diagram below (where the costs are estimated as the total cost of medication, office visit, ear check, and hours of lost work) to answer the following. *Source: Journal of Pediatric Infectious Disease.*

(a) Find the expected cost of using each antibiotic to treat a middle ear infection.

(b) To minimize the total expected cost, which antibiotic should be chosen?

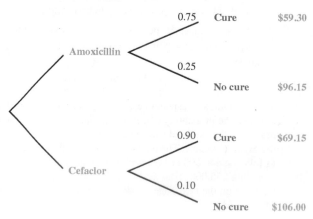

38. Hospitalization Insurance An insurance policy pays an individual $100 per day for up to 3 days of hospitalization and $25 per day for each day of hospitalization thereafter. The number of days of hospitalization, X, is a discrete random variable with probability function

$$P(X = k) = \begin{cases} \dfrac{6 - k}{15} & \text{for } k = 1, 2, 3, 4, 5 \\ 0 & \text{otherwise.} \end{cases}$$

Calculate the expected payment for hospitalization under this policy. Choose one of the following. *Source: Society of Actuaries.*

(a) $85 (b) $163 (c) $168 (d) $213 (e) $255

Social Sciences

39. Education Recall from Exercise 57 in Section 8.4 that a study from Cleveland Clinic reported that 74% of very-low-birth-weight babies graduate from high school by age 20. If 250 very-low-birth-weight babies are followed through high school, how many would you expect to graduate from high school? *Source: The New England Journal of Medicine.*

40. Cheating Recall from Exercise 56 in Section 8.4 that a poll conducted by *U.S. News and World Report* reported that 84% of college students believe they need to cheat to get ahead in the world today. If 500 college students were surveyed, how many would you expect to say that they need to cheat to get ahead in the world today? *Source: U.S. News and World Report.*

41. Samuel Alito When Supreme Court Justice Samuel Alito was on the U.S. Court of Appeals for the 3rd Circuit, he dissented in the successful appeal of a first-degree murder case. The prosecution used its peremptory challenges to eliminate all African Americans from the jury, as it had in three other first-degree murder trials in the same county that year. According to a majority of the judges, "An amateur with a pocket calculator can calculate the number of blacks that would have served had the State used its strikes in a racially proportionate manner. In the four capital cases there was a total of 82 potential jurors on the venires who were not removed for cause, of whom eight, or 9.76%, were black. If the prosecution had used its peremptory challenges in a manner proportional to the percentage of blacks in the overall venire, then only 3 of the 34 jurors peremptorily struck (8.82%) would have been black and 5 of the 48 actual jurors (10.42%) would have been black. Instead, none of the 48 jurors were black. Admittedly, there was no statistical analysis of these figures presented by either side in the post-conviction proceeding. But is it really necessary to have a sophisticated analysis by a statistician to conclude that there is little chance of randomly selecting four consecutive all white juries?" *Source: findlaw.com.*

(a) Using binomial probability, calculate the probability that no African Americans would be selected out of 48 jurors if the percentage of African Americans is 9.76%.

(b) Binomial probability is not entirely accurate in this case, because the jurors were selected without replacement, so the selections were not independent. Recalculate the probability in part (a) using combinations.

(c) In his dissent, Judge Alito wrote, "Statistics can be very revealing—and also terribly misleading in the hands of 'an amateur with a pocket calculator.' . . . Although only about 10% of the population is left-handed, left-handers have won five of the last six presidential elections. Our 'amateur with a calculator' would conclude that 'there is little chance of randomly selecting' left-handers in five out of six presidential elections. But does it follow that the voters cast their ballots based on whether a candidate was right- or left-handed?" Given the figures quoted by Judge Alito, what is the probability that at least 5 out of the last 6 presidents elected would be left-handed?

(d) The majority of the judges, in disagreeing with Judge Alito, said, "The dissent has overlooked the obvious fact that there is no provision in the Constitution that protects persons from discrimination based on whether they are right-handed or left handed." Furthermore, according to *Chance News*, only 2 of the last 6 men elected president were left-handed. What is the probability that at least 2 out of the last 6 presidents elected would be left-handed? *Source: Chance News.*

Physical Sciences

42. **Seeding Storms** One of the few methods that can be used in an attempt to cut the severity of a hurricane is to *seed* the storm. In this process, silver iodide crystals are dropped into the storm. Unfortunately, silver iodide crystals sometimes cause the storm to *increase* its speed. Wind speeds may also increase or decrease even with no seeding. Use the table below to answer the following. *Source: American Association for the Advancement of Science.*

(a) Find the expected amount of damage under each option, "seed" and "do not seed."

(b) To minimize total expected damage, what option should be chosen?

	Change in wind speed	Probability	Property damage (millions of dollars)
	+32%	0.038	335.8
	+16%	0.143	191.1
Seed	0	0.392	100.0
	−16%	0.255	46.7
	−34%	0.172	16.3
	+32%	0.054	335.8
	+16%	0.206	191.1
Do not seed	0	0.480	100.0
	−16%	0.206	46.7
	+34%	0.054	16.3

General Interest

43. **Zilch** In the dice game of Zilch, a player rolls up to 6 dice and receives points based upon what is rolled. If some of the dice are worth points, the player may then roll the remaining dice again. *Source: playr.co.uk.*

(a) Suppose a player rolls only two dice. The player gets 50 points for each 5 and 100 points for each 1 rolled. Find the expected value of the game. (*Hint:* There are 6 cases to consider.)

(b) Suppose a player rolls three dice. Now find the expected value of a roll with three dice. (*Hint:* There are 10 cases to consider.)

(c) The game with three dice is actually more complicated than we considered in part (b), in that three 1's, 2's, 3's, 4's, 5's, or 6's earn 1000, 200, 300, 400, 500, or 600 points, respectively. Now find the expected value of a roll with three dice.

44. **Postal Service** Mr. Statistics (a feature in *Fortune* magazine) investigated the claim of the U.S. Postal Service that 83% of first class mail in New York City arrives by the next day. (The figure is 87% nationwide.) He mailed a letter to himself on 10 consecutive days; only 4 were delivered by the next day. *Source: Fortune.*

(a) Find the probability distribution for the number of letters delivered by the next day if the overall probability of next-day delivery is 83%.

(b) Using your answer to part (a), find the probability that 4 or fewer out of 10 letters would be delivered by the next day.

(c) Based on your answer to part (b), do you think it is likely that the 83% figure is accurate? Explain.

(d) Find the number of letters out of 10 that you would expect to be delivered by the next day if the 83% figure is accurate.

45. **Raffle** A raffle offers a first prize of $400 and 3 second prizes of $80 each. One ticket costs $2, and 500 tickets are sold. Find the expected payback for a person who buys 1 ticket. Is this a fair game?

46. **Raffle** A raffle offers a first prize of $1000, 2 second prizes of $300 each, and 20 third prizes of $10 each. If 10,000 tickets are sold at 50¢ each, find the expected payback for a person buying 1 ticket. Is this a fair game?

Find the expected payback for the games of chance described in Exercises 47–52.

47. **Lottery** A state lottery requires you to choose 4 cards from an ordinary deck: 1 heart, 1 club, 1 diamond, and 1 spade in that order from the 13 cards in each suit. If all four choices are selected by the lottery, you win $5000. It costs $1 to play.

48. **Lottery** If exactly 3 of the 4 choices in Exercise 47 are selected, the player wins $200. (Ignore the possibility that all 4 choices are selected. It still costs $1 to play.)

49. **Roulette** In one form of roulette, you bet $1 on "even." If 1 of the 18 even numbers comes up, you get your dollar back, plus another one. If 1 of the 20 noneven (18 odd, 0, and 00) numbers comes up, you lose your dollar.

50. Roulette In another form of roulette, there are only 19 non-even numbers (no 00).

51. Numbers *Numbers* is a game in which you bet $1 on any three-digit number from 000 to 999. If your number comes up, you get $500.

52. Keno In one form of the game *Keno*, the house has a pot containing 80 balls, each marked with a different number from 1 to 80. You buy a ticket for $1 and mark one of the 80 numbers on it. The house then selects 20 numbers at random. If your number is among the 20, you get $3.20 (for a net winning of $2.20).

53. Contests A magazine distributor offers a first prize of $100,000, two second prizes of $40,000 each, and two third prizes of $10,000 each. A total of 2,000,000 entries are received in the contest. Find the expected payback if you submit one entry to the contest. If it would cost you $1 in time, paper, and stamps to enter, would it be worth it?

54. Contests A contest at a fast-food restaurant offered the following cash prizes and probabilities of winning on one visit. Suppose you spend $1 to buy a bus pass that lets you go to 25 different restaurants in the chain and pick up entry forms. Find your expected value.

Prize	Probability
$100,000	1/176,402,500
$25,000	1/39,200,556
$5000	1/17,640,250
$1000	1/1,568,022
$100	1/282,244
$5	1/7056
$1	1/588

55. The Hog Game In the hog game, each player states the number of dice that he or she would like to roll. The player then rolls that many dice. If a 1 comes up on any die, the player's score is 0. Otherwise, the player's score is the sum of the numbers rolled. *Source: Mathematics Teacher.*

(a) Find the expected value of the player's score when the player rolls one die.

(b) Find the expected value of the player's score when the player rolls two dice.

(c) Verify that the expected nonzero score of a single die is 4, so that if a player rolls n dice that do not result in a score of 0, the expected score is $4n$.

(d) Verify that if a player rolls n dice, there are 5^n possible ways to get a nonzero score, and 6^n possible ways to roll the dice. Explain why the expected value, E, of the player's score when the player rolls n dice is then

$$E = \frac{5^n(4n)}{6^n}.$$

56. Football After a team scores a touchdown, it can either attempt to kick an extra point or attempt a two-point conversion. During the 2013 NFL season, two-point conversions were successful 47.8% of the time and the extra-point kicks were successful 99.6% of the time. *Source: Sporting Charts.*

(a) Calculate the expected value of each strategy.

(b) Which strategy, over the long run, will maximize the number of points scored?

(c) Using this information, should a team always only use one strategy? Explain.

57. Baseball The 2013 National League batting champion was Michael Cuddyer, with an average of 0.331. This can be interpreted as a probability of 0.331 of getting a hit whenever he bats. Assume that each time at bat is an independent event. Suppose he goes to bat four times in a game. *Source: baseball-reference.com.*

(a) Find the probability distribution for the number of hits.

(b) What is the expected number of hits that Michael Cuddyer gets in a game?

YOUR TURN ANSWERS

1.
x	0	1	2
$P(x)$	6/11	9/22	1/22

2.
x	0	1	2	3
$P(x)$	1/8	3/8	3/8	1/8

3. −$3.25   4. 4.045   5. 6

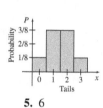

8 CHAPTER REVIEW

SUMMARY

In this chapter we continued our study of probability by introducing some elementary principles of counting. Our primary tool is the multiplication principle:

> If n choices must be made, with m_1 ways to make choice 1, and for each of these ways, m_2 ways to make choice 2, and so on, with m_n ways to make choice n, then there are $m_1 \cdot m_2 \cdot \ldots \cdot m_n$ ways to make the entire sequence of choices.

We learned two counting ideas to efficiently count the number of ways we can select a number of objects without replacement:

- permutations (when order matters), and
- combinations (when order doesn't matter).

We also considered distinguishable permutations, in which some of the objects are indistinguishable. All of these concepts were then used to calculate the numerator and denominator of various probabilities. We next explored binomial probability, in which the following conditions were satisfied:

- the same experiment is repeated a fixed number of times (n),
- there are only two possible outcomes (success and failure), and
- the trials are independent, so the probability of success remains constant (p).

We showed how to quickly calculate an entire set of combinations for binomial probability using Pascal's triangle. Finally, we introduced the following terms regarding probability distributions:

- random variable (a function assigning a real number to each outcome of an experiment),
- probability distribution (the possible values of a random variable, along with the corresponding probabilities),
- histogram (a bar graph displaying a probability distribution), and
- expected value (the average value of a random variable that we would expect in the long run).

In the next chapter, we will see how probability forms the basis of the field known as statistics.

Factorial Notation	$n! = n(n-1)(n-2)\cdots(3)(2)(1)$ $0! = 1$
Permutations	$P(n, r) = \dfrac{n!}{(n-r)!}$
Distinguishable Permutations	If there are n_1 objects of type 1, n_2 of type 2, and so on for r different types, then the number of distinguishable permutations is $$\dfrac{n!}{n_1! n_2! \cdots n_r!}.$$
Combinations	$C(n, r) = \dfrac{n!}{(n-r)! \, r!}$
Binomial Probability	$P(x) = C(n, x)\, p^x (1-p)^{n-x}$
Expected Value	$E(x) = x_1 p_1 + x_2 p_2 + x_3 p_3 + \cdots + x_n p_n$ For binomial probability, $E(x) = np$.

KEY TERMS

8.1
multiplication principle
factorial notation
permutations
distinguishable permutations

8.2
combinations

8.4
Bernoulli trials
binomial experiment

binomial probability
Pascal's triangle

8.5
random variable
probability distribution

probability function
histogram
expected value
fair game

REVIEW EXERCISES

CONCEPT CHECK

Determine whether each of the following statements is true or false, and explain why.

1. Permutations provide a way of counting possibilities when order matters.

2. Combinations provide a way of counting possibilities when order doesn't matter.

3. The number of distinguishable permutations of n objects, when r are indistinguishable and the remaining $n - r$ are also indistinguishable, is the same as the number of combinations of r objects chosen from n.

4. Calculating the numerator or the denominator of a probability can involve either permutations or combinations.

5. The probability of at least 2 occurrences of an event is equal to the probability of 1 or fewer occurrences.

6. The probability of at least two people in a group having the same birthday is found by subtracting the probability of the complement of the event from 1.

7. The trials in binomial probability must be independent.

8. Binomial probability can be used when each trial has three possible outcomes.

9. A random variable can have negative values.

10. The expected value of a random variable must equal one of the values that the random variable can have.

11. The probabilities in a probability distribution must add up to 1.

12. A fair game can have an expected value that is greater than 0.

PRACTICE AND EXPLORATIONS

13. In how many ways can 6 shuttle vans line up at the airport?

14. How many variations in first-, second-, and third-place finishes are possible in a 100-yd dash with 6 runners?

15. In how many ways can a sample of 3 oranges be taken from a bag of a dozen oranges?

16. In how many ways can a committee of 4 be selected from a club with 10 members?

17. If 2 of the 12 oranges in Exercise 15 are rotten, in how many ways can the sample of 3 include

    (a) exactly 1 rotten orange?

    (b) exactly 2 rotten oranges?

    (c) no rotten oranges?

    (d) at most 2 rotten oranges?

18. If 6 of the 10 club members in Exercise 16 are males, in how many ways can the sample of 4 include

    (a) exactly 3 males?

    (b) no males?

    (c) at least 2 males?

19. Five different pictures will be arranged in a row on a wall.

    (a) In how many ways can this be done?

    (b) In how many ways can this be done if a certain one must be first?

20. In how many ways can the 5 pictures in Exercise 19 be arranged if 2 are landscapes and 3 are puppies and if

    (a) like types must be kept together?

    (b) landscapes and puppies must be alternated?

21. In a Chinese restaurant the menu lists 8 items in column A and 6 items in column B.

    (a) To order a dinner, the diner is told to select 3 items from column A and 2 from column B. How many dinners are possible?

    (b) How many dinners are possible if the diner can select up to 3 from column A and up to 2 from column B? Assume at least one item must be included from either A or B.

22. A representative is to be selected from each of 3 departments in a small college. There are 7 people in the first department, 5 in the second department, and 4 in the third department.

    (a) How many different groups of 3 representatives are possible?

    (b) How many groups are possible if any number (at least 1) up to 3 representatives can form a group? (Each department is still restricted to at most one representative.)

23. Explain under what circumstances a permutation should be used in a probability problem, and under what circumstances a combination should be used.

24. Discuss under what circumstances the binomial probability formula should be used in a probability problem.

A basket contains 4 black, 2 blue, and 7 green balls. A sample of 3 balls is drawn. Find the probabilities that the sample contains the following.

25. All black balls

26. All blue balls

27. 2 black balls and 1 green ball

28. Exactly 2 black balls

29. Exactly 1 blue ball

30. 2 green balls and 1 blue ball

Suppose a family plans 6 children, and the probability that a particular child is a girl is 1/2. Find the probabilities that the 6-child family has the following children.

31. Exactly 3 girls

32. All girls

33. At least 4 girls

34. No more than 2 boys

Suppose 2 cards are drawn without replacement from an ordinary deck of 52. Find the probabilities of the following results.

35. Both cards are red.

36. Both cards are spades.

37. At least 1 card is a spade.

38. One is a face card and the other is not.

39. At least one is a face card.

40. At most one is a queen.

In Exercises 41 and 42, (a) give a probability distribution, (b) sketch its histogram, and (c) find the expected value.

41. A coin is tossed 3 times and the number of heads is recorded.

42. A pair of dice is rolled and the sum of the results for each roll is recorded.

In Exercises 43 and 44, give the probability that corresponds to the shaded region of each histogram.

43.

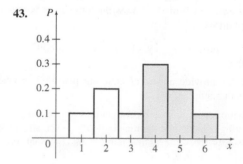

44.

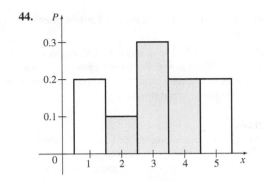

45. You pay $6 to play in a game where you will roll a die, with payoffs as follows: $8 for a 6, $7 for a 5, and $4 for any other results. What are your expected winnings? Is the game fair?

46. Find the expected number of girls in a family of 5 children.

47. Three cards are drawn from a standard deck of 52 cards.

   (a) What is the expected number of aces?

   (b) What is the expected number of clubs?

48. Suppose someone offers to pay you $100 if you draw 3 cards from a standard deck of 52 cards and all the cards are clubs. What should you pay for the chance to win if it is a fair game?

49. Six students will decide which of them are on a committee by flipping a coin. Each student flips the coin and is on the committee if he or she gets a head. What is the probability that someone is on the committee, but not all 6 students?

50. Find the probability that at most 2 students from Exercise 49 are on the committee.

51. In this exercise we study the connection between sets (from Chapter 7) and combinations (from Chapter 8).

   (a) Given a set with n elements, what is the number of subsets of size 0? of size 1? of size 2? of size n?

   (b) Using your answer from part (a), give an expression for the total number of subsets of a set with n elements.

   (c) Using your answer from part (b) and a result from Chapter 7, explain why the following equation must be true:

   $$C(n, 0) + C(n, 1) + C(n, 2) + \cdots + C(n, n) = 2^n.$$

   (d) Verify the equation in part (c) for $n = 4$ and $n = 5$.

   (e) Explain what the equation in part (c) tells you about Pascal's triangle.

In the following exercise, find the digit (0 through 9) that belongs in each box. This exercise is from the 1990 University Entrance Center Examination, given in Japan to all applicants for public universities. *Source: Japanese University Entrance Examination Problems in Mathematics.*

52. The numbers 1 through 9 are written individually on nine cards. Choose three cards from the nine, letting x, y, and z denote the numbers of the cards arranged in increasing order.

   (a) There are $\square\square$ such x, y, and z combinations.

   (b) The probability of having x, y, and z all even is $\dfrac{\square}{\square\square}$.

   (c) The probability of having x, y, and z be consecutive numbers is $\dfrac{\square}{\square\square}$.

   (d) The probability of having $x = 4$ is $\dfrac{\square}{\square\square}$.

   (e) Possible values of x range from $\square$ to $\square$. If k is an integer such that $\square \le k \le \square$, the probability that $x = k$ is $\dfrac{(\square - k)(\square - k)}{\square\square\square}$. The expected value of x is $\dfrac{\square}{\square}$.

APPLICATIONS

Business and Economics

53. Music Players A popular music player is manufactured in 3 different sizes, 8 different colors, and with or without a camera. How many different varieties of this music player are available?

54. Job Qualifications Of the 12 people applying for an entry level position, 9 are qualified and 3 are not. The personnel manager will hire 4 of the applicants.

   (a) In how many different ways can she hire the 4 applicants if the jobs are considered the same?

   (b) In how many ways can she hire 4 applicants that are qualified?

   (c) In how many ways can she hire at most 1 unqualified applicant?

   (d) In how many ways can she hire the 4 applicants if the jobs are not the same?

Identity Theft **According to a survey by Javelin Strategy and Research, 1 out of 6 adults in Arizona were victims of identity theft. Suppose that 12 adults are randomly selected from Arizona. Find the probabilities of each of the following results.** *Source: The New York Times.*

55. None of the adults were victims of identity theft.

56. All of the adults were victims of identity theft.

57. Exactly 10 of the adults were victims of identity theft.

58. Exactly 2 of the adults were victims of identity theft.

59. At least 2 of the adults were victims of identity theft.

60. At most 3 of the adults were victims of identity theft.

61. Find the expected number of victims of identity theft in a sample of 12 adults in Arizona.

62. Land Development A developer can buy a piece of property that will produce a profit of $26,000 with probability 0.7, or a loss of $9000 with probability 0.3. What is the expected profit?

63. Insurance Claims An insurance company determines that N, the number of claims received in a week, is a random variable with $P(N = n) = 1/2^{n+1}$, where $n \ge 0$. The company also determines that the number of claims received in a given week is independent of the number of claims received in any other week. Determine the probability that exactly seven claims will be received during a given two-week period. Choose one of the following. *Source: Society of Actuaries.*

   (a) 1/256   **(b)** 1/128   **(c)** 7/512   **(d)** 1/64   **(e)** 1/32

64. Injury Claims The number of injury claims per month is modeled by a random variable N with

$$P(N = n) = \frac{1}{(n+1)(n+2)}, \quad \text{where } n \geq 0.$$

Determine the probability of at least one claim during a particular month, given that there have been at most four claims during that month. Choose one of the following. *Source: Society of Actuaries.*

(a) 1/3   (b) 2/5   (c) 1/2   (d) 3/5   (e) 5/6

65. Product Success A company is considering the introduction of a new product that is believed to have probability 0.5 of being successful and probability 0.5 of being unsuccessful. Successful products pass quality control 80% of the time. Unsuccessful products pass quality control 25% of the time. If the product is successful, the net profit to the company will be $40 million; if unsuccessful, the net loss will be $15 million. Determine the expected net profit if the product passes quality control. Choose one of the following. *Source: Society of Actuaries.*

(a) $23 million   (b) $24 million   (c) $25 million

(d) $26 million   (e) $27 million

66. Sampling Fruit A merchant buys boxes of fruit from a grower and sells them. Each box of fruit is either Good or Bad. A Good box contains 80% excellent fruit and will earn $200 profit on the retail market. A Bad box contains 30% excellent fruit and will produce a loss of $1000. The a priori probability of receiving a Good box of fruit is 0.9. Before the merchant decides to put the box on the market, he can sample one piece of fruit to test whether it is excellent. Based on that sample, he has the option of rejecting the box without paying for it. Determine the expected value of the right to sample. Choose one of the following. (*Hint:* The a priori probability is the probability before sampling a piece of fruit. If the merchant samples the fruit, what are the probabilities of accepting a Good box, accepting a Bad box, and not accepting the box? What are these probabilities if he does not sample the fruit?) *Source: Society of Actuaries.*

(a) 0   (b) $16   (c) $34   (d) $72   (e) $80

67. Overbooking Flights The March 1982 issue of *Mathematics Teacher* included "Overbooking Airline Flights," an article by Joe Dan Austin. In this article, Austin developed a model for the expected income for an airline flight. With appropriate assumptions, the probability that exactly x of n people with reservations show up at the airport to buy a ticket is given by the binomial probability formula. Assume the following: 6 reservations have been accepted for 3 seats, $p = 0.6$ is the probability that a person with a reservation will show up, a ticket costs $400, and the airline must pay $400 to anyone with a reservation who does not get a ticket. Complete the following table.

Number Who Show Up (x)	0	1	2	3	4	5	6
Airline's Income							
$P(x)$							

(a) Use the table to find $E(I)$, the expected airline income from the 3 seats.

(b) Find $E(I)$ for $n = 3$, $n = 4$, and $n = 5$. Compare these answers with $E(I)$ for $n = 6$. For these values of n, how many reservations should the airline book for the 3 seats in order to maximize the expected revenue?

Life Sciences

68. Pharmacology In placebo-controlled trials of Prozac®, a drug that is prescribed to fight depression, 23% of the patients who were taking the drug experienced nausea, whereas 10% of the patients who were taking the placebo experienced nausea. *Source: The New England Journal of Medicine.*

(a) If 50 patients who are taking Prozac® are selected, what is the probability that 10 or more will experience nausea?

(b) Of the 50 patients in part (a), what is the expected number of patients who will experience nausea?

(c) If a second group of 50 patients receives a placebo, what is the probability that 10 or fewer will experience nausea?

(d) If a patient from a study of 1000 people, who are equally divided into two groups (those taking a placebo and those taking Prozac®), is experiencing nausea, what is the probability that he/she is taking Prozac®?

(e) Since 0.23 is more than twice as large as 0.10, do you think that people who take Prozac® are more likely to experience nausea than those who take a placebo? Explain.

Social Sciences

69. Education In Exercise 46 of Section 8.3, we saw that a school in Bangkok requires that students take an entrance examination. After the examination, 5 students are randomly drawn from each group of 40 for automatic acceptance into the school regardless of their performance on the examination. The drawing consists of placing 35 red and 5 green pieces of paper into a box. If the lottery is changed so that each student picks a piece of paper from the box and then returns the piece of paper to the box, find the probability that exactly 5 of the 40 students will choose a green piece of paper. *Source: The Mathematics Teacher.*

General Interest

In Exercises 70–73, (a) give a probability distribution, (b) sketch its histogram, and (c) find the expected value.

70. Candy According to officials of Mars, the makers of M&M Plain Chocolate Candies, 20% of the candies in each bag are orange. Four candies are selected from a bag and the number of orange candies is recorded. *Source: Mars, Inc.*

71. Schools In 2011, 48% of U.S. schools made progress under the No Child Left Behind mandate. Suppose 5 schools are picked at random and the number of schools making progress is recorded. *Source: The World Almanac and Book of Facts 2014.*

72. Race In the mathematics honors society at a college, 2 of the 8 members are African American. Three members are selected at random to be interviewed by the student newspaper, and the number of African Americans is noted.

73. Homework In a small class of 10 students, 3 did not do their homework. The professor selects half of the class to present solutions to homework problems on the board, and records how many of those selected did not do their homework.

74. Moneyball In the 2011 movie *Moneyball*, Billy Beane is shown reading a paper in which we see the following:

"Since Chesbro's team was 51–47, or .520, then I figured him by the formula

$$\frac{53!}{41!12!}(.520)^{41}(.480)^{12}.\text{"}$$

Based on what you've learned in this chapter, discuss what the author of the paper might have been calculating.

75. Contests At one time, game boards for a United Airlines contest could be obtained by sending a self-addressed, stamped envelope to a certain address. The prize was a ticket for any city to which United flies. Assume that the value of the ticket was $2000 (we might as well go first-class), and that the probability that a particular game board would win was 1/8000. If the stamps to enter the contest cost 49¢ and envelopes cost 4¢ each, find the expected payback for a person ordering 1 game board. (Notice that 2 stamps and envelopes were required to enter.)

76. Lottery On June 23, 2003, an interesting thing happened in the Pennsylvania Lottery's Big 4, in which a four-digit number from 0000 to 9999 is chosen twice a day. On this day, the number 3199 was chosen both times. *Source: Pennsylvania Lottery.*

(a) What is the probability of the same number being chosen twice in one day?

(b) What is the probability of the number 3199 being chosen twice in one day?

77. Lottery In the Pennsylvania Lottery's Daily Number (Evening) game, a three-digit number between 000 and 999 is chosen each day. The favorite number among players is 000, which on May 16, 2011, was the winning number for the 15th time since 1980. *Source: Pennsylvania Lottery.*

(a) Find the number of times that 000 would be expected to win in 32 years of play. (Assume that the game is played 365 days a year.)

(b) In 2003, a Daily Number (Midday) drawing was added. The number 000 has occurred four times. Find the number of times that 000 would be expected to win in 10 years of play. (Assume that the game is played 365 days a year.)

78. Lottery New York has a lottery game called Quick Draw, in which the player can pick anywhere from 1 up to 10 numbers from 1 to 80. The computer then picks 20 numbers, and how much you win is based on how many of your numbers match the computer's. For simplicity, we will consider only the two cases in which you pick 4 or 5 numbers. The payoffs for each dollar that you bet are given in the table below.

How Many Numbers Match the Computer's Numbers					
	0	1	2	3	4	5
You Pick 4	0	0	1	5	55	
You Pick 5	0	0	0	2	20	300

(a) According to the Quick Draw playing card, the "Overall Chances of Winning" when you pick 4 are "1:3.86," while the chances when you pick 5 are "1:10.34." Verify these figures.

(b) Find the expected value when you pick 4 and when you pick 5, betting $1 each time.

(c) Based on your results from parts (a) and (b), are you better off picking 4 numbers or picking 5? Explain your reasoning.

79. Murphy's Law Robert Matthews wrote an article about Murphy's Law, which says that if something can go wrong, it will. He considers Murphy's Law of Odd Socks, which says that if an odd sock can be created it will be, in a drawer of 10 loose pairs of socks. *Source: Sunday Telegraph.*

(a) Find the probability of getting a matching pair when the following numbers of socks are selected at random from the drawer.

(i) 5 socks   (ii) 6 socks

(b) Matthews says that it is necessary to rummage through 30% of the socks to get a matching pair. Using your answers from part (a), explain precisely what he means by that.

(c) Matthews claims that if you lose 6 socks at random from the drawer, then it is 100 times more likely that you will be left with the worst possible outcome—6 odd socks—than with a drawer free of odd socks. Verify this calculation by finding the probability that you will be left with 6 odd socks and the probability that you will have a drawer free of odd socks.

80. Baseball The number of runs scored in 16,456 half-innings of the 1986 National League Baseball season was analyzed by Hal Stern. Use the table to answer the following questions. *Source: Chance News.*

(a) What is the probability that a given team scored 5 or more runs in any given half-inning during the 1986 season?

(b) What is the probability that a given team scored fewer than 2 runs in any given half-inning of the 1986 season?

(c) What is the expected number of runs that a team scored during any given half-inning of the 1986 season? Interpret this number.

Runs	Frequency	Probability
0	12,087	0.7345
1	2451	0.1489
2	1075	0.0653
3	504	0.0306
4	225	0.0137
5	66	0.0040
6	29	0.0018
7	12	0.0007
8	5	0.0003
9	2	0.0001

81. St. Petersburg Paradox Suppose you play a gambling game in which you flip a coin until you get a head. If you get a head on the first toss, you win $2. You win $4 if the first head occurs on the second toss, $8 if it occurs on the the third toss, and so forth, with a prize of 2^n if the first head occurs on the nth toss. Show that the expected value of this game is infinite. Explain why this is a paradox.*

*Many articles have been written in an attempt to explain this paradox, first posed by the Swiss mathematician Daniel Bernoulli when he lived in St. Petersburg. For example, see Székely, Gábor and Donald St. P. Richards, "The St. Petersburg Paradox and the Crash of High-Tech Stocks in 2000," *The American Statistician*, Vol. 58, No. 3, Aug. 2004, pp. 225–231.

82. Pit The card game of Pit was introduced by Parker Brothers in 1904 and is still popular. In the version owned by one of the authors of this book, there are 10 suits of 9 identical cards, plus the Bull and the Bear card, for a total of 92 cards. (Newer versions of the game have only 8 suits of cards.) For this problem, assume that all 92 cards are used, and you are dealt 9 cards.

(a) What is the probability that you have one card from each of 9 different suits, but neither the Bull nor the Bear?

(b) What is the probability that you have a pair of cards from one suit and one card from each of 7 other suits, but neither the Bull nor the Bear?

(c) What is the probability that you have two pairs of cards from two different suits and one card from each of 5 other suits, but neither the Bull nor the Bear?

EXTENDED APPLICATION
OPTIMAL INVENTORY FOR A SERVICE TRUCK

For many different items it is difficult or impossible to take the item to a central repair facility when service is required. Washing machines, large television sets, office copiers, and computers are only a few examples of such items. Service for items of this type is commonly performed by sending a repair person to the item, with the person driving to the location in a truck containing various parts that might be required in repairing the item. Ideally, the truck should contain all the parts that might be required. However, most parts would be needed only infrequently, so that inventory costs for the parts would be high.

An optimum policy for deciding on which parts to stock on a truck would require that the probability of not being able to repair an item without a trip back to the warehouse for needed parts be as low as possible, consistent with minimum inventory costs. An analysis similar to the one below was developed at the Xerox Corporation.

To set up a mathematical model for deciding on the optimum truck-stocking policy, let us assume that a broken machine might require one of 5 different parts (we could assume any number of different parts—we use 5 to simplify the notation). Suppose also that the probability that a particular machine requires part 1 is p_1; that it requires part 2 is p_2; and so on. Assume also that failures of different part types are independent, and that at most one part of each type is used on a given job.

Suppose that, on the average, a repair person makes N service calls per time period. If the repair person is unable to make a repair because at least one of the parts is unavailable, there is a penalty cost, L, corresponding to wasted time for the repair person, an extra trip to the parts depot, customer unhappiness, and so on. For each of the parts carried on the truck, an average inventory cost is incurred. Let H_i be the average inventory cost for part i, where $1 \leq i \leq 5$.

Let M_1 represent a policy of carrying only part 1 on the repair truck, M_{24} represent a policy of carrying only parts 2 and 4, with

M_{12345} and M_0 representing policies of carrying all parts and no parts, respectively.

For policy M_{35}, carrying parts 3 and 5 only, the expected cost per time period per repair person, written $C(M_{35})$, is

$$C(M_{35}) = (H_3 + H_5) + NL[1 - (1 - p_1)(1 - p_2)(1 - p_4)].$$

(The expression in brackets represents the probability of needing at least one of the parts not carried, 1, 2, or 4 here.) As further examples,

$$C(M_{125}) = (H_1 + H_2 + H_5) + NL[1 - (1 - p_3)(1 - p_4)],$$

while

$$C(M_{12345}) = (H_1 + H_2 + H_3 + H_4 + H_5) + NL[1 - 1]$$
$$= H_1 + H_2 + H_3 + H_4 + H_5,$$

and

$$C(M_0) = NL[1 - (1 - p_1)(1 - p_2)(1 - p_3)(1 - p_4)(1 - p_5)].$$

To find the best policy, evaluate $C(M_0)$, $C(M_1)$, ..., $C(M_{12345})$, and choose the smallest result. (A general solution method is in the *Management Science* paper.) *Source: Management Science.*

EXAMPLE 1

Suppose that for a particular item, only 3 possible parts might need to be replaced. By studying past records of failures of the item, and finding necessary inventory costs, suppose that the following values have been found.

p_1	p_2	p_3		H_1	H_2	H_3
0.09	0.24	0.17		$15	$40	$9

Suppose $N = 3$ and L is $54. Then, as an example,

$$\begin{aligned} C(M_1) &= H_1 + NL[1 - (1 - p_2)(1 - p_3)] \\ &= 15 + 3(54)[1 - (1 - 0.24)(1 - 0.17)] \\ &= 15 + 3(54)[1 - (0.76)(0.83)] \\ &\approx 15 + 59.81 = 74.81. \end{aligned}$$

Thus, if policy M_1 is followed (carrying only part 1 on the truck), the expected cost per repair person per time period is $74.81. Also,

$$\begin{aligned} C(M_{23}) &= H_2 + H_3 + NL[1 - (1 - p_1)] \\ &= 40 + 9 + 3(54)(0.09) = 63.58, \end{aligned}$$

so that M_{23} is a better policy than M_1. By finding the expected values for all other possible policies (see the exercises), the optimum policy may be chosen.

EXERCISES

1. Refer to the example and find the following.

   (a) $C(M_0)$ (b) $C(M_2)$ (c) $C(M_3)$

   (d) $C(M_{12})$ (e) $C(M_{13})$ (f) $C(M_{123})$

2. Which policy leads to the lowest expected cost?

3. In the example, $p_1 + p_2 + p_3 = 0.09 + 0.24 + 0.17 = 0.50$. Why is it not necessary that the probabilities add up to 1?

4. Suppose an item to be repaired might need one of n different parts. How many different policies would then need to be evaluated?

DIRECTIONS FOR GROUP PROJECT

Suppose you and three others are employed as service repair persons and that you have some disagreement with your supervisor as to the quantity and type of parts to have on hand for your service calls. Use the answers to Exercises 1–4 to prepare a report with a recommendation to your boss on optimal inventory. Make sure that you describe each concept well, since your boss is not mathematically minded.

9

Statistics

To understand the economics of large-scale farming, analysts look at historical data on the farming industry. In an exercise in Section 1 you will calculate basic descriptive statistics for U.S. wheat prices and production levels over a recent decade. Later sections in this chapter develop more sophisticated techniques for extracting useful information from this kind of data.

Statistics is a branch of mathematics that deals with the collection and summarization of data. Methods of statistical analysis make it possible for us to draw conclusions about a population based on data from a sample of the population. Statistical models have become increasingly useful in manufacturing, government, agriculture, medicine, the social sciences, and all types of research. In this chapter we give a brief introduction to some of the key topics from statistical theory.

9.1 Frequency Distributions; Measures of Central Tendency

APPLY IT How can the results of a survey of business executives on the number of college credits in management needed by a business major best be organized to provide useful information?

Frequency distributions will provide an answer to this question in Example 1.

Often, a researcher wishes to learn something about a characteristic of a population, but because the population is very large or mobile, it is not possible to examine all of its elements. Instead, a limited sample drawn from the population is studied to determine the characteristics of the population. For these inferences to be correct, the sample chosen must be a **random sample**. Random samples are representative of the population because they are chosen so that every element of the population is equally likely to be selected. A hand dealt from a well-shuffled deck of cards is a random sample.

A random sample can be difficult to obtain in real life. For example, suppose you want to take a random sample of voters in your congressional district to see which candidate they prefer in the next election. If you do a telephone survey, you have a random sample of people who are at home to answer the telephone, underrepresenting those who work a lot of hours and are rarely home to answer the phone, or those who have an unlisted number, or those who cannot afford a telephone, or those who only have a cell phone, or those who refuse to answer telephone surveys. Such people may have a different opinion than those you interview.

A famous example of an inaccurate poll was made by the *Literary Digest* in 1936. Their survey indicated that Alfred Landon would win the presidential election; in fact, Franklin Roosevelt won with 62% of the popular vote. The *Digest's* major error was mailing their surveys to a sample of those listed in telephone directories. During the Depression, many poor people did not have telephones, and the poor voted overwhelmingly for Roosevelt. Modern pollsters use sophisticated techniques to ensure that their sample is as random as possible.

Frequency Distribution Once a sample has been chosen and all data of interest are collected, the data must be organized so that conclusions may be more easily drawn. One method of organization is to group the data into intervals; equal intervals are usually chosen.

EXAMPLE 1 Business Executives

A survey asked a random sample of 30 business executives for their recommendations as to the number of college credits in management that a business major should have. The results are shown below. Group the data into intervals and find the frequency of each interval.

3	25	22	16	0	9	14	8	34	21
15	12	9	3	8	15	20	12	28	19
17	16	23	19	12	14	29	13	24	18

APPLY IT

SOLUTION   The highest number in the list is 34 and the lowest is 0; one convenient way to group the data is in intervals of size 5, starting with 0–4 and ending with 30–34. This gives an interval for each number in the list and results in seven equal intervals of a convenient size. Too many intervals of smaller size would not simplify the data enough, while too few intervals of larger size would conceal information that the data might provide. A rule of thumb is to use from 6 to 15 intervals.

First tally the number of college credits falling into each interval. Then total the tallies in each interval as in the following table. This table is an example of a **grouped frequency distribution**.

Grouped Frequency Distribution		
College Credits	Tally	Frequency
0–4	|||	3
5–9	||||	4
10–14	⊬|	6
15–19	⊬ |||	8
20–24	⊬	5
25–29	|||	3
30–34			1
		Total: 30

The frequency distribution in Example 1 shows information about the data that might not have been noticed before. For example, the interval with the largest number of recommended credits is 15–19, and 19 executives (more than half) recommended between 10 and 24 credits, inclusive. Also, the frequency in each interval increases rather evenly (up to 8) and then decreases at about the same pace. However, some information has been lost; for example, we no longer know how many executives recommended 12 credits.

The information in a grouped frequency distribution can be displayed in a histogram similar to the histograms for probability distributions in Chapter 8. The intervals determine the widths of the bars; if equal intervals are used, all the bars have the same width. The heights of the bars are determined by the frequencies.

A **frequency polygon** is another form of graph that illustrates a grouped frequency distribution. The polygon is formed by joining consecutive midpoints of the tops of the histogram bars with straight line segments. The midpoints of the first and last bars are joined to endpoints on the horizontal axis where the next midpoint would appear.

NOTE   In this section, the heights of the histogram bars give the frequencies. The histograms in Chapter 8 were for probability distributions, and so the heights gave the probabilities.

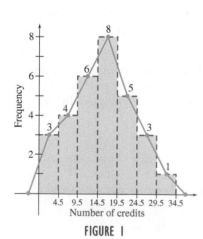

FIGURE 1

EXAMPLE 2   **Histogram and Frequency Polygon**

A grouped frequency distribution of college credits was found in Example 1. Draw a histogram and a frequency polygon for this distribution.

SOLUTION   First draw a histogram, shown in red in Figure 1. To get a frequency polygon, connect consecutive midpoints of the tops of the bars. The frequency polygon is shown in blue.

TECHNOLOGY NOTE

Many graphing calculators have the capability of drawing a histogram. On a TI-84 Plus C calculator, enter the data by selecting STAT EDIT and then typing the entries in L_1. To create a histogram, select STATPLOT and 1:Plot1. Turn the plot ON and select the histogram icon in the Type row, as shown in Figure 2(a). Be sure that L_1 is entered for Xlist.

Select WINDOW to set up the intervals, as shown in Figure 2(b). The Xscl value gives the width of each interval. To draw the histogram, select GRAPH. Figure 2(c) shows the histogram for the data of Example 1. See the *Graphing Calculator and Excel Spreadsheet Manual* available with this text.

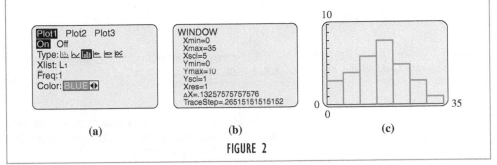

(a)   (b)   (c)

FIGURE 2

Measures of Central Tendency

As we have seen, the frequency distribution, histogram, and frequency polygon give us a picture of the data. We also use mathematics to summarize and quantify some of the characteristics or tendencies of the data.

In Example 1, business executives were asked how many college credits in management business students should complete. If we want to use these data to develop a recommendation, we would need to summarize the responses into a single number. We could look at the histogram and see that our value should be near the center of the data, which is somewhere in the range of 15 to 19 credits. Of course, the frequency distribution and the histogram don't indicate exactly what that number should be.

Three mathematical quantities are used to describe the "average" value of a set of data. These values are said to measure the central tendency of a set of data and are called the mean, median, and mode.

Mean

The most important of the measures of central tendency is the mean, which is similar to the expected value of a probability distribution.

The **arithmetic mean** (the **mean**) of a set of numbers is the sum of the numbers, divided by the total number of numbers. Recall from Section 1.3 that we can write the sum of n numbers $x_1, x_2, x_3, \ldots, x_n$ in a compact way using *summation notation*:

$$x_1 + x_2 + x_3 + \cdots + x_n = \Sigma x.$$

The symbol $\bar{x}$ (read x-bar) is used to represent the mean of a sample.

Mean

The **mean** of the n numbers $x_1, x_2, x_3, \ldots, x_n$ is

$$\bar{x} = \frac{\Sigma x}{n}.$$

Bankruptcies	
Year	Petitions Filed (thousands)
2008	1118
2009	1474
2010	1593
2011	1411
2012	1221
2013	1072

YOUR TURN 1 Find the mean of the following data: 12, 17, 21, 25, 27, 38, 49.

EXAMPLE 3 Bankruptcy

The table to the left lists the number of bankruptcy petitions (in thousands) filed in the United States in the years 2008–2013. Find the mean number of bankruptcy petitions filed annually during this period. *Source: U.S. Courts.*

SOLUTION Let $x_1 = 1118$, $x_2 = 1474$, and so on. Here, $n = 6$, since there are six numbers.

$$\bar{x} = \frac{1118 + 1474 + 1593 + 1411 + 1221 + 1072}{6}$$

$$\bar{x} = \frac{7889}{6} \approx 1315$$

The mean number of bankruptcy petitions filed per year during the given years is about 1,315,000. **TRY YOUR TURN 1**

As another example, the mean response for the number of college credits in management that a business major should have, based on the sample of 30 business executives described in Example 1, is

$$\bar{x} = \frac{3 + 25 + 22 + \cdots + 18}{30} = \frac{478}{30} = 15.93.$$

EXAMPLE 4 Mean for Frequency Distributions

Find the mean for the data shown in the following frequency distribution.

Calculations for Frequency Distribution		
Value, x	Frequency, f	Product, xf
30	6	$30 \cdot 6 = 180$
32	9	$32 \cdot 9 = 288$
33	7	$33 \cdot 7 = 231$
37	12	$37 \cdot 12 = 444$
42	6	$42 \cdot 6 = 252$
	Total: 40	Total: 1395

SOLUTION The value 30 appears six times, 32 nine times, and so on. To find the mean, first multiply 30 by 6, 32 by 9, and so on.

A new column, "Product, xf" has been added to the frequency distribution. Adding the products from this column gives a total of 1395. The total from the frequency column is 40, so $n = 40$. The mean is

$$\bar{x} = \frac{1395}{40} = 34.875.$$

The mean of grouped data is found in a similar way. For grouped data, intervals are used, rather than single values. To calculate the mean, it is assumed that all these values are located at the midpoint of the interval. The letter x is used to represent the midpoints and f represents the frequencies, as shown in the next example.

EXAMPLE 5 Business Executives

Listed below is the grouped frequency distribution for the 30 business executives described in Example 1. Find the mean from the grouped frequency distribution.

Grouped Frequency Distribution for College Credits			
Interval	Midpoint, x	Frequency, f	Product, xf
0–4	2	3	6
5–9	7	4	28
10–14	12	6	72
15–19	17	8	136
20 24	22	5	110
25–29	27	3	81
30–34	32	1	32
		Total: 30	Total: 465

SOLUTION A column for the midpoint of each interval has been added. The numbers in this column are found by adding the endpoints of each interval and dividing by 2. For the interval 0–4, the midpoint is $(0 + 4)/2 = 2$. The numbers in the product column on the right are found by multiplying each frequency by its corresponding midpoint. Finally, we divide the total of the product column by the total of the frequency column to get

$$\bar{x} = \frac{465}{30} = 15.5.$$

Notice that this mean is slightly different from the earlier mean of 15.93. The reason for this difference is that we have acted as if each piece of data is at the midpoint, which is not true here, and is not true in most cases. Information is always lost when the data are grouped. It is more accurate to use the original data, rather than the grouped frequency, when calculating the mean, but the original data might not be available. Furthermore, the mean based upon the grouped data is typically not too far from the mean based upon the original data, and there may be situations in which the extra accuracy is not worth the extra effort.

TRY YOUR TURN 2

YOUR TURN 2 Find the mean of the following grouped frequency.

Interval	Frequency
0–6	2
7–13	4
14–20	7
21–27	10
28–34	3
35–41	1

The formula for the mean of a grouped frequency distribution is given below.

Mean of a Grouped Distribution

The mean of a distribution, where x represents the midpoints, f the frequencies, and $n = \Sigma f$, is

$$\bar{x} = \frac{\Sigma xf}{n}.$$

The mean of a random sample is a random variable, and for this reason it is sometimes called the **sample mean**. The sample mean is a random variable because it assigns a number to the experiment of taking a random sample. If a different random sample were taken, the mean would probably have a different value, with some values more probable than others. If another set of 30 business executives were selected in Example 1, the mean number of college credits in management recommended for a business major might be 13.22 or 17.69. It is unlikely that the mean would be as small as 1.21 or as large as 32.75, although these values are remotely possible.

NOTE
1. The midpoint of the intervals in a grouped frequency distribution may be values that the data cannot take on. For example, if we grouped the data for the 30 business executives into the intervals 0–5, 6–11, 12–17, 18–23, 24–29, and 30–35, the midpoints would be 2.5, 8.5, 14.5, 20.5, 26.5, and 32.5, even though all the data are whole numbers.
2. If we used different intervals in Example 5, the mean would come out to be a slightly different number. Verify that with the intervals 0–5, 6–11, 12–17, 18–23, 24–29, and 30–35, the mean in Example 5 is 16.1.

We saw in Section 8.5 how to calculate the expected value of a random variable when we know its probability distribution. The expected value is sometimes called the **population mean**, denoted by the Greek letter μ. In other words,

$$E(x) = \mu.$$

Furthermore, it can be shown that the expected value of $\bar{x}$ is also equal to μ; that is,

$$E(\bar{x}) = \mu.$$

For instance, consider again the 30 business executives in Example 1. We found that $\bar{x} = 15.93$, but the value of μ, the average for all possible business executives, is unknown. If a good estimate of μ were needed, the best guess (based on this data) is 15.93.

Median   Asked by a reporter to give the average height of the players on his team, a Little League coach lined up his 15 players by increasing height. He picked the player in the middle and pronounced that player to be of average height. This kind of average, called the **median**, is defined as the middle entry in a set of data arranged in either increasing or decreasing order. If there is an even number of entries, the median is defined to be the mean of the two center entries.

Calculating the Median	
Odd Number of Entries	**Even Number of Entries**
1	2
3	3
Median = 4	4 ⎫
7	7 ⎬ Median = $\dfrac{4 + 7}{2}$ = 5.5
8	9
	15

EXAMPLE 6   **Median**

Find the median for each list of numbers.

(a) 11, 12, 17, **20**, 23, 28, 29

   SOLUTION   The median is the middle number; in this case, 20. (Note that the numbers are already arranged in numerical order.) In this list, three numbers are smaller than 20 and three are larger.

(b) 15, 13, 7, 11, 19, 30, 39, 5, 10

   SOLUTION   First arrange the numbers in numerical order, from smallest to largest.

$$5, 7, 10, 11, \mathbf{13}, 15, 19, 30, 39$$

   The middle number, or median, can now be determined; it is 13.

(c) 47, 59, 32, 81, 74, 153

   SOLUTION   Write the numbers in numerical order.

$$32, 47, \mathbf{59}, \mathbf{74}, 81, 153$$

There are six numbers here; the median is the mean of the two middle numbers.

$$\text{Median} = \frac{59 + 74}{2} = \frac{133}{2} = 66\frac{1}{2}$$

YOUR TURN 3   Find the median of the data in Your Turn 1.

TRY YOUR TURN 3

Mode   Katie's scores on ten class quizzes include one 7, two 8's, six 9's, and one 10 (out of 10 points possible). She claims that her average grade on quizzes is 9, because most of her scores are 9's. This kind of "average," found by selecting the most frequent entry, is called the **mode**.

EXAMPLE 7   **Mode**

Find the mode for each list of numbers.

(a) 57, 38, 55, 55, 80, 87, 98, 55, 57

SOLUTION   The number 55 occurs more often than any other, so it is the mode. It is not necessary to place the numbers in numerical order when looking for the mode.

(b) 182, 185, 183, 185, 187, 187, 189

SOLUTION   Both 185 and 187 occur twice. This list has *two* modes.

(c) 10,708; 11,519; 10,972; 17,546; 13,905; 12,182

SOLUTION   No number occurs more than once. This list has no mode.

EXAMPLE 8   **Seed Storage**

Seeds that are dried, placed in an airtight container, and stored in a cool, dry place remain ready to be planted for a long time. The table below gives the amount of time that each type of seed can be stored and still remain viable for planting. *Source: The Handy Science Answer Book.*

Storage Time			
Vegetable	Years	Vegetable	Years
Beans	3	Cucumbers	5
Cabbage	4	Melons	4
Carrots	1	Peppers	2
Cauliflower	4	Pumpkin	4
Corn	2	Tomatoes	3

Find the mean, median, and mode of the information in the table.

SOLUTION

Method 1
Calculating by Hand

The mean amount of time that the seeds can be stored is

$$\bar{x} = \frac{3 + 4 + 1 + 4 + 2 + 5 + 4 + 2 + 4 + 3}{10} = 3.2 \text{ years.}$$

After the numbers are arranged in order from smallest to largest, the average of the two middle numbers, or median, is found; it is 3.5.

The number 4 occurs more often than any other, so it is the mode.

Method 2
Graphing Calculator

Most scientific calculators have some statistical capability and can calculate the mean of a set of data; graphing calculators can often calculate the median as well. For example, Figure 3 shows the mean and the median for the data above calculated on a TI-84 Plus C, where the data were stored in the list L_1. These commands are found under the LIST-MATH menu. This calculator does not include a command for finding the mode.

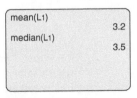

```
mean(L1)
              3.2
median(L1)
              3.5
```

FIGURE 3

⊞ **Method 3**
Spreadsheet

Using Microsoft Excel, place the data in cells A1 through A10. To find the mean of these data, type "=AVERAGE(A1:A10)" in cell A11, or any other unused cell, and then press Enter. The result of 3.2 will appear in cell A11. To find the median of these data, type "=MEDIAN(A1:A10)" in cell A12, or any other unused cell, and press Enter. The result of 3.5 will appear in cell A12. To find the mode of these data, type "=MODE(A1:A10)" in cell A13, or any other unused cell, and press Enter. The result of 4 will appear in cell A13.

The mean, median, and mode are examples of a **statistic**, which is simply a number that gives information about a sample. All three are a measure of the center, or "average," of the data.

The mean is the most commonly used measure of central tendency. Its advantages are that it is easy to compute, it takes all the data into consideration, and it is reliable—that is, repeated samples are likely to give very similar means. A disadvantage of the mean is that it is influenced by extreme values, as will be illustrated in Example 9.

The median can be easy to compute and is influenced very little by extremes. Another advantage is that the median can be found in situations where the data are not numerical. For example, in a taste test, people are asked to rank five soft drinks from the one they like best to the one they like least. The combined rankings then produce an ordered sample, from which the median can be identified. A disadvantage of the median is the need to rank the data in order; this can be difficult when the number of items is large.

The mode has the advantages of being easily found and not being influenced by data that are very large or very small compared to the rest of the data. It is often used in samples where the data to be "averaged" are not numerical. A major disadvantage of the mode is that we cannot always locate exactly one mode for a set of values. There can be more than one mode, in the case of ties, or there can be no mode if all entries occur with the same frequency.

The final example shows a situation in which one data value is much larger than the rest of the data. In this case, the median gives a truer representation than the mean.

EXAMPLE 9 **Salaries**

An office has 2 secretaries, 4 salespersons, 1 sales manager, and Jeff Weidenaar, who owns the business. Their annual salaries are as follows:

Each of the two secretaries earns $35,000;

each of the four salespersons earns $45,000;

the sales manager earns $55,000;

and the owner earns $300,000.

(a) Calculate the mean salary of those working in the office.

SOLUTION The mean salary is

$$\bar{x} = \frac{(35,000)2 + (45,000)4 + 55,000 + 300,000}{8} = \$75,625.$$

Notice that 7 people earn less than this mean and only 1 (the owner) earns more. The owner's salary is much higher than the rest of the salaries, and this extreme value has a pronounced effect on the mean. In this case, the mean does not seem very representative of the center, or "average," of the office salaries.

(b) Calculate the median salary of those working in the office.

> **SOLUTION**   The median salary is found by ranking the salaries by size:
>
> $35,000, $35,000, $45,000, $45,000, $45,000, $45,000, $55,000, $300,000.
>
> Because there are 8 salaries (an even number) in the list, the mean of the fourth and fifth entries will give the value of the median. The fourth and fifth entries are both $45,000, so the median is $45,000. In this example, the median gives a truer representation of the office salaries than the mean.   ▬

9.1   EXERCISES

For Exercises 1–4, do the following:

(a) Group the data as indicated.

(b) Prepare a frequency distribution with a column for intervals and frequencies.

(c) Construct a histogram.

(d) Construct a frequency polygon.

1. Use six intervals, starting with 0–24.

7	105	116	73	129	26
29	44	126	82	56	137
43	73	65	141	79	74
121	12	46	37	85	82
2	99	85	95	90	38
86	147	32	84	13	100

2. Use seven intervals, starting with 30–39.

79	71	78	87	69	50	63	51
60	46	65	65	56	88	94	56
74	63	87	62	84	76	82	67
59	66	57	81	93	93	54	88
55	69	78	63	63	48	89	81
98	42	91	66	60	70	64	70
61	75	82	65	68	39	77	81
67	62	73	49	51	76	94	54
83	71	94	45	73	95	72	66
71	77	48	51	54	57	69	87

3. Repeat Exercise 1 using eight intervals, starting with 0–19.

4. Repeat Exercise 2 using six intervals, starting with 39–48.

5. How does a frequency polygon differ from a histogram?

6. Discuss the advantages and disadvantages of the mean as a measure of central tendency.

Find the mean for each list of numbers.

7. 8, 10, 16, 21, 25

8. 67, 89, 75, 86, 100, 93

9. 30,200; 23,700; 33,320; 29,410; 24,600; 27,750; 27,300; 32,680

10. 38,500; 39,720; 42,183; 21,982; 43,250

11. 9.4, 11.3, 10.5, 7.4, 9.1, 8.4, 9.7, 5.2, 1.1, 4.7

12. 15.3, 27.2, 14.8, 16.5, 31.8, 40.1, 18.9, 28.4, 26.3, 35.3

Find the mean for the following.

13.

Value	Frequency
4	6
6	1
9	3
15	2

14.

Value	Frequency
9	3
12	5
15	1
18	1

15. Find the mean for the data in Exercise 1 from the grouped frequency distribution found in each of the following exercises.

(a) Exercise 1

(b) Exercise 3

16. Find the mean for the data in Exercise 2 from the grouped frequency distribution found in each of the following exercises.

(a) Exercise 2

(b) Exercise 4

Find the median for each list of numbers.

17. 27, 35, 39, 42, 47, 51, 54

18. 596, 604, 612, 683, 719

19. 100, 114, 125, 135, 150, 172

20. 359, 831, 904, 615, 211, 279, 505

21. 28.4, 9.1, 3.4, 27.6, 59.8, 32.1, 47.6, 29.8

22. 0.2, 1.4, 0.6, 0.2, 2.5, 1.9, 0.8, 1.5

Use a graphing calculator or spreadsheet to calculate the mean and median for the data in the indicated exercises.

23. Exercise 1   **24.** Exercise 2

Find the mode or modes for each list of numbers.

25. 4, 9, 8, 6, 9, 2, 1, 3

26. 16, 15, 13, 15, 14, 13, 11, 15, 14

27. 55, 62, 62, 71, 62, 55, 73, 55, 71

28. 158, 162, 165, 162, 165, 157, 163

29. 6.8, 6.3, 6.3, 6.9, 6.7, 6.4, 6.1, 6.0

30. 22.35, 14.90, 17.85, 15.46, 14.91, 17.85, 21.35

31. When is the median the most appropriate measure of central tendency?

32. Under what circumstances would the mode be an appropriate measure of central tendency?

For grouped data, the *modal class* is the interval containing the most data values. Find the modal class for each collection of grouped data.

33. Use the distribution in Exercise 1.

34. Use the distribution in Exercise 2.

35. To predict the outcome of the next congressional election, you take a survey of your friends. Is this a random sample of the voters in your congressional district? Explain why or why not.

APPLICATIONS

Business and Economics

Wheat Production   U.S. wheat prices and production figures for recent years are given in the following table. *Source: USDA.*

Year	Price ($ per bushel)	Production (millions of bushels)
2004	3.40	2157
2005	3.42	2103
2006	4.26	1808
2007	6.48	2051
2008	6.78	2499
2009	4.87	2218
2010	5.70	2207
2011	7.24	1999
2012	7.77	2266
2013	6.87	2130

Find the mean and median for the following.

36. Price per bushel of wheat

37. Wheat production

38. Salaries   The total compensation (in millions of dollars) for the 10 highest paid CEOs in 2013 is given in the table at the top of the next column. *Source: The Huffington Post.*

Person, Company	Total Compensation
Anthony Petrello, Nabors Industries	68.2
Leslie Moonves, CBS	65.6
Richard Adkerson, Freeport-McMoRan Copper & Gold	55.3
Stephen Kaufer, TripAdvisor	39.0
Philippe Dauman, Viacom	37.2
Leonard Schleifer, Regeneron Pharmaceuticals	36.3
Robert Iger, Walt Disney	34.3
David Zaslav, Discovery Communications	33.3
Jeffrey Bewkes, Time Warner	32.5
Brian Roberts, Comcast	31.4

(a) Find the mean total compensation for this group of people.

(b) Find the median total compensation for this group of people.

39. Household Income   The total income for African American households making under $250,000 in 2012 is given in the following table. *Source: U.S. Census Bureau.*

Income Range	Midpoint Salary	Frequency (in thousands)
Under $20,000	$10,000	5037
$20,000–$39,999	$30,000	3936
$40,000–$59,999	$50,000	2593
$60,000–$79,999	$70,000	1583
$80,000–$99,999	$90,000	1031
$100,000–$149,999	$125,000	1151
$150,000–$199,999	$175,000	327
$200,000–$249,999	$225,000	132

Use the table to estimate the mean income for African American households in 2012.

40. Household Income   The total income for white households making under $250,000 in 2012 is given in the following table. *Source: U.S. Census Bureau.*

Income Range	Midpoint Salary	Frequency (in thousands)
Under $20,000	$10,000	16,431
$20,000–$39,999	$30,000	20,501
$40,000–$59,999	$50,000	16,183
$60,000–$79,999	$70,000	12,780
$80,000–$99,999	$90,000	9097
$100,0000–$149,999	$125,000	12,859
$150,000–$199,999	$175,000	5186
$200,000–$249,999	$225,000	2160

(a) Use this table to estimate the mean income for white households in 2012.

(b) Compare this estimate with the estimate found in Exercise 39. Discuss whether this provides evidence that white American households have higher earnings than African American households.

41. Airlines The number of consumer complaints against the top U.S. airlines in 2013 is given in the following table. *Source: U.S. Department of Transportation.*

Airline	Complaints	Complaints per 100,000 Passengers Boarding
Southwest Airlines	397	0.34
Alaska Airlines	86	0.44
Delta Airlines	713	0.59
JetBlue Airways	192	0.63
AirTran Airways	130	0.73
SkyWest Airlines	217	0.80
Mesa Airlines	71	0.85
Endeavor Air	113	0.86
ExpressJet Airlines	319	0.96
Hawaiian Airlines	105	1.06
Virgin America	81	1.28
US Airways	806	1.42
American Eagle Airlines	303	1.70
American Airlines	1730	1.99
United Airlines	1935	2.14
Frontier Airlines	316	3.09

(a) By considering the numbers in the column labeled "Complaints," calculate the mean and median number of complaints per airline.

(b) Explain why the averages found in part (a) are not meaningful.

(c) Find the mean and median of the numbers in the column labeled "Complaints per 100,000 Passengers Boarding." Discuss whether these averages are meaningful.

42. Housing Prices An Erie, PA, newspaper advertised homes for sale in different areas of the region. In Summit Township, seven homes were advertised at the following listing prices: $199,000, $109,000, $229,000, $169,900, $219,900, $25,500, and $207,000. In the rural area south of Summit, six homes were advertised at the following listing prices: $749,000, $352,400, $314,900, $165,000, $175,000, and $215,000.

(a) Find the mean and median housing prices for Summit Township.

(b) Find the mean and median housing prices for the rural area.

(c) Discuss the differences between the mean and median for each region. Which gives a truer representation of the average housing price for each region?

43. New Housing Sales The number (in thousands) of new houses sold each month in the United States from 2010 to 2013 is given in the following table. *Source: U.S. Census.*

	2010	2011	2012	2013
Jan.	24	21	23	32
Feb.	27	22	30	36
Mar.	36	28	34	41
Apr.	41	30	34	43
May	26	28	35	40
June	28	28	34	43
July	26	27	33	33
Aug.	23	25	31	31
Sept.	25	24	30	31
Oct.	23	25	29	36
Nov.	20	23	28	32
Dec.	23	24	28	31

(a) Prepare a frequency distribution with a column for intervals and frequencies. Use six intervals, starting with 20–23.

(b) Sketch a histogram and a frequency polygon, using the intervals in part (a).

(c) Find the mean for the original data.

(d) Find the mean using the grouped data from part (a).

(e) Explain why your answers to parts (c) and (d) are different.

(f) Find the median and mode for the original data.

Life Sciences

44. Pandas The size of the home ranges (in square kilometers) of a group of pandas were surveyed over a year's time, with the following results.

Home Range	Frequency
0.1–0.5	11
0.6–1.0	12
1.1–1.5	7
1.6–2.0	6
2.1–2.5	2
2.6–3.0	1
3.1–3.5	1

(a) Sketch a histogram and frequency polygon for the data.

(b) Find the mean for the data.

45. Blood Types The number of recognized blood types varies by species, as indicated by the table below. Find the mean, median, and mode of this data. *Source: The Handy Science Answer Book.*

Animal	Number of Blood Types
Pig	16
Cow	12
Chicken	11
Horse	9
Human	8
Sheep	7
Dog	7
Rhesus monkey	6
Mink	5
Rabbit	5
Mouse	4
Rat	4
Cat	2

General Interest

46. Temperature The following table gives the number of days in June and July of recent years in which the temperature reached 90 degrees or higher in New York's Central Park. *Source: The National Weather Service.*

Year	Days	Year	Days	Year	Days
1985	4	1995	14	2005	12
1986	8	1996	0	2006	5
1987	14	1997	10	2007	4
1988	21	1998	5	2008	10
1989	10	1999	24	2009	0
1990	6	2000	3	2010	20
1991	21	2001	4	2011	17
1992	4	2002	13	2012	15
1993	25	2003	11	2013	13
1994	16	2004	1	2014	3

(a) Prepare a frequency distribution with a column for intervals and frequencies. Use six intervals, starting with 0–4.

(b) Sketch a histogram and a frequency polygon, using the intervals in part (a).

(c) Find the mean for the original data.

(d) Find the mean using the grouped data from part (a).

(e) Explain why your answers to parts (c) and (d) are different.

(f) Find the median and the mode for the original data.

47. Temperature The table at the top of the next column gives the average monthly temperatures in degrees Fahrenheit for a certain area.

Month	Maximum	Minimum
January	39	16
February	39	18
March	44	21
April	50	26
May	60	32
June	69	37
July	79	43
August	78	42
September	70	37
October	51	31
November	47	24
December	40	20

Find the mean and median for the following.

(a) The maximum temperature

(b) The minimum temperature

48. Olympics The number of nations participating in the Winter Olympic games, from 1968 to 2014, is given below. Find the following measures for the data. *Source: Sports-Reference.*

Year	Nations Participating	Year	Nations Participating
1968	37	1994	67
1972	35	1998	72
1976	37	2002	77
1980	37	2006	85
1984	49	2010	82
1988	57	2014	89
1992	64		

(a) Mean (b) Median (c) Mode

49. Personal Wealth When Russian billionaire Roman Abramovich became governor of the Russian province Chukotka (in the Bering Straits, opposite Alaska), it instantly became the fourth most prosperous region in Russia, even though its 80,000 other residents are poor. Mr. Abramovich was then worth $5.7 billion. Suppose each of the 80,000 other residents of Chukotka was worth $100. *Source: National Public Radio.*

(a) Calculate the average worth of a citizen of Chukotka.

(b) What does this example tell you about the use of the mean to describe an average?

50. Personal Wealth *Washington Post* writer John Schwartz pointed out that if Microsoft Corp. cofounder Bill Gates, who, at the time, was reportedly worth $10 billion, lived in a town with 10,000 totally penniless people, the average personal wealth in the town would make it seem as if everyone were a millionaire. *Source: The Washington Post.*

(a) Verify Schwartz's statement.

(b) What would be the median personal wealth in this town?

(c) What would be the mode for the personal wealth in this town?

(d) In this example, which average is most representative: the mean, the median, or the mode?

51. **Baseball Salaries** The Major League Baseball team with the lowest payroll in 2014 was the Houston Astros. The following table gives the salary of each Astro in 2014. *Source: ESPN.*

Name	Salary
Scott Feldman	$12,000,000
Jose Veras	$3,850,000
Chad Qualls	$2,750,000
Jason Castro	$2,450,000
Jose Altuve	$1,437,500
Jesus Guzman	$1,300,000
Matt Dominguez	$510,100
Chris Carter	$510,000
Dallas Keuchel	$508,700
Josh Fields	$506,500
Carlos Corporan	$505,300
Anthony Bass	$505,200
Marwin Gonzalez	$504,500
Robbie Grossman	$504,500
Brad Peacock	$504,300
L. J. Hoes	$502,900
Jared Cosart	$500,000

(a) Find the mean, median, and mode of the salaries.

(b) Which average best describes these data?

(c) Why is there such a difference between the mean and median?

52. **SAT I: Reasoning Test** Given the following sequence of numbers*

$$1, a, a^2, a^3, \ldots, a^n,$$

where n is a positive even integer, with the *additional assumption* that a is a positive number, the median is best described as

(a) greater than $a^{n/2}$;

(b) smaller than $a^{n/2}$;

(c) equal to $a^{n/2}$.

(d) The relationship cannot be determined from the information given.

YOUR TURN ANSWERS

1. 27

2. 19.85

3. 25

*Permission to reprint SAT materials does not constitute review or endorsement by Educational Testing Service or the College Board of this publication as a whole or of any other questions or testing information it may contain. This problem appeared, minus the *additional assumption*, on an SAT in 1996. Colin Rizzio, a high school student at the time, became an instant celebrity when he noticed that the additional assumption was needed to complete the problem. *Source: The New York Times.*

9.2 Measures of Variation

APPLY IT How can we tell when a manufacturing process is out of control?
To answer this question, which we will do in Example 6, we need to understand measures of variation, which tell us how much the numbers in a sample vary from the mean.

The mean gives a measure of central tendency of a list of numbers but tells nothing about the *spread* of the numbers in the list. For example, suppose three inspectors each inspect a sample of five restaurants in their region and record the number of health violations they find in each restaurant. Their results are recorded in the table to the left.

Each of these three samples has a mean of 4, and yet they are quite different; the amount of dispersion or variation within the samples is different. Therefore, in addition to a measure of central tendency, another kind of measure is needed that describes how much the numbers vary.

Three Sets of Data					
I	3	5	6	3	3
II	4	4	4	4	4
III	10	1	0	0	9

Range The largest number in sample I is 6, while the smallest is 3, a difference of 3. In sample II this difference is 0; in sample III, it is 10. The difference between the largest and smallest number in a sample is called the **range**, one example of a measure of variation.

The range of sample I is 3, of sample II, 0, and of sample III, 10. The range has the advantage of being very easy to compute, and gives a rough estimate of the variation among the data in the sample. It depends only on the two extremes, however, and tells nothing about how the other data are distributed between the extremes.

EXAMPLE 1 Range

Find the range for each list of numbers.

(a) 12, 27, 6, 19, 38, 9, 42, 15

SOLUTION The highest number here is 42; the lowest is 6. The range is the difference between these numbers, or $42 - 6 = 36$.

(b) 74, 112, 59, 88, 200, 73, 92, 175

SOLUTION

$$\text{Range} = 200 - 59 = 141$$

Variance and Standard Deviation

The most useful measure of variation is the *standard deviation*. Before defining it, however, we must find the **deviations from the mean**, the differences found by subtracting the mean from each number in a sample.

EXAMPLE 2 Deviations from the Mean

Find the deviations from the mean for the numbers

$$32, 41, 47, 53, 57.$$

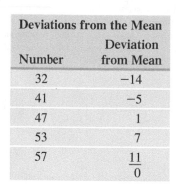

Deviations from the Mean	
Number	Deviation from Mean
32	−14
41	−5
47	1
53	7
57	11
	0

SOLUTION Adding these numbers and dividing by 5 gives a mean of 46. To find the deviations from the mean, subtract 46 from each number in the list. For example, as shown in the table to the left, the first deviation from the mean is $32 - 46 = -14$; the last is $57 - 46 = 11$.

To check your work, find the sum of these deviations. It should always equal 0. (The answer is always 0 because the positive and negative numbers cancel each other.)

To find a measure of variation, we might be tempted to use the mean of the deviations. As mentioned above, however, this number is always 0, no matter how widely the data are dispersed. One way to solve this problem is to use absolute value and find the mean of the absolute values of the deviations from the mean. Absolute value is awkward to work with algebraically, and there is an alternative approach that provides better theoretical results. In this method, the way to get a list of positive numbers is to square each deviation and then find the mean. When finding the mean of the squared deviations, most statisticians prefer to divide by $n - 1$, rather than n. We will give the reason later in this section. For the data above, this gives

$$\frac{(-14)^2 + (-5)^2 + 1^2 + 7^2 + 11^2}{5 - 1} = \frac{196 + 25 + 1 + 49 + 121}{4}$$
$$= 98.$$

This number, 98, is called the *variance* of the sample. Since it is found by averaging a list of squares, the variance of a sample is represented by s^2.

For a sample of n numbers $x_1, x_2, x_3, \ldots, x_n$, with mean $\bar{x}$, the variance is

$$s^2 = \frac{\Sigma(x - \bar{x})^2}{n - 1}.$$

The following shortcut formula for the variance can be derived algebraically from the formula above. You are asked for this derivation in Exercise 23.

Variance

The **variance** of a sample of n numbers $x_1, x_2, x_3, \ldots, x_n$, with mean $\bar{x}$, is

$$s^2 = \frac{\Sigma x^2 - n\bar{x}^2}{n - 1}.$$

To find the variance, we squared the deviations from the mean, so the variance is in squared units. To return to the same units as the data, we use the *square root* of the variance, called the *standard deviation*.

Standard Deviation

The **standard deviation** of a sample of n numbers $x_1, x_2, x_3, \ldots, x_n$, with mean $\bar{x}$, is

$$s = \sqrt{s^2} = \sqrt{\frac{\Sigma x^2 - n\bar{x}^2}{n - 1}}.$$

As its name indicates, the standard deviation is the most commonly used measure of variation. The standard deviation is a measure of the variation from the mean. The size of the standard deviation tells us something about how spread out the data are from the mean.

EXAMPLE 3   Standard Deviation

Find the standard deviation of the numbers

$$7, 9, 18, 22, 27, 29, 32, 40.$$

SOLUTION

Method I
Calculating by Hand

The mean of the numbers is

$$\bar{x} = \frac{7 + 9 + 18 + 22 + 27 + 29 + 32 + 40}{8} = 23.$$

Arrange the work in columns, as shown in the table.

Standard Deviation Calculations	
Number, x	Square of the Number, x^2
7	49
9	81
18	324
22	484
27	729
29	841
32	1024
40	1600
	Total: 5132

The total of the second column gives $\Sigma x^2 = 5132$. Now, using the formula for variance with $n = 8$, the variance is

$$s^2 = \frac{\Sigma x^2 - n\bar{x}^2}{n - 1}$$

$$= \frac{5132 - 8(23)^2}{8 - 1} \qquad \Sigma x^2 = 5132, n = 8, \bar{x} = 23$$

$$\approx 128.57,$$

rounded, and the standard deviation is

$$s = \sqrt{128.57} \approx 11.3.$$

Method 2
Graphing Calculator

The data are entered into the L_1 list on a TI-84 Plus C calculator. Figure 4 shows how the variance and standard deviation are then calculated through the LIST-MATH menu. Figure 5 shows an alternative method, going through the STAT menu, which calculates the mean, the standard deviation using both $n - 1$ (indicated by Sx) and n (indicated by σx) in the denominator, and other statistics.

YOUR TURN 1 Find the range, variance, and standard deviation for the following list of numbers: 7, 11, 16, 17, 19, 35.

```
variance(L1)
              128.5714286
stdDev(L1)
              11.33893419
```

FIGURE 4

```
1-Var Stats
x̄=23
Σx=184
Σx²=5132
Sx=11.33893419
σx=10.60660172
↓n=8
```

FIGURE 5

Method 3
Spreadsheet

The data are entered in cells A1 through A8. Then, in cell A9, type "=VAR(A1:A8)" and press Enter. The standard deviation can be calculated by either taking the square root of cell A9 or by typing "=STDEV(A1:A8)" in cell A10 and pressing Enter.

TRY YOUR TURN 1

CAUTION Be careful to divide by $n - 1$, not n, when calculating the standard deviation of a sample. Many calculators are equipped with statistical keys that compute the variance and standard deviation. Some of these calculators use $n - 1$ and others use n for these computations; some may have keys for both. Check your calculator's instruction book before using a statistical calculator for the exercises.

One way to interpret the standard deviation uses the fact that, for many populations, most of the data are within three standard deviations of the mean. (See Section 9.3.) This implies that, in Example 3, most members of the population from which this sample is taken are between

$$\bar{x} - 3s = 23 - 3(11.3) = -10.9$$

and

$$\bar{x} + 3s = 23 + 3(11.3) = 56.9.$$

This has important implications for quality control. If the sample in Example 3 represents measurements of a product that the manufacturer wants to be between 5 and 45, the standard deviation is too large, even though all the numbers in the sample are within these bounds.

We saw in the previous section that the mean of a random sample is a random variable. It should not surprise you, then, to learn that the variance and standard deviation are also random variables. We will refer to the variance and standard deviation of a random sample as the **sample variance** and **sample standard deviation**.

Recall from the previous section that the sample mean $\bar{x}$ is not the same as the population mean μ, which is defined by $\mu = E(x)$, but that $\bar{x}$ gives a good approximation to μ because $E(\bar{x}) = \mu$. Similarly, there is a **population variance**, denoted σ^2, defined by $\sigma^2 = E(x - \mu)^2$, which measures the amount of variation in a population. The **population standard deviation** is simply σ, the square root of the population variance σ^2. (The Greek letter σ is the lowercase version of sigma. You have already seen Σ, the uppercase version.) In more advanced courses in statistics, it is shown that $E(s^2) = \sigma^2$. The reason many statisticians prefer $n - 1$ in the denominator of the standard deviation formula is that it makes $E(s^2) = \sigma^2$ true; this is not true if n is used in the denominator. It may surprise you, then, that $E(s) = \sigma$ is *false*, whether n or $n - 1$ is used. If n is large, the difference between $E(s)$ and σ is slight, so, in practice, the sample standard deviation s gives a good estimate of the population standard deviation σ.

For data in a grouped frequency distribution, a slightly different formula for the standard deviation is used.

FOR REVIEW

Recall from Section 8.5 that a random variable is a function that assigns a real number to each outcome of an experiment. When the experiment consists of drawing a random sample, the standard deviation and the variance are two real numbers assigned to each outcome. Every time the experiment is performed, the standard deviation and variance will most likely have different values, with some values more probable than others.

> ## Standard Deviation for a Grouped Distribution
> The standard deviation for a distribution with mean $\bar{x}$, where x is an interval midpoint with frequency f, and $n = \Sigma f$, is
>
> $$s = \sqrt{\frac{\Sigma fx^2 - n\bar{x}^2}{n - 1}}.$$

CAUTION

In calculating the standard deviation for either a grouped or ungrouped distribution, using a rounded value for the mean may produce an inaccurate value.

The formula indicates that the product fx^2 is to be found for each interval. Then these products are summed, n times the square of the mean is subtracted, and the difference is divided by one less than the total frequency; that is, by $n - 1$. The square root of this result is s, the standard deviation.

EXAMPLE 4 Standard Deviation for Grouped Data

Find the standard deviation for the grouped data of Example 5, Section 9.1.

SOLUTION Begin by forming columns for x (the midpoint of the interval), x^2, and fx^2. Then sum the f and fx^2 columns. Recall from Example 5 of Section 9.1 that $\bar{x} = 15.5$.

Standard Deviation for Grouped Data				
Interval	x	x^2	f	fx^2
0–4	2	4	3	12
5–9	7	49	4	196
10–14	12	144	6	864
15–19	17	289	8	2312
20–24	22	484	5	2420
25–29	27	729	3	2187
30–34	32	1024	1	1024
			Total: 30	Total: 9015

YOUR TURN 2 Find the standard deviation for the following grouped frequency distribution.

Interval	Frequency
0–6	2
7–13	4
14–20	7
21–27	10
28–34	3
35–41	1

The total of the fourth column gives $n = \Sigma f = 30$, and the total of the last column gives $\Sigma fx^2 = 9015$. Use the formula for standard deviation for a grouped distribution to find s.

$$s = \sqrt{\frac{\Sigma fx^2 - n\bar{x}^2}{n-1}}$$

$$= \sqrt{\frac{9015 - 30(15.5)^2}{30-1}} \qquad \Sigma fx^2 = 9015, n = 30, \bar{x} = 15.5$$

$$\approx 7.89$$

Verify that the standard deviation of the original, ungrouped data in Example 1 of Section 9.1 is 7.92. **TRY YOUR TURN 2** ▬▬

EXAMPLE 5 Nathan's Hot Dog Eating Contest

Since 1916, Nathan's Famous Hot Dogs has held an annual hot dog eating contest, in which each contestant attempts to consume as many hot dogs with buns as possible in a set time period. The following table contains a list of each year's winners since 2000. In what percent of the contests did the number of hot dogs eaten by the winner fall within one standard deviation of the mean number of hot dogs? Within two standard deviations? Within three standard deviations? *Source: Wikipedia.*

Hot Dog Eating Contest Winners		
Year	Winner	Hot Dogs Eaten
2000	Kazutoyo Arai	25.125
2001	Takeru Kobayashi	50
2002	Takeru Kobayashi	50.5
2003	Takeru Kobayashi	44.5
2004	Takeru Kobayashi	53.5
2005	Takeru Kobayashi	49
2006	Takeru Kobayashi	53.75
2007	Joey Chestnut	66
2008	Joey Chestnut	59
2009	Joey Chestnut	68
2010	Joey Chestnut	54
2011	Joey Chestnut	62
2012	Joey Chestnut	68
2013	Joey Chestnut	69
2014	Joey Chestnut	61

SOLUTION First, using the formulas for $\bar{x}$ and s, we calculate the mean and standard deviation:

$$\bar{x} \approx 55.56 \quad \text{and} \quad s \approx 11.46.$$

Subtracting one standard deviation from the mean and then adding one standard deviation to the mean, we find the lower and upper limits:

$$\bar{x} - s = 55.56 - 11.46 = 44.10 \quad \text{(lower)}$$

and

$$\bar{x} + s = 55.56 + 11.46 = 67.02. \quad \text{(upper)}$$

In 11 of the 15 contests, the number of hot dogs eaten by the winner was between 44.10 and 67.02. Therefore, in about 73% $(11/15 \approx 0.73)$ of the recent contests, the number of hot dogs consumed by the winner was within one standard deviation of the mean.

Likewise, subtracting 2 standard deviations from the mean and adding 2 standard deviations to the mean, we get a lower limit of 32.64 and an upper limit of 78.48. In 14 of the 15 contests, or about 93% $(14/15 \approx 0.93)$ of the contests, the winning number of consumed hot dogs was within two standard deviations of the mean.

Finally, subtracting 3 standard deviations from the mean and adding 3 standard deviations to the mean gives an interval of 21.18 to 89.94. The winning numbers in all fifteen contests fall in this interval, so in 100% of the recent contests the number of hot dogs eaten by the winner was within three standard deviations from the mean. ▬

EXAMPLE 6   Quality Assurance

APPLY IT   *Statistical process control* is a method of determining when a manufacturing process is out of control, producing defective items. The procedure involves taking samples of a measurement on a product over a production run and calculating the mean and standard deviation of each sample. These results are used to determine when the manufacturing process is out of control. For example, three sample measurements from a manufacturing process on each of four days are given in the table below. The mean $\bar{x}$ and standard deviation s are calculated for each sample.

		Samples from a Manufacturing Process										
Day		1			2			3			4	
Sample Number	1	2	3	1	2	3	1	2	3	1	2	3
Measurements	−3	0	4	5	−2	4	3	−1	0	4	−2	1
	0	5	3	4	0	3	−2	0	0	3	0	3
	2	2	2	3	1	4	0	1	−2	3	−1	0
$\bar{x}$	−1/3	7/3	3	4	−1/3	11/3	1/3	0	−2/3	10/3	−1	4/3
s	2.5	2.5	1	1	1.5	0.6	2.5	1	1.2	0.6	1	1.5

Next, the mean of the 12 sample means, $\overline{X}$, and the mean of the 12 sample standard deviations, $\bar{s}$, are found (using the formula for $\bar{x}$). Here, these measures are

$$\overline{X} = 1.3 \quad \text{and} \quad \bar{s} = 1.41.$$

The control limits for the sample means are given by

$$\overline{X} \pm k_1 \cdot \bar{s},$$

where k_1 is a constant that depends on the sample size, and can be found from a manual. For samples of size 3, $k_1 = 1.954$, so the control limits for the sample means are

$$1.3 \pm (1.954)(1.41).$$

The upper control limit is 4.06, and the lower control limit is −1.46.

Similarly, the control limits for the sample standard deviations are given by $k_2 \cdot \bar{s}$ and $k_3 \cdot \bar{s}$, where k_2 and k_3 also are values given in the same manual. Here, $k_2 = 2.568$ and $k_3 = 0$, with the upper and lower control limits for the sample standard deviations equal to $2.568(1.41)$ and $0(1.41)$, or 3.62 and 0. As long as the sample means are between −1.46 and 4.06 and the sample standard deviations are between 0 and 3.62, the process is in control. *Source: Statistical Process Control.* ▬

9.2 WARM-UP EXERCISES

W1. Find the mean of the following data list: 17, 22, 19, 24, 32, 25, 29, 22, 21, 31. *(Sec. 9.1)*

W2. Find the mean from the grouped frequency distribution. *(Sec. 9.1)*

Interval	Frequency, f
0–6	5
7–13	8
14–20	10
21–27	12
28–34	9
35–41	6

9.2 EXERCISES

1. How are the variance and the standard deviation related?

2. Why can't we use the sum of the deviations from the mean as a measure of dispersion of a distribution?

Find the range and standard deviation for each set of numbers.

3. 72, 61, 57, 83, 52, 66, 85

4. 122, 132, 141, 158, 162, 169, 180

5. 241, 248, 251, 257, 252, 287

6. 51, 58, 62, 64, 67, 71, 74, 78, 82, 93

7. 3, 7, 4, 12, 15, 18, 19, 27, 24, 11

8. 17, 57, 48, 13, 26, 3, 36, 21, 9, 40

 Use a graphing calculator or spreadsheet to calculate the standard deviation for the data in the indicated exercises.

9. Exercise 1 from Section 9.1   **10.** Exercise 2 from Section 9.1

Find the standard deviation for the following grouped data.

11. (From Exercise 1, Section 9.1)

Interval	Frequency
0–24	4
25–49	8
50–74	5
75–99	10
100–124	4
125–149	5

12. (From Exercise 2, Section 9.1)

Interval	Frequency
30–39	1
40–49	6
50–59	13
60–69	22
70–79	17
80–89	13
90–99	8

Chebyshev's theorem states that for any set of numbers, the fraction that will lie within k standard deviations of the mean (for $k > 1$) is at least

$$1 - \frac{1}{k^2}.$$

For example, at least $1 - 1/2^2 = 3/4$ of any set of numbers lie within 2 standard deviations of the mean. Similarly, for any probability distribution, the probability that a number will lie within k standard deviations of the mean is at least $1 - 1/k^2$. For example, if the mean is 100 and the standard deviation is 10, the probability that a number will lie within 2 standard deviations of 100, or between 80 and 120, is at least 3/4. Use Chebyshev's theorem to find the fraction of all the numbers of a data set that must lie within the following numbers of standard deviations from the mean.

13. 3   **14.** 4

15. 5   **16.** 6

In a certain distribution of numbers, the mean is 60 with a standard deviation of 8. Use Chebyshev's theorem to tell the probability that a number lies in each interval.

17. Between 36 and 84   **18.** Between 48 and 72

19. Less than 36 or more than 84

20. Less than 48 or more than 72

21. Discuss what the standard deviation tells us about a distribution.

22. Explain the difference between the sample mean and standard deviation, and the population mean and standard deviation.

23. Derive the shortcut formula for the variance

$$s^2 = \frac{\Sigma x^2 - n\bar{x}^2}{n - 1}$$

from the formula

$$s^2 = \frac{\Sigma (x - \bar{x})^2}{n - 1}$$

and the following summation formulas, in which c is a constant:

$$\Sigma cx = c\Sigma x, \quad \Sigma c = nc, \quad \text{and} \quad \Sigma(x \pm y) = \Sigma x \pm \Sigma y.$$

(*Hint:* Multiply out $(x - \bar{x})^2$.)

24. Consider the set of numbers 9,999,999, 10,000,000, and 10,000,001.

(a) Calculate the variance by hand using the formula
$$s^2 = \frac{\Sigma(x - \bar{x})^2}{n - 1}.$$

(b) Calculate the variance using your calculator and the short-cut formula $s^2 = \dfrac{\Sigma x^2 - n\bar{x}^2}{n - 1}$.

(c) There may be a discrepancy between your answers to parts (a) and (b) because of roundoff. Explain this discrepancy, and then discuss advantages and disadvantages of the shortcut formula.

APPLICATIONS

Business and Economics

25. Battery Life Forever Power Company analysts conducted tests on the life of its batteries and those of a competitor (Brand X). They found that their batteries had a mean life (in hours) of 26.2, with a standard deviation of 4.1. Their results for a sample of 10 Brand X batteries were as follows: 15, 18, 19, 23, 25, 25, 28, 30, 34, 38.

(a) Find the mean and standard deviation for the sample of Brand X batteries.

(b) Which batteries have a more uniform life in hours?

(c) Which batteries have the highest average life in hours?

26. Sales Promotion The Quaker Oats Company conducted a survey to determine whether a proposed premium, to be included in boxes of cereal, was appealing enough to generate new sales. Four cities were used as test markets, where the cereal was distributed with the premium, and four cities as control markets, where the cereal was distributed without the premium. The eight cities were chosen on the basis of their similarity in terms of population, per capita income, and total cereal purchase volume. The results were as follows. *Source: Quaker Oats Company.*

	City	Percent Change in Average Market Share per Month
Test Cities	1	+18
	2	+15
	3	+7
	4	+10
Control Cities	1	+1
	2	−8
	3	−5
	4	0

(a) Find the mean of the change in market share for the four test cities.

(b) Find the mean of the change in market share for the four control cities.

(c) Find the standard deviation of the change in market share for the test cities.

(d) Find the standard deviation of the change in market share for the control cities.

(e) Find the difference between the means of parts (a) and (b). This difference represents the estimate of the percent change in sales due to the premium.

(f) The two standard deviations from parts (c) and (d) were used to calculate an "error" of ±7.95 for the estimate in part (e). With this amount of error, what are the smallest and largest estimates of the increase in sales?

On the basis of the interval estimate of part (f), the company decided to mass-produce the premium and distribute it nationally.

27. Process Control The following table gives 10 samples of three measurements, made during a production run.

Sample Number									
1	2	3	4	5	6	7	8	9	10
2	3	−2	−3	−1	3	0	−1	2	0
−2	−1	0	1	2	2	1	2	3	0
1	4	1	2	4	2	2	3	2	2

Use the techniques in Example 6 to find the following.

(a) Find the mean $\bar{x}$ for each sample of three measurements.

(b) Find the standard deviation s for each sample of three measurements.

(c) Find the mean $\bar{X}$ of the sample means.

(d) Find the mean $\bar{s}$ of the sample standard deviations.

(e) Using $k_1 = 1.954$, find the upper and lower control limits for the sample means.

(f) Using $k_2 = 2.568$ and $k_3 = 0$, find the upper and lower control limits for the sample standard deviations.

28. Process Control Given the following measurements from later samples on the process in Exercise 27, decide whether the process is out of control. (*Hint:* Use the results of Exercise 27(e) and (f).)

Sample Number					
1	2	3	4	5	6
3	−4	2	5	4	0
−5	2	0	1	−1	1
2	1	1	−4	−2	−6

29. Washer Thickness An assembly-line machine turns out washers with the following thicknesses (in millimeters).

1.20	1.01	1.25	2.20	2.58	2.19	1.29	1.15
2.05	1.46	1.90	2.03	2.13	1.86	1.65	2.27
1.64	2.19	2.25	2.08	1.96	1.83	1.17	2.24

Find the mean and standard deviation of these thicknesses.

30. Unemployment The number of unemployed workers in the United States in recent years (in millions) is given below. *Source: Bureau of Labor Statistics.*

Year	Number Unemployed
2004	8.15
2005	7.59
2006	7.00
2007	7.08
2008	8.92
2009	14.27
2010	14.83
2011	13.75
2012	12.51
2013	11.46

(a) Find the mean number unemployed (in millions) in this period. Which years had unemployment closest to the mean?

(b) Find the range (in millions) of the data.

(c) Find the standard deviation (in millions) for the data.

(d) In how many of these years is unemployment within 1 standard deviation of the mean?

(e) In how many of these years is unemployment within 2 standard deviations of the mean?

31. New Housing Sales In Exercise 43, Section 9.1, the number (in thousands) of new houses sold each month in the United States from 2010 to 2013 was given. *Source: U.S. Census.*

(a) Find the standard deviation of the data.

(b) In what percent of the months did new housing sales fall within one standard deviation of the mean? Within two standard deviations? Within three?

32. New Housing Sales The following grouped frequency distribution, from Exercise 43, Section 9.1, gives the number (in thousands) of new houses sold each month in the United States from 2010 to 2013. The mean of the grouped data was found to be 29.75 thousand. Find the standard deviation of the grouped data. Compare the answer with the answer to part (a) of the previous exercise. *Source: U.S. Census.*

New Houses Sold per Month (in thousands)	Midpoint, x	f
20–23	21.5	8
24–27	25.5	10
28–31	29.5	14
32–35	33.5	8
36–39	37.5	3
40–43	41.5	5

33. Home-Based Workers Because of advancements in communication and information technologies, workers are increasingly able to work at home. The following grouped frequency distribution gives the number (in millions) of employed people who work at home for various age groups in 2010. (Assume the midpoint for the last interval is 69.5.) *Source: U.S. Census Bureau.*

Age (in years)	Midpoint, x	Frequency, f
15–24	19.5	0.4
25–34	29.5	1.3
35–44	39.5	2.1
45–54	49.5	2.5
55–64	59.5	2.0
Over 65	69.5	1.0

(a) Find the mean age of employed people who work at home.

(b) Find the standard deviation for the data.

Life Sciences

34. Blood Types The number of recognized blood types between species is given in the following table. In Exercise 45 of the previous section, the mean was found to be 7.38. *Source: The Handy Science Answer Book.*

Animal	Number of Blood Types
Pig	16
Cow	12
Chicken	11
Horse	9
Human	8
Sheep	7
Dog	7
Rhesus monkey	6
Mink	5
Rabbit	5
Mouse	4
Rat	4
Cat	2

(a) Find the variance and the standard deviation of these data.

(b) How many of these animals have blood types that are within 1 standard deviation of the mean?

35. Tumor Growth The amount of time that it takes for various slow-growing tumors to double in size are listed in the following table. *Source: American Journal of Roentgen.*

Type of Cancer	Doubling Time (days)
Breast cancer	84
Rectal cancer	91
Synovioma	128
Skin cancer	131
Lip cancer	143
Testicular cancer	153
Esophageal cancer	164

(a) Find the mean and standard deviation of these data.

(b) How many of these cancers have doubling times that are within 2 standard deviations of the mean?

(c) If a person had a nonspecified tumor that was doubling every 200 days, discuss whether this particular tumor is growing at a rate that would be expected.

36. Blood pH A medical laboratory tested 21 samples of human blood for acidity on the pH scale, with the following results.

7.1	7.5	7.3	7.4	7.6	7.2	7.3
7.4	7.5	7.3	7.2	7.4	7.3	7.5
7.5	7.4	7.4	7.1	7.3	7.4	7.4

(a) Find the mean and standard deviation.

(b) What percentage of the data is within 2 standard deviations of the mean?

General Interest

37. Temperature In Exercise 46, Section 9.1, the number of days in June and July of recent years in which the temperature reached 90 degrees or higher in New York's Central Park was given. The mean was found to be 10.43 days. *Source: The National Weather Service.*

(a) Find the standard deviation of the data.

(b) In what percent of the years did the number of 90 plus degree days in June and July fall within one standard deviation of the mean? Within two standard deviations? Within three?

38. Temperature The following grouped frequency distribution, from Exercise 46, Section 9.1, gives the number of days in June and July of recent years in which the temperature reached 90 degrees or higher in New York's Central Park. The mean of the grouped data was found to be 10.67 days. Find the standard deviation of the grouped data. Compare the answer with the answer to part (a) of the previous exercise. *Source: The National Weather Service.*

Interval	Frequency, f
0–4	9
5–9	4
10–14	9
15–19	3
20–24	4
25–29	1

39. Baseball Salaries The table in Exercise 51, Section 9.1, lists the salary for each player on the Houston Astros baseball team in 2014. The mean was found to be $1,726,441. *Source: ESPN.*

(a) Calculate the range of the salaries.

(b) Calculate the standard deviation of these data.

(c) How many of the 2014 Houston Astros players have salaries that are beyond 3 standard deviations from the mean?

(d) What does your answer to part (c) suggest?

40. Box Office Receipts The table below lists the 20 films in which actor Will Smith has starred through 2013, along with the gross domestic box office receipts and the year for each movie. *Source: The Movie Times.*

Movie	Domestic Box Office Receipts
After Earth, 2013	$27,520,040
Men in Black 3, 2012	$179,020,854
Hancock, 2008	$227,946,274
Seven Pounds, 2008	$69,951,824
I Am Legend, 2007	$256,386,216
The Pursuit of Happyness, 2006	$162,586,036
Hitch, 2005	$177,575,142
Shark Tale, 2004	$161,412,000
I, Robot, 2004	$144,801,023
Bad Boys II, 2003	$138,540,870
Men in Black 2, 2002	$190,418,803
Ali, 2001	$58,200,000
The Legend of Bagger Vance, 2000	$30,695,000
Wild Wild West, 1999	$113,745,000
Enemy of the State, 1998	$111,544,000
Men in Black, 1997	$250,107,128
Independence Day, 1996	$306,124,000
Bad Boys, 1995	$65,807,000
Made in America, 1993	$44,942,000
Six Degrees of Separation, 1993	$6,410,000

(a) Find the mean domestic box office receipts for Will Smith's movies. Which movie has box office receipts closest to the mean?

(b) Find the range of the data.

(c) Find the standard deviation for the data.

(d) What percent of the movies have box office receipts within 1 standard deviation of the mean? Within 2 standard deviations of the mean?

41. Cookies Marie Revak and Jihan Williams performed an experiment to determine whether Oreo Double Stuf cookies contain twice as much filling as traditional Oreo cookies. The table below gives the results in grams of the amount of filling inside 49 traditional cookies and 52 Double Stuf cookies. *Source: The Mathematics Teacher*.

(a) Find the mean, maximum, minimum, and standard deviation of the weights for traditional Oreo cookies.

(b) Find the mean, maximum, minimum, and standard deviation of the weights for Oreo Double Stuf cookies.

(c) What percent of the data of traditional Oreo cookies is within 2 standard deviations of the Double Stuf Oreo mean? (*Hint:* Use the mean and standard deviation for the Double Stuf data.)

(d) What percent of the data of traditional Oreo cookies, when multiplied by 2, is within 2 standard deviations of the Double Stuf Oreo mean? (*Hint:* Use the mean and standard deviation for the Double Stuf data.)

(e) Is there evidence that Double Stuf Oreos have twice as much filling as the traditional Oreo cookie? Explain.

YOUR TURN ANSWERS
1. 28, 92.7, 9.628
2. 8.52

Traditional	Traditional	Traditional	Double Stuf	Double Stuf	Double Stuf
2.9	2.4	2.7	4.7	6.5	5.8
2.8	2.8	2.8	6.5	6.3	5.9
2.6	3.8	2.6	5.5	4.8	6.2
3.5	3.1	2.6	5.6	3.3	5.9
3.0	2.9	3.0	5.1	6.4	6.5
2.4	3.0	2.8	5.3	5.0	6.5
2.7	2.1	3.5	5.4	5.3	6.1
2.4	3.8	3.3	5.4	5.5	5.8
2.5	3.0	3.3	3.5	5.0	6.0
2.2	3.0	2.8	5.5	6.0	6.2
2.6	2.8	3.1	6.5	5.7	6.2
2.6	2.9	2.6	5.9	6.3	6.0
2.9	2.7	3.5	5.4	6.0	6.8
2.6	3.2	3.5	4.9	6.3	6.2
2.6	2.8	3.1	5.6	6.1	5.4
3.1	3.1	3.1	5.7	6.0	6.6
2.9			5.3	5.8	6.2
			6.9		

9.3 The Normal Distribution

APPLY IT What is the probability that a salesperson drives between 1200 miles and 1600 miles per month?

This question will be answered in Example 4 by using the normal probability distribution introduced in this section.

Suppose a bank is interested in improving its services to customers. The manager decides to begin by finding the amount of time tellers spend on each transaction, rounded to the nearest minute. The times for 75 different transactions are recorded with the results shown in the following table. The frequencies listed in the second column are divided by 75 to find the empirical probabilities.

FOR REVIEW

Empirical probabilities, discussed in Section 7.3, are derived from grouped data by dividing the frequency or amount for each group by the total for all the groups. This gives one example of a probability distribution, discussed further in Sections 7.3 and 8.5.

Teller Transaction Times		
Time	Frequency	Probability
1	3	$3/75 = 0.04$
2	5	$5/75 \approx 0.07$
3	9	$9/75 = 0.12$
4	12	$12/75 = 0.16$
5	15	$15/75 = 0.20$
6	11	$11/75 \approx 0.15$
7	10	$10/75 \approx 0.13$
8	6	$6/75 = 0.08$
9	3	$3/75 = 0.04$
10	1	$1/75 \approx 0.01$

Figure 6(a) shows a histogram and frequency polygon for the data. The heights of the bars are the empirical probabilities rather than the frequencies. The transaction times are given to the nearest minute. Theoretically at least, they could have been timed to the nearest tenth of a minute, or hundredth of a minute, or even more precisely. In each case, a histogram and frequency polygon could be drawn. If the times are measured with smaller and smaller units, there are more bars in the histogram, and the frequency polygon begins to look more and more like the curve in Figure 6(b) instead of a polygon. Actually, it is possible for the transaction times to take on any real number value greater than 0. A distribution in which the outcomes can take any real number value within some interval is a **continuous distribution**. The graph of a continuous distribution is a curve.

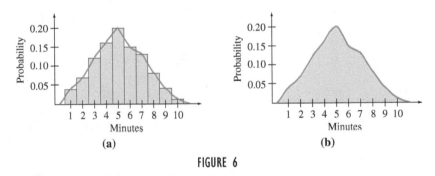

FIGURE 6

The distribution of heights (in inches) of college women is another example of a continuous distribution, since these heights include infinitely many possible measurements, such as 53, 58.5, 66.3, 72.666, . . . , and so on. Figure 7 shows the continuous distribution of heights of college women. Here the most frequent heights occur near the center of the interval shown.

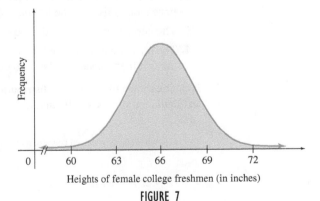

Heights of female college freshmen (in inches)

FIGURE 7

Another continuous curve, which approximates the distribution of yearly incomes in the United States, is given in Figure 8. The graph shows that the most frequent incomes are grouped near the low end of the interval. This kind of distribution, where the peak is not at the center, is called **skewed**.

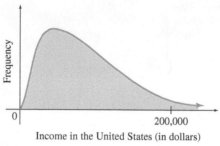

Income in the United States (in dollars)

FIGURE 8

Many natural and social phenomena produce continuous probability distributions whose graphs can be approximated very well by bell-shaped curves, such as those shown in Figure 9 below. Such distributions are called **normal distributions** and their graphs are called **normal curves**. Examples of distributions that are approximately normal are the heights of college women and the errors made in filling 1-lb cereal boxes. We use the Greek letters μ (mu) to denote the mean and σ (sigma) to denote the standard deviation of a normal distribution. The definitions of the mean and standard deviation of a continuous distribution require ideas from calculus, but the intuitive ideas are similar to those in the previous section.

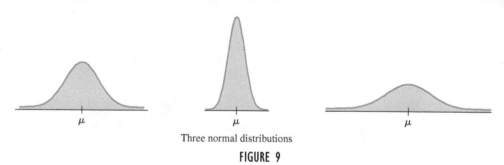

Three normal distributions

FIGURE 9

There are many normal distributions. Some of the corresponding normal curves are tall and thin and others are short and wide, as shown in Figure 9. But every normal curve has the following properties.

1. Its peak occurs directly above the mean μ.
2. The curve is symmetric about the vertical line through the mean (that is, if you fold the page along this line, the left half of the graph will fit exactly on the right half).
3. The curve never touches the x-axis—it extends indefinitely in both directions.
4. The area under the curve (and above the horizontal axis) is always 1. (This agrees with the fact that the sum of the probabilities in any distribution is 1.)

It can be shown that a normal distribution is completely determined by its mean μ and standard deviation σ.* A small standard deviation leads to a tall, narrow curve like the one in

*As is shown in more advanced courses, its graph is the graph of the function

$$f(x) = \frac{1}{\sigma\sqrt{2\pi}} e^{-(x-\mu)^2/(2\sigma^2)},$$

where $e \approx 2.71828$ is a real number.

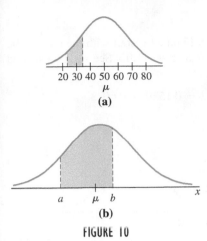

(a)

(b)

FIGURE 10

the center of Figure 9. A large standard deviation produces a flat, wide curve, like the one on the right in Figure 9.

Since the area under a normal curve is 1, parts of this area can be used to determine certain probabilities. For instance, Figure 10(a) is the probability distribution of the annual rainfall in a certain region. Calculus can be used to show that the probability that the annual rainfall will be between 25 in. and 35 in. is the area under the curve from 25 to 35. The general case, shown in Figure 10(b), can be stated as follows.

Normal Probability

The area of the shaded region under a normal curve from a to b is the probability that an observed data value will be between a and b.

To use normal curves effectively, we must be able to calculate areas under portions of these curves. These calculations have already been done for the normal curve with mean $\mu = 0$ and standard deviation $\sigma = 1$ (which is called the **standard normal curve**) and are available in a table in the Appendix. The following examples demonstrate how to use the table or a calculator or spreadsheet to find such areas. Later we shall see how the standard normal curve may be used to find areas under any normal curve.

EXAMPLE 1 **Standard Normal Curve**

The horizontal axis of the standard normal curve is usually labeled z. Find the following areas under the standard normal curve.

Method 1
Using a Table

(a) The area to the left of $z = 1.25$

SOLUTION The normal curve table (located in the Appendix) gives the area (rounded to four decimal places) under the standard normal curve to the left of a value z. To find the area to the left of $z = 1.25$, find 1.2 in the left-hand column and 0.05 at the top, then locate the intersection of the corresponding row and column. The specified area is 0.8944, so the shaded area shown in Figure 11 is 0.8944. This area represents 89.44% of the total area under the normal curve, and so the probability that $z \leq 1.25$ is

$$P(z \leq 1.25) = 0.8944.$$

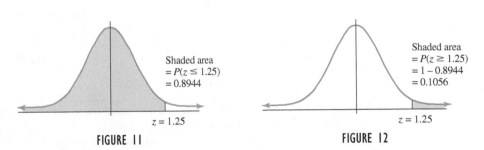

Shaded area
$= P(z \leq 1.25)$
$= 0.8944$

$z = 1.25$

FIGURE 11

Shaded area
$= P(z \geq 1.25)$
$= 1 - 0.8944$
$= 0.1056$

$z = 1.25$

FIGURE 12

(b) The area to the right of $z = 1.25$

SOLUTION From part (a), the area to the left of $z = 1.25$ is 0.8944. The total area under the normal curve is 1, so the area to the right of $z = 1.25$ is

$$1 - 0.8944 = 0.1056.$$

See Figure 12, where the shaded area represents 10.56% of the total area under the normal curve, and the probability that $z \geq 1.25$ is $P(z \geq 1.25) = 0.1056$.

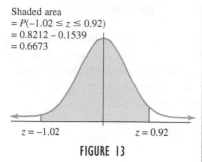

Shaded area
$= P(-1.02 \le z \le 0.92)$
$= 0.8212 - 0.1539$
$= 0.6673$

$z = -1.02$ $z = 0.92$

FIGURE 13

(c) The area between $z = -1.02$ and $z = 0.92$

SOLUTION To find this area, which is shaded in Figure 13, start with the area to the left of $z = 0.92$ and subtract the area to the left of $z = -1.02$. See the two shaded regions in Figure 14. The result is

$$P(-1.02 \le z \le 0.92) = 0.8212 - 0.1539 = 0.6673.$$

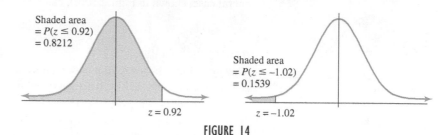

Shaded area
$= P(z \le 0.92)$
$= 0.8212$

$z = 0.92$

Shaded area
$= P(z \le -1.02)$
$= 0.1539$

$z = -1.02$

FIGURE 14

Method 2
Graphing Calculator

Because of convenience and accuracy, graphing calculators have made normal curve tables less important. On the TI-84 Plus C calculator, the area under the normal curve can be found using the `normalcdf` command in the `DISTR` menu. The `normalcdf` command requires you to enter four values: the lower bound, the upper bound, the mean (μ), and the standard deviation (σ). (If the mean and standard deviation are not entered, the calculator assumes the standard normal with $\mu = 0$ and $\sigma = 1$.)

In part (a), we are looking for the area to the left of $z = 1.25$. The lower bound is negative infinity, but the most negative value that the calculator can handle is -1×10^{99}. The area between -1×10^{99} and 1.25 is essentially the same as the area to the left of 1.25, so enter -1 EE 99 for the lower bound. (Note that only one E will show on the screen.) The upper bound is 1.25, the mean is 0, and the standard deviation is 1. See Figure 15.

In part (b), we are looking for the area to the right of $z = 1.25$. The lower bound is 1.25 and the upper bound is infinity. The largest value that the calculator can handle is 1×10^{99}, so enter 1 EE 99. Again, the mean is 0 and the standard deviation is 1. See Figure 15.

In part (c), we are looking for the area between $z = -1.02$ and $z = 0.92$. The command and solution are shown in Figure 15.

```
normalcdf(-1E99, 1.25, 0, 1)
                .894350161
normalcdf(1.25,1E99,1.25,0,1)
                .105649839
normalcdf(-1.02, .92, 0, 1)
                .6673494029
```

FIGURE 15

Method 3
Spreadsheet

Statistical software packages are widely used today. These packages are set up in a way that is similar to a spreadsheet, and they can be used to generate normal curve values. In addition, most spreadsheets can also perform a wide range of statistical calculations. For example, Microsoft Excel can be used to generate the answers to parts (a), (b), and (c) of this example. In any cell, type "=NORMDIST(1.25,0,1,1)" and press Enter. The value of 0.894350226 is returned. Notice that this value differs slightly from the value returned by a TI-84 Plus C. The first three input values represent the z value, mean, and standard deviation. The fourth value is always either a 0 or 1. For applications in this text, we will always place a 1 in this position to indicate that we want the area to the left of the first input value. Similarly, by typing "=1-NORMDIST(1.25,0,1,1)" and pressing Enter, we find that the area to the right of $z = 1.25$ is 0.105649774.

YOUR TURN 1 Find the following areas under the standard normal curve. **(a)** The area to the left of $z = -0.76$. **(b)** The area to the right of $z = -1.36$. **(c)** The area between $z = -1.22$ and $z = 1.33$.

TRY YOUR TURN 1

CAUTION

When using a table to calculate normal probabilities, it is wise to draw a normal curve with the mean and the z-scores every time. This will avoid confusion as to whether you should add or subtract probabilities.

NOTE

1. The probability that z is equal to one exact value is zero, because no area is included. For example, $P(z = 1.25) = 0$.

2. The area under the curve is the same, whether we include the endpoint or not. Therefore, $P(z \leq 1.25) = P(z < 1.25)$.

EXAMPLE 2 Finding a Value of z

Find a value of z satisfying the following conditions.

Method 1
Using a Table

(a) 12.1% of the area is to the left of z.

SOLUTION Use the normal curve table (located in the Appendix) backwards. The table gives the area (rounded to four decimal places) under the normal curve to the left of z. The total area under the curve is 1, so 12.1% of 1 is 0.121. Look in the body of the table for an area of 0.1210. The value is in the row -1.1 and the column labeled 0.07. Therefore, $z = -1.17$ corresponds to an area of 0.121.

(b) 20% of the area is to the right of z.

SOLUTION If 20% of the area is to the right, 80% is to the left. Look in the body of the table for an area of 0.8000. This value is not in the table, so we select the closest value, which is 0.7995. This area corresponds to $z = 0.84$.

Method 2
Graphing Calculator

On the TI-84 Plus C calculator, the value of z can be found using the `invNorm` command found in the `DISTR` menu. The `invNorm` command requires you to enter three values: the area to the left, the mean (μ), and the standard deviation (σ). (If the mean and standard deviation are not entered, the calculator assumes the standard normal with $\mu = 0$ and $\sigma = 1$.)

In part (a), we are looking for the value of z with 12.1% of the area to the left. We enter .121 for the area, 0 for the mean, and 1 for the standard deviation. The value of z, rounded to two decimal places, is $z = -1.17$. See Figure 16.

In part (b), we are looking for the value of z with 20% of the area to the right. The area to the left then is 80%, so we enter .8 for the area along with 0 for the mean and 1 for the standard deviation. The value of z, rounded to two decimal places, is $z = 0.84$. See Figure 16.

```
invNorm(.121, 0, 1)
                 -1.170002407
invNorm(.8, 0, 1)
                  .8416212335
```

FIGURE 16

Method 3
Spreadsheet

Microsoft Excel can also be used to generate the answers to parts (a) and (b) of this example. In any cell, type "=NORMINV(.121,0,1)" and press Enter. The value of -1.170002408 is returned. Similarly, by typing "=NORMINV(.8,0,1)" and pressing Enter, we find that the corresponding z value is 0.841621234.

YOUR TURN 2 Find a value of z satisfying the following conditions. **(a)** 2.5% of the area is to the left of z. **(b)** 20.9% of the area is to the right of z

TRY YOUR TURN 2

The key to using the normal table to find areas under *any* normal curve is to express each number x on the horizontal axis in terms of standard deviation above or below the mean. The **z-score** for x is the number of standard deviations that x lies from the mean (positive if x is above the mean, negative if x is below the mean).

EXAMPLE 3 z-Scores

If a normal distribution has mean 50 and standard deviation 4, find the following z-scores.

(a) The z-score for $x = 46$

SOLUTION Since 46 is 4 units below 50 and the standard deviation is 4, 46 is 1 standard deviation below the mean. So, its z-score is -1.

YOUR TURN 3 Find the z-score for $x = 20$ if a normal distribution has a mean 35 and standard deviation 20.

(b) The z-score for $x = 60$

SOLUTION The z-score is 2.5 because 60 is 10 units above the mean (since $60 - 50 = 10$), and 10 units is 2.5 standard deviations (since $10/4 = 2.5$).

TRY YOUR TURN 3

In Example 3(b), we found the z-score by taking the difference between 60 and the mean and dividing this difference by the standard deviation. The same procedure works in the general case.

z-Score

If a normal distribution has mean μ and standard deviation σ, then the z-score for the number x is

$$z = \frac{x - \mu}{\sigma}.$$

The importance of z-scores lies in the following fact.

Area Under a Normal Curve

The area under a normal curve between $x = a$ and $x = b$ is the same as the area under the standard normal curve between the z-score for a and the z-score for b.

Therefore, by converting to z-scores and using the table for the standard normal curve, we can find areas under any normal curve. Since these areas are probabilities, we can now handle a variety of applications.

EXAMPLE 4 Sales

Dixie Office Supplies finds that its sales force drives an average of 1200 miles per month per person, with a standard deviation of 150 miles. Assume that the number of miles driven by a salesperson is closely approximated by a normal distribution.

APPLY IT

Method 1
Using a Table

(a) Find the probability that a salesperson drives more than 1375 miles per month.

SOLUTION Here $\mu = 1200$ and $\sigma = 150$, and we must find the area under the normal distribution more than, or to the right of, $x = 1375$. We begin by finding the z-score corresponding to $x = 1375$.

$$z = \frac{x - \mu}{\sigma} = \frac{1375 - 1200}{150} = \frac{175}{150} \approx 1.17$$

From the table, the area to the left of $z = 1.17$ is 0.8790, so the area to the right is

$$1 - 0.8790 = 0.1210.$$

Therefore, the probability that a salesperson drives more than 1375 miles per month is 0.1210. See Figure 17.

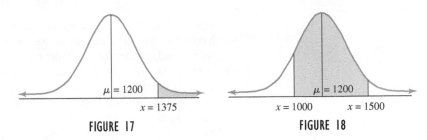

FIGURE 17   FIGURE 18

(b) Find the probability that a salesperson drives between 1000 miles and 1500 miles per month.

SOLUTION   As shown in Figure 18, z-scores for both $x_1 = 1000$ and $x_2 = 1500$ are needed.

For $x_1 = 1000,$ For $x_2 = 1500,$

$$z_1 = \frac{1000 - 1200}{150} \qquad z_2 = \frac{1500 - 1200}{150}$$

$$= \frac{-200}{150} \qquad\qquad = \frac{300}{150}$$

$$z_1 \approx -1.33. \qquad\qquad z_2 = 2.00.$$

From the table, $z_1 = -1.33$ leads to an area of 0.0918, while $z_2 = 2.00$ corresponds to 0.9772. A total of $0.9772 - 0.0918 = 0.8854$, or 88.54%, of the drivers travel between 1000 and 1500 miles per month. The probability that a driver travels between 1000 miles and 1500 miles per month is 0.8854.

(c) Find the shortest and longest distances driven by the middle 95% of the sales force.

SOLUTION   Notice that in parts (a) and (b) we were given different traveling distances and we were asked to find the corresponding probability (or area under the curve). In this part, we are given the probability (or area under the curve) and we are asked to find the distances that bound this area.

First, find the values of z that bound the middle 95% of the data. As Figure 19 illustrates, the lower z value, z_1, has 2.5% of the area to its left, and the higher z value, z_2, has 97.5% of the area to its left. Using the table backwards, we find that $z_1 = -1.96$ and $z_2 = 1.96$.

The shortest distance is, therefore, 1.96 standard deviations *below* the mean, or

$$\text{Shortest} = \mu + z \cdot \sigma = 1200 + (-1.96) \cdot (150) = 906 \text{ miles.}$$

Likewise, the longest distance is 1.96 standard deviations *above* the mean, or

$$\text{Longest} = \mu + z \cdot \sigma = 1200 + (1.96) \cdot (150) = 1494 \text{ miles.}$$

Therefore, the distances driven by the middle 95% of the sales force are between 906 and 1494 miles.

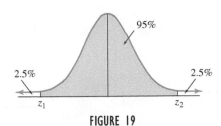

FIGURE 19

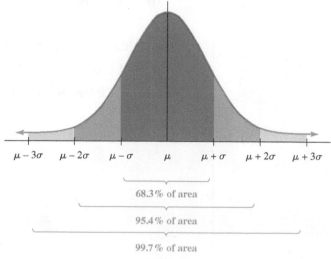

Method 2
Graphing Calculator

Graphing calculators and computers can be used to solve Example 4. Because you can enter the mean and standard deviation for any normal curve, it is not necessary to first calculate the z-score.

In part (a), to find the probability that a salesperson drives more than 1375 miles per month on the TI-84 Plus C calculator, we use the `normalcdf` command. We enter 1375 for the lower bound, 1EE99 for the upper bound, 1200 for the mean, and 150 for the standard deviation. The answer, rounded to four decimal places, is 0.1217. This is more accurate than the value of 0.1210 found using the normal curve table, which required rounding the z-score to two decimal places. See Figure 20.

In part (b), the probability that a salesperson drives between 1000 and 1500 miles per month can be found by entering the following command: `normalcdf(1000,1500,1200,150)`. As shown in Figure 20, the answer, rounded to four decimal places, is 0.8860.

In part (c), to find the shortest distance and the longest distance driven that correspond with the middle 95% of the sales force, we use the `invNorm` command. The shortest distance would have 2.5% of the area to its left, so the command would be `invNorm(.025,1200,150)`. The longest distance would have 2.5% of the area to its right, and therefore 97.5% of the area to its left. The command would be `invNorm(.975,1200,150)`. As Figure 20 shows, the distances driven by the middle 95% of the sales force are between 906 miles and 1494 miles.

```
normalcdf(1375,-1E99,1200,▶
                 .1213725608
normalcdf(1000,1500,1200, ▶
                 .8860386561
invNorm(.025, 1200, 150)
                 906.0054021
invNorm(.975, 1200, 150)
                 1493.994598
```

FIGURE 20

YOUR TURN 4 For Example 4, find the probability that a salesperson drives between 1275 and 1425 miles.

TRY YOUR TURN 4

As mentioned above, z-scores are the number of standard deviations from the mean, so $z = 1$ corresponds to 1 standard deviation above the mean, and so on. Looking up $z = 1.00$ and $z = -1.00$ in the table shows that

$$0.8413 - 0.1587 = 0.6826,$$

or 68.3% of the area under a normal curve lies within 1 standard deviation of the mean. Also, looking up $z = 2.00$ and $z = -2.00$ shows that

$$0.9772 - 0.0228 = 0.9544,$$

or 95.4% of the area lies within 2 standard deviations of the mean. These results, summarized in Figure 21, can be used to get a quick estimate of results when working with normal curves.

NOTE
The answers given to the exercises in this text are found using a graphing calculator. If you use the normal curve table or a computer program, your answers may differ slightly.

$\mu - 3\sigma$ $\quad$ $\mu - 2\sigma$ $\quad$ $\mu - \sigma$ $\quad$ μ $\quad$ $\mu + \sigma$ $\quad$ $\mu + 2\sigma$ $\quad$ $\mu + 3\sigma$

68.3% of area

95.4% of area

99.7% of area

FIGURE 21

9.3 EXERCISES

1. The peak in a normal curve occurs directly above _____.

2. The total area under a normal curve (above the horizontal axis) is _____.

3. How are z-scores found for normal distributions where $\mu \neq 0$ or $\sigma \neq 1$?

4. How is the standard normal curve used to find probabilities for normal distributions?

Find the percent of the area under a normal curve between the mean and the given number of standard deviations from the mean.

5. 1.70

6. 0.93

7. −2.31

8. −1.45

Find the percent of the total area under the standard normal curve between each pair of z-scores.

9. $z = 0.32$ and $z = 3.18$

10. $z = 0.99$ and $z = 2.37$

11. $z = -1.83$ and $z = -0.91$

12. $z = -3.13$ and $z = -2.65$

13. $z = -2.95$ and $z = 2.03$

14. $z = -0.15$ and $z = 0.23$

Find a z-score satisfying the following conditions.

15. 5% of the total area is to the left of z.

16. 1% of the total area is to the left of z.

17. 10% of the total area is to the right of z.

18. 25% of the total area is to the right of z.

19. For any normal distribution, what is the value of $P(x \leq \mu)$? $P(x \geq \mu)$?

20. Compare the probability that a number will lie within 2 standard deviations of the mean of a probability distribution using Chebyshev's theorem and using the normal distribution. (See Exercises 13–20, Section 9.2.) Explain what you observe.

21. Repeat Exercise 20 using 3 standard deviations.

APPLICATIONS

In all of the following applications, assume the distributions are normal. In each case, you should consider whether this is reasonable.

Business and Economics

Life of Light Bulbs   A certain type of light bulb has an average life of 500 hours, with a standard deviation of 100 hours. The length of life of the bulb can be closely approximated by a normal curve. An amusement park buys and installs 10,000 such bulbs. Find the total number that can be expected to last for each period of time.

22. At least 500 hours

23. Less than 500 hours

24. Between 680 and 780 hours

25. Between 350 and 550 hours

26. Less than 770 hours

27. More than 440 hours

28. Find the shortest and longest lengths of life for the middle 60% of the bulbs.

Quality Control   A box of oatmeal must contain 16 oz. The machine that fills the oatmeal boxes is set so that, on the average, a box contains 16.5 oz. The boxes filled by the machine have weights that can be closely approximated by a normal curve. What fraction of the boxes filled by the machine are underweight if the standard deviation is as follows?

29. 0.5 oz

30. 0.3 oz

31. 0.2 oz

32. 0.1 oz

Quality Control   The chickens at Colonel Thompson's Ranch have a mean weight of 1850 g, with a standard deviation of 150 g. The weights of the chickens are closely approximated by a normal curve. Find the percent of all chickens having weights in the following ranges.

33. More than 1700 g

34. Less than 1950 g

35. Between 1750 and 1900 g

36. Between 1600 and 2000 g

37. More than 2100 g or less than 1550 g

38. Find the smallest and largest weights for the middle 95% of the chickens.

39. Annual Bonuses   Salespeople of a large corporation received an annual bonus based upon their sales performance. The size of the bonuses was normally distributed with a mean of $12,000 and a standard deviation of $2500.

   (a) What percent of the salespeople received an annual bonus in excess of $10,000?

   (b) What percent of the salespeople received an annual bonus between $10,000 and $15,000?

   (c) What size bonus is exceeded by 75% of all other bonuses?

   (d) Find the smallest and largest amounts for the middle 75% of the annual bonuses.

40. Grocery Bills   At the Discount Market, the average weekly grocery bill is $74.50, with a standard deviation of $24.30.

   (a) What percent of the market's customers spend over $100?

   (b) What percent of the market's customers spend less than $50?

   (c) What percent of the market's customers spend between $0 and $50?

   (d) Based on your answers to parts (b) and (c), discuss whether the amounts that customers spend is likely to be normally distributed. Explain why this might be expected.

   (e) What are the smallest and largest amounts spent by the middle 50% of the market's customers?

41. Quality Control A machine that fills quart milk cartons is set up to average 32.2 oz per carton, with a standard deviation of 1.2 oz. What is the probability that a filled carton will contain less than 32 oz of milk?

42. Quality Control A machine produces bolts with an average diameter of 0.25 in. and a standard deviation of 0.02 in. What is the probability that a bolt will be produced with a diameter greater than 0.3 in.?

43. Grading Eggs To be graded extra large, an egg must weigh at least 2.2 oz. If the average weight for an egg is 1.5 oz, with a standard deviation of 0.4 oz, how many eggs in a sample of five dozen would you expect to grade extra large?

Life Sciences

44. Vitamin Requirements In nutrition, the Recommended Daily Allowance of vitamins is a number set by the government as a guide to an individual's daily vitamin intake. Actually, vitamin needs vary drastically from person to person, but the needs are very closely approximated by a normal curve. To calculate the Recommended Daily Allowance, the government first finds the average need for vitamins among people in the population and the standard deviation. The Recommended Daily Allowance is then defined as the mean plus 2.5 times the standard deviation. What percent of the population will receive adequate amounts of vitamins under this plan?

45. Life Spans According to actuarial tables, life spans in the United States are approximately normally distributed with a mean of about 75 years and a standard deviation of about 16 years. *Source: Psychological Science.*

(a) Find the probability that a randomly selected person lives less than 88 years.

(b) Find the probability that a randomly selected person lives more than 67 years.

46. Blood Clotting The mean clotting time of blood is 7.45 seconds, with a standard deviation of 3.6 seconds. What is the probability that an individual's blood clotting time will be less than 7 seconds or greater than 8 seconds?

Social Sciences

Speed Limits New studies by Federal Highway Administration traffic engineers suggest that speed limits on many thoroughfares are set arbitrarily and often are artificially low. According to traffic engineers, the ideal limit should be the "85th percentile speed." This means the speed at or below which 85 percent of the traffic moves. Assuming speeds are normally distributed, find the 85th percentile speed for roads with the following conditions. *Source: Federal Highway Administration.*

47. The mean speed is 52 mph with a standard deviation of 8 mph.

48. The mean speed is 30 mph with a standard deviation of 5 mph.

Education The grading system known as "grading on the curve" is based on the assumption that grades are often distributed according to the normal curve and that a certain percent of a class should receive each grade, regardless of the performance of the class as a whole. The following is how one professor might grade on the curve.

Grade	Total Points
A	Greater than $\mu + (3/2)\sigma$
B	$\mu + (1/2)\sigma$ to $\mu + (3/2)\sigma$
C	$\mu - (1/2)\sigma$ to $\mu + (1/2)\sigma$
D	$\mu - (3/2)\sigma$ to $\mu - (1/2)\sigma$
F	Below $\mu - (3/2)\sigma$

What percent of the students receive the following grades?

49. A   **50.** B   **51.** C

52. Do you think this system would be more likely to be fair in a large freshman class in psychology or in a graduate seminar of five students? Why?

Education A teacher gives a test to a large group of students. The results are closely approximated by a normal curve. The mean is 76, with a standard deviation of 8. The teacher wishes to give A's to the top 8% of the students and F's to the bottom 8%. A grade of B is given to the next 20%, with D's given similarly. All other students get C's. Find the bottom cutoff (rounded to the nearest whole number) for the following grades.

53. A   **54.** B

55. C   **56.** D

57. Standardized Tests David Rogosa, a professor of educational statistics at Stanford University, has calculated the accuracy of tests used in California to abolish social promotion. Dr. Rogosa has claimed that a fourth grader whose true reading score is exactly at reading level (50th percentile—half of all the students read worse and half read better than this student) has a 58% chance of scoring either above the 55th percentile or below the 45th percentile on any one test. Assume that the results of a given test are normally distributed with mean 0.50 and standard deviation 0.09. *Source: The New York Times.*

(a) Verify that Dr. Rogosa's claim is true.

(b) Find the probability that this student will not score between the 40th and 60th percentile.

(c) Using the results of parts (a) and (b), discuss problems with the use of standardized testing to prevent social promotion.

General Interest

58. Christopher Columbus Before Christopher Columbus crossed the ocean, he measured the heights of the men on his three ships and found that they were normally distributed with a mean of 69.10 in. and a standard deviation of 3.50 in. What is the probability that a member of his crew had a height less than 65.46 in.? (The answer has another connection with Christopher Columbus!)

59. Lead Poisoning Historians and biographers have collected evidence that suggests that President Andrew Jackson suffered from lead poisoning. Recently, researchers measured the amount of lead in samples of Jackson's hair from 1815. The results of this experiment showed that Jackson had a mean lead level of 130.5 ppm. *Source: JAMA.*

(a) If levels of lead in hair samples from that time period follow a normal distribution with mean 93 and standard deviation 16, find the probability that a randomly selected person from this time period would have a lead level of 130.5 ppm or higher. Does this provide evidence that Jackson suffered from lead poisoning during this time period?* *Source: Science.*

(b) Today's typical lead levels follow a normal distribution with approximate mean 10 ppm and standard deviation 5 ppm. By these standards, calculate the probability that a randomly selected person from today would have a lead level of 130.5 or higher. (*Note:* These standards may not be valid for this experiment.) *Source: Clinical Chemistry.*

(c) Discuss whether we can conclude that Andrew Jackson suffered from lead poisoning.

60. Mercury Poisoning Historians and biographers have also collected evidence that suggests that President Andrew Jackson suffered from mercury poisoning. Recently, researchers measured the amount of mercury in samples of Jackson's hair from 1815. The results of this experiment showed that Jackson had a mean mercury level of 6.0 ppm. *Source: JAMA.*

(a) If levels of mercury in hair samples from that time period follow a normal distribution with mean 6.9 and standard deviation 4.6, find the probability that a randomly selected person from that time period would have a mercury level of 6.0 ppm or higher. *Source: Science of the Total Environment.*

(b) Discuss whether this provides evidence that Jackson suffered from mercury poisoning during this time period.

(c) Today's accepted normal mercury levels follow a normal distribution with approximate mean 0.6 ppm and standard deviation 0.3 ppm. By present standards, is it likely that a randomly selected person from today would have a mercury level of 6.0 ppm or higher?

(d) Discuss whether we can conclude that Andrew Jackson suffered from mercury poisoning.

61. Barbie The popularity and voluptuous shape of Barbie dolls have generated much discussion about the influence these dolls may have on young children, particularly with regard to normal body shape. In fact, many people have speculated as to what Barbie's measurements would be if they were scaled to a common human height. Researchers have done this and have compared Barbie's measurements to the average 18- to 35-year-old woman, labeled Reference, and with the average model. The table at the top of the next column illustrates some of the results of their research, where each measurement is in centimeters. Assume that the distributions of measurements for the models and for the reference group follow a normal distribution with the given mean and standard deviation. *Source: Sex Roles.*

(a) Find the probability of Barbie's head size or larger occurring for the reference group and for the models.

(b) Find the probability of Barbie's neck size or smaller occurring for the reference group and for the models.

Measurement	Models Mean	Models s.d.	Reference Mean	Reference s.d.	Barbie
Head	50.0	2.4	55.3	2.0	55.0
Neck	31.0	1.0	32.7	1.4	23.9
Chest (bust)	87.4	3.0	90.3	5.5	82.3
Wrist	15.0	0.6	16.1	0.8	10.6
Waist	65.7	3.5	69.8	4.7	40.7

(c) Find the probability of Barbie's bust size or larger occurring for the reference group and for the models.

(d) Find the probability of Barbie's wrist size or smaller occurring for the reference group and for the models.

(e) Find the probability of Barbie's waist size or smaller occurring for the reference group and for the models.

(f) Compare the above values and discuss whether Barbie represents either the reference group or models. Any surprises?

62. Ken The same researchers from Exercise 61 wondered how the famous Ken doll measured up to average males and with Australian football players. The table below illustrates some of the results of their research, where each measurement is in centimeters. Assume that the distributions of measurements for the football players and for the reference group follow a normal distribution with the given mean and standard deviation. *Source: Sex Roles.*

Measurement	Football Mean	Football s.d.	Reference Mean	Reference s.d.	Ken
Head	52.1	2.3	53.7	2.9	53.0
Neck	34.6	1.8	34.2	1.9	32.1
Chest	92.3	3.5	91.2	4.8	75.0
Upper Arm	29.9	1.9	28.8	2.2	27.1
Waist	75.1	3.6	80.9	9.8	56.5

(a) Find the probability of Ken's head size or larger occurring for the reference group and for the football players.

(b) Find the probability of Ken's neck size or smaller occurring for the reference group and for the football players.

(c) Find the probability of Ken's chest size or smaller occurring for the reference group and for the football players.

(d) Find the probability of Ken's upper arm size or smaller occurring for the reference group and for the football players.

(e) Find the probability of Ken's waist size or smaller occurring for the reference group and for the football players.

(f) Compare the above values and discuss whether Ken's measurements are representative of either the reference group or football players. Then compare these results with the results of Exercise 61. Any surprises?

*Although this provides evidence that Andrew Jackson had elevated lead levels, the authors of the paper concluded that Andrew Jackson did not die of lead poisoning.

YOUR TURN ANSWERS
1. (a) 0.2236 **(b)** 0.9131 **(c)** 0.7970
2. (a) −1.96 **(b)** 0.81 **3.** −0.75 **4.** 0.2417

9.4 Normal Approximation to the Binomial Distribution

APPLY IT · What is the probability that at least 40 out of 100 drivers exceed the speed limit by at least 20 mph in Atlanta?
This is a binomial probability problem with a large number of trials (100). In this section we will see how the normal curve can be used to approximate the binomial distribution, allowing us to answer this question in Example 4.

As we saw in Section 8.4 on Binomial Probability, many practical experiments have only two possible outcomes, sometimes referred to as success or failure. Such experiments are called Bernoulli trials or Bernoulli processes. Examples of Bernoulli trials include flipping a coin (with heads being a success, for instance, and tails a failure) or testing a computer chip coming off the assembly line to see whether or not it is defective. A binomial experiment consists of repeated independent Bernoulli trials, such as flipping a coin 10 times or taking a random sample of 20 computer chips from the assembly line. In Section 8.5 on Probability Distributions and Expected Value, we found the probability distribution for several binomial experiments, such as sampling five people with bachelor's degrees in education and counting how many are women. The probability distribution for a binomial experiment is known as a **binomial distribution**.

EXAMPLE 1 Speeding

It was reported in a recent study that 40% of drivers in Atlanta exceed the speed limit by at least 20 mph. *Source: Laser Atlanta.*

(a) Suppose a state trooper wants to verify this statistic and records the speed of 10 randomly selected drivers. The trooper finds that 5 out of 10, or 50%, exceed the speed limit by at least 20 mph. How likely is this if the 40% figure is accurate?

SOLUTION We can answer this question with the binomial probability formula from the previous chapter:

$$C(n, x) \cdot p^x \cdot (1 - p)^{n-x},$$

where n is the size of the sample (10 in this case), x is the number of speeders (5 in this example), and p is the probability that a driver is a speeder (0.40). This gives

$$P(x = 5) = C(10, 5) \cdot 0.40^5 \cdot (1 - 0.40)^5$$
$$= 252(0.01024)(0.07776) \approx 0.2007.$$

The probability is about 20%, so this result is not unusual.

(b) Suppose that the state trooper takes a larger random sample of 100 drivers. What is the probability that 50 or more drivers speed if the 40% figure is accurate?

SOLUTION Calculating $P(x = 50) + P(x = 51) + \cdots + P(x = 100)$ is a formidable task. One solution is provided by graphing calculators or computers. On the TI-84 Plus C, for example, we can first calculate the probability that 49 or fewer drivers exceed the speed limit using the DISTR menu command `binomcdf(100,.40,49)`. Subtracting the answer from 1 gives a probability of 0.0271. ∎

As we saw in Example 1(b), calculators and computers can be used to compute a binomial probability with just a few keystrokes. But this high-tech method fails as n becomes

┌FOR REVIEW─────
Recall from Chapter 8 that the symbol $C(n, r)$ is defined as
$\dfrac{n!}{r!(n - r)!}$. For example,

$C(10, 5) = \dfrac{10!}{5!\,5!}$

$= \dfrac{10 \cdot 9 \cdot 8 \cdot 7 \cdot 6}{5 \cdot 4 \cdot 3 \cdot 2 \cdot 1} = 252.$

larger; the command `binomcdf(1000000,.40,50000)` gives an error message. On the other hand, there is a low-tech method that works regardless of the size of n. It has further interest because it connects two different distributions: the normal and the binomial. The normal distribution is continuous, since the random variable can take on any real number. The binomial distribution is *discrete*, because the random variable can only take on integer values between 0 and n. Nevertheless, the normal distribution can be used to give a good approximation to binomial probability.

In order to use the normal approximation, we first need to know the mean and standard deviation of the binomial distribution. Recall from Section 8.5 that for the binomial distribution, $E(x) = np$. In Section 9.1, we referred to $E(x)$ as μ, and that notation will be used here. It is shown in more advanced courses in statistics that the standard deviation of the binomial distribution is given by $\sigma = \sqrt{np(1-p)}$.

Mean and Standard Deviation for the Binomial Distribution

For the binomial distribution, the mean and standard deviation are given by

$$\mu = np \quad \text{and} \quad \sigma = \sqrt{np(1-p)},$$

where n is the number of trials and p is the probability of success on a single trial.

EXAMPLE 2   Coin Flip

Suppose a fair coin is flipped 15 times.

(a) Find the mean and standard deviation for the number of heads.

SOLUTION   Using $n = 15$ and $p = 1/2$, the mean is

$$\mu = np = 15\left(\frac{1}{2}\right) = 7.5.$$

The standard deviation is

$$\sigma = \sqrt{np(1-p)} = \sqrt{15\left(\frac{1}{2}\right)\left(1 - \frac{1}{2}\right)}$$

$$= \sqrt{15\left(\frac{1}{2}\right)\left(\frac{1}{2}\right)} = \sqrt{3.75} \approx 1.94.$$

We expect, on average, to get 7.5 heads out of 15 tosses. Most of the time, the number of heads will be within 3 standard deviations of the mean, or between $7.5 - 3(1.94) = 1.68$ and $7.5 + 3(1.94) = 13.32$.

(b) Find the probability distribution for the number of heads, and draw a histogram of the probabilities.

SOLUTION   The probability distribution is found by putting $n = 15$ and $p = 1/2$ into the formula for binomial probability. For example, the probability of 9 heads is given by

$$P(x = 9) = C(15, 9)\left(\frac{1}{2}\right)^9\left(1 - \frac{1}{2}\right)^6 \approx 0.15274.$$

Probabilities for the other values of x between 0 and 15, as well as a histogram of the probabilities, are shown in the table and in Figure 22 on the next page.

TRY YOUR TURN 1

YOUR TURN 1 Suppose a die is rolled 12 times. Find the mean and standard deviation of the number of sixes rolled.

Probability Distribution for Number of Heads	
x	$P(x)$
0	0.00003
1	0.00046
2	0.00320
3	0.01389
4	0.04166
5	0.09164
6	0.15274
7	0.19638
8	0.19638
9	0.15274
10	0.09164
11	0.04166
12	0.01389
13	0.00320
14	0.00046
15	0.00003

FIGURE 22

In Figure 22, we have superimposed the normal curve with $\mu = 7.5$ and $\sigma = 1.94$ over the histogram of the distribution. Notice how well the normal distribution fits the binomial distribution. This approximation was first discovered in 1733 by Abraham De Moivre (1667–1754) for the case $p = 1/2$. The result was generalized by the French mathematician Pierre-Simon Laplace (1749–1827) in a book published in 1812.* As n becomes larger and larger, a histogram for the binomial distribution looks more and more like a normal curve. Histograms of the binomial distribution with $p = 0.3$, using $n = 8$ and $n = 50$ are shown in Figures 23(a) and (b), respectively.

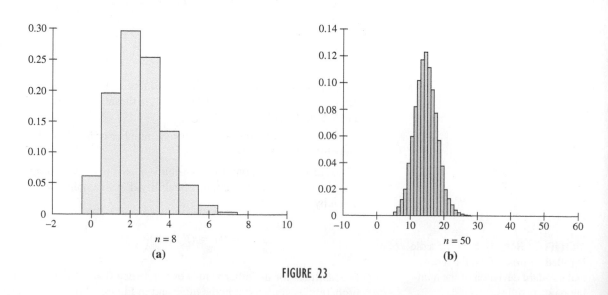

$n = 8$

(a)

$n = 50$

(b)

FIGURE 23

*Laplace's generalization, known as the Central Limit theorem, states that the distribution of the sample mean from *any* distribution approaches the normal distribution as the sample size increases. For more details, see any statistics book, such as *Elementary Statistics* (12th ed.) by Mario F. Triola, Pearson, 2014.

EXAMPLE 3 **Normal Distribution Approximation to the Binomial**

A coin is flipped 15 times. Use the normal distribution to approximate the probability of getting exactly 9 heads in 15 tosses.

SOLUTION

Method 1
Using a Table

From Example 2(b), the probability of getting exactly 9 heads in 15 tosses, or 0.15274, is the same as the area of the bar in blue in Figure 22. As the graph suggests, the area in blue is approximately equal to the area under the normal curve from $x = 8.5$ to $x = 9.5$. The normal curve is higher than the top of the bar in the left half but lower in the right half.

To find the area under the normal curve from $x = 8.5$ to $x = 9.5$, first find z-scores, as in the previous section. The mean and the standard deviation for the distribution, which we calculated in Example 2(a), are $\mu = 7.5$ and $\sigma = 1.94$.

$$\text{For } x_1 = 8.5, \qquad\qquad \text{For } x_2 = 9.5,$$
$$z_1 = \frac{8.5 - 7.5}{1.94} \qquad\qquad z_2 = \frac{9.5 - 7.5}{1.94}$$
$$= \frac{1.00}{1.94} \qquad\qquad = \frac{2.00}{1.94}$$
$$z_1 \approx 0.52. \qquad\qquad z_2 \approx 1.03.$$

From the normal curve table in the Appendix, $z_1 = 0.52$ gives an area of 0.6985, and $z_2 = 1.03$ gives 0.8485. The difference between these two numbers is the desired result.

$$P(z \le 1.03) - P(z \le 0.52) = 0.8485 - 0.6985 = 0.1500$$

This answer (0.1500) is not far from the more accurate answer of 0.15274 found in Example 2(b).

Method 2
Graphing Calculator

The TI-84 Plus C calculator can be used to find the normal approximation to the binomial. We use the `normalcdf` command, and enter 8.5 for the lower bound, 9.5 for the upper bound, 7.5 for the mean, and $\sqrt{3.75}$ for the standard deviation. The answer, 0.1519, is an even closer approximation to 0.15274 found in Example 2(b) than the answer using Method 1.

YOUR TURN 2 Use the normal distribution to approximate the probability of getting at most 10 heads in 15 tosses of a coin.

TRY YOUR TURN 2

CAUTION The normal curve approximation to a binomial distribution is quite accurate *provided that n is large and p is not close to 0 or 1.* As a rule of thumb, the normal curve approximation can be used as long as both np and $n(1 - p)$ are at least 5.

EXAMPLE 4 **Speeding**

Consider the random sample discussed in Example 1 of 100 drivers in Atlanta, where 40% of the drivers exceed the speed limit by at least 20 mph.

(a) Use the normal distribution to approximate the probability that at least 50 drivers exceed the speed limit.

APPLY IT

SOLUTION First find the mean and the standard deviation using $n = 100$ and $p = 0.40$.

$$\mu = 100(0.40) \qquad \sigma = \sqrt{100(0.40)(1 - 0.40)}$$
$$= 40 \qquad\qquad = \sqrt{100(0.40)(0.60)}$$
$$= \sqrt{24} \approx 4.899$$

As the graph in Figure 24 on the next page shows, we need to find the area to the right of $x = 49.5$ (since we want 50 or more speeders). The z-score corresponding to $x = 49.5$ is

$$z = \frac{49.5 - 40}{4.899} \approx 1.94.$$

From the table, $z = 1.94$ leads to an area of 0.9738, so

$$P(z > 1.94) = 1 - 0.9738 = 0.0262.$$

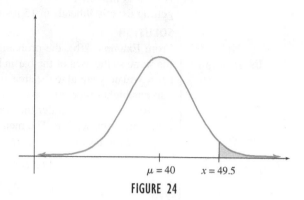

FIGURE 24

This value is close to the value of 0.0271 found earlier with the help of a graphing calculator. Either method tells us there is roughly a 3% chance of finding 50 or more speeders out of a random sample of 100. If the trooper found 50 or more speeders in his sample, he might suspect that either his sample is not truly random, or that the 40% figure for the percent of drivers who speed is too low.

(b) Find the probability of finding between 42 and 48 speeders in a random sample of 100.

SOLUTION As Figure 25 shows, we need to find the area between $x_1 = 41.5$ and $x_2 = 48.5$.

$$\text{If } x_1 = 41.5, \text{ then } z_1 = \frac{41.5 - 40}{4.899} \approx 0.31.$$

$$\text{If } x_2 = 48.5, \text{ then } z_2 = \frac{48.5 - 40}{4.899} \approx 1.74.$$

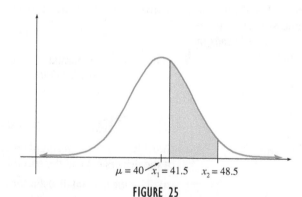

FIGURE 25

YOUR TURN 3 Suppose that a test consists of 120 multiple choice questions, each with 5 answers from which to choose. Use the normal distribution to find the probability that if you guess at random, you get at least 32 correct.

Use the table to find that $z_1 = 0.31$ gives an area of 0.6217, and $z_2 = 1.74$ yields 0.9591. The final answer is the difference of these numbers, or

$$P(0.31 \le z \le 1.74) = P(z \le 1.74) - P(z \le 0.31)$$
$$= 0.9591 - 0.6217 = 0.3374.$$

The probability of finding between 42 and 48 speeders is about 0.3374. Alternatively, the command `normalcdf` (41.5, 48.5, 40, 4.899) gives 0.3384. This is close to the value of 0.3352 found using the `binomcdf` command on a TI-84 Plus C.

TRY YOUR TURN 3 ▬

9.4 EXERCISES*

1. What must be known to find the mean and standard deviation of a binomial distribution?

2. What is the rule of thumb for using the normal distribution to approximate a binomial distribution?

Suppose 16 coins are tossed. Find the probability of getting the following results (a) using the binomial probability formula and (b) using the normal curve approximation.

3. Exactly 4 heads

4. Exactly 10 heads

5. More than 12 tails

6. Fewer than 5 tails

For the remaining exercises in this section, use the normal curve approximation to the binomial distribution.

Suppose 1000 coins are tossed. Find the probability of getting the following results.

7. Exactly 500 heads

8. Exactly 510 heads

9. 475 heads or more

10. Fewer than 490 tails

A die is tossed 120 times. Find the probability of getting the following results.

11. Exactly twenty 5's

12. Exactly twenty-four 6's

13. More than fifteen 3's

14. Fewer than twenty-eight 6's

15. A reader asked Mr. Statistics (a feature in *Fortune* magazine) about the game of 26 once played in the bars of Chicago. The player chooses a number between 1 and 6 and then rolls a cup full of 10 dice 13 times. Out of the 130 numbers rolled, if the number chosen appears at least 26 times, the player wins. Calculate the probability of winning. *Source: Fortune.*

16. (a) Try to use both the binomial probability formula and the normal approximation to the binomial to calculate the probability that exactly half of the coins come up heads if the following number of coins are flipped. You may run into problems using the binomial probability formula for part (iii).

  (i) 10   **(ii)** 100   **(iii)** 1000

(b) If you ran into problems using the binomial probability formula for part (iii), tell what happened and explain why it happened.

(c) Someone might speculate that with more coins, the probability that exactly half are heads goes up with the number of coin flips. Based on the results from part (a), does this happen? Explain the error in the speculation.

APPLICATIONS

Business and Economics

17. Quality Control Two percent of the quartz heaters produced in a certain plant are defective. Suppose the plant produced 10,000 such heaters last month. Find the probabilities that among these heaters, the following numbers were defective.

  (a) Fewer than 170   **(b)** More than 222

18. Quality Control The probability that a certain machine turns out a defective item is 0.05. Find the probabilities that in a run of 75 items, the following results are obtained.

  (a) Exactly 5 defectives

  (b) No defectives

  (c) At least 1 defective

19. Survey Results A company is taking a survey to find out if people like its product. Their last survey indicated that 70% of the population like the product. Based on that, of a sample of 58 people, find the probabilities of the following.

  (a) All 58 like the product.

  (b) From 28 to 30 (inclusive) like the product.

20. Minimum Wage A recent study of minimum wage earners found that 50.6% of them are 16 to 24 years old. Suppose a random sample of 600 minimum wage earners is selected. What is the probability that more than 330 of them are 16 to 24 years old? *Source: Bureau of Labor Statistics.*

Life Sciences

21. Nest Predation For certain bird species, with appropriate assumptions, the number of nests escaping predation has a binomial distribution. Suppose the probability of success (that is, a nest escaping predation) is 0.3. Find the probability that at least half of 24 nests escape predation. *Source: The American Naturalist.*

*The normal distribution approximations of the binomial in the exercises were calculated with a graphing calculator and rounded to four decimal places. If the approximation value is found from the normal tables, the answer may be slightly different.

22. Food Consumption Under certain appropriate assumptions, the probability of a competing young animal eating x units of food is binomially distributed, with n equal to the maximum number of food units the animal can acquire and p equal to the probability per time unit that an animal eats a unit of food. Suppose $n = 120$ and $p = 0.6$. *Source: The American Naturalist.*

(a) Find the probability that an animal consumes exactly 80 units of food.

(b) Suppose the animal must consume at least 70 units of food to survive. What is the probability that this happens?

23. Coconuts A 4-year review of trauma admissions to the Provincial Hospital, Alotau, Milne Bay Providence, reveals that 2.5% of such admissions were due to being struck by falling coconuts. *Source: The Journal of Trauma.*

(a) Suppose 20 patients are admitted to the hospital during a certain time period. What is the probability that no more than 1 of these patients are there because they were struck by falling coconuts? Do not use the normal distribution here.

(b) Suppose 2000 patients are admitted to the hospital during a longer time period. What is the approximate probability that no more than 70 of these patients are there because they were struck by falling coconuts?

24. Drug Effectiveness A new drug cures 80% of the patients to whom it is administered. It is given to 25 patients. Find the probabilities that among these patients, the following results occur.

(a) Exactly 20 are cured.

(b) All are cured.

(c) No one is cured.

(d) Twelve or fewer are cured.

25. Flu Inoculations A flu vaccine has a probability of 80% of preventing a person who is inoculated from getting the flu. A county health office inoculates 134 people. Find the probabilities of the following.

(a) Exactly 10 of the people inoculated get the flu.

(b) No more than 10 of the people inoculated get the flu.

(c) None of the people inoculated get the flu.

26. Blood Types The blood types B− and AB− are the rarest of the eight human blood types, representing 1.5% and 0.6% of the population, respectively. *Source: The Handy Science Answer Book.*

(a) If the blood types of a random sample of 1000 blood donors are recorded, what is the probability that 10 or more of the samples are AB−?

(b) If the blood types of a random sample of 1000 blood donors are recorded, what is the probability that 20 to 40 inclusive of the samples are B−?

(c) If a particular city had a blood drive in which 500 people gave blood and 3% of the donations were B−, would we have reason to believe that this town has a higher than normal number of donors who are B−? (*Hint:* Calculate the probability of 15 or more donors being B− for a random sample of 500 and then discuss the probability obtained.)

27. Motorcycles According to a recent report, 24.1% of nonfatal injuries suffered by motorcycle riders occur between 3 P.M. and 6 P.M. If 200 injured motorcyclists are surveyed, what is the probability that at most 50 were injured between 3 P.M. and 6 P.M.? *Source: Insurance Information Institute.*

Social Sciences

28. Straw Votes In one state, 55% of the voters expect to vote for Nicole Foran. Suppose 1400 people are asked the name of the person for whom they expect to vote. Find the probability that at least 750 people will say that they expect to vote for Foran.

29. Smoking A recent study found that 46.3% of all ninth grade students in the United States have tried cigarette smoking, even if only one or two puffs. If 500 ninth grade students are surveyed, what is the probability that at most half have ever tried cigarettes? *Source: Centers for Disease Control and Prevention.*

30. Weapons and Youth A recent study found that 17.5% of all high school students in the United States have carried a weapon, including a gun, knife, or club. If 1200 high school students are surveyed, what is the probability that more than 200 students, but fewer than 250, have carried a weapon? *Source: Centers for Disease Control and Prevention.*

31. Election 2000 The Florida recount in the 2000 presidential election gave George W. Bush 2,912,790 votes and Al Gore 2,912,253 votes. What is the likelihood of the vote being so close, even if the electorate is evenly divided? Assume that the number of votes for Bush is binomially distributed with $n = 5,825,043$ (the sum of the votes for the two candidates) and $p = 0.5$. *Source: historycentral.com.*

(a) Using the binomial probability feature on a graphing calculator, try to calculate $P(2,912,253 \leq X \leq 2,912,790)$. What happens?

(b) Use the normal approximation to calculate the probability in part (a).

General Interest

32. Homework Only 1 out of 12 American parents requires that children do their homework before watching TV. If your neighborhood is typical, what is the probability that out of 120 parents, 5 or fewer require their children to do homework before watching TV? *Source: Harper's.*

33. True-False Test A professor gives a test with 100 true-false questions. If 60 or more correct is necessary to pass, what is the probability that a student will pass by random guessing?

34. Hole in One In the 1989 U.S. Open, four golfers each made a hole in one on the same par-3 hole on the same day. *Sports Illustrated* writer R. Reilly stated the probability of a hole in one for a given golf pro on a given par-3 hole to be 1/3709. *Source: Sports Illustrated.*

(a) For a specific par-3 hole, use the binomial distribution to find the probability that 4 or more of the 156 golf pros in the tournament field shoot a hole in one. *Source: School Science and Mathematics.*

(b) For a specific par-3 hole, use the normal approximation to the binomial distribution to find the probability that 4 or more of the 156 golf pros in the tournament field shoot a hole in one. Why must we be very cautious when using this approximation for this application?

(c) If the probability of a hole in one remains constant and is 1/3709 for any par-3 hole, find the probability that in 20,000 attempts by golf pros, there will be 4 or more hole in ones. Discuss whether this assumption is reasonable.

9 CHAPTER REVIEW

SUMMARY

In this chapter we introduced the field of statistics. Measures of central tendency, such as mean, median, and mode, were defined and illustrated by examples. We determined how much the numbers in a sample vary from the mean of a distribution by calculating the variance and standard deviation. The normal distribution, perhaps the most important and widely used probability distribution, was defined and used to study a wide range of problems. The normal approximation to the binomial distribution was then developed, as were several important applications.

Mean	The mean of the n numbers $x_1, x_2, x_3, \ldots, x_n$ is $$\bar{x} = \frac{\Sigma x}{n}.$$
Mean of a Grouped Distribution	The mean of a distribution, where x represents the midpoints, f the frequencies, and $n = \Sigma f$, is $$\bar{x} = \frac{\Sigma xf}{n}.$$
Variance	The variance of a sample of n numbers $x_1, x_2, x_3, \ldots, x_n$, with mean $\bar{x}$, is $$s^2 = \frac{\Sigma x^2 - n\bar{x}^2}{n-1}.$$
Standard Deviation	The standard deviation of a sample of n numbers $x_1, x_2, x_3, \ldots, x_n$, with mean $\bar{x}$, is $$s = \sqrt{\frac{\Sigma x^2 - n\bar{x}^2}{n-1}}.$$
Standard Deviation for a Grouped Distribution	The standard deviation for a distribution with mean $\bar{x}$, where x is an interval midpoint with frequency f, and $n = \Sigma f$, is $$s = \sqrt{\frac{\Sigma fx^2 - n\bar{x}^2}{n-1}}.$$
Normal Distribution	The area of the shaded region under a normal curve from a to b is the probability that an observed data value will be between a and b.
z-scores	If a normal distribution has mean μ and standard deviation σ, then the z-score for the number x is $$z = \frac{x - \mu}{\sigma}.$$
Area Under a Normal Curve	The area under a normal curve between $x = a$ and $x = b$ is the same as the area under the standard normal curve between the z-score for a and the z-score for b.
Mean and Standard Deviation for the Binomial Distribution	For the binomial distribution, the mean and standard deviation are given by $$\mu = np \quad \text{and} \quad \sigma = \sqrt{np(1-p)},$$ where n is the number of trials and p is the probability of success on a single trial.

KEY TERMS

9.1
random sample
grouped frequency distribution
frequency polygon
(arithmetic) mean
sample mean
population mean
median

mode
statistic

9.2
range
deviations from the mean
variance
standard deviation

sample variance
sample standard deviation
population variance
population standard deviation
Chebyshev's theorem

9.3
continuous distribution

skewed distribution
normal distribution
normal curve
standard normal curve
z-score

9.4
binomial distribution

REVIEW EXERCISES

CONCEPT CHECK

Determine whether each of the following statements is true or false, and explain why.

1. The mean, median, and mode of a normal distribution are all equal.

2. If the mean, median, and mode of a distribution are all equal, then the distribution must be a normal distribution.

3. If the means of two distributions are equal, then the variances must also be equal.

4. The sample mean $\bar{x}$ is not the same as the population mean μ.

5. A large variance indicates that the data are grouped closely together.

6. The mode of a distribution is the middle element of the distribution.

7. For a random variable X that is normally distributed, we know that $P(X \geq 2) = P(X \leq -2)$.

8. For a random variable X that is normally distributed with $\mu = 5$, we know that $P(X > 10) = P(X < 0)$.

9. The normal curve approximation to the binomial distribution should not be used on an experiment where $n = 30$ and $p = 0.1$.

10. The expected value of a sample mean is the population mean.

11. The expected value of a sample standard deviation is the population standard deviation.

12. For a standard normal random variable Z, $P(-1.5 < Z < 0) = 0.50 - P(Z > 1.5)$.

PRACTICE AND EXPLORATIONS

13. Discuss some reasons for organizing data into a grouped frequency distribution.

14. What is the rule of thumb for an appropriate interval in a grouped frequency distribution?

In Exercises 15 and 16, (a) write a frequency distribution, (b) draw a histogram, and (c) draw a frequency polygon.

15. The following numbers give the sales (in dollars) for the lunch hour at a local hamburger stand for the last 20 Fridays. Use intervals 450–474, 475–499, and so on.

| 480 | 451 | 501 | 478 | 512 | 473 | 509 | 515 | 458 | 566 |
| 516 | 535 | 492 | 558 | 488 | 547 | 461 | 475 | 492 | 471 |

16. The number of credits carried in one semester by students in a business mathematics class was as follows. Use intervals 9–10, 11–12, 13–14, 15–16.

| 10 | 9 | 16 | 12 | 13 | 15 | 13 | 16 | 15 | 11 | 13 |
| 12 | 12 | 15 | 12 | 14 | 10 | 12 | 14 | 15 | 15 | 13 |

Find the mean for the following.

17. 30, 24, 34, 30, 29, 28, 30, 29

18. 105, 108, 110, 115, 106, 110, 104, 113, 117

19.
Interval	Frequency
10–19	6
20–29	12
30–39	14
40–49	10
50–59	8

20.
Interval	Frequency
40–44	3
45–49	6
50–54	7
55–59	14
60–64	3
65–69	2

21. What do the mean, median, and mode of a distribution have in common? How do they differ? Describe each in a sentence or two.

Find the median and the mode (or modes) for each list of numbers.

22. 12, 17, 21, 23, 27, 27, 34

23. 38, 36, 42, 44, 38, 36, 48, 35

Find the modal class for the indicated distributions.

24. Exercise 20   **25.** Exercise 19

26. What is meant by the range of a distribution?

27. How are the variance and the standard deviation of a distribution related? What is measured by the standard deviation?

Find the range and standard deviation for each distribution.

28. 22, 27, 31, 35, 41

29. 26, 43, 51, 29, 37, 56, 29, 82, 74, 93

Find the standard deviation for the following.

30. Exercise 20   **31.** Exercise 19

32. Describe the characteristics of a normal distribution.

33. What is meant by a skewed distribution?

Find the following areas under the standard normal curve.

34. Between $z = 0$ and $z = 2.17$

35. To the left of $z = 0.84$

36. Between $z = -2.13$ and $z = 1.11$

37. Between $z = 1.53$ and $z = 2.82$

38. Find a z-score such that 7% of the area under the curve is to the right of z.

39. Why is the normal distribution not a good approximation of a binomial distribution that has a value of p close to 0 or 1?

40. Suppose a card is drawn at random from an ordinary deck 1,000,000 times with replacement.

   (a) What is the probability that between 249,500 and 251,000 hearts (inclusive) are drawn?

   (b) Why must the normal approximation to the binomial distribution be used to solve part (a)?

41. Suppose four coins are flipped and the number of heads counted. This experiment is repeated 20 times. The data might look something like the following. (You may wish to try this yourself and use your own results rather than these.)

Number of Heads	Frequency
0	1
1	5
2	7
3	5
4	2

   (a) Calculate the sample mean $\bar{x}$ and sample standard deviation s.

   (b) Calculate the population mean μ and population standard deviation σ for this binomial population.

   (c) Compare your answer to parts (a) and (b). What do you expect to happen?

42. Much of our work in Chapters 8 and 9 is interrelated. Note the similarities in the following parallel treatments of a frequency distribution and a probability distribution.

Frequency Distribution

Complete the table below for the following data. (Recall that x is the midpoint of the interval.)

14, 7, 1, 11, 2, 3, 11, 6, 10, 13, 11, 11, 16, 12, 9, 11, 9, 10, 7, 12, 9, 6, 4, 5, 9, 16, 12, 12, 11, 10, 14, 9, 13, 10, 15, 11, 11, 1, 12, 12, 6, 7, 8, 2, 9, 12, 10, 15, 9, 3

Interval	x	Tally	f	$x \cdot f$
1–3	2	$\cancel{||||}\,|$	6	12
4–6				
7–9				
10–12				
13–15				
16–18				

Probability Distribution

A binomial distribution has $n = 10$ and $p = 0.5$. Complete the following table.

x	$P(x)$	$x \cdot P(x)$
0	0.001	
1	0.010	
2	0.044	
3	0.117	
4		
5		
6		
7		
8		
9		
10		

   (a) Find the mean (or expected value) for each distribution.

   (b) Find the standard deviation for each distribution.

   (c) Use the normal approximation of the binomial probability distribution to find an interval centered on the mean that contains 95.44% of that distribution.

   (d) Why can't we use the normal distribution to answer probability questions about the frequency distribution?

APPLICATIONS

Business and Economics

43. Stock Returns The annual returns of two stocks for 3 years are given below.

Stock	2014	2015	2016
Stock I	11%	−1%	14%
Stock II	9%	5%	10%

(a) Find the mean and standard deviation for each stock over the 3-year period.

(b) If you are looking for security (hence, less variability) with an average 8% return, which of these stocks should you choose?

44. Quality Control A machine that fills quart orange juice cartons is set to fill them with 32.1 oz. If the actual contents of the cartons vary normally, with a standard deviation of 0.1 oz, what percentage of the cartons contain less than a quart (32 oz)?

45. Quality Control About 4% of the frankfurters produced by a certain machine are overstuffed and thus defective. For a sample of 500 frankfurters, find the following probabilities—first by using the binomial probability formula, and then by using the normal approximation.

(a) Twenty-five or fewer are overstuffed.

(b) Exactly 25 are overstuffed.

(c) At least 30 are overstuffed.

46. Bankruptcy The probability that a small business will go bankrupt in its first year is 0.21. For 50 such small businesses, find the following probabilities—first by using the binomial probability formula, and then by using the normal approximation.

(a) Exactly 8 go bankrupt.

(b) No more than 2 go bankrupt.

Life Sciences

47. Rat Diets The weight gains of 2 groups of 10 rats fed different experimental diets were as follows.

Diet	Weight Gains									
A	1	0	3	7	1	1	5	4	1	4
B	2	1	1	2	3	2	1	0	1	0

Compute the mean and standard deviation for each group.

(a) Which diet produced the greatest mean gain?

(b) Which diet produced the most consistent gain?

Chemical Effectiveness White flies are devastating California crops. An area infested with white flies is to be sprayed with a chemical that is known to be 98% effective for each application. Assume a sample of 1000 flies is checked.

48. Use the normal distribution to find the approximate probability that exactly 980 of the flies are killed in one application.

49. Use the normal distribution to find the approximate probability that no more than 986 of the flies are killed in one application.

50. Use the normal distribution to find the approximate probability that at least 975 of the flies are killed in one application.

51. Use the normal distribution to find the approximate probability that between 973 and 993 (inclusive) of the flies are killed in one application.

Social Sciences

Commuting Times The average resident of a certain East Coast suburb spends 42 minutes per day commuting, with a standard deviation of 12 minutes. Assume a normal distribution. Find the percent of all residents of this suburb who have the following commuting times.

52. At least 50 minutes per day

53. No more than 40 minutes per day

54. Between 32 and 40 minutes per day

55. Between 38 and 60 minutes per day

56. I.Q. Scores On standard IQ tests, the mean is 100, with a standard deviation of 15. The results are very close to fitting a normal curve. Suppose an IQ test is given to a very large group of people. Find the percent of those people whose IQ scores are as follows.

(a) More than 130   (b) Less than 85

(c) Between 85 and 115

General Interest

57. Olympics The number of countries participating in the Summer Olympics since 1960 is given in the following table. *Source: Sports Reference.*

Olympic City	Year	Number of Countries
Rome	1960	83
Tokyo	1964	93
Mexico City	1968	112
Munich	1972	121
Montreal	1976	92
Moscow	1980	80
Los Angeles	1984	140
Seoul	1988	159
Barcelona	1992	169
Atlanta	1996	197
Sydney	2000	200
Athens	2004	201
Beijing	2008	204
London	2012	205

(a) Find the mean, median, and mode of the data.

(b) Find the standard deviation of the data.

(c) What percent of the data is within 1 standard deviation of the mean?

(d) What percent of the data is within 2 standard deviations of the mean?

58. Broadway A survey was given to 313 performers appearing in 23 Broadway companies. The percentage of performers injured during practice or a performance was 55.5%. If a random sample of 500 Broadway performers is taken, use the normal approximation to the binomial distribution to find the approximate probability that more than 300 performers have been injured. *Source: American Journal of Public Health.*

59. Broadway In the survey described in Exercise 58, the demographics of the Broadway performers were recorded as shown in the next column. Assume that all of these demographics follow a normal distribution, an assumption that always must be verified prior to using it in real situations. *Source: American Journal of Public Health.*

   (a) Find the probability that a female dancer is 35 years old or older.

   (b) Find the probability that a male dancer is 35 years old or older.

   (c) Compare your answers to parts (a) and (b).

	Mean	Standard Deviation
Dancer's Age (female)	28.0	5.5
Dancer's Age (male)	32.2	8.4
Height (in m) (female)	1.64	0.08
Duration as Professional in yr (female)	11.0	8.9
Total No. of Injuries as Performer (female)	3.0	2.2

   (d) Find the probability that a female performer is 1.4 m tall or taller.

   (e) Find the probability that a female performer has a career duration that is more than 1.5 standard deviations from the mean.

   (f) Would a female who has more than 6 injuries during her career be considered a rare event? Explain.

EXTENDED APPLICATION

STATISTICS IN THE LAW—THE *CASTANEDA* DECISION

Statistical evidence is now routinely presented in both criminal and civil cases. In this application we'll look at a famous case that established use of the binomial distribution and measurement by standard deviation as an accepted procedure.*

Defendants who are convicted in criminal cases sometimes appeal their conviction on the grounds that the jury that indicted or convicted them was drawn from a pool of jurors that does not represent the population of the district in which they live. These appeals almost always cite the Supreme Court's decision in *Castaneda v. Partida* [430 U.S. 482], a case that dealt with the selection of grand juries in the state of Texas. The decision summarizes the facts this way:

> After respondent, a Mexican-American, had been convicted of a crime in a Texas District Court and had exhausted his state remedies on his claim of discrimination in the selection of the grand jury that had indicted him, he filed a habeas corpus petition in the Federal District Court, alleging a denial of due process and equal protection under the Fourteenth Amendment, because of gross underrepresentation of Mexican-Americans on the county grand juries.

The case went to the Appeals Court, which noted that "the county population was 79% Mexican-American, but, over an 11-year period, only 39% of those summoned for grand jury service were Mexican-American," and concluded that together with other testimony about the selection process, "the proof offered by respondent was sufficient to demonstrate a prima facie case of intentional discrimination in grand jury selection. . . ."

The state appealed to the Supreme Court, and the Supreme Court needed to decide whether the underrepresentation of Mexican Americans on grand juries was indeed too extreme to be an effect of chance. To do so, they invoked the binomial distribution. Here is the argument:

> Given that 79.1% of the population is Mexican-American, the expected number of Mexican-Americans among the 870 persons summoned to serve as grand jurors over the 11-year period is approximately 688. The observed number is 339. Of course, in any given drawing, some fluctuation from the expected number is predicted. The important point, however, is that the statistical model shows that the results of a random drawing are likely to fall in the vicinity of the expected value. . . .

*The *Castaneda* case and many other interesting applications of statistics in law are discussed in Finkelstein and Levin, *Statistics for Lawyers*, New York, Springer-Verlag, 1990. U.S. Supreme Court decisions are online at www.findlaw.com/casecode/supreme.html. In addition, most states now have important state court decisions online.

The measure of the predicted fluctuations from the expected value is the standard deviation, defined for the binomial distribution as the square root of the product of the total number in the sample (here 870) times the probability of selecting a Mexican-American (0.791) times the probability of selecting a non-Mexican-American (0.209) . . . . Thus, in this case the standard deviation is approximately 12. As a general rule for such large samples, if the difference between the expected value and the observed number is greater than two or three standard deviations, then the hypothesis that the jury drawing was random would be suspect to a social scientist. The 11-year data here reflect a difference between the expected and observed number of Mexican-Americans of approximately 29 standard deviations. A detailed calculation reveals that the likelihood that such a substantial departure from the expected value would occur by chance is less than 1 in 10^{140}.

The Court decided that the statistical evidence supported the conclusion that jurors were not randomly selected, and that it was up to the state to show that its selection process did not discriminate against Mexican-Americans. The Court concluded:

The proof offered by respondent was sufficient to demonstrate a prima facie case of discrimination in grand jury selection. Since the State failed to rebut the presumption of purposeful discrimination by competent testimony, despite two opportunities to do so, we affirm the Court of Appeals' holding of a denial of equal protection of the law in the grand jury selection process in respondent's case.

EXERCISES

1. Check the Court's calculation of 29 standard deviations as the difference between the expected number of Mexican-Americans and the number actually chosen.

2. Where do you think the Court's figure of 1 in 10^{140} came from?

3. The *Castaneda* decision also presents data from a $2\frac{1}{2}$-year period during which the State District Judge supervised the selection process. During this period, 220 persons were called to serve as grand jurors, and only 100 of these were Mexican-American.

   (a) Considering the 220 jurors as a random selection from a large population, what is the expected number of Mexican-Americans, using the 79.1% population figure?

   (b) If we model the drawing of jurors as a sequence of 220 independent Bernoulli trials, what is the standard deviation of the number of Mexican-Americans?

   (c) About how many standard deviations is the actual number of Mexican-Americans drawn (100) from the expected number that you calculated in part (a)?

   (d) What does the normal distribution tell you about the probability of this result?

4. The following information is from an appeal brought by Hy-Vee stores before the Iowa Supreme Court, appealing a ruling by the Iowa Civil Rights Commission in favor of a female employee of one of their grocery stores.

   In 1985, there were 112 managerial positions in the ten Hy-Vee stores located in Cedar Rapids. Only 6 of these managers were women. During that same year there were 294 employees; 206 were men and 88 were women.

   (a) How far from the expected number of women in management was the actual number, assuming that gender had nothing to do with promotion? Measure the difference in standard deviations.

   (b) Does this look like evidence of purposeful discrimination?

5. Go to the website WolframAlpha.com and enter "normal probability." Use the results to calculate the probability of being 12.3 standard deviations below the mean, as calculated in Exercise 3(c). Compare this result with the result using a graphing calculator and using Excel.

DIRECTIONS FOR GROUP PROJECT

Suppose that you and three other students are serving as interns at a prestigious law firm. One of the partners is interested in the use of probability in court cases and would like the four of you to prepare a brief on the Castaneda *decision. She insists that you describe the case and highlight the mathematics used in your brief. Be sure to use the results from the case along with the results of Exercises 1–3 in preparing your brief. Also, make recommendations of other types of cases in which probability may be used in law. Presentation software, such as Microsoft PowerPoint, should be used to present your brief to the partners of the firm.*

APPENDIX B

Tables

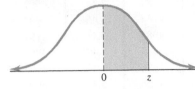

Table 2 Areas under the Normal Curve

The column under A gives the proportion of the area under the entire curve that is between $z = 0$ and a positive value of z.

z	A	z	A	z	A	z	A
.00	.0000	.48	.1844	.96	.3315	1.44	.4251
.01	.0040	.49	.1879	.97	.3340	1.45	.4265
.02	.0080	.50	.1915	.98	.3365	1.46	.4279
.03	.0120	.51	.1950	.99	.3389	1.47	.4292
.04	.0160	.52	.1985	1.00	.3413	1.48	.4306
.05	.0199	.53	.2019	1.01	.3438	1.49	.4319
.06	.0239	.54	.2054	1.02	.3461	1.50	.4332
.07	.0279	.55	.2088	1.03	.3485	1.51	.4345
.08	.0319	.56	.2123	1.04	.3508	1.52	.4357
.09	.0359	.57	.2157	1.05	.3531	1.53	.4370
.10	.0398	.58	.2190	1.06	.3554	1.54	.4382
.11	.0438	.59	.2224	1.07	.3577	1.55	.4394
.12	.0478	.60	.2258	1.08	.3599	1.56	.4406
.13	.0517	.61	.2291	1.09	.3621	1.57	.4418
.14	.0557	.62	.2324	1.10	.3643	1.58	.4430
.15	.0596	.63	.2357	1.11	.3665	1.59	.4441
.16	.0636	.64	.2389	1.12	.3686	1.60	.4452
.17	.0675	.65	.2422	1.13	.3708	1.61	.4463
.18	.0714	.66	.2454	1.14	.3729	1.62	.4474
.19	.0754	.67	.2486	1.15	.3749	1.63	.4485
.20	.0793	.68	.2518	1.16	.3770	1.64	.4495
.21	.0832	.69	.2549	1.17	.3790	1.65	.4505
.22	.0871	.70	.2580	1.18	.3810	1.66	.4515
.23	.0910	.71	.2612	1.19	.3830	1.67	.4525
.24	.0948	.72	.2642	1.20	.3849	1.68	.4535
.25	.0987	.73	.2673	1.21	.3869	1.69	.4545
.26	.1026	.74	.2704	1.22	.3888	1.70	.4554
.27	.1064	.75	.2734	1.23	.3907	1.71	.4564
.28	.1103	.76	.2764	1.24	.3925	1.72	.4573
.29	.1141	.77	.2794	1.25	.3944	1.73	.4582
.30	.1179	.78	.2823	1.26	.3962	1.74	.4591
.31	.1217	.79	.2852	1.27	.3980	1.75	.4599
.32	.1255	.80	.2881	1.28	.3997	1.76	.4608
.33	.1293	.81	.2910	1.29	.4015	1.77	.4616
.34	.1331	.82	.2939	1.30	.4032	1.78	.4625
.35	.1368	.83	.2967	1.31	.4049	1.79	.4633
.36	.1406	.84	.2996	1.32	.4066	1.80	.4641
.37	.1443	.85	.3023	1.33	.4082	1.81	.4649
.38	.1480	.86	.3051	1.34	.4099	1.82	.4656
.39	.1517	.87	.3079	1.35	.4115	1.83	.4664
.40	.1554	.88	.3106	1.36	.4131	1.84	.4671
.41	.1591	.89	.3133	1.37	.4147	1.85	.4678
.42	.1628	.90	.3159	1.38	.4162	1.86	.4686
.43	.1664	.91	.3186	1.39	.4177	1.87	.4693
.44	.1700	.92	.3212	1.40	.4192	1.88	.4700
.45	.1736	.93	.3238	1.41	.4207	1.89	.4706
.46	.1772	.94	.3264	1.42	.4222	1.90	.4713
.47	.1808	.95	.3289	1.43	.4236	1.91	.4719

Table 2   (*continued*)

z	A	z	A	z	A	z	A
1.92	.4726	2.42	.4922	2.92	.4983	3.42	.4997
1.93	.4732	2.43	.4925	2.93	.4983	3.43	.4997
1.94	.4738	2.44	.4927	2.94	.4984	3.44	.4997
1.95	.4744	2.45	.4929	2.95	.4984	3.45	.4997
1.96	.4750	2.46	.4931	2.96	.4985	3.46	.4997
1.97	.4756	2.47	.4932	2.97	.4985	3.47	.4997
1.98	.4762	2.48	.4934	2.98	.4986	3.48	.4998
1.99	.4767	2.49	.4936	2.99	.4986	3.49	.4998
2.00	.4773	2.50	.4938	3.00	.4987	3.50	.4998
2.01	.4778	2.51	.4940	3.01	.4987	3.51	.4998
2.02	.4783	2.52	.4941	3.02	.4987	3.52	.4998
2.03	.4788	2.53	.4943	3.03	.4988	3.53	.4998
2.04	.4793	2.54	.4945	3.04	.4988	3.54	.4998
2.05	.4798	2.55	.4946	3.05	.4989	3.55	.4998
2.06	.4803	2.56	.4948	3.06	.4989	3.56	.4998
2.07	.4808	2.57	.4949	3.07	.4989	3.57	.4998
2.08	.4812	2.58	.4951	3.08	.4990	3.58	.4998
2.09	.4817	2.59	.4952	3.09	.4990	3.59	.4998
2.10	.4821	2.60	.4953	3.10	.4990	3.60	.4998
2.11	.4826	2.61	.4955	3.11	.4991	3.61	.4999
2.12	.4830	2.62	.4956	3.12	.4991	3.62	.4999
2.13	.4834	2.63	.4957	3.13	.4991	3.63	.4999
2.14	.4838	2.64	.4959	3.14	.4992	3.64	.4999
2.15	.4842	2.65	.4960	3.15	.4992	3.65	.4999
2.16	.4846	2.66	.4961	3.16	.4992	3.66	.4999
2.17	.4850	2.67	.4962	3.17	.4992	3.67	.4999
2.18	.4854	2.68	.4963	3.18	.4993	3.68	.4999
2.19	.4857	2.69	.4964	3.19	.4993	3.69	.4999
2.20	.4861	2.70	.4965	3.20	.4993	3.70	.4999
2.21	.4865	2.71	.4966	3.21	.4993	3.71	.4999
2.22	.4868	2.72	.4967	3.22	.4994	3.72	.4999
2.23	.4871	2.73	.4968	3.23	.4994	3.73	.4999
2.24	.4875	2.74	.4969	3.24	.4994	3.74	.4999
2.25	.4878	2.75	.4970	3.25	.4994	3.75	.4999
2.26	.4881	2.76	.4971	3.26	.4994	3.76	.4999
2.27	.4884	2.77	.4972	3.27	.4995	3.77	.4999
2.28	.4887	2.78	.4973	3.28	.4995	3.78	.4999
2.29	.4890	2.79	.4974	3.29	.4995	3.79	.4999
2.30	.4893	2.80	.4974	3.30	.4995	3.80	.4999
2.31	.4896	2.81	.4975	3.31	.4995	3.81	.4999
2.32	.4898	2.82	.4976	3.32	.4996	3.82	.4999
2.33	.4901	2.83	.4977	3.33	.4996	3.83	.4999
2.34	.4904	2.84	.4977	3.34	.4996	3.84	.4999
2.35	.4906	2.85	.4978	3.35	.4996	3.85	.4999
2.36	.4909	2.86	.4979	3.36	.4996	3.86	.4999
2.37	.4911	2.87	.4980	3.37	.4996	3.87	.5000
2.38	.4913	2.88	.4980	3.38	.4996	3.88	.5000
2.39	.4916	2.89	.4981	3.39	.4997	3.89	.5000
2.40	.4918	2.90	.4981	3.40	.4997		
2.41	.4920	2.91	.4982	3.41	.4997		

Answers to Selected Exercises

Chapter 1

Section 1.1 (Page 8)

1. True   **3.** Answers vary with the calculator, but 2,508,429,787/798,458,000 is the best.   **5.** Distributive property   **7.** Identity property of addition   **9.** Associative property of addition   **11.** Answers vary.   **13.** -39 **15.** -2 **17.** 45.6   **19.** About .9167   **21.** -12 **23.** 0   **25.** 4   **27.** -1 **29.** $\dfrac{2040}{523}, \dfrac{189}{37}, \sqrt{27}, \dfrac{4587}{691}, 6.735, \sqrt{47}$ **31.** $12 < 18.5$ **33.** $x \geq 5.7$ **35.** $z \leq 7.5$ **37.** $<$ **39.** $<$ **41.** a lies to the right of b or is equal to b.   **43.** $c < a < b$ **45.**

47.

49.

51. -3 **53.** -19 **55.** $=$ **57.** $=$ **59.** $=$ **61.** $>$ **63.** $7 - a$ **65.** Answers vary.   **67.** Answers vary.   **69.** 1   **71.** 9   **73.** 7   **75.** 49.9   **77.** 3.8   **79.** 35.7   **81.** 2005, 2006, 2008, 2010, 2011   **83.** 2007, 2008, 2009, 2010, 2011

Section 1.2 (Page 16)

1. 1,973,822.685   **3.** 289.0991339   **5.** Answers vary.   **7.** 4^5 **9.** $(-6)^7$ **11.** $(5u)^{28}$ **13.** Degree 4; coefficients: 6.2, -5, 4, -3, 3.7; constant term 3.7   **15.** 3   **17.** $-x^3 + x^2 - 13x$ **19.** $-6y^2 + 3y + 6$ **21.** $-6x^2 + 4x - 4$ **23.** $-18m^3 - 54m^2 + 9m$ **25.** $12z^3 + 14z^2 - 7z + 5$ **27.** $12k^2 + 16k - 3$ **29.** $6y^2 + 13y + 5$ **31.** $18k^2 - 7kq - q^2$ **33.** $4.34m^2 + 5.68m - 4.42$ **35.** $-k + 3$ **37.** $R = 5000x$; $C = 200,000 + 1800x$; $P = 3200x - 200,000$ **39.** $R = 9750x$; $C = -3x^2 + 3480x + 259,675$; $P = 3x^2 + 6270x - 259,675$ **41. (a)** \$265 million   **(b)** About \$212 million   **43. (a)** \$948 million   **(b)** About \$883 million   **45.** About \$1712 million   **47.** About \$1163 million   **49.** False   **51.** True   **53.** .866   **55.** .505   **57. (a)** Approximately 60,501,067 cu ft   **(b)** The shape becomes a rectangular box with a square base, with volume b^2h.   **(c)** Yes   **59. (a)** 0, 1, 2, 3, or no degree (if one is the negative of the other)   **(b)** 0, 1, 2, 3, or no degree (if they are equal)   **(c)** 6   **61.** Between 40,000 and 45,000 calculators

Section 1.3 (Page 23)

1. $12x(x - 2)$ **3.** $r(r^2 - 5r + 1)$ **5.** $6z(z^2 - 2z + 3)$ **7.** $(2y - 1)^2(14y - 4) = 2(2y - 1)^2(7y - 2)$ **9.** $(x + 5)^4(x^2 + 10x + 28)$ **11.** $(x + 1)(x + 4)$ **13.** $(x + 3)(x + 4)$ **15.** $(x + 3)(x - 2)$ **17.** $(x - 1)(x + 3)$ **19.** $(x - 4)(x + 1)$ **21.** $(z - 7)(z - 2)$ **23.** $(z + 4)(z + 6)$ **25.** $(2x - 1)(x - 4)$ **27.** $(3p - 4)(5p - 1)$ **29.** $(2z - 5)(2z - 3)$ **31.** $(2x + 1)(3x - 4)$ **33.** $(5y - 2)(2y + 5)$ **35.** $(2x - 1)(3x + 4)$ **37.** $(3a + 5)(a - 1)$ **39.** $(x + 9)(x - 9)$ **41.** $(3p - 2)^2$ **43.** $(r - 2t)(r + 5t)$ **45.** $(m - 4n)^2$ **47.** $(2u + 3)^2$ **49.** Cannot be factored   **51.** $(2r + 3v)(2r - 3v)$ **53.** $(x + 2y)^2$ **55.** $(3a + 5)(a - 6)$ **57.** $(7m + 2n)(3m + n)$ **59.** $(y - 7z)(y + 3z)$ **61.** $(11x + 8)(11x - 8)$ **63.** $(a - 4)(a^2 + 4a + 16)$ **65.** $(2r - 3s)(4r^2 + 6rs + 9s^2)$ **67.** $(4m + 5)(16m^2 - 20m + 25)$ **69.** $(10y - z)(100y^2 + 10yz + z^2)$ **71.** $(x^2 + 3)(x^2 + 2)$ **73.** $b^2(b + 1)(b - 1)$ **75.** $(x + 2)(x - 2)(x^2 + 3)$ **77.** $(4a^2 + 9b^2)(2a + 3b)(2a - 3b)$ **79.** $x^2(x^2 + 2)(x^4 - 2x^2 + 4)$ **81.** Answers vary.   **83.** Answers vary.

Section 1.4 (Page 29)

1. $\dfrac{x}{7}$ **3.** $\dfrac{5}{7p}$ **5.** $\dfrac{5}{4}$ **7.** $\dfrac{4}{w + 6}$ **9.** $\dfrac{y - 4}{3y^2}$ **11.** $\dfrac{m - 2}{m + 3}$ **13.** $\dfrac{x + 3}{x + 1}$ **15.** $\dfrac{3}{16a}$ **17.** $\dfrac{3y}{x^2}$ **19.** $\dfrac{5}{4c}$ **21.** $\dfrac{3}{4}$ **23.** $\dfrac{3}{10}$ **25.** $\dfrac{2(a + 4)}{a - 3}$ **27.** $\dfrac{k + 2}{k + 3}$ **29.** Answers vary.   **31.** $\dfrac{3}{35z}$ **33.** $\dfrac{4}{3}$ **35.** $\dfrac{20 + x}{5x}$ **37.** $\dfrac{3m - 2}{m(m - 1)}$ **39.** $\dfrac{37}{5(b + 2)}$ **41.** $\dfrac{33}{20(k - 2)}$ **43.** $\dfrac{7x - 1}{(x - 3)(x - 1)(x + 2)}$ **45.** $\dfrac{y^2}{(y + 4)(y + 3)(y + 2)}$ **47.** $\dfrac{x + 1}{x - 1}$ **49.** $\dfrac{-1}{x(x + h)}$ **51. (a)** $\dfrac{\pi x^2}{4x^2}$ **(b)** $\dfrac{\pi}{4}$ **53. (a)** $\dfrac{x^2}{25x^2}$ **(b)** $\dfrac{1}{25}$ **55.** $\dfrac{-7.2x^2 + 6995x + 230,000}{1000x}$ **57.** About \$2.95 million   **59.** No   **61.** \$3.99   **63.** \$10,537.68

Section 1.5 (Page 41)

1. 49   **3.** $16c^2$ **5.** $32/x^5$ **7.** $108u^{12}$ **9.** $1/7$ **11.** $-1/7776$ **13.** $-1/y^3$ **15.** $9/16$ **17.** b^3/a **19.** 7   **21.** About 1.55   **23.** -16 **25.** $81/16$ **27.** $4^2/5^3$ **29.** 4^3 **31.** 4^8 **33.** z^3 **35.** $\dfrac{p}{9}$ **37.** $\dfrac{q^5}{r^3}$ **39.** $\dfrac{8}{25p^7}$ **41.** $2^{5/6}p^{3/2}$ **43.** $2p + 5p^{5/3}$ **45.** $\dfrac{1}{3y^{2/3}}$ **47.** $\dfrac{a^{1/2}}{49b^{5/2}}$ **49.** $x^{7/6} - x^{11/6}$ **51.** $x - y$ **53.** (f)   **55.** (h)   **57.** (g)   **59.** (c)   **61.** 5   **63.** 5   **65.** 21   **67.** $\sqrt{77}$ **69.** $5\sqrt{3}$ **71.** $-\sqrt{2}$ **73.** $15\sqrt{5}$ **75.** 3   **77.** $-3 - 3\sqrt{2}$ **79.** $4 + \sqrt{3}$ **81.** $\dfrac{7}{11 + 6\sqrt{2}}$ **83. (a)** 14   **(b)** 85   **(c)** 58.0   **85.** About \$10.2 billion   **87.** About \$10.6 billion   **89.** About 180.6   **91.** About 168.7   **93.** About 5.8 million   **95.** About 7.3 million   **97.** About 30.4 million   **99.** About 87.1 million

Section 1.6 (Page 50)

1. 4   **3.** 7   **5.** $-10/9$ **7.** 4   **9.** $\dfrac{40}{7}$ **11.** $\dfrac{26}{3}$ **13.** $-\dfrac{12}{5}$ **15.** $-\dfrac{59}{6}$ **17.** $-\dfrac{9}{4}$ **19.** $x = .72$ **21.** $r \approx -13.26$ **23.** $\dfrac{b - 5a}{2}$ **25.** $x = \dfrac{3b}{a + 5}$ **27.** $V = \dfrac{k}{P}$ **29.** $g = \dfrac{V - V_0}{t}$ **31.** $B = \dfrac{2A}{h} - b$ or $B = \dfrac{2A - bh}{h}$ **33.** $-2, 3$ **35.** $-8, 2$ **37.** $\dfrac{5}{2}, \dfrac{7}{2}$ **39.** 10 hrs   **41.** 23°   **43.** 71.6°   **45.** 2010

47. 2015   **49.** 2010   **51.** 2016   **53.** 2012   **55.** 2016
57. 4779 thousand   **59.** 3074 thousand   **61.** $205.41
63. $21,000   **65.** $70,000 for first plot; $50,000 for the second

67. About 409,091 per month   **69.** 25,772,733   **71.** $\frac{400}{3}$L

73. About 105 miles   **75.** 83 mph   **77.** 2.9 gallons of premium and 12.7 gallons of regular

Section 1.7 (Page 58)

1. $-4, 14$ **3.** $0, -6$ **5.** $0, 2$ **7.** $-7, -8$ **9.** $\frac{1}{2}, 3$

11. $-\frac{1}{2}, \frac{1}{3}$ **13.** $\frac{5}{2}, 4$ **15.** $-5, -2$ **17.** $\frac{4}{3}, -\frac{4}{3}$ **19.** $0, 1$

21. $2 \pm \sqrt{7}$ **23.** $\frac{1 \pm 2\sqrt{5}}{4}$ **25.** $\frac{-7 \pm \sqrt{41}}{4}$; $-.1492, -3.3508$

27. $\frac{-1 \pm \sqrt{5}}{4}$; $.3090, -.8090$ **29.** $\frac{-5 \pm \sqrt{65}}{10}$; $.3062, -1.3062$

31. No real-number solutions   **33.** $-\frac{5}{2}, 1$ **35.** No real-number

solutions   **37.** $-5, \frac{3}{2}$ **39.** 1   **41.** 2   **43.** $x \approx .4701$ or 1.8240

45. $x \approx -1.0376$ or $.6720$ **47. (a)** 30 mph   **(b)** About 35 mph
(c) About 44 mph   **49. (a)** 2007   **(b)** 2009
51. (a) About $7.6 trillion   **(b)** 2007   **53.** About 1.046 ft
55. (a) $x + 20$ **(b)** Northbound: $5x$; eastbound: $5(x + 20)$ or $5x + 100$
(c) $(5x)^2 + (5x + 100)^2 = 300^2$ **(d)** About 31.23 mph and 51.23 mph
57. (a) $150 - x$ **(b)** $x(150 - x) = 5000$ **(c)** Length 100 m; width 50 m
59. 9 ft by 12 ft   **61.** 6.25 sec   **63. (a)** About 3.54 sec   **(b)** 2.5 sec
(c) 144 ft   **65. (a)** 2 sec   **(b)** 3/4 sec or 13/4 sec   **(c)** It reaches the given height twice: once on the way up and once on the way down.

67. $t = \frac{\sqrt{2Sg}}{g}$ **69.** $h = \frac{d^2\sqrt{kL}}{L}$

71. $R = \frac{-2Pr + E^2 \pm E\sqrt{E^2 - 4Pr}}{2P}$ **73. (a)** $x^2 - 2x = 15$

(b) $x = 5$ or $x = -3$ **(c)** $z = \pm\sqrt{5}$ **75.** $\pm\frac{\sqrt{6}}{2}$

77. $\pm\sqrt{\dfrac{3 + \sqrt{13}}{2}}$

Chapter 1 Review Exercises (Page 61)

Refer to Section	1.1	1.2	1.3	1.4	1.5	1.6	1.7
For Exercises	1–18, 81–84	19–24, 85–88	25–32	33–38, 89–90	39–60, 91–92	61–68, 93–94	69–80, 95–100

1. $0, 6$ **3.** $-12, -6, -\frac{9}{10}, -\sqrt{4}, 0, \frac{1}{8}, 6$

5. Commutative property of multiplication   **7.** Distributive property
9. $x \geq 9$ **11.** $-|3 - (-2)|, -|-2|, |6 - 4|, |8 + 1|$ **13.** -1
15.

$-\frac{7}{9}$ **19.** $4x^4 - 4x^2 + 11x$ **21.** $25k^2 - 4h^2$

23. $9x^2 + 24xy + 16y^2$ **25.** $k(2h^2 - 4h + 5)$
27. $a^2(5a + 2)(a + 2)$ **29.** $(12p + 13q)(12p - 13q)$
31. $(3y - 1)(9y^2 + 3y + 1)$ **33.** $\frac{9x^2}{4}$ **35.** 4   **37.** $\frac{(m - 1)^2}{3(m + 1)}$
39. 5^3 or $\frac{1}{125}$ **41.** -1 **43.** 4^3 **45.** $\frac{1}{8}$ **47.** $\frac{7}{10}$ **49.** $\frac{1}{5^{2/3}}$
51. $3^{7/2}a^{5/2}$ **53.** 3   **55.** $3pq\sqrt[3]{2q^2}$ **57.** $-21\sqrt{3}$
59. $\sqrt{6} - \sqrt{3}$ **61.** $-\frac{1}{3}$ **63.** No solution   **65.** $x = \frac{3}{8a - 2}$

67. $-38, 42$ **69.** $-7 \pm \sqrt{5}$ **71.** $\frac{1}{2}, -2$ **73.** $-\frac{3}{2}, 7$

75. $\pm\frac{\sqrt{3}}{3}$ **77.** $r = \frac{-Rp \pm E\sqrt{Rp}}{p}$ **79.** $s = \frac{a \pm \sqrt{a^2 + 4K}}{2}$

81. 111%   **83.** $1118.75   **85. (a)** 2009   **(b)** 2012
87. 52.66 million   **89. (a)** 9.8824 million   **(b)** 2013
91. (a) About $19.79 billion   **(b)** About $31.27 billion   **93.** 11%
95. (a) 7182   **(b)** About 13.61 million   **97.** 3.2 feet
99. About 7.77 seconds

Case Study 1 (Page 64)

1. $218 + 508x$ **3.** Electric by $1880   **5.** $1529.10 + 50x$
7. LG by $29.10

Chapter 2

Section 2.1 (Page 72)

1. IV, II, I, III   **3.** Yes   **5.** No
7.
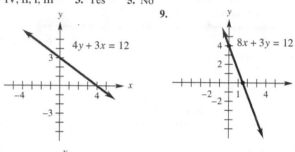
9.

11.
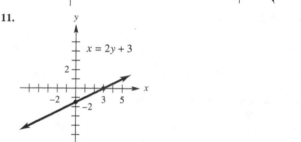

13. x-intercepts $-2.5, 3$; y-intercept 3   **15.** x-intercepts $-1, 2$;
y-intercept -2 **17.** x-intercept 4; y-intercept 3   **19.** x-intercept 12;
y-intercept -8 **21.** x-intercepts $3, -3$; y-intercept -9
23. x-intercepts $-5, 4$; y-intercept -20
25. no x-intercept; y-intercept 7
27.
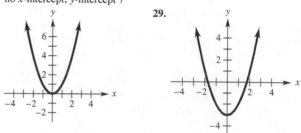
29.

31.
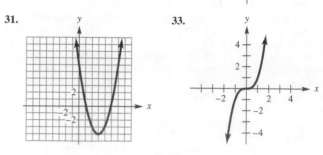
33.

35.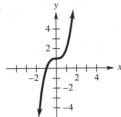

37.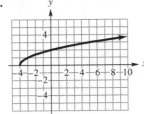

31.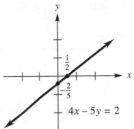

39.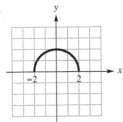

41. 2008; 20 million pounds **43.** 2011
45. (a) About $1,250,000 **(b)** About $1,750,000
(c) About $4,250,000 **47. (a)** About $500,000
(b) About $1,000,000 **(c)** About $1,500,000 **49.** Beef: about
59 pounds; Chicken: about 83 pounds; Pork: about 47.5 pounds
51. 2001 **53.** About $507 billion **55.** 2008–2015
57. $16.5; $21 **59.** $17.25; Day 14 **61.** No

63.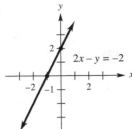

65.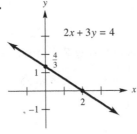

67.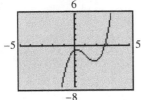

69. No;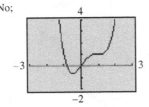

71. $x \approx -1.1038$ **73.** $x \approx 2.1017$ **75.** $x \approx -1.7521$
77. About $6.99 trillion **79.** About $45.41 trillion

Section 2.2 (Page 84)

1. $-\dfrac{3}{2}$ **3.** -2 **5.** $-\dfrac{5}{2}$ **7.** Not defined **9.** $y = 4x + 5$

11. $y = -2.3x + 1.5$ **13.** $y = -\dfrac{3}{4}x + 4$ **15.** $m = 2; b = -9$

17. $m = 3; b = -2$ **19.** $m = \dfrac{2}{3}; b = -\dfrac{16}{9}$ **21.** $m = \dfrac{2}{3}; b = 0$

23. $m = 1; b = 5$ **25. (a)** C **(b)** B **(c)** B **(d)** D

27.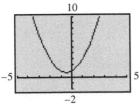

29.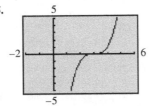

33. Perpendicular **35.** Parallel **37.** Neither **39. (a)** $\dfrac{2}{5}, \dfrac{9}{8}, -\dfrac{5}{2}$

(b) Yes **41.** $y = -\dfrac{2}{3}x$ **43.** $y = 3x - 3$ **45.** $y = 1$

47. $x = -2$ **49.** $y = 2x + 3$ **51.** $2y = 7x - 3$ **53.** $y = 5x$
55. $x = 6$ **57.** $y = 2x - 2$ **59.** $y = x - 6$ **61.** $y = -x + 2$
63. $1330.42 **65.** $6715.23 **67. (a)** $202.05 billion
(b) $270.5 billion **(c)** 2015 **69. (a)** 384.6 thousand
(b) 366.6 thousand **(c)** 2019 **71. (a)** $(5, 35.1), (11, 29.7)$
(b) $y = -.9x + 39.6$ **(c)** $31.5 billion **(d)** 2016
73. (a) $y = .035x + .40$ **(b)** $.82 **75. (a)** $y = -964.5x + 36{,}845$
(b) 31,058 **77. (a)** The average decrease in time over 1 year; times
are going down, in general. **(b)** 12.94 minutes

Section 2.3 (Page 93)

1. (a) $y = \dfrac{5}{9}(x - 32)$ **(b)** 10°C and 23.89°C **3.** 463.89°C

5. $y = 4.66x + 173.64; 210.92; 243.54$
7. $y = .0625x + 6; 6.625$ million **9.** 4 ft
11. (a) 22.2, -23.2, -12.6, 6.0, 7.6; -22.6, -41.4, -4.2, 41.0, 69.2;
sum $= 0$ **(b)** 1283.6; 8712 **(c)** Model 1 **13.** Yes
15. (a) $y = 5.90x + 146.59$ **(b)** $235.09 billion
17. (a) $y = -3.96x + 73.98$ **(b)** $10.62 billion
19. (a) $y = 2.37x - 2.02$ **(b)** $26.42 billion; $31.16 billion
21. (a) $y = -2.318x + 55.88$ **(b)** 41.972 thousand **(c)** early 2012
(d) $r \approx -.972$

Section 2.4 (Page 100)

1. Answers vary.
3. $[-4, \infty)$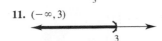

5. $(-\infty, 0)$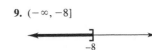

7. $\left(-\infty, \dfrac{10}{3}\right]$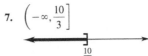

9. $(-\infty, -8]$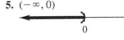

11. $(-\infty, 3)$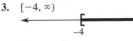

13. $(-1, \infty)$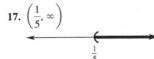

15. $(-\infty, 1]$

17. $\left(\dfrac{1}{5}, \infty\right)$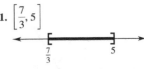

19. $(-5, 7)$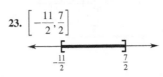

21. $\left[\dfrac{7}{3}, 5\right]$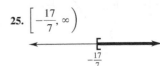

23. $\left[-\dfrac{11}{2}, \dfrac{7}{2}\right]$

25. $\left[-\dfrac{17}{7}, \infty\right)$

27. $x \geq 2$ **29.** $-3 < x \leq 5$ **31.** $x \geq 400$ **33.** $x \geq 50$

35. Impossible to break even

37. $(-\infty, -7)$ or $(7, \infty)$

39. $[-5, 5]$

41. All real numbers

43. $\left(-\dfrac{3}{2}, \dfrac{5}{2}\right)$

45. $\left(-\infty, -\dfrac{3}{2}\right]$ or $\left[\dfrac{1}{4}, \infty\right)$

47. $76 \leq T \leq 90$ **49.** $40 \leq T \leq 82$

51. (a) $25.33 \leq R_L \leq 28.17; 36.58 \leq R_E \leq 40.92$

(b) $5699.25 \leq T_L \leq 6338.25; 8230.5 \leq T_E \leq 9207$ **53.** $35 \leq B \leq 43$

55. $0 < x \leq 8700; 8700 < x \leq 35{,}350; 35{,}350 < x \leq 85{,}650;$
$85{,}650 < x \leq 178{,}650; 178{,}650 < x \leq 388{,}350; x > 388{,}350$

Section 2.5 (Page 108)

1. $\left[-4, \dfrac{3}{2}\right]$

3. $(-\infty, -3)$ or $(-1, \infty)$

5. $\left[-2, \dfrac{1}{4}\right]$

7. $(-\infty, -1)$ or $\left(\dfrac{1}{4}, \infty\right)$

9. $[-6, 6]$

11. $(-\infty, 0)$ or $(16, \infty)$

13. $[-3, 0]$ or $[3, \infty)$ **15.** $[-7, -2]$ or $[2, \infty)$

17. $(-\infty, -5)$ or $(-1, 3)$ **19.** $\left(-\infty, -\dfrac{1}{2}\right)$ or $\left(0, \dfrac{4}{3}\right)$ **21.** No.

23. $(-.1565, 2.5565)$ **25.** $[-2.2635, .7556]$ or $[3.5079, \infty)$

27. $(.5, .8393)$ **29.** $(-\infty, 1)$ or $[4, \infty)$ **31.** $\left(\dfrac{7}{2}, 5\right)$

33. $(-\infty, 2)$ or $(5, \infty)$ **35.** $(-\infty, -1)$ **37.** $(-\infty, -2)$ or $(0, 3)$

39. $[-1, .5]$ **41.** $(8, \infty)$ **43.** $[52, 200]$ **45.** 2010 or higher

47. $[2006, 2011]$

Chapter 2 Review Exercises (Page 110)

Refer to Section	2.1	2.2	2.3	2.4	2.5
For Exercises	1–10	11–34	35–38	39–54	55–68

1. $(-2, 3), (0, -5), (3, -2), (4, 3)$

3.

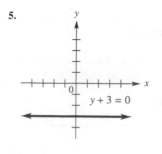

$5x - 3y = 15$

5.

$y + 3 = 0$

7.

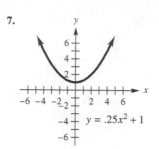

$y = .25x^2 + 1$

9. (a) About 11:30 AM to about 7:30 PM   **(b)** From midnight until about 5 AM and after about 10:30 PM   **11.** Answers vary.   **13.** -3

15. $-\dfrac{1}{4}$ **17.** 3   **19.** 0   **21.** -3

23.

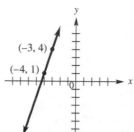

$(-3, 4)$
$(-4, 1)$

25. $3y = 2x - 13$ **27.** $4y = -5x + 17$

29. $x = -1$ **31.** $3y = 5x + 15$

33. (a) $y = .55x + 11.25$ **(b)** Positive; exports increased

(c) 18.95 million hectoliters

35. (a) $y = 1919x + 47{,}059$ **(b)** $y = 1917.38x + 47{,}051.26$

(c) $\$68{,}168; \$68{,}142.44$; least–squares regression line is closer;

(d) $\$75{,}811.96$

37. (a) $y = 10.72x + 98.8$

(b)

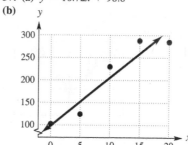

(c) Yes   **(d)** $r \approx .953$ **39.** $\left(\dfrac{3}{8}, \infty\right)$ **41.** $\left(-\infty, \dfrac{1}{4}\right]$

43. $\left[-\dfrac{1}{2}, 2\right]$ **45.** $[-8, 8]$ **47.** $(-\infty, 2]$ or $[5, \infty)$

49. $\left[-\dfrac{9}{5}, 1\right]$ **51. (d)**   **53. (a)** $y = 75.4x + 1496$ **(b)** 2013

55. $(-3, 2)$ **57.** $(-\infty, -5]$ or $\left[\dfrac{3}{2}, \infty\right)$

59. $(-\infty, -5]$ or $[-2, 3]$ **61.** $[-2, 0)$ **63.** $\left(-1, \dfrac{3}{2}\right)$

65. $[-19, -5)$ or $(2, \infty)$ **67.** 2011 and 2012

Case Study 2 Exercises (Page 113)

1. $y = -146.1x + 2330$

3. $-389.8, -212.7, 96.4, 331.5, 525.6, 195.7, -41.2, -221.1, -217.0,$
$-137.9, 73.2$

5. $y = .343x - 20.65$ **7.** $\hat{y} = \$-.07$; Cannot have a negative wage
9. $y = 0$; answers vary.

Chapter 3

Section 3.1 (Page 121)

1. Function   **3.** Function   **5.** Not a function   **7.** Function
9. $(-\infty, \infty)$ **11.** $(-\infty, \infty)$ **13.** $(-\infty, 0]$
15. All real numbers except 2   **17.** All real numbers except 2 and -2
19. All real numbers such that $x > -4$ and $x \neq 3$ **21.** $(-\infty, \infty)$
23. (a) 8 (b) 8 (c) 8 (d) 8   **25.** (a) 48 (b) 6 (c) 25.38
(d) 28.42   **27.** (a) $\sqrt{7}$ (b) 0 (c) $\sqrt{5.7}$ (d) Not defined
29. (a) 12 (b) 23 (c) 12.91 (d) 49.41   **31.** (a) $\dfrac{\sqrt{3}}{15}$
(b) Not defined **(c)** $\dfrac{\sqrt{1.7}}{6.29}$ **(d)** Not defined   **33.** (a) 13 (b) 9
(c) 6.5 **(d)** 24.01   **35.** (a) $6 - p$ (b) $6 + r$ (c) $3 - m$
37. (a) $\sqrt{4 - p}$ $(p \leq 4)$ (b) $\sqrt{4 + r}$ $(r \geq -4)$ (c) $\sqrt{1 - m}$ $(m \leq 1)$
39. (a) $p^3 + 1$ (b) $-r^3 + 1$ (c) $m^3 + 9m^2 + 27m + 28$
41. (a) $\dfrac{3}{p - 1}$ $(p \neq 1)$ (b) $\dfrac{3}{-r - 1}$ $(r \neq -1)$ (c) $\dfrac{3}{m + 2}$ $(m \neq -2)$
43. 2   **45.** $2x + h$
47.

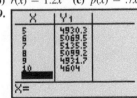

49. (a) \$1070 (b) \$4542.30 (c) \$8420.18   **51.** (a) \$-6.744 billion
(loss) **(b)** \$14.448 billion   **53.** (a) \$2347.9 million
(b) \$2299.9 million   **55.** $2050 - 500t$ **57.** (a) $c(x) = 1800 + .5x$
(b) $r(x) = 1.2x$ **(c)** $p(x) = .7x - 1800$
59.

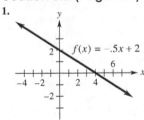

Section 3.2 (Page 131)

1.

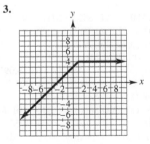

$f(x) = -.5x + 2$

3.

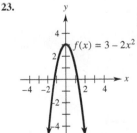

$f(x) = \begin{cases} x + 3 & \text{if } x \leq 1 \\ 4 & \text{if } x > 1 \end{cases}$

5.

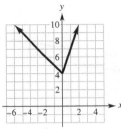

$y = \begin{cases} 4 - x & \text{if } x \leq 0 \\ 3x + 4 & \text{if } x > 0 \end{cases}$

7.

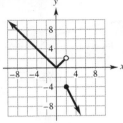

$f(x) = \begin{cases} |x| & \text{if } x < 2 \\ -2x & \text{if } x \geq 2 \end{cases}$

9.

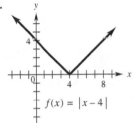

$f(x) = |x - 4|$

11.

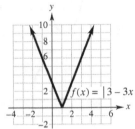

$f(x) = |3 - 3x|$

13.

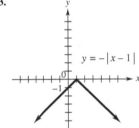

$y = -|x - 1|$

15.

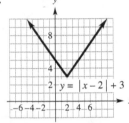

$y = |x - 2| + 3$

17.

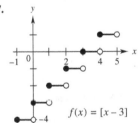

$f(x) = [x - 3]$

19.

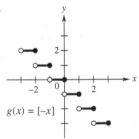

$g(x) = [-x]$

21.

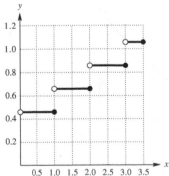

23.

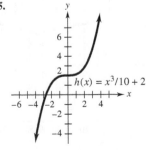

$f(x) = 3 - 2x^2$

25.

$h(x) = x^3/10 + 2$

27.

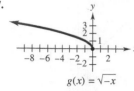

$g(x) = \sqrt{-x}$

29.

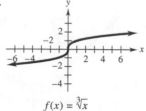

$f(x) = \sqrt[3]{x}$

31.

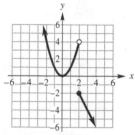

33. Function   **35.** Not a function   **37.** Function

39.

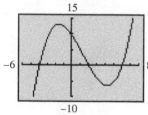

41. $(1, -1)$ is on the graph; $(1, 3)$ is not on the graph

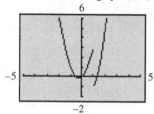

43. $x = -4, 2, 6$ **45.** Peak at $(.5078, .3938)$; valleys at $(-1.9826, -4.2009)$ and $(3.7248, -8.7035)$

47.

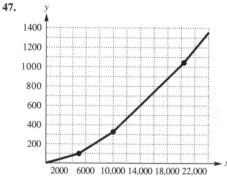

49. (a)

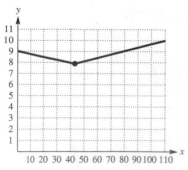

(b) \$7.879   **51. (a)** $f(x) = \begin{cases} 2x + 15.1 & \text{if } 0 \le x \le 30 \\ 10.5x - 240.1 & \text{if } x > 30 \end{cases}$

(b)

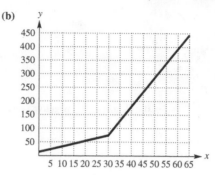

(c) 326.9   **(d)** 442.4   **53. (a)** No   **(b)** 1998, 2002, 2009   **(c)** 2009
55. (a) Yes   **(b)** The years 1990–2010   **(c)** [7750, 15400]
57. (a) 33; 44   **(b)** The figure has vertical line segments, which can't be part of the graph of a function. (Why?) To make the figure into the graph of f, delete the vertical line segments; then, for each horizontal segment of the graph, put a closed dot on the left end and an open circle on the right end (as in Figure 3.7).   **59. (a)** \$34.99   **(b)** \$24.99   **(c)** \$64.99
(d) \$74.99

(e)

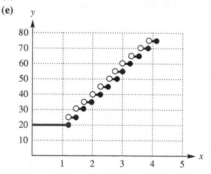

61. There are many correct answers, including

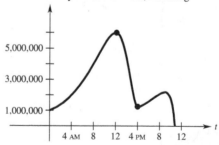

Section 3.3 (Page 142)

1. Let $C(x)$ be the cost of renting a saw for x hours; $C(x) = 25 + 5x$.
3. Let $C(x)$ be the cost (in dollars) for x half hours; $C(x) = 8 + 2.5x$.
5. $C(x) = 36x + 200$ **7.** $C(x) = 120x + 3800$ **9.** \$48, \$15.60,
\$13.80   **11.** \$55.50, \$11.40, \$8.46   **13. (a)** $f(x) = -1916x + 16,615$
(b) 7035   **(c)** \$1916 per year   **15. (a)** $f(x) = -11,875x + 120,000$
(b) [0, 8]   **(c)** \$48,750   **17. (a)** \$80,000   **(b)** \$42.50   **(c)** \$122,500;
\$1,440,000   **(d)** \$122.50; \$45   **19. (a)** $C(x) = .097x + 1.32$
(b) \$98.32   **(c)** \$98.42   **(d)** \$.097, or 9.7¢   **(e)** \$.097, or 9.7¢
21. $R(x) = 1.77x + 2,310,000$ **23. (a)** $C(x) = 10x + 750$
(b) $R(x) = 35x$ **(c)** $P(x) = 25x - 750$ **(d)** \$1750
25. (a) $C(x) = 18x + 300$ **(b)** $R(x) = 28x$ **(c)** $P(x) = 10x - 300$
(d) \$700   **27. (a)** $C(x) = 12.50x + 20,000$ **(b)** $R(x) = 30x$
(c) $P(x) = 17.50x - 20,000$ **(d)** $-\$18,250$ (a loss)   **29.** $(3, -1)$
31. $\left(-\dfrac{11}{4}, -\dfrac{61}{4}\right)$ **33. (a)** 200,000 policies ($x = 200$)

(b)

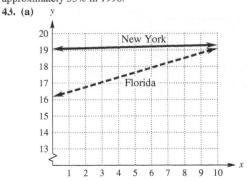

(c) Revenue: $12,500; cost: $15,000   **35. (a)** $C(x) = .126x + 1.5$
(b) $2.382 million   **(c)** About 17.857 units   **37.** Break-even
point is about 467 units; do not produce the item.   **39.** Break-even
point is about 1037 units; produce the item.   **41.** The percentage is
approximately 53% in 1998.

43. (a)

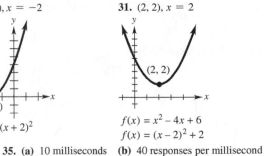

(b) No   **(c)** Yes; Late 2010   **45.** $140   **47.** 10 items
49. (a) $16   **(b)** $11   **(c)** $6   **(d)** 8 units   **(e)** 4 units   **(f)** 0 units
(g)

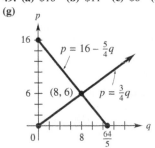

(h) 0 units   **(i)** $\frac{40}{3}$ units   **(j)** $\frac{80}{3}$ units   **(k)** See part (g).   **(l)** 8 units

(m) $6
51. (a)

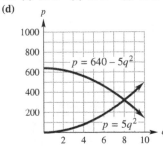

(b) 125 units   **(c)** 50¢   **(d)** [0, 125]   **53.** Total cost increases when
more items are made (because it includes the cost of all previously made
items), so the graph cannot move downward. No; the average cost can
decrease as more items are made, so its graph can move downward.

Section 3.4 (Page 154)
1. Upward   **3.** Downward   **5.** (5, 7); downward
7. (−1, −9); upward   **9.** i   **11.** k   **13.** j   **15.** f

17. $f(x) = \frac{1}{4}(x - 1)^2 + 2$ **19.** $f(x) = (x + 1)^2 - 2$ **21.** (−3, 12)

23. (2, −7)   **25.** x-intercepts 1, 3; y-intercept 9
27. x-intercepts −1, −3; y-intercept 6

29. (−2, 0), $x = -2$

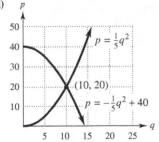

$f(x) = (x + 2)^2$

31. (2, 2), $x = 2$

$f(x) = x^2 - 4x + 6$
$f(x) = (x - 2)^2 + 2$

33. 54   **35. (a)** 10 milliseconds   **(b)** 40 responses per millisecond
37. (a) 27 cases   **(b)** Answers vary.   **(c)** 15 cases
39. (a) About 12 books   **(b)** 10 books   **(c)** About 7 books   **(d)** 0 books
(e) 5 books   **(f)** About 7 books   **(g)** 10 books   **(h)** about 12 books
(i)

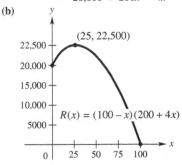

41. (a) $640   **(b)** $515   **(c)** $140
(d)

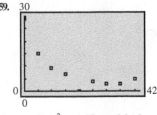

(e) 800 units   **(f)** $320   **43.** 80; $3600   **45.** 30; $1500
47. 20   **49.** 10
51. (a) $R(x) - (100 - x)(200 + 4x)$
    $= 20,000 + 200x - 4x^2$
(b)

(c) 25 seats   **(d)** $22,500   **53.** 13 weeks; $96.10/hog
55. (a) $.013(x - 20)^2$ **(b)** About 4
57. (a) $f(x) = 3.9375(x - 4)^2 + 57.8$ **(b)** About $309.8 billion
59. 30   **61.** 200

$f(x) = .034x^2 - 1.87x + 26.16$;
about 4

$f(x) = 1.808x^2 - 5.185x + 50.72$;
about $248.85 billion

63. **(a)** 11.3 and 88.7 **(b)** 50 **(c)** $3000 **(d)** $x < 11.3$ or $x > 88.7$
(e) $11.3 < x < 88.7$

Section 3.5 (Page 165)

1.
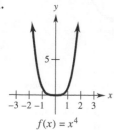
$f(x) = x^4$

3.
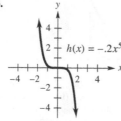
$h(x) = -.2x^5$

5. **(a)** Yes **(b)** No **(c)** No **(d)** Yes **7.** **(a)** Yes **(b)** No
(c) Yes **(d)** No **9.** d **11.** b **13.** e

15.
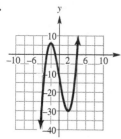

17.
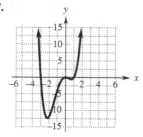

19.
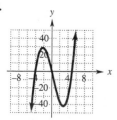

21.
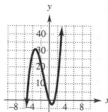

23. $-3 \le x \le 5$ and $-20 \le y \le 5$ **25.** $-3 \le x \le 4$ and
$-35 \le y \le 20$ **27.** **(a)** $933.33 billion **(b)** $1200 billion
(c) $1145.8 billion **(d)** $787.5 billion

(e)
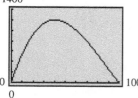

29. **(a)** $54.785 million; $64.843 million; $99.578 million

(b)
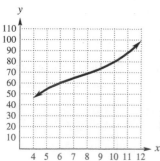

(c) Yes, because the slope is always positive.
31. **(a)** $53.615 million; $63.505 million; $97.33 million

(b)
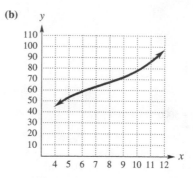

(c) Yes, the slope is always positive
33. $P(x) = .006x^3 - .13x^2 + .99x - 1.28$; $2.248 million

35. **(a)**
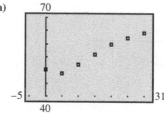

(b) $g(x) = -.0016x^3 + .0765x^2 - .425x + 50.0$

(c)
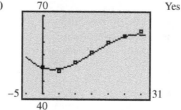
Yes

(d) 62.9528 million
37. **(a)** $R(x) = -.0668x^3 + 1.708x^2 - 12.15x + 120.1$

(b)
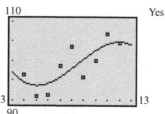
Yes

39. $P(x) = -.0313x^3 + .773x^2 - 4.83x + 17.1$

Section 3.6 (Page 175)

1. $x = -5, y = 0$

3. $x = -\dfrac{5}{2}, y = 0$

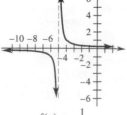
$f(x) = \dfrac{1}{x+5}$

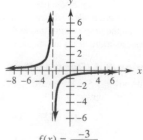
$f(x) = \dfrac{-3}{2x+5}$

5. $x = 1, y = 3$

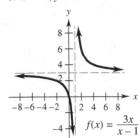

$f(x) = \dfrac{3x}{x-1}$

7. $x = 4, y = 1$

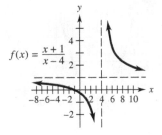

$f(x) = \dfrac{x+1}{x-4}$

(e)

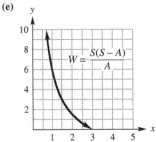

$W = \dfrac{S(S-A)}{A}$

(f) W becomes negative. The waiting time approaches 0 as A approaches 3. The formula does not apply for $A > 3$ because there will be no waiting if people arrive more than 3 min apart.

27.

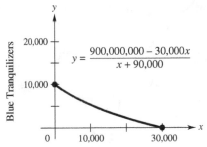

$y = \dfrac{900,000,000 - 30,000x}{x + 90,000}$

30,000 reds; 10,000 blues

9. $x = 3; y = -1$

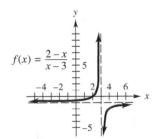

$f(x) = \dfrac{2-x}{x-3}$

11. $x = -2, y = \dfrac{3}{2}$

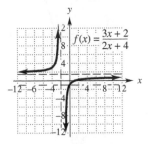

$f(x) = \dfrac{3x+2}{2x+4}$

29. (a) $C(x) = 2.6x + 40,000$

(b) $\overline{C}(x) = \dfrac{2.6x + 40,000}{x} = 2.6 + \dfrac{40,000}{x}$

(c) $y = 2.6$; the average cost may get close to, but will never equal, $2.60.

31. About 73.9

33. (a)

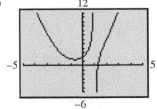

13. $x = -4, x = 2, y = 0$

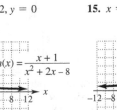

$h(x) = \dfrac{x+1}{x^2 + 2x - 8}$

15. $x = -2, x = 2, y = 1$

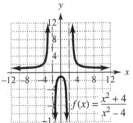

$f(x) = \dfrac{x^2 + 4}{x^2 - 4}$

(b) They appear almost identical, because the parabola is an asymptote of the graph.

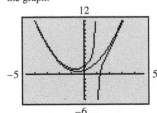

17. $x = -2, x = 1$ **19.** $x = -1, x = 5$
21. (a) $4300 **(b)** $10,033.33 **(c)** $17,200 **(d)** $38,700
(e) $81,700 **(f)** $210,700
(g) $425,700 **(h)** No
(i)

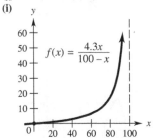

$f(x) = \dfrac{4.3x}{100 - x}$

23. (a) $[0, \infty)$

(b)

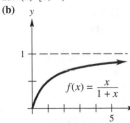

$f(x) = \dfrac{x}{1+x}$

(c)

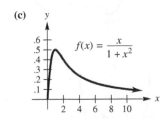

$f(x) = \dfrac{x}{1+x^2}$

(d) Increasing b makes the next generation smaller when this generation is larger.   **25. (a)** 6 min **(b)** 1.5 min **(c)** .6 min **(d)** $A = 0$

Chapter 3 Review Exercises (Page 177)

Refer to Section	3.1	3.2	3.3	3.4	3.5	3.6
From Exercises	1–12	13–24	25–36	37–60	61–70	71–80

1. Not a function   **3.** Function   **5.** Not a function
7. (a) 23 **(b)** -9 **(c)** $4p - 1$ **(d)** $4r + 3$
9. (a) -28 **(b)** -12 **(c)** $-p^2 + 2p - 4$ **(d)** $-r^2 - 3$
11. (a) -13 **(b)** 3 **(c)** $-k^2 - 4k$ **(d)** $-9m^2 + 12m$
(e) $-k^2 + 14k - 45$ **(f)** $12 - 5p$

13.

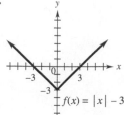

$f(x) = |x| - 3$

15.

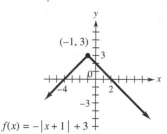

(−1, 3)

$f(x) = -|x+1| + 3$

17.

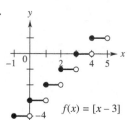

$f(x) = [x - 3]$

19.

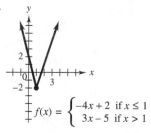

$f(x) = \begin{cases} -4x + 2 & \text{if } x \le 1 \\ 3x - 5 & \text{if } x > 1 \end{cases}$

21.

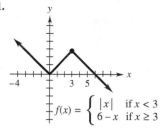

$f(x) = \begin{cases} |x| & \text{if } x < 3 \\ 6 - x & \text{if } x \ge 3 \end{cases}$

23.

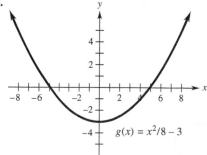

$g(x) = x^2/8 - 3$

25. (a)

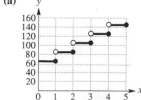

(b) Domain: $(0, \infty)$; range: $\{65, 85, 105, 125, \ldots\}$ **(c)** 2 days
27. (a) decreasing; relatively flat   **(b)** $f(x) = -1.4x + 30$ **(c)** 13.2%
29. (a) $C(x) = 30x + 60$ **(b)** $30   **(c)** $30.60
31. (a) $C(x) = 30x + 85$ **(b)** $30   **(c)** $30.85
33. (a) $18,000   **(b)** $R(x) = 28x$ **(c)** 4500 cartridges   **(d)** $126,000
35. Equilibrium quantity is 36 million subscribers at a price of $12.95 per month.   **37.** Upward; (2, 6)   **39.** Downward; (−1, 8)

41.

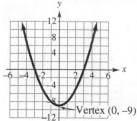

Vertex (0, −9)

43.

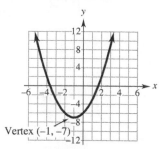

Vertex (−1, −7)

45.

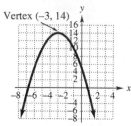

Vertex (−3, 14)

47.

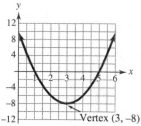

Vertex (3, −8)

49. Minimum value; −11   **51.** Maximum value; 7
53. 161 weeks; $97.16   **55.** 2027; about 1391 million
57. (a) $f(x) = 25.82(x - 5)^2 + 3672$ **(b)** $44,984
59. (a) $g(x) = 9.738x^2 + 389x + 1096$
(b) 35,000

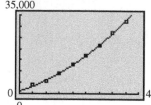

(c) $38,320.45

61.

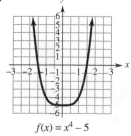

$f(x) = x^4 - 5$

63.

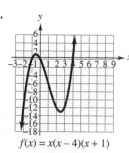

$f(x) = x(x - 4)(x + 1)$

65.

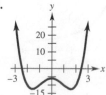

$f(x) = x^4 - 5x^2 - 6$

67. About 313,152; about $690.72 per thousand
69. (a) $404,963 million

(b) $373,222 million   **(c)** $297x^3 - 6901x^2 + 50,400x - 79,159$
(d) $31,741 million; $45,113 million
71. $x = 3, y = 0$ **73.** $x = 2, y = 0$

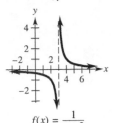

$$f(x) = \frac{1}{x - 3}$$

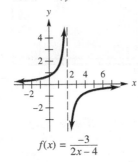

$$f(x) = \frac{-3}{2x - 4}$$

75. $x = -\dfrac{1}{2}, x = \dfrac{3}{2}, y = 0$

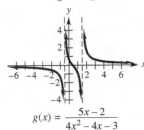

$$g(x) = \frac{5x - 2}{4x^2 - 4x - 3}$$

77. (a) About $10.83   **(b)** About $4.64   **(c)** About $3.61
(d) About $2.71
(e)

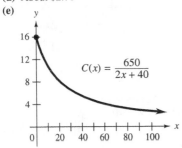

$$C(x) = \frac{650}{2x + 40}$$

79. (a) $(10, 50)$

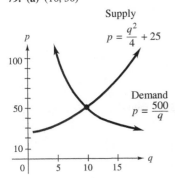

Supply

$$p = \frac{q^2}{4} + 25$$

Demand

$$p = \frac{500}{q}$$

(b) $(10, \infty)$ **(c)** $(0, 10)$

Case Study 3 Exercises (Page 182)

1. $f(x) = \dfrac{-20}{49}x^2 + 20$

3. $g(x) = \sqrt{625 - x^2}$; 50 ft

5. $h(x) = \sqrt{144 - x^2} + 8$; 8 ft   **7.** It will fit through the semicircular arch and Norman arch; to fit it through the parabolic arch, increase the width to 15 ft.

Chapter 4

Section 4.1 (Page 189)

1. Exponential   **3.** Quadratic   **5.** Exponential
7. (a) The graph is entirely above the x-axis and falls from left to right, crossing the y-axis at 1 and then getting very close to the x-axis.
(b) $(0, 1), (1, .6)$ **9. (a)** The graph is entirely above the x-axis and rises from left to right, less steeply than the graph of $f(x) = 2^x$.
(b) $(0, 1), (1, 2^{.5}) = (1, \sqrt{2})$ **11. (a)** The graph is entirely above the x-axis and falls from left to right, crossing the y-axis at 1 and then getting very close to the x-axis.   **(b)** $(0, 1), (1, e^{-1}) \approx (1, .367879)$

13.   **15.**

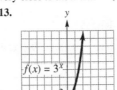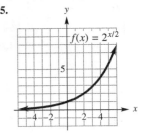

17.

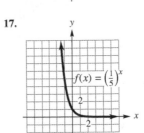

19. (a)–(c)

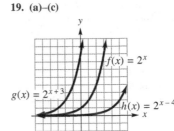

(d) Answers vary.   **21.** 2.3   **23.** .75   **25.** .31
27. (a) $a > 1$ **(b)** Domain: $(-\infty, \infty)$; range: $(0, \infty)$
(c)

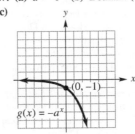

(d) Domain: $(-\infty, \infty)$; range: $(-\infty, 0)$
(e)

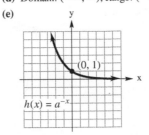

(f) Domain: $(-\infty, \infty)$; range: $(0, \infty)$ **29. (a)** 3   **(b)** $\dfrac{1}{3}$ **(c)** 9   **(d)** 1

31.

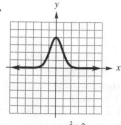

$$f(x) = 2^{-x^2+2}$$

33.

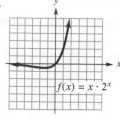

$$f(x) = x \cdot 2^x$$

(b)

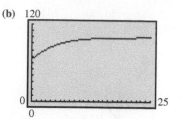

(c) No

35. (a)

t	0	1	2	3	4	5	6	7	8	9	10
y	1	1.06	1.12	1.19	1.26	1.34	1.42	1.50	1.59	1.69	1.79

(b)

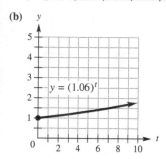

37. (a) About \$141,892 **(b)** About \$64.10
39. (a) About 175 million **(b)** About 321 million
(c) About 355 million **41. (a)** About .97 kg **(b)** About .75 kg
(c) About .65 kg **(d)** About 24,360 years **43.** \$34,706.99
45. (a) About 6.2 billion **(b)** About 6.5 billion **(c)** About 8 billion
(d) Answers vary. **47. (a)** China: About \$12.4 trillion; U.S: About
\$15.6 trillion **(b)** China: About \$27.2 trillion; U.S: About \$22.4 trillion
(c) China: About \$515.3 trillion; U.S: About \$86.3 trillion **(d)** 2016
49. (a) About 13.72 million **(b)** About 28.9 million
(c) First quarter of 2012 **51. (a)** About 1.2 billion
(b) About 2.1 billion **(c)** Fourth quarter of 2012
53. (a) About 12.6 mg **(b)** About 7.9 mg **(c)** In about 15.1 hours

Section 4.2 (Page 197)

1. (a) \$752.27 **(b)** \$707.39 **(c)** \$432.45 **(d)** \$298.98
(e) Answers vary. **3. (a)** 2540 **(b)** About 9431 megawatts; about
59,177 megawatts **5. (a)** $f(t) = 1000(1.046)^t$ **(b)** \$3078.17
(c) 2005 **7. (a)** $f(t) = 81.1(1.067)^t$ **(b)** About \$260.6 billion
(c) About \$410.3 billion **9. (a)** Two-point: $f(t) = (.9763)^t$;
regression: $f(t) = .998(.976)^t$ **(b)** Two-point: \$.70; \$.65; regression:
\$.69; \$.64 **(c)** Two-point: 2038; regression: 2037
11. (a) Two-point: $f(t) = 257.6(.964)^t$; regression: $f(t) = 257.4(.963)^t$
(b) Two-point: about 165.9; about 143.3; regression: about 163.7; about
140.8 **(c)** Two-point: 2025; regression: 2025 **13. (a)** About 6 items
(b) About 23 items **(c)** 25 items **15.** 2.6° C **17. (a)** .13
(b) .23 **(c)** About 2 weeks
19. (a) About \$594.0 billion; about \$802.4 billion
(b) 1000

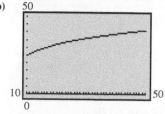

(c) 2011
21. (a) About \$91.89 billion; about \$96.86 billion

Section 4.3 (Page 207)

1. a^y **3.** It is missing the value that equals b^y. If that value is x, the
expression should read $y = \log_b x$ **5.** $10^5 = 100,000$ **7.** $9^2 = 81$
9. $\log 96 = 1.9823$ **11.** $\log_3\left(\dfrac{1}{9}\right) = -2$ **13.** 3 **15.** 2

17. 3 **19.** -2 **21.** $\dfrac{1}{2}$ **23.** 8.77 **25.** 1.724
27. -4.991 **29.** Because $a^0 = 1$ for every valid base a.
31. $\log 24$ **33.** $\ln 5$ **35.** $\log\left(\dfrac{u^2 w^3}{v^6}\right)$ **37.** $\ln\left(\dfrac{(x+2)^2}{x+3}\right)$

39. $\dfrac{1}{2}\ln 6 + 2\ln m + \ln n$ **41.** $\dfrac{1}{2}\log x - \dfrac{5}{2}\log z$ **43.** $2u + 5v$
45. $3u - 2v$ **47.** 3.32112 **49.** 2.429777
51. Many correct answers, including, $b = 1, c = 2$.
53. **55.**

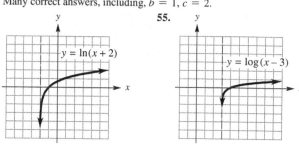

57. Answers vary. **59.** $\ln 2.75 = 1.0116009$; $e^{1.0116009} = 2.75$
61. (a) 17.67 yr **(b)** 9.01 yr **(c)** 4.19 yr **(d)** 2.25 yr
63. (a) \$2219.63
(b) 2500

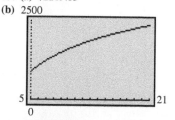

(c) Gradually increasing
65. (a) About 31.99 million; about 37.67 million
(b) 50

(c) Gradually increasing **67.** 1.5887
69. (a) About \$441.15 billion; about \$737.74 billion **(b)** 2027
71. (a) About 24.8 gallons; about 21.9 **(b)** 2021

Section 4.4 (Page 216)

1. 8 **3.** 9 **5.** 11 **7.** $\dfrac{11}{6}$ **9.** $\dfrac{4}{9}$ **11.** 10

13. 5.2378   **15.** 10   **17.** $\dfrac{4+b}{4}$ **19.** $\dfrac{10^{2-b}-5}{6}$

21. Answers vary.   **23.** 4   **25.** $-\dfrac{5}{6}$ **27.** -4 **29.** -2

31. 2.3219   **33.** 2.710   **35.** -1.825 **37.** .597253

39. $-.123$ **41.** $\dfrac{\log d + 3}{4}$ **43.** $\dfrac{\ln b + 1}{2}$ **45.** 4

47. No solution   **49.** $-4, 4$ **51.** 9   **53.** 1   **55.** $4, -4$
57. ± 2.0789 **59.** 1.386   **61.** Answers vary.   **63.** (a) 2009
(b) 2012   **65.** (a) 1992 $(x \approx 92.1518)$ (b) Mid-2007 $(x \approx 107.7364)$
(c) Mid-2041 $(x \approx 141.6168)$ **67.** (a) 1995   (b) 2022
69. (a) 25 g   (b) About 4.95 yr   **71.** About 3689 yr old
73. (a) Approximately $79{,}432{,}823 i_0$ (b) Approximately $251{,}189 i_0$
(c) About 316.23 times stronger   **75.** (a) 21   (b) 100   (c) 105
(d) 120   (e) 140   **77.** (a) 27.5%   (h) $130.14

79. (a)

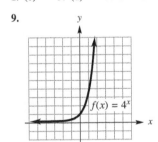

(b) 2002

Chapter 4 Review Exercises (Page 219)

Refer to Section	4.1	4.2	4.3	4.4
For Exercises	1–10	13–14, 55–58, 61–64	11–12, 15–40, 65–66	41–54, 59–60

1. (c)   **3.** (d)   **5.** $0 < a < 1$ **7.** All positive real numbers

9.

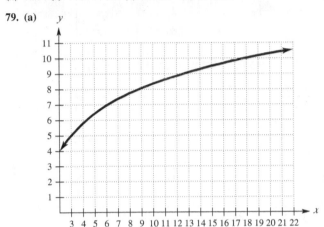

$f(x) = 4^x$

11.

$f(x) = \ln x + 5$

13. (a) About 412 thousand   (b) June 2012   **15.** $\log 340 = 2.53148$
17. $\ln 45 = 3.8067$ **19.** $10^4 = 10{,}000$ **21.** $e^{4.3957} = 81.1$

23. 5   **25.** 8.9   **27.** $\dfrac{1}{3}$ **29.** $\log 20x^6$ **31.** $\log\left(\dfrac{b^3}{c^2}\right)$

33. 4   **35.** 97   **37.** 5   **39.** 5   **41.** -2 **43.** -2
45. 1.416   **47.** -2.807 **49.** -3.305 **51.** .747
53. 28.463   **55.** (a) C   (b) A   (c) D   (d) B   **57.** (a) 10 g
(b) About 140 days   (c) About 243 days   **59.** (a) $10{,}000{,}000 i_0$
(b) $3{,}162{,}278 i_0$ (c) About 3.2 times stronger   **61.** $81.25°$ C
63. (a) $f(x) = 500(1.067)^x$ (b) $f(x) = 474.8(1.075)^x$
(c) Two-point: about 896 minutes; regression: about 910 minutes
(d) Two point and regression: May, 2013.

65. (a) $f(x) = 18 + 21.07 \ln x$ (b) $f(x) = 15.21 + 20.47 \ln x$
(c) Two point: about 64%; regression: about 60%
(d) Two point: 2016; regression: 2019

Case Study 4 Exercises (Page 224)

1.

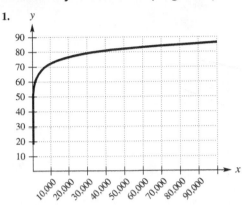

3. 66.6 years   **5.** About $1383

7.

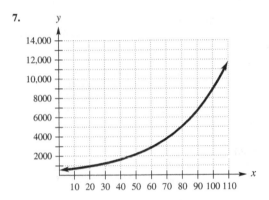

9. About $2131; about $8899

11.

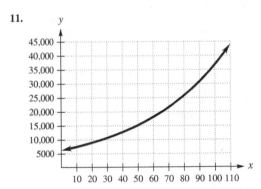

13. About $18,168; about $44,329

Chapter 5

Section 5.1 (Page 230)

1. Time and interest rate   **3.** $133   **5.** $217.48   **7.** $86.26
9. $158.82   **11.** $31.25; $187.50   **13.** $234.38; $4687.50
15. $81.25; $1625   **17.** $12,105   **19.** $6727.50
21. Answers vary.   **23.** $14,354.07   **25.** $15,089.46
27. $19,996.25; about .07501%   **29.** $15,491.86; about .105087%
31. $19,752; about 5.0223%   **33.** $15,117.92; about 5.0545%

35. (a) $9450 **(b)** $19,110   **37.** $3056.25   **39.** 5.0%
41. 4 months   **43.** $1750.04   **45.** $5825.24   **47.** 3.5%
49. About 11.36%   **51.** About 102.91%. Ouch!   **53.** $13,725; yes
55. (a) $y_1 = 8t + 100$; $y_2 = 6t + 200$
(b) The graph of y_1 is a line with slope 8 and y-intercept 100. The graph of y_2 is a line with slope 6 and y-intercept 200.

(c)

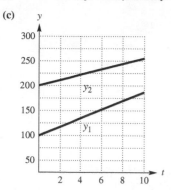

(d) The y-intercept of each graph indicates the amount invested. The slope of each graph is the annual amount of interest paid.

Section 5.2 (Page 241)

1. Answers vary.   **3.** Interest rate and number of compounding periods
5. Answers vary.   **7.** $1265.32; $265.32   **9.** $1204.75; $734.75
11. $9297.93; $2797.93   **13.** $10,090.41; $90.41
15. $5081.63; $81.63   **17.** $107,896.09; $7,896.09   **19.** 3.75%
21. 5.25%   **23.** $23,824.92; $3824.92   **25.** $31,664.54; $1664.54
27. $10,000   **29.** $20,000   **31.** 4.04%   **33.** 5.095%
35. $8954.58   **37.** $11,572.58   **39.** $4203.64   **41.** $9963.10
43. $4606.57   **45.** $465.85   **47.** $1000 now   **49.** $21,570.27
51. Treasury note   **53.** $1000 now   **55.** 3.59%
57. Flagstar, 4.45%; Principal, 4.46%; Principal paid a higher APY
59. About $2,259,696   **61.** About $21,043   **63.** 23.4 years
65. 14.2 years   **67.** About 11.9 years   **69. (a)** $16,659.95
(b) $21,472.67   **71. (a)**

Section 5.3 (Page 249)

1. 21.5786   **3.** $119,625.61   **5.** $23,242.87   **7.** $72,482.38
9. About $205,490   **11.** About $310,831   **13.** $797.36
15. $4566.33   **17.** $152.53   **19.** 5.19%   **21.** 5.223%
23. Answers vary.   **25.** $6603.39   **27.** $234,295.32
29. $26,671.23   **31.** $3928.88   **33.** $620.46   **35.** $265.71
37. $280,686.25   **39. (a)** $173,497.86 **(b)** $144,493.82
(c) $29,004.04   **41. (a)** $552,539.96 **(b)** $854,433.28
43. $32,426.46   **45.** $284,527.35   **47. (a)** $256.08 **(b)** $247.81
49. $863.68   **51. (a)** $1200 **(b)** $3511.58   **53.** 6.5%
55. (a) Answers vary. **(b)** $24,000 **(c)** $603,229 **(d)** $84,000
(e) $460,884

Section 5.4 (Page 261)

1. Answers vary.   **3.** $8693.71   **5.** $1,566,346.66
7. $11,468.10   **9.** $38,108.61   **11.** $557.68   **13.** $6272.14
15. $119,379.35   **17.** $97,122.49   **19.** $48,677.34
21. $15,537.76   **23.** $9093.14   **25.** $446.31   **27.** $11,331.18
29. $589.31   **31.** $979.21   **33.** $925.29
35. $594.72; $13,818.25   **37.** $947.69; $151,223.33   **39.** $6.80
41. $42.04   **43.** $30,669,881   **45.** $24,761,633
47. (a) $1465.42 **(b)** $214.58   **49.** $2320.83
51. $414.18; $14,701.60   **53. (a)** $2717.36 **(b)** 2
55. (a) $969.75 **(b)** $185,658.15 **(c)** $143,510
57. About $8143.79   **59.** $406.53   **61.** $663.22

63.

Payment Number	Amount of Payment	Interest for Period	Portion to Principal	Principal at End of Period
0	–	–	–	$4000.00
1	$1207.68	$320.00	$887.68	3112.32
2	1207.68	248.99	958.69	2153.63
3	1207.68	172.29	1035.39	1118.24
4	1207.70	89.46	1118.24	0

65.

Payment Number	Amount of Payment	Interest for Period	Portion to Principal	Principal at End of Period
0	–	–	–	$7184.00
1	$189.18	$71.84	117.34	7066.66
2	189.18	70.67	118.51	6948.15
3	189.18	69.48	119.70	6828.45
4	189.18	68.28	120.90	6707.55

Chapter 5 Review Exercises (Page 265)

Refer to Section	5.1	5.2	5.3	5.4
For Exercises	1–14	15–28, 65–66, 71	32–41, 67–70, 75–76	29–31,42–64, 72–74,77–79

1. $292.08   **3.** $62.05   **5.** $285; $3420   **7.** $7925.67
9. Answers vary.   **11.** $78,742.54   **13.** About 4.082%
15. $5634.15; $2834.15   **17.** $20,402.98; $7499.53   **19.** $8532.58
21. $15,000   **23.** 5.0625%   **25.** $18,207.65   **27.** $1088.54
29. $9706.74   **31.** Answers vary.   **33.** $162,753.15
35. $22,643.29   **37.** Answers vary.   **39.** $2619.29   **41.** $916.12
43. $31,921.91   **45.** $14,222.42   **47.** $136,340.32
49. $1194.02   **51.** $38,298.04   **53.** $3581.11   **55.** $435.66
57. $85,459.20   **59.** $81.98   **61.** $502.49
63. (a) $7,233,333.33 **(b)** $136,427,623.40
65. $2298.58   **67.** $24,818.76; $2418.76   **69.** $12,538.59
71. $5596.62   **73.** $3560.61   **75.** $222,221.02   **77.** (d)

Case Study 5 Exercises (Page 268)

1. (a) $22,549.94 **(b)** $36,442.38 **(c)** $66,402.34
3. (a) $40,722.37 **(b)** $41,090.49 **(c)** $41,175.24 **(d)** $41,216.62
(e) $41,218.03   **5. (a)** About 4.603% **(b)** About 5.866%
(c) About 7.681%

Chapter 7 Sets and Probability

Exercises 7.1 (page 308)

For exercises . . .	5–19	21–24,63,69	25–44	47–50,74–76,78,79	53–56,59–62,64–68, 71–76,78,79	70
Refer to example . . .	2	4	5,6,7	9	8	3

47. All students in this school not taking this course   **48.** All students in this school taking this course or taking accounting   **49.** All students in this school taking accounting and zoology   **50.** All students in this school not taking accounting and not taking zoology   **53.** B' is the set of all stocks on the list with a closing price below $40 or above $105; $B' = \{$AT&T, Costco$\}$ **54.** $A \cap B$ is the set of all stocks on the list with a high price greater than $80 and a closing price between $40 and $105; $A \cap B = \{$McDonald's, Pepsico, Walt Disney$\}$ **55.** $(A \cap B)'$ is the set of all stocks on the list that do not have both a high price greater than $80 and a closing price between $40 and $105; $(A \cap B)' = \{$AT&T, Coca-Cola, Costco$\}$ **56.** $(C \cup D)'$ is the set of all stocks on the list that do not have either a positive price change or a low price less than $40; $(C \cup D)' = \{$Costco$\}$ **59.** $\{$Berkshire Hathaway, Wells Fargo$\}$ **60.** $\{$Berkshire Hathaway, Google, Microsoft, Wells Fargo$\}$ **61.** $\{$Apple, Apache, DIRECTV, Texas Instruments$\}$ **62.** $\{$Apple, Google, Microsoft, Verizon$\}$ **74.** $\{$TBS$\}$; the set of networks launched before 1985 that also have more than 99.5 million viewers.   **75.** $\{$TNT, USA, TBS$\}$; the set of networks that features sports or that have more than 99.5 million viewers.   **76.** $\{$Discovery, TLC$\}$; the set of networks that do not feature sports.   **78. (a)** The set of states whose name contains the letter "e" or who are not both more than 4 million in population and more than 40,000 square miles in area.   **(b)** $\{$Alaska, Hawaii, Indiana, Kentucky, Maine, Nebraska, New Jersey$\}$ **79. (a)** The set of states who are not among those whose name contains the letter "e" or who are more than 4 million in population, and who also have an area of more than 40,000 square miles.

Exercises 7.2 (page 316)

For exercises . . .	1–8,25–28	11–20,29–32,38,39	21–24	41,46,47	40	42,43,48, 49,51–61	44,45,50,62,63
Refer to example . . .	1	2	6	4	5	7	8

1.
$B \cap A'$

2.
$A \cup B'$

3.
$A' \cup B$

4.
$A' \cap B'$

5.
$B' \cup (A' \cap B')$

6.
$(A \cap B) \cup B'$

7.
$U' = \emptyset$

8.
$\emptyset' = U$

11.
$(A \cap B) \cap C$

12.
$(A \cap C') \cup B$

13.
$A \cap (B \cup C')$

14.
$A' \cap (B \cap C)$

15.
$(A' \cap B') \cap C'$

16.
$(A \cap B') \cap C$

17.
$(A \cap B') \cup C'$

18.
$A' \cap (B' \cup C)$

19.
$(A \cup B') \cap C$

20.
$A' \cup (B' \cap C')$

25.

26.

27. **28.** **29.** 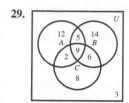 **30.** 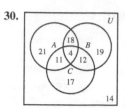 **31.**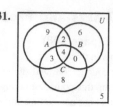

32.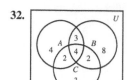

38. One possible answer: 1: Jane Austen; 2: Pele; 3: Bruce Springsteen; 4: Franklin Delano Roosevelt; 5: Tony Blair; 6: Margaret Thatcher; 7: Hillary Clinton; 8: Lady Gaga

Exercises 7.3 (page 326)

For exercises . . .	3–10,13–18	13–18	19–24	25–34	35–40,53,62,63	41–48,56,57–61	51,55,56
Refer to example . . .	1	2,3	6	7	6,7	8	4

9. $\{(h, 1), (h, 2), (h, 3), (h, 4), (h, 5), (h, 6), (t, 1), (t, 2), (t, 3), (t, 4), (t, 5), (t, 6)\}$ **10.** $\{(1, 1), (1, 2), (1, 3), (1, 4), (1, 5),$ $(2, 1), (2, 2), (2, 3), (2, 4), (2, 5), (3, 1), (3, 2), (3, 3), (3, 4), (3, 5), (4, 1), (4, 2), (4, 3), (4, 4), (4, 5), (5, 1), (5, 2), (5, 3),$ $(5, 4), (5, 5)\}$ **13.** {AB, AC, AD, AE, BC, BD, BE, CD, CE, DE}, 10, yes **14.** {(CA, CO, NJ), (CA, CO, NY), (CA, CO, UT), (CA, NJ, NY), (CA, NJ, UT), (CA, NY, UT), (CO, NJ, NY), (CO, NJ, UT), (CO, NY, UT), (NJ, NY, UT)}, 10, yes **(b)** {(CA, CO, NJ), (CA, CO, NY), (CA, NJ, UT), (CA, NY, UT), (CO, NJ, NY), (NJ, NY, UT)} **(c)** {(CA, NJ, NY), (CO, NJ, NY), (UT, NJ, NY)} **15.** $\{(1, 2), (1, 3), (1, 4), (1, 5), (2, 3), (2, 4), (2, 5), (3, 4), (3, 5), (4, 5)\}$, 10, yes **(b)** $\{(1, 2), (1, 4), (2, 3), (2, 5), (3, 4), (4, 5)\}$ **16.** {www, wwc, wcw, cww, ccw, cwc, wcc, ccc}, 8, yes **17.** {hh, thh, hth, tthh, thth, htth, ttth, ttht, thtt, httt, tttt}, 11, no **18.** $\{(1, 1), (1, 2), (1, 3), (1, 4), (1, 5), (2, 1), (2, 2), (2, 3), (2, 4), (2, 5) (3, 1), (3, 2),$ $(3, 3), (3, 4), (3, 5), (4, 1), (4, 2), (4, 3), (4, 4), (4, 5)\}$, 20, yes **(a)** $\{(2, 1), (2, 2), (2, 3), (2, 4), (2, 5), (4, 1), (4, 2), (4, 3),$ $(4, 4), (4, 5)\}$ **(b)** $\{(1, 2), (1, 4), (2, 2), (2, 4), (3, 2), (3, 4), (4, 2), (4, 4)\}$ **51. (a)** Worker is male. **(b)** Worker is female and has worked less than 5 years. **(c)** Worker is female or does not contribute to a voluntary retirement plan. **(d)** Worker has worked 5 years or more. **(e)** Worker has worked less than 5 years or has contributed to a voluntary retirement plan. **(f)** Worker has worked 5 years or more and does not contribute to a voluntary retirement plan. **55. (a)** Person is not overweight. **(b)** Person has a family history of heart disease and is overweight. **(c)** Person smokes or is not overweight. **56. (a)** Person smokes or has a family history of heart disease, or both **(b)** Person does not smoke and has a family history of heart disease. **(c)** Person does not have a family history of heart disease or is not overweight, or both.

Exercises 7.4 (page 335)

37. Not possible; the sum of the probabilities is less than 1.

For exercises . . .	9–20,23,24,54,55,	21,22,47,52,53,	27–32,48,65,70	35–40,49–51,56,	60,71
		57–59,61–64		66–69	
Refer to example . . .	1,2,3,4	9	5	8	6,7

38. Not possible; the sum of the probabilities is greater than 1. **39.** Not possible; a probability cannot be negative. **40.** Not possible; a probability cannot be negative and the sum of the probabilities is not one. **60.** Gore: 1/3; Daschle: 1/5; Kerry: 1/5; Dodd: 1/5; Lieberman: 1/6; Biden: 1/6; Leahy: 1/7; Feingold: 1/9; Edwards: 1/10; Gephardt: 1/16. The probabilities add up to 1.68, but the sum of the probabilities of all possible outcomes cannot be greater than 1. **66. (a)**

	A	B	C	D
O	0.0779	0.0616	0.0433	0.0068
E	0.2676	0.2380	0.2296	0.0628
M	0.0036	0.0042	0.0047	0.0000

Exercises 7.5 (page 349)

For exercises . . .	1–12	13–16	23,24,44–46,49–53,63,	43,69,86	36–40,47,54–60,	29,30,41,42,	48,61,68,78,
			71,72,79–82,84,87–89		62,64–67, 69,73,74,77	75,76	83,85,86
Refer to example . . .	3,4	8	5,6,7	2	1	9	10

32. (a) It is better to switch, for a probability of winning of 1/6, as opposed to a probability of 1/7 of winning if you don't switch. **36.** The probability of a customer cashing a check, given that the customer made a deposit, is 3/4. **37.** The probability that a customer cashing a check will fail to make a deposit is 1/3. **38.** The probability of a customer not cashing a check, given that the customer did not make a deposit, is 1/4. **39.** The probability that a customer making a deposit will not cash a check is 1/4. **40.** The probability of a customer not both cashing a check and making a deposit is 1/2.

Exercises 7.6 (page 360)

For exercises . . .	1,2,9,10–13,23–26, 29–32,36,39	3–8,14–17,19 27,28	18,20–22,33–35, 37,38
Refer to example . . .	1	2	3

Chapter 7 Review Exercises (page 365)

For exercises . . .	1–5,13–28, 59,103,106	6,43–52,60,61,69,70, 104,106,119,120	7,8,53,54,65–68, 71–73,77,78,81–85, 107,109,111,112	9–11,55–58,62, 63,74–76,86–96, 102,106,110, 117,118,123,124	12,79,80, 97–101,105, 113,114	39–42,108,115, 121,122,125
Refer to section . . .	1	3	4	5	6	2

33. All female employees in the accounting department   **34.** All sales employees who have MBA degrees   **35.** All employees who are in the accounting department or who have MBA degrees   **38.** All employees who are not either in the sales department or female, that is, all male employees not in the sales department

39. 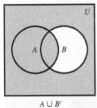   **40.** 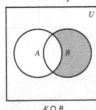   **41.** 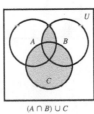   **42.**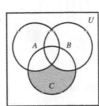

$A \cup B'$ $A' \cap B$ $(A \cap B) \cup C$ $(A \cup B)' \cap C$

44. {ace, 2, 3, 4, 5, 6, 7, 8, 9, 10, J, Q, K}   **45.** {0, 0.5, 1, 1.5, 2, . . . , 299.5, 300}   **46.** {*hhhh, hhht, hhth, hthh, thhh, hhtt, htht,* *htth, thht, tthh, thth, httt, thtt, ttht, ttth, tttt*}   **47.** {(3, *r*), (3, *g*), (5, *r*), (5, *g*), (7, *r*), (7, *g*), (9, *r*), (9, *g*), (11, *r*), (11, *g*)}
48. {(7, *r*), (7, *g*), (9, *r*), (9, *g*), (11, *r*), (11, *g*)}   **49.** {(3, *g*), (5, *g*), (7, *g*), (9, *g*), (11, *g*)}

Chapter 8 Counting Principles; Further Probability Topics

Exercises 8.1 (page 380)

For exercises . . .	1–4,37,39,54,55	5–12,19,20,32,34,40	13–16,30,31,35,43–53	19–24	23,24,33,36, 38,41,42
Refer to example . . .	4,5	6	1	9,10	8

Exercises 8.2 (page 388)

For exercises . . .	3–10,39,48,58	11,12,26(a),33, 35,36,40–42, 45,54–56	14,32,37,43, 44,49,53	15,16,26(b)	17–24	17–24,29–31, 34,38,46,47, 50–52,57
Refer to example . . .	1	6	2,3	7	4	5

Exercises 8.3 (page 400)

For exercises . . .	1–10,36–41,45, 47,65,66,68–71,73	11–18,46–64	19–22,42–44,46,72	25–28,33	29–32
Refer to example . . .	1,2,3	4	5	6	7

Exercises 8.4 (page 407)

For exercises . . .	1–4,9–12,25–33,35–38,51–55	5–8,13,14,20–24,34,39–43,46–50	44,45,56–59
Refer to example . . .	2	3	5

Exercises 8.5 (page 418)

For exercises . . .	1–4	5–8,29	9–16,30,32,36,37,42	17,18,26,45,56	19–25,29,31,38,43,44,47–54,57	33,39,40,55,56
Refer to example . . .	1	2	3	5	4,7	8

1.

Number of Heads	0	1	2	3	4
Probability	1/16	1/4	3/8	1/4	1/16

2.

Number of Points	2	3	4	5	6	7	8	9	10	11	12
Probability	1/36	1/18	1/12	1/9	5/36	1/6	5/36	1/9	1/12	1/18	1/36

3.

Number of Aces	0	1	2	3
Probability	0.7826	0.2042	0.0130	0.0002

4.

Number of Black Balls	0	1	2
Probability	2/5	8/15	1/15

5.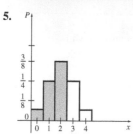

6.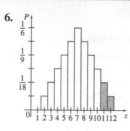

7.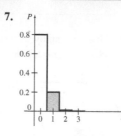

8.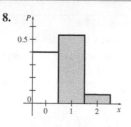

19. (a)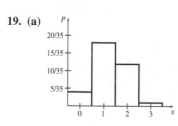

20. (a)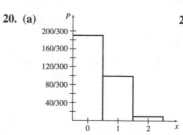

21. (a)

x	0	1	2	3	4
P(x)	625/1296	125/324	25/216	5/324	1/1296

29. (a)

Sum	5	6	7	8	9
Probability	1/6	1/6	1/3	1/6	1/6

(b)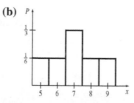

44. (a)

Number of Letters Delivered the Next Day	0	1	2	3	4	5	6	7	8	9	10
Probability	0.0000	0.0000	0.0000	0.0003	0.0024	0.0141	0.0573	0.1600	0.2929	0.3178	0.1552

57. (a)

x	0	1	2	3	4
P(x)	0.2003	0.3964	0.2942	0.0970	0.0120

Chapter 8 Review Exercises (page 423)

For exercises . . .	1,3,13,14,19,20,53	2,15–18,21,22,54	4–6,25–30,35–40, 69,76,78,79,82	7,8,31–34,49,50, 55–60,67,68,70–74	9–12,41–48,61,62, 67,70–73,75,77,78, 80,81
Refer to section . . .	1	2	3	4	5

41. (a)

Number of Heads	0	1	2	3
Probability	0.125	0.375	0.375	0.125

(b)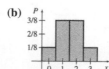

42. (a)

Number	2	3	4	5	6	7	8	9	10	11	12
Probability	1/36	1/18	1/12	1/9	5/36	1/6	5/36	1/9	1/12	1/18	1/36

(b)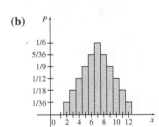

(c) 7 **70. (a)**

Number	0	1	2	3	4
Probability	0.4096	0.4096	0.1536	0.0256	0.0016

(b)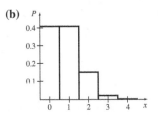

(c) 0.8 **71. (a)**

Number of Schools	0	1	2	3	4	5
Probability	0.0380	0.1755	0.3240	0.2990	0.1380	0.0255

(b)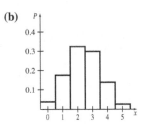

(c) 2.4 **72. (a)**

Number	0	1	2
Probability	10/28	15/28	3/28

(b)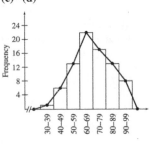

(c) 3/4

73. (a)

Number Who Did Not Do Homework	0	1	2	3
Probability	1/12	5/12	5/12	1/12

(b)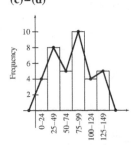

(c) 3/2

Chapter 9 Statistics

Exercises 9.1 (page 439)

For exercises ...	1(a)(b), 2(a)(b), 3(a)(b), 4(a)(b), 43(a), 46(a)	1(c)(d), 2(c)(d), 3(c)(d), 4(c)(d), 43(b), 44(a), 46(b)	7–12,23,24, 43(c),46(c)	13–16,39, 40,43(d), 44(b), 46(d)	17–24, 43(f), 46(f)	25–30, 43(f), 46(f)	36–38,41, 45,47,48	42, 49–51
Refer to example ...	1	2	3	4,5	6	7	8	9

1. (a)–(b)

Interval	Frequency
0–24	4
25–49	8
50–74	5
75–99	10
100–124	4
125–149	5

(c)–(d)

2. (a)–(b)

Interval	Frequency
30–39	1
40–49	6
50–59	13
60–69	22
70–79	17
80–89	13
90–99	8

(c)–(d)

3. (a)–(b)

Interval	Frequency
0–19	4
20–39	5
40–59	4
60–79	5
80–99	9
100–119	3
120–139	4
140–159	2

(c)–(d)

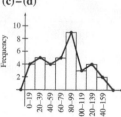

4. (a)–(b)

Interval	Frequency
39–48	6
49–58	13
59–68	20
69–78	19
79–88	13
89–98	9

(c)–(d)

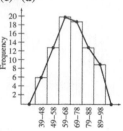

43. (a)

New Houses Sold per Month (in thousands)	f
20–23	8
24–27	10
28–31	14
32–35	8
36–39	3
40–43	5

(b)

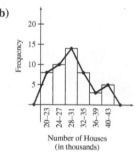

Number of Houses
(in thousands)

44. (a)

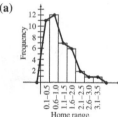

Home range

46. (a)

Interval	Frequency
0–4	9
5–9	4
10–14	9
15–19	3
20–24	4
25–29	1

(b)

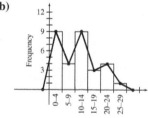

Exercises 9.2 (page 450)

For exercises . . .	3–8,30, 39,40	9,10,25, 26,29	11,12,32, 33,38	27,28	30,31, 34–37,39, 40,41
Refer to example . . .	1,3	3	4	6	5

Exercises 9.3 (page 463)

For exercises . . .	5–14	15–18	22–62
Refer to example . . .	1	2	4

Exercises 9.4 (page 471)

16. (b) Your calculator may have given you an error message. $C(1000, 500)$ is too large for many calculators

For exercises . . .	3–34
Refer to example . . .	4

Chapter 9 Review Exercises (page 474)

For exercises . . .	4,6,10, 13–25	3,5,11, 26–33	7,8,12,34–38,44, 52–56,58,59	1,2,9,39–41, 45,46,48–51	43,47,57
Refer to section . . .	1	2	3	4	1,2

15. (a)

Sales	Frequency
450–474	5
475–499	6
500–524	5
525–549	2
550–574	2

(b)–(c)

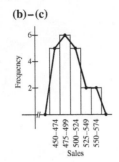

16. (a)

Credits	Frequency
9–10	3
11–12	6
13–14	6
15–16	7

(b)–(c)

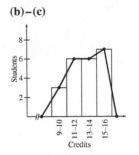

Photo Credits

Text Credits

CHAPTER 7:   327–328 Exercise 50: Excerpt from "Three Slips of Paper Puzzler" from Cartalk.com, Tappet Brothers. Copyright © 2007. **336** Exercise 26: Quote by Roger Staubach from *First Down, Lifetime to Go*. Published by Word Books. Copyright © 1976. **337** Exercise 45: From *Everybody's an Expert: Putting Predictions to the Test* by Louis Menand. Published by *The New Yorker*. Copyright © 2005; Exercise 46: From Sample Exam P, Education and Examination Committee of the Society of Actuaries. Copyright © Society of Actuaries, 2005. Used by permission of Society of Actuaries. **338** Exercise 57: From Sample Exam P, Education and Examination Committee of the Society of Actuaries. Copyright © Society of Actuaries, 2005. Used by permission of Society of Actuaries; Exercise 58: From Sample Exam P, Education and Examination Committee of the Society of Actuaries. Copyright © Society of Actuaries, 2005. Used by permission of Society of Actuaries. **339** Exercise 59: From Sample Exam P, Education and Examination Committee of the Society of Actuaries. Copyright © Society of Actuaries, 2005. Used by permission of Society of Actuaries. **350** Exercise 31: Excerpt from "Ask Marilyn" by Daniel Hahn. Copyright © *Parade* magazine, 1994. Used by permission of *Parade* magazine. **352** Exercise 69: From Sample Exam P, Education and Examination Committee of the Society of Actuaries. Copyright © Society of Actuaries, 2005. Used by permission of Society of Actuaries. **360** Exercise 18: From Course 1 Examination, Education and Examination Committee of the Society of Actuaries. Copyright © Society of Actuaries, 2003. Used by permission of Society of Actuaries. **361** Exercises 19–20: From Sample Exam P, Education and Examination Committee of the Society of Actuaries. Copyright © Society of Actuaries, 2005. Used by permission of Society of Actuaries. **362** Exercise 27: From Course 1 Examination, Education and Examination Committee of the Society of Actuaries. Copyright © Society of Actuaries, 2003. Used by permission of Society of Actuaries; Exercises 28–30: From Sample Exam P, Education and Examination Committee of the Society of Actuaries. Copyright © Society of Actuaries, 2005. Used by permission of Society of Actuaries. **366** Exercise 64: From "Ask Marilyn" by Marilyn Savant from *Parade* magazine (September 9, 1990). Copyright © *Parade* magazine, 1990. Used by permission of *Parade* magazine; Exercise 78: From Sample Exam P, Education and Examination Committee of the Society of Actuaries. Copyright © Society of Actuaries, 2005. Used by permission of Society of Actuaries. **367** Exercises 81–95: Exercises by Michael Cohen. Used by permission of Michael Cohen. **368** Exercise 107: From Course 1 Examination, Education and Examination Committee of the Society of Actuaries. Copyright © Society of Actuaries, 2003. Used by permission of Society of Actuaries; Exercises 108–109: From Sample Exam P, Education and Examination Committee of the Society of Actuaries. Copyright © Society of Actuaries, 2005. Used by permission of Society of Actuaries; Exercise 110: From Course 1 Examination, Education and Examination Committee of the Society of Actuaries. Copyright © Society of Actuaries, 2003. Used by permission of Society of Actuaries; **369** Exercise 113: From Sample Exam P, Education and Examination Committee of the Society of Actuaries. Copyright © Society of Actuaries, 2005. Used by permission of Society of Actuaries. **370** Exercise 120: From *Optimal Strategies on Fourth Down* by Virgil Carter and Robert E. Machol. Copyright © Institute for Operations Research and the Management Sciences, 1978. Used by permission of Institute for Operations Research and the Management Sciences; Exercise 124: Excerpt from *Debt of Honor* by Tom Clancy. Published by G. P. Putnam's Sons (Penguin books). Copyright © 1994. **371** Exercise 125: From Course 1 Examination, Education and Examination Committee of the Society of Actuaries. Copyright © Society of Actuaries, 2003. Used by permission of Society of Actuaries.

CHAPTER 8:   409 Exercise 34: From Sample Exam P, Education and Examination Committee of the Society of Actuaries. Copyright © Society of Actuaries, 2005. Used by permission of Society of Actuaries. **419** Exercise 32: From Sample Exam P, Education and Examination Committee of the Society of Actuaries. Copyright © Society of Actuaries, 2005. Used by permission of Society of Actuaries. **420** Exercise 35: From Sample Exam P, Education and Examination Committee of the Society of Actuaries. Copyright © Society of Actuaries, 2005. Used by permission of Society of Actuaries; Exercise 38: From May 2003 Course 1 Examination, Education and Examination Committee of the Society of Actuaries. Copyright © Society of Actuaries, 2003. Used by permission of Society of Actuaries. **421** Exercise 42: From *The Decision to Seed Hurricanes* by Howard, R. A., J. E. Matheson, and D. W. North. Copyright © American Association for the Advancement of Science, 1972. Used by permission of American Association for the Advancement of Science. **425** Exercise 52: From "Japanese University Entrance Examination Problems in Mathematics," edited by Ling-Erl Eileen T. Wu. Copyright © Mathematical Association of America, 1993. Used by permission of Mathematical Association of America; Exercise 63: From Sample Exam P, Education and Examination Committee of the Society of Actuaries. Copyright © Society of Actuaries, 2005. Used by permission of Society of Actuaries. **426** Exercise 64: From Sample Exam P, Education and Examination Committee of the Society of Actuaries. Copyright © Society of Actuaries, 2005. Used by permission of Society of Actuaries; Exercises 65–66: Course 130 Examination, Operations Research from Society of Actuaries (November 1989). Copyright © Society of Actuaries, 1989. Used by permission of Society of Actuaries; Exercise 69: From "Media Clips," *The Mathematics Teacher*, Vol. 92, No. 8, 1999. Copyright © National Council of Teachers of Mathematics, 1999. Used by permission of National Council of Teachers of Mathematics.

Photo Credits

CHAPTER 7:   301 Jupiterimages/Liquidlibrary/Getty Images **371** Alexander Raths/Shutterstock

CHAPTER 8:   373 Stephen Coburn/Shutterstock **428** Lisa F. Young/Shutterstock

CHAPTER 9:   430 Kletr/Shutterstock **478** Moodboard/Fotolia

Index of Companies, Products, and Agencies

Index of Applications

Economics

Education

Finance

General Interest

Health

Health And Life Sciences

Natural Science

Physical Science

Social Sciences

Subject Index

7.3 Basic Probability Principle

Let S be a sample space of equally likely outcomes, and let event E be a subset of S. Then the probability that event E occurs is

$$P(E) = \frac{n(E)}{n(S)}.$$

7.4 Union Rule

For any two events E and F from a sample space S,

$$P(E \cup F) = P(E) + P(F) - P(E \cap F).$$

7.5 Product Rule

If E and F are events, then $P(E \cap F)$ may be found by either of these formulas.

$$P(E \cap F) = P(F) \cdot P(E|F) \qquad \text{or} \qquad P(E \cap F) = P(E) \cdot P(F|E)$$

7.6 Bayes' Theorem

$$P(F_i|E) = \frac{P(F_i) \cdot P(E|F_i)}{P(F_1) \cdot P(E|F_1) + P(F_2) \cdot P(E|F_2) + \cdots + P(F_n) \cdot P(E|F_n)}$$

8.2 Permutations and Combinations

Permutations Different orderings or arrangements of the r objects are different permutations.

$$P(n, r) = \frac{n!}{(n - r)!}$$

Clue words: arrangement, schedule, order
Order matters!

Combinations Each choice or subset of r objects gives one combination. Order within the group of r objects does not matter.

$$C(n, r) = \frac{n!}{(n - r)!r!}$$

Clue words: group, committee, set, sample
Order does not matter!

8.4 Binomial Probability

If p is the probability of success in a single trial of a binomial experiment, the probability of x successes and $n - x$ failures in n independent repeated trials of the experiment, known as binomial probability, is

$$P(x \text{ successes in } n \text{ trials}) = C(n, x) \cdot p^x \cdot (1 - p)^{n-x}.$$

8.5 Expected Value

Suppose the random variable x can take on the n values $x_1, x_2, x_3, \ldots, x_n$. Also, suppose the probabilities that these values occur are, respectively, $p_1, p_2, p_3, \ldots, p_n$. Then the expected value of the random variable is

$$E(x) = x_1 p_1 + x_2 p_2 + x_3 p_3 + \cdots + x_n p_n.$$

9.2 Variance and Standard Deviation

The variance of a sample of n numbers $x_1, x_2, x_3, \ldots, x_n$, with mean $\bar{x}$, is

$$s^2 = \frac{\Sigma x^2 - n\bar{x}^2}{n - 1}.$$

The standard deviation of a sample of n numbers $x_1, x_2, x_3, \ldots, x_n$, with mean $\bar{x}$, is

$$s = \sqrt{\frac{\Sigma x^2 - n\bar{x}^2}{n - 1}}.$$